A2
LEVEL
Psychology

the student's textbook

Nigel Holt and Rob Lewis

LIBRARY
TEL NO,
01443 810032
YSTRAD MYNACH

Crown House Publishing Ltd
www.crownhouse.co.uk
www.crownhousepublishing.com

First published by
Crown House Publishing Ltd
Crown Buildings, Bancyfelin, Carmarthen, Wales, SA33 5ND, UK
www.crownhouse.co.uk

and

Crown House Publishing Company LLC
6 Trowbridge Drive, Suite 5, Bethel, CT 06801, USA
www.crownhousepublishing.com

British Library of Cataloguing-in-Publication Data
A catalogue entry for this book is available
from the British Library.

ISBN 978-184590093-9

LCCN 2008923497

Printed and bound by
Cambridge University Press, Cambridge

Contents

INTRODUCTION

A2 PSYCHOLOGY: THE STUDENT'S TEXTBOOK

AUTHORS: NIGEL HOLT AND ROB LEWIS

Nigel Holt is a Senior Lecturer in Psychology at Bath Spa University. He has a PhD in experimental cognitive psychology and is an active researcher in perception and cognition and e-learning. He is a team leader examiner with a major exam board and an external examiner at two English universities. He talks regularly to psychology teachers and students at conferences around the UK. Nigel is the co-author of a leading University-level introductory psychology textbook, a guide to research methods and GCSE level psychology textbook.

Rob Lewis is an extremely experienced teacher and examiner. He has held senior examining posts and consultancy positions with several examination boards and is closely involved in specification development and delivery. He is also involved in INSET and continuing professional development. He talks to students at many different events across the UK and currently holds a senior examining post at a major examination board. In addition to this, Rob has taught at both undergraduate and postgraduate level and has particular interests in neuropsychology and anomalistic psychology, although as an A level lecturer he teaches the full range of topics in this book. In addition to this A2 book, and the associated AS textbook and study guides, Rob is also the co-author of a GCSE level psychology textbook.

ACKNOWLEDGEMENTS

We thank Kate and Nic for their amazing support and understanding during the production of this book. We promise to make sure that we will take time off from now on and we will do our best to remind ourselves that home and work are two different things. We also thank our workmates for putting up with our moods, anxieties and general elusiveness during the production of this book. Our contributors have all been extremely understanding and all accepted editing of their work with good humour and patience. The army of people involved in the production of a book like this are too numerous to name, but the excellent team at Crown, and our consticulous roof-reader John Rogers, have made a rocky road easier, so our thanks go to them also. Finally, thanks go to our students: this book is for you.

WHAT IS PSYCHOLOGY?

If you are reading this book for interest you may be interested to find out that psychology is one of the broadest and newest of the sciences. It is extremely popular, both in school and college and at university. Psychology is best described as 'the science of mind and behaviour'. If you are reading this book as part of your studies towards an A2 qualification then you should already know what psychology is! This is because you will have taken the preceding AS course in psychology and so have some idea, we hope, of what to expect.

WHO IS THIS BOOK FOR?

First and foremost, this book is for students. We know teachers and those interested in psychology from other professions read books like this, but this book is designed carefully with students in mind. Specifically, it has been written for students preparing for the A2 component of their psychology A level, following specification A with the AQA examining board.

WHY HAVE WE WRITTEN THIS BOOK?

This is not a book with the bare minimum of information. We know from experience that textbooks are often written with teachers in mind, and frequently contain messages intended for teachers rather than students. Textbook authors know that teachers help students understand difficult material in the classroom and so are often guilty of not explaining things as carefully and as thoroughly as they might. We have taken an approach which we hope will encourage students to *read*, and allow students to access often hard to understand things. We are teachers ourselves and know how vital a good teacher is to education. However, we also wanted to help student understanding by providing a textbook which thoroughly covers the specification and which was accessible outside the classroom. Everything required to get a top grade in the AQA/A A2 exams is included in this book.

AS AND A2 PSYCHOLOGY

Those reading this book as part of their A2 learning will already have sat the AS component of the A level. It is very important to point out that just because the AS knowledge has already been used successfully in the AS level, you must not discard what you have learned. The AS level provides a foundation for A2 study, and a great deal of what you have learned at AS is revisited at A2. It is not a sign of weakness to have to return to AS notes to remind oneself of what has gone before. Most notably the information covered in Research Methods at AS is required knowledge at A2 and we recommend that all students spend a little while looking back to that part of their AS course to refresh their memories.

RESEARCH

Psychology is a science, and progresses through careful research. Research is central to the development of psychological understanding. A sound knowledge of how research should be designed and carried out is extremely important. The topic was introduced at AS, and we build on it here at A2. Students are required not only to *know* information they must be able to *apply* their knowledge and examiners will be looking for this skill when allocating marks. Our advice is that those intent on being the best students of psychology should build themselves a solid foundation in research methods. Once this is in place the additional information becomes a great deal easier to understand and evaluate.

FURTHER HELP

We are confident that everything needed to complete the exam successfully is included in this book. However, we know that exams are not just about knowledge. Exam technique is more than just squeezing knowledge onto the exam answer booklet. It's also about knowing how much to include of what sort of thing to give the best chance of maximum marks. Because of this we have written a comprehensive study guide that accompanies the book where exam preparation and practice take centre stage.

The study guide includes more tips on how to do well, summaries of essential information, example questions and answers, and a thorough glossary of important terms.

USEFUL FEATURES

All textbooks include features intended to develop interest or improve learning in some way. In this book we have kept features like this to a minimum because we know that they often fail in their intentions – they end up cluttering the page, they frequently contain vague or irrelevant instructions and ideas, and often distract from sustained concentration and reading. Where we have used features and boxes we have done so either because the information they contain extends information we've described elsewhere or is additional important guidance.

DIAGRAMS

Diagrams are used to help visualise an idea of a concept. We know from experience that diagrams are only helpful if the idea can be simplified and so we have used them carefully and only where appropriate. If you are fortunate to have a diagram to learn, then do so – diagrams can help you to remember things and can earn you marks in an exam.

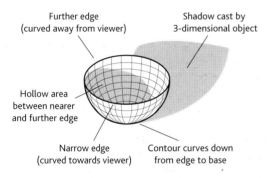

ASK AN EXAMINER

An expert perspective is always useful. In A2 psychology the experts are the examiners and so we have included 'Ask An Examiner' boxes to guide learning and help focus the reader on important information wherever appropriate.

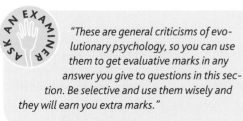

"These are general criticisms of evolutionary psychology, so you can use them to get evaluative marks in any answer you give to questions in this section. Be selective and use them wisely and they will earn you extra marks."

BOXES

Occasionally we have included boxes which give more detail of particular studies or ideas. You can read the main text without referring to the boxes, but if you want a bit more detail the box might contain information useful to you.

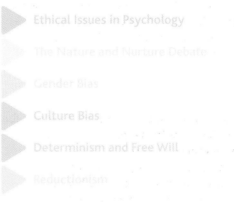

A PSYCHODYNAMIC ACCOUNT OF SLEEPWALKING

Abrams (1964) describe the case of a 42-year-old woman arrested for shoplifting from a large department store whilst sleepwalking. Her behaviour was completely at odds with her morality and character – she was described as an energetic, active member of the religious community. As a result of this experience she became depressed and anxious, afraid to leave her home. Initially, she showed no understanding of her behaviour, but after several sessions of therapy, recalled that she had been a sleepwalker all her life, and when younger had often had her leg tied to the bed at night to stop her wandering off.

The therapist interpreted the subject's shoplifting behaviour as being a result of extreme pressures and personal difficulties. Shortly before the shoplifting incident she had been very distressed at the news of a relative's serious illness. According to Abrams, the sleepwalking was basically a 'cry for help', the stealing being a reflection of her need to take control of her life. After several more sessions of therapy, the patient came to accept the interpretation, and her symptoms of depression and anxiety disappeared.

ISSUES AND DEBATES

A level students are required to show an understanding of various issues and debates. In this book we have devised a simple code for identifying where each issue is touched upon in the text so students can see quickly where the relevant information is on the page.

▶ Ethical Issues in Psychology

▶ The Nature and Nurture Debate

▶ Gender Bias

▶ Culture Bias

▶ Determinism and Free Will

▶ Reductionism

Remember though that these are only *suggestions* – there are plenty of other places where issues and debates can be applied, so don't be afraid of thinking for yourself when looking to see how you can address issues and debates.

THE A2 EXAMINATIONS

A much more detailed description of the examination, including lots of tips and advice on avoiding the pitfalls, is available in the study guide accompanying this book. A short description of the A2 examinations is given here however to help you use this book more effectively.

In order to gain a full A level students must first complete AS and then A2, each worth 50% of the full qualification. Following AS level (where Unit 1 and Unit 2 are covered), students follow the A2 course, covering Unit 3 and Unit 4.

In Unit 3, three topics are chosen from a list of eight: Biological rhythms, Perception, Relationships, Aggression, Eating behaviour, Gender, Intelligence and learning, Cognition and development. The questions require essay-style answers.

Unit 4 is a little more complicated. It is divided into three sections. In the first section you choose **one** disorder to study from four (schizophrenia, depression, anxiety – phobia, or anxiety – OCD). Exam questions require an essay-style answer. In the second section, **one** Psychology in Action topic is selected from three (Media psychology, The psychology of addictive behaviour, or Anomalistic psychology). Parted questions are used in the exam (e.g. (a), (b), (c)…). The final section is a compulsory one covering Psychological Research and Scientific Method. The exam question is structured, i.e. several questions based on a scenario.

Quality of Written Communication

Marks are awarded for Quality of Written Communication (QWC) in both Units 3 and 4. In order to gain the maximum marks reserved for QWC candidates must:

» ensure that text is legible and that spelling, punctuation and grammar are accurate so that meaning is clear

» select and use a form and style of writing appropriate to purpose and to complex subject matter

» organise information clearly and coherently, using specialist vocabulary when appropriate.

In Unit 3, QWC marks are awarded for each answer. In Unit 4, QWC marks are awarded only for the essay-style question on Psychopathology.

HOW SCIENCE WORKS

You are expected to demonstrate an understanding of how scientists investigate psychological phenomena, and marks are allocated for this knowledge. Very few How Science Works marks are available in Unit 3, and it is easiest to get them by effective use and evaluation of research studies and, where relevant, commentary on the methods used by psychologists. Many more marks are available for this in Unit 4, where there is a compulsory question on research methods. You must also be prepared to demonstrate your knowledge of How Science Works in both your Psychopathology and Psychology in Action answers, however.

ISSUES AND DEBATES

In Unit 3, students are required to have a knowledge of 'issues and debates' in psychology and how they relate to each topic being studied. These issues and debates represent a more general understanding of psychology, above and beyond any analysis and commentary relevant to the topic. Not all issues and debates are relevant to all topics, but you are expected to show understanding of them in exam answers where they are applicable.

STRETCH AND CHALLENGE

This A2 specification incorporates something called *Stretch and Challenge*. This is an initiative meant to provide the most able students with the opportunity to demonstrate their knowledge and skills. Stretch and Challenge does not influence grades A to E – these are awarded by exam boards in the usual way. However, those students who achieve 90% of the available A2 marks (and 80% of the marks overall, including the AS marks), will be seen to have responded to Stretch and Challenge and will therefore be awarded an A* grade. Students wishing to achieve an A* must have a sound and thorough understanding of the content of psychology at this level. They must write clearly and coherently, demonstrate an understanding of how science works, and incorporate issues and debates effectively. Everything you need for Stretch and Challenge is included in this book, and we

	Unit 3	Unit 4
Paper value	25% of total A level marks	25% of total A level marks
Exam length	1 hour 30 minutes	2 hours
Exam format	Three essay-style questions	Three sections: Psychopathology (one essay-style question) Psychology in Action (one parted question) Research Methods (one compulsory structured question)
Quality of written communication (QWC)	Assessed in each essay question	Assessed in the psychopathology essay

Summary of the A2 examinations.

believe that using this book will give you the best possible chance of achieving this A* grade.

IMPORTANT RESOURCES

Additional help is available in various places online. We know that students (and indeed teachers) often use bulletin boards on the internet to discuss problems they may have and seek assistance with their peers and this is fine in some ways as it provides a feeling of social support for the often lonely process of learning and revising information. However, we urge caution. A quick glance over many of these online bulletin boards reveals that incorrect and misleading information is extremely common. You should use these and other online resources with great care in the knowledge that you do so at your own risk. You will not go wrong with relying on the information in this book and the study guide.

www.aqa.org.uk

This is the homepage of The Assessment and Qualifications Alliance (AQA). It is they who write the specification and organize the examination, and it is they who employ examiners to mark the completed papers. At this site you will find the Specification A for Psychology GCE. The site also includes some helpful points on how the examination is marked, and other resources like past papers. Remember, if it's not in the specification you will not be tested on it. Similarly, if it is in the specification it is very possible that it may be included in the examination.

www.askanexaminer.com

Ask An Examiner includes information and links related to the exam. There is also a facility whereby questions can be asked of experienced examiners who will provide you with a personal answer.

www.bps.org.uk

The British Psychological Society (BPS) is the professional body for psychologists working in the UK. Their website provides a huge amount of information on all areas of psychology for those interested in taking psychology further, such as information on psychology as a career, university courses, and links to other websites. Also on the site is useful information on how psychologists are expected to behave professionally in terms of ethical guidelines and concerns. These are central to good research practice and are part of the research methods component of this course.

CONTRIBUTORS

Andrea Ackland

Andrea Ackland works as a Psychology Lecturer at Coleg Gwent. She is an experienced teacher and examiner, and has a background in applied psychology research.

Gareth Griffiths

Gareth Griffiths has taught Psychology at both advanced and undergraduate levels. He teaches a wide variety of topics, but has particular interests in biological psychology and psychopathology.

Rob Irwin

Dr Rob Irwin is a Senior Lecturer in Psychology at Bath Spa University. Amongst other things Rob is a qualified nurse and holds qualifications in counselling. His teaching and research specialisms are in counselling psychology and the psychology of health, where his expertise in eating disorders is put to great use.

Chris Roe

Dr Chris Roe is a Senior Lecturer in Psychology at the University of Northampton, and a member of the university's *Centre for the Study of Anomalous Psychological Processes*. He is Editor of the *Journal of the Society for Psychical Research* and is currently a Board Member of the Parapsychological Association, Council Member of the Society for Psychical Research, and International Affiliate for England for the Parapsychology Foundation.

Nicola Taylor

Nicola Taylor has considerable experience and success both as a teacher and examiner for AS / A level Psychology. She is currently Head of Social Science at Monmouth Comprehensive School.

Ian Walker

Dr Ian Walker is a lecturer and cognitive psychologist working at the University of Bath. He has lectured at the Dyslexia Institute and has worked as a professional researcher at the Max Planck Institute for Human Cognitive and Brain Sciences in Leipzig. His research is in how different road users interact, most notably cyclists, motorcyclists and drivers of cars.

Claire Williams

Dr Claire Williams is a Lecturer in Psychology at the University of Reading where she specialises in biological psychology. She is actively involved in researching addiction, nutrition and animal welfare.

ETHICAL ISSUES IN PSYCHOLOGY

In psychology we study a huge range of subject matter, from the activity of a single brain cell, to the behaviour of large groups of football fans. Where research is not carried out with sufficient care for its participants we say that it has not been carried out ethically. Examples of research in psychology where human participants may well have suffered psychological damage include Milgram's obedience research where participants were deceived into believing they were giving electric shocks to another person. As a result of such studies, ethical guidelines have been produced which govern the behaviour of researchers. Ethical guidelines extend to the use of animals in research, meaning that researchers have an ethical obligation to do their best to ensure that suffering is minimised. A great deal of ethically questionable research has been carried out in psychology. For example, in Harry Harlow's research, young Rhesus monkeys removed from their mothers clearly suffered anxiety and trauma as a result.

These days, all research in the UK is subject to very strict ethical controls. Researchers wishing to use animals must go through a demanding process of applying for a licence to do so. The welfare of animals is important in a laboratory setting since the responses of psychologically healthy animals are of much more use to researchers than those of terrified or traumatised animals. So it is in the interest of the teams conducting the work to keep the animals carefully and in good condition. How psychologists maintain ethically acceptable research is partly through law and partly through guidance from the British Psychological Society (BPS). Professional researchers must submit an outline of their proposed research to a committee who decide whether participants will be harmed in any way. These committees assess the research on the basis of the BPS ethical guidelines. Ethical considerations to include issues of informed consent, deception, debriefing, the right of participants to withdraw, confidentiality and the right of participants to protection from physical and psychological harm. If research is not carried out ethically, researchers risk being expelled from the BPS and so will find it difficult or impossible to conduct research in the future. As a result they risk losing their jobs.

It is almost impossible to conduct psychological research which does not in some way raise an ethical issue. It is important to have methods of dealing with such issues, should they arise. Researchers may for example deal with deception by informing participants of the true nature of the study after they have taken part and then offering them the chance to withdraw any information gathered as a result of their participation. Ultimately, psychologists must ask themselves whether, in their research, the ends justify the means. By this we mean that all research using human or non-human animals must be considered in terms of the value of the results when compared to the cost (both moral and financial) of carrying out the work. If chimpanzees are subjected to research with drugs and possibly surgery, and the result is a cure for cancer, then many would say that the means (experimenting with chimpanzees) are justified, or made acceptable, by the ends (the cure to a horrible and often lethal disease). It could be argued that if the Russians had not sent Laika the dog into space in 1957 we might not have a space shuttle and all the technological benefits that space research has brought; and if Pavlov and Skinner had not conducted research with animals we might not understand the principles of learning as well as we now do.

THE NATURE AND NURTURE DEBATE

What's more important – what you are born with or what you learn during your development?

The two sides of the argument are summed up in the words *nature* and *nurture*.

The nature part of the debate refers to those of our abilities, strengths, weaknesses and characteristics that are determined by our genes. These are the characteristics that we inherit from our parents, and are determined not by our experiences but by our biology. People who strongly support the nature argument are called 'nativists' and in psychology we can identify a number of 'nativist' approaches. The clearest of them are those that argue for a genetic basis for behaviour, such as evolutionary and biological explanations. Biological approaches are those that explain behaviour in term of genes, hormones and brain structure, which are not due to environmental influences.

The nurture part of the debate refers to the influence of our experiences after we are born. These influences may be both physical (and refer to the environments in which we live), and social (referring to our interactions with those around us). Supporters of the nurture argument are described as 'empiricists'. Empiricists say that our characteristics are shaped by our experience. The most typical empiricist argument is expressed by those who take the extreme view that behaviour is purely a result of the environment. An example of this is behaviourism (or learning theory), which says that everything we are and everything we know is learned through conditioning.

We see this nature/nurture argument repeatedly in psychology. For example, in developmental psychology there is a debate about whether our biology and genetics or our experiences after birth are most important in the formation of our attachment bonds. On the one hand there is the evolutionary approach, which argues that attachment is instinctive; whilst on the other we have the view of learning theory, which suggests that attachments are conditioned.

The nativist and empiricist approaches, of course, represent extremes. In reality most psychologists take an interactionist view and accept that behaviour is influenced by *both* nature *and* nurture. As can be seen in the important influence of culture on attachment and the differences in attachment types, a full understanding of attachment can only be achieved through consideration of both views. The debate in psychology is about the *relative* contribution of nature and nurture, not whether something is exclusively due to one or the other. It is limiting to describe behaviour solely in terms of either nature or nurture, and attempts to do this underestimate the complexity of human behaviour.

For instance, Bandura would say that we know how to be aggressive because we learn, from watching others be aggressive. Similarly, we know that some behaviours are acceptable and others are not, because we learn from watching other people behave: we learn that we are rewarded if we do good or acceptable things, and that we are punished if our actions are bad or unacceptable. In short, behaviourists argue that we are what we are because we have learned from our experiences to be that way.

GENDER BIAS

If research is biased towards men or women, it does not provide a clear view of the behaviour that has been studied. A dominantly male perspective is known as an *andocentric* bias, and this can have two forms. An *alpha-bias* is an andocentric bias in which the differences between males and females are exaggerated and so stereotypically male and female characteristics may be emphasised. Freud's theory, for example, can be considered to have an alpha-bias. A *beta-bias* is seen when the differences between males and females are minimised so that only the male view is considered and applied to both genders. This means that life experiences which are unique to female experience are ignored.

In psychology, gender biases can also arise because of the way the research has been carried out. An example of this is where an entirely male sample of participants is generalised to the whole population, including females. There are many examples of this in psychology, such as the research of Asch, Milgram and Zimbardo, who never tested females. Some psychologists would argue that methodological biases are also found in the techniques used in psychology. 'Male preferred' techniques include carefully controlled and manipulated experimental methods. Females, however, prefer a less controlled, person-centred approach, such as interviews, where results come from personal participation and experience.

The way in which the research is reported is also important. For instance, Bowlby's work on maternal deprivation implies that women should remain at home and look after children or risk maternal deprivation and long-term problems. The way in which the results of research are used and applied can also be influential with respect to gender bias. Maternal deprivation research for example might have been used to encourage new mothers not to return to work, so increasing gender inequality in society. When considering articles for publication, editors of scientific journals prefer data that show differences between groups. A finding where a difference is not found is called a *null-result* and data which show this are usually not published. This means that research that reveals a difference between men and women is much more likely to be published than research that finds no difference.

We may ask, however, whether any action to reduce gender bias is necessary, and indeed, whether gender bias is a problem at all. Maccoby and Jacklin (1974) investigated the problem of gender differences in research and found that in most areas there was no gender bias. It would therefore be wrong to assume that all research has a gender bias. There are real differences between the way men and women perform on certain tasks, but these are mostly quite subtle and appear after averaging a lot of data. Maccoby and Jacklin show that women generally perform better on verbal tasks, and men on visual and spatial tasks. Schaffer (1999) says that women are more emotionally sensitive than men. An emphasis on these differences, rather than stereotypical ones, might help to clarify the real differences and similarities in the sexes.

The subtle differences that do exist between men and women may be exaggerated, to support the view that men and women are very different from one another. This encourages gender bias and can be used to maintain the gender supremacy of men in powerful positions in society. For instance, data suggesting that women are unreliable and relatively expensive to employ because they miss work due to problems of menstruation, pregnancy and childcare may not be challenged by research. To do so would threaten the position of the mainly male workforce.

CULTURAL BIAS

Culture can be described as all the knowledge and values shared by a society. Cultures may differ from one another in many ways, so that the findings of psychological research conducted in one culture may not apply directly to another. For example, research produced in *individualistic* cultures may be designed, analysed and interpreted differently from research carried out in *collectivist* cultures. An individualist culture is one where importance is placed on individual achievement, whereas a collectivist one is where there is an emphasis on the social group above the individual.

Ethnocentric approaches to research can result in ethnocentric bias. Such a bias occurs where a culture is judged and assessed in terms of the norms of another culture. This can exaggerate differences between cultures and lead to a distorted view of their differences. Similarly, an ethnocentric bias may arise because most research (approximately two thirds of all psychological research in the world) is carried out in North America. If we base our understanding of human nature and human behaviour on this body of research alone without assessing other cultures our view will be biased towards the behaviour of North Americans. These ethnocentric biases limit the validity of research findings. Similarly, the vast majority of research carried out involves white North American or European participants, with less than 5% of participants being from other cultures. The results may well reflect this bias and so limit the validity of the findings for other ethnic groups. The antidote to ethnocentrism is *cultural relativism*, which is an approach to treating each culture as unique and worthy of study.

The *etic/emic* distinction should be considered when thinking about cultural bias. *Etic* refers to the study of a culture from the perspective of another culture. For instance, studying Eastern cultures from a Western vantage point can cause a distorted view and reduced validity of findings. An example of this is the application of the Strange Situation to measure attachment in infants. Based on data from this test one might come to an erroneous negative conclusion about the child-rearing skills of Japanese parents since they seem to produce so many infants with insecure attachments. The concepts underlying the Strange Situation however are rooted in a Western perspective – it is an idea reflecting ideals and norms of Western culture, so must be treated with caution in cultures other than this.

An *emic* approach refers to the investigation of a culture from within the culture itself. This means that research of European society from a European perspective is emic, and African society by African researchers in Africa is also emic. An emic approach is more likely to have ecological validity as the findings are less likely to be distorted or caused by a mismatch between the cultures of the researchers and the culture being investigated. An example of an etic approach which produces bias might be the imposition of IQ tests designed within one culture on another culture. If a test is designed to measure a European's understanding of what intelligence is it may not be a valid measure of an African's, or Asian's intelligence. An emic approach would be to design a test specific to the culture being tested to provide more validity to the research method used and therefore more ecological validity to the findings. Studies of attachment which have taken an emic approach have reduced the cultural bias in the Strange Situation by adjusting it for use within specific cultures. Rothbaum et al (2007) for example introduced the uniquely Japanese concept of amae into his revamped version of the Strange Situation which also does not involve separation of the mother and infant.

Culturally biased research nonetheless has been common in psychology, not least because the vast majority of research is carried out in the West. The consequences of cultural bias are far reaching, and ultimately only serve to exaggerate cultural differences and misunderstandings.

DETERMINISM AND FREE WILL

The free will / determinism debate revolves around the extent to which our behaviour is the result of forces over which we have no control or whether people are able to decide for themselves whether to act or behave in a certain way. A deterministic view is one which describes behaviour as not being under the control of the individual. A determinist point of view would say that behaviour is 'determined' by external and internal forces – that is, by the environment and by our biology. If something is not under our control, it is determined by something else. If something is automatic, it is not under our control. One of the most radical determinists was Skinner, who said that we do not have free will at all. Instead, behaviours are determined by our learning experiences, that is, what we are is a result of an accumulation of conditioned responses. Another example of a deterministic approach would be explanations which focus on the role of genetics in mental illness.

By arguing that humans can make free choices, the free will approach appears to be quite the opposite of the deterministic one. Psychologists who take the free will view suggest that determinism removes freedom and dignity, and devalues human behaviour. By creating general laws of behaviour, deterministic psychology underestimates the uniqueness of human beings and their freedom to choose their own destiny.

There are important implications for taking either side in this debate. Deterministic explanations for behaviour reduce individual responsibility. A person arrested for a violent attack for example might plead that they were not responsible for their behaviour – it was due to their upbringing, a bang on the head they received earlier in life, recent relationship stresses, or a psychiatric problem. In other words, their behaviour was *determined*. The deterministic approach also has important implications for psychology as a science. Scientists are interested in discovering *laws* which can then be used to predict events. This is very easy to see in physics, chemistry and biology. As a science, psychology attempts the same thing – to develop laws, but this time to predict behaviour. If we argue against determinism, we are in effect rejecting the scientific approach to explaining behaviour.

Studying human behaviour presents psychologists with a problem not shared by the natural sciences – that is, the unpredictability of its subject matter. Human behaviour appears to be only *somewhat* predictable. If you visit a shopping centre then you can be confident that, as long as other people play their roles, the experience will be unremarkable – it is predictable. There are occasions, however, when events do not follow this script, and you see someone behaving in a surprising (i.e. unpredictable) way. The vast complexity of human behaviour means that psychologists can never offer a complete explanation for behaviour which is 100% certain. This means that behaviour is not *absolutely* determined, and also means that it is not random and entirely unpredictable either. Clearly, a pure deterministic or free will approach does not seem appropriate when studying human behaviour. Most psychologists use the concept of free will to express the idea that behaviour is not a passive reaction to forces, but that individuals actively respond to internal and external forces. The term *soft determinism* is often used to describe this position, whereby people do have a choice, but their behaviour is always subject to some form of biological or environmental pressure.

REDUCTIONISM

Reductionism is the belief that human behaviour can be explained by breaking it down into smaller component parts. Reductionists say that the best way to understand why we behave as we do is to look closely at the very simplest parts that make up our systems, and use the simplest explanations to understand how they work.

Behaviourists such as Skinner explain all behaviour as being a result of past learning. The relationships between stimuli and our responses to them are the basis for all we know and how we behave. This is a reductionist view because complex behaviour is being reduced to a simple stimulus and response relationship. We might also consider the biological approach to abnormality as reductionist. The biological approach says that psychological problems can be treated like a disease and so are often treatable with drugs. Identifying the source of someone's mental illness as an imbalance of chemicals in the brain is being reductionist.

Reductionism operates at different *levels*. The lowest level of reductionism offers physiological explanations: these attempt to explain behaviour in terms of neurochemicals, genes and brain structure. At the highest socio-cultural level, explanations focus on the influence on behaviour of where and how we live. Between these extremes there are behavioural, cognitive and social explanations.

Supporters of a reductionist approach say that it is scientific. Breaking complicated behaviours down

to small parts means that they can be scientifically tested. Then, over time, explanations based on scientific evidence will emerge. However, some would argue that the reductionist view lacks validity. For instance, we can see how the brain responds to particular musical sounds by viewing it in a scanner, but how you *feel* when you hear certain pieces of music is not something a scanner can ever reveal. Just because a part of the brain that is connected with fear is activated while listening to a piece of music does not necessarily mean that you *feel* afraid. In this case, being reductionist is not a valid way of measuring feelings. It is also argued that reductionist approaches do not allow us to identify *why* behaviours happen. For example, they can explain that running away from a large dog was made possible by our fear centres causing a stress response to better allow us to run fast, but the same reductionist view cannot say *why* we were afraid of the dog in the first place. In effect, by being reductionist we may be asking smaller, more specific questions and therefore not addressing the bigger issue of why we behave as we do.

It has been suggested that the usefulness of reductionist approaches depends on the purpose to which they are put. For example, investigating brain response to faces might reveal much about how we recognise faces, but this level of description should not perhaps be used to explain human attraction. Likewise, whilst we need to understand the biology of mental disorders, we may not fully understand the disorder without taking account of social factors which influence it. Thus, whilst reductionism is useful, it can lead to incomplete explanations.

Interactionism is an alternative approach to reductionism, focusing on how different levels of analysis interact with one another. It differs from reductionism since an interactionist approach would not try to understand behaviour from explanations at one level, but as an interaction between different levels. So for example, we might better understand a mental disorder such as depression by bringing together explanations from physiological, cognitive and socio-cultural levels. Such an approach might usefully explain the success of drug therapies in treating the disorder; why people with depression think differently about themselves and the world; and why depression occurs more frequently in particular populations.

Biological rhythms and sleep

ROB LEWIS

You are expected in the examination to show both the skills of knowledge and understanding and the skills of analysis and evaluation in relation to the topic Biological rhythms and sleep.

Where opportunities for their effective use arise, you will need to demonstrate an appreciation of issues and debates. These include the nature/nurture debate, ethical issues in research, free-will/determinism, reductionism, gender and culture bias, and the use of animals in research.

You will also need to demonstrate an understanding of How Science Works. You can do this through the effective use of studies in your answer (as description or evaluation) or where appropriate by evaluating methodology and findings.

WHAT YOU NEED TO KNOW

BIOLOGICAL RHYTHMS

- Circadian, ultradian and infradian rhythms, including the role of endogenous pacemakers and of exogenous zeitgebers
- The consequences of disrupting biological rhythms, e.g. shift work, jet lag

SLEEP STATES

- The nature of sleep
- Functions of sleep, including restoration theory and evolutionary explanations
- Lifespan changes in sleep

DISORDERS OF SLEEP

- Explanations for insomnia, including primary and secondary insomnia and factors influencing insomnia, e.g. apnoea, personality
- Explanations for other sleep disorders, including narcolepsy and sleepwalking

BIOLOGICAL RHYTHMS

CIRCADIAN, ULTRADIAN AND INFRADIAN RHYTHMS

The body has rhythms of many different frequencies. Some rhythms may last only milliseconds, such as those found in individual nerve cells, whilst others may last minutes or hours, such as in changes to core body temperature. These biological rhythms that happen more than once every 24 hours are called *ultradian rhythms*. Many of the most observable rhythms are those that recur on a daily basis. Rhythms that run to a 24 hour cycle, such as sleep and waking, are called *circadian rhythms*. When rhythms occur less than once in every 24 hours they are known as *infradian rhythms*, for example the monthly menstrual cycle in women and the seasonal migration of some animals.

Quite how these rhythms are controlled is still a matter of research and debate. These time keeping systems are assumed to be controlled by endogenous (internal) pacemakers, which are in turn influenced to a greater or lesser degree by exogenous (external) cues, sometimes called zeitgebers (from the German 'time-giver'). Endogenous pacemakers and exogenous zeitgebers interact in often complex and obscure ways to synchronise the many biological rhythms.

ASK AN EXAMINER

"You are expected to know about the role of endogenous pacemakers and exogenous zeitgebers in the various rhythms. They are referred to in the individual sections that follow. Remember, any clue to time which comes from the environment is exogenous, whilst any kind of biology is endogenous."

CIRCADIAN RHYTHMS

It is often assumed that, other than for very obvious things like sleep, we remain basically the same throughout the day. However, many of our behaviours, cognitions and aspects of physiology change, or modulate, over a 24 hour cycle. These cycles that take about 24 hours to complete are called circadian rhythms, after the Latin circa dies ('about one day'). This appears to be the case for all organisms, from humans to bacteria, and from plants to fungi. All organisms are exposed to fluctuations in light and dark in an alternating 24 hour rhythm because of the rotation of the Earth, and this has a profound effect on them.

There are many circadian rhythms in human behaviour, and whilst some, like the sleep and wake cycle, are obvious and unavoidable, others are subtle and go unnoticed (e.g. temperature, hormone secretion). These, like the rhythms in other animal species, have evolved to cope with 24 hour rhythms in the environment. Animals which lose the ability to adjust to such natural cycles do not survive as long as those that can adjust. For example, DeCoursey and Krulas (1998) found that chipmunks that had had their endogenous clock surgically damaged so that they lost their normal rest–activity cycles were more prone to predation in the wild.

That many circadian rhythms are controlled endogenously has been established by observations of organisms kept in constant environmental conditions, since the cycles continue in the absence of exogenous cues. In order to examine the nature of human internal clocks, a number of studies have attempted to isolate individuals from all exogenous cues that might indicate time. Some research has involved people spending extended periods in continuously lit cave chambers. Going deep into caves has the advantage of reducing the impact of geomagnetic and electromagnetic influences that also fluctuate on a daily basis. Possibly the most famous study of this kind was conducted by French cave explorer Michel Siffre. He spent three lengthy periods isolated underground, in 1962, 1972 and finally in 2000. The longest was his 1972 stay in Midnight Cave, Texas which lasted 205 days. Whilst he could choose to illuminate his living quarters when he wanted, he had no way of knowing the time in the outside world. Researchers studying his progress found that at first his sleep pattern was erratic but soon settled into a regular free-running rhythm, whilst his day shifted to 25 hours in length.

A more controlled series of studies has been conducted by Jürgen Aschoff and colleagues at the Max Planck Institute in Germany. In one study they had participants spend up to a month living in specially designed underground laboratories. These 'bunkers' were built to shield participants from any external influence which might affect their daily rhythms, including time of day. Participants were allowed to sleep or engage in any activity they wanted. It was noted that the participants kept a regular cycle of activity, confirming the idea of an internal biological clock. However, their cycles soon began to drift. After about two weeks, participants were found to be half a day out of synchrony with the outside world. This is because our body's natural rhythm is around 25 hours, not 24. This means that after one day without knowing the time participants went to bed an hour later, then the next day two hours, and so on. After 25 days in such an environment a participant will have had the psychological experience of 24 days. Whilst the sleep–wake cycle is maintained, it becomes 'free-running' – that is, it is not bound to the 24 hour light–dark cycle.

Further research has suggested that the lighting used in these studies artificially lengthens circadian rhythms, and the actual free-running rhythm is closer to 24.2 hours (Lavie, 2000). In any case, it seems clear that the endogenous body clock tends to run to only an approximate 24 hour day and because of this requires a daily adjustment to the light–dark cycle by some external zeitgeber in order to entrain (reset) it to the natural environment. It appears though that even in free-running conditions endogenous clocks are incredibly accurate. Richter (1968) recorded the rest–activity cycles of a blinded squirrel monkey for over three years. Whilst its cycles became 'free-running' the rest–activity cycles themselves varied by only a few minutes during this time.

"Remember to note any references to endogenous and exogenous factors – you may need to make explicit reference to them in the exam!"

The vital importance of light as an exogenous zeitgeber can be seen in the circadian rhythms of totally blind individuals. Because light does not reach the circadian clock in the brain, the internal pacemaker runs in and out of synchrony with the 24 hour day. Consequently, many behavioural rhythms become desynchronised, such as the sleep–wake cycle, temperature and hormonal rhythms, and cycles of alertness. The majority of blind people thus suffer from non-24 hour sleep–wake disorder, which is characterised by disrupted sleep cycles and excessive day naps (Skene et al, 1999).

The search for the location of an internal 'body clock' began in earnest in the 1960s. One of the pioneers was Curt Paul Richter. In 1967 he reported having succeeded in eliminating certain rhythmic behaviours by lesioning (damaging) the front part of the hypothalamus in the brains of laboratory rats. It was Stephan and Zucker (1972), however, who discovered a specific region of the hypothalamus as the site of the circadian clock. They found that lesions to a group of cells called the suprachiasmatic nucleus (SCN) affected a number of circadian rhythms in rats, including hormone secretion and drinking and wheel-running.

Moore (1973) discovered the crucial link between the SCN and its primary zeitgeber, light, by identifying a neural pathway from the eyes to the SCN. It was this route that provides the light information which entrains the cells in the SCN to fluctuations of light and dark. Subsequent research discovered that light–dark information is perceived by specialised photoreceptors in the retina and it is this information which is passed directly to the SCN.

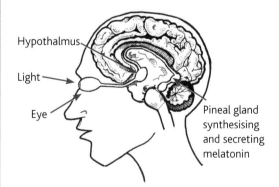

The brain indicating the light pathways from the eyes to hypothalamus, and the pineal gland.

That the SCN has a rhythm of its own which is entrained by zeitgebers was demonstrated in a study by Inouye and Kawamura (1979). They kept animal SCN tissue alive in an organ culture so that it was isolated from all other brain activity and found that, even in the absence of light information from the eyes, the SCN tissue continued to exhibit circadian rhythms.

One of the most important studies of the role of the SCN was conducted by Ralph et al (1990). They took the SCN from a golden hamster (the tau mutant) which had a circadian rhythm which was mutated to a shortened 20.2 hours, and transplanted it into another hamster with a normal 24 hour circadian rhythm which had had its SCN removed to make it arrhythmic. They found that, on recovery, the recipient exhibited a circadian rhythm very similar to that of the donor. This change in rhythm could only be attributed to the transplanted SCN. Further research suggested that individual cells in the SCN could sustain circadian rhythms. Welsh et al (1995) found that there was substantial variation in the rhythms maintained by individual cells, ranging from 21.25 to 26.25 hours. According to Liu et al (1997) the circadian rhythm seen in animal behaviour corresponds to the average rhythm across large numbers of SCN cells.

There is some debate about how individual cells communicate and synchronise their oscillations with those of other cells. According to Maywood et al (2006), a hormone called vasoactive intestinal polypeptide (VIP) might be important for establishing synchrony. Circadian rhythms in substantial numbers of SCN cells are either abolished or desynchronised in mice which are deficient in VIP. Kept in constant conditions, they show abnormal behavioural activity rhythms.

ASK AN EXAMINER

"Don't be put off by a few biological terms. There are lots in psychology – after all, humans are biological organisms and much of our behaviour is dictated by our biology. A little effort and patience getting used to scientific language will pay off."

Research with a number of animal species suggests that circadian oscillators are not restricted to structures in the central nervous system, but may also exist in peripheral organs. It has been suggested that an important function of the SCN is to maintain synchrony between these peripheral oscillators. A widely accepted view is that the SCN is entrained by exogenous light zeitgebers and, from its position at the top of a 'circadian hierarchy', it uses neural and hormonal signals to entrain the various peripheral, or 'organ', clocks.

However, whilst the SCN does seem to perform a coordinating role for some rhythms, research suggests that the peripheral oscillators are more than just responsive slaves. Stokkan et al (2001) showed that cells in the liver keep time independently of those in the SCN. They kept rats in continuous darkness, but only fed them for a restricted period each day. They found that a four hour restricted feeding regime shifted the rhythm of liver cell oscillators by up to ten hours within two days. The SCN remained unaffected by this feeding regime and maintained a rhythm related to the light cycle. This suggests that the circadian oscillators in the liver which are entrained by feeding are separate from those in the SCN entrained by light.

Whilst a principal circadian pacemaker has been found in the brains of many species, it is not always restricted to the SCN. For example, the circadian clock appears to be located in the optic lobes of the cockroach and the cricket (Page, 1982). In aplysia (or sea slugs) however, the ciracdian pacemaker appears to be located in the retina. There are even some species where, as yet, no central clock has been found. For example, Cahill (2002) points out that whilst many cells and tissues of the zebrafish contain circadian clocks, there appears to be no central clock in this animal.

It seems that the SCN does not work alone in keeping biological time. Research has discovered that the SCN has important connections to

THE CIRCADIAN RHYTHM OF MELATONIN

Whilst other rhythms such as changes in core body temperature have been taken as key indicators of a circadian clock, according to Klerman et al (2002) the most reliable circadian indicator is dim light melatonin onset (DLMO). Released by the pineal gland in the brain, the hormone melatonin is suppressed by light. It is nearly absent during the daytime, but concentrations begin to rise in the evening with dimming light (the DLMO phase of the circadian cycle). Levels of melatonin stay fairly constant throughout the night, as long as it remains dark – research shows that even normal room light can suppress melatonin (Boivin and James, 2002). Levels of melatonin decline towards the time of natural waking. The point of decline is known as DLMOoff, and is another conspicuous aspect of the circadian cycle of melatonin. The morning light suppresses melatonin and the cycle starts over.

PHOTORECEPTORS IN THE POPLITEAL REGION

According to Campbell and Murphy (1998), whilst mammals have evolved a preference for the eyes as a source of light information, there remain vestiges of our distant ancestral past when other, non-visual, systems were used.

Taking place in a sleep laboratory with artificial lighting, their study involved 15 healthy volunteer participants taking part in 33 trials, each lasting four consecutive days and nights. At each trial, participants were randomly assigned to the control or experimental condition. On the second night of each trial, experimental participants had light shone on the popliteal region (backs of their knees) for three hours. This area of the body was chosen because it has a rich blood supply. Participants in the control condition had exactly the same experience except that they did not receive the light. Compared to a control group, the core body temperature and melatonin levels of test participants consistently shifted by as much as three hours. They suggest that light sensitive substances in the blood such as haemoglobin have an influence in the production of melatonin.

This research was hailed at the time as a top scientific discovery with life-transforming potential. Based on this, a number of circadian sleep disorder patents were registered. For example, one was for a chair which illuminated the knees during flight in order to combat the effects of jet lag. Another patent involved exposing any non-ocular region of the body to intense bright light in order to enhance alertness and performance.

There are a number of problems with this study however. The results could have been confounded by participants being exposed to light whilst the knee was illuminated. Also, changes in melatonin were not recorded in control participants for comparison. In a follow-up study, contrary to predictions, Campbell and Murphy (2000) were unable to produce phase shifts in sleeping participants by using light in this way. In a replication of this study which eliminated the confounding variables in the Campbell and Murphy (1998) study, Wright and Czeisler (2002) could find no changes in melatonin levels. It seems that there is insufficient evidence to support the argument that, in humans, light signals can be carried in the blood supply from the knees to the brain, thus influencing the body's circadian rhythm. Indeed, few if any researchers in the field now take the idea seriously.

another part of the brain called the pineal gland. The pineal gland regulates the manufacture and release of a hormone called melatonin, an important hormone which helps to control sleep cycles. Light information travels from the photoreceptors in the eyes to the SCN, and then travels along a pathway to the pineal gland. In this way, light influences the release of melatonin from the pineal gland. Melatonin is secreted during darkness, making us sleepy, peaking at around 3 a.m. in a normal night's sleep. During daylight the level of melatonin is at its lowest, its release being inhibited by light signals to the pineal gland. Thus, levels of melatonin rise and fall through the day in a circadian cycle, governed by the exogenous zeitgeber, light.

Whilst light is an important zeitgeber, its influence is not restricted to the eyes. There is substantial evidence showing that a wide range of animal species have specialised non-visual photoreceptors. For example, mice selectively bred to be blind and non-responsive to light can be entrained to a light–dark cycle (Foster et al, 1991). Cells sensitive to light appear throughout the body of many animals. Liu et al (1997) removed the head of a fruit fly and found that circadian cycles continued in the body for up to three days, suggesting that the head and brain did not contain the sole circadian clocks. Yang et al (1998) found that they could influence the circadian rhythm of fruit flies that had been selectively bred to have no eyes, whilst Weber (1995) found that cells sensitive to light within the skin of cockroach legs serve as a circadian clock.

ULTRADIAN RHYTHMS

Ultradian rhythms are those that have cycles which last less than 24 hours. There are many ultradian cycles, the majority occurring without our noticing them, such as temperature regulation, hormone secretion and heart rate. Ultradian rhythms are very largely under endogenous control, although everyday observation clearly indicates exogenous influence. For example, probably the most obvious ultradian rhythm we have is the rhythm of sleep. As will be discussed later in this chapter, sleep rhythms are certainly controlled by endogenous pacemakers. However, body heat seems to one factor that influences this rhythm, either that generated (endogenously) through our own thermo-regulation or (exogenously) by the environment. This might be why hot days and warm baths make us sleepy, and sometimes change the quality of our sleep.

The ultradian rhythm of REM/NREM sleep

Sleep is part of a general circadian cycle, dictated by an internal biological clock influenced by exposure to light – we sleep at night and are awake during the daytime. Sleep however also has its own identifiable ultradian rhythm. The two basic sub-phases of sleep which make up this rhythm are REM (rapid eye movement) and NREM (non-rapid eye movement). When we first go to sleep we enter the first of four stages of NREM sleep. Stages 3 and 4 of NREM together are known as slow-wave sleep (SWS). After about 20 minutes in SWS we enter REM sleep. For the remainder of the night, sleep shifts between these two phases of sleep in an approximate 90 minute cycle. The first bout of REM sleep might last 20 to 30 minutes, before a switch to 60 to 70 minutes of SWS making up the 90 minute cycle. As the night's sleep progresses, SWS gets shorter, with the REM stage getting longer but still maintaining the 90 minute cycle, so that a later cycle might consist of 30 to 40 minutes of REM and 50 to 60 minutes of SWS. By the morning awakening, a typical night's sleep of eight hours might have contained five cycles of NREM and REM sleep.

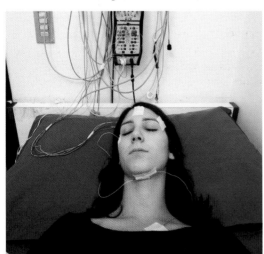

Ultradian sleep rhythms being monitored by electroencephalogram (EEG).

The regularity of the 90 minute cycle suggests that there must a brain mechanism alternately causing REM and NREM. A considerable body of research has established that this endogenous switching mechanism is in the brain stem. It has been shown that destruction of an area just below a structure called the locus coeruleus in the brain stem of cats would permanently destroy their REM sleep (Jouvet, 1972). Since then, technological advances have allowed more selective destruction of neurons in this area, and as a result it is now thought that cholinergic cells in this area in particular are critical for REM sleep ('cholinergic' means that they use the neurotransmitter *acetylcholine*). This is supported by research which shows that the loss of REM sleep is proportionate to the number of cholinergic cells destroyed (Webster and Jones, 1988).

The REM/NREM ultradian cycle is thought to be generated by the contrasting activities of REM-on and REM-off cells in the pontine reticular formation of the brain stem (Hobson et al, 1975). REM-off cells include groups of monoaminergic cells (that is, cells which use monoamine neurotransmitters) located in the locus coeruleus and raphe nuclei, which are most active when awake. The activity of these REM-off cells inhibits the activity of REM-on cells.

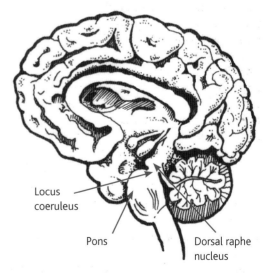

Locus coeruleus

Pons

Dorsal raphe nucleus

As a person falls asleep, the REM-off cells' activity declines, reducing the level of inhibition which is preventing the firing of REM-on cells. The decline in activity of REM-off neurons is thought to be caused by the release from nearby cells of the neurotransmitter GABA, although other factors are certain to contribute. As REM-on cells become disinhibited, they increase their activity.

This disinhibition is associated with an increase in the firing of cholinergic neurons. It is this activity which leads to the various manifestations of REM sleep, for example rapid eye movements and loss of muscle tone. The increase in cholinergic activity triggered by REM-on cells in turn eventually contributes to the inhibition of REM-on cells by monoaminergic neurotransmitters. REM sleep is thus terminated and NREM sleep returns.

The Basic Rest Activity Cycle (BRAC)

Based on his observation that infant feeding intervals coincided with REM sleep cycles, Kleitman (1961) proposed a basic rest activity cycle (BRAC). This theory assumes that the 90 minute REM/NREM cycle that occurs during sleep continues over the 24 hours of the day and includes arousal and behavioural activity of the waking person. In effect, the REM/NREM cycle is the nocturnal fragment of a 24 hour BRAC. Kleitman actually speculated that the BRAC might actually be a feeding rhythm. This notion received some support from a study which found greater gastric secretions during REM than NREM sleep (Kales and Tan, 1969) and from Friedman and Fischer (1967), who found 90–120 minute cycles of 'oral' waking behaviour, such as eating, drinking and smoking. Hiatt and Kripke (1975) inflated balloons in the stomachs of fasting participants in order to measure gastric contractions. They found a clear ultradian rhythm over an eight hour period of measurement. For them, this was further evidence of an oral cycle.

However, subsequent research failed to find a relationship between REM/NREM cycles and gastric contractions. Furthermore, 60–90 minute gastric contraction rhythms have been found in dogs, sheep and rabbits, all of which have REM/NREM cycles of 20–30 minutes (Grivel and Ruckebusch, 1967). It seems as though the earlier studies found a gastric ultradian cycle, but in error associated it with REM/NREM and thus a BRAC cycle. These two cycles clearly have separate origins.

There was also support for Kleitman's idea that the BRAC would be seen in fluctuations of daytime arousal. Kripke and Sonnenschein (1978) found 90–120 minute cycles in vivid daydreaming, and Lavie (1979) found evidence for fluctuations in alertness and people's ability to fall asleep. Participants attempting to fall asleep every 20 minutes showed a rhythm of stage 1 sleep approximately every 100 minutes. Okudaira et al (1983), however, could find no evidence of 90–100 minute rhythms in their study. They had ten healthy participants wear apparatus for monitoring skeletal

motor activity in their wrists, ankles and forehead for 24 hours. They concluded that whilst there may be cycles in other aspects of functioning, one does not exist in levels of bodily activity.

Neubauer and Freudenthaler (1994) searched for an ultradian rhythm in human cognitive performance. They gave their sixty participants a basic cognitive task every ten minutes for nine hours, and also rated alertness and mood, and measured heart rate during the task. They could not find any evidence for a 90 minute cycle in any variables they measured, and suggest that the BRAC may emerge both from analysis of data and because of the statistical methods used.

Whilst there is evidence to support ultradian cycles in the body during waking (for example, in neurochemical activity and urine flow), no support has emerged for the notion that they have a common BRAC mechanism. It is thought highly unlikely by most researchers that a mechanism controlling REM/NREM cycles could also be governing so many divergent cycles within a general BRAC. Rather than a BRAC, it is generally accepted now that there are a number of rest–activity cycles which are independent of, and at best only partially associated with, the 90 minute REM/NREM cycle.

Ultradian rhythm in neurochemical activity

A number of studies have reported ultradian rhythms in neurochemical activity. Kennedy et al (2002) measured the levels of tryptophan (TRP) and 5-hydroxy indoleacetic acid (5-HIAA) in the cerebrospinal fluid (CSF) of 12 healthy volunteers. Using lumbar puncture, they removed 1ml of fluid for analysis every 10 minutes over a 24 hour period. Accounting for factors like food intake which might affect these chemicals, they found evidence for ultradian rhythms in the concentrations of both TRP and 5-HIAA. Kennedy et al point out that this may have significance for the understanding of mental problems in which these chemicals are implicated. 5-HIAA and TRP for example are essential in the production of the neurotransmitter serotonin. Serotonin is understood to play a role in both the cause and treatment of a range of problems including anorexia, bulimia, obsessive compulsive disorder and depression. Salomon et al (2005) investigated neurochemical ultradian rhythms in people with depression. They took CSF samples from 15 depressed patients at 10 minute intervals for 24 hours before and after anti-depressant treatment. A change in ultradian cycle length of 5-HIAA was observed following treatment, suggesting that abnormal ultradian rhythms are part of the general pathophysiology of depression.

Ultradian rhythm in urine flow

Mandell et al (1966) found evidence of an ultradian rhythm in urine flow. They catheterised seven male participants and measured the urine flow over 11 nights. Because of the catheter, urine would not be held by the bladder but would continuously pass into a measuring container. All periods of REM sleep recorded during this study were associated with changes in urine flow. Within two minutes of the onset of REM sleep the quantity of urine from the catheter decreased. At the end of the REM phase urine flow increased again. They suggest that these changes were a result of changes in renal function associated with REM sleep, in particular, secretion of anti-diuretic hormone (ADH) occurring rhythmically with REM sleep onset and offset. It is possible however that urine flow was altered by changes to bladder tone and compression to the catheter tube caused by penile erection, which occurs during REM sleep. Indeed, Rubin et al (1975) could find no evidence of a correlation between ADH and sleep cycles. Lavie and Kripke (1977) looked for evidence of waking ultradian rhythms in the flow of urine. Avoiding the use of a catheter, they asked their participants to drink a constant set amount of liquid over a ten hour period. Participants were asked to urinate as much as possible every ten minutes. Lavie and Kripke reported a prominent ultradian rhythm of 80 to 133 minutes in the urine flow of their participants, concluding that this was due to a rhythmic secretion of ADH.

INFRADIAN RHYTHMS

As the seasons change so do the lengths of days, and organisms adjust their 24 hour cycles accordingly. These adjusted cycles are greater than 24 hours and are known as infradian rhythms. There are many variations in such biological rhythms. For example, some occur on a monthly cycle, whilst others appear to follow tidal rhythms. Many behaviours appear to have a much longer rhythm, cycling on a seasonal or annual basis.

These are often referred to as circannual rhythms. Pengelley et al (1978) kept golden-mantled ground squirrels under constant 24 hour light and 34°C temperature for three years and measured their body weight, something that normally fluctuates with the seasons. They found that the animals' body weight and food consumption rhythm followed a circannual cycle independent of temperature and light. The free-running nature of the body weight cycle in these ground squirrels suggests that whilst the rhythm is endogenous, exogenous cues such as light and temperature act as important synchronising zeitgebers for the biological clocks.

> **ASK AN EXAMINER**
>
> "This is a biological rhythm clearly under both endogenous and exogenous control – as with the other rhythms, watch for reference to biology and environment and be prepared to mention these factors in an exam answer."

Such seasonal rhythms have been discovered in many animal species. Alexander and Brooks (1999) kept Rinkhal's Spitting Cobra at a constant temperature (25°C) and photoperiod (12 : 12 h, meaning 12 hours' daylight and 12 hours of darkness) for a period of seven years. They found that periods of lowest food acceptance and least likelihood of skin-shedding were during the winter months, as with wild snakes. Since the most likely exogenous cues (light and temperature) were controlled for in these studies, this is good evidence that these seasonal patterns of behaviour are under endogenous control. Some circannual rhythms appear to be clearly associated with particular exogenous zeitgebers. For example, Goss (1977) found that the annual shedding of sika deer antlers was very closely associated with lengthening days. Fawns were kept under controlled light conditions and, whilst the antlers began growing at the usual expected age, they were encouraged to renew half a year early by manipulating the light available to the animal.

> **ASK AN EXAMINER**
>
> "We've been very thorough here, providing you with three examples of infradian rhythms. Two understood really well or three or four used more briefly could get you good marks. We are quite sure that using this section from this book will make you a bit of an expert when it comes to an exam question compared to those that use other textbooks! A question specifically on infradian rhythms could appear in the exam – know your stuff!"

Hibernation

A number of animals that experience a combination of long cold winters and reduced food availability go through periods of reduced feeding and activity, a sort of 'deep sleep', called hibernation. This can last up to seven or eight months, and whilst smaller animals such as the dormouse occasionally 'wake up' and snack, larger ones such as the bear tend to hibernate continuously for up to eight months, living off the fat stores accumulated the previous autumn. Hibernation involves significant changes to bodily functions – for example to kidney function, metabolism, heart rate and circulation. It has been suggested that these changes are guided by hormones, which in turn influence the hibernation processes of preparation, initiation, maintenance, and final arousal.

Some evidence indicates that these hormonal changes are a result of endogenous mechanisms, with the obvious environmental changes to light and temperature associated with periods of hibernation acting as zeitgebers. Such endogenous timers enable animals to anticipate and prepare for the onset of the harsh winter months. Animals which might normally hibernate do not do so if their environment does not give them appropriate cues. Black bears for example inhabit a wide area of North America and only hibernate when resident in the extreme climates of the northern regions. Captive black bears do not hibernate as long as they have a constant food source, but do become less active, sleep more and eat less when the weather becomes cold.

Some of the earliest clear evidence for endogenous factors in hibernation came from Dawe and Spurrier (1968). They transfused blood from hibernating ground squirrels into awake active ones and noted that within 48 hours these active squirrels began hibernating, even though it was spring (a time they would not normally hibernate). Although it hasn't been isolated or analysed, it seems that there is a chemical in the blood of some animals which induces hibernation. This has been called the *hibernation induction trigger* or HIT. One idea is that this substance becomes active when triggered by zeitgebers (e.g. days becoming cooler and shorter), inducing the animal to prepare for hibernation.

Myers et al (1981) demonstrated that HIT can have effects on the behaviour of animals that do not hibernate, such as the Macaque and Rhesus monkey. In one study, Macaque monkeys received, directly into their brains, injections of a substance that had been derived from the blood plasma of hibernating 13-lined ground squirrels. For up to 36 hours afterwards the monkeys exhibited reductions in appetite, heart rate and temperature (typical symptoms of hibernation). Plasma from non-hibernating ground squirrels had no observable effects on the monkeys. It has been suggested that HIT acts like an opiate to suppress the activity of systems in the central nervous system, especially ones which control such things as body temperature and metabolism.

The exact way in which HIT induces hibernation remains unknown, however. Indeed, some researchers have failed to find evidence of effects similar to those of HIT, in other animals. For example, Wang et al (1988) compared the effects of active summer plasma and hibernating plasma derived from Richardson's ground squirrel on the summer hibernation behaviour of both Richardson's and 13-lined ground squirrels. They found that whilst 13-lined ground squirrels readily entered hibernation, the type of injection received – whether plasma, warm saline, or even sham injection – had no effect on either the length or quality of hibernation. In contrast, none of the Richardson's ground squirrels either entered hibernation or showed any other effects from the various types of injection. This study both casts doubt on the existence of blood-borne 'trigger' substances and suggests that responses to such chemicals may only apply to specific species.

Kondo et al (2006) identified another hormone called HP20c, which is found in increased levels in the brain of chipmunks during hibernation. To eliminate the possibility that these increased levels of HP20c were a result of changes in heat and light, they kept chipmunks in a controlled environment of constant temperature and regular 24 hours cycles of day and night. They found that levels of HP20c continued to fluctuate on a seasonal basis, suggesting that they were under circannual endogenous control. Moreover, chipmunks that were unable to increase their levels of HP20c were also unable to lower body temperature in order to initiate hibernation. The researchers suggest that this hormone is a key regulator of hibernation, although so far it has not been found in other hibernating animals.

Seasonal affective disorder (SAD)

Some people experience annual episodes of depression which seem to occur on a seasonal basis, with the problem worse in winter and lessening or disappearing entirely during the spring and summer. This disorder, known as seasonal affective disorder (SAD), is relatively common, being estimated to affect 6%, or 11 million people, in the United States. It is not evenly distributed, however, with rates ranging from 1.4% in the southern state of Florida to over 10% in the more northerly state of Maine. The important factor underlying this dispersion appears to be the decreased amount of daylight in northern latitudes during the winter months compared to the south.

Sufferers of SAD have a number of circadian abnormalities, including sleep disturbance, increases in core body temperature, and disturbances in cortisol and melatonin secretion. Many researchers have pointed to the key part played by the melatonin, since this substance has a role in the seasonal behaviour of many animals. This hormone is only released during the hours of darkness and excess secretions of melatonin during the darker winter months were thought to explain the symptoms of SAD. However, it appears that this may not be the case, since research suggests that people with SAD secrete melatonin normally. It is curious then that SAD is helped by the administration of bright light.

Studies demonstrating the effective treatment of some patients by exposure to bright light are often cited as evidence for the link between light fluctuation and SAD. For example, Eastman et al (1998) treated SAD patients either with bright light (6000 lux) or a placebo. They found that those treated with bright light were more likely to respond with a partial or full remission of symptoms. According to Postolache et al (1998) however, treatment with artificial light does not produce as complete a remission of symptoms as occurs during normal summer time. Despite being given light treatment at least equivalent to that administered in other clinical trials, patients scored higher on measures of depression after light therapy in winter than during the following summer. This may be due

to a number of factors associated with the quality of light, such as light intensity, photoperiod and amount of UV radiation. The researchers also suggest, however, that variables which differ between summer and winter – such as personal finances, temperature and lifestyle (e.g. reduced social contact) – may also have an effect.

Patients with SAD appear to have circadian rhythms which are phase-delayed relative to the light–dark cycle, and this may be the principal cause of the disorder. This is supported by Lewey et al (1998). They suggest that treating patients with a phase advance of light period (i.e. producing a backward shift in the circadian clock by giving patients morning bright light) may be more effective than a phase delay of light (i.e. producing a forward shift in the circadian clock with evening bright light).

The menstrual cycle

The clearest infradian rhythm in human behaviour is the monthly menstrual cycle. The menstrual cycle is a series of physical and hormonal changes that prepare a woman's body for pregnancy. At the beginning of the menstrual cycle, levels of the hormone oestrogen rise, causing the lining of the uterus (also called the endometrium) to thicken. At around the middle of the cycle, ovulation occurs, whereby an egg is released by an ovary. The egg travels down the fallopian tubes to the uterus. If the egg is fertilised it attaches to the uterus and develops: otherwise the thick lining is not needed and it begins to shed in preparation for another chance of pregnancy the following month. This is menstruation, which usually lasts from three to five days. The average menstrual cycle is 28 days from the start of one to the start of the next, although it can range from 21 days to 35 days. The equivalent in other mammals, varying considerably in length according to species, is the oestrous cycle (the differences being that other mammals reabsorb their endometrium).

It is a widespread belief that women who spend an extended time together will synchronise their menstrual cycles. Arden et al (1999) reported that 80% of women in their study believed that synchrony exists, with 70% claiming it to be a pleasant experience. In 1971 Martha McClintock published the results of her research into synchronising menstrual cycles, triggering decades of research and debate. She studied 135 women aged 17 to 22 living in all-female university halls of residence. They were asked to recall previous menstrual periods over the last year, how much time they spent each week in male company, and with the females they considered best friends and had spent most time with. According to McClintock (1971), the menstrual cycles of the women who spent extended time together tended to synchronise.

Weller and Weller (1993) suggest that menstrual synchrony is affected by the closeness of the relationship between women, particularly those who spend prolonged time in each other's company. They found a significant degree of synchrony between mothers and daughters residing in the same home. They have also found greater degrees of menstrual synchrony among women who work together, who share accommodation, among women basketball players, and in lesbian couples.

According to McClintock (1971), synchrony is produced by pheromones. Pheromones are chemicals, detected by olfaction (smell) that trigger certain behaviours. Whilst they appear widespread in animals, there is considerable disagreement about whether human pheromones exist. The first study that directly investigated the influence of pheromones on the menstrual cycle was conducted by Russell et al (1980). They wanted to know if olfactory cues from one woman could influence the timing of menstrual onset of another. They collected odour by placing cotton pads in the armpits of donors for 24 hours. The donors were told not to use deodorants or wash their armpits during this time. This cotton pad, now carrying the odour of perspiration, was then rubbed on the upper lip of participants, who were told not to wash their faces for six hours. This happened three times a week for six months. Russell et al report that participants shifted their menstrual cycles significantly, to resemble the donor's monthly cycle. There have been many subsequent studies like this. In a similar study, Jacob et al (2004) found that the menstrual cycle length of participants could be influenced by exposure to pads odourised in the nursing brassieres of breastfeeding donors.

Whilst the findings of McClintock, and Russell et al, have been replicated and broadly supported by a number of studies, the theory that menstrual cycles can be entrained by pheromones has met with considerable opposition. Wilson (1992) has shown mathematically that menstrual synchrony could in any case be expected to occur in half the cases in a sample studied after three to four cycles, and that claims of apparent synchrony are in fact a result of the research method and techniques used, rather than an accurate observation of menstrual behaviour. He points out major methodological problems with the research he criticises, in that it tends to observe cycles over too short a time, and tends to exclude from data analysis those participants who 'don't fit'. Wilson also argues that apparent increases in synchrony are due to errors in calculating menstrual onset. Apparently, McClintock also used invalid statistical tests, which calls into question the significance of her findings. Wilson asserts that these studies gave an exaggerated image of synchrony because the data were pre-biased towards asynchrony. Furthermore, Schank (2000) points out that some research has also assumed that women basically have the same stable cycle length, whereas in reality it varies considerably, both within and between females.

Many studies directly contradict the theory of menstrual synchrony. In a recent study, and the largest of its kind, Yang and Schank (2006) looked at the occurrence of menstrual cycles in 186 Chinese women living in university accommodation over the course of one year. Avoiding the methodological errors of previous research, they found no evidence beyond chance level that women synchronise their cycles. They suggest that women's perception of synchrony is due to the fact that cycle variability will inevitably lead to repeated cycle convergences, giving the impression of synchrony where none exists.

A number of studies in the 1980s reported oestrous synchrony in animals such as tamarins, rats and chimpanzees. Ravizza and Ray (1980) for example found that a submissive hamster of a pair would synchronise its oestrous cycle to the rhythm of the dominant one. However, efforts to replicate this finding failed, and no other studies since have reported cycle synchronisation in mammals, suggesting that that these earlier studies were flawed in some way. A more recent study by Gattermann et al (2002) kept female golden hamsters living either in groups or in individual separate but connected cages. The usual golden hamster oestrous cycle has an extremely stable four-day length under constant light conditions, and phase shifts are extremely rare. They found no evidence of synchrony in either group of hamsters.

Several evolutionary explanations have been put forward to explain why menstrual synchrony might be advantageous. It has been suggested for example that males with multiple wives would be more able to detect pheromone signals of fertility, thereby increasing the probability of conception in the co-wives. It has also been suggested that menstrual synchrony increases infant survival chances, since new mothers would also have synchronised lactation. They would be able to feed each other's babies and, if a mother died, remaining babies could still be nursed. There is a lack of any firm evidence for these theories, however. Gattermann et al (2002) suggest that asynchronous cycles could be adaptive in some animals. They point out that asynchrony increases the chance of reproductive success in female hamsters. At the beginning of the breeding season in February the population is low because of winter mortality. Males patrol burrows widely, in search of females to mate with. A female stands a better chance of being visited if she has less competition from other (synchronous) females. Thus, asynchrony in this instance is advantageous. It appears that both synchrony and asynchrony may increase reproductive success, depending on whether the animal is social or, like the hamster, enjoys a solitary lifestyle.

CONSEQUENCES OF DISRUPTING BIOLOGICAL RHYTHMS

A person's biological rhythm is naturally synchronised to the light–dark cycle so that activity is largely diurnal. However, our rhythms need to adapt in order to accommodate such things as night working and movement across time zones. Our central and peripheral oscillators however require time in order to adjust to new environmental synchronisers, with the result that for a period there is desynchrony in our biological rhythms. Such circadian phase shifts have potential negative consequences for our health and behaviour.

"You are expected to know several consequences of disrupting rhythms. Jet lag and shift work are covered here in really good detail. Don't choose between them – you should know something about both."

SHIFT WORK
Modern life causes a disruption to natural biological rhythms in many ways. In order to maximise their productivity and profits, many businesses resort to shift work. It is a very common and often unavoidable work practice, with between 15% and 20% of the working population of the US and Europe engaged in shift work in some form. Shift work can be considered any scheduled work

outside the 'normal' daytime hours of 7 a.m. to 7 p.m.: it can be either fixed (for example, regular night, evening or day shift) or rotating (for example, a combination or cycle of these shifts). Whilst there are many different shift work patterns, they have a common effect – they disrupt an individual's biological clock. Basically, the biological clock is designed to prepare the body for activity during daylight and inactivity at night. Shift work disrupts this natural pattern of behaviour so that workers have difficulty establishing a regular circadian rhythm of day–night activity.

Research suggests that some shift work schedules appear to be more disrupting than others. The most taxing ones are those that go against the body's natural inclination to adapt to a longer day of about 25 hours, and those that include night work. Fixed shift work schedules are usually considered best as they allow the body the best chance to adapt to a new rhythm. If shift work schedules are to rotate, however, then it is best if they rotate in a clockwise rather than counter-clockwise direction. The problem with counter-clockwise rotating shifts, especially rapidly rotating ones, is that they cause greatest disruption to circadian rhythms and result in shortened sleep.

Day	Clockwise shift rotation		Counter-clockwise shift rotation	
	Hours at work	Hours to next shift	Hours at work	Hours to next shift
Monday	0600–1400	16	1400–2200	16
Tuesday	0600–1400	24	1400–2200	8
Wednesday	1400–2200	16	0600–1400	16
Thursday	1400–2200	24	0600–1400	8
Friday-Sat	2200–0600	48	2200–0600	80

Adapted from Cruz et al (2003).

Traditionally, shift work changes go in a counter-clockwise direction, but also shift patterns tend to last only between one and two weeks at most before they change. This also causes problems for our internal clocks, since on a traditional eight-hour counter-clockwise shift pattern it would take approximately sixteen days for the body to adjust. In effect, the body never adapts to its current rhythm before it has to readjust to a new one.

Given the opportunity, our biological clocks will eventually adjust to altered patterns of day–night activity. This rarely happens however, even in people on a permanent shift, because the normal pattern of everyday life continues, regardless of shift work. Life goes on as usual for everyone else, with more noise during daytime making relaxation more difficult, and social routines and responsibilities at odds with working hours. Light also causes a problem – it suppresses melatonin production, which is important for sleepiness.

That shift direction and rotation length are important was demonstrated by Czeisler et al (1985). They were asked to devise a new work schedule for police officers in Philadelphia. Officers were reporting significant sleep and work problems as a result of their eight-day counter-clockwise shift rotation. For example, officers working nights were having four times as many accidents as day shift workers. The new schedule devised by Czeisler et al involved a change of rotation length (so that officers spent 18 days on each shift before changing) and a change in shift direction to clockwise. Significant benefits resulted – for example accidents during night shift fell by 40%, and officers reported greater satisfaction in their personal lives.

A range of health problems has been associated with night and rotating shift work, such as hypertension, coronary heart disease and cancer. People who work at night can suffer considerable sleep deprivation. It has been suggested that people who work night shifts experience on average two hours' less sleep a day than those working day shifts. Sleep deprivation has been shown to cause deficits in cognitive and physical performance, and is associated with a range of serious health problems resulting from disrupted metabolism. Research has linked sleep deprivation to problems such as type II diabetes, hypertension, gastro-intestinal complaints, and immune system suppression. Knutsson et al (1999) for example found that night shift work increased the risk of heart attack by 30% compared with that found in day workers. This was the case for both men and women who had been exposed to shift work for 16 to 20 years.

Kubo et al (2006) suggest that people working rotating shifts are particularly vulnerable to cancer. They studied the cancer risk in 14,052 Japanese male workers. Controlling for lifestyle factors such as smoking, alcohol consumption, stress and type of work, they found that men who worked some kind of night shift (with rotating or regular schedules) were four times as likely to develop prostate cancer than men who worked fixed day shifts. However, another recent study contradicts this. In a long-term study of the health of 3.2 million Swedish workers, Schwartzbaum et al (2007) compared the incidence of cancer in occupational groups with at least 40% shift work with that in groups that had less than 30% shift work. The researchers found no relationship between shift

CIRCADIAN RHYTHMS IN SPACE

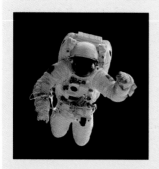

Research has shown that endogenous circadian cycles tend to deviate from a precise 24 hour rhythm and whatever produces these cycles needs regular entrainment from zeitgebers, such as light changes with sunset or sunrise. This poses a particular problem for astronauts on space missions which do not involve geostationary orbit, as in these circumstances the sun rises every 90 minutes. In effect, astronauts experience constant daytime. There are also unique environmental factors in space which might further affect circadian rhythms, such as space motion sickness and weightlessness.

Gundel et al (1993) investigated the experiences of a Russian astronaut on a solo eight day mission. They found clear evidence for a circadian phase delay of 2–3 hours, during the mission, in core body temperature and subjective alertness. However, because the mission only lasted eight days they could not be sure that the phase delay did not mark the beginning of a circadian free-run. In another study, Gundel et al (1997) found evidence for similar phase delay in four astronauts staying aboard the Russian space station MIR. However, they found no evidence of a circadian free-run during the 30 days in space. They suggest that a combination of low-intensity light changes and non-light-related zeitgebers (e.g. clocks) aboard the orbiting spacecraft may have been responsible for synchronising the circadian system to a 24 hour day.

Both studies, however, found evidence of sleep disturbance among the astronauts. Sleep was shorter and more disturbed than on earth, and the structure of REM/non-REM cycles was altered. They speculated that this might be due to a combination of factors, including altered circadian cycles and changes in physical activity due to weightlessness.

work and increased risk of developing cancer. The study has, however, been criticised because of the way that it defined shift work and how it combined many different jobs with different degrees of shift work. This had the effect of 'averaging out' the effects of individual jobs and shift work schedules with particularly high risk.

The Schwartzbaum et al study also contradicts many others which have found a link between cancer and specific occupations. Schernhammer et al (2001) used data gathered as part of a 10 year study following the health of 78,562 US nurses. Accounting for potential confounding variables like alcohol consumption, use of oral contraception, weight, and post-menopausal hormone use, they found that the risk of breast cancer increased significantly with the number of years working rotating night shifts.

If we are to work at night, of course, artificial light is necessary. Exposure to this, however, disrupts a natural rhythm which appears essential for a range of physiological functions. One important hormone which has a very distinct pattern of production is melatonin. It follows a very strict circadian rhythm, with almost all melatonin produced by the pineal gland in the brain when it is dark. Melatonin concentrations in the body normally peak in the middle of the night. Exposure to light, whether natural or artificial, alters the release of melatonin so that almost none is produced. Neither is melatonin quick to recover after disruption. It has been found that it can take over two weeks for levels to recover after night-time light exposure, and even then full recovery only occurs when there has been a period of constant day–night circadian rhythm (Zeitzer et al, 2000).

Those workers with disrupted biological rhythms caused by their shift-working secrete lower levels of melatonin, a hormone which previous research suggests is associated with anti-cancer properties.

It has been proposed that the link between night work and melatonin is mediated by the reproductive hormone oestrogen. Reduction in melatonin leads to increases in levels of a range of hormones, particularly a type of oestrogen called oestradiol. This hormone is responsible for the growth of hormone-sensitive cells in the breast, and elevated levels of oestradiol have been associated with increased risk of breast cancer (Swerdlow, 2003). Schernhammer and Hankinson (2003) point out that blind women, who do not have their melatonin levels suppressed by light, experience a lower incidence of breast cancer. Whilst Spiegel and Sephton (2002) agree that cancer is associated with disruption of biological rhythms, they argue that this association is not due solely to a reduction in melatonin secretion. They suggest that increased risk is actually caused by disruption of diurnal rhythms in the hormone cortisol. Levels of this hormone peak in the early morning and decline through the rest of the day, and the loss of this normal variation, according to Spiegel and Sephton, is related to early death from breast cancer.

JET LAG

Jet lag occurs when normal circadian rhythms are disrupted by travelling across time zones. When we cross time zones there is a shift in zeitgebers, which causes a conflict between external cues (such as light and temperature), and endogenous circadian clocks. Basically, our body is telling us that it is one time, and environmental cues are telling us that it is a different time. Generally, eastward flights (where there has been phase advance of the circadian rhythm, i.e. a backward shift in the 24 hour cycle) cause greater problems than travelling west (where there is phase delay, i.e. a forward shift in the 24 hour cycle). Jet lag is less of a problem when travelling west because the body finds it less dificult adjusting to a slightly longer day than to a slightly shorter one.

GAINING TIME →

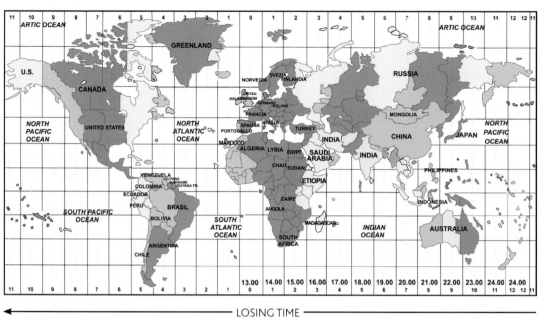

Time zones start at the Prime Meridian (Greenwich, in London) and divide the world into 24 zones: each zone crossed involves a change in time of one hour, either backwards or forwards, depending on the direction of travel.

People with jet lag show a wide range of symptoms, including fatigue, concentration problems, reduced alertness, clumsiness, memory difficulties, and lethargy (Spitzer et al, 1997). One of the main after-effects of jet lag is disturbed sleep, with problems going to sleep after eastward travel and problems with premature waking, having travelled west. The severity of jet lag and the amount of time needed for recovery depend on the direction of flight and the number of time zones covered. A general rule of thumb is that, for each time zone passed, one day of recovery is needed. Recovery from jet lag involves a re-entrainment of the circadian rhythm back to the regular rhythm of daylight and darkness that we are used to. Even though the SCN can readjust and reset its clock within a day, the effects of jet lag can last up to a month because internal clocks, (for example in the lungs, liver and muscles), entrain at different speeds. This means that central and peripheral clocks remain uncoordinated for some time.

Given the range of symptoms, it is often assumed that the effects of jet lag might be most visible in those who might subsequently have to perform activities regardless of the effects of travel. There has been considerable research, for example, into the potential consequences of jet lag on the performance of trained athletes. One of the earliest studies was by Sasaki (1980). He reported on the performance of the Soviet Union volleyball team after travelling to play in Japan. The team lost matches during the first three days but won by increasing margins over the next six. Sasaki put this change down to the re-entrainment of the Soviet team to the Japanese time zone. Such conclusions, however, overlook the influence of individual performance on that of the team, and the varying quality of the opposition. Also, there was no baseline score for comparison. Such methodological problems are very common with research which looks at team performance in this way, making the conclusions drawn about the effects of jet lag unreliable.

Some studies have made retrospective assessment of the impact of jet lag based on accumulated data

← LOSING TIME

of team performance over one or more seasons. For instance, Recht et al (1995) looked at the effects of jet lag on the performance of baseball teams. They studied three complete season records (1991–93) of 19 North American Eastern or Pacific time zone based baseball teams. To play each other these teams would have to travel over three time zones. They found that home teams won 56% of the games, but the chances of winning depended on whether the visiting team had travelled eastward. When this was the case, home teams could also expect to score 1.24 more runs than the visitors. The researchers found no such home field advantage when the visiting team had travelled westward. This is consistent with what might be expected, as jet lag is generally more severe travelling west to east and so should have a greater impact on performance than westward travel. However, these studies also have many flaws. For example, they suffer from problems with the selection of data for analysis; there is a lack of control over the behaviour of team members en route which may affect performance (e.g. alcohol consumption, amount of rest); and they tend to overlook the significant impact on team performance of non-playing individuals like coaches.

A number of studies have looked at the effects of jet lag on individual athletic performance. O'Connor et al (1991) looked at the effects of travelling across four time zones on competitive swimmers. They assessed the swimmers individually on their favourite stroke and could find no significant evidence of a drop in performance that could not be put down to a lack of training due to travel. More recently, Lemmer et al (2002) investigated the performance of thirteen athletes who had travelled westward over six time zones (Frankfurt to Atlanta) and six who had travelled eastward over eight time zones (Munich to Osaka). They found that training performance of all athletes was disturbed by jet lag on the first day after arrival,

with jet lag symptoms persisting until day six for the westward group and day seven for the eastward. Contrary to what might be expected, they found training performance was worst in the first four days for the westward group, although they did suggest that this might be due to the relatively small sample in the eastward group making the data especially vulnerable to individual differences. Overall, it seems that there is a lack of convincing evidence that jet lag significantly impairs athletic performance.

Evidence suggests that chronic jet lag can contribute significantly to the development of cancer – for instance Rafnsson et al (2001). Using data gathered from 1,500 female flight attendants, they found that those who had been flying for over five years had double the risk of breast cancer. Whilst a number of studies support a link between working as flight crew and breast cancer, there is considerable disagreement about the cause. A number of explanations were proposed, including the effects of regularly working at high altitude, flight dehydration, greater exposure to cosmic radiation and magnetic fields, as well as disturbed biological rhythms. A number of studies, however, could find no link at all. For example, Kojo et al (2005) found no increase in risk of breast cancer among cabin attendants that could not be attributed to established risk factors, such as family history of cancer. In their study, there was no clear evidence that disruption of circadian rhythms due to repeated jet lag was linked to breast cancer risk.

Research by Filipski et al (2004) on the other hand provides a potential animal model for the relationship between disrupted biological rhythm caused by jet lag and cancer. They re-created the effects of chronic jet lag in mice by repeatedly phase advancing the light–dark cycle by eight hours every two days. They found that the desynchronised animals experienced accelerated cancer tumour growth, and suggested that this acceleration was caused by uncoordinated central and peripheral circadian clocks. Gauger and Sancar (2005) suggest that it is the role of light rather than rhythm disturbance itself that causes cancer. Light produces a reduction in melatonin level, and it is these low levels of melatonin that are linked to development of cancer. A great deal of research has recorded an association between reduced levels of melatonin and patients suffering from cancer. For example, Blask et al (2005) studied rats xenografted with human breast cancer tissue (xenografting is the technique of grafting tissues from different species). They found that blood collected from human donors during a normal night's sleep (when melatonin is at its highest concentration) had the effect of slowing down cancer cell growth in the rats. On the other hand, blood collected during daytime or during bright light exposure at night did not have this effect.

According to Cho (2001) constant travel across time zones has been found to increase the amount of the stress hormone cortisol in the body. He suggests that these increased cortisol levels caused by repeated jet lag have physical effects on the brain. Participants in his study were 20 healthy women aged 20–28 employed by international airline companies for five years. Half the women had a short jet lag recovery period of less than five days between transmeridian flights that crossed seven time zones. The other half were a long recovery group that had 14 days between transmeridian flights, during which time their flights were short and did not involve large time shifts. All the participants had MRI scans which were used to assess brain structure, and psychological tests of cognitive functioning. He found that the short recovery group had noticeably smaller temporal lobes and scored lower on visuo-spatial tests. One important implication of this research is that temporal lobe atrophy associated with prolonged jet lag might be reduced by introducing periods of jet lag recovery.

"There is loads of research into the effects of jet lag and shift work. Don't restrict yourself – show breadth of understanding by considering a range of effects. Plenty of information is provided here to enable you to show off your knowledge and gain lots of marks."

SLEEP STATES

THE NATURE OF SLEEP

Sleep is a behaviour seen in all mammals, with something resembling mammal sleep occurring in all other species. Sleep is obviously important since when sleep is lost most animals appear to try to make up for lost time by engaging in more sleep. Animals make a considerable commitment to this behaviour. Humans for example, in the course of a normal healthy lifetime, can expect to spend around 190,000 hours sleeping – about a third of our lives. Quite what sleep *does* for us however (other than provide us with several – hopefully enjoyable – hours of relaxation and dreams) is still a topic of considerable debate.

"If you are asked a question on the nature of sleep, don't worry. Anything which tells us about sleep is telling us something about its nature. You can use information from any part of this chapter as long as it is about sleep – for example, ultradian rhythms, lifespan changes and functions of sleep, even sleep disorders. How straightforward is that?!"

THE CIRCADIAN RHYTHM OF SLEEP

"Circadian rhythms were covered earlier in this chapter. This is just a summary here, but in an answer to a question on the nature of sleep you should take from that earlier section information which is a bit more research-based and also evaluative."

Sleep follows a regular 24 hour cycle and forms part of a broader circadian timing system. A part of the hypothalamus called the suprachiasmatic nucleus (SCN) acts like a master clock. Cells in this brain region have clock proteins which go through a 24 hour biochemical cycle, setting time for many bodily rhythms, including sleep. The SCN receives light signals from the retina, so that it is linked to the outside world's day–night cycle. The SCN provides signals to the lateral hypothalamus which have neurons that release a substance called hypocretin, which directly influences sleep and arousal states. Light information which affects the SCN also influences the pineal gland in its production of melatonin, the release of which is affected by light.

Unless inhibited by light, levels of melatonin rise shortly after dark and fall again just before dawn. The biological clock determines the timing of sleep rather than sleep itself, so that when exogenous cues like light and temperature are absent, sleep still occurs but in a more fragmented way as a series of shorter episodes. Melatonin thus helps to regulate circadian sleep cycles.

THE ULTRADIAN RHYTHM OF SLEEP

"Whilst it is useful to know about ultradian rhythms in sleep, don't make them the focus of your answer to an exam question on the nature of sleep. It is much easier to gain evaluative marks by concentrating on the other four topics in this section."

A great deal of what is known about sleep comes from research measuring the electrical activity of the brain. These signals are recorded by a device called an electroencephalogram (EEG), which represents the brain activity as waveforms. Although sleep is traditionally broken up into a series of stages, the EEG basically shows a series of brain waves indicating that the brain is slowing down. When we are awake and alert, the EEG shows a pattern of *beta* waves. As you relax and feel more drowsy, however, *alpha* waves are seen. As sleep deepens, *theta* and then *delta* waves appear.

Stage 1 of sleep is seen soon after a person settles to sleep. On the EEG it resembles relaxed wakefulness, except that *theta* waves make an appearance. Observation of someone in this stage will see them open and roll their eyes, and there are often sudden body jerks. These are called myoclonic jerks, and are frequently accompanied by sensations of falling.

After about ten minutes, sporadic bursts of brain activity called sleep spindles appear on the EEG, indicating that the person has entered **Stage 2** of NREM sleep. Muscles are relaxed, breathing is steady and a person looks as though they are soundly asleep. However, if woken now they will typically deny having been asleep.

After another ten minutes or so a significant change is seen on the EEG, with the appearance of large, slow waves called *delta* waves. This signifies that a person is in **Stage 3** sleep. Once the EEG shows predominantly delta wave activity, the

person will have entered **Stage 4** sleep. These two stages are sometimes referred to collectively as *slow-wave sleep* (SWS). Other than for occasional twitches of the hands and feet, a person appears very still. A person is now in a deep sleep and is difficult to wake up, and when woken generally acts groggy.

About 30 minutes after the onset of **Stage 4** sleep, the EEG changes again, moving rapidly back through stages 3 and 2 to show activity resembling the beta activity of an active awake person. This new type of sleep is REM sleep, and it is quite distinct from the other stages. A close inspection of an asleep person at this stage will reveal eyeballs moving around behind closed lids, breathing that has become more rapid, and an increased heart rate. The body appears to have flaccid paralysis, so that it is 'floppy' and, unlike in slow-wave sleep, does not readily respond to being touched. If a person in REM is woken up they are likely to report having been dreaming (REM is sometimes referred to as 'dream sleep').

For the rest of the night, sleep alternates between periods of slow wave and REM, with periods of REM becoming longer as the night progresses, at the expense of time in SWS. Of course, sleep does not occur in exactly the same way every night, which will change the look of the EEG recording. Some nights we are so very tired that we 'crash', and our descent into sleep is very rapid. On other nights we may struggle to relax and our sleep is more fitful.

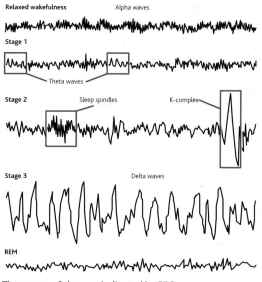

The stages of sleep as indicated by EEG.

However, in a typical night's sleep, going to sleep follows a very particular pattern. Psychologists distinguish between two kinds of sleep – REM (rapid eye movement) and non-REM sleep (non-rapid eye movement, or NREM). When we first go to sleep we are in NREM sleep. This consists of a series of stages identified by distinct patterns of brain waves. We progress through these stages until we enter a period of REM sleep.

WHY DO WE SLEEP?

"Elsewhere in this chapter you will find much more information on the various theories about why we sleep. They tell us a great deal about 'the nature of sleep' and can be used to good effect in a general question of this kind."

There is no simple explanation for why we sleep, and whilst psychologists can't agree why we do so, there is agreement that sleep is absolutely necessary. From an evolutionary standpoint, sleep makes sense, as it allows an animal both to conserve energy and to avoid danger. Many animals are simply not attuned for night vision and are therefore vulnerable during the hours of darkness. Animals that can hide away for security during this time do so, whilst others that can't, because of their habitat and their size, must stay awake for longer, relatively still but alert to danger. Many of the sleep patterns of animals can be understood simply by considering their ecological niche. On the other hand, it could be that since being awake involves wear and tear on the body, sleep is a period during which restoration can take place. Of course, these functions are not necessarily mutually exclusive. Even if sleep evolved for one purpose, there is no reason why during the course of evolution it did not come to serve many functions. So for example, it may have evolved as a means of energy conservation, but during a period of relative calm it came to be an ideal time to carry out restorative functions.

SLEEP AND AGEING

"How sleep changes over a lifespan is covered in more detail elsewhere in this chapter. Lifespan changes become a lot easier to remember and use effectively in a question on the nature of sleep if the material is organised – for example, infant sleep, adolescent sleep, and adult sleep."

Changes to sleep occur naturally as we age. Investigating the sleep patterns of babies in the womb is very problematic, but research has shown that behaviours resembling sleep are identifiable in the foetus by about 32 weeks' gestation. After birth, babies sleep in 3 to 4 hour bouts for 17 hours or more a day. At least 50% of this is REM sleep. Sleep decreases to about 13 hours by the end of the first year, and also more closely follows a circadian rhythm. Sleep continues to decline towards adolescence, by which time the typical pattern of adult sleep has emerged. Sleep changes in adulthood happen largely because of social and life changes: for example a new baby is estimated to cause at least 400 to 750 hours of lost sleep in the first year alone. As a person gets older, subtle changes can be observed, however, such as decreases in the amount of SWS and increases in stage 1 and stage 2 sleep. Two of the key changes in older adults are the greater degree of awakening during the night, and increases in daytime napping.

DISORDERED SLEEP

"Sleep disorders are covered in their own section later in the chapter. Here is just an outline, but in an answer to a question on the nature of sleep you should take from the disorders section information which is a bit more research-based and also evaluative."

Disorders of sleep are among the most common health problems, but more often than not go undiagnosed or untreated. The most common sleep problem is insomnia. This is where people have difficulty falling asleep, or once asleep wake up and can't get back to sleep again. This results in excessive sleepiness, which increases the likelihood of accidents as well as generally affecting the quality of life. One cause of insomnia is apnoea, which is a cessation of breathing during sleep. Apnoea is also a sleep disorder in its own right. The most common type is obstructive sleep apnoea, where the upper airway is blocked, causing arousal from sleep. This prevents a sufferer from entering the deeper stages of sleep, leaving them tired and unsatisfied with their night's sleep. Narcolepsy is another sleep disorder where people suffer sleep attacks during the day, causing them suddenly and irresistibly to fall asleep. Fortunately quite rare, the condition is debilitating and can be quite dangerous. It is caused by the loss of neurons in the hypothalamus which contain the neurotransmitter hypocretin. Some disorders occur when phenomena associated with waking intrude into sleep states. Sleepwalking is one example of this, where muscle tone is maintained during REM sleep when there would normally be flaccid paralysis.

FUNCTIONS OF SLEEP

Despite the fact that everyone sleeps, no one is entirely sure why we do it. Attempts to explain the function of sleep have generally fallen into one of two camps. They either suggest that our bodies need time at night to rest and recuperate after daytime physical and mental exertion, or they take the view that sleep is a behaviour which evolved because it serves some kind of adaptive function.

RESTORATION THEORIES OF SLEEP

ASK AN EXAMINER

"Whilst there is more than one restoration theory of sleep, all have in common the notion that sleep is for rest and repair. It is a good idea to know about more than one for your examination and collectively call them 'restoration theory', simply because it gives you more to write about!"

According to the *cell-repair hypothesis*, one function of sleep is to minimise the effects of oxidative stress. The body is constantly burning energy to maintain itself. Whenever the body metabolises oxygen in this way it produces chemicals called free radicals, which are harmful to cells in the body – the damage they cause is known as oxidative stress. In effect, high metabolic rates increase damage to cells in the body. For most parts of the body this damage can be dealt with by simply replacing old cells with new ones, and this can happen in any state of rest. However, the brain is largely unable to do this – the brain cells we have at birth must last us a lifetime. This theory suggests that NREM sleep provides the ideal opportunity to repair the damage to brain cells that these free radicals cause. During NREM the brain is in a relatively inactive state, and the brain temperature during this time is ideal for enabling enzymes to repair cells more efficiently, or for new enzymes to be produced to replace those themselves damaged by free radicals. One particular enzyme that can break down free radicals and render them harmless is called superoxide dismatuse (SOD).

Ramanathan et al (2002) found a link between oxidative stress and sleep deprivation. They kept twelve healthy rats awake for between five and eleven days and found evidence of decreased activity of SOD in the hippocampus and brain stem. This may be because the constant awake activity of the rat degraded these enzymes. The researchers speculate that over time this would result in damage to brain structures caused by the action of these free radicals. This is supported by Eiland et al (2002) who, in an investigation of changes in the brains of rats, caused by sleep deprivation, found damage to cells in the hypothalamus due to reduced activity of SOD. Presumably, since these cells were only damaged and not dead, sleep might still serve to repair them and so reverse the damage.

The cell repair hypothesis is also supported by observations of animal sleep. In general, larger animals require less sleep that smaller ones. The increased sleep in smaller animals might be necessary to counteract the increased free radicals produced by their higher metabolisms. So an elephant, which has a low metabolism, needs less sleep to neutralise free radicals (about three hours a night) than a cat, which has a higher metabolism (and sleeps for about twelve hours a day).

Another restorative function of sleep according to Guzmán-Marín et al (2003) is *neurogenesis* (the formation of new brain cells). Whilst most brain cells do not regenerate, research has found that some do, particularly in a part of the hippocampus called the dentate gyrus. The hippocampus is a brain region important for the storage of memories. When they deprived rats of sleep for four days the researchers found that the number of new cells in the dentate gyrus was reduced by 50%. Further research by Guzmán-Marín et al (2005) showed that hippocampal cells that form during sleep deprivation don't mature normally. They suggest that not only does sleep deprivation reduce the number of new cells produced, but it also decreases the number of cells that fully develop into neurons. They did not find in either study an increase in corticosterone (a stress hormone) in the rats and the rats did not look worse for wear after the sleep deprivation. However, it was impossible to rule out the idea that the stress caused by the forced exercise used to keep them awake contributed to the finding.

One of the earliest restoration theories was proposed by Oswald (1980). His *growth and repair hypothesis* suggests that the patterns of brain activity change during sleep to allow restoration. REM sleep allows the restoration and reorganisation of the nervous system. NREM on the other hand involves the restoration and repair of the body through the release of growth hormone (GH). GH is essential for growth and repair and whilst it is released in small bursts throughout the day, it is released in more significant amounts during SWS. That the release of GH is tied to SWS is demonstrated in studies which disrupt sleep cycles – a phase delay or phase advance in the sleep cycle so that SWS is moved will also cause a corresponding move in the release of GH. This idea has been developed by Horne (1988). He says that sleep can be divided into core sleep (which includes REM and SWS) and optional sleep (everything else). It is during core sleep that repair and restoration takes place. In the absence of core sleep (which provides the ideal conditions) restoration can occur during optional sleep, and can even happen during relaxed wakefulness.

The theories of both Oswald and Horne predict that the amount of sleep needed will vary according to the amount of repair required following periods of awake activity. Both these ideas have been investigated in sleep deprivation studies.

Resoration theory and total sleep deprivation studies

Pitcher and Huffcutt (1996) conducted a meta-analysis of 19 total sleep deprivation studies. Participants had either experienced short-term total deprivation (less than 45 hours without sleep), long-term total deprivation (more than 45 hours) or partial sleep deprivation (sleeping for no more than five hours for one or more nights). Sleep loss affected all three groups of participants: it was found to affect mood most, followed by cognitive then physical abilities.

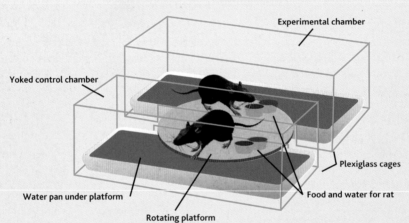

SLEEP DEPRIVATION IN RATS

Experimental chamber

Yoked control chamber

Plexiglass cages

Water pan under platform

Food and water for rat

Rotating platform

Rechtschaffen et al (1983) studied pairs of rats deprived of sleep by keeping them on a platform suspended above cold water. The EEG pattern of one rat was monitored and when sleep patterns were recognised, a motor was switched on, which rotated the platform. If the rat did not wake and begin to walk it would be pushed into the water by the dividing barrier. This technique reduced sleep by 92% in the 'connected' experimental rat, and by 23% in the yoked control. Being 'yoked' meant that this rat experienced exactly the same thing as the experimental rat: it was there for comparison, to ensure that results were not influenced by the method used to monitor sleep.

The experimental rats soon began to look ragged and unkempt. Despite the fact that they doubled their consumption of food, by the end of the study they had lost a fifth of their body weight. The first rat died after 13 days, and all the experimental rats were dead after 21 days. Post-mortem examination could find no clear cause of death – it appeared as though the rats had 'just died' from a lack of sleep.

This study is a good experiment. The environment was controlled: e.g. light, noise and temperature. Plenty of food and water was provided and there was a 'yoked' control rat for comparison. The study does, however, have limitations. It is unclear how far the findings based on rats can be applied to humans. For instance, it could be that sleep serves a slightly different function in humans and rats. Secondly, despite the use of a control rat, it is still difficult in this study to separate the stressful effects of the method used to keep rats awake from the effects of sleep loss.

ETHICS   NATURE/NURTURE   GENDER   CULTURE   DETERMINISM   REDUCTIONISM

For ethical reasons, most sleep deprivation studies with humans last less than five days. There are however instances where people have voluntarily stayed awake for much longer. In 1964, 17-year-old Randy Gardner set a world record by staying awake for 11 days (264 hours). As the time without sleep lengthened, Randy tended to show increasing signs of sleepiness and impaired functioning – for example, he experienced mild hallucinations and concentration problems. When he did eventually sleep, he did so for 15 continuous hours and within a week he appeared to return to a normal sleeping routine. Whilst he only caught up a small fraction of the total sleep he had lost, closer inspection showed that over two thirds of this SWS and just over half the lost REM were made up. This extra sleep supports the idea of recovery through sleep, and also indicates that SWS and REM are particularly important for recuperation. This is a poorly controlled and recorded case study so care should be taken about basing too many conclusions on it. It is not even clear what the true extent of sleep deprivation was, since unless participants in these conditions are observed carefully they can engage in frequent microsleeps, unnoticed even by the participants.

Such studies with humans ultimately do little more than *suggest* a restorative function for sleep as they lack the precise measurement and observation of controlled laboratory experiments. Unfortunately, it would not be ethical to conduct such scientific studies with humans. However, studies have been undertaken using animals to discover the effects of very long-term sleep deprivation. For example, it has been shown that adult dogs tend to die after about 13 days without sleep, whilst puppies die much sooner, after about six sleepless days (Coren, 1996). Cirelli et al (2005) found that drosphila which had been selectively bred to engage in less sleep had a much reduced lifespan. The researchers suggest that a lengthened time of awake activity in these flies causes greater wear and tear, and the reduced opportunity for repair because of reduced sleep caused premature death.

One of the most influential studies of its kind was conducted by Rechtschaffen et al (1983). He found that sleep deprivation over a prolonged period had serious consequences for his experimental rats, with all animals dying at between 13 and 21 days of deprivation.

Although the findings of Rechtschaffen et al seem to suggest that sleep performs some kind of vital physiological function, they do not make it exactly clear what the restorative function might be. One possibility they suggest is that, following prolonged sleep deprivation, the body loses its ability to maintain normal temperature. It was observed that the body temperature of experimental rats dropped steadily before death, despite increased eating. It seems that this over-eating might be a strategy to maintain body temperature but that this only works for a while. Eventually, body fat is used up (resulting in the observed weight loss)

THE MUCH MISUNDERSTOOD CASE OF RANDY GARDNER

In 1964, 17-year-old Randy Gardner stayed awake for 11 consecutive days as part of a high school science project. Popular myth has it that he suffered no negative side effects as a result of his record-breaking feat. However, according to Ross (1965), who conducted medical examinations, Randy had quite a tough time during his non-sleep marathon.

Day 2 – Trouble focusing eyes and subtle signs of astereognosis.

Day 3 – Some evidence of trouble with physical coordination, and some moodiness.

Day 4 – Increased moodiness and some paranoia, problems with memory and concentration, perceptual distortions (e.g. the 'head band' effect).

Day 5 – Randy appeared better than on day four, but he did experience hypnagogic hallucinations.

Day 6 – A return of day four problems, plus increased astereognosis, physical weakness and lack of coordination.

Day 7 & 8 – Memory and concentration problems became more apparent, and there was increased moodiness/irritability. Speech appeared sluggish and slurred.

Day 9 & 10 – Concentration became very difficult, with many lapses on even very ordinary tasks. Blurred vision worsened. Significant episodes of paranoia appeared on day ten.

Day 11 – A full medical revealed that, other than a light tremor, physical coordination and balance were normal. Speech was slurred and monotone, and vision was blurred. A slight heart murmur was detected that later disappeared. On a psychological level, concentration was limited and his mental abilities diminished.

and the rat fails to create enough body heat so goes into terminal decline and dies.

This is supported by Horne (1988), for whom a key factor in the relationship between sleep and restoration is brain temperature. He points out that whilst the exact mechanism is unclear, other studies with human participants have also noted both increased eating behaviour without weight gain and decreased body temperature. It has also been shown that those participants who suffer the most severe side effects of sleep deprivation are also those who experience the most significant drops in body temperature.

On the face of it, animals appear to fare less well than humans in sleep deprivation studies. The raised levels of stress hormone cortisol in sleep-deprived rats suggest that this may be because effects are mediated by cognition. Humans participating in sleep deprivation studies are aware that their welfare is important for the researcher, which might reduce stress. Rats of course have no such insight, so as a result they experience higher levels of stress, which in turn reduces the effectiveness of the immune system, leading to ill health. This view seems to be supported by observations of sleep deprivation used as a form of torture, when several people might experience equivalent amounts of deprivation, but with very different and individual consequences.

Restoration theory and increased exercise

If sleep serves a restorative function then it might be expected that sleep would be influenced by the amount of daytime activity. That is, sleep would increase at times of increased wear-and-tear and, conversely, decrease during times of inactivity.

Shapiro et al (1981) studied the sleep patterns of ultra-marathon runners before and after a 56 mile race. Such excessive activity would presumably create a big need for subsequent repair, and indeed overall sleep increased significantly the following two nights. However, much more impressive changes occurred in the content of sleep, with increases in SWS of 40% and 45% on the first and second night respectively. This was at the expense of REM sleep, suggesting that SWS is particularly important for repair and recuperation. Whilst this seems to support the restoration theory, other research suggests that reduced activity does not result in less sleep at night. Adey et al (1968) looked at the sleep patterns of people who were paralysed. If the logic of restoration theory is carried through, being completely immobile should mean little need for sleep, as there is no subsequent need to repair after activity. The researchers found little difference in overall sleep and only a small reduction in SWS. Whilst this does not prove restoration theory wrong, it does suggest that the relationship between sleep and restoration is not a simple one. It could be for example that, regardless of overt activity, the body has a need for a minimum amount of sleep, maybe for natural wear-and-tear as a result of day-to-day functioning or perhaps for some other purpose.

According to Horne (1988), even in a state of physical inactivity, such as with the participants in the Adey et al study, the brain is active and this requires some amount of sleep for recovery. With physical exercise, such as in the Shapiro et al participants, it isn't the effect that exercise has on the body that necessitates increased sleep, but the effect exercise has on the brain. Physical exercise creates body heat which causes a hot brain. This results in increased brain activity and a greater need subsequently for SWS to aid recovery. This is supported by a study by Horne and Horley (1989). They increased the brain temperature of some of their participants by approximately 1% by warming their heads with a hair drier. Even though there were no significant differences in the daytime activities of their participants, those that had received the warm air increased their subsequent amounts of SWS.

EVOLUTIONARY THEORIES OF SLEEP

All animals appear to enter periods of quiescence which might be described as sleep, and although the actual behaviour varies considerably across species, all mammals engage in something identifiable as sleep (Cirelli and Tononi, 2008). For example, whilst an elephant can do it standing up and cats can do it with their eyes half open, both animals are clearly sleeping. Some animals sleep for prolonged uninterrupted periods whereas others sleep in shorter bursts. The content of sleep also varies, with animals differing in the amount of REM and NREM, and others still seemingly only having NREM. Some animals, such as dolphins, cannot sleep in the conventional sense because they have to keep moving, so have evolved a way of allowing one half of the brain to go to sleep at a time – something called unihemispheric sleep.

The fact that sleep evolved in all animals suggests that the strong evolutionary pressures shaping this behaviour must have been similar for them all. Since each animal species faces its own set of evolutionary pressures, the many variations in sleep observed across species may reflect differing adaptive responses to these pressures.

A number of evolutionary explanations for sleep have been proposed, which focus on issues such as the benefits of reduced energy expenditure during sleep, responses to predation, and adaptive functions of certain types of sleep. What they all have in common, however, is the assumption that sleep evolved because it served some purpose useful to the fitness of the species.

ENERGY CONSERVATION THEORY

Webb (1982) claims that the function of sleep is similar to that of hibernation. It is a mechanism which has evolved to force animals to conserve energy at times when it would be relatively inefficient to be awake. Animals which are adapted to diurnal (daytime) activity and eat during the daytime would be wasting valuable energy at night when they would be awake and unable to eat. Sleep then reduces the amount of energy expended by an animal. According to Berger (1995), sleep helps to offset the greater cost of being endothermic (warm-blooded). Extended bouts of sleep reduce metabolic pressures on an animal – an endothermic animal at rest has a metabolic rate up to 10 times greater than an ectotherm (cold-blooded animal) in a similar state.

Evaluation

This theory is supported by the observation that torpor and hibernation, which undoubtedly serve energy conservation functions, resemble SWS. Indeed, some people refer to this as the *hibernation theory* of sleep. It has also been found that, in some animals, food restriction results in larger bouts of SWS.

Support for this theory also comes from the foraging behaviour of some animals. Zepelin et al (2005) found that diet is strongly correlated with sleep time, with herbivores (e.g. sheep) sleeping the least, and carnivores (e.g. lion) the most. Herbivore diets are relatively poor in nutrients so they must spend more time eating (and consequently less time sleeping). Carnivores on the other hand eat highly nutritious food so eat less often. This gives them the opportunity to sleep more. Omnivores (e.g. baboon) eat both diets and, appropriately it seems, have sleep habits somewhere between the two.

The ecological habits and lifestyles of some animals also point to an energy conservation function. For example, Lee and Martin (1990) describe the sleep behaviour of the koala, a slow-moving animal which sleeps up to 19 hours a day. Its sole diet (eucalyptus leaves) is scarce and has low nutritional value. For these animals, wasting energy unnecessarily can be very costly indeed. Similar conclusions can be drawn from the behaviour of other animals with poor diets, such as sloths and giant pandas.

SLEEP RESEARCH: A WARNING FROM SLOTHS

Three-toed sloth wearing a mini EEG.

Rattenborg et al (2008) have conducted the first study recording the electrophysiology of sleep in a wild free-roaming animal. They attached a mini EEG to three-toed sloths, worn as a cap on their head, and monitored their movements high in the tropical forests wherever they live, with a radio telemetry system. Sloths are often used as examples of lengthy sleepers. Over a three to five day period the researchers found that these sloths slept an average of 9.63 hours per day – 6 hours less than records from captive sloths indicate.

It is suggested that wild animals sleep less than captive animals because they have to be more concerned about predation, and spend more of their time foraging. Relative to the total number, only a very few have had their sleep behaviours recorded – according to Coren (1996) around 200 species – and all of these have been captive animals, or fairly crude observations of sleep behaviour. This finding, however – that captive animals can extend sleep – has implications for theories and research that are based on data from these animals. It also suggests that research with wild animals is more likely to reveal the true functions of sleep.

The theory is also supported by the extended amounts of sleep observed in many newborn animals. Younger animals have a high ratio of surface to body mass, which makes energy conservation through sleep particularly important. As body size increases, they get less energy conservation benefit from sleep, and so there is a decrease in sleep time.

There is a major question mark, however, over whether sleep is actually an effective way of conserving energy. Whilst there is a reduction in body temperature during sleep, according to Shapiro et al (1984) sleep saves at most about 15% on energy, and even then this figure would depend on such things as nutrition and lack of disturbance during sleep. In fact, it is hard to see how some animals save any energy at all during sleep. For example, dolphins must remain active at all times, otherwise they will drown. It seems that whilst sleep might provide a way of conserving energy in some animals, in others it must be serving some other function.

Another version of conservation theory is *energy restriction theory*. Whilst on the face of it they are similar theories, energy restriction theory has a different emphasis. Here, sleep serves to prevent the exhaustion of energy supplies by putting a limit on activity. According to this theory, sleep serves to force rest on an animal who will then as a result *expend energy at an affordable level*. The larger an animal's body, the greater the energy reserves: according to Calder (1955) the proportion of body fat to body mass increases with size, ranging for example from 5% in mice to 30% in cows. Also, as size increases the ratio of surface to body mass decreases, as does the thickness of fur. This means that larger animals lose less heat to the environment relative to size. Larger animals then can afford to eat proportionately less than very small animals, who will quickly die if they go without food for even a short time. Many small species thus need to sleep more in order to avoid exhausting energy supplies. This is supported by the observation that sleep varies across species according to body size. Smaller animals may need to sleep as much as possible to conserve energy due to a relatively high ratio of surface area to body mass, which makes it costly to maintain body temperature.

PREDATION THEORY

This theory suggests that sleep provides a survival advantage because it reduces environmental threat (Meddis, 1975). Night-time presents a number of problems for diurnal animals that depend on vision. Poor night vision puts them at greater risk during the hours of darkness both from injury and from attack by nocturnal predators. Animals in this situation have evolved responses which involve changing sleep patterns or developing strategies to evade predators. Some prey animals reduce the risk of predation, for example, by living in burrows. The increased security offered by something like a burrow means that these animals can sleep more. Grazing animals which would otherwise be vulnerable to predation sleep very little. Being still during sleep increases survival chances because it means that an animal reduces the risk of being spotted by predators. For instance, a small burrowing animal like a rat sleeps much longer than a large grazing animal like a cow. Predators on the other hand generally sleep more than the animals they prey upon, although the amount of sleep in predators varies considerably according to where on the food chain they lie – many predatory

---

PRESTON ET AL (2009) – IMMUNE THEORY OF SLEEP

The relationship between sleep and the immune system is well established, with research showing both immune system functions impaired by sleep loss, and sleep being altered when the immune system is having to work hard to fight off disease. This has led some researchers to speculate that sleep may be part of an initial immune response to infection (Krueger and Majde, 1990).

Preston et al propose that sleep is an adaptive response to possible infection. They counted the white cells in blood samples from 26 mammals and found a highly significant correlation between sleep time and immune function: those species that sleep more had higher numbers of white blood cells. Increases in white blood cells should mean improved resistance to parasitic infection, and an analysis of parasitic load confirmed this. They found that animals that sleep for longer have substantially reduced levels of parasite infection.

They argue that 'sleep fuels the immune system'. Awake activity places many demands on an animal's energy resource which largely disappear during sleep, such as foraging and parental care. These resources are then allocated to the body's natural defences. Some animals have evolved longer sleep time specifically to increase their investment in immune defence, reducing the impact of parasites which would otherwise have a significant effect on fitness.

animals are also prey to other, larger predators. It is also argued that animals which are immature at birth benefit from sleeping more as this reduces their exposure to danger. Indeed, it is the case that, as young animals mature and become better able to fend for themselves, there is a corresponding decrease in sleep time.

Evaluation

This theory is supported by Allison and Cicchetti (1976) who found that an analysis of the sleep patterns of 39 animal species revealed a relationship between risk of predation and amount of sleep. Animals with a high risk of predation slept less than those at lower risk – although there are exceptions to this rule, suggesting that this theory may only apply to some animals.

This theory is also supported by the sentinel hypothesis of REM sleep (Snyder, 1966). This argues that, because an animal still has an active brain during REM sleep and could rouse itself quickly if necessary, this sleep phase allows an animal to be ready to escape in the event of an attack. This is supported by studies which have shown that some animals especially prone to predation are not only very alert when awoken from REM sleep (Horner et al, 1997), but are also very sensitive to external stimuli during REM sleep (Cote et al, 2002).

The problem with this theory is that, when remaining awake but inactive would serve the same predator-avoidance purpose, it is hard to see why such a physiologically complex behaviour as sleep should exist at all, if it only served such a function. Prey animals are more vulnerable to predation during sleep because they are less sensitive to the approach of predators during this time. This is supported by the observation that prey animals sleep less than predators, since they have to be alert as much as possible to avoid predation. Giraffes, for example, are thought to sleep less than 2½ hours a day. If sleep served no other function than predator avoidance then logic dictates that giraffes would do best to dispense with this meagre ration of sleep entirely.

THREAT SIMULATION THEORY

Sleep is not a unitary condition, but is made up of several distinct states. This has led several theorists to consider possible evolutionary functions for these individual states, the logic being much the same as with theorists who have looked for separate restorative and/or evolutionary functions for REM and NREM sleep.

According to Revonsuo (2002), the dreams that occur during REM sleep have an evolutionary function. He argues that the brain did not begin to dream by accident: rather it has a biological adaptive function formed because the environment presented challenges to our hunter-gatherer ancestors that were extreme threats to reproductive success. The response to this threat was to develop a mechanism for simulating threatening situations and rehearsing threat-avoidance responses – dreaming. Revonsuo points out that in contrast to the widely held view that dreams are nothing more than a random and disorganised by-product of some neurobiological process, dreams are the result of active, organised processes. They involve all the senses, and the visual appearance of dreams is mostly like the real world. In effect, dreaming provides us with an 'off-line' model of the world. Just as with the development of any skill where training and repetition improves performance, so realistic rehearsals of threat perception and avoidance in dreams improve our chances of surviving subsequent real-life experiences.

Evaluation

To support the idea that dreaming simulates threat, Revonsuo points out that dream content is often biased towards threatening events, with animals and male strangers appearing most frequently as enemies. This is interpreted as being a vestige of ancestral environments in which carnivores and poisonous animals presented a survival threat. And whilst encounters now with unfamiliar males are very rarely aggressive or threatening, intergroup violence over territory and resources would once have been common.

Further support comes from the widely recognised tendency for actual threats to become incorporated into dreams. For example, post-traumatic nightmares are common in people who have experienced catastrophes, horrible accidents etc. Brenneis (1994) points out that such dreams initially closely replicate the events and, whilst they might reduce in frequency and exactness, dreams about the event might last for years. According to Revonsuo, these real threats activate the threat simulation system, and intensify the physiological processes underlying dream sleep. This is supported by Williamson et al (1995) who point out that stressful real-life events tend to increase the intensity of REM sleep. We are not dreaming about traumatic experiences in order to resolve emotional problems, however, but because these situations represent threats to survival and reproductive success. In this case it is in our interests that the dream production system selects the event from long-term memory as a theme for threat simulation.

The idea that dreaming is an ancient threat-simulation system is supported by studies of the dream content of hunter-gatherer populations. Gregor (1981) reports that males from the Mehinaku Indians of Central Brazil dream significantly more about animals, killing animals and physical aggression. The theory's prediction that threatening events should be over-represented in dreams is borne out by the content of Mehinaku dreams. Only about 20% of 276 dreams reported by men had non-threatening and non-aggressive content. However, disproportionate to the real daytime risk, about 60% of dreams consisted of some kind of threat.

LIFESPAN CHANGES IN SLEEP

There are significant individual differences in how much people sleep, and age is one important factor influencing this variation.

PRENATAL AND INFANT SLEEP

It is difficult to assess exactly when sleep patterns emerge in the developing foetus. For instance, it is impossible to measure the brain activity of a human foetus in the womb, directly, for both ethical and practical reasons. EEG measures of premature babies are not reliable either, as they are not taken *in utero*, so may not resemble normal developmental patterns of sleep. An alternative source of information about foetal sleep comes from observations of foetal eye movements. Okai et al (1992) used ultrasound scanning to investigate possible sleep patterns in the unborn children of 30 normal pregnant women between 20 and 40 weeks of gestation. By identifying phases of eye movement and body movement they found that, before 28 weeks, REM phases were hard to identify, but by 32 weeks of gestation REM/NREM cycles could be distinguished. Their results suggest that the critical point in gestation is at 32 weeks. This is supported by correlation between these sleep changes and the development of the brain. For instance, the brain stem reaches a high developmental level between 28 and 31 weeks. Neural systems within this brain structure are known to be important for the control of REM/NREM ultradian cycles.

Newborn full-term infants spend approximately 17 hours a day sleeping, with about 50% of this time spent in REM sleep. Newborn infants generally enter REM very quickly after falling asleep, with the usual adult pattern of NREM/REM not emerging for several months.

In newborns, sleep is interrupted every three to four hours by short bouts of wakefulness. As the child develops, sleep behaviour stabilises so that by 6 months of age long sleep – wake cycles replace the earlier short cycles. This is partly achieved through entrainment by the parents, who attempt to establish regular night-sleep and day-wake rhythms. This sleep period gradually extends to about six hours and, under the influence of the circadian clock, shifts towards night-time sleep. The number of night-time awakenings becomes fewer and shorter as the infant grows, and daytime wakefulness becomes less frequently interrupted by naps.

The amount of REM sleep continues to decline during the first year of life, with a general decrease in the total sleep time to about 13 hours (Sheldon, 1996). By 12 months the amount of REM sleep has declined from about eight hours a night at birth to about four or five hours. Whilst toddlers usually continue to nap during the daytime, they do so much less often than when they were babies.

A number of factors can interrupt the normal pattern of sleep in infants. Armitage et al (2009) studied the sleep of 18 healthy full-term infants at monthly intervals to 6 months of age. Eleven of the infants were born to mothers diagnosed with depression. They found that infants of depressed mothers took longer to fall asleep, and had sleep patterns that were different from those experienced by the offspring of non-depressed mothers. For example, they had more short sleep episodes during the daytime. Although the exact mechanisms of the relationship are unclear (it could for example be a result of maternal hormones, or of genetics, or both), it seems that infant sleep is associated with maternal depression.

A relationship between maternal depression and infant sleep was also indicated by Baird et al (2009). They suggest that another factor affecting infant sleep is whether or not mothers experienced anxiety or depression prior to pregnancy. They measured pre-conceptual psychological distress using the General Health Questionnaire – and when their infants were 6 and 12 months of age the mothers were asked to report the sleep habits of their infants for the previous two weeks. Baird et al found that pre-conceptual distress was associated with a 23% increased risk of waking between midnight and 6 a.m. At 12 months there was a 22% increased risk. They point out that this is important because night waking during the first year is associated with sleep problems at 3 years of age. Such disruption is also related to later behavioural problems and might even affect learning abilities.

From about the age of 5 years to early adolescence the total amount of sleep time continues to decline to about eight hours a night. It is usual, however, for younger children to sleep deeply at the start of the night, with two bouts of NREM sleep before the usual REM/NREM cycle begins. It is also usual for pre-teens to wake quite suddenly in the morning and feel refreshed. The more familiar difficult awakening and sluggish start to the morning is something that emerges in most people during their teens.

SLEEP IN ADOLESCENTS

There are no significant changes in sleep patterns due to maturation during adolescence through to adulthood. Sleep changes that do occur are mostly the result of increasing social pressures causing more irregular sleep patterns – for example, staying up later and sleeping longer at weekends. Reduced parental influence at this time of life also appears to be a key factor.

Crowley et al (2007) note that sleep patterns in adolescents vary according to the school year. They identified several environmental factors that influence bedtime on school nights: for example, increased homework and extra-curricular activities such as sports and club memberships. Other activities blamed for later nights include watching TV, and using the computer. Crowley et al note that sleep is typically reduced during the school week and is compensated for by sleeping on at weekends. By doing this, the teenagers are resetting their circadian clock to a later time, pushing back the brain's cue to be awake nice and early on Monday morning. In effect, teenagers are giving themselves jet lag over the weekend which results in feelings of tiredness and poor school performance at the beginning of the week.

This supports earlier research by Wolfson and Carskadon (1998). In a survey of 3,000 high school students (equivalent of Year 12/13 in the UK), they found that respondents were on average getting only 7.3 hours of sleep a night, with a quarter getting 6.5 hours or less. The researchers found that students who achieved mostly A's in their progress grades went to bed earlier and slept on average an hour longer each night than those getting mostly low grades. There are of course many factors contributing to academic performance, but delayed sleep and wake cycles appear to be key contributors. This is supported in a recent study by Pagel (2007) who found that adolescents who experience sleep disturbances are more likely to receive bad grades in school.

During adolescence the brain is going through a critical phase of cortical development and cognitive change, and sleep is crucial in ensuring that these changes occur efficiently (Dahl and Lewin, 2002). The impact of school on sleep cycles has led some researchers (for example, Hansen et al, 2005) to suggest that this age group has a special need in terms of sleep and that school start times should be adjusted to accommodate this need.

SLEEP FROM ADULTHOOD TO OLD AGE

In a meta-analysis consisting of data from 2,391 healthy adults aged 19 to 102, Ohayon et al (2004) found a number of age-related changes in sleep, including decreases in total sleep time and also changes in the structure of sleep, with shifts in NREM and REM sleep. Their findings are summarised in the table below.

	Adults 19–102 years	Older adults 60–102 years
Total sleep time	⇓	⇔
Sleep latency (time from full wakefulness to sleep)	⇔	⇔
WASO (wake after sleep onset)	⇑	⇔
Sleep efficiency (the amount of sleep time actually spent sleeping)	⇓	⇓
Percent stage 1	⇑	⇔
Percent stage 2	⇑	⇔
Percent SWS	⇓	⇔
Percent REM	⇓	⇔
REM latency (amount of time before REM sleep begins)	⇔	⇔

Adapted from Vitello (2006).
Key: ⇔ *= remains the same;* ⇓ *= decreases;* ⇑ *= increases*
Summary of significant findings from Ohayon et al (2004).

Contrary to the widely held view that sleep in the elderly is poor, Ohayon et al's data shows that sleep does not change much after the age of 60, and that the bulk of the change occurs in the

THE IMPACT OF SCHOOL SCHEDULES ON SLEEP

Hansen et al (2005) had sixty senior high school students (equivalent to Year 12/13 in the UK) keep a sleep diary, beginning in August before the start of school and continuing until two weeks after the September start of term. Diaries were also kept for a further one month in November and one month in February. The students were given psychological tests for such things as vigilance and logical reasoning for two consecutive days at the beginning of November and February. This testing occurred three times a day: 6.30 – 8.00 a.m., 11.30 a.m. – 1 p.m., and 3 – 4.30 p.m.

The test results showed that the students performed better in the afternoon than in the morning, with them reporting greater weariness and having to expend more effort during testing in the morning. Analysis of sleep time showed that the students lost nearly 120 minutes of sleep per night during the week after starting school, and weekend sleep was approximately 30 minutes longer than before the start of term. Although total sleep time increased from September to February, there was no evidence that things like mood and performance adapted to school schedules. However, a number of factors may have affected this, such as the effect of term breaks and seasonal changes in light.

Hansen et al suggest that the weekend sleep is an attempt to return to a circadian rhythm that is lost during the week because of imposed school schedules. They recommend changing school start times and avoid all testing before 10 a.m. They also strongly recommend education of adolescents and all key groups that work with them, to raise awareness of the potential health and social problems associated with sleep loss. Hansen et al point out that parents might also benefit from realising that weekend sleeping is part of their child's inborn cycle, and not lazy or anti-social behaviour.

years of adulthood before this age. One of the advantages of this study compared to others of its kind is the careful screening of participants for good health prior to inclusion, and a comparison of age effects in the older half of the sample. In contrast to this, Redline et al (2004) found from their meta-analysis that sleep continued to change with age. However, they did not look for older age effects, nor were they as selective in their choice of healthy participants for analysis.

As healthy adults age, the amount of night-time sleep declines slightly, and sleep satisfaction also diminishes. The older a person gets, the longer it takes to get to sleep, and there are more incidences of night-time awakenings. Older adults for example are more easily awoken by night-time noise (Zepelin et al, 1984). In fact, the number of times a person wakes up after falling asleep seems to be one of the key changes in sleep associated with age (Vitello, 2006). Although older adults tend to get up earlier, overall time in bed is not decreased because they go to bed earlier. Whilst the feeling of being refreshed on waking up increases with advancing age, daytime drowsiness and fatigue during the day also increases. Poor sleep can lead to a number of problems in adulthood, such as depressed mood, memory problems, excessive daytime sleepiness, and a greater use of over-the-counter sleep aids.

The frequency and duration of daytime naps increase significantly with age. Possible reasons for greater napping during the daytime in older adults were investigated by Goldman et al (2008). They hypothesised that napping might be related to deficiencies in night-time sleep. They monitored the night-time and daytime sleep of 235 people with an average age of 80 years, over a seven night period. They found that the people most likely to nap were those who had experienced disturbed sleep, although disturbed sleep and nap duration were not related. Vitelli (2006) suggests that regular napping is strongly associated with the presence of other problems, for example medical problems. Healthy older adults are much less likely to report napping. According to Ancoli-Israel et al (2008), poor sleep in the elderly is not a result of aging as such, but caused by illnesses and the medications used to treat them. They point out that older adults who are healthy rarely have sleep problems.

"Three identifiable lifespan changes in sleep are outlined here – prenatal and infant sleep, adolescence and adulthood/old age. Organise your learning like this – it will really help."

DISORDERS OF SLEEP

EXPLANATIONS FOR INSOMNIA

Insomnia means literally a total lack of sleep. In practice however, since everyone sleeps for some amount of time, insomnia refers to a reduction in sleep. Even then, the definition is unclear since some people who claim to suffer insomnia don't experience a reduction in total sleep as such, but a reduction in the quality of their sleep. Some people complain of having difficulty getting to sleep (*sleep onset insomnia*); others complain of not staying asleep, frequently waking during the night (*sleep maintenance insomnia*); and others still are troubled because they wake up long before they need to (*terminal insomnia*). Then there are those people who sleep but deny that they do so, and those who spend excessive amounts of time in bed trying to get to sleep.

The matter is further complicated by the fact that there is no absolute amount of sleep that we all need, and these individual variations in sleep lead many people to believe, erroneously, that they are getting less sleep than they actually require, resulting in perceptions of insomnia. Clearly, insomnia is a complex and often subjective problem which is not going to lend itself to a simple definition. In a National Sleep Foundation survey in the US in 2002, 58% of respondents reported experiencing insomnia at least a few nights a week, whilst 35% had experienced insomnia almost every night over the previous year. The rate of clinically identifiable insomnia is said to be around 9% to 12% of the population, although this is very much an estimate. Insomnia is more common among women, and is said to increase with age (Weyerer and Dilling, 1991). In a longitudinal study involving 388 adults, Morin et al (2009) found that 79% reported symptoms of insomnia which lasted for at least one year, and 46% reported problems over the duration of the three year study. 54% of the participants who reported insomnia at the start said that they had recovered from the condition, though 27% reporting eventually relapsing. This study suggests not only that insomnia is quite widespread, but also that it is a persistent problem.

Insomnia can be *primary* or *secondary* in nature, and in terms of duration can be *acute* (it is transient, lasting four weeks or less); *subacute* (it is relatively transient, lasting more than four weeks but less than six months); or *persistent* (it is chronic, lasting six months or longer).

PRIMARY INSOMNIA

Primary insomnia is said to be caused by something other than a disease process, so that the sleep disturbance is not the result of either medical, psychiatric or environmental causes. Primary insomnia is usually associated with increases in a number of physiological measures over a 24 hour cycle, such as body temperature, heart rate and metabolic rate. Indeed, many insomniacs feel less sleepy during the day than non-insomniacs, even though they may sleep less at night. This has led many researchers to suggest that insomniacs are in a state of hyper-arousal. Higher levels of physiological arousal during the day mean that they feel less sleepy during this time than they might normally, and at night this continued higher arousal means that they have difficulty sleeping. This is supported by Vgontzas et al (2001) who found that insomniacs have increased levels of adrenocorticotropic hormone (ACTH) and cortisol, both of which are associated with stress and arousal.

Research by Nofzinger et al (2004) implicated particular brain regions in this state of hyper-arousal. The transition from wakefulness to sleep is usually associated with a decrease in activity in the brain stem, thalamus and prefrontal cortex. Using PET scans, Nofzinger et al showed that insomniacs experienced a smaller decline in such activity when going to sleep, perhaps partially explaining the difficulties that some insomniacs have in getting to sleep. Whilst sleep deprivation produces reduced activity in these brain areas in normal sleepers (which fits with the impaired cognitive and physical functioning usually seen after deprivation), Nofzinger et al found elevated levels of activity in the brains of insomniacs. These findings appear to be consistent with the idea that people with insomnia are in a state of hyper-arousal during sleep. It has even been suggested that hyperarousal is the key defining element of insomnia, rather than sleep loss and sleep deprivation.

According to Winkelman et al (2008), insomnia may be caused by specific changes in brain chemistry. They found that people who had been suffering with insomnia for more than six months have reduced levels in their brain of the neurotransmitter GABA. This is an inhibitory transmitter, which means that it reduces activity in the brain. Reductions in GABA therefore mean that the brain is not being quietened down at night, which might account for the common complaint amongst insomniacs that they are sometimes unable to sleep because they can't seem to 'switch off' their thoughts at night.

There is growing evidence of a possible genetic predisposition towards primary insomnia. Beaulieu-Bonneau et al (2007) reported that 34.9% of insomniacs surveyed indicated that they had a first degree relative with a current or recent problem with insomnia. Mothers were most likely to be identified as sufferers (19.7%), followed by sisters (11.1%), fathers (7.5%), and brothers (5.9%). This seems to support earlier research on insomnia in twins. In a study of 1,042 monozygotic (identical) twins and 828 dizygotic (non-identical) twins, Watson et al (2006) found that monozygotic twin insomnia was highly correlated (0.47). Dizygotic twin insomnia on the other hand was poorly correlated, at 0.15. This suggests that, whilst genes don't absolutely predict insomnia, they have a strong influence on the disorder.

Some research is pointing to the precise nature of this genetic influence. Joho et al (2008) studied mice who displayed behaviour very similar to human sleep maintenance insomnia. These mice sleep only 50 – 60% as much as normal mice, an effect which appears to be caused by their difficulty staying asleep. This sleep pattern did not change even after sleep deprivation. Joho et al found mutations in the genes that control electrical excitability in a part of the brain called the thalamic reticular nucleus. Neurons in this brain area, thought to play a role in the timing of slow-wave sleep, were found to be overactive, causing mice to enter slow-wave sleep for only short periods before waking up.

The influence of personality on insomnia

A number of studies have suggested that certain personality characteristics are associated with insomnia. We are talking here about primary insomnia, because personality is a relatively stable attribute of a person rather than something resulting from medical, psychiatric or environmental conditions. One of the earliest and most influential studies was conducted by Kales et al (1976). They used a personality test called the Minnesota Multiphasic Personality Inventory (MMPI) to test 128 insomniacs and found that they had certain personality traits in common. In particular, the insomniacs had a tendency to handle stress and

conflict by internalising rather than expressing emotions.

Recognising that this study was flawed due to a lack of a control group and a small biased sample, Kales et al (1983) tested a more representative sample of 300 insomniacs. This time they also included a control group of 100 non-insomniacs for comparison purposes. They found results similar to those of the 1976 study. The tests suggested a cluster of traits indicating such things as neurotic depression, obsessiveness, inhibition of anger, and negative self-image. These are all strong indicators of internalising tendencies. According to Kales et al (1983), the internalising personality characteristics possessed by insomniacs mean that they are in a fairly constant state of emotional arousal. The consequence of this is that they exhibit higher levels of physical arousal, for example increased heart rate and temperature. This means that they have much greater difficulty getting to sleep, staying asleep, and returning to sleep if they wake in the night. There is in effect a cycle of emotional and physiological arousal, since this experience of sleep makes them feel more anxious about sleep, which in turn increases their arousal levels.

"Insomnia is very common. Try not to lose any sleep over it."

In their study, de Saint-Hilaire et al (2005) used the Temperament and Character Inventory (TCI) developed by Cloninger (1986). In the TCI, temperament refers to biases in automatic emotional responses, which are thought to be genetically based and stable throughout life. These are Harm Avoidance (HA), Novelty Seeking (NS), Reward Dependence (RD) and Persistence (P).

Research has shown that the HA in particular is closely related to aspects of brain activity which have some relevance to insomnia (Cloninger et al, 1993). The character dimension refers to individual differences shaped by socio-cultural influences, and comprises Self-Directedness (SD), Cooperativeness (C) and Self-Transcendence (ST). de Saint-Hilaire et al compared the sleep patterns of 32 adult participants with chronic primary insomnia with 216 volunteer participants with no history of sleep disturbance or psychiatric illness. All participants had their sleep assessed in a sleep laboratory and, whilst there, also completed the TCI. The researchers found that insomniacs scored higher on HA and lower on SD compared to the normal controls. High HA people are described by the TCI as shy, easily fatigued, fearful, and pessimistic worriers. A low SD refers to a reduced ability to control and adapt behaviour.

Ong et al (2007) investigated whether insomnia was related to a particular chronotype. A chronotype is a term used to refer to a person's preference for activity and sleep, the three main chronotypes being *morning types* (or 'larks', who prefer activity early in the day), *evening types* (or 'owls', who prefer activity later in the day), and the largest category, *intermediate types* (who are not strongly owls or larks).Whilst chronotype categorising is usually associated with circadian rhythm research and used with people suffering circadian rhythm sleep disorders, there is growing evidence that circadian factors are important in insomnia. For example, Morris et al (1990) found that sleep onset insomniacs have a phase delay pattern in rhythms of body temperature (their temperature changes later than it should), whist terminal insomniacs have a phase advance problem in temperature rhythm (their temperature changes sooner than it should). Ong et al used the Morningness-Eveningness Composite Scale (MECS) to categorise 312 people attending therapy sessions for insomnia as either morning types, evening types, or intermediate types. They found that evening types were most likely to report problems with sleep, suggesting that there is some kind of interaction between personality, circadian rhythms and insomnia.

SECONDARY INSOMNIA

Secondary insomnia is said to be an insomnia precipitated, or made worse, by a disease process, disorder or substance. Insomnia in this sense is a symptom associated with physical illness and disease, psychiatric disorder and personality factors.

A range of medical conditions has been shown to be associated with insomnia. For example, problems associated with chronic pain (e.g. arthritis), respiratory disease (e.g. asthma), gastrointestinal disorders (e.g. ulcers), and endocrine conditions (e.g. thyroid problems). These don't cause insomnia as such: rather the medical conditions and sometimes the drugs used to treat them produce symptoms which disturb normal sleep. Katz et al (2002) conducted a study involving 3,445 patients with a diagnosis of one or more of five chronic medical conditions – hypertension, congestive heart failure, myocardial infarction, diabetes mellitus, and clinical depression. Responses to self-administered questionnaires showed that 50% of them reported symptoms indicative of insomnia, such as difficulty initiating and maintaining sleep. Insomnia was rated as mild in 34% of the patients and severe in 16%. Their findings also suggested that insomnia had a significant negative effect on the quality of life of the patients, beyond the effects due to their other illnesses.

"*You are expected to know about both primary and secondary insomnia. You could be asked a general question on insomnia, or about either one. Personality is a factor influencing primary insomnia, whilst here drugs, mental health, brain injury, vitamins and apnoea are given as factors influencing secondary insomnia.*"

Insomnia and drugs

Medications and leisure drugs are also associated with insomnia. For example, Bardage and Isacson (2000) found that 20% of their participants using drugs to treat their hypertension reported side effects of insomnia. It has also been found that medication taken to help with insomnia, such as sedatives, can also have negative side effects. The use of sleeping medication can quickly cause dependency and tolerance. The consequence is that withdrawal results in a 'rebound' insomnia, which reinforces the sufferer's belief that medication is necessary, leading to increased dependence on drugs for sleep, even when the medication is no longer effective (Kales et al, 1978). This type of insomnia has been referred to as an iatrogenic disorder, since it is medical treatment that is largely responsible for the disorder. Philips and Danner (1995) found that smokers were more likely than non-smokers to report a range of sleep problems, including insomnia, and whilst alcohol can increase the speed at which you go to sleep, it is known to cause disruption to the second half of the sleep period.

Insomnia and mental health

Insomnia is a well known additional symptom in many people with mental health problems. Weiss et al (1962) found that 72% of psychiatric patients in their study reported sleep disturbance, compared to 18% of their control sample. According to Kamerow (1989), insomnia is ten times more likely as a result of mental health problems than it is after physical health problems. In a major study by Ohayon and Roth (2003), 14,195 participants representative of the general populations of the UK, Italy, Portugal, and Germany were interviewed over the telephone about their psychiatric history and current sleep patterns. The study found that people with insomnia were six times more likely to report a mental health problem such as depression or anxiety than participants without insomnia. There is also some suggestion that the more severe the mental health problem, the more severe the insomnia (Sweetwood et al, 1980).

Insomnia is so closely associated with depression that it is included as a criterion for diagnosis. Because they so closely co-occur, it has been suggested that they may share common underlying mechanisms. Benca and Peterson (2008) suggest a number of potential mechanisms. Insomniacs and depressives may have similar abnormalities in their biological clocks. Patients with depression who have been found to have an abnormality in the genes that govern circadian pacemakers are more likely to experience severe insomnia (Serretti et al, 2003). Another possibility is that insomnia and depression have shared neurochemical imbalances. Many of the neurochemicals that have been found to be important to depression are also involved in aspects of sleep. For example, the cycle of REM sleep may be initiated by decreases in serotonin. People with depression have reduced levels of serotonin and spend more time in REM sleep and enter this phase of sleep more quickly. Anti-depressant drugs which increase levels of serotonin in the brain reverse these changes. The role of the hypothalamic-pituitary-adrenal (HPA) axis in depression is well established, with research suggesting that depression is linked to increased levels of cortisol. The HPA system is closely involved in the body's response to stress (Steiger, 2007). Whilst the principal hormones secreted by the HPA (ACTH and cortisol) normally reach their lowest concentrations in the body

during the first few hours of sleep, in depressed people their levels remain elevated. This fits in well with the idea that insomnia may be caused by hyper-arousal. The relationship between insomnia and mental health problems such as depression is not however a straightforward one. For example, whilst insomnia may certainly cause or contribute to the symptoms of depression, it is also equally the case that depression may contribute to insomnia. Conversely, many people with insomnia do not have depression, and vice versa.

Insomnia and brain injury

Brain injury is also a common cause of secondary insomnia (Baumann et al, 2007). Cohen et al (1992) compared the sleep complaints of 22 patients hospitalised with brain injury with those of 77 discharged patients who had sustained brain injury 2 to 3 years previously. They found rates of 72.7% and 51.9% respectively, much higher than would be expected from the general population. Ayalon et al (2007) estimate that between 40% and 65% of people who suffer mild traumatic brain injury subsequently complain of insomnia. In their study, they assessed 42 people who claimed to experience insomnia following head injury. Fifteen of them were found to have circadian rhythm sleep disorder (CRSD), which is a problem with the timing of the sleep–wake cycle. Unlike insomniacs who lose sleep, people with CRSD are able to get enough sleep if allowed. Unfortunately, because their sleep cycle does not coincide with normal daily life and all its distractions and demands, they have disturbed sleep and hence feel sleep-deprived and complain of insomnia. This study suggests that many people may be being misdiagnosed with insomnia after head injury when in fact they have another disorder with different origin and treatment. Medicines to treat insomnia are not going to benefit people with, for example, CRSD, since they are not going to influence the primary complaint – a circadian rhythm that needs resetting.

Insomnia and vitamins

Recent research has indicated a possible role of vitamins in disturbed sleep. Minerals and vitamins are not usually associated with either sleep gain or loss, although Baldewicz et al (1998) have suggested that a supplement of B vitamins might be helpful for insomnia, to counteract low levels of vitamin B6, which have been found to cause disturbed sleep. Lichstein et al (2007) had 517 participants complete questionnaires about health, daytime functioning and vitamin use, and keep a sleep diary for two weeks. Content analysis of the diaries revealed poorer sleep in those people taking multivitamin or single vitamin supplements. Controlling for age, gender and ethnicity, there was a tendency for vitamin users to wake up more in the night and subsequently stay awake longer, to make more use of sleep medications, and generally to show a higher risk for insomnia. They proposed a number of possible explanations for this finding. It could be that poor sleep is caused by certain vitamins, or by an interaction between several vitamins. Alternatively, insomnia could result from another unidentified factor which both promotes vitamin use and results in poor sleep. Equally, it could be that someone is already a poor sleeper and seeks vitamins to help address the problem, as they see it.

The final possibility is that the study is flawed. There are, indeed, some problems with it: for example the study was unable to judge the effect of vitamin dose and timing, and analysis of the potential contribution of particular vitamins was not possible. Furthermore, the possibility that participants had been taking herbal supplements was not investigated. None of the flaws however completely explains the findings, and no doubt many more researchers will be attracted to the hypothesis that, in some people, vitamin supplements contribute to insomnia.

THE INFLUENCE OF APNOEA ON INSOMNIA

The term 'apnoea' simply refers to a cessation of breathing. Apnoea is a form of sleep disordered breathing (SDB), and has been long assumed to be a cause of insomnia, although it is a primary sleep disorder in its own right.

There are two types of apnoea, obstructive sleep apnoea (OSA) and central sleep apnoea (CSA). OSA is the most common form of sleep disordered breathing, and is the most common cause of insomnia. The International Classification of Sleep Disorders (ICSD) defines it as "characterised by repetitive episodes of upper airway obstruction that occur during sleep, usually associated with a reduction in blood oxygen saturation". The main thing that distinguishes OSA from CSA is that with OSA, respiratory muscles continue to work, i.e. a person continues to attempt to breathe. OSA most often occurs in those who are loud snorers, and is typically caused by a blockage to the upper airway (usually the back of the throat) during sleep. The subsequent lack of air going into the lungs causes a drop in blood oxygen levels (hypoxaemia) with the result that the person wakes up. Athough a complete cessation of airflow might not occur, it can be that breath is not taken for several seconds, which ends with gasps, loud snores, moans, and movements, that frequently cause the person to wake up. These brief arousals are not necessarily noticed by the individual, however, and may happen many times during a typical night's sleep (in the worst cases they can occur up to 100 times for each hour of sleep). The consequence is that the person feels excessively sleepy the next day. OSA is thought to occur in about 2% to 4% of working age adults, 1% to 3% of children, and in about 20% of the over 65s.

There are many reasons why an airway might become blocked during sleep, among them medical conditions involving nasal congestion, growths and deformities in the neck, and enlarged tonsils. Because of this, treatments for OSA are usually mechanical (e.g. devices to improve breathing), or surgical (e.g. to reduce airway obstruction). Whilst such interventions do not cure all cases of OSA, they have a high success rate and can contribute significantly to reducing sleep disturbance. One important risk factor for OSA is obesity, since fat tissue may narrow the airway. Obesity is also the primary cause of another form of SDB called obesity hypoventilation syndrome, although this is different from apnoea in that fluctuations in blood oxygen levels due to breathing difficulties occur while awake or asleep (Ahmed et al, 1991).

Another more serious form of apnoea is central sleep apnoea (CSA), which according to the ICSD is "characterised by a cessation of ventilator effort during sleep and is usually associated with oxygen desaturation". Snoring is less common than with OSA, and people have greater trouble staying asleep, waking up gasping or choking. CSA is much less frequent than OSA, and is caused by a reduced respiratory drive from the central nervous system to the muscles in the body that create respiration – unlike OSA, the airway remains open but there is a lack of respiratory effort. CO_2 produced by the activity of the body is carried by the blood to the lungs and is exhaled during normal breathing. There are chemoreceptors in the body sensitive to concentrations of elevated levels of arterial carbon dioxide ($PaCO_2$), and increases in these levels cause the brain centres responsible for breathing to increase the rate of respiration. This reduces $PaCO_2$, and subsequently respiration slows down again. This process is helped when we are awake because of our awareness of our own breathing. However, if we are insensitive to CO_2 levels then when we sleep breathing can become irregular with associated fluctuations in CO_2 levels. In some people this can cause breathing to slow so much it can stop. Whilst the two forms of apnoea have slightly different origins, OSA and CSA share common consequences, such as excessive daytime sleepiness, changes in mood, reduced concentration, morning headaches, and loss of libido.

Cheyne-Stokes syndrome is often considered to be synonymous with CSA, although it has slightly different characteristics. It is seen most often in people with central nervous system damage, for example due to stroke and heart failure: breathing effort appears to stop after a deep in-breath and out-breath. There is usually arousal or snoring. A crucial distinguishing feature is that Cheyne-Stokes respiration does not occur during REM sleep.

NARCOLEPSY

Narcolepsy is a sleep disorder characterised by excessive daytime sleepiness, which Mitler and Gujavarty (1982) compared with the "sleepiness one feels when trying to complete a boring task at 3 a.m. after 72 hours of total sleep deprivation." In addition to feelings of extreme sleepiness during the daytime, people with narcolepsy can also exhibit symptoms such as cataplexy, disturbed night-time sleep, sleep attacks, hypnogogic (sleep onset) hallucinations, hypnopompic (sleep offset) hallucinations, and sleep paralysis. These additional symptoms can occur immediately, or they can develop over a number of years after the appearance of excessive sleepiness and can be

very debilitating, interfering with work, education, personal relationships, and quality of life in general. Broughton et al (1981) reported that 80% of their narcoleptic sample had experienced falling asleep at work on several occasions. In a study by McMahon et al (1982), compared to a sample of 2,406 non-sufferers, narcoleptics reported more family problems (21%), social isolation (35%) and physical/emotional health impairments (25%). Narcolepsy is not however a common disorder, affecting somewhere between 0.03% and 0.18% of the general population (Nishino et al, 2000). Whilst narcolepsy usually begins in the late teens or early twenties, around 25% of sufferers do not experience onset until after the age of 40 (Honda et al, 1983).

ASK AN EXAMINER

"The specification requires you to know about two sleep disorders in addition to insomnia – narcolepsy and sleepwalking. Learn about them both, and be prepared to write exam answers specifically on one or the other of these if required. Plenty of detail is provided here on both disorders to help you."

The sleep attack, which is the tendency to fall asleep at an inappropriate time, is the main symptom of narcolepsy. Attacks most frequently happen at times of physical inactivity or boredom and are often preceded by drowsiness. They can however

NARCOLEPSY AS A RESULT OF BRAIN DAMAGE

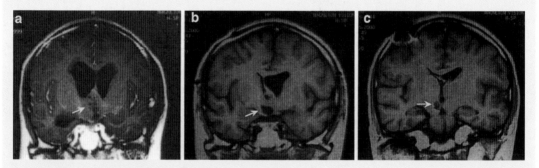

MRI scan showing damage to the region of the hypothalamus.

Arii et al (2001) report a case study of a 16-year-old girl who underwent brain surgery for the removal of a tumour from the region of her hypothalamus. Although she had no history of sleep-related problems prior to surgery, afterwards she experienced intense urges to sleep during the daytime, and often fell asleep during monotonous tasks and whilst watching television. Cerebrospinal fluid (CSF), extracted from her spine, was compared with CSF obtained from control participants undergoing assessments for other problems. It was found that her CSF contained reduced levels of Hcrt. MRI scans indicated that surgery to remove the tumour had caused damage to her hypothalamus. Arii et al suggest that Hcrt neurotransmission had been disturbed by damage to the Hcrt-producing cells in the hypothalamus.

occur at any time, suddenly without warning, and have for example been reported to occur whilst waiting at traffic lights, eating a meal, and skiing. Sufferers are easily awoken, feel refreshed, and are then unlikely to experience a sleep attack for several hours. Cataplexy is a brief and sudden loss of muscle tone, without any loss of consciousness. These symptoms can vary widely in severity and frequency, from a mild physical sense of weakness to complete collapse that can happen a couple of times in a lifetime to several times a day. The most common trigger for an attack is a sudden emotion, such as surprise, laughter, or anger. Sleep paralysis involves a sudden but temporary inability to move any muscles, and occurs in some narcoleptics in the periods between sleep and waking. Sleep paralysis is often accompanied by hypnogogic and hypnopompic hallucinations, which are vivid dream-like experiences: it is as though the person is awake but still dreaming. These experiences usually last anywhere from seconds to about 20 minutes, and a person is easily aroused from this state by noise and touch.

Neural explanations of narcolepsy

One of the first indications that narcolepsy was associated with the functioning of a particular brain region came in 1916 when von Economo correctly suggested that his patients with *encephalitis lethargica*, the symptoms of which include muscle weakness and extreme sleepiness, had damage to the hypothalamus and midbrain. Evidence for narcolepsy being caused by brain damage is, however, scarce. Scammell et al (2001) report the case of a 23-year-old who acquired narcolepsy following damage to his hypothalamus because of a stroke. Tests of his cerebrospinal fluid (CSF) showed reduced levels of a brain chemical called hypocretin, or Hcrt (also known as orexin). This is supported by Arii et al (2001) who report the case of someone who showed signs of narcolepsy as a result of a tumour.

The role of hypocretin (Hcrt) in narcolepsy

Scammell et al and Arii et al both suggest that narcolepsy is caused by the loss of cells in the hypothalamus that secrete Hcrt. There is direct evidence for the role of the hypothalamus in narcolepsy from studies with animals. Gerashchenko et al (2003) destroyed the cells in the lateral hypothalamus in rats with a neurotoxin. They found a relationship between the number of cells lost and a decline in the levels of Hcrt in the CSF. A 73% decline in Hcrt neurons resulted in a 50%

reduction in CSF Hcrt. They suggest that since humans with narcolepsy have more than 80% reduction in CSF Hcrt, this must mean that either virtually all Hcrt neurons are lost, or that surviving neurons are increasing their output of Hcrt.

Further support for the role of Hcrt comes from studies of people with Parkinson's disease. This is a degenerative brain disorder which involves the loss of cells in many brain areas. People with Parkinson's disease show sleep complaints that strongly resemble narcolepsy. Thannickal et al (2007) conducted a post-mortem analysis of the brains of people who had suffered Parkinson's disease and found that the brains had lost up to 62% of the cells that contain Hcrt. This is supported by other research which has shown reduced levels of Hcrt in the CSF drawn from the ventricles of people with Parkinson's disease (Fronczek et al, 2009).

Genetic explanations for narcolepsy

Research has indicated a clear genetic contribution to narcolepsy. It was discovered in the 1970s that certain breeds of dog appeared to have an inherited form of narcolepsy. This led to the establishment of a breeding colony of narcoleptic dogs and a concerted effort to find the gene or genes responsible for the disorder. Nishino and Mignot (1997) found that narcoleptic Doberman Pinschers have a genetic mutation affecting Hcrt, but unfortunately further research indicated that this genetic defect did not apply to humans.

Despite the insights gained from animal research, the search for mutations responsible for narcolepsy in humans has been less successful. It seems highly unlikely that narcolepsy in humans is absolutely genetic. It is the exception rather than the rule that narcolepsy runs in families – although there is an increased risk of narcolepsy above general population figures, most narcoleptics do not have relatives with the disorder. Sixteen identical twin pairs with at least one narcoleptic in each pair have been reported in research, but in only four of these pairs did both twins have the condition (Mignot et al, 1998). In all likelihood, narcolepsy is caused by a combination of genetic susceptibility and one or more environmental triggers, such as hormonal changes, infection, trauma, or immune system dysfunction.

Despite the lack of genetic abnormality in the Hcrt system in humans, 90% of narcoleptics have levels of Hcrt so low that they are almost or completely undetectable (Nishino et al, 2000). Although narcolepsy may be well established as a disorder of the neurotransmitter Hcrt, caused by reduced numbers of Hcrt cells, the question of what causes this reduction has until recently remained unanswered. The finding that over 90% of narcoleptics carry particular subtypes of a human leukocyte antigen (HLA) gene indicates that Hcrt neurons may be being destroyed as part of an autoimmune response (Overeem et al, 2008). HLA is part of the immune system and plays a vital role in recognising foreign antigens. One possibility is that the Hcrt-producing cells in the hypothalamus are selectively destroyed in susceptible people by the immune system (Thannickal, 2009). However, as yet there is no direct evidence for this hypothesis.

SLEEPWALKING

Sleepwalking, or somnambulism, is a condition where some phenomenon of both waking and of sleeping occur at the same time. Sleepwalking usually occurs during the first two hours of sleep during slow-wave sleep, and is indicated on an EEG with a sudden burst of slow-wave activity. Sleepwalking appears to be a result of an abnormal transition from NREM to REM sleep. Normally, a shift from SWS to REM sleep would involve a loss of muscle tone, preventing movement during REM sleep. However, this does not seem to occur with sleepwalkers, so that the elements of one sleep state (NREM muscular control) intrude upon the other (REM dream sleep). REM and muscle tone occurring at the same time makes it appear as though sleepwalkers are responding to events in their dreams.

A sleepwalking individual wanders around in a dazed and uncoordinated fashion, which can last

anywhere from a few seconds to 30 minutes or more. When woken, sleepwalkers experience a period of 'mental confusion' before they regain full waking consciousness. This is supported by Broughton (1968). He aroused people from SWS by suddenly standing them up and questioning them. When this happened during REM sleep the participants became lucid almost immediately. Arousal during SWS on the other hand resulted in symptoms including mental confusion, slurred speech, and non-responsiveness. Whilst both sleepwalkers and control participants had a period of poor responsiveness when woken from SWS, this effect lasted longer in sleepwalkers.

Sleepwalking can appear at any age after a person learns to walk, but is most common in 4 to 6-year-old children. As the young person matures, the proportion of SWS at the start of sleep reduces, and so do the incidences of sleepwalking. Whilst becoming far less frequent in adulthood, the habit is still not uncommon, with up to 3% of adults sleepwalking (Partinen, 1994). Sleepwalkers also experience complete or partial amnesia for the sleepwalking event. This was again demonstrated by Broughton (1968), who induced sleepwalking by giving his participants a large drink of water before bedtime. When suddenly aroused from SWS, participants generally wandered to the toilet and then back to bed. When asked about the event later, they showed no memory of the experience.

Psychodynamic explanation of sleepwalking

Some of the earliest explanations of sleepwalking were psychodynamic, focusing on the idea that sleepwalking is the expression of unresolved unconscious conflicts. The sleepwalker is, in effect, 'acting out' repressed conflicts. The later finding that sleepwalking occurs during SWS was seen to support the psychodynamic theory, since the conditions of SWS are ideal for this to happen – the likelihood of recalling harmful repressed memories is minimal during this phase of sleep.

There is no scientific evidence to support psychodynamic explanations of sleepwalking however. Neither is there any clear evidence for a pure psychological explanation for sleepwalking. For example, the results of most personality studies suggest that there is no specific personality type which is prone to sleepwalking, and those personality types that have been suggested are subtle and difficult to identify. According to Cartwright (2004), the only personality traits which appear associated with sleepwalking are the tendencies to have compulsive behaviours and over-control of emotions, and these may only apply to a particular form of sleepwalking involving violent acts. Most researchers now agree that the disorder is the result of underlying biological mechanisms.

Genetic explanations of sleepwalking

There is some evidence that sleepwalking may be genetic. Bakwin (1970) studied the frequency of sleepwalking in 19 monozygotic (MZ) twins and 14 dizygotic (DZ) twins. He found a concordance rate of 47% for MZ and 7% in DZ twins. He also found a tendency within families for sleepwalking. Far more siblings of MZ somnambulists walked in their sleep than would be expected from the general population. The data also suggested a much greater likelihood of this sleep disorder in near relatives of sleepwalkers than in more distant ones. This is supported by Hublin et al (1997). They investigated sleepwalking in a large sample of 1,045 MZ and 1,899 DZ twin pairs. From responses to questions about the frequency of sleepwalking during childhood and adulthood, they suggest that there is a substantial genetic influence on sleepwalking, with the disorder

---

A PSYCHODYNAMIC ACCOUNT OF SLEEPWALKING

Abrams (1964) describe the case of a 42-year-old woman arrested for shoplifting from a large department store whilst sleepwalking. Her behaviour was completely at odds with her morality and character – she was described as an energetic, active member of the religious community. As a result of this experience she became depressed and anxious, afraid to leave her home. Initially, she showed no understanding of her behaviour, but after several sessions of therapy, recalled that she had been a sleepwalker all her life, and when younger had often had her leg tied to the bed at night to stop her wandering off.

The therapist interpreted the subject's shoplifting behaviour as being a result of extreme pressures and personal difficulties. Shortly before the shoplifting incident she had been very distressed at the news of a relative's serious illness. According to Abrams, the sleepwalking was basically a 'cry for help', the stealing being a reflection of her need to take control of her life. After several more sessions of therapy, the patient came to accept the interpretation, and her symptoms of depression and anxiety disappeared.

WRITING E-MAILS IN YOUR SLEEP

A

Subj: !HELP ME P-LEEEEESE
Date: 12/7/2004:24 Eastern Standard Time
From: DUCKANDJOE
To: Docksea

i don't get it. please esplain LUCY!!
cOME TOMORROW AND SORT THIS HELL HOLE Out!!!!!

dinner & drinks, 4;00 pm shars house. Wine and caviar to bring only. everything else, a guess?   MANANA XXOO D

B

Subj: I DON'T GETIT
Date: 12/7/2004 11:50:07 PM   Eastern Standard Time
From: DUCKANDJOE
To: Suetheshoe13

WHAT THE?

Siddiqui et al (2008) report what they claim to be a unique case of somnambulism in a 44-year-old woman who began sleepwalking after increasing her dosage of Zolpidem (a drug prescribed to help with her insomnia). During one episode, she walked to her computer, switched it on and connected to the internet by logging on using her ID and password. She sent a friend three e-mail invitations to dinner: one at 11.47 p.m, another at 11.50 p.m. and a final one at 11.53 p.m. She had no recollection of this and was shocked when next day the friend contacted her to accept the invitation, and when she found copies of her e-mails in her sent folder. When she followed advice to reduce her dosage of Zolpidem, the sleep-walking stopped.

This case is unusual because of the complex information processing skills involved. Although the subject had amnesia for the event, she had full cognitive capabilities needed for the high level processing displayed in her behaviour.

showing a continuity through life: 88.9% of adult males and 84.5% of adult female sleepwalkers had a history of sleepwalking as children. The exact nature of the genes underlying sleepwalking is unclear as yet, although Bassetti (2002) suggests that it may be related to the same HLA gene abnormality associated with narcolepsy. He found that 50% of sleepwalkers he tested had a version of the HLA gene found in only 24% of non-sleepwalkers. Of course, this doesn't explain sleepwalking in half his participants without this variant of the gene. Neither does it explain why 25% of his sample who had this gene were not sleepwalkers.

Neural explanations of sleepwalking

Brain imaging studies have indicated that the brain is in a different state during a sleepwalking episode. Bassetti et al (2000) suggest that sleepwalking is the result of selective activation of some brain areas (the thalamocingulate circuits) at the same time as an inhibition of other brain areas (thalamocortical arousal systems). Increased cerebral blood flow (indicating increased brain activity) was observed in the cingulate cortex, a brain area thought to be important for the regulation of emotional behaviours. Decreased blood flow was found in the prefrontal cortices, which is consistent with the lack of awareness and insight observed in sleepwalkers.

Oliviero (2008) has suggested an explanation for sleepwalking based on what we already know about physiological mechanisms controlling sleep. Usually, the release of the neurotransmitter

GABA during sleep serves to prevent activity in the brain's motor system, causing a loss of muscle tone. Sleepwalking is more frequent in children because this inhibitory system is underdeveloped, so that insufficient quantities of GABA allow motor activity. Oliviero further speculates that adult sleepwalking is a result of this inhibitory GABA mechanism somehow remaining underdeveloped in certain individuals.

According to Dexter (1986), there is an association between sleepwalking and migraine headache. He found that 55 of his 100 patients with migraine reported sleepwalking, a rate much higher than in the control participants. Sleepwalking has also been related to temporal lobe epilepsy. Atay and Karaean (2000) found abnormal brain activity in the temporal lobes of 12 of the 22 sleepwalkers studied – and in 11 of these, sleepwalking completely disappeared following anti-convulsive medication.

Whilst sleepwalking is a primary sleep disorder in its own right, it can occur as a result of other factors, such as drug use, alcohol consumption, head injury, and general illness. Sleepwalking can be caused by a variety of prescription medications, such as anxiolytics (sedatives to help with anxiety), antihistamines (drugs to help counter allergies), and beta-blockers (to control arrhythmic heart conditions). Sleepwalking can even be caused by drugs which are intended to help improve sleep (Siddiqui et al, 2008).

Violent sleepwalking – a special case of sleepwalking

Many cases have been reported of violence committed whilst sleepwalking. Howard and d'Orban (1987) report a case from 1933 of a man who "woke to find himself battering his wife's head with a shovel. The shock was so great he fainted and, when he realised his wife had died, attempted suicide". Whilst this is an extreme example, it is not an isolated incident and many instances exist where pleas of diminished responsibility due to somnambulism have been made by defence lawyers in cases of sleepwalking violence. What all these cases have in common is how out-of-keeping with the normal behaviour of a person this violent sleepwalking is.

According to Ohayon et al (1997), sleep-related aggression is surprisingly common, occurring in about 2.1% of the population. The fact that little violent sleepwalking is reported suggests that most aggression in sleep occurs at a mild level. Bonkalo (1974) points out that adult sleepwalking violence is almost exclusively a male phenomenon (47 out of 50 cases he investigated); that it falls in the 27 to 48 age range; and that it most often occurs when there is a family history of sleepwalking. Bonkalo notes that the main difference between sleepwalking in childhood and in adulthood is the greater degree of purposeful behaviour seen in adults. In the case of violent sleepwalking, this is particularly purposeful and goal-directed.

It is unclear why, given that incidences of sleepwalking lessen with maturity, relatively benign instances should become violent events. There is no evidence to indicate that mechanisms underlying violent sleepwalking are different from those underlying normal sleepwalking. Evidence does suggest, however, that additional environmental factors may trigger this behaviour. A number of researchers have pointed to the role played by substance abuse and certain medications. Huapaya (1979) for example reports a number of cases of violent sleepwalking in which substance abuse appeared to play a key role. Hormones have also been implicated. Many reports of sleepwalking violence indicate that the sleepwalker had experienced periods of stress prior to the violent episode. Cartwright (2000) points out that in this context the observation that sleepwalking aggression resembles a fight-or-flight response to threat makes sense.

Perception

IAN WALKER

You are expected in the examination to show both the skills of knowledge and understanding and the skills of analysis and evaluation in relation to the topic Perception.

Where opportunities for their effective use arise, you will need to demonstrate an appreciation of issues and debates. These include the nature/nurture debate, ethical issues in research, free-will/determinism, reductionism, gender and culture bias, and the use of animals in research.

You will also need to demonstrate an understanding of How Science Works. You can do this through the effective use of studies in your answer (as description or evaluation) or where appropriate by evaluating methodology and findings.

WHAT YOU NEED TO KNOW

THEORIES OF PERCEPTUAL ORGANISATION

- Gibson's bottom-up/direct theory of perception and Gregory's top-down/indirect theory of perception

DEVELOPMENT OF PERCEPTION

- The development of perceptual abilities, e.g. depth/distance, visual constancies, face processing
- Infant and cross-cultural studies of the development of perceptual abilities
- The nature-nurture debate in relation to explanations of perceptual development

FACE RECOGNITION AND VISUAL AGNOSIAS

- Bruce and Young's theory of face recognition, including case studies and explanations of prosopagnosia

The world is a very busy place with many things happening around us all the time. In order for us to interact safely and effectively with the things and people in the world we must have an idea of what is happening. You know what is going on around you because you *perceive* it. Perception is a way of making sense of sensory information, to get knowledge about what is happening in the environment through the senses. That is not to say perception is the only way you can learn things about the world – you can also learn things by reasoning, or working them out for yourself, for example – but perception is a very important way for both humans and non-human animals to get information about their surroundings.

Perceiving things is not the same as sensing them. You sense things using vision, hearing, touch and your other senses, but this is just the first step in perceiving. Think about the picture shown below. As long as you look at it, the image entering your eyes stays the same – in other words, the information you are *sensing* stays the same. But what you actually *perceive* does not: one moment you might perceive a duck and the next moment you might perceive a rabbit. So perception is not the same thing as seeing, or hearing, or touching. Rather, when we perceive the world we take information from our senses and actively use it to build an understanding of what is happening around us.

THEORIES OF PERCEPTUAL ORGANISATION

Place your hand on top of this page and think about what you can see. The chances are you perceive your hand on top of a page. There's nothing surprising about that. Or is there? You perceive what you do because the light that bounces off the page and your hand into your eyes doesn't keep the hand and the page separate. Instead, the light entering your eyes has the page and the hand all mixed together. In fact, what goes into your eyes is a constant confusion of lines, curves, coloured areas etc. Your perceptual system, however, is able to tell which bits of the scene are the page and which bits are your hand. This is a skill known as *figure-ground separation* – the ability to separate objects from their backgrounds.

PERCEPTUAL ORGANISATION

The ability to separate objects from their backgrounds – as well as from one another – is an extremely important aspect of perception. Have a look at the picture of the busy street scene. Here, even though there is just a big messy mixture of lines, curves and colours, you can separate out all the objects – you see them as individual cars, people and buildings, even though this isn't what your eyes started with. We need this ability to separate the world into distinct objects because it is objects we deal with day-to-day: if you are hungry you want to find a sandwich, which is an object; if you are being chased by a tiger you need to be able to run away from it, and this means being able to tell which parts of the world around you are a tiger and which are not. This ability to separate objects from their backgrounds and from one another seems effortless to us, but it is proving incredibly difficult to make computers do it, showing just how complex the task really is.

This ability to take messy, mixed-up signals from your senses and separate them into individual objects is called *perceptual organisation*. We experience the world around us as being filled with people and objects. Perceptual organisation is the way our minds separate out these people and objects from one another, even though they arrive at our sense organs all mixed together.

There is a nice example of perceptual organisation in the diagram below. What arrives at your eyes is simply a set of lines, but you probably don't perceive the picture that way. Rather, your perceptual system organises the lines into objects. Do you perceive the picture as a line going behind a rectangle? Most people do, thanks to the way information from the senses is organised into objects.

"You will need to able to describe and evaluate each of two theories of perceptual organisation. One is a top-down theory (Gregory's theory) and the other is a bottom-up theory (Gibson). Using examples from perception illustrating aspects of each theory is a good way of getting descriptive marks."

ASK AN EXAMINER

BOTTOM-UP AND TOP-DOWN PROCESSING

Although we clearly organise our perceptions, separating the world around us into lots of separate 'objects', not everybody agrees about how we do this. There have been two main approaches to understanding the way perception happens. Some researchers have said our minds perceive the world around us by interpreting sensations. This is known as *bottom-up processing*, because it sees us starting at the bottom, with information from our senses, and working up to a finished perception. Bottom-up perception progresses in two stages: first we get information from the senses; then after we have got the information, we interpret it to work out what is going on around us. The two stages are separate, and always happen in the same order.

Other researchers have rejected the idea that perception happens in stages like this. They say that when we perceive the world we use information that we already have, to help us. This is known as

top-down processing, as information already stored in your memory is being used to interpret sensations. For example, because you know what dogs look like, this stored knowledge helps you perceive a dog each time you see one. Top-down processing helps you make sense of the busy world in which you live because you use this stored information. People who feel that top-down processing is important say that our perceptions are affected by our existing beliefs and expectations. This means that if we expect to perceive something in the environment, we are more likely to find it than if we do not expect to do so.

GIBSON'S BOTTOM-UP/DIRECT THEORY OF PERCEPTION

The American psychologist James Gibson argued that there is enough information to make sense of our surroundings simply by using whatever arrives at our senses. Gibson said that sensations provide us with all the clues we need to make sense of what we are seeing. He developed his theory when working with pilots who, he noticed, used visual clues from outside their plane to decipher the world.

The scene a pilot saw from the cockpit contained, according to Gibson, all the information they needed to understand the plane's speed, whether it was turning, whether it was accelerating or slowing down and so on. For example, if a pilot looks down to the ground and sees a tree in a certain place, and a second later the tree is perceived to have moved a certain amount, then Gibson said that the mind should be able to work out how fast the plane is moving and also in which direction it is travelling.

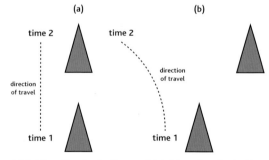

(a) At 'time 1' a pilot looking out of the window would see the tree below and to the right. At 'time 2', a second or two later, the tree is in the same place, telling the pilot he has flown in a straight line

(b) At 'time 1' a pilot looking out of the window would see the tree below and to the right. At 'time 2', a second or two later, the tree is much further away below, on the right and slightly behind, telling the pilot he has flown forwards and to the left

When we look at something moving past our eyes, we are using an 'optic array' to make sense of it. The optic array is the collection of elements or things we can see at any one time. As we move, or as the objects move, the pattern of the array changes. As things rush through our visual field, each part of the scene produces an image that moves across the retina. This movement is described as the 'optic flow'. The optic flow is caused by the fact that we, the observer, are moving differently from the scene we are looking at. An absence of optic flow means an absence of movement. The parts of the optic array that are important for us to perceive the world do not change during this movement. In this sense they are described as 'invariants'. The things that do not change in the array provide us with information upon which to base our bottom-up view of the world. Think about the pilot flying over the lines of trees. As the pilot turns the pattern of the trees changes and optic array provides useful information about our movement. Elsewhere in the environment however, some things remain the same. The mountains on the horizon for instance do not change. The mountains are an 'invariant' in the array – they stay the same. The invariants provide information about the terrain, the flowing objects in the array provide information about the pilot's movement over the terrain.

Texture gradients: The wheat and the stones near to us seem larger and further apart than the wheat and the stones further away. Gibson said we use this information when we perceive 'depth' and distance.

Gibson suggested the light we collect with our eyes contains all sorts of other clues which help us understand what we are seeing. For example, one of these clues is the *texture gradient*. Imagine standing at the edge of a field full of wheat. How do you tell which parts of the field are close to you and which are far away? One way to do this may be to compare how the different areas appear. In the areas near you, the wheat looks less tightly packed, whereas further away it looks smaller and more densely arranged, helping you judge the distance. Similarly, on a rocky beach, the stones nearer to you look larger and less closely packed than the stones further away, that look smaller and closer together.

Another common perceptual clue used in bottom-up processing is *motion parallax*. When we look out of a window and move our head from side to side we see that the window frame, which is close to us, seems to move around much more than objects outside the window, which are further away. This is one of the clues telling us the frame is closer than the objects outside.

Gibson identified various other clues like this, where the information we see or hear might give us clues to guide our perception. Perhaps the most intriguing of these clues is what Gibson called *affordance*. For example, if somebody hands you a knife, how do you know what to do with it? Many people would argue that you know how to use the knife because someone has shown you or told you in the past. In other words, you know how to use the knife because you have existing knowledge about knives. Gibson on the other hand argued that the information about how to use an object comes from the object itself. That is, you know you should use the knife for cutting because the knife 'affords' – or lends itself to – cutting. In other words, the knife's appearance suggests to you that this is an object which can be used for cutting. Similarly, Gibson might argue, the appearance of a cup suggests to you that this is an object which affords being filled with a liquid.

Many objects will afford more than one use – a large plastic box can be used as a container, or as something to stand on. This might help explain how people can come up with creative new uses for objects.

If the light entering our eyes contains all the information we need to perceive the world, as Gibson suggested, then we might ask what is happening with the ambiguous duck/rabbit picture we saw earlier. This is just one of many visual illusions where the same image can be perceived in two different ways. Surely this shouldn't happen, if our eyes receive all the clues we need? Gibson argued that visual illusions such as this are artificial images that only exist because psychologists have made them, and that such ambiguous scenes do not exist in the real world.

GREGORY'S TOP-DOWN/INDIRECT THEORY OF PERCEPTION

Whereas Gibson felt the world around us gave us the information we needed to perceive it, Richard

Gregory argued that we rely much more on what we already know to help us make sense of our surroundings. In other words, you don't just perceive the world passively, like a video camera. Instead, you are actively working with what you already know when you perceive the world.

Gregory, and other researchers interested in top-down processing, disagree with Gibson's idea that the light falling into our eyes contains all the perceptual information we need. Rather, they argue, the light entering our eyes is usually confusing and ambiguous, and we can only make sense of it by using existing knowledge to work out what we are seeing.

For Gregory, perception is a process of both forming and testing hypotheses. We do not rely on sensory information alone because it is unreliable: instead we form hypotheses, or 'best guesses', about what we sense. We combine what we have sensed and what we have learned through experience, to form an overall interpretation. This is our *perception*. Perception then is an active, constructive process of giving meaning to, and thus understanding, sensory information.

A classic example of how our knowledge can guide perception can be seen below. The middle letter in each word is identical, and is part-way between being A and H. It is ambiguous, and could be either letter. However in the first word you perceive it as an H and in the second you perceive it as an A, even though *it looks exactly the same* in both. The reason you do this is that you already know the words 'cat' and 'the', and your knowledge of the words helps you make sense of the ambiguous letter.

TAE CAT

You have probably heard the phrase 'I'll believe it when I see it'. One researcher jokingly referred to the top-down approach by saying 'I'll see it when I believe it', which nicely sums up how what we perceive might depend on what we already believe or know. This could explain why an expert architect will see a building differently from somebody who knows nothing about buildings – their knowledge about architecture guides their perception.

You can get a very good idea of how top-down processing works in perception if you listen to somebody speaking a language you don't know. When you hear somebody speaking English, or any other language you know well, it feels as

though each word is completely separate: it's almost like the words are written down, with a nice little gap between each word making it stand out from those on either side. But when you hear somebody speaking a foreign language, suddenly it becomes quite clear that the words areallsquashed-togetherlikethis with no gaps between them at all. The reason the words all sound nice and separate when you hear a very familiar language is because of top-down processing: you already know the words, and so can separate them from one another. In other words, your knowledge of the words helps you perceive them. When you lack this knowledge, as when you hear a foreign language, you cannot perceive the words. The reason hearing a foreign language feels different from hearing one you know is all about top-down processing.

"One very effective way to evaluate is to use another theory as a contrasting view. This is very straightforward here because Gibson and Gregory are opposites! The way that we are presenting evaluative material here means that you can readily compare top-down and bottom-up theories."

EVALUATING GIBSON'S BOTTOM-UP THEORY

Gibson's theory showed how important clues from the environment can be for guiding our perceptions. This is particularly true for the clues which help us perceive movement, such as motion parallax, which we all use daily as we move around, and some people, like drivers and pilots, make great use of as they control their vehicles.

We encounter many things in our world, even on a daily basis, that we have not come across before.

Stored knowledge is not always going to be available to use to make sense of these things. A bottom-up approach has a common-sense feel to it in these situations – how can we use a top-down process if we don't have the stored knowledge? It seems that it must be possible, at least sometimes, for perception to work without stored knowledge, that is, it must be possible to 'make sense' of something just from the information coming into your senses, without any use of top-down information.

Gibson's theory does, however, have its problems. For instance, the bottom-up approach does not readily explain effects like the THE / CAT picture shown earlier. It cannot account for how the same image, in this case the 'H' like shape in the centre of each word, can be perceived in different ways. If Gibson's theory is correct, we should only work with what we see, and not what we think might be the case because we are accessing information from our reading experience. Clearly, context, i.e. top-down information, is sometimes very important in perception. In much the same way, a bottom-up approach has difficulty explaining why hearing a familiar language is so different from hearing an unfamiliar one. The language we know is perceived as separate and neatly formed, whereas words in an unfamiliar language are very difficult to tell apart. The only difference in either case is stored knowledge of the language. Our past experiences and knowledge must be playing a role in our perception, although the bottom-up approach says that this cannot be the case.

EVALUATING GREGORY'S TOP-DOWN THEORY

Gregory's theory explains how we might perceive ambiguous or difficult-to-interpret situations. For example, the words 'recognise speech' sound almost exactly the same as 'wreck a nice beach' (try saying both phrases out loud quickly). If somebody just said one of these phrases to you out of the blue, you would probably struggle to decide what you had heard, as it could be either phrase. But if you had some knowledge to guide you – for example, if you knew you were having a conversation about going to the coast – it would be easy. This stored knowledge – the top-down information – would help you make sense of the ambiguous sounds you heard.

The top-down approach explains how different people often view the same scene or the same object in different ways. For example, imagine two people looking at a wooden box. One of them is told they are looking at a 'container' and the other is told they are looking at a 'platform'. The first person is more likely to put things into the box and the second person is more likely to stand on it. Gregory's approach allows for people to see objects in different ways like this thanks to their ideas about those objects, whereas a bottom-up approach, like Gibson's, does not. If perception is purely bottom-up, every person who sees an object should perceive it in exactly the same way, and what they know about objects shaped in that way shouldn't make a difference to what they perceive.

There are, of course, problems with the top-down approach. For instance, if perception relies heavily on using stored knowledge to make sense of what we see, how can we explain our ability to perceive something we have never encountered before? For example, look at the picture below. You've never seen this thing before, but you have no trouble perceiving it, even though you have no stored knowledge about the thing you are seeing.

Chimera

Bottom-up vs top-down processing

Both the Bottom-up and top-down processing theories have arguments for and against them. Both theories are strongly supported by research, and both have something sensible to tell us about how perception works.

Perceptual set theory

Perceptual set theory provides a difficulty for bottom-up processing, and supports the idea of top-down processing. The theory says that we perceive things in a certain way because we have a readiness to do so – this is our 'perceptual set'. Take the following example:

A I3 C

When you look at the 'letters' here, most people read them immediately as A, B, C. What is really presented is A, 13, C. We see the number 13 as the letter B because it is squashed between two letters, A and C. The position of the number 13 places it in a perceptual set of letters: past experience tells us that a letter is more suited in this position and so we are more likely to see the letter B than the number 13.

Bottom-up theorists, like Gibson would say that we would process the letters and numbers as they appear, and not with reference to what we know, so say that we should perceive the central number as a '1' and a '3', not as a B. If this were the case then mistaking the number 13 for a letter B should not happen. Top-down theorists, such as Gregory, would say that it is our knowledge of letters and numbers that leads us to perceive the letter B. We are using our past knowledge, of experiencing the letters ABC written in a string like this, to influence our perception.

VISUAL ILLUSIONS

One of the places where psychologists really debate the role of top-down and bottom-up processing is when looking at visual illusions. Below is a very famous illusion known as the Necker Cube. This is clearly a picture of a cube, but are you looking at it from the front, or from below? Usually, as you stare at the picture, you will find your view of it keeps flipping between the two possibilities – one moment you're seeing the cube from the front; the next moment you're seeing it from below. You probably had a similar experience with the ambiguous duck-rabbit we saw earlier.

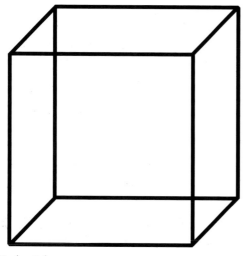

Necker Cube

Let's say perception all takes place using just bottom-up processing, as Gibson suggested. In other words, let's say light goes into your eyes and you use this information – and only this information – to decide what you are seeing. As you stare at the Necker Cube, the information going into your eyes doesn't change. As such, if perception just used bottom-up information, your perception of the cube shouldn't change either. If perception just uses bottom-up information then your perception of what you are seeing should only change when the scene changes.

Because of this, many people have said that illusions such as the Necker Cube prove we cannot just use bottom-up processing, and that we must also use top-down processing when we view the world. Your mind knows what cubes look like. As you look at the Necker Cube image, your mind is using this knowledge about cubes to try to make sense of the image. It is, in other words, using top-down processing to try to perceive the object. The flipping back and forth between the two interpretations shows your mind trying to make a fit between what it is seeing and what it knows about the world, when what it is seeing is confusing.

However, the fact the Necker Cube flips between two different views doesn't *prove* we use top-down processing in perception, because there may be another explanation. Visual illusions, such as the Necker Cube, have their effect because they are totally ambiguous. Let's say for a moment your mind processes the image in a completely bottom-up way, using only the information coming from the page. In this case, your mind could reach two different conclusions when looking at the Necker Cube – it could reach the conclusion you are seeing the cube from the front, or from below. The flipping back and forth between the two perceptions might not show us that top-down processing is happening; rather, the flipping might happen because your mind is processing the image using a bottom-up system, over and over, but getting different results each time. Both of these interpretations of the picture, top-down and Bottom-up, are *equally good*.

So it is difficult to know what visual illusions like this are telling us. They could be telling us we use top-down processing to guide our perception and make sense of the world, or they could be telling us we use just bottom-up processing, as Gibson suggested, but that with 100% ambiguous images we'll keep reaching different conclusions about what we are seeing. Because it is so difficult to know what visual illusions like the Necker Cube are telling us about the roles of top-down and bottom-up processing, many psychologists argue they are fun, but a 'dead end' when it comes to understanding how perception normally works. Supporters of bottom-up processing explanations in particular like to say that ambiguous illusions are very artificial, and in the real world we do not see objects like this, which are genuinely completely ambiguous. Counter to this, however, psychologists who think top-down processing is important often suggest that much of what we see every day *is* quite ambiguous and confusing, and that it is only by using our knowledge about the world and the objects we see in it – as perhaps we do when looking at the Necker Cube – that we can work out what we are seeing.

So, to summarise, it is really difficult to know whether visual illusions tell us anything useful about how perception takes place. What evidence we have fits both explanations, and whether a given psychologist feels visual illusions are useful or not tends to depend on whether they like the idea of bottom-up perception or top-down perception. So, ironically, the evidence on ambiguous images is itself ambiguous and is viewed differently by different people!

The integrative approach

Both the top-down and bottom-up approaches have strengths and weaknesses. Most contemporary researchers however see perception as using both top-down and bottom-up processes together. Sometimes we will rely more on our stored knowledge and other times we will rely more on analysing the scene we are looking at – the balance changes depending on what we are viewing. This is called an *integrative approach* and helps explain how we are able to perceive things we have never encountered before: it also explains how we deal with ambiguous scenes, and how our knowledge and beliefs can affect our perceptions.

"The integrative approach can be used as an evaluation of either top-down or bottom-up approaches, or both, even if you are writing about both!"

One of the most influential integrative approaches comes from David Marr. In 1982, Marr produced his *computational model* of visual perception. In his theory, Marr says that the perception of objects occurs in three stages, called primal sketch, 2½ D sketch, and 3 D model.

Primal Sketch

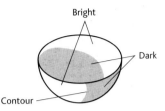

At this stage, our perception of an object is like a very simple quick sketch of it. Here all we have is very simple light and shade and edges.

2 ½ D Sketch

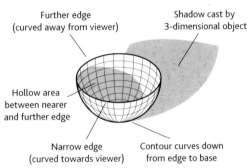

Here we begin to fill in the detail that provides richer information. At this stage we are only able to recognise the object from the viewpoint we see it from. If we were to come at it from another angle it would seem as if it were a completely new object.

3 D Model

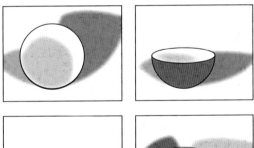

This is the final stage, when all the information is combined to form a solid representation. At this stage, the angle at which we view the object no longer matters. We are able to recognise it from any number of angles. We have formed a 'model' of it in our minds and are able to mentally manipulate and rotate it as much as we like.

Marr's computational model combines aspects of both bottom-up and top-down processing. It begins from basics, taking simple information about edges and constructing this into the primal sketch. This is bottom-up information, building a representation of the world from the simplest information received by the visual system.

Next, we begin to develop our perception by adding shading and details that allow us to understand the distances between different parts of the object. In our diagram for instance we begin to see the real shape of the object, and can understand the width of the bowl from edge to edge. In order to do this, we must begin to use information that helps us understand how light and shade work, and that solid objects normally behave in a certain way. This is the start of top-down processing. We are beginning to use stored information to help us understand how things might or should be. When we reach the 3 D model we approach the object using stored information which is part of a top-down process.

Marr's integrative approach provides us with a middle way, a combination of bottom-up and top-down processing. Later researchers, including Biederman (1990), have criticised Marr's model in much the same way as bottom-up processing models have been criticised in general. For example, Marr does not really explain how top-down processing works: it is just claimed to happen. Marr also fails to explain the very subtle abilities we have. For instance, his model can be used to explain how different 'classes' of objects (mugs, bowls, trees etc.) might be identified, but his model cannot tell us how we identify individual items within those classes, such as our favourite mug, the bowl we like our cereal in, or the tree in our garden.

DEVELOPMENT OF PERCEPTION

THE DEVELOPMENT OF PERCEPTUAL ABILITIES

When a baby is born, its vision is much poorer than an adult's: its eyes are focused at a fixed distance of about 30 centimetres in front of its face – which might be why we instinctively hold babies at about this distance when we interact with them. Interestingly, it is also roughly the distance between the baby's head and the mother's head when she' is breastfeeding, so that mother

and baby are able to focus on one another. Soon, this changes and the child is able to focus on near and far objects alike, just like anybody else. As well as these changes in a child's basic visual system, there are also lots of changes that take place in perception as the child develops. A major issue for psychologists and one which has led to a lot of debate over the years, is whether we are born with the ability to perceive the world around us or whether we need to learn this ability. The 19th-century American psychologist William James described the newborn's world as a "blooming buzzing confusion". He thought that to a young child nothing makes any sense at all. Others, however, believe a child is born with most of the skills it needs to perceive, and that these skills appear naturally as the child grows older.

"You could be asked questions about the development of perceptual abilities, infant studies of perceptual abilities, the nature-nurture debate in relation to perceptual development, and cross-cultural research. This might sound a lot, but it really isn't. There is a lot of crossover between these topics, so what you learn can be used in several different questions. We'll help you out here by suggesting how the content could be used in each of the four questions."

Here we will focus on three very important aspects of perception that have attracted particular attention from researchers. The first is our ability to tell how far away objects are (depth and distance); the second is the notion of 'constancy', which is our ability to understand that objects stay the same even though they change in appearance; and the third is face processing ability.

"Three perceptual abilities are presented here – distance-depth-visual constancies, and face processing. There is enough detail here for you to write a very thorough response to a question which asks you about the development of perceptual abilities."

PERCEPTUAL DEVELOPMENT: DEPTH AND DISTANCE PERCEPTION

Distance perception simply refers to your ability to tell how far away something is. You use this ability all the time. For example, whenever you reach out to pick an item up you are using distance perception to guide your hand to the object. Depth perception is a special use of your distance perception skill. You use depth perception to work out how far back things are in the distance, or how far below you a surface is. For example, when you stand at the top of some steps you use depth perception to work out how far down you have to move when you walk forwards. Depth and distance perception make use of lots of different clues from the scene you are looking at. Many of these clues are the sorts of things Gibson talked about, such as texture gradients. Other important clues we use for working out how far away things are include *superposition*, which refers to our understanding that when one object blocks part of another it must be closer. For example, if a tree stops us seeing part of a hill, we know the tree must be closer than the hill. We also use monocular and binocular depth cues.

Infants need an understanding of depth and distance in order to perform many of the simple tasks that are important to them, such as reaching out for something or judging the drop to the floor. Research suggests that infants begin to use binocular depth cues at around 4 months of age and monocular depth cues at around 6 months. The first cues to depth used by an infant however are *kinetic cues* at around 3 months (Bornstein et al, 1992). Kinetic cues are those provided by the movements of the body, eyes, head etc. and by the motion of objects in the environment. Studies using the *visual cliff* apparatus suggest that kinetic cues are important in infants who are able to crawl.

Using the visual cliff, Gibson and Walk (1960) found that young children old enough to crawl would not venture onto a glass shelf overhanging a drop, thus clearly showing an understanding of depth.

MONOCULAR AND BINOCULAR DEPTH CUES

Interestingly, many of the clues we use to work out how far away things are only need one eye to work – they are *monocular cues*. Monocular depth cues include *linear perspective, shading and lighting, interposition* and *motion parallax*. Linear perspective can be understood by imagining two people standing about five metres in front of us, one metre apart. Now, imagine they turn their backs to us and walk directly away – their images on our retinas get closer and closer together even though they are staying the same distance apart. Eventually, as they approach the horizon they eventually come together as one image. This is called the 'vanishing point', and is a very useful cue to perspective used by artists for centuries to give their paintings 'depth'. Shading and lighting provide another powerful monocular cue – the nearer an object is to a light source, the brighter it will appear to be. Interposition simply indicates that an object which blocks our view of another object will be perceived to be closer. Motion parallax is easy to demonstrate. Close one eye tight and move your head from side to side. You'll notice that objects nearer to you appear to move about faster than objects further away from you. However, most of the time people use two eyes to judge distance and depth, as using two eyes gives us more information. Probably the best example of this extra information is *retinal disparity,* which means the retina on the back of the left eye sees something slightly different from the retina on the back of the right eye. You can easily see retinal disparity in action by holding one hand out in front of yourself at arm's length with your thumb up. Close one eye then the other, and keep swapping between using your left eye and your right. You should notice that as you move from one eye to the other your thumb, which is quite close to you, seems to move around a lot, whereas objects which are further away move around less. So retinal disparity gives you information about how far away objects are: when an object appears to be in a very different location in each eye, you know it must be quite close; when an object appears to be more or less in the same location in each eye you know it must be far away – try the experiment again but this time looking at something in the distance.

Another important binocular cue is *binocular convergence.* Hold up your thumb again and this time, move it slowly towards yourself, until it is almost touching your nose, trying to focus on your thumbnail the whole time. You should notice that when your thumb gets really quite close to your face you can feel your eyes swiveling inwards as they both try to remain locked onto your thumb. Indeed, when your thumb gets really close to your face you might even find it starts to get uncomfortable, as the muscles which move your eyes get strained. This sort of information from your eye muscles also helps you judge how far away is the object you are focusing on. So distance and depth perception use a mixture of monocular and binocular cues to help us work out how far away objects are. Both are useful, although as anybody with one eye will tell you, it is possible to do pretty good distance perception without binocular cues. Indeed, some people have gone so far as to suggest that the main reason we have two eyes is not to give us extra binocular cues for judging depth, but so that we have a spare in case one gets damaged!

GIBSON AND WALK'S VISUAL CLIFF

Gibson and Walk built an apparatus which consisted of a sheet of strong glass held up about a metre off the ground on a frame. Underneath the glass was a sheet of checkered paper. Under half the glass, the paper was just beneath the surface. The paper then dropped down suddenly so that, under the other half of the glass, it was about a metre below the surface – the drop was the 'cliff'. From above, the view was of a continuous checkered pattern. The logic of the study was that if babies did crawl over the 'cliff', then they must not be able to tell that the patterned sheet fell away at that point, and this would suggest they cannot perceive depth.

Infants were placed on the middle of the glass sheet and their parent called to them from the 'deep' or 'shallow' side. This was done with 36 infants between 6 and 14 months of age. Twenty seven of the infants would crawl to their parents over the shallow side, with only three of these also crawling to the parent over the deep side. Nine infants refused to move at all. A number of infants became distressed when called from the deep side, and some infants actually crawled away from the parent. It is clear then that babies showed a clear aversion to crawling over the edge of the 'cliff'. Gibson and Walk concluded that they must have had good enough perceptual skills to notice the change in depth. This shows babies of just a few months have reasonably good depth perception.

Gibson and Walk also tested a number of animals on the apparatus, apparently demonstrating that they too have an innate depth perception. For example, chicks would wander to the edge of the cliff but venture no further, and lambs placed directly onto the deep side refused to get to their feet. Rats would happily wander onto the deep side over the cliff, but they did this because information from their whiskers gave them additional non-visual information of a solid surface. When their whiskers were removed they too were reluctant to cross the cliff edge to the deep side.

ASK AN EXAMINER

"Be warned – you may be asked specifically for infant studies in the exam. Several are presented in this section, in enough detail to get you good marks if you use them effectively."

The Gibson and Walk study suggests that infants can tell how far away a surface is, and so must have good depth perception. It also tells us babies have a fear of depths – they somehow know that a drop is dangerous. However, firm conclusions about the innateness of depth perception cannot be made based on these findings. It is plausible that we are born with a fear of falling, as this fear would be very useful for helping babies survive, but again this study cannot tell us this. In order to take part in the study babies would have to be mobile, and most babies do not start to crawl until after 6 months of age. It could be argued that by this time they could have had ample time and experience to learn depth perception and the dangers of falling.

In an intriguing variation of the Gibson and Walk study, Campos et al (1970) used the visual cliff to investigate depth perception in infants too young to crawl. They placed 2 to 3-month old infants face down on either the deep or shallow side whilst at the same time measuring their heart rate. Being too young to crawl and escape what they felt was a dangerous drop, these infants should show anxiety with an increased cardiac response. They found that heart rate actually decreased on the deep side, the babies seeming quieter and more engaged. This suggests that babies can identify depth but have not learned to associate it with danger so show no anxious response to it. In fact it seems that they find the deep side more interesting that the shallow, perhaps because it *was* more interesting – it offered more visual stimulation.

Another way of investigating whether depth and distance abilities are innate is to see how young infants and animals react to 'looming' objects. When an object suddenly comes towards us, our normal reaction is to move to avoid the collision. Schiff (1965) reared chicks in complete darkness from hatching. He rear-projected a 'looming' (that is, a rapidly enlarging) shadow onto a translucent screen and, despite this being their first visual experience, all chicks exposed to this stimulus responded defensively. Náñez (1988) conducted a similar study with human infants and found that, as young as 3 to 6 weeks of age, infants produced avoidance behaviours, such as blinking and backward head movement. Moreover, they do not show this behaviour if the looming object appears as though it is going to 'miss'. Babies younger than 3 weeks do not show this avoidance behaviour however, suggesting either that it is quickly learned or that the visual system is not sufficiently mature at this age to respond to these cues. Support for the latter position comes from Petterson et al (1980), who found that premature infants display this collision reaction several weeks later than full-term infants (i.e. at similar points in maturation).

Granrud and Yonas (1984)) looked at how infants use 'interposition' as a cue for depth. Interposition is a monocular depth cue where objects nearer to us obscure part or all of an object that is further away. For instance, we perceive a man standing in front of a tree as closer to us because he blocks, or obscures, our view of part of the tree. Their research suggests that, whilst some aspects of depth perception appear very early on in life, they may not be innate.

PERCEPTUAL DEVELOPMENT: VISUAL CONSTANCIES

Visual constancy is your ability to know that an object remains the same, even when what you are seeing seems to change. Imagine watching a door being opened. What arrives at your eyes as the door opens might indicate that the shape of the door itself is changing: however, you perceive its shape as *constant* in your mind – even though what your eyes are seeing has changed. This is known as *shape constancy*.

As the door opens its appearance would suggest that it has changed shape, but we perceive its shape as constantly oblong.

Your mind is able to deal with many sorts of visual constancy. The example we saw with the door is known as shape constancy – the ability to know that an object's shape stays the same as you view it from different angles. Other forms of visual constancy include *colour constancy*. If you take a sheet of white paper and view it first in daylight and then under artificial lighting, the light reaching your eyes from the page is very different. However, your perceptual system allows for this, and no matter how the lighting changes, you continue to perceive the paper as white, even though it might really look yellow, blue or pink, depending on the light. *Size constancy* is linked to distance perception. It is the ability to know that an object doesn't change size as it gets further away from you. When

INTERPOSITION IN INFANTS

Granrud and Yonas (1984) presented two groups of children aged 5 and 7 months with the following two-dimensional images and their behaviour was closely observed. The children had one eye covered at all times to avoid any use of binocular cues to depth.

If infants perceived depth by 'interposition', then the left most part of image (a) would appear nearer than the middle of (a), which in turn would appear nearer than the right most part of (a). In image (b) there is no depth information by interposition. Image (c) was a control image where the parts are identical to (a) but expanded horizontally.

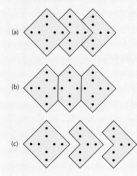

Granrud and Yonas found that children aged 7 months reached significantly more often to the left hand side of image (a) than image (b) suggesting that they considered it to be nearer to them. It might have been that the left hand side of the image is 'bigger' in some way, so Granrud and Yonas repeated the task with images (a) and (c) which had identical component parts.

The 7-month-old infants responded the same as they had before, reaching more often for the left part of (a) than (c). However, the 5-month-old infants' behaviour was different, as they spent the same amount of time reaching for the left parts of (a) and (c). Since 7 month olds understood and could use 'interposition' as a cue to depth but 5 month olds could not, Granrud and Yonas concluded that this ability develops between 5 and 7 months of age.

a person walks away from you, they get much smaller on the back of your eye. But even though the image you are seeing is shrinking, thanks to size constancy you don't feel that the person is shrinking!

All these forms of constancy are important, as without them we could not deal with our environments successfully. For instance, without constancy the objects around you would seem to change dramatically every time you moved your head. An understanding of shape constancy is important as we do not always look at the same objects from exactly the same angles, and when presented from a different angle an object may appear to be a very different shape. If we did not have shape constancy most things we saw would appear to be new to us.

Bower (1966) investigated shape constancy in infants. He wanted to know whether infants were born with this ability or whether it was learned through childhood. In his study, Bower encouraged infants to become familiar with a rectangle shape. Then, in a later session, the shape was again presented to the infants, but at an angle. This means that the infants saw a shape that was slightly different from the one to which they had previously become accustomed. The research found that even very young infants between 50 and 60 days old displayed some understanding of shape constancy. The infants showed that they were familiar with the rectangle shape even when it was presented at a different angle, suggesting that they knew that the same item may appear to be a different shape in different situations. Morrison and Slater (1985) produced data that imply that even younger infants have the same understanding. This suggests that we are either born with the ability to understand the concept of shape constancy or learn it very early indeed.

"Usually, an understanding of what researchers did and what they found is all you need, but it is sometimes worth knowing a bit of detail. In Perception, you can be given a question asking about infant studies. Learn a couple of studies really well (one each for depth/distance, visual constancy and face processing) and you will be well prepared."

"All the research in this section is also relevant to questions which ask you about nature and nurture. When you learn about the development of perceptual abilities, be sure to pay particular attention to what the research say about whether the ability is inborn or due to experience."

Bower's research was carefully conducted in a laboratory setting. He controlled variables such as distance from the object, and the physical size of the object very carefully. We can say with confidence that great care was taken to eliminate all confounding variables, and so the validity of the data is strong. His findings have also been replicated by other researchers.

Slater and Morison (1985) for example found similar results, supporting Bower's claims. Their research was not a replication of Bower's work, but it did address very similar questions. Slater and Morison tested extremely young children, very near to birth, and used a technique called habituation to test what they perceived. In this method, children are presented with a stimulus (in their case, a trapezoid) over and over again, until the young child becomes bored with it and their attention begins to wander. At this point the child is said to be habituated to the object. If a different object is now presented, the child will only attend carefully to it if they think it to be different from the habituated object. In other words, if the child can tell the difference between an habituated object and a new object she will 'tell' the researchers this by looking longer at the new object. Slater and Morison found that infants generally responded not to the shape an object made on their retina, but rather, to the physical shape of the object, just as Bower found. Their results showed that infants habituated to a trapezoid at a certain angle were just as bored with it if it was presented to them at different angles, suggesting that they knew that the object at a different angle was exactly the same as the habituated object.

In another study, Bower (1966) investigated size constancy in infants aged between 6 and 12 weeks. The babies were placed one metre away from a 30cm cube hidden by a screen. When the screen was removed so the infant could see the cube, from the side of the infant the mother played a peek-a-boo game. The aim was to condition the infant to look to one side whenever the cube appeared. There were three experimental

SHAPE CONSTANCY IN INFANTS – BOWER (1966)

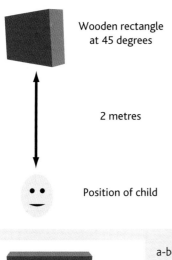

Wooden rectangle at 45 degrees

2 metres

Position of child

Bower set up a series of now classic studies to investigate whether or not visual constancies were innate or learned. In one study he looked at whether very young infants understood shape constancy.

The first part of Bower's study on shape constancy involved conditioning his infant participants.

Bower first presented children aged between 50 and 60 days old with a wooden rectangle measuring 25 by 50cm. The rectangle was placed 2 metres directly in front of the child and angled at 45 degrees.

Because the rectangle was presented at 45 degrees, the shape received by the child's eyes was not a rectangle. Instead it looked as it does in this diagram, more of a 'trapezoid' with the furthest away edge being 'shorter' than the nearest edge.

Each child was 'conditioned' to be familiar with this stimulus by using a game of 'peek-a-boo'. Every time the stimulus was presented a researcher 'rewarded' the child with an enjoyable 'peek-a-boo!'. After time, the child began to associate the presentation of the 45 degree wooden rectangle image with the exciting peek-a-boo reward.

In the second stage of the experiment, Bower presented infants with three different stimuli. If the child understood the idea of shape constancy, stimuli 1 and 2 should appear to them to be the same as the conditioned rectangle.

Stimulus 1 is the same as the conditioned rectangle but at a different angle. Even though it may produce a different shape in the children's eyes, they will know – if they understand shape constancy – that it is the same, and so will respond as if presented with a 'peek-a-boo' reward. Stimulus 2, a trapezoid presented straight on to the child, makes a shape in the children's eyes that is exactly the same as the conditioned rectangle, and *should not*, if the child understands shape constancy, produce the 'peek-a-boo' response. Stimulus 3 is a completely different shape, rotated to 45 degrees. It does not make the same shape in the eyes of the children, and so *should not*, if the child understands shape constancy, bring about the 'peek-a-boo' response.

Bower found that infants tended to respond more to stimulus 1 (the original rotated image):

The conditioned rectangle produced 51 'peek-a-boo' responses.

Stimulus 1 produced 45 'peek-a-boo' responses.

Stimulus 2 produced 28 'peek-a-boo' responses.

Stimulus 3 produced 26 'peek-a-boo' responses.

The results showed that the children responded to the physical shape of the object, not to the shape the object produced in their eyes. Bower was able to conclude that even these very young children were able to understand the concept of shape constancy – that even though something is presented at a different angle, and the eyes tell us the shape may be different, we know that physical shape remains constant even at different angles.

Stimulus 1:
The conditioned rectangle presented straight on to the child *not rotated at all*.

Stimulus 2:
A 'Trapezoid' *presented straight on. NOT rotated at all* that made the same shape in the child's eyes as the conditioned rectangle

Stimulus 3:
A 'Trapezoid' *rotated to 45 Degrees*, in the same way that the conditioned rectangle was rotated.

conditions. First, the 30cm cube was placed three metres from the babies. The second condition involved a 90cm cube being placed three metres from the babies, which would create the same size retinal image as the 30cm cube at one metre. Third, the 90cm cube was placed one metre from the babies, making the 30cm cube look three times as big. Bower found that the children demonstrated size constancy by turning their heads most times to the 30cm cube at three metres. They turned their heads less than half the number of times to the 90cm cube at three metres, showing that they were not always fooled into thinking that the same retinal image size meant the same object. For Bowlby, this demonstration of size constancy was evidence that certain visual skills are present at birth.

PERCEPTUAL DEVELOPMENT: FACE PROCESSING

Research suggests that human beings have a particular talent for recognising and distinguishing faces, a skill which is critical to human survival. There has been considerable debate among psychologists about whether face processing is a special perceptual process already organised at birth, or whether it is part of a more general-purpose object recognition system that becomes specialised with experience.

"Just as with depth/distance and visual constancies, although this section is put here in the context of the development of perceptual abilities, there is a lot you can use in a nature-nurture question. Just watch out for what the research says about face perception being inborn or due to experience."

According to Johnson and Morton (1991), humans have an innate face detection mechanism which they call a 'Conspec' (short for conspecific, which means of the same species). The purpose of this device is to direct a neonate's visual attention to faces, which are biologically important stimuli. That attending to faces may be a basic,

THE LOOKING CHAMBER – FANTZ (1961)

Fantz (1961) was interested in whether very young infants had a preference for looking at particular things. He developed a looking chamber which enabled him to present babies with various visual stimuli whilst at the same time monitoring what it was they preferred to look at.

Fantz tested babies with several different images: simple shapes, stripes, solid blocks of colour, chessboard patterns, concentric rings, and faces. These were presented two at a time and, with much testing, Fantz could tell how long, on average, babies spend looking at each type of picture.

The logic of the study was that if the baby could not tell the two pictures apart, or had no preference for one over the other, they should spend more or less the same amount of time looking at each. But because babies tend to look at things they find interesting, if the baby could tell the two pictures apart and also spent more time looking at one than the other, this would indicate one of the pictures was more interesting to, or held more significance for, the baby.

Babies of just a few days old can tell different patterns and shapes apart. They also prefer looking at complex patterns rather than simple patterns. In particular, they seem to prefer looking at faces more than anything else: Fantz believed that this showed we are born with some knowledge that faces are important.

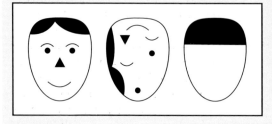

perceptually hard-wired skill is supported by Goren et al (1975), who found that infants as young as 9 minutes old would turn their head and eyes to follow a moving face-like pattern. They were less likely to do this for one in which the features were scrambled.

Early perception research suggested that babies were born with the ability to recognise human faces. Fantz placed babies face-up on a crib contained in a chamber, through the top of which he could present visual stimuli. The gaze of the infant was monitored and it was found that babies younger than 6 months old, showed a clear preference for looking at 'realistic' faces rather than scrambled faces (or, indeed, any other sort of pattern).

Fantz's research shows us that babies, even when only a few days old, can tell different images apart. As such, these very young babies (often referred to as neonates) must have reasonably good visual perception abilities.

Fantz's research also suggests that very young children might know what faces are, which might suggest they are born with this knowledge. However, the babies Fantz tested had not just been born. They all had at least a few days' visual experience – and in particular, experience of seeing their parents' faces. They might thus have learnt during this time that faces are interesting. In other words, the study still doesn't prove babies are born with these abilities or preferences – they might develop in the first days after birth. Also, the faces Fantz used were quite cartoonish and artificial. It is possible the babies looked at the faces so much not because they were faces, but because they were strange faces. Indeed, other research suggests that babies are attracted to things which are novel, so this may indeed be an alternative explanation for some of Fantz's findings.

Research with infants soon after birth, however, suggests that the ability to recognise faces is innate. Bushnell et al (1989) ensured that neonates could use only visual information to recognise their mothers by spraying a strong air-freshener, and found that infants as young as 4 days old looked longer at their mother's face than at a stranger's. Salapatek et al (1975) recorded the eye movements of 1- and 2-month-old infants as they were shown faces of people. Results showed that younger infants paid more attention to the hairline and chin, whilst the older children scanned more of the face, focusing attention on the eyes and mouth. Pascalis et al (1995) supported both

Bushnell et al and Salapatek et al. They found that neonates could not recognise their mothers if the hairline was covered by a scarf. This difficulty was overcome, however, after 4 months of age. It appears that newborn infants rely on edges and lines when they scan a face for recognition, but by about 3 months they start to rely more on internal features of a face for recognition, especially the eyes.

Research into face processing has found that even fairly young infants are capable of making quite sophisticated judgments about faces. By 9 months of age infants can tell apart some facial expressions and adjust their behaviour according to their affective meaning (Serrano et al, 1995), and as early as 3 months of age can distinguish one unfamiliar face from another (Barrera and Maurer, 1981). Fagan and Singer (1979) found that 6-month-old infants can distinguish between similar faces on the basis of age and sex. There is also evidence to suggest that babies have a built-in preference for attractive faces. Langlois et al (1987) showed two groups of infants aged 2 – 3 months and 6 – 8 months pairs of colour slides of adult caucasian women's faces. The faces had previously been rated by adults for attractiveness, and were projected so as to be life-size. Observers measured the amount of time infants spent looking at a particular face as an indication of preference. Results from both groups of infants showed that they looked longer at attractive than unattractive faces when shown in attractive/unattractive pairs. For Langlois et al this clearly indicated that infants were able to tell the difference between female faces according to adult-rated attractiveness.

These findings contradict a general assumption that such preferences are learned as part of the socialisation process, and reflect cultural and historical trends in what is or is not attractive. It is highly unlikely that 2-month-old infants would have learned to prefer attractive faces with so limited experience and in so short a time. This research therefore suggests that infants have an innate 'template' for a prototypical face. Whilst very young infants prefer faces which are prototypical because they are easier to classify as faces, age and experience in the form of culture and socialisation influences the shape and configuration of the template. That infants have an adjustable protypical face is supported by Quinn et al (2002) who found that 3-month-old infants prefer to look at female faces. They suggest that this gender bias is a result of their social environment, in which females are the primary caregivers. Indeed, they found that in cases where the fathers were the primary caregivers, infants had a preference for male faces.

Studies of infants, then, show that face processing may be an innate perceptual skill, with the ability to recognise faces developing gradually over the first 6 months. At different ages, infants attend to specific facial regions, first to edges and borders (e.g. hairline) and then to internal features (eyes then mouth). Not until about 5 months do infants begin to integrate features into a whole face pattern (Caron et al, 1985).

CROSS-CULTURAL STUDIES OF THE DEVELOPMENT OF PERCEPTUAL ABILITIES

No matter where people are born, the biology of their visual perceptual systems (the eye and the brain) is the same. However, we all go through different experiences in life and these might shape the perceptual systems we end up with. Blakemore and Cooper (1970) reared kittens in environments with very little visual stimulation and found they developed different visual systems, even to the extent of showing differences in their brains. It is possible that something similar happens with people. Humans grow up in many different cultures and environments and the different experiences people have in these environments may affect the development of their perceptual systems. In other words, had you been born in another part of the world, it is possible that you might have a fundamentally different perceptual system from the one you now have.

"Cross-cultural research can tell us a great deal about the nature and nurture of perception because it gives us an indication of how important the environment is in shaping perception. If people from different cultures perceive things differently then this is evidence for the nurture view."

Researchers such as Deregowski (1989) have investigated this issue by looking at the perceptual abilities of people from different cultures. This work suggests that people, although they have a lot in common, also show some important differences in how they perceive depending on where in the world they live. Deregowski says that these differences may come about because of the different environments in which people develop.

Look at the picture below. How would you describe what you are seeing? Gregory and Gombrich (1973) asked people from Europe and East Africa to describe this picture and showed that the viewers' life experiences had a big impact on what they saw. Most Europeans who saw this picture said the woman was sitting under a window, whereas most of the Africans said the woman was balancing a box on her head. As everybody, both Europeans and East Africans, was seeing exactly the same picture, their different interpretations of it must have been the result of their using different knowledge as they perceived the picture – a clear example of top-down processing.

"Here is a good example of why you must not compartmentalise your learning too much. Research can often be used in more than one way. This cross-cultural research is also a good example of top-down processing. Be confident enough in what you learn to use your knowledge wherever it might earn you marks: don't confine your learning to specific topics!"

There were also other cultural differences in how people perceived this picture. The Africans usually saw the group sitting outside under a tree whereas the Europeans saw them indoors. This again can be explained in terms of the different environments common to Europe and East Africa. Sitting indoors is much more likely in a European society, whereas sitting with your friends and family in the shade of a tree is more common in an East African community. The different experiences of the different groups explains why they perceive the picture differently.

Another interesting cultural difference in perception can be seen when we consider how people view paintings, drawings and photographs. In our Western culture we see two-dimensional images like drawings and photographs every day, and are used to making sense of these flat pictures through perception. It is easy to forget that photographs and paintings are really quite artificial: they are really only in 2 dimensions, but our world is rich, moving and in three dimensions. Paintings, then, are only artificial representations of a much richer world. Hudson (1960) showed tribal African people the picture below and asked them what the hunter was about to shoot.

Most people living in Western countries would almost certainly say the deer. However, Hudson found that people who had no real experience of seeing flat pictures like this, perceived things very differently. Most of the African people felt the hunter was about to shoot the elephant – because the elephant is closer to the arrow on the picture. Indeed, many of the tribal Africans whom Hudson tested referred to it as a 'baby' elephant – they knew it was smaller in the picture but took this difference in size at face value, not perceiving it as a depth cue meant to show the elephant as far away. So the tribal Africans perceived the picture differently from Europeans because they had had different developmental experiences. In this case they did not have the Europeans' experience of interpreting flat two-dimensional pictures as three-dimensional scenes. (But do note that the tribal Africans' perceptions of the picture were not 'wrong'. Their perceptions might be different from what the artist intended, but the artist has created an artificial image; the elephant is smaller than the deer in the picture, so it is fair to perceive it as a small elephant.)

It can be seen from this that differences in how people perceive a picture can be a result of their different perceptual experiences. An interesting debate has unfolded over the years about whether there might also be cultural differences in our ability to perceive certain visual illusions. If people from different backgrounds see illusions differently,

this would suggest that our tendency to be fooled by such illusions might be a result of different environmental experiences.

Below is a famous visual illusion known as the Müller-Lyer illusion. Even though both vertical lines are really the same length, we perceive one as longer than the other because the diagonal end-pieces affect our perceptions.

Many psychologists believe that the effect of the Müller-Lyer illusion is particularly strong in Western people. The argument goes that because people in the West tend to live in 'carpentered' environments with lots of straight lines and angles, we are used to seeing shapes like the Müller-Lyer, as in the inside and outside corners of rooms and buildings (look at the picture below to see examples of this).

It is this increased frequency of exposure to Müller-Lyer style lines and angles which makes people more likely to be fooled by the illusion. In effect, people in carpentered environments become less sensitive to subtle differences in lines and angles.

If this explanation for the Müller-Lyer illusion is correct then we should expect that people who grow up in a rounder, less carpentered environment will see the Müller-Lyer illusion differently. Sure enough, when people from cultures who live, for example, in round houses are shown the Müller-Lyer images, they tend to perceive the two lines as being the same length, not as different lengths – as do people who live in houses with straight lines and sharp corners. (Deregowski, 1989; Segall et al, 1966). It looks as though the

THE MÜLLER-LYER ILLUSION IN ZAMBIA AND THE UNITED STATES

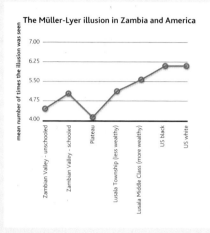

The Müller-Lyer illusion in Zambia and America

Stewart (1973) wanted to compare the extent of illusion experienced by people brought up in different parts of Zambia with that experienced by Americans. To do this he developed an apparatus that required participants to adjust the length of one part of the illusion (the section with the arrow heads) so that its perceived length matched that of the other half of the illusion. The motivation for the research came from previous thinkers who had said that 'race' was the most important factor in our experience of the illusion, and that black African people saw it differently because they were a different race from white Europeans. Stewart felt that environment rather than 'race' was more likely to be the most important factor, and so tested black Zambian people from different areas and environments and socio-economic classes across Zambia and compared their responses with black and white American participants.

Susceptibility to the illusion appeared to depend on the characteristics of the environment in which participants lived. The least susceptible were the people from the Zambezi Valley and the people of the Plateau region of Zambia, described by Stewart as a 'very uncarpentered environment', where people lived in a very traditional environment without the sharp corners and edges familiar to people in the West. He noticed that the amount of schooling seemed to influence the effect, as did the socio-economic status of the people, with middle class Zambians (who tended to live in more 'carpentered' towns) being more susceptible that less well-off Zambians living a more rural lifestyle.

Both black and white Americans were more susceptible to the illusion than any of the Zambians, leading the researchers to conclude that it is environment and culture, and not race, that most influence experience of the Müller-Lyer illusion.

illusion of one line being longer than the other might arise because of the environment in which we learnt to perceive.

Segall et al (1999) report a summary of the experiments that have investigated the illusion in different cultures and show that Europeans and North Americans are by far the most likely to experience the illusion, with the bushmen of the Kalahari, and the Bété people of the Ivory Coast being the least likely to experience the illusion. The evidence is clear. There is a cross-cultural difference in our experiences of the illusion, and it is our experiences of growing and developing in different cultures which dictates our perception.

So it appears that people who grow up in different cultures sometimes seem to perceive scenes differently. This could not happen if we were born with our perceptual systems fully developed. The fact that people from different cultures can look at the same image and perceive it differently shows that some of our perceptual ability must be learnt. If it were not, every human should perceive things in exactly the same way, and it would not matter what experiences they have during development. Clearly some of our perceptual abilities are innate – we are all born with eyes and brains which work

in much the same way. However, cultural differences show us there is a role for learning too.

THE NATURE-NURTURE DEBATE

A very long-standing debate in perception research revolves around whether babies and other young animals are able to perceive as soon as they are born, (in other words perception is something they have inherited), or whether they have to learn to perceive as they grow. This is a version of the nature-nurture debate.

One way of investigating the nature-nurture debate has been to study the perceptual abilities of newborn babies and animals. Gibson and Walk's research suggests that young infants and animals show evidence of depth perception very early on in life, but does not provide conclusive evidence that this skill is innate. Bower found good shape and size constancy skills in young babies. They made errors in judgement but, given how young they were, their performance was much better than one might expect if they had had to learn these skills. This led Bower to favour a nature explanation for visual constancies. Studies indicate that there may be inbuilt face processing mechanisms which are subsequently influenced by

A VERTICAL WORLD

In order to investigate the development of kittens' visual systems Blakemore and Cooper (1970) kept kittens in the dark except for a few hours each day where they would be placed into a 'vertical world'. This was a drum painted on the inside with vertical black and white stripes. The kittens also wore a special collar which prevented them from seeing backwards, to their own bodies. This meant that they spent their whole life seeing only vertical lines.

When the kittens were 5 months old, Blakemore and Cooper used micro-electrodes to examine the cells in the visual cortex of the cats' brains. These microelectrodes allowed the researchers to record how individual brain cells responded as the kitten looked at different images. They found that kittens raised only ever seeing vertical lines did not have any cells which responded to horizontal lines – in effect these kittens could not see horizontal lines. To demonstrate this was true, Blakemore and Cooper showed that a kitten raised seeing only vertical lines could react to a stick if it was held vertically but, when the stick was held horizontally they acted as if it had become invisible – which, to them, it had.

experience. And cross-cultural studies point very clearly to the important role played by the environment in how people perceive the world.

One problem with research into the innateness of perceptual skills however is that even if an infant doesn't show a particular ability early on it could still be innate. Some skills develop as a result of maturation, which means that whilst the ability is inborn it does not show itself until an infant reaches a particular age. Designing an experiment to investigate the importance of the environment on human perceptual development presents insurmountable practical and ethical problems. For this reason, many researchers have turned to using animals, as humans have many perceptual tasks and skills in common with them. One way in which the contribution of learning and environment has been assessed is by depriving animals of certain types of environmental experience. If a perceptual ability was entirely innate and biological then it should be unaffected by this environmental change.

Studies of this kind were conducted by A. N. Reisen during the 1950s and 1960s. He reared chimpanzees in complete darkness for the first 16 months of their life and found that when they were introduced to light their visual and learning skills were seriously impaired. One chimpanzee was kept in normal light and showed recovery of visual skills over several months. Another chimpanzee was returned to darkness for a further 16 months and when tested after this time showed the same visual impairments it had earlier, from which it never fully recovered. This study seems to suggest that perception is not entirely innate and that some environmental experience is necessary for normal development.

Blakemore and Cooper (1970) took kittens and raised them in artificial environments. Some of the kittens grew up only ever seeing horizontal lines; others grew up only ever seeing vertical lines.

Blakemore and Cooper found that after a few months growing up in these environments, the vertical-line kittens had no ability to see horizontal lines, and the horizontal-line kittens had no ability to see vertical lines. Further investigation showed that the kittens' brains did not develop normally. Brains normally have cells which are 'tuned' to see vertical lines and cells which are 'tuned' to see horizontal lines. A kitten raised without any horizontal lines simply did not develop the horizontal-line cells. Likewise, a kitten raised without any vertical lines did not develop the vertical-line cells. This study suggests that the kittens were not born with their brains fully developed and ready to see the world around them. The ability to perceive the world could only develop with experience of sight during the first few months of life. There seems to be a sensitive period during which experience must be normal if the brain is to develop a normal ability to perceive. This is clear evidence of the importance of the environment in the development of perception.

Blakemore and Cooper's study suggests that the ability to perceive isn't entirely inborn – we also need experience of seeing the world, especially during a certain period in our development, for our brains to develop normal perceptual abilities. In many ways, this study reflects the state of the nature-nurture debate today: it is really one of the *relative* importance of heredity and environment, and most psychologists view perceptual development as the result of an interaction between nature and nurture.

FACE RECOGNITION AND VISUAL AGNOSIAS

Most people have no difficulty at all working out the complicated mix of visual images that we are constantly bombarded with. In a crowded room we can pick out individual faces and decide who to talk to and who to avoid. When handed a sketch book and a pencil we can attempt a drawing to reproduce something we see in front of us. Most of us have no difficulty at all in identifying the difference between the wonderful array of colours we may experience every day, and remembering what our loved ones look like is not something we worry about – it just happens.

Some people however have great difficulties with all of these things. The inability to make sense of an otherwise normal visual stimulus is known as an agnosia, which literally means 'not knowing'.

Agnosias are usually caused by a head trauma of some kind, for example by a brain tumor, where the growth is in a region of the brain important for visual processing. Other common causes are carbonmonoxide poisoning, where brain regions are starved of vital oxygen, and stroke, whereby the blood supply to a part of the brain is somehow interrupted.

ASK AN EXAMINER

"Be prepared to say what an agnosia is: a knowledge of a couple of types of agnosia, with examples of the problem, will help you to get the point across. If you are asked a general question on agnosia, you would write mainly about a specific type of agnosia called prosopagnosia, which is described in detail later in this section."

There are different types of agnosia, according to the kind of recognition problem which the survivor of brain damage shows. Because of the type of brain damage it causes, people that survive carbon monoxide poisoning may be left with *apperceptive agnosia*. This is often described as a problem of putting the individual parts of a visual stimulus together, since whilst people with this condition can understand individual sensory elements (what size, colour or shape something is) they can't combine these into a perceptual whole. Here, people may be able to describe the physical features of an object but have difficulty identifying it. They also have difficulty copying objects.

A similar (and some say overlapping) problem is *associative agnosia*. This is where objects are correctly perceived but they have lost their meaning. So for example, such an agnostic could name an object but would have difficulty saying what it does, or putting it into a category with other objects of similar meaning. Unlike apperceptive agnostics, associative agnostics have no difficulty copying objects.

THE GENETICS OF FACES AND PLACES

Research by Polk et al (2007) suggests that face and place processing are at least partially determined by genetics. Twenty four sets of fraternal and identical twins had their brain activity measured with fMRI whilst they were shown a series of images (e.g. a face, a place, a word, or an object), as well as the images in a very degraded scrambled form as a baseline measure.

Polk et al found greater similarity in the brain activity of identical twins than fraternal twins when looking at the pictures of faces and places. They suggest that this is strong evidence for a genetic basis to some perceptual abilities. Identical twins are genetically the same, whilst fraternal twins share 50% of their genes like any other sibling pair. The lower similarity of responses to words is a result of words being more a consequence of experience than genetics. This is because face and place recognition are much older on an evolutionary scale and offer a selective advantage for animals. Polk et al support this by pointing out that, unlike reading, face and place processing is a skill shared by other animals.

THE APPERCEPTIVE AGNOSIA OF DF (GOODALE AND MILNER, 1991)

Adapted from Milner and Goodale (1995).

DF was a 35-year-old woman who suffered carbon monoxide poisoning from a faulty water heater in her bathroom, causing brain damage in part of her visual system: as a result she was unable to recognise real or drawn objects. DF's difficulties were not only to do with recognising objects, however. She was also unable to identify the size and orientation of visual objects, and she was unable to copy simple drawings of them. Interestingly, she was able to draw objects from memory, but was unable to identify the objects she was drawing. This is illustrated below.

DF was able to shape her hand to the right size and orientation when reaching out to pick up objects even though she did not recognise the object. This means that she is able to use her perception of the physical features of objects when guiding her movements to pick them up, so she must be able to perceive the object to some extent. This shows that we are not consciously aware of some of the processes of perception that go on in the brain.

Another kind of agnosia is *simultagnosia*. Those who suffer with this problem find the visual world hard or impossible to see as a whole. If you look around you right now, what you are seeing contains many visual objects, but you will not see the environment as composed of separate parts. However, if you had simultagnosia you would perceive one part of the scene at a time and then be unable to link the separate parts together to make a meaningful perception. This means that simultagnosics find the world a quite confusing place. For example, because they can't simultaneously process objects when faced with a busy scene, they appear slow because they are processing objects in a serial fashion.

Other types of agnosia include *shape agnosia* (where people have difficulty copying and discriminating between simple shapes), and *colour agnosia* (the inability to recognise colours). There is one type of object however, which appears to be different from any other, and that is the human face. Loss of the ability to recognise faces is called *prosopagnosia*.

A great deal of research has been carried out with people with shape agnosias. Many of them have suffered with carbon monoxide poisoning, which causes random, diffuse damage to the cortex on the brain. It could be that this spread-out damage may result in patients having lots of different areas of reduced sensitivity in the visual fields, with the result that their perceptions are fragmented. In effect, what they see is odd shapes and contours (Humphreys and Riddoch, 1987).

People with colour agnosia (also known as cerebral achromatopsia) have difficulty recognising colours even though the eye is not damaged at all. The problem occurs because of damage to a part of the brain that processes visual colour information and can greatly influence quality of life. Bornstein and Kidron (1959) report the case of a patient with colour agnosia who reported that the sky always looked cloudy, and the sun appeared to be 'dirty'. Colour agnosia can also influence object identification. One colour agnosic described by Pallin (1955) reported that everything was in shades of grey. All his shirts appeared dirty. He had difficulty saying whether lights were on or off and, from a distance, whether the fire in a room was burning. He also reported having trouble identifying some foods on his plate until he tasted or smelled them. Some things could be identified from their size and shape, for instance bananas and peas looked different, but an omelet looked not unlike a piece of meat.

Face recognition is a very special case of object recognition. It is probably one of the most demanding tasks we set our visual system – to identify one specific instance of an object. Faces are all pretty much the same – they all have similar features (mouth, nose, eyes, ears) arranged in the same way. The differences between faces are actually quite subtle, yet we are able to recognise thousands of individual faces. It is a skill which requires a combination of bottom-up processing (since we must know that what we are looking at is a face) and top-down processing (in that we apply prior knowledge to recognise a face, such as context, age etc.).

It looks as though when we see people's faces, our minds don't treat these like any other object. Rather, our minds see faces as a completely different type of object, which require special processing. It is as though there is something very basic about our tendency to respond to faces. This idea makes quite a lot of sense. We humans live in groups – we live in families, and communities. Such communal living only works if we can recognise other individuals, and the way we recognise individuals relies very heavily on looking at their faces (unlike dogs, say, which rely much more on scents).

BRUCE AND YOUNG'S THEORY OF FACE RECOGNITION

Vicki Bruce and Andrew Young (1983) suggested that we recognise faces in a series of three stages. In the first stage, we don't see a face as a face, but rather see a set of individual features. So in this stage our mind is processing the eyes separately from the mouth, the mouth separately from the hairline, and so on. It is at this stage we can tell whether a person is happy or sad (from analysing their mouth and eyes) and it is at this stage we can tell how old a person is (from their eyes, skin and so on). Only after we have processed the various features do we combine them to form a mental representation of the whole face. This is the second stage of face processing, and provides us with a single image of the face we are looking at. We then use this image for the third stage of processing, where we 'look up' the face in memory, and decide whether or not the person we are looking at is someone we know.

> **ASK AN EXAMINER**
>
> *"You could have a question specifically on Bruce and Young's theory, so this is a great diagram to learn – you can get a lots of marks for just reproducing it in the exam. Once you've done that it will stimulate your memory, and then it is a case of going through and explaining a little bit about what you have drawn. It really is worth the effort!"*

Bruce and Young's model of face recognition consists of a number of separate processing stages, with information passing between them. Each processing stage has a different role in face recognition.

Structural encoding – The image of the face is represented as a basic pattern. It is here that the image of the face is placed into the face processing system. This part of the model is split into two parts:

View-centred descriptions – Here the system calls on expression analysis, facial speech analysis and directed visual processing to help describe the image.

Expression-independent descriptions – Here the structural encoding system identifies features of the face that do not change with expressions: for instance, the overall size, the physical sizes of the nose and jaw etc.

Expression analysis – It is here that we decide how a person is feeling by reading the information in their face. A frown or a smile, for instance, suggests different emotional states.

Facial speech analysis – We might think of this as lip-reading. Here we use the information in a person's face to help us decipher speech. We look at a person's mouth a lot when we listen to them speak, as it gives us a clue as to what they are saying. For instance, when we see the lips close when the person is speaking, they must have produced a 'b', a 'p' or an 'm' sound.

Directed visual processing – This is where we focus on particular aspects of a face. Some kinds of face processing can depend on quite simple decisions. For instance, does the person have long hair; does the person have a beard; or does the person wear glasses? These are 'directed visual processing' questions. The system can be directed to check for an answer to each, which can help the person decipher the face.

Face recognition units (FRU) – Here we store structural descriptions of faces we are familiar with. For instance, we know what our best friend's face looks like and we store information about their head size, eyes, nose mouth etc. in this part of the model.

Person identity nodes (PIN) – This is where we store the biographical information we have about a person. For instance, we know what our best friend's favourite food and music are.

Name generation – Here we store the names of people, separately from all other information about them.

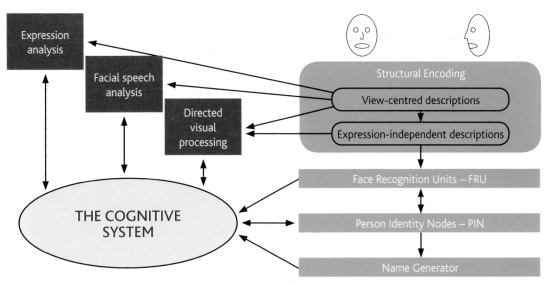

A functional model of face recognition Bruce and Young (1986).

"This diagram looks more complicated than it really is. Think of it as having four parts (as in the colours). Briefly describe what is going on in each part – first blue, then red, then green, and finally yellow. Add some detail to red and green (they are the easiest bits to remember anyway) and hey presto you have a good description which will get you loads of marks."

Cognitive system – This is the general cognitive system where for example we store all our memories. Among these would be, for instance, your memory of how people should behave in different situations. For example, you may see a person at the local swimming pool wearing a clown's nose. This is very possible on Red Nose Day, but unlikely for the rest of the year. The cognitive system would tell you this, and so influence your decision about the person's face. "Did you really see a red nose" That's very unlikely. Look again!' Similarly, you might think that you see your teacher on a beach in Spain in the summer holidays. It's possible, but the likelihood of bumping into someone you know so well so far away is quite slim. The cognitive system would help you calculate this likelihood, and perhaps alter your perception of the face of the person on the beach. This will help you notice that it is not your teacher at all – it is simply someone who bears some resemblance to them.

The structure of the model and the relationships between stages indicated by the arrows explains normal face processing skills. For example, it is a quite usual experience to see a face that we recognise, but not to recall any further information about the person – in this case, the FRU is activated by a face, giving a sense of recognition, but further information about the person including their name is not available. Similarly, a face can be recognised and biographical information retrieved, but not the person's name. Another example would be the everyday experience whereby it never seems to be the case that we remember someone's name without also recalling something else about them. This is because, as the arrows in the diagram suggest, before a name is recalled there must have been some activation of the PIN for that person, giving biographical information.

These three examples of normal face processing clearly indicate that structural descriptions of faces, biographical information and people's names are all stored separately. Separate processing mechanisms are also indicated by the kinds of deficits in face processing observed following head injury. For example, some people are left having difficulty recognising familiar faces but can still identify happy or sad facial expressions.

EVALUATION OF BRUCE AND YOUNG'S MODEL

» Bruce and Young (1993) tested the ability of soldiers who had suffered different kinds of brain damage to recognise faces and different aspects of faces. The researchers found that the types of problems the soldiers had were different from one another: for instance, some had problems identifying expressions, some matching different views of familiar faces. This suggests that face processing is indeed modular, as Bruce and Young describe. 'Modular' means that different skills (emotion, familiarity etc.) are processed in different parts of the system. The research with the soldiers shows that where one part of the system is damaged, another part may well remain intact.

» Bruce and Young's theory is supported by investigations of people with face processing problems. Bruyer et al (1983) describe the case of a man who could pick out faces from other objects and copy line drawings of faces. He could also match unfamiliar faces, so that if he was shown some photos of faces he had never seen before he would be able to select them from a larger collection of faces later on. So, he seemed to be able to perceive faces. However, he was unable to recognise famous faces, faces of friends and family, hospital staff, and even himself. He did not lose his memory for these familiar people – for example, he could recognise people from names and voices. In terms of the Bruce and Young model, this man appeared to have defective face recognition units but intact person identity nodes – he had memory for people, he could process face information of strangers, but had lost the sense of face familiarity.

» A good source of evidence that we process features separately in the early stages of face processing comes from the 'Thatcher illusion' (Thompson, 1980), a version of which is shown below. Here, the two faces (in the original version, the face of the then UK Prime Minister Margaret Thatcher was used) look pretty similar when upside down, but when turned the right way up one suddenly looks very different from the other. This shows us that we process the features of a face separately (if we did not, and only saw whole faces, we would instantly see the two images as being different). It also shows us that the second stage, where we combine facial features to get a mental image of the whole face, only works when everything is the right way up, as this is how we normally see faces.

» Bruce and Young's model has been extremely useful in developing our understanding of face processing. It has been applied in many different areas – most recently in our understanding of how the police may help people remember faces, and how face recognition may be encouraged even when small parts of a face are left visible,

such as when a criminal decides to hide their face (Frowd et al, 2008). Frowd et al build on the earlier work of Bradshaw and Wallace (1971) who investigated face perception using identikit faces. In their research, Bradshaw and Wallace made different faces out of an identikit, which allowed them to change many of the features of the face including the eyes, chin, hair, mouth and brow. They found that the more differences there were between faces, the longer it took for participants to decide whether, on balance, two identikit images were of the same face or not. This suggests that we process each feature individually and sequentially. Later research from Young et al (1987), however, concluded that we do not necessarily process each feature one at a time. It may be that when comparing two faces, we process the overall organisation of the face, described as its 'configuration'. The more features that are different between two faces, the more different is the overall configuration, and so it may have been this difference that accounted for longer processing.

This is a version of the Thatcher illusion. Both faces look relatively normal when upsidedown like this, but rather different when the book is rotated so the faces are the right way up.

» Critics of the Bruce and Young model have said that the model lacks explanation in certain areas. The 'cognitive processing' component for instance is rather vague. Bruce and Young have not fully explained the role of memory in the model, or indeed, how it may be stimulated and accessed by different parts of the face processing system. Cognitive processing is also involved, as we described earlier, in calculating likelihood and probability. For instance, seeing Angelina Jolie in your local dry-cleaner's doesn't seem likely. Bruce and Young do not explain how this calculation is done and how the many complex parts of 'cognition' – not least memory – interact.

The Bruce and Young model also has difficulty explaining covert recognition, which means that there is some familiarity with the identity of a face but without awareness. McNeil and Warrington

(1993) showed patient WJ sets of photographs containing both familiar and unfamiliar faces. When asked to select the famous faces he was unable to do so. However, performance improved significantly when the task involved questions phrased as "which one is…?" According to Bruce and Young, face familiarity occurs with the activation of FRUs, and identification of a face (by activation of PINs) should not occur without this. In other words, WJ should not be able to identify faces without some sense of familiarity, as identification occurs later in processing.

A further problem for the theory comes from the performance of a person reported by de Haan et al (1991) who could match names to famous faces but could not retrieve autobiographical information about them. This is simply not something that happens in everyday life – we never see a face and ascribe to it a name without knowing *something* else about the person. Presumably, since biographical information is the responsibility of PINs, then these must be damaged in some way in this patient. However, if Bruce and Young's theory is correct then damaged PINs should prevent information about the name from being retrieved since generating the name is later in processing and requires PIN activation. This patient should be prevented from matching names to faces, but this was clearly not the case.

Others have said that the Bruce and Young model is useful, but that the researchers have not fully explained how we learn to understand the complicated information carried, for example, in expressions, and 'facial speech'. While it does seem extremely likely that we learn these abilities as we develop, Bruce and Young do not explain how this learning occurs. Presumably, if face recognition is a skill acquired during development, then a different model of face processing is required to explain earlier face recognition skills when some of the stages in the Bruce and Young model are not yet developed.

"You may be asked specifically about prosopagnosia, so make sure you are familiar with a few case studies and can explain the problems using the Bruce and Young model. Remember, this model doesn't explain all cases of prosopagnosia, so you should be aware of alternative explanations too."

PROSOPAGNOSIA: A SPECIAL FORM OF AGNOSIA

A good source of evidence for face processing being special, and different from the processing of other objects, comes from a condition called prosopagnosia. This is where a person can recognise everyday objects but struggles to recognise faces. It is difficult to see how this could happen if faces and other objects are processed the same way (although, as we will see shortly, some people have questioned this claim). The people described in the earlier research by Bryer et al, McNeil and Warrington and de Haan et al all suffered from prosopagnosia.

Another case of prosopagnosia was Mr W (Rumiati et al, 1994). Mr W was a farmer who suffered some damage to part of his brain after an illness and who lost the ability to recognise people. When psychologists examined him, they found he was still able to process the individual features of faces normally – he could answer questions about a person's eyes, mouth and so on, could copy a drawing of a face and could tell which faces were happy and which sad. If you remember, Bruce and Young said that the first stage of face processing involves processing all the features of a person's face separately. The fact that Mr W could answer questions about individual features, and copy them one at a time in a drawing, suggests the first stage of Bruce and Young's model must have been working more or less normally: Mr W had no trouble dealing with individual features.

But what about the second stage of the model, in which the individual features are combined to create a representation of the whole face? Further investigation showed Mr W could look at photographs of people he didn't know and say which photographs showed the same person. This suggests the second stage of Bruce and Young's process was also working properly: he could combine the features to create a mental image of a face, and compare these faces across pictures.

So Mr W's problems seemed to lie specifically with the third stage, where we use these whole-face mental images to decide if the person we are looking at is familiar or not. He couldn't recognise pictures of famous people, even though he knew who they were (he could say who they were when he was told their names), and couldn't even recognise himself when shown a video recording. So Mr W provides good evidence for the model Bruce and Young suggested: two of the three processing stages seemed to be working normally and the third seemed to be impaired. The evidence all fitted the model nicely.

A DIFFERENT EXPLANATION OF PROSOPAGNOSIA

Some people have questioned Bruce and Young's multi-stage approach, however. For example, Bornstein et al (1969) found another brain-injured farmer who, after his injury, could no longer recognise faces, just like Mr W. However, Bornstein's patient also could no longer recognise the individual cows in his herd, whereas before the injury he knew every cow and could tell them apart with ease. Bruce and Young had argued that faces are, to our minds, 'special' and that we have a separate mental system for dealing with them. However, after studying the farmer, Bornstein et al suggested a very different explanation to Bruce and Young. They said that perhaps faces aren't 'special' after all, as Bruce and Young said they were, and we don't treat them completely differently to any other objects we see. Instead, perhaps patients like Mr W struggle to recognise faces simply because faces are all very similar. Cows too are very similar and he also lost the ability to tell these apart. Whereas other objects, like cars for example, can vary a great deal, faces are only very subtly different from one another – they're all pretty much the same shape and size, only come in a few colours

and so on. In other words, perhaps the problem for a prosopagnosic patient like Mr W isn't that he had lost the ability to perceive faces as such, but rather he had lost his ability to make very fine distinctions between very similar-looking objects.

Bornstein et al suggest that faces are complex objects and recognising one from another is no different to telling apart other objects which have only subtle variations.

GREEBLE TRAINING

The issue of how people process the various components which make up faces, in the way Bruce and Young described, was explored by Gauthier and Tarr (1997). They created a set of artificial objects which they called 'greebles'. These were bulbous vase-like objects with various random protuberances attached to them. Whilst greebles are not faces, the task of recognising them is very similar to the task of recognising faces.

Gauthier and Tarr trained people to recognise these greebles and discovered that, just as people are better at recognising mouths and eyes when these are seen with the rest of the face rather than on their own, people were better at recognising a greeble's various protuberances when they were seen on a greeble than when they were seen on

GREEBLE TRAINING WITH EDWARD

Duchaine (2006) studied the face processing abilities of Edward, a well-educated 53-year-old research physicist. Whilst Edward had never suffered any head injury, he had a lifelong difficulty with recognising faces: for example as a child he had difficulty recognising his father. He had what psychologists call a *developmental prosopagnosia*. When Edward was shown a variety of types of object such as horses, cars, guns etc. he could remember and distinguish between them when he was shown them again later. However, he showed particular problems when the objects were faces, indicating that his object recognition problems were specific to faces. Since Edward knew what a face was, he had no problem with the structural encoding element of Bruce and Young's theory. He could describe a face but he could not retain information *about* a face, suggesting that he had a problem with face recognition units.

Edward performed as well as normal on greeble training, suggesting that prosopagnosia was not caused by problems with fine distinction. According to Duchaine, we analyse and recognise faces in a different way from how we recognise objects, using a brain region specific to face processing.

THE DEVELOPMENT OF AN IDEA – SCIENCE IN ACTION

Bruce and Young developed their original model in 1986. Since then it has undergone a number of changes and developments. This is a good example of how science works. An idea and a theory are produced and published for the academic world to view and comment on. After publication the model was again reviewed at conferences, and other researchers were able to conduct their own research into it. As a result of this, changes were built into new versions of the model. In 1990, Mike Burton and colleagues looked again at the different parts of the model, and then in 1993, Mike Burton and Vicki Bruce together developed a new version. In their improved model, the name generation unit is removed entirely, and the person identity nodes are used in judgements about familiarity, not, as originally, the face recognition units. One way in which the models have been tested over the years is with increasingly complex computer software. These simulate the 'recognition' of faces. Computers are 'taught' to recognise faces, then different parts of these faces are changed to see how it influences the computer's performance. If the computer fails, and the failure is like that of a human, we can say that the computer is 'behaving' like a human on the task. This then allows researchers to test hypotheses about the model using the computer over and over again, carefully changing the model to achieve the best 'human-like' performance. Bruce and Stirling (2008) continue this work, identifying how computers and humans are similar in their face processing abilities and how they may be different.

their own: a very interesting parallel with face processing.

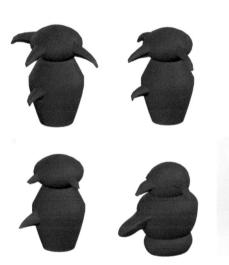

Some examples of greebles. Notice that, like faces, they differ but also have things in common.

Gauthier et al (1999) also used greebles to look directly at how people's brains process face-like information. People were trained in recognising greebles until they were good at telling individual greebles from one another. This was intended to make sure the greebles, which were all quite similar and hard to tell apart, were being processed in much the same way as faces, which are also quite similar and hard to tell apart. The participants in the study then looked at pictures of greebles and made decisions about them whilst lying in a brain scanner which could record the activity in different parts of the brain. The scans showed that the fusiform gyrus, a part of the brain which we know is used in face processing, was also being used when the greeble experts tried to recognise greebles. This is interesting, as greebles are completely artificial stimuli: whereas people might plausibly be born with a part of their brain which recognises faces, there is no way people could be born with a brain system for recognising greebles, as they are invented images. The fact that recognising faces and greebles used the same brain region suggests that that region might not be a specialised face-processing system at all. Rather, Gauthier et al suggested, it might be a system in the brain which is used for fine discrimination – that is, telling apart similar objects.

So Gauthier et al suggest that telling apart individual faces and individual greebles is really the same process and uses the same brain mechanisms. If they are correct in saying this, we should expect that a person who has difficulty telling faces apart must also have trouble telling apart greebles. However, it turned out this is not the case. Duchaine et al (2004) found a patient with prosopagnosia who was good at learning to recognise greebles and at telling them apart. If this patient, who couldn't recognise individual faces, could recognise individual greebles, then faces and greebles cannot be processed using exactly the same mechanisms after all. There must be more to prosopagnosia than simply an inability to tell apart very similar objects: it must be something particular to faces.

Relationships

ANDREA ACKLAND

You are expected in the examination to show both the skills of knowledge and understanding and the skills of analysis and evaluation in relation to the topic Relationships.

Where opportunities for their effective use arise, you will need to demonstrate an appreciation of issues and debates. These include the nature/nurture debate, ethical issues in research, free-will/determinism, reductionism, gender and culture bias and the use of animals in research.

You will also need to demonstrate an understanding of How Science Works. You can do this through the effective use of studies in your answer (as description or evaluation) or where appropriate by evaluating methodology and findings.

WHAT YOU NEED TO KNOW

THE FORMATION, MAINTENANCE AND BREAKDOWN OF ROMANTIC RELATIONSHIPS

- Theories of the formation, maintenance and breakdown of romantic relationships: e.g. reinforcement/affect theory, social exchange theory, sociobiological theory

HUMAN REPRODUCTIVE BEHAVIOUR

- The relationship between sexual selection and human reproductive behaviour
- Evolutionary explanations of parental investment: e.g. sex differences, parent–offspring conflict

EFFECTS OF EARLY EXPERIENCE AND CULTURE ON ADULT RELATIONSHIPS

- The influence of childhood and adolescent experiences on adult relationships, including parent–child relationships and interaction with peers
- The nature of relationships in different cultures

THE FORMATION, MAINTENANCE AND BREAKDOWN OF ROMANTIC RELATIONSHIPS

How and why relationships form and how they are then maintained is a substantial area of research in psychology, and a number of theories have been developed to explain this process. Some theories tell us that relationships are formed and maintained on the basis of an exchange of some kind between those taking part. These are known as 'economic' theories. Another approach focuses on evolutionary pressures that play a vital role in our relationships. Before we address these, though, we'll discuss an important theory that indicates that relationship formation and maintenance is essentially a learning process – the reinforcement/affect theory.

THE REINFORCEMENT/AFFECT THEORY

The reinforcement/affect theory developed by Byrne and Clore (1970) is based on learning theory, that is, classical and operant conditioning. Classical conditioning involves learning by association, whilst operant conditioning involves learning by consequences – we are more likely to do things that are reinforced and less likely to do things that are punished. The two forms of learning are not entirely separate: they tend to co-occur. So, for example, we might initially make a pleasurable association between two events (classical conditioning) and then, because the association was pleasurable, engage in similar behaviours again (operant conditioning).

> **ASK AN EXAMINER**
>
> *"Having a good knowledge of learning theory will be very useful in everything you cover on the A2 course. You will have come across it on your AS course – if you didn't get it then, now is the time to really put the effort in to ensure that you do 'get it'. Get it?"*

The theory has a *reinforcement* component (something which increases the likelihood of a behaviour occurring again) and an *affect* component (an emotion or feeling). In simple terms, the reinforcement/affect theory suggests experiences in the relationship may or may not 'reinforce' a positive affect. We are attracted to people and wish to form relationships with them if their company is rewarding to us in some way, making us feel good, and when their company is no longer rewarding the relationship may well come to an end as we no longer feel good in the relationship.

Interestingly, this theory also suggests that a person does not have to be the direct cause of the positive feelings in order to benefit from the positive association. For instance, if you meet somebody under pleasant circumstances then you are more likely to have positive feelings towards them than if you meet them under unpleasant circumstances because you associate a person with

LEARNING THEORY

Classical conditioning says that animals learn by association. It is a simple passive form of learning, based on reflexes. The original research was by Pavlov, who demonstrated that dogs salivated to the sound of a bell because they 'associated' the sound with the presentation of food. He showed that if each time food was presented a bell was also sounded then eventually the sound of the bell itself could make dogs salivate. This salivation is new learning, called the conditioned response. Emotions are also sensitive to classical conditioning, so that humans might learn a new association between a stimulus and an emotion. In this case we call the new learning a conditioned *emotional* response.

In operant conditioning, learning is said to occur because an animal is either rewarded or punished for a behaviour. A reward is said to be *reinforcing*, (that is, it increases the likelihood of a behaviour occurring again), whilst punishment reduces the likelihood of a behaviour occurring again. This form of learning is voluntary in that an animal does something first and learns as a consequence of its behaviour.

These two kinds of learning complement one another in that they often occur together. For example, we make an initial association between two previously unrelated things – this is the classical conditioning element. Based on this initial learning we either escape/avoid these stimuli in future, or we are attracted to them. This is sometimes called two-factor learning.

FORMATION

The theory suggests that if we are experiencing positive affect (i.e. positive emotions) then we will like the people who are around us at the time. Consequently we may wish to form a relationship with these people. On the other hand, when experiencing negative affect (or negative emotions) we will dislike the people around us and will not wish to form relationships with them. The reinforcement/affect model can explain relationship formation as follows. You meet somebody and they make you laugh. This results in your experiencing positive affect. Consequently you wish to spend more time with them because you now associate them with good feelings and you wish to continue to experience these positive feelings. You now engage in behaviours (maybe courtship ones) which increase the likelihood that you will have these experiences again.

MAINTENANCE

The reinforcement/affect model says that being in a relationship that develops positive feelings (positive affect) results in your wishing to remain in that relationship. If the relationship continues to produce these feelings then it is more likely to continue. As relationships develop, those in them may require different things: for instance, companionship and flexibility may become more important than sexual gratification. The flexibility with which a relationship responds to these changes in needs will partly determine the level of reinforcement maintained.

BREAKDOWN

If the relationship no longer generates positive affect, it may begin to break down. Just as in learning theory, when the reinforced behaviour no longer generates a reward, that behaviour will not be reinforced and will not be expressed (leading to 'extinction'). For instance, a rat taught to push a lever when it sees a light may be rewarded with some food. If the food is no longer provided when the lever is pressed then the lever-pressing behaviour will no longer happen. In a relationship, loving behaviour is rewarded by happy pleasant feelings. If the loving behaviour no longer provides this positive affect, the reward reduces, the loving behaviour may cease, and the relationship may begin to break down.

the feelings you had at the time. By this argument a wedding might be a better place to strike up a friendship than a funeral. However, a funeral might provide you both with some notion of 'similarity'. You are both there for the same thing after all, to pay your last respects to the same person, and the feelings or emotions in both you and the others attending the event may provide a basis for some form of relationship. There are many things other than aspects of the environment that might influence the affective component. For example, the physical attractiveness of the person might give us a positive feeling, or having a similar attitude or opinion with someone about something.

ASK AN EXAMINER

"With each theory we present we will first describe the theory then offer separate explanations of how that theory explains formation, maintenance and breakdown. What you must do in an exam answer is explain the theory and then apply it according to the demands of the question. So, if you are asked to explain the formation of relationships, explain one theory, apply it to formation, evaluate, and so on with the other theories. Straightforward, yes?"

RESEARCH INTO THE REINFORCEMENT/ AFFECT THEORY

A good deal of this research suggests that mood can be a positive reinforcer for behaviour and in such conditions a person will be more motivated to form a relationship. It follows that a negative mood can be a negative influence on a relationship because feeling unhappy is in effect a punisher in that it does not positively reinforce a desire to be close to someone.

Research suggests that having a positive or negative affect can alter the degree to which we find someone attractive. If a happy or positive affect is generated a person feels positively towards the potential recipient of their affections; a negative mood does the opposite. May and Hamilton (1980) asked their female participants to rate photographs of attractive and unattractive males under three experimental conditions: whilst listening to rock music (meant to produce a positive affect); listening to avant-garde music (meant to produce a negative affect); or in silence. They found that assessments of physical attractiveness were influenced by the music, with photographs in the rock music condition being evaluated as more attractive than photos viewed whilst listening to avant-garde music.

IF YOU LIKE ME I'LL LIKE YOU BACK

It may not come as a surprise to learn that we tend to like those who we believe like us too. Psychologists call this *reciprocal liking*. Aronson and Linder (1965) conducted an experiment in which participants held conversations with another person; they then 'overheard' the other person giving an opinion of them to the experimenter. This happened on seven occasions, so the other person could appear to change their opinions. Finally the participants were asked how much they liked the other person. There were four conditions.

1. The other person was entirely positive
2. The other person was entirely negative
3. The other person was negative at first and then became positive
4. The other person was positive at first and then became negative

Aronson and Linder found that the other person was most liked under condition three. Overhearing an opinion that the other person had grown to like them during their conversation was attractive to the participants.

Research has found that the most popular girls in a youth detention centre were those who helped, protected and encouraged others. By definition, 'popular' means those that most people would wish to form a relationship with. Being helpful, protecting and encouraging can be regarded as rewarding behaviours and so a relationship with one of these girls would be likely to be rewarding. Presumably, if we dislike someone and are repulsed by them, then we will not wish to form a relationship with them because we do not find their company rewarding.

In a study by Griffith and Veitch (1971) statements by strangers were presented to participants who were in either uncomfortable surroundings or physically comfortable surroundings. Results suggested that in the more uncomfortable conditions, the stranger was liked less. It was concluded that the stranger's statements had become associated with the participants' negative feelings about their surroundings. In another study, Veitch and Griffith (1976) found that people who interacted with a stranger after listening to a radio programme of good news rated the stranger more positively than when they had listened to a programme of depressing news.

Rozin, Millman and Nemeroff (1986) conducted a laboratory experiment where participants were asked to smell a shirt worn by either a liked or a disliked person. They found that a shirt was considered less desirable when it was thought to have been worn by a disliked person, than when it was thought to have been worn by a liked person. (In reality the same shirt was used for all trials!)

Cunningham (1988) asked male participants to watch either a sad or a happy movie and later interact with a female confederate. Those who had watched the happy movie interacted with the confederate more positively and disclosed more information than those who had watched the sad movie.

CRITICISMS OF REINFORCEMENT/AFFECT THEORY

We can see that there is research evidence to support the idea that we form relationships with people whose presence we find rewarding. However, there are a number of criticisms that can also be made of this theory.

» The supporting evidence may lack ecological validity. Most of the research has been conducted in laboratory settings using artificial tasks. After all, how many times have you smelt the shirt of a stranger? Remember, this is social psychology and replicating a natural social environment in a laboratory may be impossible. On this basis, the research evidence could be accused of lacking validity and may be limited in its ability to explain real life behaviour.

"Watch out for the chance to make these kinds of comments. This is a methodological issue, and your examiners will be looking out for your ability to spot problems associated with how the research was carried out. Be careful though: don't just say 'It lacks ecological validity'. That's not enough – to get the best marks, you have to explain why this is a problem and what the implications may be for any conclusions based on the findings of the research."

» The reinforcement/affect theory may be culturally biased and may therefore lack generalisability. Lott (1994) suggests that men and women may find different behaviours rewarding in different cultures. In Western societies women may focus on the needs of others as they are socialised into being attentive to the needs of others such as their husbands and children. The theory also implies that we are self-centred and only form relationships which give us pleasure.

This may not be the case with all relationships in all cultures.

» It is a simple theory, maybe even simplistic. We are dealing here with extremely complex behaviours involving hard-to-investigate issues such as emotion and motivation. Reducing these behaviours to a set of rewards and associations may well oversimplify what is actually a very complex process. It could be argued therefore that this explanation is a reductionist and a deterministic one, because it suggests that not only is the process rather simple, but we have little or no control over our choice of relationships.

"This kind of thing is absolutely fine, but once again, don't just write 'It's reductionist', 'It's deterministic'. That's not nearly enough to get marks. And besides, being reductionist and deterministic isn't necessarily a bad thing! Prove to your examiner that you really know what you're talking about – explain what you mean."

SOCIAL EXCHANGE THEORY

According to Homans (1961), people weigh up the costs and benefits of an action before deciding what they do. In terms of relationships, he suggests that we consider the actual and potential past, present and future rewards and costs before deciding whether a relationship is likely to be profitable. For Homans, choices about relationships are essentially rational economic decisions.

Homans (1974) suggests that we are attracted to those who provide us with economic rewards. An important principle here is that of 'satiation', which suggests that if something is in short supply, we appreciate it more. For instance, if you are thirsty from a lack of water, then a small glass of water will be very much appreciated. In a relationship, if a partner is supplying you with something you are short of, for instance attention or social approval, then you are likely to find their company attractive.

Social exchange theory states, then, that relationships involve the exchange of resources. The extent to which a relationship develops will depend on how mutually beneficial the relationship feels, i.e. how rewarding it is.

"Careful here! It is easy to confuse social exchange with reinforcement/ affect theory, since both use some of the same concepts and terminology, like 'reward'. This is because both theories have their origins in ideas drawn from operant conditioning."

The rewards associated with relationships are anything positive which make us feel valued: this could include gaining access to money, or receiving attention, status, gratification, pleasure etc. Determinants of attraction such as similarity could also be regarded as rewarding because we feel supported by a partner if their views are similar to ours. The costs involved in relationships are anything that is unpleasant: they could be financial costs, but might equally be emotional, such as pain, disappointment, embarrassment, putting up with annoying habits etc. Sedikides et al (1994) suggested that things like happiness and feeling loved are among the most important rewards of a relationship, while stress and worry about the relationship were significant costs. Whereas females thought intimacy and self-growth were rewards, males tended to emphasise sexual gratification as a reward and monetary losses as a cost.

Sampling	People consider the potential costs and rewards of a relationship and compare it with others
Bargaining	There is a giving and receiving of rewards at the beginning of the relationship which tests whether the relationship should continue
Commitment	Focus is on the relationship and the costs and rewards are stabilised
Institutionalisation	Norms of rewards and costs are established by the partners as they 'settle down'

Thibaut and Kelley (1959) proposed that, when in a relationship, we try to minimise costs while maximising benefits (known as the 'minimax' strategy). A relationship will be maintained as long as the rewards exceed the costs. Thibaut and Kelley suggested that relationships progress through a number of stages, as can be seen in the above table.

Social exchange theory suggests that people's feelings about a relationship depend upon a number of factors.

1. How they perceive the rewards
2. How they perceive the costs
3. Perceptions about the relationship they deserve ('comparison level')
4. Perceptions about their chances of getting a better relationship elsewhere ('comparison level for alternatives')

Individuals will calculate the outcome of the relationship quite simply by using a basic formula:

Outcome = Rewards – Costs

Whether your outcome is regarded as satisfactory depends on two factors: your *comparison level* and your *comparison level for alternatives*. Your comparison level is the standard by which all other relationships are judged. It is based on past experiences of relationships, so for example if you've had a bad relationship in the past then your comparison level will be lower than if you've had some very good relationships. The comparison level for alternatives depends on whether we believe that there is an alternative relationship that can provide us with a better outcome. Our comparison levels are likely to change over time as we experience different relationships, or as the current relationship changes in terms of costs and benefits – and they may also be affected by things like our level of self-esteem.

Rusbult (1983) extended the social exchange theory into the *investment model*. She suggested that the maintenance of a relationship also depends on how much we have invested in it. Investments are defined as anything that would be lost if the relationship were to end, and could include material possessions as well as security for the future. If we feel that we have made a large investment then we may stay in the relationship, even if the rewards are low and the costs high. According to Rusbult, we are committed to a relationship if it gives us a high degree of satisfaction, if alternatives are of a low quality and if we have invested highly by making sacrifices for the sake of the relationship.

RESEARCH INTO SOCIAL EXCHANGE THEORY

Floyd et al (1994) found that commitment develops when couples are satisfied with and feel rewarded in a relationship and when they perceive that equally or more attractive alternative relationships are not available to them. Cate and Lloyd (1988) found that the level of rewards from a relationship is a determinant of satisfaction: the more rewarded we feel, the more satisfied we are.

Social exchange theory does appear to have some useful predictive value. The theory has been used to successfully predict how long a premarital relationship would last (Cate and Lloyd 1992). Sprecher (2001) found that comparison levels for alternatives were a strong predictor of commitment in a relationship and that rewards were important as a predictor of satisfaction, especially for women. The comparison level for alternatives was also found to be important in predicting relationship outcome. If an alternative relationship compares more favourably then the cost of staying in the current relationship is increased. Similarly, if alternative relationships do not compare favourably then the costs of the current relationship are reduced.

The role of available alternatives has also been investigated. Simpson et al (1990) suggest that

FORMATION	MAINTENANCE	BREAKDOWN
Economic theories tell us that relationships are formed simply on the basis of costs and rewards. In entering into a relationship we ask ourselves whether there are more rewards than costs. If there are, then the relationship may form. Similarly, if we are in a position to choose between entering a number of different relationships we consider which one will provide us with the largest difference between rewards and costs, or put more simply, which one will provide the largest and most positive outcome.	In order to maintain a relationship the balance between costs and rewards must remain favourable to each party. Once we start investing more than we get out of it we may begin to question whether it is sensible to maintain that relationship. Of course, this involves effort on both sides! It is important for each party to maintain a positive outcome, and to do this, costs must be kept down and rewards must be kept as high as possible. As long as the rewards do not fall below the costs the outcome will remain positive and the relationship may be maintained.	It may be that the costs of a relationship begin to outweigh the rewards. If this happens then the relationship may be regarded as damaging, or too costly to continue, and it may start to break down. For instance, it may begin to require a great deal of effort to gain the same feelings of happiness. When the effort gets too much, the reward (the feelings of happiness) may become so small that, overall, the outcome is negative.

members of the opposite sex are perceived differently, depending on whether we are in a relationship or not. They found that people who were dating someone viewed members of the opposite sex as less attractive than did those who were single. However, Buunk (1987) suggests that attractive alternatives are still a major contributor to the breakdown of some relationships. According to Duck (1994), the attractiveness of an alternative might be influenced by the state of the current relationship.

Rusbult (1983) used heterosexual college students in a study which lasted over seven months and involved the completion of questionnaires every few weeks. She found that people's satisfaction, alternatives and investments all predicted how committed they were to their relationship and whether it lasted. These findings have been supported by other researchers with different samples of both married couples and homosexual relationships, and also in different cultures.

Rusbult and Martz (1995) suggested that their investment model could explain why some people return to abusive relationships. Women who had sought refuge at a shelter for battered women were interviewed. It was discovered that the women who were more likely to return to an abusive partner were those who had poorer economic alternatives to the relationship; were more heavily invested in the relationship (married and had children); and were less dissatisfied with the relationship (reported less severe forms of abuse). As Rusbult's model would predict, they demonstrated more commitment to their relationships because of a greater investment.

CRITICISMS OF SOCIAL EXCHANGE THEORY

As we have seen, there is evidence to support the social exchange theory and Rusbult's extension of the theory. The theory can also account for individual differences which may result in different perceptions of costs and rewards and for people's perceptions changing over time as their circumstances change. However, criticisms of the theory have also been made.

» Costs may not be important at all stages of a relationship. Rusbult (1983) suggests that costs are of little importance during the first few months of a romantic relationship, but may become more important at other times. The theory therefore may be best suited as an explanation of the maintenance of relationships rather than of their formation, because during formation costs are, according to Rusbult, not terribly important.

» Most of the research has been based on short-term relationships, often with samples of students. This questions the validity of the research. If the results of the research relate to the short-term relationships of students they may not be applicable to longer-term relationships of non-students. The theory therefore is of limited use as the dynamics of long-term relationships are different from those of short-term ones. Also, romantic relationships are only one of many different kinds of relationship. Social exchange theory has difficulty explaining situations in which economic exchanges do not seem to apply, such as family care for children and elderly relatives.

» The model does not predict at what level a relationship becomes so unsatisfactory that we decide to leave even if there is no alternative relationship available. We can say that in this respect it is a descriptive model rather than a predictive one. The theory is good at describing how costs and rewards may change, but exactly *how* unrewarding a relationship needs to be before it breaks down is unclear; and just how much more rewarding an alternative relationship has to be before it is chosen over the current relationship is also uncertain.

» Clarke and Mills (1979) have distinguished between two types of relationship based on the norms of giving and receiving benefits. In communal relationships there is a principal concern for the other's needs and welfare, so that there is no expectation that a benefit given will be repaid. In exchange relationships, the benefits are given by one partner in response to actual or possible benefits received in return. This suggests therefore that social exchange theory, which emphasises exchange norms, only applies to certain kinds of relationship, and has less validity in relationships which do not emphasise 'economics'.

» The majority of research relating to social exchange theory has been conducted in Western individualistic cultures and may therefore be culturally biased. The perceived costs and rewards of relationships may be different around the world. For example, in some cultures where basic subsistence is a lifestyle, it may be sufficient to be in a relationship where a partner helps to provide just enough to eat. In more wealthy cultures on the other hand, a comfortable house in a good neighbourhood may be a more important consideration.

SOCIOBIOLOGICAL THEORY

A very different explanation for the formation, maintenance and breakdown of romantic relationships is the sociobiological theory, which has its origins in evolutionary theory. Sociobiology attempts to apply the principles of evolution to an understanding of social behaviours such as relationships. We have already suggested that physical attractiveness appears to play a role in the formation of relationships and the sociobiological approach attempts to explain why this should be the case. Similarly, if we are no longer attracted to the person with whom we are in a relationship, there is the possibility that the relationship may break down. According to this approach, both males and females are seeking to produce healthy offspring in order for their genes to survive into the next generation. Consequently, sexual partners will be sought who can produce and provide for healthy children.

"Whilst, technically speaking, sociobiology and evolution theory are different, in reality when talking about human behaviour, the terms mean more or less the same thing. Sociobiology is normally the term used when applying evolution theory to human social behaviours, but don't get hung up on terminology. Sociobiology/evolutionary psychology – call it what you want."

Females produce few eggs in comparison to the millions of sperm produced by males, and also invest heavily in the nine months of pregnancy, and the childbirth, lactation and child dependency period. Clearly, the male contribution to the reproductive process is minor in comparison. Females are limited in the number of children they can produce during their reproductive years whereas males can produce a seemingly unlimited number of offspring throughout their life. These biological differences have led males and females to develop different strategies and tactics to maximise their chances of reproductive success.

Females are programmed to mate with carefully chosen partners with plentiful resources, whereas males are programmed to maximise their chances of producing offspring by mating frequently and 'sowing their seed' with as many partners as possible. Promiscuity for males is a way of increasing

their chances of reproducing, whereas monogamy is a more appropriate strategy for females, who may seek older, reliable males for long-term relationships who can provide good resources for a potential family. Males may seek younger, attractive females who are likely to be more fertile and produce healthy offspring.

RESEARCH INTO SOCIOBIOLOGICAL THEORY

Males and females look for different things in their partners. Buss (1989) conducted an extensive study which involved analysing over 9,000 questionnaires completed in 37 cultures. Respondents were asked to rate the importance of a number of characteristics such as age, intelligence, physical attributes etc. in a sexual partner. The results support the sociobiological theory, as males valued physical attractiveness while females valued earning potential and occupational status. Both males and females felt the male should be the older partner in the relationship.

Both males and females seek indicators that they can reproduce successfully. Research supports the idea that men prioritise youth and beauty (taken to indicate child-bearing potential). Singh (1993) found men are attracted to women with a low waist-to-hip ratio. Even though the American beauty ideal has become increasingly thinner over the years (as measured by Miss America contestants and *Playboy* centrefolds) a low WHR has consistently been seen as more attractive. Singh suggests that this is because a low WHR (0.7) is not only considered feminine and the most attractive figure shape, but is also linked to higher conception rates.

More recently Montoya (2007) found that both males and females were interested in body parts predictive of health (eyes, skin and complexion). Males preferred body parts predictive of fertility (hips, legs, buttocks, breasts and waist) while females preferred body parts predictive of strength and overall fitness (general muscle tone, arms, shoulders, height). A male V-shaped muscular body is thought to be attractive to females because it indicates the presence of high levels of testosterone required for muscle development (Dabbs and Dabbs, 2000). Taller males are also found to be more attractive than shorter males. Dunbar et al (2000) found that childless men are on average shorter than those men with children and suggests that height preference may therefore be programmed into women's genes.

ETHICS   GENDER   CULTURE   DETERMINISM

FORMATION	MAINTENANCE	BREAKDOWN
As we have already noted, according to sociobiological theory, males and females may enter into a relationship for different reasons and each looks for something different in their chosen partner. Men seek to form relationships with women with physical indicators of fertility, who show potential to produce strong healthy children. Women on the other hand look for men with good genes who can provide for them and their potential offspring.	In order to maintain the relationship the male must continue to provide for the female and her offspring. Similarly, the woman must continue to furnish the male with the opportunity to further his genetic line. Women may opt to provide as many children as possible within their means (both physical and financial) therefore maintaining the relationship, and/or might demonstrate good nurturing skills, thus maximising the investment of the males. Men may choose to remain monogamous and devote themselves to a single relationship in order to provide for their offspring, and ensure their survival and growth to promote the genetic line.	If the male cannot offer good resources, the woman may begin to seek support elsewhere, providing children for a stronger more supportive male in a different monogamous relationship. If the woman refuses to provide children or can no longer reproduce, the male may look elsewhere, engaging in promiscuous behaviour, and ultimately damaging the relationship, often beyond repair.

In evolutionary terms it might make sense for females as well as males to have multiple sexual partners. Females could then benefit by using, for example, the genes from one partner and the resources from another. This idea might be supported by the suggestion that many fathers are thought to be bringing up children they falsely believe are biologically theirs (Brown 2000).

ASK AN EXAMINER

"There is a whole section in this chapter on human reproductive behaviour, which explains human relationships from an evolutionary perspective – you will find loads of research and evaluative material there! Don't treat the sections as entirely separate – each section contains material relevant to all other sections."

CRITICISMS OF SOCIOBIOLOGICAL THEORY

» A good theory should be testable, but unfortunately sociobiological theory cannot be tested experimentally. In order to show that evolutionary forces are governing our choice of romantic partner, a good scientist would remove evolutionary pressures to see what happens. This of course cannot be done.

» This theory has explanatory rather than predictive powers and can be accused of being non-falsifiable. By this we mean that whatever the behaviour, sociobiological theory can account for it. For instance, males who act promiscuously

are regarded as maximising their reproductive chances while males who opt for a monogamous relationship are viewed as acting to improve the chances of their offspring surviving by being in a two-parent family. Any which way, evolution theory has an answer.

» Sociobiological theory assumes that attractiveness and child bearing are linked but is this really the case? Surely a plain woman can breed as well as an attractive woman? Why are cute baby features (such as large eyes and small noses) in females often liked by males? Does having large eyes make you a good child bearer? It may well be that there is a correlation between attractiveness and healthiness, but correlation does not mean cause and so the link between good looks and potential for bearing healthy children is no certainty.

» Sociobiological theory assumes that sexual relationships are always concerned with reproduction. Consequently this theory has difficulty explaining homosexual relationships and heterosexual relationships where the partners have chosen not to have children.

» It is difficult to separate the effects of culture from those of evolution. Historically, women have had lower social status and resources than men. In order to improve their position women have to trade their youth and beauty for an older male partner with status and resources. It could be argued from a feminist perspective that women seek a wealthy partner because they are economically dependent upon men.

» It is both a deterministic and a reductionist theory because it suggests our behaviour is pre-determined by our genes and therefore we have a lack of free will.

ASK AN EXAMINER

"Remember, each of the individual theories discussed previously can explain relationship breakdown. The theories we've included here can either be used as alternatives to those earlier explanations or, perhaps more wisely, used to add breadth and depth to an exam answer."

FURTHER EXPLANATIONS FOR THE BREAKDOWN OF RELATIONSHIPS

The different theories we've already covered (reinforcement/affect, social exchange and sociobiological theory) can all explain why relationships break down. There are, however, a number of other well-known theories that can help us understand how relationships end.

Research has uncovered a number of factors which make it less likely that a relationship will succeed, for example:

» Young couples – especially if they have become parents at a young age – are more likely to get divorced than older couples.

» Lower socioeconomic groups, lower educational levels and different demographic backgrounds are all likely to result in less stable marriages.

» Having experienced a large number of sexual partners before marriage.

» Experiencing at a young age your parents getting divorced.

Duck (2001) suggests there are three categories of relationship break-up:

Pre-existing doom	Incompatibility seems almost predestined (e.g. Granny marries teenage toyboy)
Mechanical failure	This is the most common – the couple find they just cannot live together
Sudden death	Betrayal or infidelity is discovered which causes the immediate end of the relationship

DUCK'S MODEL OF RELATIONSHIP DISSOLUTION

Duck proposed a model of relationship dissolution (breakdown) which views the breakdown of a relationship as a process rather than a single event, going through a number of stages, or phases. Each phase begins when a threshold of dissatisfaction has been reached, as illustrated below.

Stage 1: The intrapsychic phase
One or both of the partners is experiencing dissatisfaction with the relationship. This stage begins when the threshold "I can't stand this any more" has been reached. This dissatisfaction might be shared with others or might remain private.

Stage 2: The dyadic phase
Reached once the threshold "I'd be justified in withdrawing" is crossed. Here the faults are brought out into the open and the partner may be confronted if it is a serious relationship. In a less serious relationship it might end informally with a "See you around" or "I'll ring you". During this phase, discussions on how to either repair or end the relationship are started.

Stage 3: The social phase
Reached when the "I mean it" threshold is crossed. Dissatisfaction and plans to break up are now openly expressed. Outside help from a counsellor or friends might be used to try to repair the relationship, or the two partners may begin creating 'their' versions of the breakdown.

Stage 4: The grave-dressing phase
Occurs when the "It's now inevitable" threshold has been crossed. During this phase a credible, socially acceptable version of the life and the death of a relationship is created. Partners are likely to place the blame for the unsuccessful relationship on their partner or on conditions that existed before the relationship – "He changed", "She never really loved me" etc.

Harvey et al (1995) have found that the version of why the relationship ended that we present to close friends can be very different from the version we give to others such as neighbours. Duck (2001) identified a number of formats for the break-up story and found that the stories are constructed so that the speaker is seen to be open to new relationships, is not too critical of others' deficiencies, is willing to work on a relationship and only ends relationships after making a real effort to make things work. For Duck, the 'official' reasons given to others for the break-up are of far more interest psychologically than the real reasons.

Duck's model suggests that certain repair strategies will be more effective during some phases of the relationship than during others. In the intrapsychic phase for instance, it is suggested that repair should concentrate on re-establishing liking for the partner rather than focusing on the negative. Duck's model thus shows how the dissolution and the repair of relationships are intertwined.

LEE'S MODEL OF RELATIONSHIP DISSOLUTION

Lee (1984) devised a model of relationship dissolution which was based on his study of premarital romantic breakdown. After surveying 112 romantic break-ups, he suggested that such relationships went through five distinct stages.

Stage 1: Dissatisfaction
One partner becomes dissatisfied with the relationship

Stage 2: Exposure
One partner reveals their dissatisfaction to the other

Stage 3: Negotiation
Discussions take place about the dissatisfaction

Stage 4: Resolution
Attempts may be made to resolve the problems

Stage 5: Termination
This is where the relationship breaks down

Lee suggested that stages 2 and 3 were the most exhausting parts of the process. Not all relationships go through all five stages. It is possible for couples to go straight from dissatisfaction to termination, for instance, if they just walk out of a relationship. Lee also suggested that those partners who spent a long time moving through each of the stages feel more attracted to their ex-partner and experience greater loneliness during the break-up.

EVALUATION OF DUCK'S MODEL AND LEE'S MODEL

As both Duck's and Lee's models are stage models they have similar strengths and weaknesses. However, the focus of the models differs slightly – Lee's emphasis is on the earlier stages when the relationship might be saved, while Duck's emphasis is more on the beginning and end rather than the middle of the process.

» As with all stage models, these two can be criticised because they cannot be applied universally. Relationships are individual and dynamic and do not necessarily all resemble each other by going through all the stages at the same speed.

» The theories can also be accused of being culturally specific, in that they only apply to certain groups of people in Western individualist cultures. It is unlikely for example that the same processes apply to arranged marriages in non-Westernised cultures.

» Breakdowns are usually studied in retrospect because it is difficult to investigate the dissolution of a relationship as it is actually happening. For ethical reasons, researchers are reluctant to investigate at such a time in case they adversely affect the relationship. Retrospective data collection can of course be problematic because it is difficult to test whether the data is objective or accurate.

» Both theories are essentially descriptive. They both view the breakdown of a relationship as a process rather than an event and therefore describe the process of breaking up rather than explaining why relationships break up or what is the starting point of the dissatisfaction. Other theories are more helpful in this regard. Femlee (1995) put forward a 'fatal attraction' hypothesis for relationship breakdown which suggests that the qualities which attract two people also contribute to the breakdown. In the initial stages of a relationship, individuals are captivated by certain attributes in a partner. This in effect 'blinds' them to undesirable qualities. As time passes it becomes more difficult to overlook these things or to see them in a more positive light. According to Argyle and Henderson (1985) *rule violation* is a reason for relationship breakdown. Some relationship rules are *prescriptive* in that they say what is expected in a relationship (e.g. respect for privacy, being polite), whilst other rules are *restrictive* in that they say what is not permissible (e.g. not keeping confidences, not providing emotional support). Argyle and Henderson suggest that violating these rules could be interpreted as a betrayal and could lead to the breakdown of a relationship.

HUMAN REPRODUCTIVE BEHAVIOUR

THE RELATIONSHIP BETWEEN SEXUAL SELECTION AND HUMAN REPRODUCTIVE BEHAVIOUR

Darwin's theory of natural selection suggests that the most successful animals will end up with characteristics which enable them to out-perform their rivals. It appears however that some animals have characteristics which do not immediately appear to be beneficial to their species. It is argued that certain physical features and behaviours evolved specifically to help make animals attractive to the opposite sex. *Sexual selection* is the process whereby individuals advertise both their own requirements in a mate and their own attractive characteristics as a mate. Selection involves attracting the mate with the greatest fitness whilst at the same time maximising the chances of being selected as 'fit' themselves. Fitness in the context of evolution theory refers to the ability to reproduce and leave offspring. How animals select their mate is crucial to the species as it has a direct effect on the gene structure within their populations, and an effect on the future of the entire gene pool.

There are two basic types of sexual selection. *Intra-sexual selection* refers to competition for reproductive success between members of the same sex – for example males competing with other males for reproductive opportunities. *Inter-sexual selection* refers to selection by female choice.

"Having a good understanding of the sociobiological theory covered in the last section will be really useful here, especially an acquaintance with evolution theory. There is a lot of overlap and you will find that knowing about sociobiological theory will pay dividends."

SEXUAL SELECTION VERSUS NATURAL SELECTION

Sexual selection and natural selection can sometimes appear to be at odds with each other. Natural selection says that an animal's behaviour is directed towards increasing reproductive fitness. Sometimes, however, sexual selection pressures seem to have given rise to the development of characteristics, usually in the male, which contradict this aspect of natural selection. For example, the peacock and mandrill have both developed physical features which make them more of a target for predators.

Also consider the case of the wolf spider. Male wolf spiders search for female spiders and court them by drumming dry leaves with their abdomen. Higher drumming rates are preferred by females, but this energetic drumming comes at a cost – not only is it highly demanding in terms of energy but also it makes them more likely to be caught by predators. So in order to appear attractive to the female the male is putting itself at risk. It seems the risky nature of this courting procedure might be the reason females find the behaviour so irresistible. It might also be that the more energetic spiders are more fertile, as demonstrated in an experiment conducted by Hoefler (2008). He starved one group of male spiders and let a second group gorge on crickets. When presented with a female, well-fed males raised their legs eight times as often as their hungry peers. After mating with a male who naturally waved his legs a lot, the females laid more eggs, their spiderlings hatched sooner and they survived better.

However, sometimes it is difficult to understand either natural or sexual selection. In the case of the *Evarcha culicivora* (an East African jumping spider) the male is bigger than the female (a reversal of the usual pattern in spiders). Larger males are more cannibalistic towards their female mates. It is therefore strange that virgin female spiders choose bigger males to mate with initially and settle for smaller mates thereafter – there seems to be little explanation for this unusual pattern of behaviour.

Natural selection refers to a struggle for survival and reproduction, and sexual selection is a special form of natural selection whereby animals struggle for reproductive success. In the animal world, there appears to be a fine balance between the benefits of sexual selection and the costs of natural selection.

	Research findings	Evolutionary advantage
Human female mating preferences	who could financially provide	Men with greater resources are better mates because access to resources can improve female reproductive success.
	who were tall, physically strong, and healthy	Typically, physically strong males would have been better hunter/gatherers and therefore successful providers for their families.
Females were looking for males:	who were older than themselves	Older men typically have greater resources therefore increasing reproductive success.
	who had symmetry of face and body.	Symmetry is associated with health, so healthy offspring are more likely and there is less genetic predisposition to ill health.
Human male mating preferences	who were younger than themselves	Female fertility declines with age, therefore younger females are more likely to be fertile.
Males were looking for women:	who were healthy and physically symmetrical	Symmetry is associated with good genes and health.
	with a good waist-to-hip ratio.	Improves chances of child-bearing – women with high waist-to-hip ratios tend to have more problems conceiving.

Summary of the findings of Buss (1989).

ASK AN EXAMINER

"It is very important that, when you are asked to describe human reproductive behaviour, you do just that. Information from non-human animal research is useful when you want to illustrate what you mean or want to support your ideas with non-human animal research – but you will be asked to talk about human reproductive behaviour, so you really should stick to research with humans."

INTER-SEXUAL SELECTION

As complex animals but animals nevertheless, humans are subject to the same laws that govern lower animal behaviour. As with other, non-human animals, the fundamental goal of human behaviour is to reproduce and pass on our genes to the next generation, and so human reproductive behaviour has also been influenced by sexual selection pressures.

Evolutionary psychologists suggest that men have evolved to be responsive to females who are young and attractive, since these are physical cues to a woman's reproductive value. Women on the other hand are sensitive to cues from a male that he has (or could get) the resources necessary for her survival and the survival of her offspring. When it comes to selecting a partner then, women seek indicators of socioeconomic status, whilst men emphasise physical appearance.

This idea is supported by Buss (1989), who conducted a large cross-cultural study investigating human mating preferences. He surveyed more than 10,000 people drawn from 37 cultures. If the evolutionary theory of human sexual selection is correct then we would expect to find differences in the characteristics favoured by males and females and we would expect to find these differences regardless of culture. Buss did indeed report consistent gender differences across cultures. The table above outlines some of his findings.

INTER-SEXUAL SELECTION AND THE 'BIOLOGICAL MARKETPLACE'

Noë and Hammerstein (1995) have likened the process of sexual selection to a 'biological marketplace'. Because it is highly unlikely that individuals will get exactly what they want, mate choice can be seen as a trade-off between what an individual wants and the demands of the pool of potential mates. This means that individuals in a strong bargaining position (i.e. they possess desirable qualities) can increase their demands and become more selective. On the other hand, those who have fewer of these desirable qualities are in a weaker position and might have to lower their demands as a consequence (i.e. become less selective).

A good insight into the mating strategies of men and women can be gained from studying the nature of personal advertisements (sometimes referred to as 'lonely hearts' ads). Using relatively few words both men and women have to portray themselves in a way which maximises their attractiveness to the opposite sex. Evolution theory would predict that men and women would advertise the qualities that have evolved to give them the best chance of attracting the most appropriate mate.

Virtually every study conducted on the content of newspaper and magazine personal advertisements has found that women with youth and beauty and men with resources are most in demand, supporting the notion of a biological marketplace. Waynforth and Dunbar (1995) for example found that the sexes tended to use different kinds of descriptions in their search for a partner. Female advertisers appeared concerned with wealth and commitment in prospective mates, whilst male preferences in their advertisements tended to reflect female fecundity. They also found evidence of advertisers adjusting their descriptions according to how they perceived their status in the marketplace, as predicted by the economics of the biological marketplace.

The idea that mate selection is determined by a perception of 'market value' is further supported by Campos et al (2002). In the personal ads they studied, they found that as women aged they became less demanding in their mate selection. Males on the other hand became more demanding in terms of partner characteristics as they aged. A very different pattern of results however was seen in a study by Strassberg and Holty (2003). They placed four 'female seeking male' advertisements on internet dating bulletin boards, differing only slightly in wording, and discovered that the most popular advertisement was the one which described the woman as "financially independent... successful...and ambitious", which received 50% more responses than the one describing her as "lovely... very attractive and slim". It seems that, amongst the perhaps atypical male internet user population at least, financial independence may be preferred to physical attractiveness.

INTRA-SEXUAL SELECTION

One consequence of males competing with each other for access to mates is *sexual dimorphism*. This refers to the observation that, in many animal species where there is intrasexual competition, the male looks different from the female. Human males for example are on average about 12 to 15% larger than human females. Our close primate cousins the great apes show greater body dimorphism, with gorilla and orang-utan males being up to 50% bigger than females. Sexual selection accounts for a great deal of dimorphism, most frequently seen as secondary sexual characteristics. In animals these take many forms, such as the long tail feathers of the peacock or the manes of lions. Examples in females include the reddening of female rhesus monkey hindquarters, and smooth pectoral fins in carp. In male humans it includes size (e.g. height, physique), facial hair and deepening voice; whilst in females it includes enlargement of breasts and changes in body fat distribution (e.g. widening hips), and smooth hairless skin.

OWNER OF A LONELY HEART

Waynforth and Dunbar (1995) were looking to see whether the content of lonely hearts advertisements reflected evolutionary pressures to promote reproductive success. This would mean that women placing adverts would be seeking men who were older than themselves, reflecting a desire for greater wealth, resources and commitment. Men on the other hand would seek younger women, with particular physical attributes indicating greater fertility.

They conducted a content analysis of personal advertisements published in four newspapers. Their sample consisted of 479 advertisements placed by males and 402 placed by females.

They found that men included indications of material wealth in their own descriptions 1.7 times more often than women, whilst women demanded wealth in a potential partner 4.5 times more often than men. These demands for wealth were most often made by women who were in their 'peak' reproductive years (20–39).

Females were twice as likely as males to provide information about their physical attractiveness, with men of 40–49 most likely to express such preferences (a time in life when personal resources were most likely to be highest).

Waynforth and Dunbar conclude that human courtship is influenced by the same rules that govern the sexual selection preferences of other (non-human) animals.

Secondary sexual characteristics are honest indicators of male reproductive fitness, as they are not expressed to the same degree in unfit males. Unfit males do not seem to be able to tolerate the physical investment that the development of secondary sexual characteristics requires. The testosterone levels needed to promote their development suppress immune system functioning and therefore increase the chances of disease and illness. Consequently, only males in prime condition are able both to develop and to carry these features. This makes them particularly attractive to females who are looking for good genes in their potential mates.

In many non-human animals, dominant males carefully control impregnation rights. In some species non-dominant males have developed strategies which will allow them to mate with the females while the dominant males are unaware. This is called 'sneak copulation'. The dominant male must attempt to stop this from happening. In elephant seals for example, one large dominant male may possess a harem of up to 50 females, and ferociously defends the exclusive right to mate with them. Sneak copulation occurs when a non-dominant male quietly joins the female harem, posing as a female. He takes the opportunity to copulate when the bull is occupied elsewhere and then retreats before he is spotted by the dominant male.

It is argued that some human behaviours can be viewed in this way. For instance, human males can display aggression if their relationship with a female is threatened in some way by another male. Daly and Wilson (1988) point out that over 90% of all same-sex murders involve men at an age when mate competition is most intense and that a large proportion of this violence is connected to sexual rivalry. Buss (1988) also found that men are significantly more likely than women to make threats of violence towards men who were perceived to have made sexual advances towards their mate. In contrast to males, females are more likely to engage in verbal rather than physical aggression towards potential rivals. Buss and Dedden (1990) indicate that it is often the attractiveness or the sexual conduct of their competitors that will be targeted. Females' verbal aggression appears to be aimed at reducing the attractiveness of their competitors in the eyes of the male.

SPERM COMPETITION THEORY

Sperm competition occurs when sperm from two or more males compete to fertilise a female's egg. This is not an uncommon phenomenon in the animal world. For example, when males of the common fruit fly copulate they not only deposit sperm but also a protein from another gland whose function appears to be either to displace sperm from previous matings or to prevent the storage of sperm from future matings (Promislow and Tatar 1997).

Sperm competition is also thought to occur in humans. Whilst humans are a largely monogamous species, they are nonetheless fairly promiscuous animals where sex with multiple partners is not uncommon, even amongst people in committed sexual relationships. Indeed, exclusive relationships are extremely rare in the animal world, where social monogamy does not necessarily indicate sexual monogamy (Burke at al 1989). Research with many animal species has shown that females actively seek multiple partners to mate with, in order to ensure that they get the best sperm possible to fertilise their eggs. It is also important however for males to ensure fidelity in their mates. Males may invest a lot of time and resources in mating and subsequent offspring care, not to mention sacrificing other mating opportunities in the process. The possibility of female infidelity therefore has put an evolutionary pressure on the male to detect and correct this infidelity. One way of doing this is to ensure that his sperm stand the best possible chance of successfully fertilising the egg.

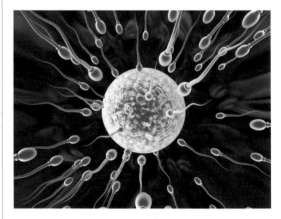

Reproductive success in females is limited by offspring production, whereas males are only limited by the numbers of available females. Whilst males produce huge numbers of sperm, their production is not limitless. This has resulted in the evolution of mechanisms whereby males can vary the ejaculate size. When males face high sperm competition they need to maximise their chances of fertilising an egg with a large ejaculate, and when they are experiencing low competition, sperm will be preserved. This is supported by the observation that larger testes, relative to body weight, have evolved in species where there is the greatest sperm competition.

Sperm are produced and stored in the testes, so it might be expected that testis size is related to the amount of sperm competition experienced by the male – the more competition, the larger the testes. This does indeed appear to be the case. The large testes however appear to have evolved as a result of female infidelity, not necessarily to allow males to impregnate as many females as possible. After all, large testes producing huge quantities of sperm would not be necessary if there was female fidelity, since after a single mating a female would have no use for further couplings and would simply retire to prepare for pregnancy. For example, female chimpanzees are extremely promiscuous and will copulate many hundreds of times with many different males for each pregnancy. Male chimpanzees have therefore as a result evolved very large testes: they produce vast quantities of sperm, and are able to ejaculate over a dozen times a day. Humans compare poorly to chimpanzees, despite their being our closest animal cousins, with human males generally unable to ejaculate more than half a dozen times a day, quickly running out of sperm. This suggests that our human ancestors experienced less sperm competition than chimpanzees and as a result evolved much smaller testes.

Where there are many opportunities to copulate, or where chance copulations are possible, it pays to be prudent with sperm allocation. Whilst the rate of sperm production is impressive (male humans for example can produce 3,000 sperm a second), the amount of sperm ejaculated with each successive copulation reduces, and as it does, so too do the chances of fertilising an egg in the face of competition from other males. Wedell et al (2002) suggest that the optimum quantity of ejaculate is a trade-off between the likelihood of sperm competition and future mating opportunities. For example, in species where there are more females than males, it pays to be economical with sperm in each ejaculate in order to increase the likelihood of fertilising as many females as possible. On the other hand, where females are fewer in number males will invest more in each ejaculate. Where there are opportunities for chance copulation, some males will keep some sperm in reserve. Evidence for sperm allocation comes from Packer and Pusey (1983) who observed that male lions, who experience competition from other males, may copulate with lionesses in their pride over 100 times a day, but only ejaculate a limited number of sperm each time.

Baker and Bellis (1993) suggest that females are more than passive providers of environments for

THE KAMIKAZE SPERM HYPOTHESIS

Competition between males can even occur after copulation has taken place. According to Baker (1996) human ejaculate consists of several different types of sperm, each with a different function. The existence of these different types of sperm suggests that humans were not monogamous in the past – otherwise the need for these different types would not have evolved. The kamikaze sperm hypothesis suggests that when there has been a 'double mating' (which must usually occur within five days), sperm from different males interact and compete with each other.

Blockers	These are the older, slow sperm which lodge themselves in the cervical channels in order to block any rival sperm entering. Approximately 100 million in the average ejaculation.
Killer sperm	These are the most common 'seek and destroy' sperm, containing chemicals which can kill rival male sperm. Approximately 500 million in the average ejaculation.
Egg-getters	These are the fewest in number and are athletic sperm whose job is to fertilise the egg. Approximately 1 million in the average ejaculation.
Family-planning sperm	These try to destroy the egg-getters because sometimes it is not in the male's interests to get the female pregnant. They are thought to be produced in greater number when the male is stressed.

Moore et al (1999) however could find no evidence for killer sperm in their study. They mixed the sperm of several human donors and could observe no significant changes in their action after one to three hours. The kamikaze sperm hypothesis therefore remains unproven and its application to human reproductive behaviour somewhat controversial.

egg fertilisation, and that they influence the sperm competition in many ways. In some non-human animals, females are actually able to eject sperm from less desirable males. The research further suggests that in humans, the female orgasm serves an important function. Orgasms are not necessary for conception so it has been suggested that they have evolved in order to manipulate the outcome of sperm competition, to ensure that the sperm from males with the highest indicators of reproductive fitness are favoured. The muscular contractions during orgasm increase the ability of sperm to remain in the reproductive tract and also serve to transport them closer to the cervix, hence increasing the probability of conception. In effect, orgasms can pull sperm closer to the egg. Therefore, the sequence and frequency with which the female copulates with competing males, and the timing, intensity and frequency with which she orgasms during copulation, all affect the outcome of sperm competition.

Shackelford et al (2000) supported the idea that the female orgasm is adaptively designed for discriminating male quality. Using a self-report method they gathered information from 388 female university students in committed hetero-sexual relationships from the United States (239) and Germany (149). The participants were asked to complete a survey containing questions about their partner (e.g. age, attractiveness) and their relationship (e.g. length of relationship, sex). Controlling for women's relationship satisfaction, relationship duration, and the ages of the woman and her partner, they found that women mated to more attractive men were more likely to report an orgasm at their most recent copulation. This study however relies on a volunteer sample with quite a limited range. A study by Pollet and Nettle (2009) on the other hand employed a large representative sample, using data gathered from the Chinese Health and Family Life Survey (a large-scale investigation of sexual attitudes and behaviour conducted in 1999/2000). They found a strong positive correlation that could not be explained by age, happiness, health, educational achievement etc. women's self-reported orgasm frequency increases with the income of their partner. This appears to support the evolutionary idea that the female orgasm is an adaptive response which pro-motes conception with higher quality males.

EXPLANATIONS FOR FEMALE MATE CHOICE

Females rather than males appear to be the more choosy sex. So why do females select some males rather than others as mates? Two evolutionary the-ories have been proposed to explain this: Fisher's 'runaway effect', also known as the 'good taste' or 'sexy sons' hypothesis; and Zahavi's handicap theory, or 'good genes' hypothesis.

The 'sexy sons' or 'good taste' hypothesis (Fisher, 1930)

This hypothesis suggests that populations of ani-mals could develop preferences for characteristics which have no particular evolutionary adaptive value. For example, a female barn swallow might arbitrarily choose a mate with a long symmetrical tail. This selection means that this characteristic is passed on to her male offspring. Since other female swallows might also find this characteristic 'sexy', these sons are more likely to be selected as mates. The tail itself need serve no purpose other than being a desirable accessory. Eventually, having long tails becomes the norm which then disadvantages those with shorter tails. By producing 'sexy sons' who will be desired by other females, the parent is enabling its genes to be passed on to future generations. If a female chooses a mate with a short tail this would result in short-tailed sons who would not be desired by other females and consequently she would have fewer descendants. Following this argument, it may well be that in humans a woman might choose a man because he has a characteristic regarded as 'sexy', such as a muscular physique. Any male children she might have would also then be more desirable to women, since they would inherit this attractive feature. Over generations of mate selection, this charac-teristic will become more and more pronounced – this is known as the 'runaway' process. The process only stops through a balance with natural selection (the trait becomes too costly) or a change in female preference.

The handicap process or 'good genes' (Zahavi, 1975)

Zahavi's hypothesis suggests that males who survive *in spite* of having a 'handicap' will be genetically superior to other males. For instance, a woman may select a partner not because he drives an expensive car but because he still manages to survive even though he has the *handicap* of run-ning an expensive car. It may be that women who prefer 'handicapped' males are selecting those who have good survival genes. This is more obvious, perhaps, in the animal world. Consider the pea-cock's tail.

Although it might initially be thought that possessing a large ornate tail reduces a male's chance of survival (because having one means it is more easily caught by predators), such a tail may also serve as a 'badge' of healthiness. Recent research by Petrie (2008) has suggested that peahens actually choose the peacock with the highest density of ocelli (the coloured 'eyed' feathers) rather than the longest tails. The density can only be assessed by the peahens when the males spread their tails during the mating ritual. The researchers involved took pictures of the displaying peacocks in order to count the number of ocelli and captured them in order to measure their tails. Petrie suggests that a high density of ocelli is thought to represent good health.

The handicap process can be seen in *parasite-mediated sexual selection*. Maintaining an effective immune system is one of the most costly activities in the body, equalled only by brain maintenance. The immune system is essential for survival as it fights off viruses and bacteria that might otherwise harm us. Another advantage in evolving an efficient immune system is that it provides defence against the weakening effects of parasites. However, the functioning of the immune system is compromised by the development of secondary sexual characteristics – the increased testosterone levels needed for this weaken the immune system, thus increasing vulnerability to parasites. It follows therefore that males with the best secondary sexual characteristics are demonstrating high levels of reproductive fitness, since it takes a great deal of strength and resilience to maintain these features whilst remaining strong and healthy. Females select these males because of the handicap of superior secondary characteristics.

*"Whilst, for the exam, the discussion must be on **human sexual selection**, you can use examples from non-human animals to support your argument. Use such examples sparingly, and when you do use them, use them **effectively**. The peacock's tail is a good example of this – parasite-mediated sexual selection is not so easy to spot in humans, so noting that ragged-tailed male peacocks are least successful at mating can usefully illustrate your point! "*

EVOLUTIONARY EXPLANATIONS OF PARENTAL INVESTMENT

Having considered how evolutionary explanations of sexual selection might affect our reproductive behaviour, we will now focus on how evolutionary explanations can be applied to parental behaviour. Sexual selection and parental investment are of course closely linked. For example the ultimate goal of sexual selection is to choose the right mate – which includes being the mate that will best satisfy the parental needs of the offspring.

"Many of the issues in the previous section on sexual selection apply here to parental investment. After all, one of the most important tasks for a female is to select the best possible mate to provide strong genes and, where appropriate, parental support. It is easy to become confused! It is probably a good idea to do what we have done here and treat them as separate issues. "

SEX DIFFERENCES IN PARENTAL INVESTMENT

Male parental investment (paternal investment) is more variable than female (maternal) investment. This is possibly due to the fact that, whilst females can always be sure that their child is biologically theirs, males can never be 100% sure of their paternity. Estimates vary, but as many as one in seven people may not be the biological child of the man he/she thinks is the father (Brown 2000). Birkhead (2000) reports one study where seventeen women who were on a long NHS waiting list for artificial insemination became pregnant before treatment began, even though their husbands produced absolutely no sperm. Paternity confidence has been found to affect the investment males make in the offspring. Cues such as physical and character similarity may be used to assess paternity, along with a perception of their mate's fidelity. Apicella and Marlowe (2004), in a London based study, found that as men's paternal resemblance and mate fidelity increases, so does the reported parental investment. However, among men who were no longer in a relationship with the mother of their children (and thus less likely to be investing in mating effort with them) paternal resemblance rather than mate fidelity predicted investment. Similarly, Anderson et al (2007) found that in their sample of men in New Mexico, low paternity confidence reduced the time fathers spent with their children, and their involvement in their education.

"The specification refers to explanations – this is a plural so you had better know about two things. We've included sex differences in parental investment and parent–offspring conflict here. Don't worry, you don't have to have a balance between the two in your examination answer (which is just as well – there is much more research on the former!)."

BATEMAN'S PRINCIPLE

An important and widely accepted explanation for the behaviour of animals during courtship is Bateman's principle. This says that "the sex which invests the most in producing offspring becomes a limiting resource over which the other sex will compete". For Bateman (1948), the origin of this unequal investment lies with the differences in the production of gametes.

For example, the human female is born with all the eggs that she will ever produce. Males produce many small gametes (sperm) while females produce fewer, larger gametes (eggs). Whilst female egg production is limited to about 300, a single male ejaculation might contain anywhere from 40 to 600 million sperm. Since the female invests more in the production of an egg than a male does a sperm, she is going to be discriminating in her choice of mate. Sperm are clearly plentiful and cheap to produce so a male is going to benefit more from mating freely and spreading them widely. From his studies of the mating behaviour of fruit flies Bateman observed that promiscuity benefited males much more than females. In effect, the reproductive success of a male increases with each female he mates with, whereas mating with more males does not increase the reproductive success of females. As a consequence, sexual selection occurs, whereby males compete with each other for females and females become more choosy about which males they mate with.

Whilst Bateman's principle became an important biological concept and still inspires a great deal of research, there are a number of problems with it.

» It is not necessarily the case that females expend more energy making gametes than do males. Although it is true that producing one egg is a greater investment than producing one sperm, many sperm are produced to ensure fertilisation of each egg: in some species with internal fertilisation this results in the male investing more in the process than females. In species that reproduce by spawning (i.e. releasing eggs and sperm into water) the investment from each sex is roughly equal.

» The assertion that all a female requires is fertilisation from one carefully selected male is also challenged by observations of some animal species which indicate that females have more offspring if they mate with a larger number of males. For example Taylor et al (2008) found that female fruit flies housed continually with males (thus with opportunities for multiple matings) produced more offspring than singly mated females housed alone or with virgin females.

» There are many examples in the animal kingdom that contradict Bateman's assertion that a male's reproductive success will depend on the number of females he mates with. The clown shrimp for example, rather than mate with as many females as possible, will spend many weeks diligently guarding a single female. The macaw is a monogamous bird and the same pair remain together for the majority of their 40 to 60 year lifespan.

» Given that a single ejaculation provides more than enough sperm to fertilise an egg, Bateman's principle has difficulty explaining the extra energy costs incurred by species that engage in multiple copulations which tip the balance towards a more equal investment. Dewsbury (1979) found that female hamsters need to be stimulated by multiple ejaculations in order to release a hormone necessary for pregnancy.

» Another problem for Bateman's principle arises with examples of sex-role reversal, where parental care is the main responsibility of the male. One example is the wattled jacana, a type of water bird where the female has the colourful plumage instead of the male. Emlen and Wrege (2004) noted that the only contribution that a female jacana makes to chick care is in defence against predators. Otherwise, females rarely intervene. Direct brood care was only observed when the male was not himself available to help (e.g. when the male died, or when the male was too busy with another brood to care for a new clutch of eggs).

"One of the most straightforward ways to address the issue of sex differences in parental investment is to describe and evaluate both Bateman's principle and Trivers' theory. They are quite similar so be careful not to confuse the two. We've provided plenty of evaluation here. Whilst an emphasis on human behaviour is good, it is not essential in this section, so don't be afraid of using non-human animal research."

TRIVERS' THEORY OF PARENTAL INVESTMENT

Trivers (1972) developed Bateman's principle so that the entire investment made by parents, such as gestation, protection, care and feeding is taken into consideration, not just their gametes. Trivers' theory of parental investment suggests that when the amount of energy that each sex must devote to reproduction and parental care is different, the sex with the greater burden will be the choosier.

This principle can be seen clearly working in the parenting behaviour of many species, especially where one sex (usually the male) makes little contribution to the rearing of offspring. For example, Hoffman et al (2007) found that female fur seals are particularly choosy when selecting a mate. Not only do they carefully discriminate between males according to size, behaviour and smell, but they are also willing to travel long distances in their search for the right mate, sometimes travelling up to 35 miles between colonies. Whilst female fur seals devote much of their adult lives to raising young, male fur seals make no contribution at all beyond mating. It is in the interests of the female in this case to get the best possible biological contribution to her offspring, and since this is all that the male is offering, females therefore select very carefully from available mates.

Trivers' theory also applies to human parental investment. The 'cost' of an egg does not stop with its production. After conception, a woman has to invest heavily in the support of her offspring with a long gestation and extended period of offspring dependency. Whilst it may be the ideal that both partners share equally the burden of offspring, it is clearly the case that in the vast majority of human cultures child-rearing responsibilities lie with the female. It has been estimated that only about 1% of men take on significant parental responsibilities by staying at home to look after children. Also, female fecundity declines rapidly after about 30 years, so the average female could expect to have a maximum of about 12 pregnancies during her lifetime. Men, however, start to produce sperm at about 13 years and continue to do so until they die. So, whilst female fertility is

"WOMEN NEED A REASON TO HAVE SEX. MEN JUST NEED A PLACE" *Billy Crystal*

In line with evolutionary predictions that men are the less choosy sex, research seems to suggest that men would have sex more often with strangers if it were easily available. Women on the other hand are generally less interested in this kind of behaviour.

This is reflected in the findings of Clark and Hatfield (1989). They had attractive confederates approach opposite-sex strangers on a university campus and ask one of three questions. The questions and main findings are summarised in the following table:

I've noticed you around and I find you very attractive...	% positive response	
	female	male
a)...would you go out with me tonight?	50	50
b)...would you come over to my apartment tonight?	6	69
c)...would you go to bed with me tonight?	0	75

Of the 96 students asked, no woman agreed to have sex; in contrast, three-quarters of the men readily consented.

It has been suggested that the lower acceptance of women was due to women's fear for their safety. However, it has been pointed out that such fears were not expressed during debriefing interviews, nor demonstrated in the behaviour of the 50% of women who were willing to date. In measuring what people actually *do* rather than what they *say* they would do, Clark and Hatfield's findings could be considered valid. They appear to demonstrate that females are somewhat more choosy than men when it comes to sex, and that indeed there may be some truth in the saying: 'women mate wisely whilst men mate widely'.

ETHICS   GENDER   CULTURE   DETERMINISM limited by egg production and age, male fertility is only limited by the number of females available to inseminate. Mistakes in mate choice then can be very costly for women, so they should be very selective.

There are, however, problems with Trivers' theory.

» Males are expected to be less demanding in their choice of a mate because they invest less than females. However, research is uncovering more and more situations where males are the choosy sex. Werner and Lotem (2003) studied sexual selection in cichlid fish. In this species, the weight of a female is positively correlated with the number of eggs spawned. Given a choice of courting two females differing in size, male cichlids preferred the larger female. This suggests that when males are not able to fertilise many females they tend to be the choosy sex.

» Male choosiness has also been shown to vary with the extent of intra-sexual competition. Bel-Venner et al (2008) studied mate selection in orb-weaving spiders. Like cichlids, the male spiders show a preference for large females. A male spider will find an immature female and guard her from other males until, with her adult moult, she reaches sexual maturity. In this way he can be the first to court her and mate. The researchers found that mate selection varied according to competitive ability. With high competition, larger males showed a preference for larger females, and smaller males smaller females. There was no size preference when competition was weak.

» Trivers' theory assumes that choosiness is the opposite of competition – if one sex is choosy, the other will compete for mates. This is not, however, always the case. There are many examples in the animal world of biparental care, where both sexes invest equally in these responsibilities. Pairs of crested auklets for instance breed once a year, nesting on sea cliffs and sharing equally in incubation and feeding of young.

When Jones and Hunter (1993) presented birds of both sexes with stuffed models, they were equally selective in preferring to mate with models with enlarged crests.

PARENT–OFFSPRING CONFLICT

Parent–offspring conflict occurs when the needs of the parent are at odds with the needs of the offspring. Parents need to treat offspring equally and divide their energy between them while the offspring want all the attention and care for themselves. Parent–offspring conflict can begin prenatally (before birth) when the interests of the mother might be in conflict with the needs of the foetus. The mother needs to maintain her own health while the foetus makes increasing demands on her body. In humans it is suggested morning sickness might be due to the foetus attempting to avoid certain food-based toxins; and pregnancy-induced diabetes might occur because the foetus requires more glucose. High blood pressure could also be a consequence of the foetus demanding more blood via the placenta, which consequently increases the mother's blood pressure and could result in kidney damage.

Another aspect of parent–offspring conflict may occur much later in life, over the choice of prospective mating partners. Evolutionary theory would suggest parents would prefer their offspring to choose mates that maximise the fitness of their grandchildren. Parents of females should be particularly choosy because mating involves greater investment for the female than the male. Mating decisions can be influenced by parents and other kin – an aspect not really considered by evolutionary approaches until recently. Parents may attempt to impose their own mating choices on their offspring while the offspring may attempt to escape this control. According to Apostolou (2008) both parents and offspring have evolved mating preferences which enable them to select those mates who maximise their inclusive fitness (i.e. the fitness of the family). Parents are thought

FEMALE INFANTICIDE

Whilst most common amongst animals, infanticide is sometimes committed by humans. Most cases of infanticide involve the killing of females, which reflects the low status of females in some parts of the world. For example, there is a long history of female infanticide in such countries as India and China. Both female infanticide and female foeticide (the selective abortion of girls in the womb) are significant issues in India, partly as a result of the patriarchal nature of Indian society. In China the One Child Policy was introduced in 1979 with the intention of keeping the population within sustainable limits. This policy of not allowing parents to have more than one child resulted in the estimated killing of more than 250,000 girls after birth between 1979 and 1984 (Ridley, 1993). Female infanticide has existed in China for a long time, however, and although the One Child Policy added to the problem, it didn't cause it.

to want their offspring to engage in long-term mating rather than short-term mating, which provides them with little if any benefits. A short-term mating strategy can be costly to the parents since it can damage the reputation of their family, while their offspring may commit their investment to an individual their parents do not approve of.

Parent–offspring conflict hypothesises that children may have a relative preference for mates with traits indicative of heritable fitness, whereas parents may have a preference for traits indicative of parental investment in their children's mates.

Parental influence on mating is supported by the 'grandmother hypothesis' which suggests that the menopause may have an evolutionary purpose. In humans it makes more sense for an older female to help care for grandchildren rather than continuing to reproduce which would be physically draining (Alvarez, 2000). If females have evolved to invest in grandchildren then it makes sense for them to maximise this investment by ensuring that their children mate with partners who can produce healthy grandchildren.

Buunk et al (2008) found in their cross-cultural research that there is likely to be some conflict between individuals and their parents over mate choice. Characteristics which indicated a lack of heritable fitness (e.g. being physically unattractive, lacking a sense of humour, having a bad smell) were considered more unacceptable to the participants themselves while characteristics which were undesirable in terms of parental investment (e.g. being divorced, being from a different ethnic background) were unacceptable to parents. This pattern was consistent across the cultures studied.

The most extreme and infrequent form of parent–offspring conflict among humans is infanticide. Infanticide occurs when parents kill infants. Conversely, it is not uncommon for non-human animals to kill and in some cases eat their young.

The killing of dependent infants by adult males is a widespread phenomenon amongst primates. Most primate infanticide seems to be caused by a colony's new dominant male killing the offspring of the usurped male. It is also know to occur in many non-primate societies. For instance, male lions will readily kill the offspring from neighbouring prides. Also, when a new male lion becomes the pride leader, it will set about systematically killing all the cubs of that pride.

According to sexual selection theory, infanticide occurs as a result of reproductive competition between males. There are several advantages for a male in killing an unrelated infant. For example, after losing a dependent infant, a female primate resumes sexual activity much sooner than a female still caring for young. This means that killing the infant increases the chances of the male fathering the next infant. This strategy only works of course if the male is not related to the infant. This is supported by the observation that cases of males deliberately killing their own offspring are very rare indeed in the animal world. Hardy (1979) has noted that females sometimes use this as a strategy to protect their offspring against infanticide. She suggests that female langur monkeys use promiscuity as a defence against infanticide, since this confuses issues of paternity. Male langurs would therefore be increasing the risk of destroying their own genetic line by infanticide and are thus less likely to kill infants.

COMMENTARY ON EVOLUTIONARY EXPLANATIONS FOR HUMAN BEHAVIOUR

» Evolutionary psychology has been used to explain human sexual selection, parental investment and parent–offspring conflict. The general prediction that males prefer younger, fertile women and females prefer older, higher-status males has been supported in many cross cultural studies. We are, however, *generalising* here and talking in terms of behavioural trends – there will always be many individual cases which appear to contradict the predictions of evolutionary theory.

"These are general criticisms of evolutionary psychology, so you can use them to get evaluative marks in any answer you give to questions in this section. Be selective and use them wisely and they will earn you extra marks."

» Many criticisms can be made of evolutionary explanations when they are applied to human behaviour. One of the major criticisms of evolutionary psychology is that it largely ignores or at least underestimates the social and cultural influences on behaviour. Whilst reproductive behaviours may be part of our biological inheritance, the way that these are expressed may be changed significantly by environmental pressures, almost to the point where the instinctive nature of the behaviour becomes unrecognisable.

» Human sexual behaviour and attitudes towards sex have changed dramatically over the past few decades – and the changes have not been accounted for by evolutionary psychology. For example, homosexuality is now becoming increasingly more acceptable in many societies. Why should some humans be homosexual and form relationships where they will never be able to procreate? Such behaviour poses difficulties for evolutionary explanations.

» Evolutionary explanations on the face of it are common sense. They do however suffer from *non-falsifiability* – how can such explanations be proved false? It has been pointed out that when empirical evidence contradicts some evolutionary principle, then the theory is adjusted to fit the data. For example, the evidence suggests that most men are monogamous, which is at odds with the important evolutionary premise that men are naturally promiscuous. Monogamy is therefore explained away as an atypical behaviour resulting from men not having the required 'market value' to compete successfully for women.

» Many evolutionary claims are difficult to test directly, under controlled conditions, so we can never be sure that these explanations are the best, or that alternative explanations are not just as relevant. Weiderman and Allgeier (1992) for example point out that human female mate choice might just as readily be explained as a rational choice made in the light of their lacking the economic resources that males possess.

» Evolutionary psychology has been accused of lacking parsimony – that is, of overlooking more plausible explanations for behaviour. For example, Wright (1975) explains that people who are infertile should, according to evolution theory, be psychologically disinclined to have sex since sexual behaviour in these individuals serves no adaptive purpose. He cites as evidence for this the reduced sex drive of nursing mothers, but does not seem to consider a rational explanation – that nursing a young child is exhausting.

» There are many aspects of human behaviour that cause difficulties for evolutionary psychologists. For example, how can evolutionary explanations account for women having affairs if they have already chosen a mate with resources? Why should older females choose younger males (with fewer resources) as partners, and why would such 'toy boys' have older females as partners especially if they are unable to provide them with offspring? Why do many women choose not to have children, and why do some men invest greatly in step-children?

» Most of the evidence cited in favour of evolutionary explanations of human behaviour comes from surveys, statistics, anecdotal evidence from anthropology and comparative observations of lower animal species. These methods are problematic and often not very scientific. It has been suggested that generating universal rules of behaviour from such evidence is flawed science.

EFFECTS OF EARLY EXPERIENCE AND CULTURE ON ADULT RELATIONSHIPS

THE INFLUENCE OF CHILDHOOD AND ADOLESCENT EXPERIENCES ON ADULT RELATIONSHIPS

Our early experience in childhood and adolescence may well shape our experiences of adult relationships. Some psychologists suggest that we form certain kinds of relationships as children, and this influences how we approach relationships for the rest of our lives. The first kind of relationship we form as children is with our parents and caregivers, but as we get older, relationships with peers become more and more important to us. Both kinds of relationship, with parents and peers, have significant influences on our later romantic relationships.

"You need to be aware of the influence of parent–child relationships and interaction with peers which occur in childhood and adolescent experiences. This makes four distinct questions you could be asked in the exam. Whilst you might also be asked more general questions on childhood and adolescence, we have organised this section in such a way that it makes what you need to know in either case as clear as possible."

THE INFLUENCE OF CHILDHOOD EXPERIENCES ON LATER ADULT RELATIONSHIPS

What happens to children has consequences throughout their lives. The first few years after

Attachment style	Caregiver and infant behaviour	Adult behaviour
Secure attachment style (Type B)	Caregivers are responsive to the infant's needs. Infants trust their caregivers and are not afraid of being abandoned.	Develop mature trusting and long lasting adult relationships
Anxious/avoidant insecure attachment style (Type A)	Caregivers are distant and do not want intimacy with the infant. Infants want to be close to the caregiver but learn that they are likely to be rejected.	Difficulty with trusting others and developing trusting intimate relationships
Anxious/resistant insecure attachment style (Type C)	Caregivers are inconsistent and overbearing in their affection. Infants are anxious because they never know when and how the caregivers will respond.	Want to be close to partners but worry that their partners will not return their affections
Disorganised/disorientated insecure attachment style (Type D)	The child does not know whether to approach or avoid the caregiver when they have been absent. A mixture of type A and C	Chaotic; insensitive; explosive; abusive; untrusting even while craving security

Attachment style and adult relationship behaviour.

birth are a time of rapid social and emotional growth and development, and the experiences of the child provide the building blocks for later life. At first, a child is dependent on caregivers for these experiences, but as the child matures and becomes more independent it is possible to see the increasing influence of other important people, especially peers.

Parent–child relationships

One theory dominant in psychology is that our adult relationships are based on the kinds of relationships we developed with our main caregivers early in life. Attachment theory suggests that the attachment styles we learn as infants and young children become an *internal working model* for what we believe relationships are like. Bowlby's classic studies of mothers and infants suggested we develop an *attachment style*. An attachment style consists of two attitudes. First is an attitude about ourselves, termed *self-esteem*. Second is an attitude about other people – termed *interpersonal trust*. These two attitudes develop from and are based on our earliest interactions with caregivers. If our caregiver leads us to believe that we are highly valued and that they are dependable and reliable then we are likely to develop high self-esteem and to trust other people. This is the basis of a secure attachment style. The absence of these conditions might result in the development of an insecure attachment style.

> **ASK AN EXAMINER**
>
> *"Remember this? Attachment was an AS topic, but here it is again. This is a good reminder that A level psychology is a whole course, not two individual halves. You are expected to bring to the A2 course what you learned at AS. Don't be afraid of using all your knowledge, as long as it is relevant."*

In their research, Ainsworth et al (1978) suggested there were three types of relationships between infants and their mothers. (A fourth attachment type – Type D – was added by Main and Solomon, 1986). Later research suggests that these early attachment relationships might affect adult behaviour as demonstrated in the table above.

There have been few studies which have investigated Bowlby's claim that attachments developed in infancy remain relatively stable over a lifetime. One reason for this is that attachment theory and methods of assessing attachment are relatively new ideas, so it is only in recent times that longitudinal research of this kind could be conducted. Waters et al (2000) retested adults for their attachment style 20 years after having first assessed them at 12 months old. They found a high degree of stability, with 72% of adults receiving the same classification from adult attachment tests as they did in infancy from the Strange Situation. Lewis et al (2000) on the other hand reported much lower attachment stability from their longitudinal study. They compared the attachment classification of children at 1 year of age with their classification at 18 years of age. With a stability of 42%, no strong evidence for consistency over time was found.

CHILDHOOD ATTACHMENT AND ADULT LOVE STYLES

Hazan and Shaver (1987) argued that the patterns of attachment described by Ainsworth were similar to the 'love styles' seen among adults, and could thus be seen to have a significant effect on the way that adults think, feel and act in relationships.

They asked readers of *The Rocky Mountain News* (a newspaper in Denver, Colorado) to complete a questionnaire on their attitudes towards love. Participants were asked to complete a three part questionnaire, assessing love style, gathering details about their current and past relationships, and measuring attachment style and history.

Participants were required to read the three paragraphs below and reflect on their history of romantic relationships to select which of the three descriptions best summed up their general experience of relationships:

"I am somewhat uncomfortable being close to others; I find it difficult to trust them completely, difficult to allow myself to depend on them. I am nervous when anyone gets too close, and often, others want me to be more intimate than I feel comfortable being."

"I find it relatively easy to get close to others and am comfortable depending on them and having them depend on me. I don't worry about being abandoned or about someone getting too close to me."

"I find that others are reluctant to get as close as I would like. I often worry that my partner doesn't really love me or won't want to stay with me. I want to get very close to my partner, and this sometimes scares people away."

The first described an avoidant attachment style, the second secure and the third a resistant one.

After analysis of over 600 questionnaires the researchers found that the distribution of categories was similar to that observed in infancy. In other words, about 56% of adults classified themselves as secure, about 24% described themselves as avoidant, and about 20% described themselves as anxious/resistant.

Participants with these different attachment styles differed in their experiences of romantic love. Securely attached adults readily trusted others and had satisfying romantic relationships. Anxious/avoidant style adults were uncomfortable being close to others and found them hard to trust; while adults with anxious/resistant styles were likely to be possessive and preoccupied about their relationships. These individuals want to be loved and needed, and Hazan and Shaver describe the relationships of these people as characterised by "emotional extremes, jealousy, obsessive preoccupation, sexual attraction, desire for union, desire for reciprocation, and falling in love at first sight." Basically, they are "over-ready for love".

Whilst these two studies disagreed on the degree of change, they did agree that change, when it occurred, was most often associated with negative life events. For Lewis et al (2000) the key life event was parental divorce. The effect of divorce on the child was not linked to any specific attachment classification, so that divorce had an impact regardless of whether an infant was securely or insecurely attached.

Whilst there is some evidence that early relationships can affect those we form as adults, much of the research comes from studies which have examined the correlation between attachment and adult relationship styles as measured by self-report questionnaires. One such study was conducted by Hazan and Shaver (1987), who suggest that infants and caregiver and adult romantic partners share similar relationship features such as feeling safe when the other is nearby, engaging in close contact, and feeling insecure when the other is unavailable.

Whilst concerns have been expressed about the methodology adopted by Hazan and Shaver, these findings have received some support from other researchers. Generally, those adults who were securely attached as children are more likely to have successful long-term relationships than adults with other attachment styles. It appears that it might also be helpful if both partners shared the same attachment style. In a German study of the relationship between attachment type and marital satisfaction, satisfaction was highest in those couples where both partners had Type B (secure) attachment styles (Banse 2004).

Those with an anxious/resistant attachment as children have the most short-term romantic relationships, often entering into relationships quickly and becoming angry when their love is not reciprocated. Indeed, Senchak and Leonard (1992) found that anxious/resistant men acquired their marriage licences after shorter courtships than secure or anxious/avoidant men. Better marital adjustment was seen in relationships where both partners were securely attached than when one or both partners were insecurely attached.

Finally, anxious/avoidant individuals are the least likely to enter into a romantic relationship: they are most likely to keep their distance and the most likely to say that they've never been in love (Campbell et al 2005). McCarthy et al (1999), in their follow-up study of women who had been assessed in childhood, found that Type Ds fared worst in all relationships.

There is some evidence to suggest that attachment styles have an effect on the quality of a relationship. Collins and Fenney (2004) found that attachment styles affected couples' behaviour and interpretation of their partners' behaviour. Secure individuals were unlikely to be affected when their partners appeared unsupportive, but anxious and avoidant participants were particularly upset, interpreting such unsupportive behaviour as evidence that their partner could not be relied upon (avoidant individuals) or was likely to reject them (resistant individuals).

Whilst attachment styles might affect adult relationships, individuals with very different styles of attachment can become partners. Kirkpatrick and Davis (1994) point out that anxious/avoidant and anxious/resistant individuals can be attracted to each other because resistant people expect to invest greatly in a relationship while avoidant people expect to be less committed than their partners. According to Morgan and Shaver (1999), if the female is the resistant partner and the male the avoidant partner, then their relationship is likely to be stable: otherwise the relationship is unlikely to be either satisfying or long-lived.

Another factor to consider is that attachment styles might change as a consequence of experiencing different relationships. It is possible that we might display different attachment styles in different relationships. Whilst having one kind of partner might result in our displaying a secure attachment style, experiencing a partner of another type might make us more anxious (Campbell and Wilson, 2003).

Childhood interaction with peers

It is not only our early relationships with our families that affect our adult relationships – early childhood interaction with our peers can also have a significant influence. Whilst the family is the most important factor in socialisation during the early years, as the child grows the impact of friends and peers becomes noticeable. In childhood, and especially after school begins, friendships become central to healthy social and emotional development. Friendships with peers provide children with important information about the world during a time of rapid development. They are a means for developing important life-long social skills. Peers can be an important source of emotional support, and provide information about rules and values, about what is or is not acceptable behaviour.

There is a growing body of research which suggests that difficulties with peers during childhood, such as the failure to form close friendships, can have implications for the adjustment we are able to make as adults. According to Parker and Asher (1987), the friendships between peers during childhood are 'training grounds' for important adult relationships, including marriage. They distinguished between *rejected* children (those who are actively disliked by their peers) and *neglected* children (those who are neither especially liked nor disliked). It is the rejected child, with the lower peer status who feels the greatest sense of loneliness, and who is most likely to suffer negative long-term outcomes as a result. According to Hartup (1989), adults who spent lonely childhoods have lower self-esteem and are less capable

EARLY PEER BEHAVIOUR AND LATER ROMANTIC RELATIONSHIPS

Ostrov and Collins (2007) conducted a 29-year prospective longitudinal study. The original sample of 267 women were recruited in 1975–1977 from a prenatal health clinic in a large American city. The sample were ethnically diverse and, because they were living in poverty, were considered 'at risk'. A sub-sample of 70 children (and their partners) of the original sample were used in the 2007 study.

The original participants had previously been assessed at the age of 5 by their classroom teachers for social–emotional and behavioural problems. At age 20–21 they were invited to participate in a 30-minute observational session with their romantic partners. In this session they had to complete two problem-solving tasks, and during this their behaviour was coded by experts in terms of tone, hostility, conflict resolution and overall relationship quality.

It was found that early peer behaviour was linked to later romantic relationship interactions. Children who had exhibited social–emotional problems with their peers when young were socially dominant (e.g. controlling and manipulating) in their later romantic relationships. No significant gender differences were observed.

of maintaining intimate relationships than adults who had close peer friendships in their early years.

Whilst some children are rejected by their peers, others have unavoidable life experiences which prevent them developing the relationships with peers that are available to most other children. One such disadvantaged group are those children that suffer long-term chronic illness, which has the effect of denying them important peer-related experiences at critical stages in their development. Thompson et al (2008) investigated whether childhood cancer survivors experience difficulties in later romantic relationships. They found that, whilst survivors of childhood cancer do not in general suffer less "satisfaction with, conflict in, and duration of romantic relationships", they tend to report fewer relationships and a sense of greater distress when relationships break down than control participants. Moreover, these feelings are greatest with those who have experienced the most severe treatments during childhood. Such treatments usually involve multiple hospitalisations and extended school absences, reducing opportunities for peer interactions and friendships. This appears to support other research in this area which suggests lower rates in marriage and cohabi-

tation, and older age at first romantic relationship and marriage (Dolgin et al 1999).

There are clearly many factors influencing later adult romantic relationships. Zimmer-Gembeck et al (2004), for example, considered the effects of friendship *quality* during childhood. They found that the quality of friendships in sixth grade (i.e. at around 11 years) has a direct effect on the age of first romantic relationship: children who have more intimate friendships in middle childhood form romantic relationships earlier than those who have not experienced such earlier friendships.

It also appears that being a bully during childhood can have long-term effects: studies of both male and female middle school children who were identified as bullies showed that in later years they were more likely to report using physical aggression with a romantic partner (Connolly et al 2000). In turn, those who have been bullied or teased are also likely to feel the effects in later romantic relationships. Ledley et al (2006) explored the relationship between childhood teasing and later social and emotional functioning. The sample consisted of 414 volunteers in university psychology classes. The students completed a number of questionnaires – some of which

FAMILY CLIMATE AND ADOLESCENCE

Bell and Bell (2005) looked at the importance of the family environment during adolescence. The researchers wanted to know whether family climate during adolescence had an effect on young people's well-being as adults.

Structured home interviews were held in the 1970s with 99 families with adolescents. Families were recruited through three high schools in one white, middle class, suburban district. There were further controls for family health, parents' education, family size, and position of identified adolescent (e.g. oldest, middle, youngest).

Family interactions were taped and coded in order to measure two things:

- *connection* (empathic and responsive caregiving from parents which encourages the development of internal working models that are carried through to later relationships).
- *individuation* (caregiving which encourages the development of autonomy through a family system of clear boundaries, encouragement of independent thought and speech, and acceptance of individual differences).

Twenty-five years later, telephone interviews were conducted with members of 82 of these families who were adolescents at the time. Of the original 199 participants, 174 now mid life adults were interviewed and measured for well being using Ryff's well being scale. Marital history and current marital status were also recorded.

The researchers found that the quality of the family system during adolescence was directly related to midlife well-being for both men and women. A significant positive correlation was found between family connection at adolescence and intact first marriage at midlife. There was a similar correlation for family connection and midlife well being. The effect of the family appeared to be slightly different on men and women. For women, a connected and individuated family during adolescence had an effect on marriage stability (i.e. whether at the time of the later interviews they were in an intact first marriage), whilst for men it influenced whether they would be married at all.

Bell and Bell concluded that, despite the innumerable life experiences that occur after individuals have become independent of their families, the effects of family life during adolescence can still be seen after 25 years, and may have life-long implications.

involved questions about their past. It was found vthat those college students who recalled frequent teasing in childhood were less comfortable with intimacy and closeness, and felt less comfortable in trusting and depending on others. They also experienced a greater degree of worry about being unloved or abandoned in romantic relationships. In addition, being teased about social matters, appearance, or performance was significantly related to later attachment difficulties.

The influence of childhood peers on later relationships was also investigated by Ostrov and Collins (2007). They suggest that the kinds of social and emotional behaviours that children show with their peers during middle childhood (5–11 years) is a good predictor of some of the problems seen in their later adult relationships.

THE INFLUENCE OF ADOLESCENT EXPERIENCES ON LATER ADULT RELATIONSHIPS

Traditional theory has it that adolescence is a period of psychological and emotional turmoil, and a time of great conflict between parent and offspring. Most contemporary psychologists however reject the idea that 'storm and stress' during adolescence is universal and inevitable. For example, according to La Freniere (2000), despite rows and conflicts the bonds between adolescents and their parents are perhaps not as weak as the early research suggested. Indeed, Stalin and Klackenberg (1992) found that adolescents who had conflicts with their parents already had poor relationships with them prior to puberty. Although the number of arguments is likely to increase during adolescence, often the arguments are mild. In a review of European studies, Jackson et al (1996) found similarities in the nature of disagreement. Reasons for disagreement included:

» Parents expecting greater independence of action from their teenage offspring.
» The adolescent wanting more autonomy (freedom) than the parents will allow. (Girls experience more conflict regarding this than boys.)
» Personal tastes and preferences.

Arguments may well be seen therefore as an attempt to change the power balance from one-sided parental authority to a more equal adult relationship.

Evidence suggests that adolescents differentiate between their parents in terms of their role, and that this process is influenced by gender. Hendy et al's (1993) longitudinal study in Scotland showed that adolescents chose to discuss personal problems with friends but matters like career and school with parents. Mothers were preferred over fathers as confidantes in all areas except careers and sex (boys only) and problems with the mother (boys and girls). Most girls and nearly half of the boys in the sample chose to confide in their mother over problems with friends. Half the girls and a third of the boys discussed doubts about their own ability with their mother. Hendy concluded from his research that adolescents disengage themselves from their fathers and girls are particularly uncomfortable when it comes to discussing issues of puberty. The mother's role is in enforcing family rules and this brings her into conflict more with her teenage offspring. The mother, however, is still seen as supportive and caring, not 'distanced' like the father. The importance of the mother–child role during adolescence is emphasised by Apter (1990), who studied 65 mother–daughter pairs in Britain and the US and found that girls said their mother was still the person they were closest to and the one who provided most emotional support.

The influence of parents

Ryan and Lynch (1989) suggest that in some respects adolescents are no different from infants. Just as securely attached infants are well equipped to form relationships away from the main caregiver, adolescent independence is likely to be a result of good rather than poor family relationships. Adolescence can be seen as a period during which young people reshape the internal working models of relationships formed earlier in their childhood into new models which will affect their adult experience.

Adolescence has traditionally been regarded as a time of readjustment for both child and parents, when a renegotiation of roles occurs to allow adolescents greater independence. Relationships with parents become more equal and reciprocal and parental authority comes to be seen as open to discussion and negotiation. This is also a transitional time for parents, who may well be reassessing their ability as parents, their life goals, career and family ambitions.

Relationships within the family may well act as a 'training ground' for later adult relationships. For example, longitudinal research by Crockett and Randall (2006) has suggested an association between the quality of adolescents' family relationships and the quality of their adult romantic relationships. Through a process of socialisation, adolescents learn relationship behaviours that they carry with them into adulthood. Parent–child relationships during adolescence appeared to have a particular influence on conflict resolution tactics used in adulthood. Adolescents who experienced less physical and verbal conflict with parents tended to show interpersonal behaviours which enhanced the quality of their adult romantic relationship, such as greater use of discussion to resolve discord.

Some studies have found associations between the quality of parent–adolescent conflict resolution and styles of conflict resolution in later romantic relationships. For example, Reese-Weber and Bartle-Haring (1998) point out that parents try to minimise the effects of their arguments on their children by avoiding such behaviour in front of them. However, it seems that what parents do to each other is much less important than what adolescents directly experience. In their study, parental conflict had much less of an impact on later relationships than parent/child conflict. So, if parents and adolescents adopted an attacking, avoiding or compromising style of conflict resolution, this approach was more likely to be used in later romantic relationships.

Generally, evidence suggests that adolescents achieve independence and competence best when within a secure family environment where the exploration of alternative ideas, identities and behaviour is allowed and encouraged. If parents are highly critical or rejecting, then adolescents can become negative about their own identity (Curry, 1998). Feldman et al (1998) found in a US sample that adolescents' reports of family interaction patterns predicted their happiness and distress in romantic relationships in early adulthood. This is supported by Seiffge-Krenke et al (2001) who conducted a six year longitudinal study in western Germany which involved annual surveys with 72 adolescents. The participants were visited in their own homes and took part in semi-structured interviews on parents, peers and romantic relationships. The results showed that the quality of relationships with parents at age 14, 15 and 17 was related to the quality of romantic relationships at age 20. Closeness and trust with parents were found to be directly related to positive aspects of romantic relationships. Similarly Joyner and Campa (2006) found adolescents' ratings of the quality of their relationships with parents were associated with the quality of their own romantic and sexual relationships as adults. Boys who reported close relationships with their parents had

higher self-esteem whilst girls who reported close relationships had fewer sexual partners, both leading to higher quality romantic relationships.

Conger et al (2000) found that having the experience of supportive, involved parents during adolescence was associated with greater commitment and satisfaction at age 20. It seems that adolescents who experience positive family relationships have a distinct advantage in their later adult romantic relationships. Conversely, Linder and Collins (2005) found that individuals with a history of hostile parent–child interactions during early adolescence were more likely to experience romantic relationship violence as young adults. In particular, they found that parent–child boundary violation at age 13 was positively related to whether individuals would later become perpetrators or victims of aggression at age 21 and 23. They defined boundary violation as overly familiar behaviour. As examples of such behaviour they listed *spousification* in which the adolescent met the caretaking needs of the parent; *parentification*, in which the adolescent displayed nurturance or limit-setting as a parent would; and *peer-role diffusion*, in which both the adolescent and the parent acted in a manner similar to adolescents. They point out however that violence in later relationships is not solely due to these boundary violations during adolescence but is also influenced by complex interactions among a range of experiences throughout childhood, including those of families, peers and siblings.

The influence of peers

As a child grows into adolescence, peer relationships and friendships become more important. Adolescents tend to interact with their peers more frequently and for longer periods than they did when younger. It is generally accepted that adolescence is a time when the peer group assumes vital importance. Palmonari et al (1989) for example found that 90% of 16–18-year-olds identified themselves as part of a peer group. Kirchler et al (1991) say adolescents who do not develop peer relationships and remain close to their families may have trouble establishing their autonomy and forming adult relationships. Peers do not necessarily replace parents however: rather they tend to coexist with them and the adolescent moves between the two contexts.

Erikson (1968) argues that adolescence is characterised by the establishment of 'ego identity', that is, a sense of one's own identity as a separate unique person, independent of one's family. An important psychological task during this time is to avoid 'role confusion', that is, an identity crisis caused by uncertainty about one's place in the world. Erikson viewed the peer group as providing a significant ego defence against role confusion. However, over-identification with peers can occur, especially when they provide details of identity, and this can result in cliques and 'out' groups of adolescents who become divorced from mainstream society and in some cases can be involved in destructive activities (e.g. drugs, alcohol, nihilistic subcultures).

The changing dynamic in relationships between adolescents and parents is aided by changes in relationships with peers. Blos (1967) describes this as a process of separation from parents and finding substitute parents. Peers help the process of separation and individuation as they help the adolescent avoid loneliness and provide the adolescent with a secure group away from the family.

It has been suggested that relationship skills appear to be learned in the 'best friend' relationship during adolescence and that these skills can then be transferred to a later romantic relationship. Indeed it is suggested that relational styles with romantic partners correspond to those with friends rather than those with parents. For example, Meeus et al (2007) looked at the psychological importance of best friends and parents during adolescence in a longitudinal study of 1,041 adolescents and early adults aged 12–23. They suggest that commitment to a best friend is a predictor of commitment to an intimate partner six years later.

According to the 'cycle of violence' hypothesis, individuals who witness or experience violence in the family subsequently become victims or perpetrators of aggression themselves. Linder and Collins (2005) however point out that whilst family experiences have a significant effect on later relationship violence, research has tended to underestimate the role of peers in romantic relationship aggression. Connolly et al (2000) suggest that middle school children identified as bullies are more likely to report using physical violence with a partner later in life, whilst Lackey and Williams (1995) suggest that peers can moderate the effects of family violence experienced during childhood. In their research, Linder and Collins followed participants from birth to 23 years of age, examining familial and extra-familial childhood and adolescent relationships in connection with couple violence in early adulthood. They suggest peers contribute to the development of aggression in romantic relationships, above and beyond the influence of parents. Indeed, individuals who had higher quality friendships at 16 years of age reported lower levels of both initiating and suffering violence in subsequent romantic relationships at 21 years of age.

Not all research agrees with these findings however. Crockett and Randall (2006) found that peer relationships appeared to have little impact on adult romantic relationships and suggest early family relationships have a greater influence in this respect.

Critics suggest that research tends to focus on *either* family relationships *or* peer relationships,

ATTACHMENT, ADOLESCENCE AND ADULTHOOD

Simpson et al (2007) have recently conducted an interesting longitudinal study which brings together a number of factors which have been raised in this section. The researchers used 78 participants who had been studied from infancy until their mid-20s. They were investigating how early childhood attachment, relationships in school and those during adolescence might all affect our experience as adults.

● The participants were initially assessed at 12 months using the Strange Situation test.

● At age 6–8 the participants' social competence in their peer groups was measured (via ratings from the classroom teacher).

● At age 16 the quality of their behaviours with their close friends (trust, disclosure etc.) was assessed, based on a detailed interview.

● Between the ages of 20 and 23 the participants' experience and expression of emotions in romantic relationships was measured (via a rating scale and an observation).

Simpson et al found that early attachment security at 12 months predicted the children's competence with peers at age 6. School competence at age 6 predicted the closeness of friends at age 16, and this measure in turn predicted emotional experiences in adult relationships. This appears to show that early attachment experiences with caregivers influence our relationship experiences in childhood, through to adolescence and adulthood.

making it difficult to gauge their relative importance in predicting the quality of romantic relationships later in life. Simpson et al (2007) attempted to address this issue. Their findings support the idea that there is a continuity of relationship representation. They suggest that individuals are not only influenced in their current relationships by immediate issues, but also by their developmental histories. Relationship experiences during critical developmental periods are therefore meaningfully related to the emotional nature of later adult romantic relationships.

THE NATURE OF RELATIONSHIPS IN DIFFERENT CULTURES

Culture is "the collective programming of the mind which distinguishes the members of one group from another" (Hofstede, 1980). Researchers have categorised cultures according to whether they are *collectivist* or *individualist*. Moghaddam et al (1993) neatly summarised the difference in focus of these cultures: relationships in Western cultures tend to be individualistic, voluntary and temporary while those in non-Western cultures tend to be collectivist, involuntary and permanent. It has been suggested that these different types of cultures have an effect on the relationships of individuals within them. Cross-cultural studies have consistently found that beliefs about mate selection in collectivist and individualist cultures differ greatly. For example, the opinions of other people can have a significant influence on mate selection in collectivist cultures whilst in individualist cultures such decisions are more likely to be based on personal emotional issues.

From an evolutionary standpoint, the principal influence on our choice of partner, regardless of culture, is their reproductive fitness: males seek females with the greatest reproductive fitness whilst females seek males who are best able to support them and their offspring. There is a considerable body of evidence for this evolutionary view. For example, in a large-scale cross-cultural study that we have mentioned earlier in this chapter, involving nearly 10,000 participants from 37 countries, Buss (1989) found that females tended to rate industriousness, status and financial resources highly in potential male partners. Whilst both sexes indicated preferences for physically attractive partners, males tended to rate this partner trait more highly than females. It should be noted, however, that the data gathered by Buss could also be interpreted to show evidence

of significant cross-cultural variations in mate preference, independent of evolutionary pressures.

"There is material throughout this chapter relevant to the effects of culture on relationships. For example, there is frequent reference to culture in the human reproductive behaviour section. Feel free to use information from any part of this chapter which says something about the nature of relationships in different cultures!"

LOVE AND MARRIAGE

Some concepts at first sight appear universal, such as the concept of love and marriage. Anthropologists found there was some evidence of romantic love in 147 of the 166 cultures they studied (Jankowiak, 1995). However, the concept of romantic love is to some extent culturally specific, and not necessarily a prerequisite of marriage. In an interesting experiment, Kephart (1967) asked participants the following question "If someone had all the other qualities you desired in a marriage partner, would you marry this person if you were not in love?" In the original experiment, twice as many American men replied "no" to the question as did women. However, 20 years later in Simpson et al's (1986) replication, more than 80% of men and women replied "no" to this question. This same question was later asked in LeVine et al's (1993) cross-cultural study of young people in 11 countries. It was found that in the collectivist cultures there was a higher percentage of "yes" answers (e.g. India 49%) compared to the US (3.5%) and England (7.3%).

The romantic ideal of two independent loving individuals acting on their feelings certainly appears to be pervasive. Films, television programmes and songs are all dominated by the theme of romantic love. The idea that everyone should marry only when they are in love is, however, a fairly recent one when viewed historically. Indeed, for many cultures the two concepts are not necessarily related.

In collectivist cultures, marriage choices are often made by the families on the basis of alliances and economic considerations. These are known as *arranged marriages*. In Japan almost 25% of marriages are arranged (Iwao, 1993) and although 90% of all Indian marriages are arranged (Gautam, 2000) the practical arrangements vary. For example, families may often use similar criteria to those that the individuals themselves might employ, such as matching them on attractiveness. In Sri Lanka, men and women who love one another may let their parents know their wishes for marriage indirectly, and although the marriage is then arranged by the families, it is on the basis of couple choice (de Munck, 1998).

Patterns of arranged marriage	
Traditional pattern	Parents and elders choose the spouse
Modified traditional	Individual has the power to choose
Cooperative traditional pattern	Either the young person or the parents might make the selection.

Whilst it is often assumed that arranged marriages are less successful than marriages based on romantic love, there have been few comparative studies. Yelsma and Athappilly (1988) studied marriage satisfaction in 28 Indian couples in arranged marriages, 25 Indian couples in 'love' marriages and 31 American couples in companionate marriages. They found that husbands and wives in arranged marriages were more satisfied with their marital relationships than were the husbands and wives in the American sample. However, in comparison, Xiaohe and Whyte (1990) sampled married women in the People's Republic of China and found that women in arranged marriages were less satisfied than women in free-choice marriages.

More recently Myers et al (2005) compared marital satisfaction and wellness in arranged marriages in India and free-choice marriages in America. Although characteristics for marital satisfaction were rated differently in the different cultures, overall marital satisfaction was similar in both groups. In the United States sample, love and loyalty were given a high priority. In the Indian sample, love was seen as less important as a necessary precursor to marriage but love was expected to grow as the spouses learned about each other as the years went by. This was previously suggested by Gupta and Singh (1982) who found that couples in Jaipur, India who married for love reported diminished feelings of love if they'd been married for more than five years. In contrast, those who'd undertaken arranged marriages reported more love if they weren't newlyweds. It seems that, contrary to common Western beliefs, for both men and women arranged marriages can be both happy and satisfied.

Madathil and Benshoff (2008) compared marital satisfaction in three sample groups – Asian Indians in arranged marriages in India, Asian Indians in arranged marriages living in the United States, and Americans in free-choice marriages. The researchers were interested in the importance of love, loyalty, shared values and finances in these different relationships. Love was given the highest rating of importance by the arranged marriage couples in America. Both Asian Indian groups rated finances and shared values more highly than the American free-choice group, presumably because financial security and lack of debt is a key cultural value for Indians. Overall, the Indian arranged marriages in America were rated more satisfactory than the marriages in the other two groups. This is possibly because the couples enjoy the stability of an arranged marriage together with a culture that imposes fewer restraints on them than their tradi-

CROSS-CULTURAL VARIATIONS IN COURTSHIP AND MARRIAGE

In the Bassa Komo tribe of Nigeria, should a man of one family wish to marry a girl of another, then tradition has it that he must have a sister to give in exchange to his future father-in-law to replace the girl he marries. Unfortunately, if a man does not have a sister then he must find a solitary distant relation of his own to marry. He can marry as many times as he likes (i.e. polygamy) as long as he has sufficient sisters to give in return.

The Zulu of South Africa have five distinct stages of courtship and marriage.

1. Initially 'senior girls' decide when younger girls should have a boyfriend. The younger girl then tells the chosen young man of her love. The couple is then allowed to spend evenings and nights together (but no sex is allowed).

2. The girl's father builds a hut for the young couple to meet in (as he has to officially forbid the couple from meeting in his home).

3. The girl's father acknowledges the suitor by asking his daughter to "fetch some cattle from her lover".

4. The young man pays 'ten plus one' cattle to the girl's mother to compensate her for her loss.

5. The wedding ceremony, which may last for several days, then takes place.

tional culture. They may also have less interference from other family members.

A further finding was that the more involvement the people living in India had in selecting their mate, the higher the scores on marital satisfaction – but interestingly this was not the case for the Indians living in America. It appears that the length of time the Indian couples had spent in America did not affect their total satisfaction scores. So perhaps Indian married couples living in America may not be significantly influenced by American cultural values. There is also the possibility that such families spend most of their time socialising with other Indian families therefore maintaining their cultural identities.

It is clear that marital arrangements and marital satisfaction are complex issues. It could be that marriages in individualistic cultures are more pressured because marriage is expected to fulfil diverse psychological needs in such societies. DePaulo and Morris (2005) suggest that in America several social roles have merged into one relationship, so that the spouse is often also the best friend and primary social partner. The ideal 'perfect' spouse now has to perform so many functions that it is unrealistic to expect any one person to fulfil this role. This could be why divorce rates among those who marry according to parents' wishes are lower than among those who have love-based marriages and have been looking for the impossible 'perfect' partner.

Marriage is considered by Western cultures to be a permanent bond between a man and a woman which is supported by moral and legal codes. This institution of marriage also assigns rights, parental responsibilities, rules of dependency and divisions of labour. Moreover, there is a general assumption that marriage is universal and that marriage performs similar functions in all societies. However, there is evidence which clearly suggests that cultures have developed their own very different versions of marriage. The Nayar are a good example of this. The Nayar were an upper caste Hindu society of South-Western India who lived in large communal houses of up to 80 family members. The roles of men and women were very different, with men engaged in military training and the women collectively responsible for cooking and child care. The Nayar had a system of 'visiting husbands', whereby a couple did not live together, but the man would visit his partner at night in her family home (Gough, 1959).

Although the custom of marriage is thought to be universal, the Na people of the Himalayan region of China appear to be an exception. Marriage does not seem to figure in their society. Na brothers and sisters live together for their entire lives. Women tend the gardens and cook for their brothers while

Cause of divorce	% positive response						
	Africa	Circum-Mediterranean	East Eurasia	Insular Pacific	North America	South America	Total cases
Adultery	12	11	15	17	19	14	88
Sterility	18	16	13	9	12	7	75
Cruelty/maltreatment	11	8	4	7	13	11	54
Witchcraft or sorcery	10	1	1	1	0	0	13
Old age	2	3	1	0	0	2	8
Spouse favours kin	5	0	0	1	0	1	7
Absence of male children	0	2	2	0	0	0	4
Bad dream or omen	0	0	0	2	0	0	2

Some examples of regional causes of relationship dissolution. Adapted from Betzig (1989).

the men care for the herds and provide protection for their sisters and their sisters' children. However, since incest is prohibited, the men engage in night visits to the homes of other women. Although men may 'visit' women, they never form households with their lovers (Tapp, 2002).

DIVORCE

Although high divorce rates are often associated with marriages in Western cultures, in reality, divorce and failed relationships (not necessarily at a high rate) occur in all cultures. Statistics show that the divorce rate in India (which has a very high rate of arranged marriage) is approximately 1%, compared to divorce rates in the United States of 55%. Before drawing too many conclusions from this data however, it should be noted that there are many personal, social and cultural factors affecting divorce rates, beyond the happiness (or unhappiness) of the individuals involved. For example, research shows that 'arranged married' couples experience a great deal of pressure from families, friends and society as a whole, often making divorce not an option. It may be that arranged marriages endure because ending the marriage would bring shame upon the families, not because they are successful or rewarding. Also, the status of women in some non-Western societies is such that being a single independent woman is not possible. It may even be that the idea of what constitutes a 'successful' marriage differs considerably between cultures.

It has been suggested that one reason for significant increases in divorce rates in Western non-arranged marriages lies with the motivation to marry itself. The principal reasons for marriage – e.g. love, sex, beauty – are transient, things that will change over time, possibly leading to disenchantment and dissolution. Arranged marriages, however, place much greater emphasis on more practical and mundane factors, such as dependability, reliability, commitment to family etc. Love and affection, something presumed to be a consequence of marriage, therefore have a more solid foundation on which to develop. As a result, these marriages tend to last longer.

Fisher (1992) suggests that there are universal factors which are likely to end relationships. In an analysis of reasons for divorce in 186 societies, Betzig (1989) found that adultery was the most common cause for divorce across cultures, followed respectively by sterility and cruelty/maltreatment. As can be seen in the table above however, Betzig's study also shows that there are culturally specific reasons for divorce.

CULTURAL VARIATIONS IN PHYSICAL ATTRACTIVENESS

Physical attractiveness is regarded as an important determinant of attraction and subsequent relationship formation in many societies. Cunningham et al (1995) found a high degree of agreement between different races in their perception of facial attractiveness. They found that their Asian, Hispanic and white judges consistently rated highly such things as large neonate eyes, facial symmetry, small noses, dilated pupils, larger smiles and well-groomed hair. Research also suggests that there is broad cross-cultural agreement in attractiveness indicated by weight (as measured by body mass index, or BMI) and shape (assessed as waist-to-hip ratio, or WHR). Such features are usually associated with good physical health and fertility, and such findings fit in with evolutionary assumptions regarding mate preference. Humans should be sensitive to the visual cues that honestly indicate reproductive fitness, since wrong choices can have a significant effect on reproductive potential. Some features of physical attraction, however, appear harder to explain in terms of their association with

WHAT CONSTITUTES PHYSICAL ATTRACTIVENESS CAN VARY GREATLY BETWEEN SOCIETIES

In some African cultures the wearing of a lip plate is considered attractive. For example, Mursi women of Ethiopia can choose to have their lower lip pierced before they marry. The hole is gradually stretched by inserting increasingly bigger clay or wooden discs, with diameters of 15cm not being uncommon.

Scarification is widespread in African culture. In involves cutting the skin in such a way as to control the shape of the scar tissue. Sometimes the practice involves irritating the cuts to produce permanent blisters or staining them to produce darkened scarring. Women of the Nuba tribe in Sudan receive their first scars from navel to breasts at the first signs of maturity. More scars are cut on the torso at menses, and a final set cut on the arms, leg and neck after the first child is weaned. This final set of scars is so important to the woman's sense of beauty that she will end the marriage if the husband refuses to pay for them.

In Pa Dong women of Thailand and Burma, a long slender neck is traditionally considered a sign of beauty and wealth. They engage in a custom of 'neck stretching'. Metal rings are put around the necks of girls, starting at age 6, with rings regularly added, perhaps reaching 20 rings or more. The weight of the rings pushes down the collar bones to give the illusion of a very long neck.

At one time, small dainty feet were so admired in China that foot binding was practised. Foot binding involved wrapping the foot extremely tightly in cloth for many years, starting in infancy. This restricted normal bone growth, resulting in extremely small and distorted feet. This had such crippling effects that some women had to be carried around because they were unable to walk properly.

Because the above examples refer to female attractiveness it does not mean that similar customs do not apply to men! Lip plates are also popular amongst men in some cultures, and there are many examples of body scarring, tattooing and genital modifications such as penis inserts, circumcision and subincision.

good health. For example, Fessler et al (2005) investigated foot size preferences across nine distinct cultures and found a general preference for small foot size in females and average foot size in males.

According to Singh (1984), the WHR is thought to be important for males when selecting a female because a low WHR may be linked to increased fertility. Where there is cross-cultural support for this idea however it has largely come from studies carried out in industrial societies. Marlowe and Wetsman (2001) looked at WHR preferences of men from the United States and of the Hadza tribe (hunter-gatherers from Tanzania) and found that Hadza did not share American men's preferences for the lower WHR. They tended to show a preference for women with higher weight, regardless of WHR. Further evidence for cultural differences can be seen in the WHR preferences of Matsigenka Indians of Peru. Yu and Shepard (1998) found that despite belonging to the same ethnic population, the more Westernised group of Matsigenka preferred low WHR women whilst a highly isolated group considered high WHR more attractive. In both populations non-child-bearing

women had a lower WHR than childbearing women.

There is a growing body of cross-cultural research, however, which suggests that BMI is the more important predictor of attraction, with WHR acting as a secondary cue. Swami et al (2006) looked at the relative contribution of BMI and WHR to female physical attractiveness in Britain and Japan. Males from both countries were asked to rate photographs of women with varying BMI and WHR. It was found that for both populations BMI was the main determinant of physical attractiveness. There were important cultural differences however, with Japanese men preferring lower BMI than Britons and the Japanese being more reliant than the Britons on body shape as a sign of female attractiveness.

Stone et al (2008) argue that what determines cultural preference for a particular shape is level of socioeconomic development. People living in areas of low socioeconomic development face a range of living problems generally not experienced by most people from more developed areas – for example, poor health and extreme poverty. They argue that these conditions exert a significant influence on mate preference because finding a healthy partner is more difficult. They used questionnaire data gathered from a sample of 4,499 men and 5,310 women living in 36 cultures on six continents and five islands. They found that characteristics which indicate good health were more important to both sexes in less developed countries. People in more developed countries placed greater importance on "mutual attraction/love" than those in less well-developed countries. Stone et al suggest that this implies an economic transaction underlying marriage in some less developed countries where, for example, marriage involves trade in goods and livestock. This is less important in more developed countries, resulting in relationships based on companionship and emotional commitment.

Whilst culture no doubt has a strong effect on what is considered physically attractive, cross-cultural studies consistently indicate that there is general agreement about this issue. These studies suggest that ideas of attractiveness are to some extent at least inborn and part of human nature. This is further supported by research results which indicate that very young infants show some preferences for faces considered attractive by adults (Hoss and Langlois, 2003). For some psychologists this is strong evidence of an underlying evolutionary pressure on mate preference.

Aggression

NICOLA TAYLOR AND ROB LEWIS

You are expected in the examination to show both the skills of knowledge and understanding and the skills of analysis and evaluation in relation to the topic Aggression.

Where opportunities for their effective use arise, you will need to demonstrate an appreciation of issues and debates. These include the nature/nurture debate, ethical issues in research, free-will/determinism, reductionism, gender and culture bias, and the use of animals in research.

You will also need to demonstrate an understanding of How Science Works. You can do this through the effective use of studies in your answer (as description or evaluation) or where appropriate by evaluating methodology and findings.

WHAT YOU NEED TO KNOW

SOCIAL PSYCHOLOGICAL APPROACHES TO EXPLAINING AGGRESSION

- Social psychological theories of aggression, e.g. social learning theory, deindividuation
- Explanations of institutional aggression

BIOLOGICAL EXPLANATIONS OF AGGRESSION

- The role of genetic factors in aggressive behaviour
- The role of neural and hormonal mechanisms in aggression

AGGRESSION AS AN ADAPTIVE RESPONSE

- Evolutionary explanations of human aggression, including infidelity and jealousy
- Explanations of group display in humans

SOCIAL PSYCHOLOGICAL APPROACHES TO EXPLAINING AGGRESSION

SOCIAL LEARNING THEORY OF AGGRESSION

Social learning theory (SLT) evolved from operant conditioning and not only recognises the effect that reinforcement has on behaviour but also considers the role of observation of the behaviour of others in shaping our own. According to this theory, aggressive behaviour can be learned by observing and imitating the aggressive behaviour of other people.

"You need to know social learning theory in detail. There are key concepts here which will help you demonstrate a sound grasp of the theory in an exam – learn them and use them."

SLT was proposed by Albert Bandura, who used the term *modelling* to explain how humans can very quickly learn specific acts of aggression and incorporate them into their behaviour. Modelling is sometimes referred to as vicarious learning. The term vicarious means indirect; we can learn aggression without being directly reinforced for aggressive behaviour. This works when we observe aggression in others somehow being rewarded. An example would be if a child observed two of his/her peers arguing over a toy. If one child gains control of the toy through force (e.g. by hitting the other child) then the observer has witnessed positive use of aggression and has seen the act of aggression being rewarded with sole use of the toy. The aggressive behaviour has been vicariously reinforced for the observer and this may therefore lead to imitation of the aggressive act.

This process is not as simple as it first appears as there are other criteria that, according to Bandura, need to be fulfilled to make imitation of a model more likely. One of these is *self-efficacy*. This is the belief that a person has about whether the observed behaviour is within their ability to perform. If a person believes that they are capable and in possession of the necessary skills and strength to carry out the behaviour, and they believe that they are likely to achieve the desired result, then the aggressive act is more likely to be imitated. This may help explain varied responses from the same individual. According to this explanation a person will not use aggression against another person in all situations, only in those situations where they feel that they are most likely to be successful – i.e. when they believe they are superior in strength or they have an advantage in some other way. For example, a child who is challenged for a toy will not necessarily retaliate if the aggressor is much bigger than they are, but may choose to use aggression against a smaller child who attempts to take their toy.

The *characteristics of the model* are another important factor in the social learning process. An individual will not imitate a random model, but is more likely to be influenced by one which is judged to have status and power. The likelihood that a particular model will be imitated is also increased if the model is deemed to be similar to the individual in some way – for example, the same gender. Similarity also helps to increase the sense of self-efficacy, so that having, as a model, someone similar to you makes you feel more confident that you can do the same thing yourself. If we bear in mind the characteristics of a likely model as being someone powerful and similar, we can understand how, in a child's life, one of the most influential role models is the same-sex parent. Parents who use physical punishment to discipline their children are demonstrating that aggression is an appropriate way of controlling others and getting what you want. For example, a parent who scolds and hits a child because the child has hit someone else is in effect saying 'Don't do as I say, do as I do'. It is the behaviour modelled by the parent, and not what the parent says, that is the most powerful influence on the future behaviour of the child. Research shows that children subjected to physical punishment in childhood often use violence themselves in later life (Baron and Richardson, 1994). Powerful models may also be presented through the media and much concern has been expressed about the depiction of aggressive models on television, in films and in video games. Models may have a particularly powerful influence if they are seen to have gained high status or wealth through their aggression. In summary, aggressive behaviour is more likely to be imitated if an individual believes it will work and if the model has the right characteristics.

Instigation of the behaviour is only the first part of the process: for an individual to use an aggressive behaviour over time it must be maintained, and this involves the behaviour being rewarded. Aggression may be maintained by external reinforcers – for example, a violent criminal amasses wealth or goods and is therefore directly rewarded for their aggressive behaviour. Status may also act as a reinforcer for gang members who, through increasingly aggressive acts, may rise through the ranks of the gang. This provides us with an example of *reciprocal determinism*, which is

THE BOBO DOLL STUDY

Bobo doll

The aim of Bandura et al was to show that learning can occur through observation. More significantly in this case their aim was to demonstrate that children could learn aggressive behaviour through the observation of an aggressive model. They predicted that children who observed an adult model behaving aggressively towards a Bobo doll (something like an inflatable punch bag) would be more likely to show aggressive behaviour than children who had observed a non-aggressive model.

The participants in this study were 36 boys and 36 girls with a mean age of 4 years and 4 months. In each experimental condition the children were shown individually into a room containing toys and allowed to play for ten minutes. The children were divided into three conditions:

One group were exposed individually to an aggressive adult model who continuously hit, punched and kicked the Bobo doll. The model used a wooden mallet to strike the doll on the head and repeated aggressive statements such as "Hit him on the nose, or "Throw him in the air."

A second group were exposed to a non-aggressive adult model who played quietly in the corner of the room.

A third group were used as the control and were not shown a model.

A baseline test was conducted to assess existing levels of aggression in the children and they were distributed across the groups using a matched pairs design to ensure that one group of children were not already more or less aggressive than another.

After exposure to the model all the children were taken individually to another room where they were presented with some toys but prevented from playing with them. This mildly frustrating situation was designed to give all groups an equal chance of demonstrating aggressive behaviour and also to show how those exposed to the non-aggressive model may behave less aggressively. Each child was then taken into another room containing a Bobo doll and mallet and a further choice of toys such as balls, colouring materials and dolls. The children were observed through a one-way mirror for 20 minutes and their behaviour was recorded.

The observations revealed that the children who had been exposed to the aggressive model showed more imitation of the model's behaviour than the children in the other two groups. Some of the specific aggressive acts displayed by the children who had been in the first group were very close imitations of the behaviour modelled by the adult. Children who had observed the non-aggressive model demonstrated very little aggression – although this was not always significantly less than was shown by those in the control group. Bandura suggested that the close imitation shown by the children of the model's behaviour was clear evidence of learning through observation.

Bandura's work has not escaped criticism however, some of it focused on the methodology used. In the experiment just described, it would have been difficult to standardise the behaviour of each model. Even with clear instructions and strict timing, each child would still have witnessed a slightly different version of the Bobo doll attack. Later versions of the experiment used film footage to overcome this issue. A further concern over the method relates to the artificiality of the situation of an adult showing aggression towards a Bobo doll: this was an unexpected form of behaviour for an adult, that could have frightened some of the children. There are of course ethical issues such as informed consent and protection from harm to consider.

Despite these concerns the study remains a classic and is accepted as an example of imitation of aggressive behaviour that has important implications for the effect of media violence on children's behaviour.

another important factor in social learning theory. Reciprocal determinism describes the two-way relationship between an individual and their environment. In this instance the gang member carries out an act of violence that is recognised and praised within the gang. This increases his status but also impacts upon his future behaviour as he becomes more violent in order to maintain the achieved status. Aggressive behaviour will not necessarily continue without reward and if aggression is punished then its occurrence may decrease.

Throughout this description of social learning theory we can see the importance of cognition in the acquisition of learning. Bandura recognises the importance of thought processes in assessing the model, the self and the situation in order to ascertain whether aggression will be imitated. Another cognitive process important to this model is memory, as the individual needs to be able to recall situations when aggression was a successful tactic, and those where it was unsuccessful, in order to judge when and where to use aggression again. Bandura summarised social learning in terms of four essential conditions for an individual to model the behaviour of someone else:

Attention	A person has to pay some attention to the behaviour of the model in order for it to be imitated. A number of factors influence the attention given to the model, including as already mentioned the status, similarity and attractiveness of the model.
Retention	The behaviour has to be remembered if it is going to be imitated.
Reproduction	The observer has to be able to replicate (i.e. copy) the behaviour.
Motivation	The observer must want to imitate the behaviour.

EVALUATION OF SOCIAL LEARNING THEORY

» In the early 1960s Bandura and his colleagues conducted a series of experiments designed to demonstrate the imitation of aggression. They became known as 'The Bobo Doll Studies' due to the use of a large inflatable doll in the shape of a skittle that sprang back when hit. The experiments were conducted under different conditions including observing an adult model in the same room or via a film. In the version of the study using a film, the adult model was seen by some children as being rewarded for his

or her behaviour by receiving praise and sweets and chocolate; while another group observed the model being punished and told off for aggression towards the Bobo doll. The children who had witnessed the model being rewarded were more likely to display aggressive behaviour towards the doll than those children who observed punishment for such behaviour.

"One of the most common mistakes that students make with social learning theory is using one of the variations of the Bobo doll studies to describe the theory – don't! They are evaluation only: remember that."

» In another study to support social learning theory, Bandura et al (1961) focused on the effects of observing aggressive behaviour being rewarded or punished. A group of nursery age children were shown a television programme in which one character, Johnny, refuses to let another character, Rocky, play with some toys. In one version of the programme Rocky retaliates by hitting Johnny and throwing toys at him. In the final scene the voice-over declares Rocky victorious and he departs, taking some of Johnny's toys with him. In a second version of the programme, events are changed so that when Rocky tries to retaliate, Johnny prevents him by hitting him. Children who had observed these films were recorded playing for 20 minutes. Those children who had seen Rocky rewarded for his aggressive behaviour used far more aggression in their play than the children who had not witnessed the aggression being rewarded.

One of the major limitations of this and other studies by Bandura is that they are measuring forms of play. The Bobo doll in particular is designed to be hit and bounce back up, so demonstration of this behaviour in children would not necessarily cause concern. A parent who bought a Bobo doll for their child to play with would expect to see them hitting it repeatedly as the toy is designed to encourage this action. It is unlikely that the parent would have cause for concern and interpret this behaviour as aggressive. It could therefore be argued that Bandura's study is measuring imitation of play behaviour and not necessarily aggression.

» The measurement of 'real' aggression under controlled conditions is difficult as it poses major issues, particularly with regards to ethics. Deliberately inducing aggression in one person towards another is unethical. Instead we may consider instances where individuals have already developed aggressive behaviour and try to ascertain the cause of their behaviour. Patterson et al (1982) studied a group of 19 male and female children ranging from 3 to 12 years old whose problem behaviour had been defined as 'social aggression'. Their parents often described the children as 'out of control' with frequent temper tantrums and hitting out at other children and adults, and the children had all been referred to specialist services for help. Initial analysis of the children showed stable levels of aggression over time and demonstrations of aggressive behaviour across a range of situations. Family analysis also revealed that parents had modelled aggressive behaviour by administering physical punishment to the children. They also frequently gave in to tantrums, thus rewarding the aggressive behaviour in their children. Experts at the learning centre were able to help the parents to change their behaviour so that they became positive models for their children. This meant training the parents to model appropriate behaviour, to use positive reinforcement and praise their children when they behaved well. They were also taught more appropriate forms of discipline, such as the use of a 'naughty step'. The parents reported the treatment as "very effective". This clearly demonstrates a positive application of social learning theory in changing aggressive behaviour in children.

» A more recent discovery concerns the role of biology in the imitation of others' behaviour. In the 1990s Rizzolatti and colleagues discovered a group of cells in the brain that they named 'mirror neurons'. Mirror neurons become active not only when we perform an action but also when we see another person perform an action. In fact, the neurons that activate during this observation are the same ones that would be active if we were to engage in the behaviour ourselves. Another important thing about motor neurons is that they only respond to meaningful actions, so that they would not be active for example in response to a hand grasping an 'invisible' apple, but would if there was a 'real' apple being grasped. It has been suggested that mirror neurons allow us to experience what others are doing and feeling, so that everything we watch someone else doing we also rehearse in our own minds.

The discovery of mirror neurons has major implications for our understanding of the social learning of aggression. For example, mirror neurons explain how we are able to understand the pleasure that someone experiences when they are victorious after a fight and empathise with that emotion to the point where we can understand what it would be like to experience the pleasure ourselves. In some respects, mirror neuron theory is providing a biological basis for social learning theory. Potentially, the discovery of mirror neurons is a major breakthrough in understanding human behaviour – although it must be remembered that the theory is still in the early stages of research.

DEINDIVIDUATION THEORY OF AGGRESSION

To become deindividuated means to lose one's sense of individuality and identity. This can occur in two main ways: an individual may become part of a crowd; or may identify with a particular role (often aided by the wearing of a uniform or mask). Psychologists have discovered that these experiences have an effect on our behaviour.

ASK AN EXAMINER

"You need to know two theories of aggression for your exam. If you are only asked to write about one, then you should probably chose social learning theory. Deindividuation applies specifically to aggression which occurs when in a group – be sure to mention that."

Early work by Le Bon (1896) pointed to the notion that when part of a large anonymous group, individuals are more likely to behave in an anti-social and aggressive manner. In crowds, a 'collective mindset' is created and the group acts as one: Le Bon termed this a 'mob'. More recent research supports Le Bon's idea that often the presence of other people weakens constraints against acting in anti-social ways.

Research suggests that when an individual becomes submerged in a group they feel less identifiable, and this in some circumstances can lead to less inhibited behaviour. Loss of inhibition means the individual is not so constrained by their normal internal standards of acceptable behaviour, leading a person perhaps to engage in behaviours that they would not consider while alone. The normal constraints that prevent aggressive behaviour may be lost in a crowd of people where the individual is not identifiable and is therefore at less risk of social disapproval for their actions. The shared responsibility for action reduces the sense of guilt if the action results in violent behaviour and harm to other people or to property.

Things that reduce personal identity, such as uniforms, can also create anonymity and contribute to aggressive behaviour as the individual identifies with the role created by the uniform and loses their sense of individuality. Uniforms are often used by groups whose intention is to behave in an aggressive manner – for example the Ku Klux Klan (a secret militant organisation in the US which is aggressively pro-white American).

Central in understanding why deindividuation occurs is the concept of self-awareness. This is important since awareness of our own attitudes, feelings, and behaviour is used for self-regulation. An example of self-regulated behaviour influenced by beliefs is someone who has strong Christian beliefs 'turning the other cheek' rather than retaliating with aggression.

According to Diener (1980), deindividuation occurs when self-awareness is blocked by environmental events. When this occurs people *feel* different – for example, they get caught up in the present, they are less able to consider consequences, and perception of time becomes distorted. Factors critical for a deindividuated state to occur include strong feelings of group membership, increased levels of arousal, and a focus on external rather than internal events, as well as feelings of anonymity.

According to Diener, someone in a deindividuated state is less concerned about what others think of their actions, and they are not thinking clearly, so rational planning is affected. In addition, because they are focusing on external events rather than their own feelings and because they are now more impulsive, there is a greater risk that they will behave in dangerous and aggressive ways.

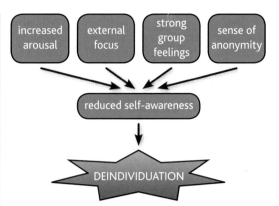

Diener's theory of deindividuation.

Prentice-Dunn and Rogers (1982) have modified Diener's theory to distinguish between two types of self-awareness: public and private. Whilst reductions in either can result in aggressive behaviour, they suggest that only reductions in private self-awareness lead to genuine deindividuation. Other researchers however consider a loss of either can produce this outcome (e.g. Postmes and Spears, 1998).

Public self-awareness

This is a concern over the impression of yourself that you are presenting to others when you know that you are being judged. The level of anonymity that may occur when part of a crowd can reduce a person's level of public self-awareness. Believing that you cannot be identified and publicly held accountable for your actions can increase the level of aggressive behaviour: for instance, during a riot individuals may smash shop windows to loot goods since they are not likely to be picked out from the crowd – i.e. they can 'get away with it'. The anti-social behaviour in this instance may be behaviour that ordinarily the individual is too afraid to carry out as it brings the risk of being labelled by others as criminal. Diener (1980) describes this lack of public self-awareness as disinhibition rather than deindividuation.

Private self-awareness

This relates to the individual's own sense of self, including thoughts, feelings, values and morals. This is a personal sense of who you are – your own internal set of standards that govern behaviour. You may behave 'out of character' and lose your own set of internal standards as you lose yourself in the crowd. Individuals can take their cues for how to behave from the crowd they have become a part of, rather than thinking for themselves. In this situation people may be no longer capable of making rational decisions and as they become swept up by the crowd they may be more likely to aggress if the crowd becomes violent. Most people can recall times in their life when they have lost their inhibitions whilst in a crowd at a concert, festival or football match and behaved out of the ordinary. Whilst this does not automatically lead to anti-social behaviour, aggression is more likely to occur in these conditions than when the individual is self-governing and in control of their actions.

EVALUATION OF DEINDIVIDUATION AS AN EXPLANATION OF AGGRESSION

"Beware! You may come across research into deindividuation which looks at anti-social behaviour rather than aggression. An example would be research into the naughty behaviour of children wearing trick-or-treat costumes. Do not use this! It is not specifically about aggressive behaviour and is therefore not relevant."

» Zimbardo (1973) used deindividuation to explain in part the rapid degeneration of behaviour in his Stanford Prison Experiment. The 'prison' was actually a simulation, set up in the basement of Stanford University, with students recruited to play the role of prisoner or guard. The experiment, which was supposed to run for two weeks, was stopped after six days because of the level of aggression shown by the guards and the inhumane treatment of the prisoners. During the study the participants did not address one another by name: instead the prisoners were called by number and the guards addressed as 'Mr Correctional Officer'. The guards were given uniforms to wear including reflective sunglasses which prevented the prisoners from making direct eye contact. The prisoners wore smocks and stockings over their hair. Both sets of clothes increased the anonymity of individuals and, combined with the fact that the participants were unaware that they were being closely observed throughout the experiment, contributed to their deindividuation and escalation of aggressive behaviour. (A full description of the Stanford Prison Experiment can be found in the next section on explanations of institutional aggression.)

"Zimbardo's Stanford Prison Experiment is an incredibly useful study to know about – it can be used in many different ways. You will see it referred to several times in this chapter."

» In an earlier experiment, Zimbardo (1969) explored the effects of deindividuation on female undergraduates. The women were divided into two groups. The first group were dressed in loose fitting white laboratory coats and asked to put hoods over their faces to disguise their individuality. The second group were given large name tags to wear. All the participants were asked to observe a woman being interviewed and to evaluate her performance. In some instances the interviewee was a mild-mannered, pleasant woman and in another condition participants saw an interviewee who was rude and obnoxious. The participants evaluated the interviewee by administering electric shocks (these were of course fakes and the interviewee was a confederate). The participants who were identifiable by name shocked the rude interviewee more than the pleasant interviewee; however, the deindividuated participants shocked both interviewees equally. Zimbardo concluded that deindividuation increased the level of aggressive behaviour and also that the aggressive behaviour was indiscriminate and not influenced by the characteristics of the individual receiving the aggression.

» Another study to support deindividuation was conducted by Dodd (1985). He asked his students "If you could be totally invisible for 24 hours and were completely assured that you could not be detected or held responsible for your actions what would you do?" Responses were gathered from 229 students, 26 of whom were taking part in a college programme in prison. Thirty six percent of the actions described by the students were categorised by independent raters as anti-social and there was no significant difference between the responses given by the students at the university and those studying in prison. Acts of extreme aggression were mentioned infrequently, but did include murder, rape, vandalism and political assassination. Dodd concluded that, given the chance to remain anonymous and non-identifiable, even 'normal' college students could be capable of extreme anti-social behaviour.

» A field experiment carried out by Ellison et al (1995) suggested that drivers in convertible cars with the tops up sounded their horns at a vehicle remaining stationary at a green light more than convertible drivers with their tops down. Ellison interpreted the horn honking as aggressive behaviour and felt that anonymous drivers (i.e. those with their tops up) were more likely to display aggression than identifiable drivers with their tops down. He tested his hypothesis in a driving simulation experiment using 289 psychology students as participants. Their levels of aggressive driving were judged by the speed at which they drove, the number of red lights they ran, the number of collisions and the number of pedestrians they ran over. The participants were told to imagine they were either non-identifiable in a convertible car with the top up or identifiable with their convertible top down. The participants drove more aggressively when in the anonymous condition. Research such as this could have interesting implications in helping us to understand the causes of aggressive driving and road rage. However, caution must be exercised in applying these simulated findings to the real world. The participants were obviously aware that the driving test was like a computer game and might also have easily inferred from the instructions the expected behaviour in relation to anonymity.

» A meta-analysis of 60 studies into deindividuation concluded that anonymity to outsiders was the key to increasing the likelihood of aggressive behaviour (Postmes and Spears, 1998). This supports the concept of the loss of public self-awareness as a major factor in increasing the likelihood that deindividuation will lead to anti-social behaviour. Although they found that loss of identity to people outside of the group was consistent with the risk of aggressive behaviour the risk was only slight. This also highlights the

fact that people can gather in large crowds and become part of the group without this leading to aggression. Many crowds gather peacefully and induce a sense of belonging such as at festivals or religious gatherings.

» Most of the research into deindividuation discussed so far has taken place under controlled laboratory conditions, with participants being asked to perform actions that are unfamiliar or unlikely to happen in their everyday lives. Rehm et al (1987) addressed this issue by conducting research in a real-life context, focusing on aggression in sport and assessing the aggressive acts of 11-year-old children in a handball game. Deindividuation was created by giving one team bright orange shirts to wear and allowing the other team to remain in their own shirts which varied in style and colour. Thirty different games were observed across three schools. Nineteen of the games involved boys-only teams and eleven featured girls-only teams. The uniformed teams displayed more aggressive acts than the non-uniformed teams. However, this effect was only apparent for the boys' teams: there was no difference in the levels of aggression shown by the female teams. In 14 out of the 19 boys' games, the greater amount of aggression was judged to have come from the orange shirt-uniformed team. The researchers concluded that the uniform created similarity amongst the members of the team and that the loss of individuality led to deindividuation and higher levels of aggression. The same effect, however, could be explained using social identity theory. Wearing the uniform could enhance the cohesion within the group and create a social identity which leads to the team working harder as a group. The occurrence of aggressive acts could be a by-product of greater efforts to fulfil the group norm. This explanation could also account for the gender differences between the teams, in that it showed that male and female norms were different – i.e. the male norm allowed for levels of aggression in a bid to win the game which were different from those of the female norm.

» Very few studies have looked at the effects of deindividuation on violent physical aggression in the real world. One study which has attempted to do this was a cross-cultural study by Watson (1973). The findings across 24 cultures showed that in conflict situations warriors who concealed their identity by wearing face and body paint were more aggressive than those who were identifiable. The anonymous warriors were significantly more likely to kill, mutilate and torture captured prisoners. In a more recent study, Silke (2003) examined the relationship between anonymity and aggression in violent assaults that occurred in Northern Ireland. Of the 500 cases studied, 206 were carried out by offenders wearing masks or disguises. Those offenders that were anonymous inflicted more serious physical injuries, attacked more people at the scene of the offence and carried out more acts of vandalism than offenders who were identifiable. The findings from both of these studies seem to suggest that anonymity contributes to deindividuation and that higher levels of aggression result.

EXPLANATIONS OF INSTITUTIONAL AGGRESSION

When aggression and violence occur within an institutionalised setting it often attracts the attention of the media. This is due to the fact that rules and expectations of behaviour have been transgressed. Institutions are often created to maintain order and combat anti-social behaviour so when this goes wrong questions are raised about the effectiveness of these institutions. Reports of aggressive behaviour in schools, hospitals and prisons, and within the armed forces and police, seem to be on the increase. Even the office is not exempt, with reports of disgruntled workers inflicting harm on work colleagues in response to being sacked or to being repeatedly harassed by a superior (Blair, 1991).

Aggression in educational settings

Aggressive behaviour in schools and colleges is becoming more common. In United States schools in 1974 there were a reported 900 rapes, 12,000 armed robberies, 204,000 reports of aggravated assault and 270,000 burglaries (Brickman, 1976). Students and teachers at all academic levels are victims of physical assault, verbal threat, theft and vandalism of property and reports of these incidents are worldwide. In extreme cases teachers have been murdered by their pupils. On the 11 March 2009 Tim Kretschmer shot dead three teachers at his former school in Germany. He also killed ten of his classmates before turning the gun on himself.

Aggression in healthcare settings

Workers and patients in healthcare institutions are also at risk of violence and abuse – particularly carers and nurses who work with the mentally ill. Recent statistics suggest that injuries to healthcare workers from patient assaults exceed injuries to construction workers, whose jobs are considered to be far more risky. Healthcare settings have provided easy targets for serial killers. Beverley Allitt murdered four children and injured five others whilst working as a State Enrolled Nurse on the children's ward of a Lincolnshire hospital. One of Britain's most notorious murderers was Dr Harold Shipman: he is thought to have killed up to 250 of his patients, 80% of whom were women, usually elderly.

Aggression in the police and prisons

Violence is an expected event in policing. It has been suggested that the aggression experienced by police officers can be categorised into three types: witnessing violence in others, aggressive acts against the police and aggressive acts initiated by the police (Anderson and Bauer, 1987). Yarney (1988) reports that the police in the United States shoot over 400 criminals each year and that over 100 officers die in the line of duty. Most police murders studied by Yarney took place in cities where the crimes being investigated involved the use of guns, and police were found to be more at risk during robberies than when investigating domestic disputes. In the policing of the G20 protests against global warming in 2009 a man died after being pushed to the ground by a police officer. Over 120 complaints were made against the police at this event, by people who had claimed to have witnessed or suffered police brutality.

A detailed study was conducted into deaths in Canadian penitentiaries (prisons) from 1967 to 1981 and, of the 65 deaths related to assaults, 6 involved members of the prison staff (Jaywardene and Doherty, 1985).The perpetrator was most likely to be a young male with a history of violent behaviour who committed the act of aggression when there were less likely to be any witnesses. Most assaults occurred in high security blocks during the day, with prison wardens of less than one year's experience at the greatest risk. A report in *The Guardian* from 2003 highlighted abuse of prison inmates at Wormwood Scrubs. Prison officers subjected inmates to sustained beatings, mock executions, death threats, choking and torrents of racist abuse. At least 122 separate instances of assault were recorded between 1995 and 1999 and left some inmates with broken bones and mental trauma. On several occasions officers psychologically tortured prisoners by threatening to hang them and bragging that they had done this to other inmates without being caught.

EXPLANATIONS OF INSTITUTIONAL AGGRESSION

"You'll find research relevant to each of these explanation in examples of institutional aggression to follow. How you get your descriptive and evaluative marks is up to you – how you say things in an exam is often as important as what you say."

Deindividuation

The loss of personal identity that results from wearing a uniform – either as a police officer or prison guard – may go some way towards explaining the likelihood that people will display aggression. Removing an individual's own clothes and replacing them with a uniform plays a major part in depersonalising them within an institutional setting. Deindividuation may also occur amongst prisoners whose heads are shaved and who are given matching clothing to wear. However, the removal of individuality in this instance is more likely to dehumanise the prisoners and make them targets of aggression. Police in riot gear are difficult to identify because partial masks and visors cover their faces. Officers in the 2009 G20 protests were criticised for covering up their individual identity numbers in order to make themselves even more anonymous. Anonymity may encourage aggression by lessening the likelihood of being caught or through the loss of personal values and morals. The anonymity of police officers, particularly when in large groups, may also make them seem less human, and this fact in turn may be more likely to incite violence from a rioting crowd so that they become the victims of assault.

Identification with a role

Uniforms can also help to define roles. A person's behaviour may change in accordance with the expectations afforded to the role they have adopted, and the wearing of a uniform can help them to 'feel the part'. Uniforms are synonymous with institutions whether in hospitals, the police force, prisons or schools. Even colleges and universities adopt the use of scarves or sweatshirts to denote membership of a particular house or fraternity.

Ecological explanations – situational variables

Characteristics of an environment in which an institution is housed may contribute to aggressive behaviour. Although overcrowding in schools and prisons is a factor to be considered, these institutional characteristics may not necessarily be physical – they may be more to do with the set of rules or norms created within the institution. Institutions often have an 'us and them' hierarchy: teachers and pupils, health workers and patients, prisoners and guards. This means that one group has power over the other group, leading to social inequality. Each person's role is instantly identifiable by what they are wearing, with people in positions of power often denoted by a uniform that bears symbols of their status and authority. Even in schools, teachers may wear identity badges that symbolise their authority; and guards in prisons may carry batons and keys. There may also be a pecking order within each identifiable group, with in-groups and out-groups appearing particularly in schools, colleges and prisons.

RESEARCH INTO INSTITUTIONAL AGGRESSION

"Remember, research can be used as description or evaluation. It can be used to support an explanation, in which case it is evaluative. A piece of research can also be presented as description and evaluated by considering its strengths and limitations."

Institutional aggression – prisons

Support for the role of deindividuation in institutional aggression comes from Zimbardo's Stanford Prison experiment (1973). Loss of personal identity was experienced by both guards and prisoners. This can be seen from the way in which they addressed one another either by number if they were a prisoner or by the title 'Mr Correctional Officer' if they were a prison guard. The uniforms worn by the guards were designed to increase anonymity. They wore khaki military style uniforms, carried batons and wore reflective sunglasses to hide their eyes. The prisoners' uniforms were designed to reflect their loss of status and identity. Prisoners wore smocks with their prisoner number clearly visible, and covered their hair with stockings to create a uniform appearance. The uniforms could also have assisted in the identification with the role the students were playing. Evidence suggests that the students very quickly 'became' prisoners or guards. Even the prisoners referred to one another by number and their conversations were wholly concerned with activities within the prison: they did not discuss their lives prior to taking part in the simulation. The guards responded similarly, in that they discussed only prison business and even volunteered to do extra shifts within the prison. The students selected to take part in the experiment were chosen for their emotional stability and yet the study had to be stopped after only six days when it should have run for two weeks. The reason for this was the brutality and humiliation experienced by the prisoners at the hands of the guards. Instances included the imposition of solitary confinement, removal of basic rights such as food and toileting and forcing prisoners to clean toilets with their bare hands.

Visible signs of stress emerged in some patients, including bodily rashes – and some prisoners also showed symptoms of depression. Zimbardo concluded that what makes acts of evil happen in a prison setting is nothing to do with the prisoners or guards as individuals but everything to do with the powerful influence of the institutional set-up and the power attributed to the role of guard,

THE STANFORD PRISON EXPERIMENT (ZIMBARDO ET AL, 1973)

The Stanford prison experiment.

What the researchers did

Twenty-four men were recruited from the student population of Stanford University, including two reserves, and paid $15 a day. Each was checked carefully for both physical and psychological well-being, and each was assigned randomly to the role of either prisoner or guard. The ten 'prisoners' were arrested unexpectedly in a realistic fashion by the local police department and taken blindfolded from their homes to the mock 'prison' that had been set up in a basement at the university. They were subjected to all the things that real prisoners would be, including delousing and the removal of personal possessions. Their clothes were taken and they were given a prison smock to wear bearing their number.

To all intents and purposes they were prisoners, and lived constantly like this. For example, they were mostly confined to cells, and allowed only three supervised trips a day to the toilet. The 'guards' were given mirror sunglasses and official-looking uniforms to wear, along with whistles and clubs. They worked in shifts attending to the prisoners. This was all part of the deindividuation process where personal identity was being reduced, a sense of group identity was being increased, and individuals were given powerful roles to occupy. The guards and prisoners experienced life in these roles for six days until the study was halted early. This was due to both the increasingly tyrannical behaviour of the guards and the deteriorating psychological condition of the prisoners.

Implications

It was clear to Phillip Zimbardo that the situation in which the participants found themselves influenced their behaviour more than their dispositions (i.e. what kind of people they were). Although conducted over 35 years ago, the study still raises important issues. At the end of the Iraq war, shocking images were revealed showing instances of disrespect and torture of Iraqi prisoners by their American guards at Abu Ghraib prison. The parallels between this and the prison study were all too clear. Zimbardo says that although the behaviour of the guards was inexcusable, it was not inexplicable. In his 2007 book *The Lucifer Effect: Understanding How Good People Turn Evil* Zimbardo points out that it is all too easy to blame the guards in instances like this. He says it is not the bad apple in the barrel that you need to blame, but rather the bad barrel. By this he means that it is not the individuals who are at fault in the first instance, but the system (i.e. the institution) that the individuals are part of.

Zimbardo's view on the Abu Ghraib images is that they were inexcusable but not inexplicable.

aided by the wearing of a uniform. This seemed the most likely explanation, since the guards and prisoners within the prison simulation were all 19-year-old college students with no previous convictions or history of violence. The likelihood is that if those students playing prisoners had been guards the outcome would have been no different.

Zimbardo's study is the closest we can come to using controlled conditions to study the effects of imprisonment. The very fact that this research is a simulation, however, raises questions about how far we can generalise the findings to help us understand the effects of imprisonment. The 'prisoners' in the experiment had not committed a crime nor were they going to be locked away from society for more than a period of days or weeks. Aspects of prison life that cannot be studied under experimental conditions are the homosexual liaisons and sex pressure situations sometimes experienced by inmates. These situations frequently incite aggression and some prisoners respond with violence when solicited for sex (Nacci and Kane, 1984).

A study conducted in the United States found that two in every ten prison inmates had been sexually assaulted (Lockwood, 1980). Most of these victims were heterosexual as were their assailants. Lockwood claims that within the prison institution participation in homosexual activity does not 'count' towards sexual identity. In some assaults the victim must appear like a woman to the rapist and they see him as taking on a female identity in an institutionalised world that is devoid of females. Nacci and Kane (1984) noted common characteristics amongst both prisoners who were victims of rape and those who were willing participants in homosexual activity. Both groups tended to be physically thinner and less muscular than other inmates and had a more effeminate appearance. Although generally heterosexual, they had more positive attitudes towards homosexuality compared with more negative attitudes from most prisoners. When questioned by Nacci and Kane about how conflicts should be resolved they exhibited a tendency to view all conflicts as best resolved using greater levels of violence. This is perhaps a reflection of their personal insecurities regarding their thin and effeminate appearance. These inmates might have learned that if they did not strike first and hardest in a fight their inferior strength might work against them and they could be exploited. This helps to explain the violent reaction of some inmates when solicited for sex. Some sexual assaults in prisons may be used as an appropriate form of degradation and punishment

after an argument. The rapist increases his power and status in the eyes of the other inmates and he may establish a higher position in the prison hierarchy. According to Lockwood, sex is the reason behind 25% of conflicts that occur within prisons: however, within the prison system sexual aggression is not perceived as sexual behaviour. The motivation behind many of the assaults is not sexual gratification but social control. Two types of rape have been identified, according to the social roles they fulfil. Role-expressive rape occurs due to participation in a group and may result in gang rapes: such rapes do not take place for sexual gratification. Role-supportive rape happens in order to maintain membership of a particular group. Both types can only occur in groups such as prison hierarchies that condone the use of force in achieving their goals.

Institutional aggression – educational settings

In stark contrast to prison institutions are the fraternities and sororities established as support networks for undergraduate students within the United States college system. Despite the contrast, surprising similarities exist between these two forms of institution. Fraternities in particular have been criticised for the use of force in their initiations and in condoning the sexual assault of women. The tradition known as 'hazing' is the ritualistic harassment or abuse of an individual or a group. Acts can include burning and branding, kidnapping, drugging and sexual abuse. Probationary members may experience mental and physical stress over periods of weeks or months as a way of proving that they are worthy of membership to a particular fraternity or sorority. According to research by Nuwer (1990) hazing has contributed to more than 50 deaths in college fraternities and many physical injuries including paralysis. In most states across America, hazing is now illegal and campaigns are under way to try to curb these brutal practices. The extreme behaviour that occurs in these groups can be explained using the theory of identification. Young men and women are prepared to take part in potentially life-threatening activities in order to belong to a group. Many of the groups have high status, and acceptance can have implications that reach far beyond the students' life at university. Fraternities and sororities are often shrouded in secrecy: this makes them difficult to control, but also makes their victims more vulnerable, as members are unwilling to speak out for fear of breaking the code.

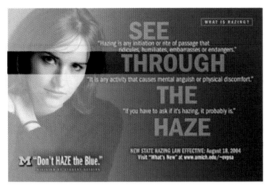

Campaign poster to stop hazing, from the University of Michigan.

Martin and Hummer (1989) studied sexual assault in fraternal life and concluded that fraternities as social institutions actively encourage sexual violence against women as an acceptable norm. "Preoccupation with loyalty, group protection, secrecy and the illegal use of alcohol combined with an involvement in violence, emphasis on competition and superiority create an atmosphere conducive to rape." (Martin and Hummer, 1989). The researchers aimed to discover the extent to which this aspect of fraternal behaviour had impacted on women in sororities who would mix with the fraternal males during social gatherings. They conducted a questionnaire by mail and received only a 28% response which they deduced was due to the secrecy surrounding the sororities and the need to uphold the code of the institution. Half of the respondents to Martin and Hummer's questionnaire had experienced some form of sexual coercion: 24% cited incidents of attempted rape and 17% claimed to have been victims of full rape. Over half of these rapes had occurred in a fraternity house and over half at a fraternity function. The study supports the theories of ecology and identification, as in order to be accepted as a member of a fraternity a young man would have to prove himself worthy by upholding the norms of the group. There is no evidence, however, for the role played by deindividuation in encouraging aggression. In fact this scenario goes against the theory as the attackers would be known to their victims and would be likely to have further contact with them at future social gatherings.

An ecological perspective can be applied to address the question of how school size and structure may influence social dynamics (Garabino, 1977). 13-year-old students in the 7th grade of school were given questionnaires to assess their perception of anonymity and levels of danger within their schools (Blyth, 1980). They also asked the participants whether they had been victims of bullying. The children were divided into a victim or non-victim category. The victims, who comprised 34% of the sample, had experienced at least one instance of bullying. Seventh graders from both junior high schools and elementary schools took part in the study. Within the junior high, 7th graders would be amongst the youngest pupils; whereas in an elementary school 7th graders would be the older children within the school. More of the children questioned had experienced bullying in the junior high schools than in the elementary schools, suggesting that the children's experiences were affected by their position within their school. The children attending junior high also reported higher degrees of anonymity related to the larger size of the school and greater number of pupils on roll. The victims were pupils who felt isolated from others in their schools and had less protection from support networks.

Institutional aggression – healthcare settings

Violence in healthcare settings is most commonly associated with psychiatric units particularly as aggression is a recognised component of some psychiatric disorders. Biological factors may underpin the likelihood of aggression but these

FRATERNITIES AND SORORITIES

These single-sex organisations exist within the American college system and are primarily made up of under-graduate students. Fraternities are for males and sororities for females (the words come from the Latin for 'brother' and 'sister'). Their primary goal is to provide academic and social activities for students and opportunities to contribute to their community. It is not unusual for fraternities and sororities to be involved in holding charitable events to raise money for local and national charities. Some have houses providing residential and dining facilities for their members. Many of them have names represented by Greek letters such as Gamma Phi or Alpha Delta. They are characterised by symbolic traditions such as initiation ceremonies, songs, passwords and handshakes. Members are often instantly identifiable by special clothing bearing their Greek letter names and symbols. When a new student wants to join a sorority or fraternity they make a 'pledge' and may be asked to prove their worth through a series of challenges that take place over weeks or months before full membership is bestowed upon them.

SITUATIONAL VARIABLES IN INSTITUTIONAL AGGRESSION

Other aspects of the environment in institutions can also contribute to the tendency to show aggression. Experiences of crowding in college dormitories and prisons may be associated with higher levels of aggression. Crowding is the feeling created by density whilst density is the number of people occupying a particular space. Matthews et al (1979) manipulated the sense of crowding by placing individuals in high density situations with lots of others or in low density settings with room to move. He then gave them a task to complete that was either competitive or cooperative. The findings revealed that those in high density situations (i.e. with an increased sense of crowding) asked to compete with one another actually showed a lower tendency to aggress. Matthews suggested that there was a curvilinear relationship between the experience of crowding and the tendency to exhibit aggressive behaviour.

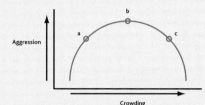

As crowding increases so does aggression (a), but only up to point (b). After this, further increases in crowding lead to decreases in aggression.

Crowding would increase levels of aggression, but only up to a certain point. When the density becomes such that people find it difficult to move they are less likely to display aggressive behaviour. Isolation can also be a contributory factor. Prisoners deprived of stimuli by being detained in small and limited environments as a form of punishment reported several effects of their deprivation. These included increased irritability and aggression directed at themselves and others (Drtil, 1969). Favazza, (1987) suggests that self-harm serves to provide stimulation especially in psychopathic inmates.

factors also interact with social and environmental influences (Tupin, 1988). Rosenhan (1973) found that labelling someone as mentally ill impacted upon the way they were treated by healthcare staff. In his famous study Rosenhan instructed eight mentally sane people to attempt to gain admission to a psychiatric unit by reporting that they were hearing voices. Once admitted they were told to stop any signs of abnormal behaviour to see if the nurses and psychiatrists could detect that they were not really mentally ill. The 'patients' spent their time observing and writing notes. None of the participants was actually detected as false and they remained in the psychiatric institution for an average of 19 days before being discharged with schizophrenia in remission. The false patients found their experience unpleasant and frustrating and they witnessed situations which could easily incite aggressive behaviour from patients. These included a loss of identity and powerlessness as a result of deprivation of human rights – for example a lack of privacy, from having to use toilets without doors. The participants were often frustrated when their simple requests were ignored as if the patient was invisible. This happened in 88% of recorded cases, when nurses moved away from the patient with their heads turned away as if they had not heard them speak. Staff also displayed aggressive behaviour towards the patients and some ward orderlies were brutal to patients in full view of others but stopped once other staff approached.

"Don't just describe examples of institutional aggression, explain them. Three examples have been given here – prison, education and health settings – with deindividuation, identification and situational variable explanations applied as appropriate."

BIOLOGICAL EXPLANATIONS OF AGGRESSION

THE ROLE OF GENETIC FACTORS IN AGGRESSIVE BEHAVIOUR

Genes do not directly cause aggression but influence elements of our biology that contribute to it. Some of these effects are considered structural, that is, the genes contribute elements necessary for aggression, such as muscle and bone development. Other genetic effects can be considered functional – that is, they influence neurochemical, hormonal and sensory systems. It is a combination of these structural and functional effects that contribute to an animal's aggressive behaviour (Renfrew, 1997).

"You could get a question in the exam specifically on genetic explanations of aggression. Don't worry – a technical understanding of genetics is not necessary, for you to do well, though it is probably best that you become acquainted with some of the terminology."

Selective breeding

Selective breeding involves choosing animals with desirable characteristics and mating them with similar other animals in order to enhance these particular traits. Selective breeding of some animals for aggression has been carried out for many years. For example, bulls (Spanish fighting bulls), chickens (fighting cocks), fish (Siamese fighting fish), and dogs (pit bull terriers) have all been selectively bred for high levels of aggression. The structural influence of genes on aggression can be seen in all these animals. For instance, compared to a regular cockerel, the fighting cock is larger, has much stronger wing muscles and legs, and well-developed claws for damaging opponents.

There have been many laboratory-based selective breeding studies. One of the most influential has been by Lagerspetz (1979), carried out in Turku, Finland. She isolated mice immediately after weaning. Mice reared in isolation tend to be aggressive when later placed with other mice. Based on ratings of aggression when placed with another mouse (such as attacking, biting response

speed), she classified them as either Turku aggressive (TA) or Turku non-aggressive (TNA). These mice were interbred so that by the nineteenth generation rates of aggressive biting behaviour in the TA mice were 52% whilst in TNA mice were only 5%. It was also noted that these TA mice had heavier testes and forebrains and altered levels of the neurochemical serotonin in the forebrain and noradrenaline in their brainstem, supporting the notion that genes influence both the structural and functional aspects of an animal's biology.

Lagerspetz (1981) does make the point however that genetic factors do not absolutely determine aggressive behaviour, but that environmental factors are also very important. For example, she points out that both strains of mice can be conditioned to make them less aggressive. This should come as no surprise given the great deal anecdotal evidence of wild animals which would otherwise be dangerously aggressive becoming tamed, such as wolves, bears and big cats.

Twin studies

Understanding the influence of genes on human aggression is a much more difficult task than it is with lower animals. Not only are humans much more complex organisms anyway because of our highly evolved brains, but we live in complex environments which influence behaviour in many and often unpredictable ways. Discriminating between genetic and environmental influences is very difficult.

Whilst selective breeding and rearing in isolation might theoretically address the problem, it is obviously not practical or ethical to do so with humans. An alternative approach has been to investigate a naturally occurring population with known genetic factors – identical (or monozygotic, MZ) twins. Because they are genetically identical, any similarities in aggressiveness might be attributable to shared genes, whilst differences in aggression between them could be ascribed to environmental variables. A strong argument could be made for genetic components in aggression, if MZ twins separated at an early age and reared apart (hence having different environments) were found to have similarities in aggression.

Findings from twin studies however have been extremely variable. For example, Canter (1973) found a correlation of 0.14 for MZs reared together, whilst for the same kind of population O'Connor (1980) found a correlation of 0.72. Slightly less variability emerges from the analysis of correlations in aggressiveness of MZ twins reared

THE PROBLEM OF DEFINING HUMAN AGGRESSION

"Thus far we have only used the general term 'aggression'. In this biological section you will come across a range of terms to describe different types of aggression so it is necessary to clarify their meaning before we move on."

According to McEllistrem (2004) much of the literature on aggression is problematic because researchers have not been sufficiently clear about the type of aggression they are investigating. Aggression is an extremely complex behaviour. Some researchers argue that 'aggression' is a term for a collection of behaviours which emerge in response to many different kinds of environmental factors. Whilst animal research has been reasonably consistent in its use of terms and definitions, a problem arises with human research as no standardised terminology for describing aggressive behaviour in humans has emerged.

Kingsbury et al (1997) prefer aggression to be categorised as either *instrumental* or *hostile*. Instrumental aggression occurs for some kind of reward, such as recognition by other gang members. Hostile aggression applies to behaviours where the goal is specifically to harm another person, for example in response to a threat or insult. This classification is based on a social–psychological perspective for application in clinical settings. Based on the frustration-aggression model of aggressive behaviour, Berkowitz (1994) distinguishes between *instrumental* aggression (which is purposeful and goal-directed and may result from social learning) and *reactive* aggression (emotional, unregulated aggression which occurs in response to frustration). Aggression is commonly subdivided into *affective* (also called *reactive*) and *predatory* (or *proactive*) aggression. McEllistrem argues that this is a particularly important distinction because the two types have different biological origins, and encompass the various other attempts to classify aggression. *Affective* aggression is that which might be understood as appropriate to the species, for example instantly responding to provocation or threat. *Predatory* aggression however is more goal-directed and premeditated, and is often associated with crimes such as assault, murder and rape.

apart. However, whilst the correlations vary, what remains constant across all studies is a greater association of aggressiveness with MZ than with DZ (dizygotic, non-identical) twins, whether reared together or apart (see table below). This is strongly indicating a genetic contribution, even if there is disagreement about its magnitude.

Identical (MZ) twins		Non-identical (DZ) twins	
Reared together	Reared apart	Reared together	Reared apart
0.72	0.64	0.42	0.34
0.39	0.46	0.42	0.06
0.14	0.53	0.30	0.39

Table summarising correlations for MZ and DZ twins reared apart and together. Adapted from Miles and Carey (1997).

From a meta-analysis of twin and adoption studies, Miles and Carey (1997) suggest a heritability measure of aggression of 50%. This is a very high estimate compared to an earlier meta-analysis of eleven twin studies by Plomin et al (1990), who found a small heritability for aggression. The average concordance rate for MZ twins was 0.32 and for DZ twins was 0.14. It appears that different sources of evidence produce different estimates of the heritability of aggression. Rhee and Waldman (2002) suggest that the variability may be due at least in part to the methods of assessing aggressive behaviour in the various studies. Their meta-analysis of 51 twin and adoption studies indicated significant differences in the magnitude of genetic and environmental effects according to how aggression was measured. They found that heritability varied according to the assessment method used, with 39% for self-reported aggression and 53% when reported by others.

The XYY syndrome

Some of the earliest efforts to determine the genetic basis of aggression involved studying the XYY syndrome. This is where men have an extra Y male sex chromosome. Since males are considered more aggressive than females, then having an extra male chromosome suggests that XYY males might be more aggressive. Jacobs et al (1965) found that the incidence of XYY syndrome among inmates of institutions was approximately 3% whereas it is estimated to occur in 0.1% of the normal population. Further studies indicated that these men were taller, had higher levels of testosterone and lower levels of intelligence than non-XYY people. Whilst the link between XYY and aggression was widely accepted, a number of researchers challenged the relationship. A large-scale study by Witken et al (1976) could find no link between XYY syndrome and increased aggressiveness. They did however support previous findings that XYYs had lower levels of intelligence. Whilst they were more likely to commit crimes, closer inspection of their offences showed that their crimes were generally not violent in nature. What the criminal records also revealed was that XYYs were often not very good at being criminals. Witken et al concluded that their lower IQ made them more likely to get caught and convicted for their crimes, hence the higher density of XYYs in the prison population. Whilst Witken et al seem to lay to rest a causal link between XYY syndrome and aggression, a role for XYY syndrome in aggression however cannot be discounted.

MAOA gene and aggression

Attention has turned recently to the issue of identifying particular genes underlying aggressive behaviour. Most recent research has focused on a gene called monoamine oxidase A (MAOA), since a number of studies have found a link between this gene and aggression. MAOA gene regulates an enzyme in the brain also called monoamine oxidase A (enzymes are substances in the body that either break down molecules or join others together). This enzyme is known to break down several neurotransmitters, such as serotonin, noradrenaline and dopamine. By removing excess amounts of these neurotransmitters, monoamine oxidase A helps neurons to communicate with each other more efficiently. The association with aggression makes sense because research has already established that these neurotransmitters are related to mood, and a build-up of these chemicals can cause people to respond excessively (and often aggressively) to stressful situations.

Studies with humans have also indicated a link between MAOA gene and aggression. Brunner et al (1993) discovered a mutation in the MAOA gene in a Dutch family. Family records showed a history of violence in only male members, often associated with stressful events. Investigation indicated that the defective MAOA gene was passed onto problem men from the X (female) chromosome of their mothers. The aggressive problem only affects men since they have only one X chromosome, so show symptoms whenever they inherit the gene. Even though women too might inherit the gene, they don't show aggressive symptoms of the males because they have a second X chromosome

carrying a good copy of the gene. This is supported in ground-breaking research by Cases et al (1995). They disabled the MAOA gene in an X chromosome of mice and found that males became highly aggressive. Females were unaffected by the procedure. Whereas males lacked the monoamine oxidase A enzyme, thereby increasing levels of dopamine and serotonin, females still had a functioning gene in their other X chromosome to do the job. Significantly, restoring the function of the gene had the effect of returning the male mice to a normal state.

Different forms of the MAOA gene have been identified. One form of this gene is a low-activity one (MAOA-L) which produces less of the monoamine oxidase A enzyme which gets rid of excess neurotransmitters. There is also a high-activity form of this gene (MAOA-H) which produces more of this enzyme. Research suggests that it is having the MAOA-L gene in particular which predisposes an individual to anti-social and aggressive behaviour.

In a large longitudinal study of 1,037 children followed over 25 years, Caspi et al (2002) found that males who had been severely maltreated as boys were more likely to engage in anti-social behaviour, including violence as adults. However, males with the MAOA-L gene were more than twice as likely to have been diagnosed in adolescence with a conduct disorder as were those with the MAOA-H gene, and three times more likely to have been convicted of violent crime by 26 years of age. Only 12% of the sample had a combination of maltreatment and the MAOA-L gene: this third subgroup was found to have committed 44% of the crimes. The results indicate the importance of an interaction between genes and environmental influence. Neither having the MAOA-L gene nor the experience of maltreatment alone predicted later aggressive behaviour, but having them both did.

Research has suggested that the MAOA-L variant may be linked to structural changes in the brain. Meyer-Lindberg et al (2006) conducted an fMRI (functional magnetic resonance imaging) study using healthy participants. They found significant reductions in volume of several areas of the brain, including the amygdala and prefrontal cortex in MAOA-L compared to MAOA-H participants. These structures are known to be involved in emotion and are often found to be impaired in anti-social individuals. Furthermore, McDermott et al (2008) showed that participants in their study with the MAOA-L gene displayed higher levels of aggression in response to provocation than those

THE MAOA GENE AND RESPONSE TO PROVOCATION

A study by McDermott et al (2009) demonstrated in controlled experiment conditions a relationship between MAOA-L and actual behavioural aggression. Their study took place over a computer network, so that participants did not actually meet. Each participant first took part in a vocabulary task which earned them money. They were then told that another participant linked to them over the network could if they wished take some of this money away from them – either 20% or 80% of it. If a participant who had lost money wanted to punish the other one for this act, they could do so by forcing them to eat very hot chilli sauce. However, this retaliation would cost some of the money earned in the vocabulary task – the more sauce used in the retaliation the more it would cost. In effect, participants were paying to harm someone. In reality, the set-up was a ruse. In the vocabulary task, there was only one participant each time: the other participant was in fact a computer which was manipulated by researchers to influence the frequency and the amount of money taken. Neither did anyone eat chilli sauce.

They found that participants with the MAOA-L gene demonstrated higher levels of aggression, as measured by hot sauce punishment, than MAOA-H participants. Supporting Caspi et al (2005), McDermott et al also found evidence for a gene/environment interaction. There was evidence in their study that aggressive responses were moderated by environmental factors – when the amount of money taken was high (i.e. there was high provocation), those with MAOA-L gene were much more likely to be aggressive than when provocation was low (i.e. a low amount of money was taken).

with MAOA-H variant. This appears to be evidence for a direct link between genetic variation and willingness to engage in acts of physical aggression.

THE ROLE OF NEURAL AND HORMONAL MECHANISMS

"You are expected to know about neural and hormonal mechanisms – we've separated the two in this section to make things a little clearer."

NEURAL MECHANISMS AND AGGRESSION

Research in the 1930s pointed to the involvement in emotional behaviours, including aggression, of a circuit of structures deep in the brain (Papez, 1937). Whilst some of the structures identified by Papez and others are no longer considered as important in aggressive behaviour, subsequent research has clearly indicated a key role for several of them. Decades of research with non-human animals is beginning to lead to a consensus of opinion that normal aggressive behaviour is not dependent on separate and independently functioning brain areas but on the interaction of a system of structures. Specifically, there is a circuit of brain structures involved in aggression running from the areas of the amygdala, down to the hypothalamus, and from there to the periaqueductal grey (PAG) (Balir and Charney, 2003). This system appears to be organised in a hierarchical way, so that aggressive responses originating higher up the circuit depend on those

structures below functioning normally, while those structures lower down the circuit do not depend on the functioning of those higher up. For example, aggressive responses produced from the amygdala depend on the normal functioning of the hypothalamus and PAG, but the PAG does not depend on the normal operation of the hypothalamus and amygdala. At the highest level of control, this circuit appears to be moderated by the prefrontal cortex. It is the role of the prefrontal cortex to control the outward expression of aggression. Research suggests that this circuit works in a similar way to control human aggression. For example, structures within this circuit appear to be involved in psychiatric disorders where there is a heightened risk of aggression, and damage due to such things as stroke or tumour growth also produces changes in aggressive behaviour. Most research has focused on the role in aggression of two of these structures in particular – the amygdala and the prefrontal cortex.

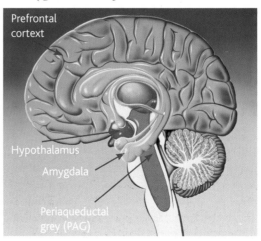

The role of the amygdala in human aggression

The amygdala has long been associated with aggressive behaviour in both animals and humans. One of the earliest links was established by Kluver and Bucy in the 1930s when they removed part of the temporal lobes of rhesus monkeys (thus destroying the amygdala). The behavioural changes resulting from this procedure (known as the Kluver-Bucy syndrome) included a loss of fear and a marked taming effect. Many other studies have confirmed the important role of the amygdala, and findings from animal studies have been used to justify targeting this area for destruction in psycho-surgery aimed at reducing aggression. Narabayashi et al (1972) reported that 43 out of 51 patients who received operations to destroy their amygdala showed more normal social behaviour afterwards, including reduced aggression. Heimburger et al (1978) report that following similar operations, 48 out of 58 patients showed an improvement in aggressive behaviour.

Sustained electrical stimulation of the amygdala in laboratory animals usually results in fear and rage responses (LeDoux, 1996). Humans have been found to behave similarly in response to stimulation. Mark and Ervin (1970) describe the case of a female patient who, during electrical stimulation of the amygdala, at first exhibited facial grimacing, then became very angry, and ultimately flung herself at the wall, beating it with her fists. On another occasion, she picked up her guitar and threw it in the direction of the psychiatrist. This is supported by observations of people experiencing temporal lobe epilepsy becoming aggressive towards those close by, even attacking furniture and other objects (Ashford, 1980).

A number of studies have found that the size of the amygdala is reduced in criminals with violent tendencies (e.g. Wong et al, 1997). In a study of aggressive patients with temporal lobe epilepsy, Van Elst et al (2000) found that the amygdala had lost approximately 20% of its volume. These findings are supported by studies which have found reduced activity in the amygdala, which is what one might expect when a brain structure is reduced (Birbaumer et al 2005). Findings by Müller et al (2003) contradict this however. They showed six male psychopaths and six normal male controls a series of positive and negative pictures whilst measuring their brain activity using fMRI. Results indicated increased activity in several brain areas, including the amygdala.

The exact role of the amygdala in aggression is as yet unclear and the issue has generated considerable debate. For example, it has been suggested that certain areas of the amygdala are 'wired' to produce aggression, whilst other brain areas, especially the prefrontal cortex, offer some control of these aggressive responses. In essence, research is indicating that aggression is an interaction between top-down control via the prefrontal regions and bottom-up signals generated by structures within the limbic system, such as the amygdala (Zuckerman, 2005).

The role of the prefrontal cortex in human aggression

The prefrontal brain regions are directly connected with limbic system structures. They are thought to regulate the amygdala-driven emotional responses, and in this way exercise some form of emotional control. Damage to the prefrontal cortex results in a range of responses, including loss of control, impulsivity, immaturity and altered emotionality, all of which are associated with aggressive acts (Damasio et al, 1994). Anderson et al (1999) have shown that individuals with damage to the frontal cortex during infancy are at an increased risk of aggressive behaviour as adults. They conducted case studies on two individuals who had received damage to their frontal lobes before the age of 16 months. Both cases showed a range of anti-social behaviours, including aggression, beginning in childhood and extending into adulthood. Whilst their behaviour closely resembled that of a comparison group of 25 patients with adult-onset damage, the two early-onset patients were distinct in a number of ways. For instance, the adult-onset patients did not have the degree of anti-social behaviour seen in the early-onset patients, such as stealing and violence against people and property. One particularly significant difference was that the early-onset patients performed very poorly on tests of social and moral reasoning, showing levels characteristic of 10-year-olds. Anderson et al suggest that the adult-onset patients had an intact prefrontal cortex during a critical time in development when rules of social behaviour are formed, and had many years of practice in these skills before brain damage. The early-onset patients however had damaged their prefrontal cortex at a crucial time, thereby disrupting the normal development of social and moral behaviour. This is consistent with other research which suggests that brain impairments in individuals, leading to disrupted moral thinking, predisposes them to anti-social behaviour (Raine, 2008).

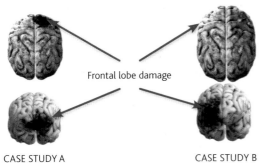

CASE STUDY A   CASE STUDY B

Reconstructions of the brains of the two case studies,
showing damage to their prefrontal cortices.
(Adapted from Anderson et al, 1999).

Neuroimaging studies have consistently found
reductions in prefrontal brain tissue in people
with anti-social and aggressive tendencies. Particular subgroups of aggressive individuals have
been found to have impaired functioning of the
prefrontal cortex. Raine et al (1997) for example
investigated the brain activity of 41 murderers
using positron emission tomography (or PET)
scans. PET scans are used to assess brain activity
by measuring glucose uptake by brain cells – glucose is used as energy by cells so the more glucose
they take up (or metabolise) the more active they
are. They found reduced glucose metabolism in
the prefrontal cortex. Along with the amygdala
and hippocampus, where Raine et al also found
reduced glucose metabolism, the prefrontal
cortex makes up part of the limbic system, which
has long been implicated in the expression of
emotions. These are also critical brain areas for
learning, memory and attention. This fits in with
suggestions that violent offenders have difficulty
forming conditioned emotional responses and
learning from experience (e.g. Cleckley, 1976).
This research is also supported by Soderstrom et
al (2000) who found frontal and temporal lobe
dysfunction in impulsive and violent prisoners.
Volkow et al (1995) looked at the cerebral blood
flow (CBF) of eight violent psychiatric patients.
Cerebral blood flow is used as a measure of brain
activity, since the more active a particular part of
the brain is then the more nutrient-rich blood
supply it needs. They found that, compared with
normal controls, the psychiatric patients were
found to have reduced cerebral blood flow to the
prefrontal cortex. As research had consistently
implicated this brain area in aggressive behaviour,
they speculate that dysfunction in the prefrontal
cortex contributed to the repetitive violent behaviour of their patients.

HORMONES AND AGGRESSION

Observations of behaviour across many species
reveal that aggression more often occurs in males
than females. This sex difference in aggression
is usually attributed to the effects of the male
sex hormone, testosterone. It is one of a class of
hormones called androgens which are important
in producing sperm and developing secondary
sexual characteristics. These hormones also exert
an influence on a range of behaviours, including
aggression.

"Research into hormones can get very com-
plicated if you let it. Here, we have focused
largely on the male hormone testosterone,
and also attempted to keep the technical
jargon to a minimum. Don't worry though: there is
still more than enough here for that top grade!"

Noting the differences in aggressiveness in female
laboratory rats, Vom Saal (1983) investigated the
possibility that this was due to their *in utero* experience (i.e. experience in the womb). Rats can have
around twelve young at a time, which are posi-
tioned close together in two rows in the womb.
Those gestating closest to the ovaries would be
exposed to more oestrogen (female hormone)
than those lying further away. Also, those female
rats gestating next to brothers would be exposed
to testosterone as the testes of their brothers
developed. He found that when they were born,
the female rats which gestated closest to male rats
were the most aggressive female rats in the litter.

Castration has been used as a technique for making domestic and farm animals more manageable
for many years, although the causal link between
the effects of this surgery and testosterone
were not known until relatively recently. Early
observations of animals noted the relationship
between testosterone and increased aggression in
various species, especially at mating season, and
laboratory studies later established the involvement of testosterone in increased aggression at
puberty. Beeman (1947) castrated male mice
and found that their aggressiveness reduced. He
demonstrated the important role of testosterone
in producing this behaviour by later injecting the
mice with testosterone and re-establishing their
aggressiveness. Subsequent studies however found
that castration only reduces aggression in mice if it
is done before puberty, which is the age at which
the animal begins to behave aggressively. It seems

that testosterone contributes to the development of aggression and once it has accomplished this, its effects become relatively permanent and largely unaffected by the subsequent loss of testosterone.

Adult Nazca Booby

Evidence of the effects of hormones on aggression in the behaviour of wild animals was also recently observed by Müller et al (2008) in the aggressive behaviour of Nazca booby bird chicks. When a parent lays two eggs, one chick always kills the other soon after hatching. They took blood samples from Nazca booby chicks in one- and two-egg nests within 24 hours of hatching and analysed them for hormones. They also took blood samples from a near relative for comparison, one that does not engage in this form of aggressive behaviour, the blue-footed booby. The Nazca chicks were found to hatch with levels of circulating testosterone up to three times higher than blue-footed boobies. When the Nazca chicks grow and become mobile they wander the colony bullying other chicks, and when they grow up they are more aggressive than boobies who did not kill a sibling. Müller et al suggest that having a nest mate results in exposure to testosterone at a sensitive time in development. Whilst this confers benefits on the chick early on in that it helps them fight for their survival, it also causes a long-term change in the bird. This thinking fits in with Vom Saal's *organisation/activation model* of aggression. According to Vom Saal, (1983) exposure to androgen during the prenatal period serves to organise the neural networks involved in aggressive behaviour. Later, usually in early adulthood (but sometimes much earlier, for example in the Nazca booby), these neural networks are activated by further exposure to testosterone, resulting in increases in aggressive behaviour. The theory also suggests that, as

early androgen exposure sensitises an animal to its effects, less hormone is needed later in life to activate aggressive behaviour. The theory also suggests that if there is no later burst of hormone (for example, due to castration), then these networks are not activated, with the result that there is less aggressive behaviour.

The role of testosterone in aggression is clear in the behaviour of lower animals, but there is strong evidence that it contributes to human aggression too. For ethical reasons, androgens cannot be given to people in order to see if changes in aggression occur. They would need to be administered over a period of time, which carries a health risk. An alternative approach has been to investigate testosterone levels in people who are displaying aggressive behaviours. Dabbs et al (1995) investigated the relationship between testosterone, crime and prison behaviour. They measured the testosterone in the saliva of 692 adult male prisoners, and found that those who had committed crimes involving sex and violence had higher testosterone levels than inmates who had committed crimes like burglary and theft. The high testosterone males also violated more prison rules involving confrontation. In another study, Dabbs et al (1996) looked at the relationship between testosterone levels and fraternity behaviour. Their argument was that since people affiliate with others like themselves, then high testosterone levels may be a characteristic of groups as well as individuals. Shared interests and activities may serve to intensify pre-existing characteristics. They measured the testosterone levels of 240 members of twelve fraternities in two universities, and compared this to descriptions of fraternity behaviour. They found less smiling and generosity and lower academic achievement in high testosterone fraternities. Members of fraternities with highest levels of testosterone were described as boisterous and macho, whilst those in the lowest testosterone fraternities were attentive and helpful.

These are many problems with studies such as these, which investigate testosterone levels in individuals who may be displaying aggressive behaviours. For one, this kind of research is correlational, and correlation does not mean causation. Also, measurements of aggression are often unreliable, as behaviours are open to interpretation. In Dabbs's fraternity study for example, a lack of smiling was deemed a negative trait associated with being less friendly. Clearly, smiling occurs for many reasons, as does a lack of it, and it may not be related to testosterone at all. Neither does it mean that aggression is only seen in men with high testosterone levels, as aggression can occur for many reasons other than hormone levels.

Whilst women have less testosterone than men, its effects are considered to be just the same. Dabbs et al (1988) looked at the criminal history and measured the testosterone levels of 84 female prison inmates. They found testosterone levels were related to criminal violence, although this relationship was not straightforward. Testosterone was highest in cases of unprovoked violence but lowest where violence was defensive (for example, abused wives who had retaliated). Dabbs et al point out that this seems at odds with the finding of Olweus (1983) who reported higher testosterone levels in participants engaged in what could be called defensive aggression. This raises the problematic issue in aggression research of how exactly aggression is operationalised. Olweus for example referred to 'provoked' aggression when participants were frustrated or restricted in some way. In fact most of the inmates in the Dabbs et al study could be considered to have been

AN INTERACTIONIST APPROACH TO AGGRESSION

For Viding and Frith (2006), research confirms that there are genetic factors underlying individual differences in aggressive behaviour. However, rather than genes being directly responsible for aggressive behaviour, they create variations in brain functioning which in turn determine *predispositions* towards aggression. Whether or not an individual behaves aggressively will depend to some extent on environmental factors.

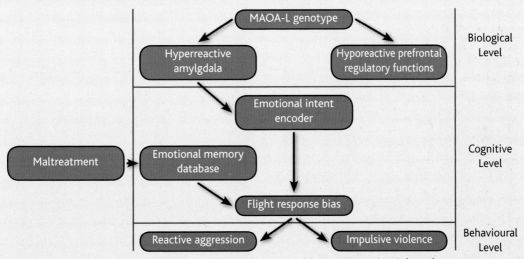

A model of gene-brain-cognition-behaviour interactions. Adapted from Viding and Frith (2006).

At the biological level, the MAOA-L gene affects the development of the prefrontal cortex, which normally regulates emotional responses. This deficiency in the MAOA-L gene means that the prefrontal cortex is now *hyporeactive* (i.e. less responsive), whilst the amygdala is *hyperreactive* (i.e. more responsive) and is therefore more likely to trigger emotional responses during emotional arousal. These brain mechanisms express themselves at a cognitive level through something called the emotional intent encoder. This is the point at which some attempt is made to interpret and understand these aggressive responses.

Environmental effects operate at all three levels. For example, at the behavioural level a brain injury might lead to emotion regulation problems in the prefrontal cortex. At the cognitive level prior experience (and hence memories) of violence might lead to a bias towards a fight response rather than alternative non-aggressive reactions. Childhood maltreatment is a particularly important environmental factor working at the cognitive level, since it produces powerful, emotionally-charged memories. The biological and cognitive levels interact to produce reactive and impulsive aggression.

provoked to violence, by either other people or circumstances.

AGGRESSION AS AN ADAPTIVE RESPONSE

"It is very clear what is needed in this section. The term 'adaptive response' is very specifically related to evolutionary theory, so make sure that you restrict your answers to this if a question comes up in the exam on evolutionary explanations of aggression, or explanations of group display."

EVOLUTIONARY EXPLANATIONS OF HUMAN AGGRESSION

From an evolutionary perspective, the fact that human aggression exists must mean that it has survival value. On the face of it this seems contradictory, as often aggression involves risk of harm or possibly even death. Regardless of the risks involved, research suggests that humans have aggressed against one another for a very long time. Prehistoric remains show signs of physical aggression between early humans. Skulls and ribs have been discovered with evidence of wounds inflicted by man-made weapons designed to cut and stab (Vandermeersch and Leveque, 2002). Traditional hunter-gatherer societies do not have possessions to fight over but are still involved in status conflicts and altercations over access to mates. High levels of violence have been noted in the !Kung San of the Kalahari desert who have murder rates four times higher than those recorded in the United States (Lee, 1979).

The high incidence of aggressive behaviour across cultures and through time has led evolutionary psychologists to conclude that the adaptive and functional benefits of aggressive behaviour must outweigh the possible costs (Buss and Duntley, 2006). From an evolutionary perspective humans are most likely to survive if they have access to resources (food, water and territory); if they can defend their resources and protect their families; and if they can attract or gain access to mates. Aggressive behaviour seems to have evolved to

support the human race in achieving all of these primary goals.

"The specification explicitly requires you to talk about human aggression. Only discuss animal aggression if it can be made clearly relevant to humans."

Not all aggressive behaviour involves direct physical contact. Aggression amongst humans can be indirect (consisting of gossiping, spreading rumours and ostracising people from a group) and can therefore pose little threat to the perpetrator. Even amongst animals aggression is not indiscriminate and fighting generally ceases or diminishes at the end of the mating season. This indicates that access to females is a greater motivating factor in aggression than acquisition or defending of resources such as food. Aggression therefore does have an adaptive value. Aggressive displays that ward off potential rivals also enhance status and therefore attract females. In turn this provides greater opportunities for mating and the birth of more offspring to continue the genes of the successful male. Evolutionary psychologists have concluded that aggression is tactically calculated to help increase the chances of reproduction and survival in both humans and animals. The fight or flight response has an adaptive function and both animals and humans will not stand and fight if outnumbered. They will flee to survive – self preservation being the all important motivating factor.

Aggression in males

Acquisition of status is a primary motivator in male aggression. The motivation to gain high status is driven by both natural selection and sexual selection. High status males have access to resources necessary for survival and females necessary for breeding and producing offspring. In the days when humans lived as hunter-gatherers fitness in males was directly related to success as a hunter and warrior. Good hunters accrued resources and skilled fighters could ward off rival males. These successful males were attractive to females as they were seen as good providers and protectors. To a female who needs to be sure that her mate will be able to guarantee the survival of her and her children the good hunter is an attractive prospect. His desirability in the eyes of the female also serves to enhance the status of the male and ensure his reproductive success. Men in many cultures use aggression as a means of ascending hierarchies and achieving status. Higher status men receive more attention and are more desirable as mates (Li and Kenrick, 2006). It can therefore be costly to male fitness not to engage in conflict. High status men will monopolise more than their fair share of females, leaving low status men at risk of not producing any offspring. Low status males may then indulge in high risk strategies to compete for status and to enhance their chances of reproducing. We can therefore predict that individuals most likely to commit aggressive acts are low status males with few resources and no mate. This prediction is supported by Daly and Wilson (1985). Their review of conflicts that resulted in murder in Detroit throughout 1972 revealed that the motive behind most of these conflicts was status. The victims and the offenders were most likely to be unemployed and unmarried young men – i.e. low status and without a mate. These young men had more to gain through the potential success of a risky act of extreme aggression than a high status male. It is also interesting to note that most victims and offenders knew each other and therefore had an understanding of the status of their rival. Those of equal status were more likely to resort to aggression in a bid to rise above their opponent in their local community hierarchy.

Sexual jealousy and infidelity in males

Daly and Wilson (1985) also noted that in 58 of the 214 cases of murder studied, sexual jealousy was the underlying factor. This involved two men contesting a female partner. The attempt by males to constrain female sexuality by the threat or use of aggression appears to be cross-culturally universal (Daly and Wilson, 1982). This suggests that the use of aggression for this purpose is an adaptive trait that has evolved in males to give them greater confidence of paternity and serve as a warning to potential rival suitors. As females have evolved to carry the offspring during gestation, a woman can always be 100% confident of her genetic relationship to the child. Males, however, can never be 100% sure of their paternity and have therefore evolved behaviour to try to improve their level of certainty. The male is reluctant to expend energy and resources in raising the offspring of another male. In some species (e.g. in lions) young sired by other males are systematically killed (Bertram, 1975).

"You could be asked specifically about infidelity and jealousy, so make sure you learn and don't gloss over this."

Sexual jealousy has therefore evolved to help a man protect his lineage and ensure that the investment he is making in offspring is to his benefit. The concept of male sexual jealousy can be witnessed throughout history with legal systems often supporting the male as the injured party against an adulteress. Historically and cross-culturally sexual intercourse between a woman and a man outside of her marriage is an offence. The husband is portrayed as the victim, entitled to revenge, damages and divorce. Henry VIII executed his second wife, Anne Boleyn, for alleged crimes of incest and adultery. The king expected his brides to be unsullied virgins yet it was acceptable for him to have mistresses and father illegitimate children.

Male aggression against females is designed to deter the female from indulging in behaviour that is not in the interests of the male. This may include adultery and bearing another man's child. Data compiled by Bellis and Baker (1990) suggests that 7% to 14% of children are not fathered by the mother's husband or partner. In a sample of 80 murders where the victim and murderer were married or living together, the victims were 44 husbands and 36 wives, and 29% of these conflicts were deemed to have arisen as a result of sexual jealousy (Daly and Wilson, 1982). The statistics are interesting as they show more husbands murdered by their wives. Evidence from these cases, however, points to the fact that the conflict was instigated by the husband and that the wife killed him in self-defence. This is supported by the convictions: there were fifteen husbands convicted for murder compared with five wives, from the sample studied. Care must be exercised when using this data as evidence to support the prevalence of sexual jealousy in murder cases as psychologists are reliant upon testimonies gathered by police at the time of the crime. Although sexual jealousy may be the prime motive, alcohol and drug abuse, along with low socio-economic status, all correlate highly with abuse of a spouse.

More reliable data may be gathered directly from the victims themselves. Of 44 battered wives living in a women's hostel in Ontario, Canada, 55% cited jealousy as the reason for their husband's aggressive behaviour (Miller, 1980). Actual infidelity on the part of the woman was the reason for the assault in eleven of the cases but the beatings were often motivated by suspicion or fear of adultery. Husbands sometimes objected to their wives going out with friends and in extreme cases they were not even allowed out to go shopping without their husbands. In Western cultures this extreme behaviour may be termed 'morbid' jealousy, with the person showing this level of jealousy deemed to be in need of treatment. In some cultures, however, female confinement is the norm. In Greece the worst form of disgrace experienced by a husband is brought upon him by an adulterous wife. A husband who tolerates this behaviour is seen as unmanly and weak.

Experimental evidence also supports the evolutionary prediction of male aggression in response to threat from a rival suitor. Young (1978) asked students to describe their likely reactions to a jealousy-inducing situation shown in a film. Men predicted that they would respond angrily and become drunk and threaten their rival. Women on the other hand anticipated their reaction to be crying, pretending not to care or trying hard to increase their own attractiveness in order to regain the attention of the male.

Aggression in females

The experimental evidence above highlights the difference in levels of aggression shown by men and women. Females are generally viewed as less aggressive. Evolutionary theory explains lower levels of female aggression by considering the impact that aggressive behaviour may have on the female. In any situation, aggression is a high risk strategy. For males the risk may be outweighed by the possible gains of resources, status and access to fertile females. However, for females the costs of aggressive behaviour exceed the benefits. Lower levels of aggression in the female reflect an adaptive behaviour motivated by the importance of her survival. The mother's presence is more critical to the survival of offspring than the father's (Campbell, 2002). Among the Ache of Paraguay children are five times more likely to die if the mother dies, but only three times more likely on the death of the father. If the mother dies before the child reaches the age of 1, the mortality rate for the infant is 100% (Hill and Hurtado, 1996). Even in Western cultures the mother is more likely to gain custody of children in a marriage breakdown and is the parent primarily responsible for raising the offspring. If a woman wants her children to survive she must be concerned with her own survival.

"Aggression is not restricted to males! Don't forget to also discuss female aggression, as it shows a good rounded understanding of the issue."

Evidence for the female's concern for her own survival can be seen in studies of fear and phobic reactions in women. The things that women are frightened of correspond to specific dangers faced by humans during the time of evolutionary adaptation when humans lived as hunter-gatherers (Marks and Nesse, 1997). Phobias concerning animals – particularly dogs, snakes and insects – are far more common in women, as are fear of injury, blood and medical procedures. Agoraphobia is more prevalent amongst women, reflecting a time when open spaces would have meant vulnerability to attack by predators and would have threatened survival. Women also perceive more danger when assessing a situation compared with assessment of the same situation by men. A meta-analysis of 127 laboratory studies found that women saw aggressors as being in greater danger as a result of displaying because, in so doing, they were possibly inciting aggression in an opponent (Bettencourt and Miller, 1996).

A woman has nothing to gain by exhibiting aggressive behaviour. High status, dominant aggressive females are not preferred as mates so this kind of behaviour has no adaptive value for the woman. The woman's main aim is to secure a valuable male who can support both her and her offspring. To this end she may be in competition with other females to secure the best mates but she is more concerned with her own mortality. This has led to the development of low risk and indirect strategies in disputes and conflict. Women are more likely to use gossiping, name calling and ostracising, aimed at decreasing the attractiveness of the competing female – tactics which reduce the risk of physical injury. Meta analyses have shown that sex differences in aggression exist for both direct physical aggression and indirect, verbal and psychological aggression. Men exhibit more physical aggression than women from the age of 2 (Simon and Baxter, 1989) but females exceed males in the use of indirect aggression (Archer, 2004).

Recent research – both under laboratory conditions and using self-report techniques in naturalistic settings – confirms sex differences in types of aggression (Griskevicius et al, 2009). A survey of

153 college students confirmed that males were four times more likely to use direct physical aggression than women. In a further study students were asked how they would respond to a situation that could provoke aggression – e.g. a person of the same sex spilling a drink on the participant at a party and not apologising. The majority of men said they would be likely to respond with direct physical aggression (e.g. pushing the other man). In the same circumstances women were most likely to walk away. (See table below.)

Response	Male	Female
Direct aggression	43%	25%
Walk away	39.8%	34.9%
Indirect aggression	9.7%	29%
Other	7.5%	11.1%

Male and female responses to a situation likely to provoke aggression (Griskevicius et al, 2009).

Griskevicius et al (2009) also conducted a series of laboratory experiments to test male and female aggression. The experiments were designed not only to look at the differences between sexes when it comes to aggressive behaviour but also to consider the influence of context – i.e. where they are and who is watching. Findings suggested that status was the key factor in provoking a direct physical aggressive response from a man. Interestingly, this was tempered if the man was in a courtship situation – i.e. out on a date – when provoked to aggress, especially if the audience was female. It seems as though in Western cultures women are not attracted to men who are physically aggressive in public (Sadalla et al, 1987). "An audience of prospective mates leads a man to control his aggression when he is motivated to make a romantic impression" (Griskevicius et al, 2009).

Women fight over food shortages.

However a further experiment by Griskevicius et al (2009) showed that even in a courtship scenario, men would display more direct aggression

if the audience was male. The researchers also found that if the motivation was competition for resources then direct physical aggression might have high benefits for both men and women. In this scenario behaviour is driven by the need to survive. Women may be more inclined to use direct aggression when they are competing for the resources that will aid their survival. This effect was more distinct in a scenario where the woman was single and without children. If the woman imagined she was married with children she was less likely to involve herself in risky aggressive tactics that could leave her children without a mother.

EXPLANATIONS OF GROUP DISPLAY IN HUMANS

In animals, display behaviour occurs in a specialised pattern which is used for intimidation or to communicate courtship intentions. It is a public exhibition using bodily gestures and sound. The behaviour is most often linked to the survival of the species. In animals for example, males fight to gain reproductive access to females or show off colourful plumage to attract their attention. Territorial display behaviour that involves warding off neighbouring groups helps to preserve foraging and hunting sites. It has been argued that similar motivating factors apply to group display behaviour in humans.

ASK AN EXAMINER

"Make sure you can explain two examples of group display in humans – here we have chosen to cover group display in sporting events and war."

Group display in humans can be understood by studying behaviour at sporting events. Research has been carried out to study the actions of the players in a team and those of their supporters. Competitive team games such as rugby and football are often the focus of studies. From an evolutionary viewpoint it is easy to see why men would aspire to succeed in these games that offer top players the opportunity to earn high wages and gain access to resources, status and women. High profile contests are covered by the media so although the benefits may outweigh the costs, in competition the risks are high. A lost game or contest can mean loss of status and public humiliation. At its most extreme group display can mean battle and war. In lower animals war is rare and

AGGRESS TO IMPRESS

Griskevicius et al (2009) had 178 college students read a scenario designed to activate a competitive, courtship or neutral motivational state. The students in the competitive condition were asked to imagine themselves in a situation where they were in competition against two other people of the same sex for a top job. The job was a high level promotion offering a bonus and a posh office. They were asked to try to imagine themselves in the scenario, feeling the emotions of the person. In the courtship condition students were asked to imagine how they would feel in a situation where they had just been on the perfect first date and were keen to see the person on future occasions. A questionnaire was used to examine whether the participants had fully identified with the expected feelings generated by the scenario. Each group of students were then asked to state how they would respond if they were publicly insulted. The insult designed to provoke an aggressive response was a scenario where a person of the same sex spills a drink on them in a bar and does not apologise. A questionnaire

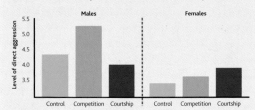

Competition and courtship results when responding to an insult with direct aggression. (Adapted from Griskevicius et al, 2009.)

was used to assess the feelings and responses to the insult. The researchers wanted to find out whether aggressive tendencies would be influenced by the competition or courtship motives. They found that men were more inclined to aggress when motivated by competition and status and were more likely to use direct aggression. Men were less inclined to behave aggressively when motivated by courtship, showing that mating motives did not boost the level of direct aggression in men. In both motivational states women were more indirectly aggressive.

only occurs in social species such as dolphins, chimpanzees and humans. War in this context refers to the formation of coalitions to attack others within the same species. Group display does not have to mean physical display. Verbal aggression can be used in discussion to outwit an opponent and win a contest. There can be just as much at stake for a political party contesting an election.

GROUP DISPLAY AND WAR

Only the most intelligent species opt for this extreme course of action, which is highly likely to end up in injury or death. This seems contradictory to survival of the species: therefore from an evolutionary perspective it must be assumed that the benefits of forming coalitions for aggressive ends outweigh the costs. Aggressive group display is likely to cost individuals their lives but there is a greater chance of survival afforded by acting as part of a group, compared with acting alone. Groups are more powerful and offer greater protection to individuals. Men are only willing to fight as part of a coalition if they are confident of victory and the odds of their being killed are relatively low. They also need to see that much can be gained from entering into conflict. Warfare exists among many modern-day tribal societies and some, such as the Maori of New Zealand and the Yanomamo of the Amazon Rainforest, place particular emphasis on warrior culture. Fighting often occurs within the tribe but between local villages.

When this happens the only possible advantage a village can have is manpower, as their access to weaponry and level of skill is equal. For this reason the Yanomamo are obsessed with the size of their villages and are constantly forming alliances and reorganising as they know that small villages are easy targets (Chagnon, 1968).

Yanomamo male

One of the most frequent causes of conflict amongst branches of the Yanomamo people is the abduction of women. According to local missionary reports cited by Chagnon (1968) there was constant fighting between branches of the Yanomamo for access to women or to improve the status of one tribe over another. Success in battle can give a warrior status and thus increase his attractiveness to females and improve his chances of reproducing offspring to continue his genetic line. Amongst the Yanomamo, successful warriors had more wives and children than those who were less successful in battle. Most young men who had killed were married; most young men who had never killed were not (Chagnon, 1968). According to Pinker (1997) even in modern-day war men fight to secure access to women. In more recent wars such as World War II, the Germans invading Eastern Europe carried out systematic acts of rape and women in concentration camps were often abused. More than 20,000 Muslim girls and women were raped during the religiously-motivated atrocities in Bosnia, the former Yugoslavia. This took place as part of an organised Serbian programme of cultural genocide. One aim was to make the women pregnant, and raise their children as Serbs. The fact that the children carried half Muslim blood was not seen as a problem due to what the Serbs saw as the overpowering supremacy of the Serbian blood within the children. A second aim was to terrorise the women so that they would flee from their land (Allen, 1996).

From this example we can see how evolutionary theory offers an explanation for this behaviour that allows one group status over another, giving them access to land and resources and their women. It also follows that those men who are more aggressive and stronger will win wars and survive to pass on their genes. This could then lead to the emergence of an increasingly aggressive species who have evolved due to the essential benefits of war (Lehmann and Feldman, 2008). According to Lehmann and Feldmann two traits have evolved in humans that determine the likelihood that conflict will occur. The traits are 'belligerence', which is the trait that raises the probability of one tribe attacking another; and 'bravery', which is the trait that increases the likelihood that a tribe will win a war, whether as attackers or the attacked. Bravery is therefore the most highly prized trait as it has advantages when tribes are on both the offensive and the defensive. Tribes with males high in both qualities are most likely to go to war and win, thus passing on their warrior traits. War is a risky activity and those high in belligerence and bravery stand a higher chance of dying. These traits may therefore benefit the group more than the individual, as warrior genes can be passed on indirectly through kin. In evaluation of this explanation of war it is difficult to provide evidence for the existence of genetic traits for belligerence and bravery. Warrior behaviour could just as easily be passed on culturally rather than inherited.

The evolutionary theory considered so far offers an explanation for tribal warfare involving mainly raid tactics. Raids on neighbouring villages are unlikely to result in too many casualties and the rewards are great. This kind of aggressive group display therefore has an adaptive value. In recent human history aggressive conflict between groups has often consisted of escalating and prolonged warfare. This usually results in significant losses on both sides. Military incompetence – i.e. losing when you expect to win – is a common feature in battles (Wrangham, 1999). Wrangham argues that military incompetence is a result of adaptive self-deception. Humans have adopted the strategy of deceiving themselves into thinking they can win in conflict. In individual contests when opponents are closely matched they may be fighting a mental rather than a physical battle. For example if players in a tennis match are judged to be of equal skill the eventual victor may be the player who has more self-belief and the greater will to win. This also applies to war. Positive illusions about winning will make the group more successful by improving cohesion and cooperation. Self-deception also leads to opponent deception as it prevents a group signalling weakness to the opposition. Therefore the opposition are bluffed into thinking that their opponents are better than they actually are. In terms of survival of the species, it would appear that self-deception has positive benefits for groups because it makes them more effective. However, it may also lead to inaccurate assessment of your own and your opponent's ability. Therefore conflicts may occur more often and be more severe than if sides in a potential war were realistic about the possible outcome and avoided the loss of life and resources. In this sense, positive self-deception appears disadvantageous to human survival as a whole. Strategies of positive illusion are only adaptive to humans if they succeed often enough for the benefits to outweigh the costs.

Veteran soldiers displaying medals – symbols of their bravery.

Evolutionary theory also explains why some individuals choose not to fight. Humans have evolved to recognise that group conflict should be avoided if the costs outweigh the possible advantages. A third of Yanomamo males die during battle, leading some men to reflect on the futility of the feuds and make it publicly known that they will have nothing to do with inter-tribe conflict (Chagnon, 1968). In some instances when the risks are high, passive behaviour may be more advantageous to survival than aggressive behaviour. Women are also rarely involved in war. There is no reason why women should form alliances to raid neighbouring villages to gain access to men because female reproductive success is not affected by the number of available males (Pinker, 1997). To involve themselves in such risky behaviour would be disadvantageous to the survival of women.

GROUP DISPLAY AND SPORTS EVENTS

It has been claimed that, in modern society, tribal warfare has been replaced by sporting events in which different teams represent their 'tribes' – e.g. countries, towns or schools. Rarely are there any fatalities amongst either players or supporters. In this ritualised form of aggression therefore all the benefits of success are still available to competitors but with reduced risk of physical harm or death.

In the game of rugby union the New Zealand All Blacks begin their matches with a unique form of group display known as the Haka. Performance of the Haka involves moves and chants designed to intimidate the opposing team. It originates from the Maori people of New Zealand and was originally performed by warriors before going into battle.

Group display behaviour such as the Haka serves to indicate the importance placed on winning a team event. Ultimately in modern society the winning team will be seen as holding high status, making the individual members of the team desirable mates. In a game such as rugby union a certain level of aggression is sanctioned (i.e. allowed according to the rules). Moves such as tackling or being part of a scrum require a great deal of strength and athleticism. These allow for displays of behaviour attractive to females as they are related to hunting skills and the ability to provide. Team games show these skills off to their best advantage and, like hunters before them, the men are most successful working cooperatively. Some players, however, may resort to unsanctioned aggression – i.e. acts that fall outside of the rules. A study conducted in Hong Kong aimed

to assess why some players use unsanctioned acts of aggression deliberately designed to cause harm to opponents (Maxwell and Viscek, 2009). One hundred and forty four rugby union players were questioned about their use of aggression in the game. The researchers also took account of a number of other factors including professionalism. Players high in professionalism placed more emphasis on winning the game than on playing fair and displaying skill. The players most likely to use unsanctioned aggression were those who scored high on professionalism. These players even learned how to execute illegal moves designed to take out opponents without being detected. This behaviour could be interpreted in evolutionary terms. Evolutionary theory supports the concept of cheating as adaptive. Teams who learn to deploy illegal moves without getting caught will ultimately win and achieve the status and rewards that victory brings. The methodology used by Maxwell and Viscek can be criticised as the use of self-report technique may be subjective and not entirely reliable. Objective measures of aggression are needed or less subjective reports from linesmen, referees and coaches.

Victory in matches brings status not only to the players but also to their fans. Cialdini et al (1976) termed this 'basking in reflected glory'. They found that after a university football team had done well the students showed a greater tendency to wear clothes that identified them as belonging to that particular university. According to Cialdini et al the students were displaying their connection with the winning team to enhance their image in the eyes of observers. Interestingly although the supporting students were not directly involved in causing the team to win they acted as if their presence did have a direct effect on the outcome of the match. This was apparent in the supporters' tendency to use the pronoun 'we' to describe successful outcomes, e.g. "We're number one!" By using the word 'we' the students are able to

THE HAKA

This traditional Maori dance is a ritual that was originally designed to invoke the god of war. It involves actions which are designed to show strength and prowess. These include contorting the face, sticking out the tongue and showing the whites of the eyes, as well as foot stamping and slapping of hands against the thighs, arms and chest. As the dance is performed the men also chant words and emit a series of cries and grunts. The Haka must be performed in complete unison to be most effective: if anybody is out of step this is considered bad luck. Since 2005 the New Zealand All Blacks rugby team have sometimes performed a new version of the Haka called the 'Kapa o Pango', though the version most commonly performed is the Ka Mate.

The Ka Mate Haka opens with a set of five preparatory instructions shouted by the leader, before the whole team joins in:

Leader:	Ringa pakia	Slap the hands against the thighs
	Uma tiraha	Puff out the chest
	Turi whatia	Bend the knees
	Hope whai ake	Let the hip follow
	Waewae takahia kia kino	Stamp the feet as hard as you can
	Ka mate, ka mate	I die, I die
Team:	Ka ora' Ka ora'	I live, I live
Leader:	Ka mate, ka mate	I die, I die
Team:	Ka ora' Ka ora'	I live, I live
All:	Tēnei te tangata pūhuruhuru	This is the hairy man
	Nāna i tiki mai whakawhiti te rā	Who caused the sun to shine again for me
	Upane... Upane	Up the ladder, Up the ladder
	Upane Kaupane"	Up to the top
	Whiti te ra!	The sun shines
	He!	He!

associate themselves with the successful group. If the team was unsuccessful, supporters were more likely to distance themselves from the failure, using phrases such as "They lost" and thus disassociating themselves from a group with lowered status.

Football in Europe has generated extensive research into associated 'hooliganism'. Marsh (1978) suggests that football hooliganism is the human equivalent of ceremonial conflict that occurs within an animal species. Comparisons can be drawn between animals and humans in that the group displays of hooliganism are exclusively male and involve trials of strength over territory but are also restrained by the desire to minimise physical harm and death. Football hooligans are usually young males expressing their physical prowess who travel to away matches to invade the opposition's territory. Group cohesion and loyalty are all important for the group to be seen as powerful. According to Marsh, humans develop social systems and rules that rely on culture to transmit them from one generation to the next. Human displays are different from those of animals as they do not rely on instinct to read another's non-verbal behaviour and adopt an appropriate response. The aggressive behaviour displayed by football hooligans is described by Marsh as a form of ritualised aggression which is actually very orderly and rarely seriously violent. Most groups conform to the norm of 'Defend if attacked but do not start a fight'. Symbolic aggression usually involves the display of power and weapons but not actual physical contact or use of weapons. Interviews conducted with football hooligans suggest that the fans' intention is to humiliate the opposition and secure submission but not cause actual harm. Evolutionary theory can explain this form of ritualised group display as a way of securing power and status and therefore access to resources without threatening the survival of group members, and thus preserving the species.

Eating behaviour

ROB IRWIN

You are expected in the examination to show both the skills of knowledge and understanding and the skills of analysis and evaluation in relation to the topic Eating behaviour.

Where opportunities for their effective use arise, you will need to demonstrate an appreciation of issues and debates. These include the nature/nurture debate, ethical issues in research, free-will/determinism, reductionism, gender and culture bias, and the use of animals in research.

You will also need to demonstrate an understanding of How Science Works. You can do this through the effective use of studies in your answer (as description or evaluation) or where appropriate by evaluating methodology and findings.

WHAT YOU NEED TO KNOW

EATING BEHAVIOUR

● Factors influencing attitudes to food and eating behaviour, e.g. cultural influences, health concerns, mood and stress
● Explanations for the success or failure of dieting

BIOLOGICAL EXPLANATIONS OF EATING BEHAVIOUR

● The role of neural mechanisms involved in controlling eating and satiation
● Evolutionary explanations of food preference

EATING DISORDERS

● Psychological explanations of one eating disorder: e.g. anorexia nervosa and obesity
● Biological explanations, including neural and evolutionary explanations, for one eating disorder: e.g. anorexia nervosa and obesity

Eating is a necessity and, for many people, a source of immense pleasure. Indeed, the only activities of daily life rated more highly than 'a fine meal' in one study are spending time with the family, holidays, and sex (Westenhoefer and Pudel, 1993). Many magazines on food and cooking exist, and many more have sections on recipes, healthy eating and restaurant reviews. Some of the most popular programmes on television revolve around some aspect of food, cooking and eating. Clearly, eating is a behaviour that most of us take very seriously indeed.

EATING BEHAVIOUR

A number of physiological processes influence food choice, and nutritional research has examined how the properties of food influence long-term patterns of consumption. The brain monitors the body's nutritional status and drives and directs eating behaviours. However, the effects of these physiological processes are mediated by psychological and social processes.

From a developmental perspective, food preferences emerge as a consequence of innate predispositions for certain taste preferences and learning during early childhood. Newborns demonstrate unlearned, reflexive reactions to basic tastes: sweet and salty tastes are generally preferred, whereas bitter and sour tastes tend to be rejected. Although a varied and balanced diet is necessary for growth and health, young children tend to show fear and avoidance of novel foods (sometimes referred to as neophobia). This neophobic response is reduced by repeated opportunities to consume new foods (a process referred to as exposure) and generally decreases with age. Food preferences also develop through associative learning: that is learning based on the pairing of certain foods with particular experiences and contexts such as is seen in classical conditioning (Birch, 1999). For instance, if you experience profuse projectile vomiting immediately after eating a certain type of food, it's likely that you'll avoid this food in the future!

However, the findings of large-scale surveys indicate that many different motivations influence food choice, including convenience (of purchasing and preparation); sensory appeal; costs to health; weight control; mood regulation; and ethical concerns related to the production of food (Steptoe et al, 1995). This suggests that attitudes and related cognitions are key psychological variables in determining food choice and eating behaviour.

FACTORS AFFECTING ATTITUDES TO FOOD AND EATING BEHAVIOUR

ASK AN EXAMINER

"You are expected to know about several factors (i.e. more than one), that influence our attitudes to food. Here we cover attitudes, culture, health concerns and mood. Make sure you have a good understanding of more than one of them!"

ATTITUDES TO FOOD

Expectancy value theory is a model of human decision making which proposes that we are motivated to maximise chances of desirable outcomes whilst minimising the chances of undesirable ones. If this is true, then when we are given a choice between two foods, we should choose the one with the most desirable attributes or outcome (Conner and Armitage, 2002). The evaluation of any object (sometimes referred to as the 'attitude object') comprises two factors: the perceived likelihood of that object having certain attributes or leading to certain outcomes, and the value (positive or negative) attached to each of these attributes/outcomes.

So, if asked to choose between two cakes, you may consider the following before making your choice: the ingredients of each cake; whether the cake is shop-bought or home-made; and if the cake is high or low in calories. Each of these attributes would attract a particular evaluation (for example, the presence of chocolate in a cake may be seen as good; the fact that the cake was shop-bought may be viewed as bad, etc.). These evaluations of likely attributes can then be added up to form an overall evaluation (or attitude) to each of the cakes. The cake with the greatest number of positively-valued attributes is, according to expectancy value theory, the one you would most likely choose to eat!

Attitude objects may also be eating behaviours, such as eating five items of fruit and vegetables a day. There are a number of likely attributes/ outcomes associated with such behaviour. An individual may consider the likelihood that eating five pieces of fruit and vegetables a day extends the preparation time required for meals, causes inconvenience as it entails more frequent visits to the shops, reduces the likelihood of health-related problems, costs more, helps to control weight, and so on. Again, to each of these attributes is attached either a positive or negative evaluation. The sum of these beliefs about eating five pieces of fruit and vegetables a day will constitute an individual's global evaluation or attitude to this eating behaviour. There are, of course, a number of possible attributes and outcomes associated with particular foods or eating behaviours, but it is the beliefs that have the greatest relevance at the time that are thought to be the most important determinants of behaviour.

Although research has demonstrated the usefulness of expectancy value theory for predicting attitudes related to food choice (Towler and Shepherd, 1992; Armitage and Conner, 1999), one problem with this model is that it assumes the appraisals we make of food are exclusively positive or negative. However, as Ogden (2003) notes, sometimes we simultaneously attach both negative and positive values to a particular food. This ambivalence can be seen in our evaluations of food choices as 'naughty but nice' or tasty but fattening. Research by Sparks et al (2001) suggests that attitudes are less likely to be translated into an intention to eat a particular food if an individual holds both positive and negative appraisals of that food.

CULTURAL INFLUENCES

Food choice "takes place within a network of social meanings" (Ogden, 2003). That is to say,

FOOD AND RELIGION

Our relationship with food can be strongly influenced by religion.

Religion	Influences on eating behaviour
Judaism	● Food must be prepared in the right way, for it to be 'Kosher' – for example, animals must be slaughtered in a manner the religion demands. ● Certain foods, such as dairy and fish, are carefully controlled; and eating or preparing meat and dairy together is forbidden. ● There are fasting days (such as Yom Kippur) and ritual feasting days (such as Passover). ● Some foods symbolise aspects of the religion's beliefs. For instance, eating bitter herbs during Passover symbolises the suffering of the Israelites during their enslavement by the Egyptians.
Christianity	● Food, particularly bread and wine, is symbolic during certain rituals. Bread, for instance, is believed, by some, to transform into the body of Christ during communion. ● Mormons do not take caffeine or alcohol. ● Easter and Christmas are set aside as feasting days. ● Seventh Day Adventists do not eat meat or dairy. ● Roman Catholics are taught to fast for one hour before taking communion.
Islam	● Food regulations are called 'Halal' and forbidden foods are called 'Haram'. These forbidden foods include pork, alcohol, bread and bread products that include dried yeasts. Those who eat Haram foods are said to be ignored by the creator. ● Certain religious days, such as Eid al-Fatir are set aside for fasting. ● During the month of Ramadan, Islam prescribes fasting during daylight hours. ● Caffeine is occasionally considered as Haram and products containing gelatine (a product made from pork) must not be eaten. These include many sweets and some yoghurts.

eating behaviour cannot be reduced merely to the biopsychology of the individual. Choice of foods and eating behaviours are an act of social communication, providing information about an individual's identity, particularly their cultural identity. Perhaps the most obvious example of this occurs in relation to religion. Most religions forbid the eating of certain foods, or require that certain items of food are prepared in particular ways. Fasting – abstention from all or certain kinds of food or drink – is a common form of religious observance.

The consumption of food plays a central role in social interaction: group identity is in part created and maintained through food. Types of food are often described as 'the traditional family meal' or 'the national dish' (Ogden, 2003). Cultural influences determine to a significant extent what foods are deemed palatable and how such foods are prepared and consumed. Food can be used for several purposes: to affirm or develop personal relationships – as indicated in the commonly used term 'a romantic meal for two'; to demonstrate personal wealth (e.g. eating in expensive restaurants); and – through controlling access to food – to influence others.

For children in particular, mealtimes provide important opportunities for social learning regarding food preferences and eating behaviour (Bandura, 1997). Parental eating behaviours, attitudes and child-feeding practices (which are in large part culturally determined) strongly influence children's food acceptance patterns.

Through the process of modelling, both adults and peers exercise considerable influence in inducing children to eat unfamiliar or initially disliked foods (Birch, 1999).

Eating or not eating certain types of food is one (but certainly not the only) way in which people seek to change their body size or shape so that it better accords with cultural ideals. Evidence for the influence of culture on body dissatisfaction comes from a number of sources. In Western societies (where, since the Second World War, food shortages have been relatively uncommon), thinness in women has been increasingly portrayed as the ideal and studies indicate that over the second half of the 20th century women became increasingly dissatisfied with their body image (Feingold and Mazzella, 1998). Furthermore, comparative studies reveal that discrepancies between actual and ideal body weight and size are less pronounced in cultures where less emphasis is placed on thinness (Toriola et al, 1996). Advertising has been implicated in the promotion of thinness as a cultural ideal for women, and there is some evidence that men's satisfaction with their bodies is increasingly influenced by media-generated messages. For instance, Lorenzen et al (2004) report that brief exposure to advertisements showing muscular males decreases body satisfaction for men, but this does not occur when such advertisements feature men of average build. Men living in countries where there is less exposure to explicit Western messages about muscular body image report fewer body image concerns than their Western counterparts (Akiba, 1998; Yang et al, 2005).

THE WEIGHTING GAME

From left: national average; size 16, men's ideal; size 12, women's ideal; size 8

In 2008 *Fabulous* magazine conducted its UK Body Survey. When asked about the 'ideal' female body size, most women answered size 8, whilst men answered size 12. The national average is size 16, although only 20% of male respondents knew this. Sizes 12 and 14 accounted for 64% of male guesses. To the question "How often do you worry about your appearance?" only 18% of women claimed never to do so. Six percent of women claimed never to look at themselves in the mirror, and 56% said they would consider plastic surgery.

HEALTH CONCERNS

Food choices and eating behaviour are linked to health in many ways. First, what and how much we eat may make us more or less likely to develop certain diseases. Second, restricted consumption of particular foods may form an important part of the long-term management of some chronic diseases, such as diabetes or coronary heart disease. Third, food may make us feel unwell: some people experience allergic reactions

LOW SELF-ESTEEM, IMPULSE BUYING AND UNHEALTHY EATING

Verplanken et al (2005) conducted a survey using an opportunity sample of 214 adults who were travellers at an airport in Norway. Participants' self-esteem, dispositional mood, impulse buying tendency, snacking habits, and 'eating disturbance propensity' were measured.

The findings of this survey indicated that low self-esteem and the dispositional negative affect (i.e. negative feelings) associated with it, were strongly related to impulse buying tendency. Although low self-esteem and dispositional negative affect were not directly related to snacking habits, a strong snacking habit was associated with more serious eating disturbances, and these in turn were associated with low self-esteem. The pattern that emerges from these findings is one in which impulse buying coincides with unhealthy eating behaviours through their association with low self-esteem and dispositional negative affect.

The authors of this study speculate that impulse buying and the consumption of snack foods may be attempts to cope with the emotional distress associated with low self-esteem. However, as this was a correlational study, it is not possible to draw any conclusions about cause and effect relationships between the variables it investigated.

(occasionally life threatening) to certain foods, or complain of intolerances to certain types of food or ingredients. Deficiencies in certain nutrients may impair the function of the immune system, making us more susceptible to infections. Many of us will experience the unpleasant consequences of food poisoning at some time. Finally, healthy eating is associated with the prevention of chronic diseases and the promotion of general health and well-being.

A healthy diet would normally comprise five or more servings of fruit and/or vegetables a day; plenty of complex (preferably high fibre) carbo-hydrate foods (e.g. bread, pasta, potatoes); and moderate amounts of meat, fish, milk and dairy products. It is recommended that fatty and sugary foods are consumed infrequently and in small amounts. However, research into the diets of children, and of young and older adults, indicates that in general people do not eat a healthy diet (Ogden, 2007). Some findings do indicate that concern for appearance may cause people to make healthy dietary choices (Hayes and Ross, 1987). The importance of health as a motive for food choice appears to increase with age in women but not in men (Steptoe et al, 1995). It has been suggested that for some people unhealthy eating habits are

HELPING CHILDREN TO EAT MORE FRUIT AND VEG

In this study, Gratton et al (2007) randomly allocated 198 children from a secondary school in England to either a control group or one of two intervention groups. All participants were asked to keep a food diary for seven days and were then asked to fill in a questionnaire. At the beginning of the second week, participants in the first intervention group were asked to form an implementation intention by writing down how, when and where they would eat five portions of fruit and vegetables over the next week. Participants in the second intervention group were asked to complete a health education activity sheet, which asked questions about their beliefs concerning eating five portions of fruit and vegetables a day. Participants in the control group were asked to form an implementation intention, by writing down when and where they would do their homework for that week. At the end of the second week, participants in all three groups were asked to keep a food diary for another seven days and to complete a follow-up questionnaire.

In this study, the first intervention (forming the implementation intention) was a *volitional* intervention, whereas the second intervention (completing the health education activity) was a *motivational* intervention. Both types of intervention led to an increase in fruit and vegetable consumption.

Although this is an important finding, there are a number of limitations with this study. Perhaps the most important is the fact that data collection (which was based on self-reports after the interventions took place) lasted for only one week. Although the children's consumption of fruit and vegetables may have changed in the week following the interventions, this does not mean that any changes observed were maintained in the long-term.

associated with low self-esteem and the distress this creates (see Verplanken et al, 2005).

Helping individuals to eat more healthily is of particular interest to health psychologists. Increasing fruit and vegetable consumption is the second most important cancer prevention strategy identified by the UK's Department of Health (2000) – the first, by the way, is stopping smoking. But people seem reluctant to eat fruit and vegetables on a regular basis. It has been suggested that the relatively low energy density of these foods puts them at a disadvantage, given that we seem predisposed to choose high-energy foods (Steptoe and Wardle, 2004). However, a number of studies undertaken by psychologists suggest that getting people to specify their 'implementation intentions' – that is, asking them to state how, when, where they could eat more fruit and vegetables – may lead to a healthier diet (Armitage, 2007).

MOOD AND STRESS

Studies seeking to investigate the effect of mood and distress on eating often look for evidence of either hypophagia (i.e. excessive under-eating) or hyperphagia (i.e. excessive overeating), as well as changes in patterns of consumption and food preferences.

A sustained decrease or increase in appetite can be an important symptom of depression and other mood disorders (Davey, 2008). Ogden (2007) notes that dieters who overeat in response to low mood may be seeking to mask their negative mood (sometimes referred to as dysphoria) with a temporary heightened mood induced by eating – a phenomenon she refers to as the masking hypothesis. Certainly, studies indicate that dieters eat more than non-dieters when anxious regardless of how palatable the food is (Polivy et al, 1994).

There is also some evidence to suggest that certain people experience an irresistible desire to consume sweet or starchy foods in response to a low mood state. This has been labelled carbohydrate-craving syndrome. It has been suggested the eating of carbohydrates specifically appears to trigger an improvement in mood. One explanation for this is that carbohydrates are an important source of the amino acid tryptophan, an essential building-block for serotonin. Serotonin is a neurotransmitter associated with mood enhancement. It has been suggested that people who crave carbohydrates prefer to eat foods rich in carbohydrates as a means of 'self-medicating' their low mood. Support for the existence of a carbohydrate craving syndrome comes from a recent experimental trial by Corsica and Spring (2008).

Stress is commonly thought to occur when the perceived demands made of an individual exceed, or threaten to exceed, the perceived resources available to that individual to cope with such demands (Lazarus and Folkman, 1984). In the transactional model of stress developed by Richard Lazarus and colleagues, cognitive appraisal is considered the first step in the stress response. This means that responses to 'stressors' will be idiosyncratic, dependent on the primary appraisal made by an individual (whether a situation or event is benign, neutral or a threat) and their secondary

DO CARBOHYDRATES HELP TO IMPROVE LOW MOOD?

Corsica and Spring (2008) sought to test whether a preference for carbohydrates and mood enhancement were linked, by carrying out a double-blind, placebo-controlled trial.

The participants in this trial were 21 overweight women (as determined by their Body Mass Index) who described themselves as carbohydrate cravers. On six separate days over a period of two weeks, participants attended the researchers' laboratory in the afternoon after consuming a standardised meal. Baseline measures were then taken of mood and hunger. A feeling of dysphoria was induced by asking participants to recall autobiographical sad memories and to listen to sad music. Participants' mood was again assessed to ensure that a dysphoric mood had been achieved. On one day of the week participants were served a carbohydrate drink; on another they received a protein-rich drink; and on the third day (the 'test' day) they were asked to choose the drink that had made them feel better in the earlier exposure. Ratings of mood, hunger and craving were assessed at baseline, immediately post-mood induction and between 45 minutes and 180 minutes after the ingestion of each drink. The drinks used were taste-matched and calorie-matched, and neither the participants nor the research assistants knew the content of drinks on any of the days (hence the description of the trial as 'double-blind').

As predicted, the results of this trial indicated that the carbohydrate drink had a significantly greater 'antidepressant' effect and, when given a choice of drinks, participants chose the carbohydrate drink over the protein-rich drink. These findings are consistent with the theory that people who crave carbohydrates 'self-medicate' low mood by eating foods that are high in carbohydrates.

STRESS AND EATING – A COMPLEX RELATIONSHIP

Oliver et al (2000) designed an experiment to investigate whether acute stress changes food choice during a meal. The eating attitudes and food preferences of sixty-eight healthy men and women were measured before participants were allocated to either a stress or control condition. In the stress condition, participants were asked to prepare a 4-minute speech on a controversial topic, which, they were informed, would be filmed and assessed after a midday meal. By contrast, the control group listened to a piece of neutral text before eating the meal.

A combination of physiological measures (such as raised blood pressure) and self-reported measures were used to confirm the effectiveness of the stressor. The measures used to assess the effects of stress were: (1) appetite for range of foods, assessed immediately before eating the meal; and (2) food intake during the meal. For their buffet lunch, participants could select from sweet, salty or bland high- or low-fat foods.

Although stress did not alter overall intake of food or measures of appetite, stressed emotional eaters in this study consumed more sweet, high-fat foods and ate a more 'energy-dense' meal than unstressed and non-emotional eaters. Women also scored more highly on emotional eating than men.

Oliver et al suggest that the increased consumption of sweet fatty foods by emotional eaters during stress may indicate how stress can harm the health of susceptible individuals (i.e. emotional eaters) through changes in food choice.

appraisal of the resources available to deal with that particular event or situation. Thus stress, like beauty, is in the eye of the beholder.

Conner and Armitage (2002) observe that two general hypotheses have been investigated in relation to stress and eating behaviour. The first – the general effect hypothesis – proposes that stress changes the consumption patterns of food in general; the second – the individual difference hypothesis – emphasises that stress leads to changes in eating behaviour only in certain groups.

The general effect hypothesis suggests that stress produces physiological changes that explain changes in eating behaviour. Studies to examine this hypothesis have usually entailed exposing animals, particularly rats, to physical stressors (such as 'tail-pinching' and electric shocks) and observing changes in eating behaviours. In general such research has produced results that provide some support for this hypothesis, although not consistently so (Conner and Armitage, 2002). Isolation, a chronic stressor, does appear to increase both consumption of food and weight in rats, but studies with human participants have produced mixed results (Greeno and Wing, 1994).

By contrast, the individual difference hypothesis suggests that differences in biology, attitudes to eating, and learning history, produce variations in vulnerability to the effects of stress. Those with a high vulnerability respond to stress by effecting an environmental or psychological change that encourages eating, whereas those individuals with a low vulnerability make psychological or

STRESS AND SNACKING: A DIARY STUDY OF DAILY HASSLES AND BETWEEN-MEAL SNACKING

Conner et al (1999) asked a sample of 33 female and 27 male students to keep a daily record of the number and severity of daily hassles and the number of snacks consumed over a period of 7 days. Hassles were defined as problems or difficulties associated with everyday life. Participants were also asked to complete a questionnaire that assessed three dimensions of eating behaviour: restrained eating, emotional eating and external eating. Analysis of the diaries kept by participants revealed that the number of hassles reported by participants was correlated with the number of snacks consumed. However, this relationship was moderated by an individual difference variable: external eating. For participants who scored highly on measures of external eating, there was a statistically significant positive relationship between hassles and snacking. By contrast, no significant relationship between these two variables was found for participants who were rated low on external eating. In addition, no significant results were found for other possible moderators of the hassles-snacking relationship such as emotional eating and restrained eating. The findings of this study therefore support externality theory.

This study differed from much previous research in this area in that it focused on the effects of everyday stressors (as perceived by participants) on eating behaviour in real-life situations over a prolonged period of time. While this design increases the ecological validity of the study, its major limitation is that the data obtained were self-reported and therefore susceptible to social desirability effects.

ALEXITHYMIA, DISTRESS AND OVEREATING

A better understanding of some of the possible mechanisms underlying emotional eating is provided by van Strien and Ouwens (2007). In this study 86 female participants recruited at a Dutch university were randomly allocated to either an experimental condition or a control condition. Participants were asked to complete measures of impulse regulation, alexithymia, hunger, and mood state. In the experimental condition participants were led to believe they would have to deliver a five minute talk to three observers on a topic that would be revealed after they had completed a taste test. The amount eaten by participants in both the experimental and control conditions – the dependent variable – was assessed using a bowl of savoury crackers that was weighed before and after the taste test.

The findings indicate that there was no significant difference between the amount of food consumed by participants in the experimental and control conditions. Although the researchers predicted that the relationship between food consumption and distress would be moderated by both alexithymia and impulsivity, the results indicate that this relationship was moderated only by alexithymia (i.e. lower levels of alexithymia were associated with eating less food and higher levels with eating more food). Females with higher levels of alexithymia ate more in the experimental 'distress' condition than those in the control condition. This suggests that distress may lead to overeating in individuals who find it difficult to identify and describe to others what they are feeling.

environment changes that do not encourage eating (Conner and Armitage, 2002). A number of high vulnerability/low vulnerability groupings have been suggested, including:

» External and internal eaters

» Restrained and non-restrained eaters

» Emotional and non-emotional eaters.

According to externality theory (Schachter et al, 1968), people who are external eaters eat in response to food related stimuli, irrespective of whether they feel hungry or full. By contrast, internal eaters respond more to internal cues to hunger when deciding when and what to eat. It is assumed that when we are stressed, our internal cues to hunger are reduced and our attention to external cues is heightened. If this assumption is correct, increased levels of stress should reduce eating in internal eaters, but increase eating in external eaters. Research by Conner et al (1999) provides some support for this theory.

People who use self-control processes to try to suppress their intake of food are referred to by some psychologists as *restrained eaters*. According to restraint theory, if these self-control processes are undermined by stressful events, disinhibition of eating is more likely to occur, leading to an excessive intake of food (see the discussion of the 'boundary model' later in this chapter). Certainly, the findings of a number of studies appear to support the hypothesis that stress produce's a greater increase in eating in restrained eaters, compared to non-restrained eaters (Herman et al, 2005). However, as Conner and Armitage (2002) note,

these findings are almost exclusively in relation to young women.

Emotional eaters tend to increase their intake of food when they are anxious or emotionally aroused. By contrast, non-emotional eaters do not show such a response to emotion. The way in which stress is thought to lead to increased food consumption in emotional eaters is through a failure to distinguish between anxiety and hunger (Conner and Armitage, 2002). There is only a limited number of studies investigating the impact of emotional eating on the relationship between stress and overeating: the findings of a few studies offer some support for this hypothesis (e.g. Oliver et al, 2000), whereas the findings of others do not (e.g. Conner et al, 1999). A recent study by van Strien and Ouwens (2007) suggests that alexithymia, (that is, difficulty identifying and describing feelings), may be an important moderating factor in the link between distress and overeating.

EXPLANATIONS FOR THE SUCCESS OR FAILURE OF DIETING

"There's a plural here – explanations. Here you will find several reasons why dieting might succeed or fail. It is best to have an understanding of more than one explanation - just to prepare for an exam question which might require two or more."

The findings of twin and adoption studies suggest that body weight is strongly influenced by genetic factors, with some studies estimating that heredity accounts for anywhere between 40% - 70% of weight (Stroebe, 2000). How this genetic predisposition is expressed isn't entirely clear, although genes may influence factors such as appetite regulation, metabolic rate, and the number of fat cells that a person has. The potential of behavioural interventions like dieting to bring about weight loss has to be viewed in this context. Furthermore, research looking at the health and illness of populations (sometimes referred to as epidemiological studies) indicates that the prevalence of obesity has increased at a similar rate to decreases in physical activity (Ogden, 2007). The clear message from this is that being overweight is not simply a product of overeating.

People who are overweight are not only at greater risk of a wide spectrum of diseases including ischaemic heart disease, type 2 diabetes and some cancers, but also have to contend with considerable prejudice and discrimination in modern-day Western societies (Ashmore et al, 2008).

While health concerns may be important they may not necessarily be the primary motivation for dieting. By contrast, *body dissatisfaction* is consistently related to dieting and attempting to eat less (Ogden, 2007). Although some environmental pressures such as increases in portion sizes of meals promote overeating in virtually everyone, there is evidence that certain factors only promote overeating in people who diet. Herman and colleagues (2005) identify three such factors.

The first factor is *distress*, which triggers overeating in restrained eaters, but has no, or the opposite, effect in people who are not concerned about their eating. A study by Herman and Polivy (1975) examined the eating behaviour of restrained and unrestrained eaters when participants were led to believe that they would receive an electric shock. Restrained eaters ate more, whereas their unrestrained counterparts ate less. This general pattern of results has been repeatedly found in studies investigating the effects of distress on eating behaviour. What is more, Herman et al, (2005), observe that overeating in dieters is more pronounced when distress is 'personal' rather than 'physical': that is, overeating is more likely to occur in response to low mood or negative affect than in response to physical threats (such as an electric shock).

A second factor that seems to promote overeating disproportionately among dieters is *craving*. Although cravings are highly subjective states, and their potential to induce overeating is not restricted to restrained eaters, dieters seem particularly prone to experiencing them. The reason for this remains uncertain: it is difficult to determine whether cravings induce restrained eating in those who experience them, or whether they are the consequence of being deprived of certain food choices when dieting. As Herman et al (2005) note, cravings appear to be accentuated by both internal factors (such as deprivation) and external factors (such as exposure to food cues).

Pre-loading is the final factor discussed by Herman et al (2005). This refers to a portion of food that participants in experiments are asked to eat (referred to in the research literature as the 'pre-load') before, for instance, they are given free access to other foods. In theory, pre-loading should suppress appetite and in non-dieters it does indeed reduce the subsequent intake of food. However, in dieters, pre-loading appears to reverse this normal regulatory process. Why then does pre-loading, like distress, seemingly disinhibit eating in dieters? One suggestion is that once a large or perceived high-calorie 'pre-load' has been consumed, restrained eaters take the view that

THE HARMFUL EFFECTS OF WEIGHT-BASED STIGMATISATION

Data from a number of studies have indicated the harmful effects of weight-based stigmatisation. Ashmore et al (2008) studied the impact of weight-based stigmatisation on eating behaviour. Ninety-three obese adults (24 men and 69 women) who had referred themselves for help with weight loss completed three questionnaires: a Stigmatising Situations Inventory, Brief Symptoms Inventory, and a Binge Eating Questionnaire.

Correlational analysis was used to evaluate the relationships between measures of stigmatising experiences, psychological distress, and binge-eating behaviour. The results indicated that stigmatising experiences predicted binge eating and overall levels of psychological distress. In particular, psychological distress associated with stigmatising experiences appeared to be an important influence in the relationship between weight-based stigmatisation and binge-eating behaviour.

Although causal relationships cannot be determined from the data in this study, these findings do point to the possibility that psychological distress associated with weight-based stigmatisation may lead to further weight gain in those who experience such a stigma, by encouraging binge-eating behaviour.

their diet is no longer worth maintaining for that day (Herman and Mack, 1975) – an 'oh, what the heck!' response – and eat more while there is this particular opportunity to do so.

A biopsychological explanation for this restraint-disinhibition phenomenon is provided by the *boundary model* (Herman and Polivy, 1984). A central premise of this model is that food consumption is regulated by biological pressures to maintain food intake within a set range (specifically physiologically-determined boundaries for hunger and satiety). The unpleasant qualities of hunger help to keep food intake above a minimum level, whereas the unpleasant qualities of satiety help to keep food consumption below its maximum level. Therefore eating is viewed as being determined by biofeedback, with a zone of biological indifference existing between the hunger boundary and satiety boundary. Within this zone of biological indifference, eating is largely regulated by social and environmental influences. In restrained eaters this physiological control of food intake is undermined in two ways:

» First, restrained eaters impose a cognitively-determined diet boundary within their zone of biological indifference – food intake is no longer regulated through biological cues but cognitively. If this cognitive boundary is actually breached, dieters tend to consume food until deterred from doing so by their satiety boundary.

» Second, frequent oscillation between restrained eating and overeating is thought to widen the gap (the zone of biological indifference) between the boundaries of hunger and satiety, and make dieters less sensitive to hunger and satiation cues – this means that once their diet boundary is crossed, dieters are likely to eat much more than non-dieters before feeling full (Stroebe, 2000).

In addition to perceived dietary violations, factors such as distress and cravings are likely to impair the ability of dieters to prevent breaches of their 'dietary boundary'. Therefore it appears that restrained eating increases the probability of overeating in certain circumstances, and experimental research supports this link between dieting and overeating (e.g. Wardle and Beales, 1988).

IS DIETING AN EFFECTIVE WEIGHT LOSS STRATEGY?

While many overweight people lose weight as a result of dieting, most eventually regain any weight lost. This may lead to a process of 'yo-yo' dieting. Studies indicate restrained eating in non-obese individuals also predicts weight fluctuation (Heatherton et al, 1991). This is important, as repeated attempts at dieting have been associated with certain adverse effects on physical and psychological health. Indeed Ogden (2007) suggests that "dieting offers a small chance of weight loss and a high chance of both negative physical and psychological consequences".

However, a small proportion of dieters do successfully maintain their weight loss in the long-term. Studies that have investigated why this is the case have tended to produce contradictory results, although regular exercise and increased physical activity appear to be important factors (Hardeman et al, 2000). The findings of research by Ogden (2000) indicate that people who maintain weight loss following dieting are more likely to endorse a psychological model of obesity (as opposed to a medical explanation). The very fact that some people do maintain the weight loss they have achieved through dieting also suggests that restrained eating

FACTORS ASSOCIATED WITH LONG-TERM WEIGHT LOSS

Ogden (2000) used a questionnaire to explore the factors associated with success in weight loss and its maintenance. Responders were categorised into three groups: stable obese (58 people); weight loss regainers (40 people); and weight loss maintainers (44 people).

The questionnaires were analysed to examine any differences between these three groups. The results showed that weight loss maintainers had been lighter before dieting, were older and had spent longer dieting than members of the other two groups. There was no difference between the groups in terms of contact with health professionals for help with weight loss, but weight loss maintainers were less likely to endorse medical explanations for obesity. They also gave greater endorsement to the psychological consequences of obesity (i.e. depression, anxiety, low self-esteem, lack of confidence) and were more likely to report that they had been motivated to lose weight for psychological reasons (e.g. to enhance their self-confidence) rather than as a result of pressure from others or for medical reasons such as relief from obesity-related symptoms.

The findings of this study suggest that weight loss and maintenance are particularly correlated with a psychological model of obesity.

does not necessarily lead to problematic outcomes for all people and in all situations.

BIOLOGICAL EXPLANATIONS OF EATING BEHAVIOUR

NEURAL MECHANISMS CONTROLLING EATING

At a very basic level, we eat in order to function and survive. When and how much we eat is largely determined by our metabolism – that is, the rate at which the body uses energy (or calories) – and this is regulated by several physiological mechanisms. These mechanisms try to keep the body in energy homeostasis (or balance).

"You need to know about neural mechanisms involved in eating and satiation. The material on satiation is further on. Be sure to learn both, just in case you are specifically asked for one or the other."

According to *set point theory*, we have a biologically determined standard around which our body weight (specifically fat mass) is regulated (Keeley, 1986). Hence if we eat too little or eat too much, homeostatic mechanisms alter our metabolism and appetite accordingly, to return us close to our original weight. However, persistent overeating or under-eating may make it increasingly more difficult for homeostatic mechanisms to do this and over time we may settle at a new weight (Passer et al, 2009).

The main area of the brain involved in the regulation of appetite is the hypothalamus. In response to stimulation, the lateral hypothalamus (LH) produces hunger: damage to this area results in dramatic reductions in food intake. By contrast, the ventromedial hypothalamus (VMH) triggers a sense of feeling full, thereby reducing appetite. Hence it is often referred to as the satiety centre. Food consumption and weight control are, according to set point theory, the result of a balance between these two parts of the hypothalamus and other metabolic processes.

"You also need to know something about neural explanations of eating disorders (you'll come across this topic later on in the chapter). The material here is directly relevant, so be sure to make the connection between the two sections."

BRAIN MECHANISMS REGULATING HUNGER AND EATING

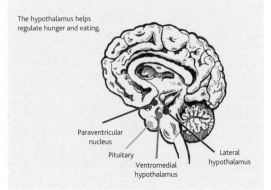

The hypothalamus helps regulate hunger and eating.

Paraventricular nucleus
Pituitary
Ventromedial hypothalamus
Lateral hypothalamus

Studies of how specific neural circuits within the hypothalamus regulate eating have found that many neuronal pathways involve the paraventricular nucleus (PVN). This is a cluster of neurons with receptors for various transmitters that stimulate or reduce appetite. The PVN integrates many short-term and long-term signals that influence metabolic and digestive processes (Berthoud and Morrison, 2008). One such signal is the peptide neurotransmitter Neuropeptide Y (NPY). Increased levels of NPY in the PVN and the regions adjacent to it, promote increases in food intake and weight. The release of NPY occurs in response to decreased levels of a hormone known as leptin which is discussed in more detail later in this section (Woods et al, 2000).

Early research suggested that the experience of hunger was largely determined by hunger pangs (that is, the muscular contractions of an empty stomach). Cannon and Washburn (1912) inserted a tube down the throat and into the stomach of a volunteer participant, so that one end was outside the mouth. Air was pumped into the pipe to inflate a balloon attached to the other end. Stomach contractions could then be measured by assessing changes in balloon air pressure. It was found that when the participant was not hungry there were no contractions, and hunger was reported at the height of the contractions,

NEURAL AND HORMONAL MECHANISMS – A BRIEF INTRODUCTION

Neural mechanisms are those structures (e.g. neurons, neural circuits, regions of the brain) and substances (e.g. neurotransmitters, hormones) that regulate behaviour and voluntary and involuntary bodily functions. The nervous system is divided into the central nervous system (the brain and spinal cord) and the peripheral nervous system (which contains all the neural structures that lie outside of the brain and spinal cord).

Food intake is controlled by a complex neural system which seeks to ensure that the body receives the nutrients it needs and that its energy supplies are kept in balance. Our understanding of the physiological processes associated with food intake and energy homeostasis is far from complete, and so it is only some of the neural mechanisms involved in these processes that are discussed below.

While many brain regions help regulate hunger and eating, the hypothalamus plays a key role. The hypothalamus consists of tiny groups of neuron cell bodies that lie at the base of the brain. It has important connections with the endocrine system – the collection of glands that make and secrete chemical messengers known as hormones. Through a direct connection with the pituitary gland (sometimes referred to as the 'master gland' of the endocrine system), the hypothalamus is able to control the secretion of hormones that help regulate metabolism. While the hypothalamus plays a crucial role in regulating eating behaviour, the cortex and limbic system (a mid-brain system of structures) are important for processing information regarding prior experience with food, reward and emotion.

The autonomic nervous system – one of the major components of the peripheral nervous system – regulates involuntary bodily functions including digestion. While the *sympathetic* branch of the autonomic nervous system inhibits the digestive system, the *parasympathetic* branch stimulates it.

suggesting that stomach contractions caused hunger. Whilst this was a dominant theory of hunger for many years, subsequent research showed that stomach contractions were not necessary for hunger. Feelings of hunger and satiety are experienced even when all the nerves from the stomach to the brain are cut, and also following surgical removal of the entire stomach (Passer et al, 2009). This indicates that other neural mechanisms must play a role in triggering hunger.

However, recent research indicates that the stomach does play some role in initiating eating behaviour. Ghrelin is a recently discovered hormone which is secreted by the mucous membrane of an empty stomach and, it has been suggested, stimulates appetite by inhibiting the activity of vagus nerve fibres (see the discussion of satiation below). The secretion of ghrelin stops when food is eaten (Berthoud and Morrison, 2008).

Once food arrives in the stomach it is broken down by digestive enzymes into key nutrients that can be used by the body. One of these is glucose, a simple sugar, which is a source of immediate fuel for the body (and especially the brain). However, while some glucose is transferred to cells to meet their energy needs, a large proportion of glucose is transported to the liver and fat cells where it is converted into other nutrients and stored. Blood glucose levels are monitored by sensors in both the liver and hypothalamus: when levels decrease, the liver responds by converting these stored nutrients back into glucose, thereby enabling blood glucose levels to rise. The liver is the primary site in the body for the delivery of glucose to the circulation when it is not readily available from

GHRELIN – THE HUNGER HORMONE

Lutter et al (2008) identified Ghrelin as an important hormone in indicating whether or not we are hungry. Ghrelin is released by an empty stomach, from where it travels to the brain, indicating that we are hungry. However, the researchers also suggest that the hormone is important in our mood. They starved mice for four days, and so increased the amount of Ghrelin in their systems because of their empty stomachs. Compared to mice who were allowed to eat freely, the mice with increased Ghrelin levels showed more anxiety and more signs of depression when carrying out tasks such as maze running. They found the same result when they increased Ghrelin levels by making the mice stressed. These findings suggest that food, hunger, stress and anxiety are all somehow associated. Happier mice have higher levels of Ghrelin, and so eat more than other mice with lower level of ghrelin. Of course, the side effect is that the mice may overeat when they are happy!

the digestive tract. According to *glucostatic theory* it is changes in the supply of glucose available to cells that generate signals to the brain which help it regulate hunger. There are, however, some problems with this theory.

First, levels of energy sources in the blood do not usually decrease to anywhere near the threshold necessary to trigger eating. Certainly a small but reliable decline in blood glucose does occur a few minutes before the initiation of spontaneous eating (Campfield et al, 1996). But this decline of blood glucose reverses just prior to the commencement of eating. Furthermore, if food is removed at this point (so no eating actually occurs) glucose levels return to the level at which they were before any decline occurred. This intriguing finding has led some researchers to suggest that it is the brain that initiates this dip in blood sugar before eating commences.

Second, in addition to fluctuations in glucose, studies of rats indicate that changes in body temperature are also associated with the initiation of eating: body temperature increases just prior to spontaneous eating, increases still further and then declines as eating stops. Alterations in metabolic rate have also been observed: this declines prior to the initiation of eating and increases when eating begins. Therefore it appears that changes in a number of physiological parameters (such as blood glucose, metabolic rate, body temperature, and probably many more), rather than just one (glucose), are associated with the initiation of eating behaviour (Woods et al, 2000).

Third, while some tissues (such as the brain) need large amounts of glucose for energy homeostasis, others such as the liver use fats, or, as in the case of skeletal muscle, use both glucose and fats depending on what is immediately available.

The liver signals to the brain reductions in fat availability and/or usage through distinct neural pathways which enter the brainstem and pass to the forebrain where they interact with controllers of energy homeostasis (Woods et al, 2000). So, separate but interacting pathways concerned with the availability of fats and glucose all influence consumption of food.

While biology plays an important part in the initiation of eating behaviour, it is important to remember that for humans the timing of meals and types of food consumed are more likely to be determined by lifestyle, convenience and opportunity. Hunger is not the only initiator of eating. Simply thinking about food has been shown to influence neural activity in parts of the brain known to be involved in the control of appetitive behaviours and this in turn leads to physiological responses such as the production of saliva, gastric acid and insulin (Berthoud and Morrison, 2008). Anticipation of eating and the actual onset of eating are also associated with increased dopamine activity in both the lateral hypothalamus and the mesolimbic dopamine system – which is the brain's primary reward centre. So the early stages of eating are also triggered and maintained by a sense of pleasure (Bennett, 2005). Learning is undoubtedly a very important factor and studies indicate that if animals are habitually fed at the same time of the day they learn to make and produce the neurotransmitters and hormones that help to regulate food intake (Woods et al, 2000). There is also evidence that the physiological processes associated with satiety, that reduce food consumption, can also be modified by learning (Goodison and Siegel, 1995)

GLUCOSE – FUEL FOR LIFE

Glucose is a simple sugar: it is vital to the body, as our cells use it for energy and metabolism, breaking it down into other important products, such as enzymes and nutrients. Glucose is the primary source of energy for the brain, and so it is extremely important in psychological processes such as attention and self-control. Fairclough and Houston (2004) have shown that mental effort, or how hard tasks appear to be, is significantly influenced when glucose levels drop. With the correct glucose levels, tasks seem more straightforward. In addition to this, Gailliot et al (2007) have shown that self-control is affected when glucose levels drop. When we have lower levels of glucose in our system than we would like, we feel less able to resist temptation, and less in control of ourselves. In other words, when we are hungry, snacking is much more likely, and eating only one piece of chocolate is extremely hard – we are much more likely to eat the whole bar!

NEURAL MECHANISMS CONTROLLING SATIATION

When we eat, this generates several body signals that cause us to feel full and stop eating (eventually!). Distension of the stomach and intestinal tract are usually signals of satiety. As the walls of these organs are stretched by the ingestion of food, vagal sensory nerves in their muscle layers, which act as 'stretch-receptors', send signals to the brain. However, satiety is not dependent on these processes alone. As with hunger, people who have had their stomachs removed, for medical reasons, still experience satiety: therefore chemical messengers must also play an important role in satiation. One such chemical is a peptide known as cholecystokinin (CCK). CCK and other peptides are released into the bloodstream by the small intestine when food arrives in the stomach. Receptors for CCK are found (among other places) on the sensory fibres of the vagus nerve near a point where food passes from the stomach into the intestine. The stimulation of these fibres sends signals to neurons in the lower brainstem that control digestive reflexes, and to other neurons in the forebrain. This in turn inhibits the intake of food (Woods et al, 2000). The neurotransmitter serotonin is another important chemical influence on satiation: its increased activity in the medial hypothalamus is associated with decreased food intake (Fetissov et al, 2000).

The release into the blood stream of leptin, a hormone secreted by fat cells, also leads to a decrease in appetite and an increase in energy expenditure. Leptin is an adiposity signal to the brain as it is secreted in direct proportion to the amount of fat stored in fat cells (known as adipocytes). (Adipose is another word for body fat). Leaner individuals secrete less leptin, whereas fatter individuals secrete more. Unlike CCK, leptin does not make us feel full but acts as a long-term background signal which moderates the effects of other satiety signals related more directly to the ingestion of food. For instance, any increase in the number of fat cells will lead to the secretion of more leptin. This may in turn mean we eat less because satiety signals make us feel full sooner. Conversely, a decline in leptin levels associated with the loss of fat cells (as occurs in dieting), stimulates motivation centres in the brain which in turn kindle our interest in food.

The importance of leptin as an adiposity signal to the brain is indicated by animals who do not produce it (such as ob/ob mice which have a mutation in the leptin gene) or who have genetic mutations that interfere with the function of leptin receptors (such as db/db mice). Characteristically, these animals consume excessive amounts of food and become extremely obese (Zhang et al, 1994).

The mouse on the left has an ob gene mutation. This means that its fat cells do not produce leptin, and it becomes overweight. Leptin injections help ob gene mice return to a normal weight.

There is growing evidence that neural pathways in the hypothalamus are particularly sensitive to the action of leptin, and, as mentioned earlier, the ventromedial hypothalamus is regarded by many to be a satiety centre. Further support for this sensitivity comes from the fact that trauma to, or tumours of, this area of the hypothalamus can cause hyperphagia and also obesity (Mayer and Thomas, 1967).

Insulin is another important adiposity signal to the brain. Secreted by the pancreas, insulin is a hormone that enables tissues to remove glucose from the blood. In fact, the secretion of insulin is directly responsive to the level of glucose in the blood. An absence or deficiency in insulin secretion (as in diabetes) is characterised by high blood glucose levels. A deficiency of insulin leads to hyperphagia (and an inhibition of satiety) as the brain strives to increase body fat. However unlike leptin-deficient individuals, people who are insulin-deficient do not become obese, as fat cells cannot store fat without insulin being present. Instead, excess calories accumulate in the blood and are often lost in the urine (Woods et al, 2000).

EVOLUTIONARY EXPLANATIONS OF FOOD PREFERENCE

ASK AN EXAMINER

"Later in this chapter there is discussion of evolutionary explanations of eating disorder. You will find useful material there to add to an exam answer on evolutionary explanations of food preference."

As discussed above, the glucostatic theory suggests that the initiation and cessation of eating is determined by levels of glucose in the blood. One problem with this theory is that if it were true it would require dangerously low levels of glucose before eating behaviour is started. From an evolutionary point of view this does not make sense. For instance, the consequences could be critical for an animal if glucose levels dipped to the threshold for initiating eating at a time when it was impossible to eat. Instead we eat when the environmental conditions (such as opportunity and availability of food) are optimal for doing so. However, there is evidence that we are born with genetic predispositions for basic tastes and that these influence food preference. We are born predisposed to prefer sweet and salty foods for instance, but to reject those foods that taste bitter and sour. Furthermore, the neophobia demonstrated by very young children indicates that we are also predisposed to be conservative in our food preferences, with new foods rejected in favour of those that are already familiar to us. Finally, we have "predisposition to learning preferences by associating foods with the context and consequences of eating them" (Birch, 1999). From an evolutionary perspective these predispositions are highly adaptive, reducing the likelihood that infants, once weaned, will ingest harmful substances (often indicated by a bitter or sour taste), therefore increasing the probability of their survival. Associative learning means that unpleasant side effects of eating something that does not agree with us make it unlikely that we will eat that food again. This too is important for survival and from an evolutionary perspective may be considered a highly adaptive response.

Given that humans are omnivores, and that eating is largely determined by environmental contingencies, some of our innate predispositions with regard to food are quickly modified as we develop – in particular, the strength of the neophobic response changes. Birch notes that at the point when a child is just starting to eat solid foods, this response appears to be minimal. She speculates that minimal neophobia during infancy may be adaptive as infants' access to food is largely controlled by adults. However, when children become increasingly independent (and capable of finding food for themselves) neophobia serves a protective function as they have not learnt the rules regarding food sourcing and preparation that reduce neophobia in adults. Associative learning not only makes us more inclined to avoid foods that have made us very ill in the past, but leads us to prefer flavours that have been previously paired with a preferred sweet taste and also flavours paired with those nutrients (such as sugar) that supply us with energy.

As we develop, we learn to prefer those flavours that are associated with high energy foods. As Birch (1999) notes, this propensity to prefer energy-dense foods over less energy-dense sources of nourishment would have been adaptive in environments where high energy foods were in short supply – a situation which has been the norm for much of human history. However, this preference for consuming energy-dense foods may now be less adaptive in many Western societies, where scarcity of food sources seldom occurs (at present) and energy expenditure (associated with physical activity) has generally diminished. The result may be over-storage of fat and obesity, an issue we discuss later.

It makes sense that our ancestors evolved by learning about the foods that provided them with good nutrition, as this would give them an evolutionary advantage over those who did not know that eating certain foods would give them strength and energy – as well as fuel for cognitive processing, such as decision making and task completion. In most cases, our ancestors would have had difficulty finding food in sufficient amounts, and so it would have paid them to learn where to find food with the maximum nutritional value. Capaldi (1996) has shown that animals in the laboratory can be taught very quickly to prefer high calorie foods, and Booth (1982) has shown a similar tendency in humans.

"You will find reference to evolution elsewhere in this chapter. Be careful though – you will need to make it relevant to food preference to get marks for it here."

It is not just high fat foods that we show a preference for. Sweet foods, high in glucose are preferred over non-sweet foods. Glucose is necessary for brain and body function, but excessive glucose will be metabolised by the body and stored, for use in times when it is harder to come by, as fat. Research from Desor et al (1973) suggests that even very tiny, 1–3-day-old infants prefer sweet flavours. Grill and Norgren (1973) showed that rats in the laboratory immediately accept foods that are sweet, and conclude that the response is almost reflex-like, in that it requires little or no decision making. The choice to eat the sweet food is automatic the moment the first taste is ingested. There is evidence from Bell et al (1973) that cultures such as the Inuit of Northern Alaska, who have traditionally lacked sweet foods in their diet, are quick to accept sweet foods into their diet when they come into contact with cultures that do eat them, even though they themselves have little or no experience of the foods.

In addition to this, there is evidence from biology that we are sensitive to sugar. The nerve that runs from our tongue to the brain, for instance, carries more fibres that are sensitive to sweet than any other flavour sensation. This evidence, together with that from rats, and the evidence from 1–3-day-old infants, who show a sweet preference, suggests that this particular preference may well be genetic and so may be explained in terms of evolution. Sugar is an extremely valuable substance that helps us survive. It provides us with fast and effective energy, and it supplies our brains with the fuel to make good and effective decisions quickly. Those with these advantages are more likely to survive than those without.

EATING DISORDERS

Disorders of eating are complex and highly distressing phenomena. A number of disorders of eating and weight are listed in both the International Classification of Diseases (ICD-10) produced by the World Health Organisation (WHO, 1992), and the Diagnostic and Statistical Manual of Mental Disorders (DSM IV-TR) published by the American Psychiatric Association (APA, 2000). Anorexia nervosa and obesity are two of the most common problems. They have a great deal in common in terms of underlying psychological processes – for example, a negative body image, chronic dietary problems, and abnormal patterns of eating and exercise.

"You only need to know about one eating disorder. We've presented a choice here, but once you've decided which one you are going to learn, don't waste any time learning about the other!"

ANOREXIA NERVOSA

The key features of anorexia nervosa include the refusal to maintain a minimally normal weight, a pathological fear of weight gain (weight gain is often equated with a loss of control) and a disturbance in the way individuals perceive their body shape that leads them to insist that they are overweight. It is not uncommon for people with anorexia nervosa to experience symptoms of depression and/or obsessive compulsive disorder (OCD) (Harrison et al, 2005).

"You will occasionally see a reference to another eating disorder in this section – bulimia nervosa. This disorder is characterised by binge eating, often with purging. It was only relatively recently (in 1979) that it was recognised as a disorder separate from anorexia, and many researchers consider bulimia and anorexia to have similar origins."

Anorexia nervosa is characterised by self-starvation and a refusal to maintain a minimally normal body weight. Weight is at least 15% below normal. There is deliberate weight loss and a pathological fear of gaining weight.

In addition to restricting drastically both the amount and type of food they eat, some individuals with anorexia nervosa also use other strategies (such as self-induced vomiting, excessive exercise, and the misuse of diuretics and laxatives) to reduce their weight. A distinction is therefore made between two forms of anorexia nervosa: restricted type (self-starvation not associated with purging) and binge-eating/purging type (APA, 2000). The physical consequences of the self-imposed starvation that characterises anorexia nervosa are serious and include: emaciation; irregular and slowed heart beat; kidney and gastrointestinal problems; dry skin and brittle hair; the development of lanugo (soft downy hair) on the back, forearms and cheeks; the absence of periods caused by disruption to the menstrual cycle (amenorrhea); and hypothermia. Between 5% - 8% of people diagnosed with anorexia nervosa die as a result of this disorder and the physical problems it causes (Davey, 2008).

PSYCHOLOGICAL EXPLANATIONS OF ANOREXIA NERVOSA

A number of factors have been implicated in the development of this eating disorder, including sociocultural factors, family factors, and a number of individual risk factors related to previous experience and dispositional differences (Polivy and Herman, 2002).

Sociocultural factors

The prevalence of eating disorders is not the same across all cultures at all times, and a preoccupation with thinness is generally only found in cultures where food is abundant. Studies suggest that the more thinness is prized by different social groups, the higher the prevalence of eating disorders within them (Striegel-Moore and Smolak, 1996). A social preoccupation with thinness may be viewed as both a precipitating and a maintaining factor for eating disorders. However, it is important to remember that even in cultures where great emphasis is placed on being slim, considerable variation exists in the extent to which people internalise their culture's valuation of thinness (Stormer and Thompson, 1996).

Family Influences

Some clinicians (usually family therapists) adopt a model of anorexia in which the individual with anorexia nervosa is viewed as a symptom of dysfunctional family relationships and structures. Minuchin et al (1978), for instance, suggest that anorexia is associated with families with at least one of the following characteristics:

» Enmeshment – where parents are intrusive and over-involved in their children's affairs, but dismissive of their children's emotional needs

» Over-protection – where members of the family are overly concerned about parenting and the welfare of others

» Rigidity – where there is a tendency to maintain the status quo within the family

» Conflict avoidance/ lack of resolution – where conflict within the family is either avoided or remains unresolved.

Adolescence tends to be a particularly stressful time, exacerbating hidden conflicts that exist between children and their parents. According to family systems theory, the development of anorexia nervosa by a young person helps to deflect attention away from other difficulties and problems located in the family structure as a whole. It is important to note, however, that evidence for this theory is largely based on the observations of clinicians who support it (Bennett, 2005).

Others have adopted a more behavioural perspective and argue that some families may help to perpetuate eating disorders by praising a person's slenderness and self-control thereby reinforcing their behaviour. It has been suggested that weight loss may provide a way of gaining acceptance from parents with high aspirations, of punishing parents, of avoiding the responsibilities (and parental expectations) associated with growing up (Bennett, 2005). But, as Polivy and Herman (2002) note, people with anorexia "do not require family approval in order to starve themselves". Furthermore, Polivy and Herman rightly point out that most studies investigating family influences are correlational and retrospective in nature. Therefore it is difficult to determine whether dysfunctional family relationships contribute to the development of eating disorders, or eating disorders lead to dysfunctional family relationships, or if there is another factor that influences both.

Experiential factors

Polivy and Herman (2002) report that trauma, abuse and teasing about one's appearance or body shape are interpersonal experiences commonly linked to the development of eating disorders. Adverse life experiences (such as the death of a family member) may be predisposing or precipitating factors for eating disorders. In one study 14% of participants with anorexia nervosa (but none of the controls) had experienced a negative life event in the three months prior to the onset of their condition (Rastam and Gillberg, 1991). An association between anorexia and the number of adverse life events experienced has also been found by other researchers, although as such studies are correlational and retrospective in nature, these findings need to be interpreted cautiously.

Although childhood sexual abuse is now generally accepted as a risk factor for eating disorders, this does not mean that everyone who is sexually abused will eventually develop an eating disorder (or that everyone with an eating disorder has experienced sexual abuse as a child). It is difficult to determine how childhood sexual abuse and other risk factors (such as emotional abuse) associated with early experience actually facilitate the development of an eating disorder (Polivy and Herman, 2002). It has been suggested that early adverse experiences may lead to other psychopathologies that are involved in the development of eating disorders (Casper and Lyubomirsky, 1997). Polivy and Herman (2002) suggest that where individuals experience continuing emotional and identity problems secondary to early adversity, focusing attention on weight, body shape, and the attainment of thinness, enables them to regain perceived control over at least one aspect of their life. As a result, the anorexic individual derives some emotional gratification from avoiding food and achieving thinness. This conceptualisation of eating disorders as coping strategies is contentious (e.g. Troop, 1998), and as Davey (2008) reminds us, while this may be an interesting view of eating disorders, further research is required to determine its validity.

Personality and dispositional factors

Findings from a number of studies indicate that eating disorders are associated with negative affect, and that mood disorders are often present at the same time as eating disorders (Davey, 2008). Stress and low mood have also been reported as antecedents of anorexia nervosa (Ball and Lee, 2000), but, as Davey (2008), notes, whether negative affect is a cause or consequence of eating disorders remains a contentious point.

Low self-esteem is also prominent among individuals who have eating disorders. This may result from a cognitive distortion concerning body weight and shape, discussed below. But there is also some evidence to suggest that low self-esteem may also play a role in the development of anorexia. As mentioned above, eating disorders have been construed as a coping strategy, a means of establishing control over at least one aspect of an afflicted individual's life – thus eating disorders may be one way some individuals seek to combat low self-esteem. Research indicates that self-esteem may moderate other factors implicated in the development of anorexia. For example women who are perfectionists and who consider themselves overweight are more likely to develop symptoms of anorexia if they have low self-esteem (Polivy and Herman, 2002).

Individuals diagnosed with anorexia nervosa score particularly highly on measures of perfectionism

EMOTIONAL RESPONSES TO FOOD AND EATING DISORDERS

McNamara et al (2008) conducted a qualitative study, the aim of which was to explore the emotional responses to different types of food of people with eating disorders.

In-depth interviews were conducted with ten women diagnosed with bulimia nervosa, anorexia nervosa or an 'eating disorder not otherwise specified'. Participants were asked to describe their thoughts while viewing slides of a range of different foodstuffs. Interviews were transcribed and a qualitative analysis was undertaken using the Framework Approach (a qualitative research approach that has been specifically designed for applied healthcare research).

Whilst a number of themes emerged from the analysis, the central theme was that of 'control'. Control encompassed 'positive control', that is, being able to influence outcome and control behaviour and the resultant emotional states associated with being able to exercise such control. 'Negative control' involved losing control of eating behaviours, associated purging, and the negative emotional reactions associated with this. All other themes that emerged from the analysis were also related to control. Positive emotional reactions to images of food were reported by participants who felt in control of their eating behaviour, whereas even the thought of losing control was enough for some participants to experience negative emotional affect towards foodstuffs and themselves.

This study is one of the first to link control with negative response to the sight of food and therefore has important implications for the treatment of eating disorders. However, a major problem is its artificiality – participants were only shown photographs of food rather than being presented with the actual foodstuffs.

ETHICS   NATURE/NURTURE   GENDER   CULTURE   DETERMINISM   REDUCTIONISM

(Bardone-Cone et al, 2007). Perfectionists characteristically set extraordinarily high standards for their own personal performance and tend also to be overly self-critical. Perfectionism may be self-orientated (seeking to attain high standards set by oneself) or other-orientated (seeking to attain high standards set by others). Not only are self-orientated and other-orientated perfectionism higher in individuals with anorexia than in non-anorexic controls (Cockell et al, 2002), but perfectionism is also highly associated with body dissatisfaction and the pursuit of thinness (Ruggerio et al, 2003). The findings of a number of studies suggest that perfectionism may be a predisposing factor for anorexia nervosa (Polivy and Herman, 2002).

Body dissatisfaction is included in almost all conceptualisations of eating disorders, as negative feelings about self are often expressed as negative feelings about the body (Polivy and Herman, 2002). Weight concern – often viewed as synonymous with body dissatisfaction – is associated with dieting, and dieting is often construed as a precipitating factor for eating disorders generally. Therefore it is often argued that body dissatisfaction has a causal role in eating disorders. Furthermore, many of the influences implicated in the development of eating disorders (such as media influences) are thought to operate through body dissatisfaction. But as Polivy and Herman (2002) observe, although body dissatisfaction is 'probably a necessary factor' in the development of an eating disorder, 'it is not sufficient' as it is possible to be dissatisfied with one's body without dieting and starving.

Cognitive factors

Several cognitive factors are associated with eating disorders, including obsessive thoughts, inaccurate judgements and rigid thinking patterns. Cognitive models of eating disorders suggest that the sociocultural influences are translated into behaviour through cognitive processes. Central to such models is the concept of weight-based schemata, that is, organised patterns of thinking about weight in which self-worth is judged on the basis of body weight and shape. Once such schemata are established, they distort an individual's subsequent perception and interpretation of experience. As a consequence, the maintenance of self-worth becomes increasingly dependent upon weight control (Bennett, 2005). Studies have certainly found that negative self (or core) beliefs are characteristic of individuals with anorexia nervosa and bulimia nervosa (Cooper, 2005)

It is also the case that individuals with eating disorders often report experiencing obsessive thoughts about food and eating, body weight and shape. Although most people try to suppress these thoughts, many report that they are not always successful in doing so and feel they have little control over such obsessions. Some individuals – particularly those with anorexia nervosa – report

A MODIFIED STROOP TEST

RED	RED	CAR	SAUSAGE
GREEN	GREEN	SHOE	DONUT
BLUE	BLUE	HOUSE	CHOCOLATE
YELLOW	YELLOW	TREE	CAKE
PINK	PINK	CHAIR	CRISPS
GREEN	GREEN	ROAD	CHIPS
RED	RED	FLOWER	PIZZA
BLUE	BLUE	BOOK	CHEESE
YELLOW	YELLOW	PENCIL	BREAD

Read the first column of words from top to bottom as fast as you can. Next, read the second column, but read out the colours of the words, not the words themselves. This is much harder because you can't help reading the words as reading is an automatic process to those that can read. This is the normal 'Stroop effect'.

Now read the third column, again reading the colours of the words. Now read the fourth column, again reading only the colours of the words. Anorexic and bulimic participants find this last task more difficult; they were faster when the words were neutral words, such as those in column three, than if they were food-related words, such as those in column four. This suggests that people with bulimia and anorexia nervosa pay more attention to food words than others.

deriving comfort from such preoccupations (Polivy and Herman, 2002).

A number of studies also indicate that people with eating disorders experience disturbances in information processing with regard to food and eating, weight and body shape stimuli (Cooper, 2005). The use of a modified Stroop procedure has revealed attentional biases in individuals with anorexia nervosa and bulimia nervosa, with greater attention given to words related to food, weight and body shape.

Individuals with anorexia nervosa exhibit a bias for food words (Polivy and Herman, 2002). Studies have also found evidence of memory bias in individuals with eating disorders – words related to food, weight, and body shape are more likely to be recalled (Cooper, 2005).

The need for control is expressed by individuals with anorexia nervosa and individuals with bulimia nervosa. However, individuals with anorexia are more capable of sustaining long-term control over their eating than those with bulimia nervosa, who tend to be more impulsive (Fairburn, 1997). Fairburn and colleagues suggest that in anorexia nervosa, once attempts to restrict eating begin, they are reinforced by three main feedback loops which help this eating disorder to become self-perpetuating (Fairburn et al, 1998). The first feedback loop is an enhanced sense of being in control derived from dietary restriction. This is a positive reinforcer of restricted eating behaviour, and control over eating gradually becomes an indicator of self-control in general and self-worth. The second feedback loop comprises the various physiological and psychological changes associated with self-starvation that encourage further dietary restriction. For example intense hunger may be interpreted as a perceived threat to control over eating thereby motivating an individual to restrict their food intake still further. In effect these changes act as negative reinforcers of further restricted eating. The third, and most culturally specific, mechanism is concerns about body shape and weight that derive from the social value attached to thinness (and the resultant imperative to avoid fatness) in Western societies.

BIOLOGICAL EXPLANATIONS OF ANOREXIA NERVOSA

Family studies have shown higher rates of anorexia in individuals who have relatives with eating disorders, indicating a genetic origin. Lilenfeld et al (1998) looked at the family history of 26 people diagnosed with anorexia and found a family vulnerability for the disorder. This vulnerability does not however necessarily emerge as full-blown anorexia. They found that relatives of anorexics were seven to twelve times more likely to show 'subthreshold' forms of anorexia (i.e. not quite meeting DSM criteria for the disorder).

Several twin studies have reported higher rates of eating disorders among identical (monozygotic, MZ) twin pairs than non-identical (dizygotic, DZ) twin pairs. For example, Holland et al (1988) found that 56% of the MZ twins in their study both had anorexia, whereas only 5% of the DZ twins both suffered. Whilst this clearly indicates that anorexia has a genetic component, the fact that the concordance was not 100% for genetically identical individuals suggests that the disorder is not entirely genetic.

Grice et al (2002) found evidence for susceptibility to anorexia on Chromosome 1. They compared DNA samples from people with anorexia with those belonging to family members. Genetic commonalities emerged when they looked at families with two or more relatives of anorexics with severe food restriction (i.e. starving rather than binge-purging). Grice et al point out that anorexia is unlikely to be caused by a single gene. It is a complex disorder with a number of genes involved, each contributing a small effect.

Given the recent dramatic increases in rates of eating disorders, it is unlikely that eating disorders

THE DIATHESIS STRESS MODEL

The diathesis-stress model is commonly used to explain the development of psychological disorders (Bennett, 2005). The word diathesis refers to an underlying vulnerability to develop a certain disorder. While this vulnerability may be biological (such as genetic predisposition), it may also refer to predisposing factors that are largely psychosocial in origin – for example, early traumatic experience, personality traits or particular cognitive schemata. For a vulnerable individual to develop a particular disorder, some form of precipitating stress is required. Once a disorder has developed, any psychological explanation for that disorder needs to account for the factors that help to maintain it. The diathesis-stress model can help us understand the development of eating disorders from a psychological perspective – it provides a framework for examining the psychosocial factors implicated in the development of these distressing (and sometimes life-threatening) disorders.

are directly inherited. It seems more likely that genetics provides a predisposition towards an eating disorder. While there is evidence of a genetic component to eating disorders – based on findings from twin and family studies – this is not yet conclusive. Polivy and Herman (2002) suggest that one problem with such studies is that it's not easy to separate genetic from environmental influences. Furthermore, research has yet to reveal how inherited dispositions increase the likelihood of developing an eating disorder. As Davey (2008) observes in relation to anorexia nervosa: "does this genetic component to anorexia simply increase the tendency to self-starve, or does it increase the vulnerability to other risk factors (such as depression or low self-esteem)?"

When thinking about changes in neural mechanisms that are associated with eating disorders, it is important to remember that the brain is neuroplastic. This means that structures (e.g. neural pathways) and functions of different areas of the brain change in response to learning, experience and environmental stimuli. Consequently, it is difficult to determine cause and effect. Any changes in neural mechanisms may be a consequence of an eating disorder rather than a cause of it. Guisinger (2003) also reminds us that although neuro-endocrine abnormalities associated with anorexia nervosa are often attributed to genetic defects or to the secondary effects of malnutrition,

> …in "normal" starvation the pattern of neuroendocrine changes is distinctly different, lead to lethargy and hunger, not hyperactivity and food refusal. Furthermore, most of these "defects" resolve with normalisation of body weight, making their role as primary etiological factors less likely…

A number of theories concerning the development of anorexia nervosa have focused on possible changes to those brain areas associated with the regulation of appetite – specifically the hypothalamus. Research has shown that damage to the lateral hypothalamus causes loss of appetite resulting in a self-starvation syndrome (Hoebel and Teitelbaum, 1966). However as Davey (2008) notes, it is unlikely that problems associated with the lateral hypothalamus are a central causal factor in anorexia. Animal studies indicate that damage to this part of the hypothalamus results in lack of hunger. By contrast those who suffer with anorexia nervosa usually report experiencing intense hunger.

"The content of the earlier sections on neural mechanisms involved in eating and satiation are directly relevant to this section on biological explanations of eating disorders. Be prepared to use relevant information from any part of the chapter!"

An alternative theory is that an excess of the neurotransmitter serotonin underlies the development of anorexia nervosa. This theory is based upon observed similarities in behavioural and cognitive traits of individuals afflicted with anorexia nervosa and individuals diagnosed with obsessive-compulsive disorder (OCD). It is known that serotonin levels influence the symptoms of OCD. One of the problems with this theory remains the issue of cause and effect: are anomalies in serotonin levels a cause or consequence of anorexia? While animal studies have shown that when serotonin is released into either ventromedial or lateral hypothalamus, animals stop eating, recent research has found lower levels of serotonergic activity during periods of starving and recovery among people with anorexia nervosa than among controls (Kaye et al, 2005). However, the similarities in the behavioural and cognitive traits associated with OCD and anorexia, continues to stimulate the interest of researchers. For instance, Steinglass and Walsh (2006) speculate that individuals with anorexia nervosa and OCD have similar deficits in their implicit learning systems associated with disturbances in the neural circuits between the cortex and basal ganglia.

More recently, Nunn et al, (2008) have suggested that anorexia nervosa can be accounted for by problems in the neural circuitry of the insula cortex, a structure that helps to integrate the functions of all the possible neural centres relevant to the features of anorexia nervosa. The failure of the insula cortex to do this could, according to Nunn et al, account for the range of symptoms associated with anorexia. The major problem with this hypothesis is that it is difficult to design tests that target the insular cortex without activating the many other areas of the brain to which it is connected, and this makes the insula hypothesis very hard to test.

EVOLUTIONARY EXPLANATIONS FOR ANOREXIA NERVOSA

ASK AN EXAMINER

"Evolutionary explanations for food preference were covered earlier – you will also find relevant material there to use in an exam question on evolutionary explanations for anorexia nervosa."

However, given the importance attached in evolutionary theory to survival and the propagation of one's genes, anorexia nervosa is from an evolutionary perspective a much more puzzling condition and aspects of it are difficult to explain (Gatward, 2007). Women who are afflicted with anorexia nervosa stop menstruating and as a consequence are temporarily unable to reproduce: some sufferers sadly do not survive. It is certainly plausible that a genetic vulnerability exists for anorexia nervosa and therefore it may be argued that aspects of this disorder may have had an adaptive function.

ASK AN EXAMINER

"If you get a general question in the exam asking for biological explanations of anorexia, you can include evolutionary explanations along with the previous biological material. Think back too to the section on biological explanations of eating behaviour – there is material you can use there too."

Guisinger (2003) has speculated that some of the most distinctive features of anorexia (restriction of food intake, denial of starvation, and hyperactivity) are likely to be evolved adaptive mechanisms. A key idea of Guisinger's Adapted to Flee Famine Hypothesis (AFFH) is that these behaviours once helped early humans to migrate in response to local famine. Many pre-agrarian human populations were nomads who foraged for food. When local sources of food were in short supply and this led to weight loss, Guisinger suggests that there would be benefits to seeking sources of food elsewhere. Guisinger argues that efficient migration was dependent upon switching off the usual adaptations to starvation (lethargy, energy conservation and hunger); and suggests that "the ability to stop foraging locally, to feel restless and energetic, and optimistically to deny that one is dangerously thin" could facilitate successful migration and, ultimately, survival (Guisinger, 2003). Although this is no longer an adaptive response, according to Guisinger's hypothesis, a very low body weight (caused by dieting or other reasons), causes some individuals' bodies to respond as though they must migrate from famine.

However, as with most explanations based on evolutionary theory, the AFFH is difficult to prove or disprove. Gatward (2007) has developed this hypothesis further by trying to explain why anorexia nervosa disproportionately affects women. Gatward frames his explanation for this in terms of social competition. Dietary restriction is considered by Gatward to be a response that is more likely to be adopted by females in the face of perceived threats of exclusion from the group, (which for our ancestors would have been very dangerous). This response only develops into anorexia nervosa when sustained weight loss triggers the ancient response to the threat of famine described by Guisinger.

Crawford (1998) describes anorexia as a *pseudopathology*. This is an illness that is brought about by an entirely intact adaptive mechanism operating in a modern environment. Whilst anorexia is a problem that both men and women suffer, it is largely and historically a problem associated with women. In terms of evolutionary adaptiveness, it is a good idea for women to be attractive to men. In the past, being attractive to men may have meant being healthy enough to care for several children at once. The environment women now live in, however, communicates the idea that being attractive to men involves being thin. It follows that there is an adaptive advantage to being thin, as it attracts men, and if it does that, a thin woman is more likely to be provided for in terms of food and safety. This adaptive mechanism, operating under today's heavy media influence, may well produce underweight or even anorexic women. As such, anorexia may be explained as an intact adaptive mechanism to the modern environment.

One of the effects on the body of anorexia is the stopping of menstruation. The body realises that the woman is not capable of carrying a healthy baby to full term and so stops producing eggs. As such the woman becomes infertile. This is obviously an evolutionary disadvantage. Being infertile means that genetic material has no chance of being passed to the next generation, since there cannot be a next generation. Wasser and Barach (1983) have suggested that this may, in fact, be an adaptive mechanism. Women are able to give birth to and look after relatively few children in the course of their lives. If they give birth in times of famine, or when there is relatively little food around, the child may not live, or the child may put pressure on other resources, making survival of existing children difficult. Infertility, brought about by the control of food intake, might have provided our ancestors with the opportunity of controlling when they were available to produce children. In times of famine, less food would be eaten, the woman would become infertile, there would be no chance of conceiving and so the scarce resources would not be put under further pressure. This means that the existing children would be more likely to survive to the next generation.

Surbe (1987) has proposed that delaying the onset of fertility to later in life provides a woman with the chance to pursue avenues of endeavour that families may find acceptable and that ultimately will allow them to provide better for a child born later in life. For instance, an anorexic in her late teens will not fall pregnant, and is able to continue with her academic studies, moving to university without the responsibility of a child. Later, when qualified and when in command of resources, the woman can begin a family, and has more chance of attracting a high-status and high-quality mate. This may explain why more and more women are choosing to have children later in life.

Voland and Voland (1989) say that anorexia may be adaptive for another reason. Research has suggested that anorexics are extremely caring and protective of their own families, and anorexic

women often come from extremely protective, and possibly over-protective, family environments (Minuchin et al, 1975). If anorexic, and therefore infertile, the woman can focus on looking after and caring for her immediate kin. The presence of this additional helper increases the likelihood that existing children in the family will survive. By giving up her own fertility, the woman ensures the survival of genes carried by other children in her own family.

OBESITY

Whilst obesity is included in the ICD-10 as a general medical condition, it does not appear in DSM IV "because it has not been established that it is consistently associated with a psychological or behavioural syndrome" (APA, 2000).

Obesity can be defined in a number of ways. These include:

Population means

Body Mass Index

Waist circumference

Percentage of body fat (which usually involves measuring skin fold thickness – around the upper arm and upper and lower back – using callipers).

There are particular difficulties with all of these definitions of obesity. For example, one problem with the 'population means' approach is that the definition of obesity depends on the population being considered and may therefore vary considerably from one country to another (Ogden, 2007). The BMI, a commonly used definition of obesity, does not allow for differences in weight between muscle and fat, so, for example, some sportsmen and women may be defined as obese on the basis of their BMI although they are incredibly fit and healthy. In general obesity is a risk factor for chronic health problems such as diabetes, cardiovascular disease, high blood pressure, some types of cancer, joint problems and back pain.

For some (but by no means all) individuals who are obese, binge-eating disorder (BED) may be the cause of their obesity. While binge eating is a characteristic of bulimia nervosa, in binge-eating disorder binges are not followed by compensatory behaviours (such as purging or fasting) to prevent weight gain. Hence, individuals are more likely to become obese (Davey, 2000).

Kopelman (1999) observes that obesity cannot be regarded as a single disorder, but is better construed as a group of varied disorders. As Prentice

(1999) notes, for obesity to occur, energy intake must remain higher than energy expenditure over a prolonged period. The causes of obesity range from the purely biological to the purely behavioural. Most cases of obesity "probably cluster towards the middle of this spectrum and can best be described as the outcome of an adverse 'obesogenic' environment, working on a susceptible genotype" (Prentice, 1999).

THE BODY MASS INDEX – HOW TO CALCULATE IT AND WHAT IT MEANS

The equation used to calculate BMI is weight (kg)/ height (m²). BMI results are interpreted as follows:

BMI of 20–24.9 = normal weight

BMI of 25–29.9 = overweight (grade 1)

BMI of 30–39.9 = clinical obesity (grade 2)

BMI of 40+ = severe obesity (grade 3)

(Source: Ogden, 2007).

PSYCHOLOGICAL EXPLANATIONS OF OBESITY

As already mentioned, there is considerable evidence that body weight is strongly influenced by genetic factors, but at present it is uncertain how this genetic inheritance expresses itself. However, the sudden rise in the prevalence of obesity in Western societies over the past three decades also indicates the importance of environmental influences and behavioural factors. A number of eating behaviours and putative eating disorders have been associated with obesity.

Emotional and restrained eating

Earlier, we considered how certain individual differences possibly mediate the relationship between stress (and specifically distress) and overeating. Among the groups suggested to be at increased risk of overeating were emotional eaters. According to the 'restraint theory' outlined by Herman and Mack (1975) emotional eating occurs as a consequence of the disinhibition of restraint by emotional arousal. An alternative explanation that has also been put forward is that overeating constitutes an escape from self-awareness in response to emotional pain (Heatherton et al, 1993). However, as reported earlier, research has produced conflicting findings regarding the influence of emotional eating in weight gain.

'Restraint theory' has significantly affected how we think about obesity, by indicating the ways in which overeating may be caused by restrained eating. Restraint theory provides an explanation

for why most people who lose weight by dieting, fail to maintain their weight loss over time. This in turn has called into question the value of dieting. But as already noted, a minority of dieters do successfully avoid putting weight back on (e.g. Ogden, 2000). This suggests that for some individuals restraint is an effective way of maintaining a healthy body weight.

Emotional problems

There is certainly a widespread view that emotional problems play a significant role in the origin of obesity. But community studies have generally failed to find a higher prevalence of psychiatric problems among obese adults (when compared to 'normal weight' adults), although there is some evidence that the incidence of depression and anxiety is higher than would be expected among obese individuals who report binge eating (Specker et al, 1994). However, this does not mean that emotional disorders are necessarily a cause of obesity brought about by binge eating. According to Wardle (1999), there is some evidence to suggest that emotional disorders among obese binge eaters are more likely to be an effect rather than the cause of their eating disorder.

Binge-eating disorder

Binge eating is defined as eating an objectively large amount of food while experiencing a subjective sense of lack of control on at least two occasions per week. This disorder usually develops during late adolescence or early adulthood, and is associated with high levels of depression, low self-esteem and body dissatisfaction (Davey, 2008). It is the absence of compensatory behaviours designed to negate the calorific effects of binges (such as purging and excessive exercise) that distinguishes binge-eating disorder from bulimia nervosa and also implicates binge-eating disorder as a cause of obesity. Although the prevalence of binge-eating disorder is between 1% and 3% in the general population, up to 30% of individuals seeking weight loss treatment complain of this eating disorder (Dingemans, et al, 2001)

FOOD ADDICTION

Many people become addicted to different types of foods such as those high in sugar and/or carbohydrates. Eating only a small amount can often trigger a binge, where the addict gorges themselves on as much as they can obtain. They may then follow the binge with purges of vomiting, and may also use laxatives to help the food leave their systems. Many food addicts are overweight and risk health problems including diabetes, heart disease, gall stones, infertility and depression. Some, however, diet obsessively to control their addiction, or involve themselves in excessive and often extreme exercise regimes where they risk physical injury as their joints and muscles may become damaged.

Food addiction

As Wardle (1999) notes, behind the food addiction explanation for obesity is a model of addiction which suggests that changes to the central nervous system occur as a result of exposure to a substance. As a consequence, symptoms of withdrawal and cravings are experienced when access to the substance is denied. According to this theory, addictions develop and are maintained as a consequence of the negative reinforcement associated with the avoidance/relief of withdrawal symptoms.

Although there are particular difficulties applying this model to food (as food consumption is normal and necessary for life), cravings for certain types of food – such as the carbohydrate craving hypothesis – are consistent with this explanation. However, in general, obese people do not eat more carbohydrates than non-obese people and obese people tend to prefer sweet, fatty foods which are not pure carbohydrates (Wardle, 1999).

Whilst many obese people report problems with cravings for certain food types which they find difficult to control, this may be partly accounted for by the palatability of modern foods. As Berthoud and Morrison (2008) observe, "the hedonistic impact of heightened palatability appears to be one of the most important factors for stimulating appetite and consumption." Wardle (1999) concludes that although popular, explanations of obesity based on addiction theories "attract a much larger following than is merited from their empirical base."

Night eating syndrome (NES)

Night eating syndrome as a cause of obesity was first described by Stunkard et al (1955). The characteristics of this syndrome are (a) evening hyperphagia: the consumption of at least a quarter of total daily calories during the period following the evening meal; (b) insomnia (especially difficulties falling asleep); and (c) morning anorexia resulting in the negligible intake of food at breakfast. A further nocturnal eating/drinking syndrome (NEDS) has also been proposed which is characterised by recurrent awakenings and an inability to fall asleep again without eating or drinking (de Zwaan et al, 2003).

Relatively little research has been undertaken in this area. Although NES appears to be more common in obese individuals who seek weight loss treatment than in community samples of people of all weights, few studies have found a positive relationship between NES and degree of obesity (e.g. Aronoff et al, 2001). As with NES, there is little evidence that a relationship exists between NEDS and increasing obesity. However, people who experience NEDS frequently report putting themselves on a diet after developing the disorder and this may increase their risk of subsequent weight gain (de Zwaan et al, 2003).

Psychological factors influencing physical activity

Obesity is associated with low levels of physical activity – but whether reduced physical activity is a cause or consequence of obesity remains unclear (Ogden, 2007). While personality traits have not been found to be strong predictors of participation in physical activity, a number of psychosocial factors have been implicated. Perceptions of competence are particularly important: by late adolescence physical self-perceptions strongly predict both the degree and type of future involvement in exercise and sport. Those individuals who perceive themselves as having little competence in sport and physical activity are much less likely to engage in future health-related physical activities. Fear of displaying the body in a public setting further deters some individuals from taking part in sport and exercise (Wardle, 1999).

BIOLOGICAL EXPLANATIONS OF OBESITY

The majority of people living in Western countries where obesity problems are greatest have a constant supply of food. Whilst it is clear that obesity seems to be a consequence of modern living, it is also clear that modern living affects people in different ways. It is only some people who store more energy as fat in these circumstances, and this may be due to genetic variations between individuals. There is strong evidence from both human and animal studies that there is a genetic contribution to obesity.

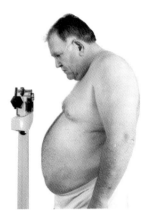

Obesity can often run in families, so that individuals with a family history may be predisposed to gain weight. In an overfeeding study lasting 100 days, Bouchard et al (1990) overfed 12 pairs of male identical twins. During this time the total excess amount consumed by each man was 84,000 calories. They found that there was three times more similarity in weight gain within pairs than between pairs, strongly suggesting that genetic factors are involved. In particular, Bouchard et al speculate that the genetic factors influenced both the tendency to store energy as fat and the expenditure of energy whilst at rest.

Some of the strongest evidence for the heritability of obesity comes from studies of identical twins reared apart, because this population is a natural control for the confounding variable of shared environments. Stunkard et al (1990) looked at 25,000 pairs of twins born in Sweden between 1886 and 1958 and estimated the heritability component of BMI in twins reared apart to be 70% for men and 66% for women.

Price and Gottesman (1991) analysed the data on body fat from a sample of 34 identical twins reared apart and compared it to that gathered from a matched sample of 38 pairs of identical twins

reared together. They found a correlation of 0.61 for the adopted twins and 0.75 for those reared together, supporting previous research. Also, these estimates of heritability did not differ significantly between the twin sets. This suggests that both genes and environment are important in accumulating body fat, and emphasises the importance of the genetic contribution to obesity since being reared apart or together appeared to have little impact on heritability.

Adoption studies are another potential source of useful information about the contribution of genes to obesity. Adoptive parents and adopted offspring (adoptees) share only their environment, whilst adoptees and their biological parents share genes but not environment. In an analysis of the data of 5,000 participants gathered from the Danish adoption register, Stunkard et al (1986) found a strong correlation between the BMI of adoptees and their biological parents, but no relationship between adoptees and their adoptive parents. A study by Sorensen et al (1989) found a strong correlation between the BMI of adoptees and biological siblings reared apart from them with their natural (biological) parents.

Some forms of obesity are known to be monogenetic (that is, caused by one gene). However, these monogenic forms of obesity account for less than 1% of all obesity cases. Obesity, in its most common form, is likely to involve both gene-gene and gene-environment interactions. Searching for a single gene, whilst complex, is relatively straightforward compared to the daunting task of finding interacting genes which offer susceptibility to obesity. This is supported by the fact that whilst over 430 genes or chromosomal regions have been implicated in the cause of obesity, only 15 of these have been replicated by multiple studies.

There is ample evidence that obesity is influenced by environmental factors. For example, in recently urbanised populations such as Fiji, there have been marked increases in obesity over the last 30 years (Ulijascek, 2005); whilst Kopelman (2000) has found that Pima Indians living in the US are each on average 25 kg heavier than Pima Indians living in Mexico. The key environmental factor appears to be the large quantities of high calorific food and much reduced need to engage in physical exercise.

The availability of sweet foods, and high-fat foods, taken together with the knowledge that evolution has designed us to find these foodstuffs desirable and attractive, is a recipe for overeating and

THE DIATHESIS STRESS MODEL

The diathesis-stress model is commonly used to explain the development of psychological disorders (Bennett, 2005). The word diathesis refers to an underlying vulnerability to develop a certain disorder. While this vulnerability may be biological (such as genetic predisposition), it may also refer to predisposing factors that are largely psychosocial in origin, for example, early traumatic experience, personality traits or particular cognitive schemata. For a vulnerable individual to develop a particular disorder, some form of precipitating stress is required. Once a disorder has developed, any psychological explanation for that disorder needs to account for the factors that help to maintain it. The diathesis-stress model can help us understand the development of eating disorders from a psychological perspective – it provides a framework for examining the psychosocial factors implicated in the development of these distressing (and sometimes life-threatening) disorders.

obesity. Controlling desires and tastes that are so heavily genetically ingrained in us from our ancestry is something that many people find extremely difficult and so we see many people in our society suffering with overeating. Early research from Nachman (1959) adds to this explanation. He showed that rats can be selectively bred to have a greater or smaller preference for sweet foods. This further suggests that such a preference may, at least in part, be influenced by our genetics. We may overeat because our parents and their parents overate. They in turn overate because their parents and their ancestors overate. This preference, possibly due to the evolutionary advantage it provided at the time, is passed down from generation to generation. Plomin et al (2008) indicate that there is significant heritability of body weight, body mass index and prevalence of obesity. This is more evidence that our eating and eating habits are genetically influenced.

Studies which have included twins, adoptees and family, confirm a strong genetic influence on weight and the distribution of fat tissue (Kopelman, 1999), but as Kopelman notes, the very rapid increase in the prevalence of obesity in the UK and many other Western societies indicates the importance also of environmental factors. However, obesity is a feature of many (albeit comparatively rare) genetic disorders in humans such as Prader-Willi syndrome (Kopelman, 1999).

When signals that inform the brain about the body's nutritional status lose their capacity to help regulate the body's energy balance, either starvation or obesity is likely to ensue. As noted earlier a number of genes and genetic mutations in rodents, associated with leptin, are linked with obesity. While extreme obesity in humans can occasionally be the result of a deficiency of leptin and is reversed by leptin treatment, research indicates that, overwhelmingly, most obese humans do not lack leptin. Somewhat paradoxically, many obese humans have high circulating-leptin

levels that are inconsistent with their obesity. Furthermore, very few respond to treatment with leptin, suggesting a state of leptin resistance. It is uncertain how this resistance develops, but obesity and leptin resistance have developed in mice and rats fed on high-fat diets, and in a number of other animals that have been discovered eating foodstuffs characteristic of a modern human lifestyles (Berthoud and Morrison, 2008).

"The content of the earlier sections on neural mechanisms involved in eating and satiation are directly relevant to this section on biological explanations of obesity. Be prepared to use relevant information from any part of the chapter!"

Obesity in humans is also associated with a number of endocrine disorders, including: hypothyroidism (in which metabolic rate is reduced, predisposing an individual to positive energy balance and weight gain); Cushing's syndrome (caused by an excess secretion of corticosteroids from the adrenal glands); ovarian disease; and certain rare diseases of the pancreas. While obesity is often attributed to 'glandular' problems generally, there is little evidence that endocrine or hormonal disorders are a common cause of obesity. Indeed, changes in endocrine function tend to be secondary to obesity itself as they are often induced by over-consumption of food and reversed by weight loss (Finer and Prentice, 1999).

EVOLUTIONARY EXPLANATIONS OF OBESITY

The human body evolved over hundreds of thousands of years to cope with a specific type of environment. Humans evolved in times of relative privation, where food availability was always limited, was likely to vary in abundance, and took a lot of effort to acquire. Genes that predispose

PRADER-WILLI SYNDROME

This is a rare condition with a prevalence of 1 per 25,000 of the population. It is usually caused by a deletion of a small part of one paternally acquired chromosome (Chromosome 15). Children with this condition initially find it difficult to feed because of weak muscle tone, but by the age of 2 or 3 years have normally developed a voracious appetite. This hyperphagia, which is accompanied by constant food-seeking behaviours, means they quickly put on weight and become obese. Children with Prader-Willi syndrome are often short in stature, and are usually blond and blue-eyed.

people to obesity may once have provided a survival advantage, in that during times of plenty our ancestors would have been able to store calories in excess of needs as fat. In an evolutionary sense, in a very short space of time people have become exposed to vast quantities of food containing lots of fat, sugar and salt. There is clearly a mismatch between modern living and our bodies, which evolution took so long to design.

"If you get a general question in the exam asking for biological explanations of obesity, you can include evolutionary explanations along with the previous biological material. Think back too to the section on biological explanations of eating behaviour – there is material you can use there too."

The types of foods we find desirable are bound up with evolution. We seem to be extremely fond of sugar and show an innate preference for it. In our evolutionary past, sugar would have been relatively scarce, provided by fruit and berries that were seasonal at best. In modern times sweet foods are everywhere. Our drinks are laced with sugar, fruit is available all year round in vast quantities to say nothing of the rows and rows of chocolate and other confectionery available everywhere. If we are naturally accepting of sweet foods, this excess availability is likely to cause some people a good deal of difficulty. Whereas in the past sugars would have been eaten sparingly and stored carefully, now they are eaten widely whenever people desire them which, as a food that gives immediate pleasure, is a good deal of the time.

Obesity may also be understood by considering the idea of *environmental uncertainty*. Our distant ancestors did not have the understanding of the environment that we have now, such as the prediction of weather systems, nor did they have technology to preserve varieties of food for long periods. This meant that food supplies were much more uncertain, and they would almost certainly live in periods of both famine and plenty. In these circumstances it would have benefited our ancestors to eat as much as they could whenever they found it simply because they did not know whether this would be their last meal of this kind. If a famine were to arrive, those most likely to survive it would be those who had stored excess energy as fat reserves when they were able.

A study of obesity in Pima Indians might, according to Chamala et al (2008), shed light on the role of genetics and evolution in obesity. Modern Pima Indians have unusually high rates of obesity. The researchers measured the metabolic rates of 200 obese Pima individuals and found that their metabolic efficiency was being influenced by single nucleotide polymorphisms (or SNP, which is a variation in a single DNA site). They suggest that this increased efficiency would have been an evolutionary advantage to Pima Indians who traditionally lived in a harsh semi-desert environment, since they would have needed to get the maximum benefit from what little food there was. Such an increased efficiency works against modern Pima Indians, however, in an environment of high calorific over-consumption. Chamala et al propose that whilst the Pima Indian example is an extreme one, the same principle could help explain obesity in any human population that evolved in a restricted calorie environment.

Gender

NICOLA TAYLOR

You are expected in the examination to show both the skills of knowledge and understanding and the skills of analysis and evaluation in relation to the topic Gender.

Where opportunities for their effective use arise, you will need to demonstrate an appreciation of issues and debates. These include the nature/nurture debate, ethical issues in research, free-will/determinism, reductionism, gender and culture bias and the use of animals in research.

You will also need to demonstrate an understanding of How Science Works. You can do this through the effective use of studies in your answer (as description or evaluation) or where appropriate by evaluating methodology and findings.

WHAT YOU NEED TO KNOW

PSYCHOLOGICAL EXPLANATIONS OF GENDER DEVELOPMENT
- Cognitive developmental theory, including Kohlberg, and gender schema theory
- Explanations for psychological androgyny and gender dysphoria including relevant research

BIOLOGICAL INFLUENCES ON GENDER
- The role of hormones and genes in gender development
- Evolutionary explanations of gender roles
- The biosocial approach to gender development

SOCIAL CONTEXTS OF GENDER ROLE
- Social influences on gender role: e.g. the influence of schools and the media
- Cross-cultural studies of gender role

PSYCHOLOGICAL EXPLANATIONS OF GENDER DEVELOPMENT

During the first days of our life, gender emerges as a way of categorising us: it becomes a fundamental element in our self concept and permeates every facet of our lives. From a very young age, children are labelled as 'boy' or 'girl' and soon learn to label themselves similarly. The terms 'boy' and 'girl' describe their genetically determined biological sex. Children also learn what it means to be 'masculine' and 'feminine.' This is their gender and it encompasses the appropriate characteristics and behaviour for males and females. Gender roles describe the expected contributions of men and women to society – i.e. the role that they play, for example, in parenting and in their occupations. These roles can lead to gender stereotypes: the expectations that society has about the way men and women should behave.

Psychologists have considered many explanations of gender development in an attempt to understand how our awareness of gender emerges and the effect that it has on our behaviour and the behaviour of those around us. In this chapter we will explore the contributions of psychological and biological research and studies into the influence of society on gender development. Psychological explanations help us to understand the development of gender through cognitive theories and provide greater insight into the concept of gender. Biological theories discuss the influence of hormones and genes on gender development, to explore how far gender behaviour is a product of nature. The study of social influences helps us to see how the media and schools can influence our gender and the similarities and differences in gender across cultures.

"You could be asked for one or more cognitive developmental theories in the exam, so make sure to learn both of the theories presented here. If you end up only describing one, remember you can use the other as evaluation."

COGNITIVE DEVELOPMENTAL THEORIES OF GENDER DEVELOPMENT

Cognitive developmental theories emphasise the importance of internal thought processes (cognition) in the development of gender. Whilst a number of theories have been put forward to explain gender development, the two which have attracted the most attention from researchers are presented here: Kohlberg's theory and gender schema theory.

KOHLBERG'S THEORY

Kohlberg (1966) proposed a staged theory of gender development. He said that as a child's cognition matures so does their understanding of gender. This means that they can only acquire concepts of gender when they are 'ready' to acquire this knowledge and this is a crucial aspect in the process of the development of sex roles. Kohlberg states that children go through three stages in the development of their gender.

Stage 1: Gender Identity (2–3 years)

When children achieve gender identity they can label their own sex correctly and can categorise other individuals as boy or girl, man or woman. At this stage children make their judgements based upon the external features that differentiate male from female (e.g. hair length or clothes) and can notice these differences from as young as 15 months. Around the age of 2 children have learned to label these different categories as male and female and at 3 years old can apply the labels to describe themselves as boy or girl. They don't yet have a full understanding of what it means to be male or female or that gender is a fixed trait – i.e. it cannot change at a later date.

Stage 2: Gender Stability (3–7 years)

At this stage children come to understand that their gender remains stable throughout life. They realise that they will stay male or female and have always been male or female. Researchers have tested this by asking children questions such as "When you were a baby were you a boy or a girl?" and "When you grow up will you be a mummy or a daddy?". On achieving gender stability a child can answer these questions correctly, demonstrating their understanding of gender as a fixed trait within themselves.

Stage 3: Gender Consistency (7–12 years)

Even when children recognise that their gender remains fixed throughout life they are confused about the gender of others, regarding change of external feature such as dress or hair length, until they acquire gender consistency. In stage 3 the child develops an understanding of the stability of gender in others regardless of external changes. They no longer use external features of individuals to make judgements about whether they are male or female. This gender consistency stage corresponds with Piaget's concrete operational stage of cognitive development and illustrates the notion of conservation. The ability to conserve means the child understands that even if an object changes externally it fundamentally remains the same. Conservation can be applied to areas such as mass, number and weight.

According to Kohlberg, children will be affected in particular ways by male and female models as they pass through the developmental stages and their cognition matures. Once children identify themselves as boy or girl they will pay more attention to same sex models and start to imitate their behaviour. Maccoby and Jacklin (1974) have termed this *self-socialisation* as it is a process that is independent of other influences such as parental reinforcement. As children achieve gender stability and consistency they are motivated to learn the behaviour that is appropriate and expected of their gender, and sex roles become internalised. Society plays a powerful part in determining what is acceptable and appropriate behaviour for males and females – although it must be remembered that Kohlberg believed gender consistency was the cause of the acquisition of gender stereotypes, not the effect. In other words the child will not respond to societal influences, no matter how powerful, until the right cognitive structural changes have taken place. Only when consistency is achieved and children understand the true difference between male and female will they acquire gender stereotypes.

EVALUATION OF KOHLBERG'S THEORY

Thompson (1975) found that children demonstrated behaviour consistent with Kohlberg's stages. Children aged between 2 and 3 years old were tested on their ability to apply gender labels correctly to themselves and others. The children who were only just 2 could identify different sexes correctly but struggled to label their own gender. The oldest children in the sample could apply gender labels correctly and recognise the category of gender they belonged to. These findings are consistent with Kohlberg's gender identity stage and show the cognitive maturation that takes place as the child ages.

Slaby and Frey (1975) provide support for the sequential order of Kohlberg's stages of gender development but raise questions regarding the age at which children reach the consistency stage and the differences between boys and girls when attending to same sex models. The researchers used interviews to test the stage of development reached by each child and also used a split-screen method to assess their attention to same-sex models. Their findings showed that children as young as five may have already acquired gender consistency and that boys who have reached the consistency stage spend more time attending to same-sex models than do girls at the same stage.

It seems that the understanding of gender consistency has different implications for boys' and girls' self-selection of models. According to social learning theory (Bandura et al, 1963) this may be due to the characteristics of the model, whose impact will be greater if it is perceived to be both powerful and similar to the observer. The children may hold strong stereotypes about the 'power' of the male model and this may affect the extent to which the model is imitated. Thus the boys who had achieved consistency were observing a male model that was both powerful and similar, whereas the girls' female model was perceived as similar but not powerful. This suggests that girls identify less strongly with the female sex role than boys with the male sex role, and it may account for the significant amount of attention paid by the boys to the male in the split-screen method.

Thompson (1975) also found that children as young as two could categorise certain items as belonging to males or females, thus showing an understanding of sex-role stereotyping long before they achieved consistency. A study by Kuhn et al (1978) echoes Thompson's findings, demonstrating that children at 2 years old showed substantial knowledge of sex-role stereotypes. Children were shown one male and one female paper doll and asked to point to the doll that would say 'I am a boy/girl'. They were then asked to point to the doll that would say 'I am strong', or 'When I grow up I will fly an aeroplane'. The strong sex-role stereotypes that the children held were consistent with those prevailing in Western culture.

It is more likely that internal cognitive development and external influences on children's gender development are mutually reinforcing. Much of the research conducted to test Kohlberg's theory supports the idea that children's achievement of gender identity is necessary for them to begin to both identify with the opposite sex and pay attention to same-sex models. However, it is difficult to separate internal and external influences on a child's behaviour. We cannot prove that sex-role stereotyping occurs as a consequence of gender identity and consistency when cognitive influences and external influences are occurring simultaneously throughout the child's life. Kuhn (1978) argues that observations of sex-role differences are apparent from birth, when the treatment of boys and girls by their parents is different because of their gender.

Martin and Little (1990) considered the methodology used to test Kohlberg's theory and concluded that the ways in which gender consistency is tested may seriously underestimate a child's level of understanding. Generally questions are asked about sex change – either of the child themselves or of a picture shown to the child. For instance, children are asked if a child could change sex if wearing opposite-sex clothes or playing with opposite-sex toys. Further research conducted with children aged between 4 and 6 (Martin and Halverson, 1983) showed that children typically respond with a 'pretend response' bias. This suggests that they are considering the questions in a more complex way and answering the question according to the sex the child is pretending to be rather than the true sex.

GENDER SCHEMA THEORY

Kohlberg believed a sophisticated level of understanding of gender was an important influence on a child's motivation to learn appropriate sex roles. Gender schema theory challenges this by claiming

TESTING KOHLBERG'S THEORY – SLABY AND FREY (1975)

The aim of Slaby and Frey's research was to test gender identity; to assess gender stability over time; and to look for evidence of consistency across situations. They used 55 children aged between 2 and 5½ years and gave them an interview to test identity, stability and consistency of gender.

Identity questions: Whilst showing children images of people or dolls they asked: "Is this a boy or a girl?" They also asked the children: "Are you a boy or a girl?"

Stability questions: "When you were a baby were you a little boy or a little girl?" "When you grow up will you be a mummy or a daddy?"

Consistency questions: (To boy): "If you wore a dress would you be a boy or a girl?" (To girl): "If you played football would you be a boy or a girl?" "Could you be a boy/girl if you wanted to be?"

Between two and six weeks after the interview the children were tested again using a different method. They were shown a five minute silent but coloured film split into two screens depicting a male image on one side and a female image on the other. Each was engaged in the same activity at the same time, e.g. playing a musical instrument. The screen hung in front of a one-way mirror, behind which sat an observer who recorded the amount of time the child spent looking at each side of the screen.

Of the 55 children tested, aged between 2 and 5½ years:

97% had achieved gender identity

75% had achieved gender stability

50% had achieved gender consistency

Calculations are based upon the correct answers to the questions asked in the interviews.

All children who had achieved gender stability had also achieved gender identity and likewise for identity and stability if they had achieved gender consistency. Children who had achieved gender consistency were more likely to spend time attending to the same-sex models in the film. It was also found that, among the children who had achieved gender consistency, the boys spent much more time focusing on the same-sex models than the girls did.

The study shows that stages of gender development are sequentially ordered as Kohlberg suggested, and are age-related. However, the findings also show that gender consistency may be acquired earlier than stated in Kohlberg's original work.

Slaby and Frey tried to ensure the reliability of the observer used to judge the focus of each child's attention in the split-screen method through the use of a double-blind procedure. The observer was not aware of the nature of the film or of which level of gender development the child was assessed to be through the interviews.

To help control any possible extraneous variables that might affect gender development, the researchers used a sub-sample of 15 boys and 20 girls to show that there was no correlation between birth order, family size and number of male/female siblings and stage of gender development.

that a child's understanding of gender need only be very basic for them to learn sex stereotypes and show strong preferences for gender-appropriate toys and activities. Both Bem (1981) and Martin and Halverson (1981) propose that a child begins to form a gender schema as soon as they notice that people are organised into categories of male and female. They may be able to make this distinction from as early as 18 months.

Martin and Halverson (1981) describe two types of sex-related schema; the 'in-group, out-group' schema and the 'own-sex' schema. Children begin with the simple in-group, out-group schema: this contains general information about male and female categories – such as behaviour, objects and particular traits or roles as being 'for males' or 'for females'. For instance, a child may make the distinction 'A doll is for a girl' and 'A train is for a boy'. The 'own-sex' schema is a more specific and personalised version consisting of objects, behaviour, traits and roles that are appropriate to their own sex. For example, a child can move the schema on from 'A doll is for a girl' to 'A doll is for a girl. I am a girl: a doll is for me'.

It is believed that schemata develop because children have a tendency to group information and form rules to help them make sense of the complex world around them. This process also helps them to understand where they fit in and is an important step towards establishing a self-identity. The process of developing a complex gender schema becomes more apparent once the child has moved from broad categorisation of people into male and female to placing themselves in one of the categories. They recognise that they belong to the 'in-group' (same sex) and not the 'out-group' (opposite sex). Children also evaluate their 'in-group' and their associated behaviour and activities as positive; and members of the 'out-group' and their associated behaviour and activities as negative. Once the child has established their own group they are motivated to learn more about the behaviour of both groups. They establish behaviour consistent with their own sex and learn to recognise that which is inconsistent. This helps the child to acquire information related to their own-sex schema so that this becomes increasingly more elaborate, containing 'sex-appropriate plans of action' that direct their behaviour. The girl acts consistently with her own sex by playing with dolls but avoiding the train or fire engine. Plans of action become increasingly detailed as the child develops: for instance a boy knows that boys like football so in order to remain consistent with this schema he will need to learn to play football. From this we can see how a child's behaviour is guided and influenced by gender schemata.

Schemata also influence the selection of information for encoding into memory. Information that is consistent with a child's gender schema becomes important and is therefore remembered better than information that is not. Schemata can also be responsible for inaccuracies in recall, as children may 'remember' information that relates to their schema rather than that which they initially observed. For example, on witnessing a woman fixing a car they may recall this event as the woman cleaning the car, as a woman fixing a car is not consistent with their gender schema.

SCHEMATA

A schema (plural schemata) is a cognitive structure that contains information about people, events or experiences. It begins as a basic and simple structure and becomes increasingly complex through experience as information is evaluated and added or rejected. It is like scaffolding that starts out with a few basic pieces and then grows to become detailed and intricate. Once we have a schema we can use it to help organise information and make sense of new experiences. In relation to gender we can use children's drawings as an example to help us understand how a gender schema may grow in complexity. Early figures contain the key elements of a person, namely basic facial features and possibly a few limbs! As children's experience of people increases, the pictures become more developed and include features that distinguish male from female. Later pictures therefore include hair and clothes. As the schema becomes more complex we can see evidence of further gender-related information such as boys playing football, girls with long eyelashes and carrying handbags. These schemata help children make sense of the world and predict what is likely to happen in various situations. Information that matches their schema is added to memory so that the information is organised and new information is related to what is already known.

EVALUATION OF GENDER SCHEMA THEORY

Much of the research carried out to test children's gender development points to the fact that children even as young as two demonstrate knowledge of sex-role stereotypes (Kuhn et al, 1978). This confirms that gender identity and the ability to apply labels correctly is enough for children to develop knowledge of gender stereotypical behaviour. Further research by Martin and Little (1990) supports the concept of the acquisition of only basic gender knowledge prior to an understanding of sex stereotypes. They studied the toy preference of children aged between 2 years 9 months and 5 years 4 months by showing them novel objects. These consisted of everyday items such as a garlic press, hole punch and pizza cutter. The researchers labelled these items as 'objects girls like' or 'objects boys like' and then asked the children to rate which they would like to play with using a smiley faces scale. The labelling encouraged strong sex-typed preferences, with boys and girls choosing the items labelled as appropriate to their sex.

Gender schema theory claims that children apply negative evaluations to the opposite sex and positive evaluations to their own sex once they have established an 'in-group, out-group schema'. Kuhn et al (1978) found that as children come to recognise their gender as permanent and irreversible they tend to describe their own gender characteristics as good and those traditionally associated with the opposite sex as bad. When describing attributes of the opposite sex, girls said that boys fight and they are mean and boys said girls cry and they are slow. Neither boys nor girls described themselves as having these negative attributes.

Research by Liben and Signorella (1993) supports gender schema theory by providing evidence that an established gender schema leads to a better memory for gender consistent stereotypes. They tested children between 5 and 10 years old by showing them black and white line drawings of men and women involved in household chores, leisure activities or at work. The pictures showed both men and women in stereotypical and non-stereotypical roles. Each child was shown 60 pictures at a rate of one per second and then after five minutes was asked to free recall as many of the pictures as they could. Images included fighting fire, washing dishes and chopping wood. The children had higher recall of traditional pictures of men depicted in masculine pursuits than of non-traditional pictures of men in feminine roles.

Jennings (1975), however, argues for the influence of distinctive information on recall, as research has shown that a novel item in a scene is often easily remembered. This may only affect short-term recall as, in the long-term, information would be transformed to be schema-consistent.

In terms of the effect that gender schemata have on memory the theory also predicts that information that is not consistent with a gender schema will be subject to distortion and reconstruction. As part of Carter and Levy's (1988) research, children aged between 3 and 5 were shown 16 pictures of males and females. Half of the images for each sex were consistent with gender stereotypes and the other half were inconsistent. In their recall of these images, children with a developed gender schema made transformational errors. In other words the gender schemata held by the children biased their processing of the images to transform the gender-inconsistent images to memories consistent with the established gender schema. Therefore an image of a woman fixing a car would be transformed to become recalled as a man fixing a car.

Although gender schema theory explains the strength and persistence of stereotypes it does not explain why boys have a much more rigid gender concept than girls. Bauer's (1993) research considers the impact of gender schemata on recall, but highlights differences between very young boys and girls. Twenty-five-month-old boys and girls were shown videos of male and female stereotypical and gender-neutral activities. Girls' recall was equal for all the activity films viewed but boys demonstrated far superior recall of stereotypical male activities at the expense of the stereotypical female activities. This shows that by 25 months, boys are making more use of their gender schemata to recall gender-consistent images and activities. Even babies as young as 3 months old have been found to pay more attention to male faces and activities than to ones that are female, regardless of their own sex (Shirley and Campbell, 2000).

As their gender schema develops, boys show stronger and earlier preferences for typically male activities and are more avoidant of the opposite sex and things associated with the opposite sex than girls. Girls develop more flexible gender concepts (Archer, 1989). This is not necessarily consistent with gender schema theory. Explanations for these differences could be social, biological or evolutionary. Martin and Halverson (1981) admit it is possible that children could show 'sex-typing of behaviour' before an age at which schemata are present. They suggest that to explain this we would need to consider biological tendencies that could be present in children from a very young age. Bem (1993) supports the idea that men and women are biologically different and will naturally have different roles to play, with women as nurturers and men as providers. She says that "the distinction between male and female serves as a basic organising principle for every human culture". She claims that there may be a biological tendency for humans to develop a gender schema since gender has evolved to be such a fundamentally important way for humans to categorise themselves. Sex is biologically determined but the attributes associated with each sex are also culturally determined. From birth, gender provides a key distinction, with boys dressed in blue and girls in pink. Early socialisation through parenting often provides boys with a different experience from girls. Research suggests that boys are spoken to more loudly and handled in a more robust manner than girls. In Western culture, females are allowed a more flexible gender concept, with the image of a 'tom-boy' being acceptable. The boundaries for boys are more rigidly drawn, however, and this could account for earlier and stronger gender schemata in males. Benenson et al (1998), suggest that there may be an evolutionary basis for stronger gender schemata in boys. In our evolutionary past, boys may have been under more pressure to form bonds with other males in order to become an organised and successful hunting group. The success of the hunt meant survival for the whole group, whereas females would benefit more from forming relationships and bonds with relatives in supporting the survival of offspring.

EXPLANATIONS FOR PSYCHOLOGICAL ANDROGYNY

Research into cognitive developmental theories of gender provides evidence of high sex-stereotyping from a very young age. Despite this evidence and the tremendous influence from society in maintaining these stereotypes there are individuals who are not highly sex-stereotyped (Bem, 1974). Traditionally these people may have been judged as not only atypical but as exhibiting some sort of mental disorder. More recent theories have recognised the restriction that traditional masculine and feminine roles may exert on a person's individuality and ability to adapt successfully to the demands of the environment. Bem (1974) questioned the polarisation of masculinity and femininity which

argued that to be masculine meant an individual was lacking in feminine traits and to be feminine meant an individual was lacking in masculine traits. She proposed that individuals could possess high levels of both masculinity and femininity and that this could apply to both men and women. She labelled such persons 'androgynous'. According to Bem the expression of these masculine and feminine traits may depend upon the 'situational appropriateness' of these behaviours. So a person, regardless of their biological sex, may be assertive when necessary or supportive and nurturing if the situation demanded. This co-existence of masculine and feminine traits within the same individual results in an ability to respond appropriately and effectively to the demands of the environment. Bem predicted that the adaptability of the androgynous person compared to the non-androgynous person made them more psychologically healthy and have a higher self-esteem.

Androgyny is based on how the individual perceives themselves and is not related to their gender schema (Bem, 1974). A woman may have a schema for the norms of feminine behaviour and understand the traditional stereotype of 'female', but still recognise traditionally masculine traits within herself. Thus androgyny is part of the self-concept and could be termed 'self-schema' rather than gender schema. Androgyny is therefore about traits and resulting behaviour. Fashion and popular media present images of 'androgynous individuals'. These are often women in men's suits with short hair or men wearing make-up and flamboyant clothes. Psychological androgyny is not about ambiguous physical appearance: it is about the high levels of both masculine and feminine traits that an individual is able to recognise within themselves.

The measurement of androgyny

Bem (1974) developed the the Bem Sex Role Inventory (BSRI) to measure an individual's sex-role type. Characteristics were categorised as male or female according to their social desirability within the American culture. For instance a characteristic was judged as masculine if it was deemed a more desirable trait in a man than in a woman and vice versa for females. Bem also listed a set of neutral traits that were judged to be neither masculine nor feminine but could apply equally to both sexes. Sixty characteristics in all were listed with 20 feminine, 20 masculine and 20 neutral. The individual is asked to indicate on a 7 point scale how well each of the characteristics describes him or herself. A score of 1 indicates that the particular characteristic is never or almost never true and a score of 7 indicates the characteristic as always or almost always true.

MASCULINE	FEMININE	NEUTRAL
Aggressive	Tender	Conscientious
Ambitious	Loves children	Happy
Independent	Shy	Reliable
Athletic	Affectionate	Tactful
Dominant	Understanding	Truthful

Table showing examples of masculine, feminine and neutral traits (Bem, 1974).

On the basis of their response each person has a score for masculinity, femininity and androgyny. The scores reflect the relative amounts of masculine and feminine traits a person includes in their description of themselves. According to Bem, this test reveals four basic sex-role types:

Masculine – this person scores high on masculine traits but low on feminine traits.

Feminine – this person scores high on feminine traits and low on masculine traits.

Androgynous – this person scores high on both masculine and feminine traits.

Undifferentiated – this person scores low on both masculine and feminine traits.

		MASCULINITY SCORE	
		High	Low
FEMININITY SCORE	High	Androgynous	Feminine
	Low	Masculine	Undifferentiated

The classification of sex-typing using the BSRI.

The BSRI attempts to measure gender objectively but gender is flexible and may even change over time – unlike a person's sex, which is biologically determined and can therefore be measured objectively.

Bem (1975) conducted a study to demonstrate the adaptability of androgynous individuals compared with masculine and feminine sex-typed individuals. The sex-typed person is motivated to behave in a way that is consistent with their stereotype for masculine and feminine behaviour. This stereotype is internalised and governs their responses to situations so that they suppress any behaviour that is deemed to be undesirable or inappropriate for their sex. Bem (1975) constructed a study which showed that the androgynous person is free of these constraints and behaves in a way that is most effective for the situation they are in. Using conditions to facilitate typical masculine and feminine behaviour (i.e. demonstrating independence and playful behaviour) she found that androgynous individuals of both sexes responded well to both situations. Thus the androgynous individual was able to adapt their behaviour to the situation rather than behave according to the constraints of gender stereotypes.

Further evidence for the psychologically healthy and well adjusted androgynous person comes from Rose and Montemayor (1994). The aim of their study was to examine the relationship between sex-type and self-esteem in adolescents. They measured the gender orientation of participants aged 12–18 years using the Children's Sex Role Inventory (Bodizar, 1991). This is a simplified version of the BSRI, adapted to use language that is more accessible to young people. The participants also completed a perceived self-competency questionnaire, rating themselves in areas such as academic performance, athleticism, social competency and global self-worth. The ones assessed as androgynous scored consistently higher in all areas compared with those classified as masculine, feminine or undifferentiated. The findings support the hypothesis that androgynous people are psychologically healthier and have a higher self-esteem than those with a traditional sex type.

THE DEVELOPMENT OF PSYCHOLOGICAL ANDROGYNY

How psychological androgyny develops is a difficult question to answer. Certainly there is very little evidence to show signs of androgyny in children younger than 10 years old. It would appear that, until this point, children's sex-role ideas are still very rigid. Martin and Halverson (1981) discuss the possibility that children may learn appropriate behaviour for both sexes but only display behaviour that is reinforced. Since generally the environment does not reinforce

TESTING THE PSYCHOLOGICAL HEALTH OF ANDROGYNOUS ADULTS

Bem (1975) aimed to demonstrate the adaptability and psychological health of androgynous individuals when compared with traditional sex-typed individuals. Her participants were students at Stanford University studying psychology. They were all asked to complete the BSRI to determine their sex-role type. The participants selected for the study were nine masculine, nine feminine and nine androgynous individuals of each sex. Her study used two separate situations: one to stimulate a typically masculine response and the second to encourage typical feminine behaviour.

Masculine condition:

In the first situation participants were placed in a soundproof booth with headphones and asked to rate a series of cartoons for how funny they found them. Prior to giving their own rating they could hear the responses of 'others' through the headphones (these were actually recorded, not 'live'). The test was designed to see how much the participant would conform to the recorded responses when giving their own rating. This demonstrates each participant's willingness to exert independent behaviour; a typically masculine trait. As predicted, those subjects previously sex-typed as masculine and androgynous conformed on fewer trials and therefore showed greater independence than the participants sex-typed as feminine.

Feminine condition:

In the second situation participants were observed playing with an 8-week-old kitten under two conditions; one when they were instructed to interact with the kitten and in a second condition when they had a choice of activities including playing with the kitten. This was designed to elicit playfulness and nurturing behaviour – typical feminine traits. The most significant findings were amongst the androgynous males, who were involved far more in playing with the kitten than the masculine males.

Bem concluded that androgynous individuals of both sexes showed high levels of masculine independence and feminine playfulness and thus demonstrated behaviour that matched the situation rather than typical sex-role stereotypes.

inappropriate behaviour, it is not performed. This opposes the gender schema theory which states that it is lack of knowledge of how to perform this behaviour that prevents the behaviour from being displayed. Flexibility in gender behaviour can only occur if the individual has learned how to perform non-stereotypical, inappropriate behaviour. Gender schema theory also claims, however, that sex-stereotyping is not easily modified even when the child is exposed to new and contradictory evidence. So it would seem that gender schema, once established, is very difficult to influence and change.

In considering the development of androgynous behaviour in individuals, it is important to remember the nature of schemata. They become more complex as they are used to make sense of new situations. It is therefore possible that for some individuals their schemata become more flexible as they widen their experiences. As children grow older and develop in their cognitive maturity, they also become involved with more social groups and this adds to their self-image. They may add information to their self schemata to define themselves as good musicians, students or actors. These traits could equally apply to both male and female and cut across the gender groups so the growing child learns that, rather than being strictly defined, the

rules regarding gender become more blurred. Older children lose the in-group, out-group aspect of stereotyping and sex roles become less central to their thinking. "As schemas become more differentiated there will be more overlap between 'male' and 'female' things and consequently less evaluation will be associated with being consistent with their own sex schema" (Martin and Halverson, 1981). It seems as though a flexible view of sex-typing is only possible once a certain level of cognitive development has been reached. This explains why only older children show androgynous behaviour as younger children's concrete thinking does not allow for this flexibility. In this approach to explaining androgyny, there are two key elements: firstly, the child must be at a stage of cognitive development that allows flexibility of thinking; secondly, the appropriate reinforcement must be available in the environment if the child is to display behaviour that is inappropriate to their sex.

EVALUATION OF PSYCHOLOGICAL ANDROGYNY EXPLANATION

Bem (1983) considered the role of society in teaching children about gender and set about explaining how parents could manipulate the environment to create a gender-aschematic child. This involved suggestions such as parents eliminating sex-stereotyping of chores, ensuring that the child had a range of toys to play with appropriate to both boys and girls and censoring books and television programmes. She believed that eliminating cultural influence could slow down the formation of the network of information that forms the gender schema. According to Bem the concept of gender should be based upon biology and not culture. Therefore a child should be taught that gender should be defined by anatomy – i.e. whether one is male or female only makes a difference within the context of reproduction. This supports the idea of environmental influence on gender behaviour, although Bem herself criticises this approach for its attempts to create an androgynous individual who has to be successful as both a male and a female. This androgynous individual now has two potential sources of inadequacy as opposed to the traditional one source. This also criticises the idea that the androgynous person is more psychologically healthy than the traditionally sex-typed person, who only has to be successful as either a male or a female.

A review of research into androgyny (Sedney, 1987) concludes that whilst androgynous parents do not produce androgynous children, the children themselves often grow up to be androgynous adults. A longitudinal study conducted by Block et al (1973) supports the idea that androgyny is a long-term consequence of non-sex-typed parenting. Information was obtained from interviews and observations of parents and their children and then compared with data collected from the 'children' when in their 30s. Two key factors emerged that encouraged the development of androgyny: first, a warm and supportive family atmosphere with psychologically healthy parents who were satisfied with their life and marriage; and second, flexibility in the definition of social roles with parents demonstrating androgynous personality styles. According to Sedney (1987) the effects of parental influence are delayed and although the young child may be raised in an androgynous environment at home they still opt for stereotypical behaviour. The combined forces of the child's cognitive immaturity and the strength of cultural pressure mean that parental influence at this stage has little visible impact. Huston (1983) claims that stereotypically sex-typed behaviour may be a result of processes that are much more complex than society. This can be shown in the way that children use gender as a means of organising information from a very early age and need little direct instruction in order to do so.

Research by Guastello and Guastello (2003) challenges the idea of parental influence on psychological androgyny in adulthood, as their research revealed a difference in levels of androgyny across generations. They examined 576 students and their parents on levels of androgyny, gender-role behaviour and emotional intelligence. They found that sons were more androgynous than their fathers but that daughters showed a 1.2% decline in androgyny compared with their mothers. Interestingly, the daughters demonstrated an increase in masculine gender-typing of 20.4% when compared with their mothers. This shows that there are factors at work other than parental influence in the formation of androgyny in adulthood. This research also supports early criticisms of androgyny as a sign of mental health in an individual. Instead, the research suggested that it was masculine traits that were positively associated with mental health and high self-esteem. However, Guastello and Guastello (2003) also found significant correlations between indicators of androgyny and emotional intelligence in both generations. This is interesting, as we know that an androgynous individual scores high on both masculine and feminine traits and that emotional intelligence is related to positive mental health. It should follow, therefore, that the androgynous person is psychologically healthy.

EMOTIONAL INTELLIGENCE

According to Salovey and Mayer (1990) emotional intelligence is an ability to accurately assess, express and regulate your own emotions and accurately appraise and respond to the emotions of others. Basic emotional intelligence involves being able to detect and decipher emotions accurately through facial expression and tone of voice. More sophisticated levels of emotional intelligence involve understanding the subtleties of emotion and how they change over time and require an ability to manage emotions in ourselves and others. Negative emotions can be harnessed in a positive way to achieve goals and emotions can be used to facilitate thought and solve problems. According to Guastello and Guastello (2003) emotionally intelligent people express a wider range of gender-role behaviour than people who are not as emotionally knowledgeable. Traditionally sex-typed individuals have rigid and simplistic expectations about emotional expression and do not have a flexible repertoire of social actions: these characteristics make them less adaptive than androgynous and emotionally intelligent people.

EXPLANATIONS FOR GENDER DYSPHORIA

Gender dysphoria is also known as *gender identity disorder*: it is characterised by a mismatch between the external appearance of a person and the way they feel with regard to their gender. With a 'normal' male or female, outward appearance is unambiguous. People with gender identity disorder have a normal outward appearance, which is unambiguously male or female – but they are uncomfortable with that appearance.

"You could be asked about either psychological androgyny or gender dysphoria in the exam. Prepare for this!"

They feel as though they have been born the wrong sex. In the past this was known as transsexualism and although the individual may cross-dress to feel more comfortable, the condition is distinct from transvestism as the person achieves no sexual arousal from dressing as the opposite sex. Dysphoria means unease or unhappiness and, in their attempts to alleviate the distress caused by the disorder, some individuals opt for sex reassignment surgery to change their external genitalia and appearance to those of the opposite sex. Gender identity disorder may be apparent in children from around 2 years old when they may express a desire to be the opposite sex and show a preference for clothes and toys belonging to the opposite sex. As they get older they may avoid games and activities traditionally associated with their sex and may even express disgust with their genitalia, particularly when going through puberty.

CASE STUDY 1

William, a boy approaching 4 years old with an IQ of 111, was referred because of parental and teacher concern regarding his gender identity development. Prior to the age of 2, he developed an 'obsessional' interest in women's shoes and clothing. He loved to walk around in his mother's shoes. He often placed items of clothing, such as sweatpants, on his head, to simulate long hair. He often would wear his mother's T-shirts during the day and to bed. Because they were so big on him, he appeared to experience the T-shirt as a dress. At the time of the assessment, William preferred to play with girls, although his parents were concerned that at times he was SO absorbed in fantasy play that he took little interest in other children. He was preoccupied with witches. He cross-dressed daily at nursery school. His toy and role interests were predominantly feminine. He only enjoyed books whose central characters were female. He showed little interest in rough-and-tumble play. Most concerning to his parents was William's repetitive insistence for the past six months that he was a girl and that he had a 'hole', not a penis. During the clinical interview, William displayed a rigid, constricted preoccupation with femininity, talking about wicked witches and his belief that he was a girl.

DSM IV CRITERIA FOR GENDER DYSPHORIA (GENDER IDENTITY DISORDER) IN CHILDREN

It is important to remember that physical abnormalities of the sex organs are rarely associated with GID. It's also important not to confuse this disorder with the phenomenon of intersex children, who will be discussed in the next section of the chapter.

DSM stands for Diagnostic and Statistical Manual. The DSM criteria, listed below, provide a way of categorising and listing symptoms of psychological abnormalities.

A.   A strong and persistent cross-gender identification (not merely a desire for any perceived cultural advantages of being the other sex). In children, the disturbance is manifested by four (or more) of the following:

    1.   repeatedly stated desire to be, or insistence that he or she is, the other sex

    2.   in boys, preference for cross-dressing or simulating female attire; in girls, insistence on wearing only stereotypical masculine clothing

    3.   strong and persistent preferences for cross-sex roles in make-believe play or persistent fantasies of being the other sex

    4.   intense desire to participate in the stereotypical games and pastimes of the other sex

    5.   strong preference for playmates of the other sex.

B.   Persistent discomfort with his or her sex or sense of inappropriateness in the gender role of that sex.

C.   The disturbance is not concurrent with a physical intersex condition.

D.   The disturbance causes clinically significant distress or impairment in social, occupational or other important areas of functioning.

"Be aware that the terms gender dysphoria and gender identity disorder basically mean the same thing, although the latter is in more common usage these days."

CASE STUDY 2

Alice, a 4-year-old girl with an IQ of 125, was referred because of parental and teacher concern regarding her gender identity development. Around the age of 2, Alice's parents reported that she reacted with great upset to her exclusion from rough-and-tumble play by her older male cousins. Ostensibly, this was because Alice was prone to severe asthma attacks and they did not want her to get very over-stimulated.

In any case Alice began to insist on wearing stereotypically masculine clothing (e.g. corduroy pants, shirts) and rejected with vehemence any clothing that was typical for girls (e.g. dresses, bows etc.). Her toy and role interests were masculine. Her kindergarten teacher mistook her for a boy because of her physical appearance (hairstyle and clothing cues). What most concerned Alice's parents was her insistence that she was a boy and that she was preoccupied with acquiring a penis. She would cry when told that she could not use scissors to cut off her younger brother's penis and attach it to herself.

Prevalence of gender dysphoria in males and females

The rate of gender identity disorder, although relatively low, is five times greater in males than in females. This is based upon statistics for those diagnosed according to the DSM IV criteria. It is interesting to consider why this might be. Zucker and Green (1992) suggest that it may be due to greater biological vulnerability in boys during the early stage of foetal development. During this stage the development of a male foetus depends upon the production of the hormone androgen. If appropriate androgen secretion does not occur, or if the cell receptors do not respond to androgen, then the foetus will develop as a female. Put simply, partial secretion or partial response to secretion of androgen could lead to incomplete male development. Zucker and Green (1992) also consider the importance of society in explaining the difference in the statistics as figures are based upon those who have reported their condition

and been diagnosed. It may be that society is less tolerant of cross-gender behaviour in boys and so they are more likely to refer themselves or be referred by their parents when they are children. Girls may need to show more extreme opposite sex behaviour than boys before they are referred. So it may be that there are just as many females as males meeting the criteria for the disorder but that fewer female cases are reported. Consideration of the differences in statistics raises the question of how gender identity disorder develops and already we can see that explanations are diverse, ranging from biological to social.

Explanations of dysphoria: separation anxiety

Coates and Person (1985) suggested that separation anxiety plays an important role in the development of gender identity disorder in boys. They claim that the anxiety caused by separation must be severe to result in feminine behaviour, which they say is an attempt to 'restore a fantasy tie to the physically or emotionally absent mother'. In an attempt to soothe the anxiety created by maternal separation the boy demonstrates cross-gender behaviour but in imitating his mother he confuses being her with the experience of her comfort or presence. In their study of 25 boys with gender identity disorder Coates and Person (1985) found that 15 of them (60%) also met the criteria for separation anxiety disorder. Further research to support these findings comes from Lowry and Zucker (1991) who found that, from a sample of 29 boys with gender identity disorder, 16 (55%) were diagnosed with separation anxiety. It is difficult to infer a causal relationship from these studies as both disorders were diagnosed at the same time. We cannot therefore claim that separation anxiety could cause gender identity disorder – only that there is a possible relationship between the two disorders. Support is provided for the idea that boys with gender identity disorder often show difficulties in their attachment relationships with their mothers. Bailey and Zucker (1995) noted, however, that children frequently suffered from other behavioural problems including depression in childhood and argued that this could be a result of the stigma attached to a child with gender identity disorder and the subsequent stress involved.

Explanations of dysphoria: parental influences

Case histories of boys with gender identity disorder reveal details of reinforcement of traditionally feminine behaviour – for example mothers giving young boys attention for dressing in girls' clothes and declaring them 'cute'. (Rekers and Lovaas, 1974). This has led to research into the area of parental influence as an explanation for gender identity disorder. Early research by Green (1974) found that in a sample of 'feminine' boys 15% had been dressed in girls' clothes during infancy and as toddlers. Stoller (1975) studied the facial features of boys with gender identity disorder and found that when asked to describe their sons' facial features in infancy, the mothers typically used terms to express feminine beauty. Stoller's research revealed that often these boys were physically attractive. Although he emphasised the importance of parental influence on the child's behaviour, he thought it more likely that the attractiveness of the boy acted as a trigger for parental feminisation particularly from the mother. Behavioural signs of gender identity disorder appear early and are often apparent in toddlers and pre-school children. It is difficult, however, to ascertain whether these behavioural differences are shaped by the parents' behaviour or whether the parents are responding to differences that already exist. Green (1987) studied a group of 'feminine' boys and a control group. He asked the parents of both groups of boys to recall the faces of their children in infancy and describe their appearance. The parents of the 'feminine' boys were more likely to use terms such as 'beautiful' and 'feminine' than the parents of the control group. Green did consider that, as this was a retrospective study, the parents' recall could be distorted by the current feminine appearance of their sons. In children with gender identity disorder the pattern of opposite sex behaviour is so distinct that it would need extreme environmental responses to explain its existence. Parents would not just have to be tolerant of their child's cross-sex behaviour: they would need to be actively and consistently promoting it. To assess the impact of parental influence, it is necessary to study parents of both 'normal' children and a sample whose children have gender identity disorder, to compare their reactions to their child's cross-sex behaviour. This is very difficult, however, as 'normal' children rarely show cross-sex behaviour (Roberts et al, 1987).

Explanations of dysphoria: biology

The idea of the influence of sex hormones during foetal development has already been discussed as a possible explanation for higher prevalence of gender identity disorder amongst males. Most of the research to support this proposal comes from studies of non-human animals. Female foetuses exposed to male levels of androgens (male hormones) during development in the womb typically demonstrate masculine behaviour when born. Similarly if a male foetus is under-exposed to the necessary levels of androgens his behaviour will become feminised (Dixson, 1998). Research like this cannot be carried out on humans and any evidence of hormones as an explanation for gender identity disorder comes from inter sex children whose external genitalia have been affected by hormonal anomalies. Abnormality of the external genitalia is not characteristic of gender identity disorder, however: studies conducted with female rhesus monkeys show masculinisation can occur in behaviour without altering external appearance. This supports the assumption that if it can occur in primates it could possibly explain gender identity disorder in humans.

A study by Zucker et al (2001) attempted to find a relationship between gender identity disorder and neurobiological abnormality by studying the link between boys with gender identity disorder and their handedness. There are two possible explanations for left-handedness: one is genetic and the other refers to pre-natal stress (Staz, 1973). Pre-natal stress could include exposure to ultrasound, smoking, premature birth or birth stress. Developmental instability refers to the degree of vulnerability of a foetus to environmental stressors during development and has been associated with various indicators of Darwinian fitness – e.g. resistance to disease, rate of growth and reproductive success. Yeo and Gangestad (1998) have noted that left-handedness is associated with indicators of reduced fitness including lower birth weight. It is possible that left-handedness in boys provides an indication of general instability in neurodevelopment. In the study by Zucker et al (2001) they compared 205 boys with gender identity disorder with 205 controls: 19.5% of the gender identity disorder group were found to be left-handed, compared with 8.3% of the controls. This provides evidence that left-handedness may be a behavioural marker indicating an underlying neurobiological process associated with gender identity disorder. Interestingly, Zucker et al (1999) also found, in a comparison of boys with gender identity disorder and a control group, that the former weighed significantly less at birth – supporting the idea of a link between developmental instability in the foetal stage and gender identity disorder.

Another biological explanation is known as brain-sex theory and it relates to the difference in size between particular brain structures in males and females. Allen and Gorski (1990) compared the brains of 26 age-matched male and female human subjects. They found an area of the brain known as the bed nucleus of the stria terminalis (BNST) which is thought to influence sexual behaviour. The volume of the BNST was 2.47 times greater in males than females. Zhou et al (1995) studied the brains of transsexuals and found the BNST to be the same size in male-to-female transsexuals as it was in females. This is supported by Kruijver et al (2000) who found that the number of neurons in the BNST of male-to-female transsexuals was similar to that of females; and the neuron number of a female-to-male transsexual was found to be in the normal male range. These results support the hypothesis that gender identity develops as a result of an interaction between the developing brain and sex hormones – although the BNST may be only one of many structures involved in gender identity.

BIOLOGICAL INFLUENCES ON GENDER

Biology has already played a part in helping us to understand gender identity disorder. The brain-sex theory and exposure to pre-natal hormones explains why some individuals feel as though they are trapped inside the wrong body. It makes sense, therefore, to explore the role of biology in 'normal' gender development, particularly in helping us to understand *how* gender develops and *why* gender roles are different for males and females.

THE ROLE OF HORMONES AND GENES IN GENDER DEVELOPMENT

When we refer to an individual's biological sex we are identifying a person as male or female chromosomally, i.e. whether they are XX female or XY male. A person's biological sex is determined at the time of conception by the father's sperm. As females have two X chromosomes, the ovum (egg) that the woman produces contains the X chromosome. Men have two different sex chromosomes so half of the male sperm contain X chromosomes and the other half contain Y chromosomes. Whether the resulting foetus is male or female is therefore determined by which sperm fertilises the ovum (egg).

The X and Y chromosomes responsible for determining biological sex.

The Y chromosome controls the development of the glands that produce male sex hormones. Up until the sixth week of development in the womb, both foetuses have identical gonads (sex glands). These have the potential to develop into ovaries or testes. The factor that determines the direction of their development is contained within the Y chromosome. In the sixth week of pre-natal development the Y chromosome produces a protein which causes the undifferentiated gonads to become testes and sets the path of male development for the foetus. If the protein is not present (i.e. if the fertilising sperm did not contain a Y chromosome) the gonads become ovaries. Once the gonads have developed, further sexual development is triggered by the release of sex hormones. Up until the sixth week all foetuses, regardless of their genetic potential, contain the same internal sex organs, which have the potential to grow into either male or female sex organs. Thus in effect they are bisexual. There are two parts to the undifferentiated gonads, called the Mullerian system and the Wolffian system. The Mullerian system has the potential to develop into the female sex organs and the Wolffian system is the precursor to the male sex organs. During the third month of foetal development only part of this system develops and the other part dies away. The part that develops is determined by the release of hormones from the testes. If testes are present male hormones (androgens) are released and the Wolffian system develops; if androgens are not present the Mullerian system develops. No release of hormones from the ovaries is necessary for the female sex organs and reproductive system to develop. There are two different androgens responsible for masculinisation: these are called testosterone and dihydrotestosterone. Their role is two-fold: pre-natally they influence the development of the male sex organs and masculinise the brain; and

A STUDY OF NATURALLY OCCURRING SEX CHANGE – IMPERATO-MCGINLEY ET AL (1974)

The researchers discovered a rare genetic disorder amongst 24 individuals across 13 families in the village of Salinas in the Dominican Republic. The individuals studied ranged in age from 18 months to 60 years. The frequency of normal to affected males in the village, where the population was 4,300, was 90:1. The 24 individuals studied were born with ambiguous external genitalia and raised as girls until at puberty their voices grew deeper, muscle mass increased, testes descended and the clitoral-like phallus enlarged to become a fully functional penis. By studying across an age range, the researchers were able to see that as these individuals grew older they never developed acne or receding hair, had very little or no beard growth, and a small or non-existent prostate gland. It was thought that these physical changes were likely to be absent due to the lack of metabolism of dihydrotestosterone and that it was the lack of the action of this hormone in the womb that also accounted for the female like external appearance of the individuals at birth. During puberty the flood of testosterone produced enough dihydrotestosterone for the normal male appearance to be generated. The researchers concluded that both testosterone and dihydrotestosterone are necessary for the complete emergence of male features. What is particularly interesting from a gender development point of view is the fact that the men had a male sexual orientation even though they had been raised as girls for the first 12 years of life. They were able to change their gender identity successfully at the time of puberty so that they considered themselves male and were sexually attracted to females. This suggests that exposure to testosterone in the womb and at puberty is the dominant factor in determining gender identity.

post-natally they are responsible for activating the sex organs during puberty. In summary the development of biological sex is determined by the Y chromosome which, if present, is responsible for the interruption of natural female development. This idea was proposed by Jost (1970) based upon his research with rats and rabbits. He discovered that if the ovaries are removed from an embryo a female offspring is still the end result, whereas if the testes are removed the embryo reverts to female development.

"Biology! The specification requires you to know about the role of genes and hormones and sometimes there is no getting away from the fact that you just have to put the effort into coming to terms with this stuff. You could be asked an exam question on biological influences – what are you going to talk about then if not the biology?!"

It is clear that pre-natal exposure to hormones, particularly androgens, impacts upon biological development: however we also need to consider whether their influence affects behaviour. The major question to be considered in gender development is whether gender-appropriate behaviour is a product of hormonal influence or whether socialisation is the overriding factor in determining gender-related behaviour. One way of answering this question would be to take a child of one sex and raise it as the opposite sex to see how it eventually ended up. This has obvious ethical implications: however, rare case studies of

unusual individuals (including those carried out by Imperato-McGinley and Money) have aided psychologists in this quest.

"Case studies can be used in lots of ways. They are useful ways to illustrate a point thereby gaining you descriptive marks or they can be used as evaluation to support or criticise something."

The case studies of Imperato-McGinley et al and Money provide persuasive evidence that biology is the most powerful factor in determining both physical and psychological gender development. The influence of genes and hormones, it would seem, cannot be overridden by socialisation. The way that we develop as males and females, with the different attributes that this brings, must therefore be understood from a biological approach.

The biologist Milton Diamond also believes that, like animals, humans are born with an instinctive set of behaviours to act male or female. During the 1950s he was involved in experiments with animals that showed the influence of testosterone on gender development. Pregnant rats were injected with testosterone and the effect on the female offspring was that their genitals were male-like in appearance and they attempted to mate with other female rats. Naturalistic studies of humans offer some support for the role of testosterone. Money and Ehrhardt (1972) studied children born with androgenital syndrome due to hormone treatment received by their mothers while pregnant.

Female foetuses exposed to androgens in utero later showed more masculine behaviour than a control group comparison. In this study however, we cannot rule out the effects of socialisation. Children with androgenital syndrome are often born with genital abnormalities and therefore behaviour towards the child or even the child's own behaviour may be affected as a result. Gorski (1980) supports the idea of testosterone affecting a structure in the brain – namely the hypothalamus. He identified an area in the brain of rats called the sexually dimorphic nucleus which is twice as big in males as it is in females. He repeated Diamond's experiments and injected pregnant female rats with testosterone and again the resulting female offspring exhibited male-like behaviour. Gorski also examined the rats' brains and found the female rats had a sexually dimorphic nucleus which resembled that of a male in size. The nucleus had been affected by the levels of testosterone whilst still in the womb. The difficulty with this research is that it was conducted with animals and though Gorski hypothesised that the same difference in

the structure of the sexually dimorphic nucleus would be apparent in humans, he could not prove that this was the case.

More convincing evidence comes from the study of human brains (Swaab, 1997). Post-mortems of human brains revealed a sexually dimorphic nucleus in males that was twice the size of that in females. However, this only shows that male and female brains are structurally different: it does not explain the differences in gender identity. In order to discover whether our gender identity is contained within the sexually dimorphic nucleus, Gorski studied the brains of transsexuals. These people are unique in that their physical appearance is normal but they feel as though they are trapped in the wrong body. Gorski wanted to know whether this was because they were born with the 'wrong' nucleus and after much painstaking research he found this to be the case. Male transsexuals were found to have a sexually dimorphic nucleus that resembled a female. It seems as though this area of the hypothalamus in the brain is responsible for our sense of gender identity. Can

THE CIRCUMCISION THAT WENT WRONG – JOHN MONEY (1972)

David Reimer

In 1965 in Winnipeg, Canada, identical twin boys Bruce and Brian Reimer were born. At 6 months old they had trouble urinating and doctors advised circumcision to relieve the problem. During the operation an unfortunate accident meant that Bruce's penis was completely burnt off. For months the twins' parents did not know what to do until they saw John Money giving an interview on television. He was a pioneer in sex change surgery for intersex children. Money believed that gender identity was not programmed by genes and hormones but by how we are socialised. He claimed that children's brains were malleable up until the age of 2 and that any effects of pre-natal hormonal exposure could be overridden by socialisation. His work with intersex children supported this idea. Intersex children are exposed to an imbalance of hormones in the womb so chromosomal females may be born with the external appearance of a male and vice versa. This gave the Reimers hope that there might be a life for their son as a girl. At 22 months old Bruce's testes were removed and there followed a succession of reconstructive operations and hormone treatment. He was renamed Brenda and raised as a girl. The case was declared a success. However, by the age of 13 Brenda was deeply troubled and felt 'wrong' as a girl. Her parents decided that it was time to reveal her true sex at birth and within months she decided to become David and had hormone treatment and a penis reconstruction. In 1998, when it came to light that the original treatment had been unsuccessful, Money attempted to explain why this might be. He claimed that at 22 months the child might have been too old for a successful gender reassignment to take place. He also said that having an identical twin brother could have increased the sense of abnormality that 'Brenda' felt and that the trauma experienced by the parents could have impacted upon successful transition. However the fact remains that David was born a normal boy with a normal balance of hormones during pre-natal development and a fully masculinised brain – unlike the intersex children, whose exposure to hormone imbalance could have not only altered their physical appearance but also affected the development of sex areas in the brain. The exposure to normal levels of androgens during pre-natal development seems to have been the most important factor in determining David's gender identity.

this then also explain differences in gender behaviour such as are seen in levels of aggression and in skills such as language and spatial ability?

Biological explanations of differences in gender identity

Pre-natal exposure to androgens is thought not only to affect the structure of the sexually dimorphic nucleus in the hypothalamus but also to influence the organisation of the central nervous system (Gorski, 1980). Differences in structure and organisation may impact upon abilities and behaviour. Females with androgenital syndrome who have been exposed to high levels of testosterone in the womb are often more likely to engage in rough-and-tumble play and 'tomboyish' behaviour (Money and Ehrhardt, 1972). However, parents of these girls are aware of their masculinised appearance and may have tolerated or even encouraged this male-like behaviour.

During puberty boys tend to exhibit more aggressive behaviour. This is thought to be because of elevated levels of testosterone during this stage of their development. However, according to Hood et al (1987), levels of hormones fluctuate in response to environmental changes and in stressful situations testosterone levels decrease. Research with non-human males led Hood to conclude that there is no direct link between aggression and hormones, as increases in androgens often *follow* rather than *precede* an aggressive encounter. If hormones do affect gender-related behaviour, perhaps their effects are more subtle and complex than they at first appear. Research by Jacklin et al (1988) illustrates this point. The researchers tested 127 babies for their physical strength, to try to determine whether physical strength in boys is hormone related or whether social pressure on boys to perform strength-related activities is a more important factor. Samples of umbilical cord blood were taken at birth and analysed for levels of testosterone and progesterone (a female hormone). The boys had higher levels of testosterone than the girls but, surprisingly, this was not related to physical strength. The babies were tested at birth and at 3, 6, 9 and 12 months, by measuring their grip strength. The boys' average strength scores were higher at every age than the girls'. Interestingly the boys with above average grip strength had high levels of progesterone and the strongest girls had low progesterone levels. We need to be careful in interpreting these findings as they are correlational and only attempt to show a relationship. The high levels of progesterone in boys may be entirely unrelated to their physical strength. Low levels of progesterone in girls correlates negatively with high strength: this is easier to interpret, as this female hormone has been found to be an anti-androgen in male rats. In other words, when male rats were injected pre-natally with progesterone they were de-masculinised and behaved in a more feminine way (Hull, 1981). So it makes sense that females with low levels of progesterone may exhibit more masculine traits.

The relationship between hormones and behaviour is obviously a complex one. From this research we can only conclude that perhaps males and females metabolise (process) hormones in different ways, resulting in different effects on their behaviour.

Another gender difference that has been considered from a biological viewpoint is the difference in cognitive skills in males and females. Men are generally thought to perform better on tasks involving spatial ability, and females on tasks that test verbal ability. Waber (1976) explored the biological variable of physical maturation in relation to these skill differences. Females tend to reach physical maturity earlier than males and Waber hypothesised that this may be related to mental abilities, as brain lateralisation may affect cognitive skills. The brain is divided into left and right hemispheres, each thought to be responsible for different functions. Levy (1969) claimed that using both hemispheres for language increases the probability that language will interfere with spatial processing which is attributed to the right hemisphere. Waber proposed that the female brain is lateralised in this way due to early maturation. He tested a sample of adolescents and compared the cognitive skills of early maturers with those of late maturers. Regardless of sex the early maturers performed better on tests of verbal rather than spatial ability. Waber concluded therefore that it is better to compare differences in abilities between the sexes on a physical continuum rather than directly between the sexes.

EVOLUTIONARY EXPLANATIONS OF GENDER ROLES

Evolutionary psychology is a way of explaining behaviour through the processes of natural selection and sexual selection.

Evolutionary psychologists argue that much of human behaviour has been generated through adaptation to environmental problems in order to promote the survival of the species. For example' humans have evolved particular mental functions that allow them to acquire language at a stage in their development and at a rate which appears almost automatic: the assumption is therefore that the development of language is advantageous for the survival of the species.

Previous research on gender already considered in this chapter hints at the rapidity and strength of the acquisition of gender roles at a very early age. Children as young as 2 demonstrate substantial knowledge of sex-role stereotypes and can categorise items as belonging to males and females (Thompson, 1975; Kuhn et al, 1978). What is also clear from this research is that children have very defined gender roles and that these gender roles are different for males and females. Masculinity and femininity are defined by a clear set of traits. In the study by Kuhn et al (1978) 2 and 3-year-olds believed that girls like to cook and clean; that they like to talk a lot and give kisses; and that, although they sometimes cry, they never hit or fight. Beliefs about boys were that they like to fight, climb trees and build things; that they never cry; and that they are more likely to say things like 'I can hit you'. Bem's research (1973) also shows that adults have clear expectations about the roles acceptable to men and women and about the behaviours that are most appropriate. Traits included on the femininity scale of Bem's Sex Role Inventory include 'loves children' and 'eager to soothe hurt feelings', whereas masculinity is defined by 'competitive', 'aggressive' and 'willing to take risks'.

According to the evolutionary approach, the fact that these differences in gender exist must be because they have evolved and therefore must be advantageous to each sex. They must somehow enhance their 'fitness'. Buss (1995) supports this idea. He says that men and women differ in psychological domains where they have faced different adaptive problems over human evolutionary history. Where adaptive problems have presented the same challenge for both men and women their evolutionary solution is the same. An example of this is temperature regulation. Both sexes have sweat glands as they have both responded to the challenges of temperature change and the need to respond effectively to heat and cold. On the other hand, women have evolved mechanisms such as the release of the hormone oxytocin during childbirth which stimulates contraction of the uterus. This response is unique to women due to the challenge faced by them of giving birth.

Men and women face different challenges in ensuring reproductive success. As with many mammals, fertilisation and gestation occur internally in the human female. This means that the female can be 100% certain that the offspring is hers. Males, however, face what Buss (1995) describes as 'paternity uncertainty' as a man cannot be absolutely sure that the offspring carried by the female is his. This presents an adaptive challenge to the male that is different from that presented to the female. The male also faces the challenge of having to find and secure mates. This in itself poses

SEXUAL AND NATURAL SELECTION

The theory of evolution was developed by Charles Darwin. He set out some of the basic 'rules' which explain how evolution progresses, one of which is natural selection. Basically, this says that animals produce many more young than could possibly survive. There will be natural variations in these young, some of which will help the animal adapt to their environment. This makes them more likely to survive, thus to breed and pass on these same traits to the next generation. Over many generations, these traits become widespread in the population. This is the basis for the idea of 'survival of the fittest', 'fitness' referring to the ability to reproduce and pass on genes. Sexual selection is the process of attracting a mate with evolutionary fitness whilst also maximising the chances of being selected as a mate. One consequence of sexual selection is sexual dimorphism caused by the development of secondary sexual characteristics. These are indicators of fitness, which in males include size (e.g. height and physique) and facial hair, whilst in females they include enlargement of breasts and an optimum waist-hip ratio.

problems for the male as merely finding a willing female is not enough to ensure reproductive success: he also needs to know that she is fertile. Female fertility declines with age, and ovulation is concealed in women, thus limiting the opportunities for men to reproduce successfully. No such problem exists for the woman, as men remain fertile into old age. The challenge for the female lies in identifying a man who will invest his resources in her offspring to maximise their chance of survival. The woman who can identify such a man will have an evolutionary advantage but to secure access to his resources she will need to be able to convince him of his paternity. The greatest chance of survival for the female and her offspring is not only with a man who is willing to provide but also with one who is able. This makes the man with resources – a good provider – the most attractive prospect. This reliance on a male provider stems from the fact that the human gestation period is nine months, during which time the female is vulnerable and may not be able to provide for herself. Attempting to do so would not give her offspring the best chance of survival. She also knows that as a parent she will have to invest far more time and energy in raising her offspring than the man. Such differences in adaptation faced by males and females, and the consequences for their behaviour, may explain why the male gender role is typically of the strong provider and the female gender role is of the nurturing carer.

The ideas presented here may seem outmoded by modern standards but it is important to recognise that they are a product of evolution and that, as a species, humans have spent most of their time on this planet living as hunter-gatherers. This time in our history is known as the environment of evolutionary adaptation (EEA) and it is during this time that humans evolved to respond to the differences they faced in adaptive challenges. It is the legacy of these adaptations that still echo in our behaviour today.

Men: aggressive, competitive, risk-takers

It is generally accepted that men are more aggressive than women and that their aggression is usually directed at other men. This readiness to aggress is a reflection of the competitiveness that men need in order to gain access to the best females. Eagly and Steffen (1986) conducted a meta-analysis of studies into adult aggression and confirmed that men were more likely to aggress than women and that this effect was more pronounced with regard to physical aggression.

Wilson and Daly (1985) carried out a study to review conflicts resulting in murder in Detroit in 1972. They found that the majority of murder cases involved elements of status and competition between young men. Reasons for killing often seemed trivial – such as jostling, an insult or the owing of a small debt.

The majority of these murders appeared to be spontaneous acts of passion rather than premeditated events: however, the individuals involved behaved as if far more was at stake than, for example, the loss of a place in a queue. Clearly the men's willingness to participate in deadly conflict had far more to do with preventing loss of status. They would rather risk death than risk 'losing face'. Both victims and offenders were most likely to be unemployed, unmarried young men who therefore had less to lose and more to gain by engaging in risky behaviour. They also tended to know each other, suggesting that they would have some knowledge of the background and current status of their opponent. Of the cases noted in the Detroit study, a significant number involved sexual jealousy, where two men were contesting a female partner. Many of these were described as 'trivial altercations' that escalated into opportunities to show off and try to outdo one another in front of witnesses. Wilson and Daly note that these 'trivial altercations' in America bear a strong resemblance to 'affairs of honour' that are described in other cultures. The initial trigger for the altercation seems petty but it is usually a deliberate provocation and therefore constitutes a public challenge that cannot be dismissed. This is particularly pronounced when the males are of equal status but where one sees the other as trying to rise above his station. Where there is a greater difference in status, the high status male may reject a challenge from a low status male without losing face, almost as if it is beneath him to accept. To the female, status is attractive, as high status males often have access to the resources a woman seeks to promote her fitness.

Many research studies have been conducted into aggression in humans and the majority do support the hypothesis that men show more aggression than women – particularly physical aggression. Steffen and Eagly (1986) point out, however, that care must be taken in interpreting these findings. Their meta-analysis concluded that differences in levels and types of aggression were more pronounced in laboratory experiments when aggression was required or directly requested as opposed to those conducted in the field, where the participants had free choice. They also found that many studies of aggression used children as their participants. The gender differences in levels and types of aggression were far more pronounced in children than they were in adults.

> "An exam question could well require you to evaluate evolutionary explanations of gender roles. There are loads of studies in this section which can be used either descriptively or as evaluation. Think about it, plan your answer, and you can't go wrong!"

Risk-taking in males seems evident from a young age. Ginsberg and Miller (1982) conducted a naturalistic observation of children aged between 3 and 11 at San Antonio Zoo. They identified four different scenarios involving an element of risk: an elephant ride, feeding a burro, a petting zoo and a steep embankment near the river. On the day of the observation 480 children were admitted to the zoo, with roughly equal numbers of boys and girls. The researchers conducted frequency counts for 30 minutes at each of the identified risk-taking activities, noting the number of girls and boys involved in each one. They only included children who took part in the tasks without parental intervention. Results showed that significantly more boys than girls involved themselves in risk-taking behaviour. This was particularly apparent on the steep embankment: 74% of the children playing there during the 30-minute observation were boys. Successful risk-taking evokes admiration from females as gaining access to the best resources may involve an element of risk. Wilson and Daly (1985) equate this with modern day gambling, which is a predominantly male activity (especially where large stakes are involved) and

winning means gaining a huge amount in terms of resources and status.

Women: passive, nurturing, carers

The female anatomy is designed to provide internal fertilisation and a safe environment for the foetus to grow and develop over the nine month gestation period, and to provide sustenance for the helpless but rapidly growing offspring. This means that the woman has to invest a lot of time and energy in her children and this has led to her role as nurturer and carer. Living as hunter-gatherers during the time of EEA, women would have remained together in a social group caring for the children while the men left the group to hunt. Modern day hunter-gatherers studied by Hill and Hurtado (1989) give us some idea of their lifestyle. The division of labour among the Ache of Paraguay clearly shows the difference in gender roles. Ache men devote over seven hours a day to hunting and processing food and working to clean and improve their weapons and tools. They are the providers, generating 87% of the total diet and 100% of the fat and protein requirement for the group. In contrast, the women spend only two hours each day gathering food, two hours moving camp and eight hours in light work and child care. The caring and communal qualities traditionally associated with women can be understood therefore by looking at the amount of time women invest in looking after offspring and socialising with other women. Hill and Hurtado conclude that in reflecting on this contrast between the genders we need to assume that hunter-gatherers will spend time on activities that lower the mortality rates of their children and improve chances of reproduction. Therefore the differences in the gender roles enhance the survival of the group.

The traditional roles played by women help us to understand why women are less likely to aggress than men. The emphasis for the female is on avoiding physical harm (Steffen and Eagly, 1986). This makes sense when we consider the consequences of harm to the female for her offspring. Females also seem to be able to empathise with their victim as, according to Steffen and Eagly, compared with men, women report feeling more guilt and anxiety about possible harm that could befall a victim. They also point out, however, that women are more often victims of aggression – perhaps because of their inferior physical strength and lower social status.

This is an interesting point to consider as men, although the aggressors, also have the role of protector. These two behaviours appear contradictory. It may be that men assault their wives to deter them from pursuing other males, as the last thing the male wants is to invest in another man's offspring.

A finding that seems incongruent with the female role of carer is highlighted by research on family violence which suggests that mothers and fathers are roughly equal in their tendency to participate in child abuse (Breines and Gordon, 1983). However, the amount of time a woman spends looking after the offspring must be taken into account. She has far more exposure to provocation from the children and greater opportunity to respond in an aggressive way.

Gender differences in cognitive ability and problem solving

The cognitive skills associated with gender roles are also different. Men's visuo-spatial skills are thought to be superior to women's, whereas women are more developed in their language ability than men. These skill differences can be understood by examining traditional gender roles within the EEA. The men were the providers and therefore spent a significant proportion of their time hunting and thus developing coordination for aiming and throwing, and improving spatial abilities through building a cognitive map of the terrain and remembering the way home. Male cognitive ability in spatial rotation is thought to be related to their ability to hunt. Masters and Sanders (1993) found men to be particularly adept at mentally rotating three-dimensional figures when compared with women. Men are able to throw over a greater distance and with more speed and accuracy than women. In the EEA, skilled hunters would have made the best providers and therefore would have been particularly sexually attractive to women: this

can still be seen in current traditional tribal societies (Hill and Hurtado, 1989).

Women's skills developed through their role as nurturer and carer and also through their communal abilities. A woman would have spent a lot of time in large social groups of women working together to raise the children and tend the camp. Good communication skills would therefore have been essential and this may explain why women have superior language skills to men. Halpern (1992) found that women show more skill on measures of verbal fluency – for example, tests requiring production of words or sentences meeting certain requirements of meaning. Women also excelled in tests of speech production, demonstrating rapid and accurate speech.

The female legacy of communal living also seems evident in the way women solve problems when part of a team. In Charlesworth and Dzur's research (1987) 4–5-year-old boys and girls were tested on their ability to solve problems in same-sex groups. They were presented with the task of working out how to operate a machine that would allow them to view a cartoon. The task involved working together to turn a handle and push a button simultaneously, to allow the cartoon to be viewed. The boys and girls were equally successful in their resolution of the problem based upon the length of viewing time achieved but the methods they used highlighted clear differences. In working together the girls used more verbal behaviour than the boys, whose methods were more physical. The girls discussed turn-taking and offered to swap positions to allow each child to view the cartoon. The boys touched and pushed each other more during their negotiations. This physical behaviour from the boys may lead us to conclude that they are more competitive than the girls, who seem to demonstrate more cooperative behaviour. It may however be a popular misconception, as in this task the children achieved the same goal with equal success but through the use of different approaches, which suggests that they were no more or less competitive than each other.

Gender differences in attitudes to sexual relationships

In attitudes towards sexual relationships men are typically regarded as more permissive than the traditionally selective and choosy female. In the formation of human relationships it is the man who does the chasing and the woman who does the choosing. A comparison of parental investment helps us to understand how these differences in attitude and behaviour have emerged. As mentioned previously, the female anatomy dictates the female role and her investment from conception to birth and beyond is immense when compared with that of the male. In reality he need only invest as much time as it takes to copulate and will certainly have very little input at least until the child is born. The risk to the female in embarking on a sexual relationship is much greater than that to the male and it is therefore easy to understand why she is selective in her choice of mate. She needs to be sure that the man can and will provide, that he has healthy genes and that he will support her in raising the child and not invest in other women. Long-term investment offers the best chance of survival for the female and her offspring whereas, for the male, promiscuity offers the best chance of reproductive success.

Oliver and Hyde's research (1993) supports these differences in attitudes towards sexual relationships. They conducted a meta-analysis of 177 studies of gender differences on 21 measures of sexual attitudes and behaviour and found that generally men had more permissive attitudes to sex. In the US, active sexuality was part of the male gender role, with men talking openly and freely about sex with other men. Clark and Hatfield's study (1989) confirmed male promiscuity as, when approached by an attractive stranger of the opposite sex, men will consent to a request for sex 75% of the time compared with 0% for women.

Changing times, changing roles

Research into gender differences in attitudes to sex seems to suggest that over a lifespan men will have more sexual partners than women. However, Oliver and Hyde (1993) found that from the 1960s to the 1980s gender differences had narrowed quite considerably. Recent findings showed that there was actually little difference in the number of sexual partners accrued over a lifetime by each sex. According to Oliver and Hyde these changes may in part be explained by the invention of the contraceptive pill. When sexual activity does not involve reproduction the female can have as many partners as the male as the risk of long-term investment is removed. This explanation, however, assumes a cognitive approach in making a decision about sexual behaviour that is absent from an evolutionary explanation.

In Western culture there is a growing acceptance of the nurturing role of the father. This is reflected in changes in legislation allowing new fathers to take paternity leave and to be more involved in the rearing of their offspring – behaviour that would have been considered as 'unnatural' decades ago. Men therefore are capable of nurturing behaviour but have been discouraged in the past by socialisation practices (Fogelet et al, 1986). Environmental conditions change with the advancement of technology so that it is no longer necessary for men to hunt or fight in hand-to-hand combat. These advancements bring with them changes in socialisation practices and ultimately impacts on the male and female gender roles e.g. female soldiers. This change in gender role reflects the importance of culture in defining social practice and thus raises the question of whether gender roles are defined by biology or culture. Perhaps the two are inextricably bound, in which case the more likely explanation may be one that acknowledges both – a biosocial approach.

THE BIOSOCIAL APPROACH TO GENDER DEVELOPMENT

The biosocial approach focuses on the interaction of biological and social factors in explaining the development of gender. In this explanation, biology is the foundation upon which social factors are built. The inborn traits and physical characteristics of a newborn baby affect the way carers behave towards them. Carers behave in different ways towards their newborn babies depending on whether the babies are male or female. Biosocial theory presents the idea that a child's gender identity is consistent with the way that the child has been raised. However, it also emphasises the importance of the influence of the newborn's behaviour on the carer's response to them.

"This is one of those theories explicitly named in the spec that you really need to know about! Let's be honest, it isn't the easiest of theories to get a handle on, but all your effort will be paid off when it comes up in the exam!"

Thus children influence their own development by the way they look and act. Moss (1967) found that at 3 weeks old, boys were more irritable and were harder to pacify than girls. This may be a biological predisposition for the male baby: however, according to biosocial theory the carer responds by applying the social expectation that 'boys don't cry' and therefore does not respond so readily to the infant boy's cries. This expectation then perpetuates the temperament of the baby, as a slow response from the carer will provoke further irritability. Thus, the biological cues provided by the male infant prompt a reaction from the carer that is consistent with the expectations of society.

Money and Ehrhardt (1972) take a biosocial approach to gender development as they believe 'anatomy is destiny' and how an infant is labelled at birth (i.e. either as a boy or a girl) determines how it is socialised. They also suggested that social factors have a greater influence on gender identity than biological factors but that there is a period of flexibility when a child's gender is still malleable. Their argument was that it is possible to change the sex and thus the gender identity of a child without causing psychological damage as long as the child is less than 3 years old. This claim is supported by the case study of Mr Blackwell

(Goldwyn, 1979) who at birth was taken to be a boy and raised to form a male gender identity. At puberty he began to develop breasts and he was found to have an active ovary on one side of his body and an active testicle on the other. He had both a penis, a vagina and a small uterus and was able to ovulate and menstruate from the age of 14. This unusual condition, known as hermaphroditism, occurs when 2 sperm, one containing the X chromosome and one containing the Y chromosome, fertilise the ovum at the same time. It is thought that Mr Blackwell's brain was not fully masculinised, yet he thought of himself as masculine and elected to remain male by having his female parts removed. He lived a successful life as a fully functional male and it is reported that he never displayed any behaviour that could be described as feminine. According to Money and Ehrhardt it would have been too late for Mr Blackwell to adopt a female gender identity at the age of 14 without the change causing psychological damage, as the window of opportunity to make this transition successfully had already passed. So it seems that in this case the early socialisation was the most powerful influence on his gender identity. The surgeon who operated on Mr Blackwell also treated 25 other patients of a similar disposition, who all adopted the gender assigned to them at birth regardless of their biological make-up. This supports the biosocial theory, as it shows that biology alone cannot determine gender development. The anatomical and behavioural cues generated at birth and by the subsequent labelling and socialisation prompted the future gender identity of the hermaphrodites.

Smith and Lloyd's research (1978) emphasises the importance of cues and labelling in the socialisation of infants. The adults in their study treated babies according to the gender the adults perceived them to have, showing how an infant's supposed biology determines his or her social environment. The researchers tested this by taking a sample of 6 month old infants and dressing and naming some of them as the opposite sex. They then asked adults unknown to the babies to play with them. They found that the adults used the cues of clothing and name to prompt their interaction and toy choice when playing with the baby. Babies perceived as boys were more likely to be given a squeaky hammer to play with, whereas those perceived as girls were typically given a doll.

A more recent version of the biosocial theory has been proposed by Wood and Eagly (2002). They argue that physical differences between men and

MATERNAL BEHAVIOUR TOWARDS BABIES DRESSED AS THE OPPOSITE SEX

Smith and Lloyd (1978) wanted to show the difference in socialisation experienced by males and females from a very early age. Their participants were 32 first time mothers of infants aged 5 to 10 months. They used four actor babies, all aged around 6 months. In some trials the babies were cross-dressed: whether they were male or female they were dressed in clothes of the opposite sex.

The participants were seated in front of a table with a range of toys that were stereotypically male (e.g. a squeaky hammer) or stereotypically female (e.g. a doll). A range of neutral toys was also included, such as a rattle. The participants were told that the study was about analysing play and they were asked to play with a baby for a period of ten minutes. The actor baby was presented by its own mother and given a name appropriate to how it was dressed. The baby was left alone with the participant and observed through a one-way mirror. The observers were looking for each participant's initial toy choice for the baby and the duration of play with each toy as well as the verbal and non-verbal behaviour of the participant.

The researchers found that only the babies perceived as girls were offered the doll and those perceived as male were offered the hammer or the rattle. The perceived boys were also given more verbal encouragement toward physical activity and expected to be more vigorous in their play.

The researchers concluded that the participants showed strong stereotypes about sex-appropriate behaviour – although it could be argued that this does not fully support the biosocial theory, as the participants responded to the perceived sex of the baby, not the actual biological sex. They were not able to pick up on the subtle cues that may have been generated by the biological sex of the baby. This could be explained by the demand characteristics of the experiment, which may have influenced the participants to interact in a more sex-appropriate manner with a strange infant than they would with their own child in their home environment. It must be remembered, however, that the participants were not aware that the research was into sex-typing.

women cause psychological differences. This is because of the interaction between the physical attributes of males and females and the social contexts in which they interact. Roles are assigned to males based upon their physical strength, size and speed and therefore they are seen as more efficient hunters and providers. Women's roles are based upon their physical ability to give birth and feed their young, therefore the raising of the offspring can be more efficiently accomplished by the woman. Each sex must therefore develop psychological characteristics that equip them for the tasks their sex typically performs. Wood and Eagly claim that these characteristics then become gender stereotypical. If women are involved in domestic activities then the associated skills and values such as caring and nurturing become part of the female gender stereotype. As men are involved in economic productivity and acquisition of resources they then become associated with traits such as aggression and competitiveness. So it seems as though the roles occupied by men and women, determined by their biological make-up, then guide their social behaviour. Because these roles are complementary it is more efficient for men and women to engage in a division of labour.

EVALUATION OF BIOSOCIAL THEORY

To support the biosocial approach, Wood and Eagly examined cross-cultural research to assess both similarities and differences in sex-differentiated behaviour. If the gender behaviour is common across many cultures then it must be very important to human beings. Differences in behaviour between cultures would indicate less essential behaviour that may be moderated by the society people live in. For example, newborn infants in Western societies may be bottle-fed and therefore less dependent on their mother, thus freeing her to pursue more characteristic male activities. A mother may be able to go out to work soon after her baby is born as the role of feeding can be shared with the male. Consequently this also allows the male to be more involved in child care than his counterparts in more traditional cultures. Across industrialised societies, changes in women's status have emerged in recent times due to the greater control women now have over reproduction. Contraception and safe abortions have led to a decline in the birth rate and an increase in the number of women in positions of power (Reskin and Padavic, 1994). According to biosocial theory this should mean that as women take on male-dominated roles their psychological attributes change in parallel. Konrad et al (2000) found that women increasingly value leadership, power and prestige, which are attributes more commonly associated with men. Despite these changes, women are still the only sex that can reproduce and therefore may not be able to efficiently combine production with reproduction. Thus cross-cultural research shows that most societies are still patriarchal, with men dominating the positions of power and status. In conclusion, Wood and Eagly state that gender behaviour is constrained by the physical attributes of males and females but is still flexible to a degree and can respond to cultural influences – and this is why a biosocial theory is the best explanation for both the consistencies and differences in gender roles and behaviour across cultures.

Luxen (2007) criticises Wood and Eagly's biosocial theory, claiming that it is incompatible with evolutionary theory. This is especially apparent, according to Luxen, in Wood and Eagly's claim that evolution is responsible for physical development only and not the development of the brain. Luxen says that psychological development is just as important to survival as physical development, and claims that there is no reason why evolution cannot design different psychological mechanisms in males and females to respond to the different adaptive problems they have encountered.

Luxen also points out that biosocial theory does not explain the role of hormones in pre-natal development or the impact of hormone cycles in causing differences in behaviour between the sexes, such as the menstrual cycle in women. Hines et al (2002) found a relationship between levels of testosterone during pregnancy and masculine behaviour of the resulting female offspring at 3–4 years of age. Higher pre-natal levels of testosterone were related to more masculine behaviour in the young girls.

In a further criticism Luxen claims the biosocial theory fails to explain the overlap between human sex differences and findings from studies of animal behaviour and the behaviour of young children. He says research finds that from as early as 18 months children show strong preferences for sex-typed toys at a point in their development when the influence of sex roles is limited. The strength of their preference at this stage, when their exposure to social influence has been so brief, cannot be explained by biosocial theory. Animal research also shows very similar sex differences between males and females in terms of their sex-role allocation, with females nurturing and males providing and competing for choosy females. These psychological differences that occur in animals cannot be due to sex-role allocation based on biology because animal culture is not that sophisticated.

According to Luxen, biosocial theory fails to explain the excellent fit between partner choice in males and females and potential reproductive success. Men are highly specialised in detecting fertility cues in females, such as a waist-to-hip ratio of 0.7. This can be seen across many cultures, along with a preference for symmetry which indicates good genes. Humans are also influenced by hormone cycles: women show more interest in male faces when they are at the peak of their fertility (Little et al, 2002).

The advantages of biosocial theory over the evolutionary approach are that it intuitively seems to make sense and has ethical appeal as sex roles are perceived as products of the interaction between biology and society and as such are more flexible than if they were just biological. The social component of the biosocial theory may also be useful in explaining differences in gender behaviour across cultures by referring to the powerful influence of society.

SOCIAL CONTEXTS OF GENDER ROLE

SOCIAL INFLUENCES ON GENDER ROLE

The biosocial theory clearly highlights the need to consider the impact of social factors on the development of gender. Attempting to explain gender development through social factors alone would not provide us with a sufficient explanation, but the influence of society is important in helping us to understand how gender roles have changed over time and across cultures. Considering the social context of gender roles is also important in helping us to explain why some gender differences have persisted. Social factors within a society lay down the boundaries for acceptable and unacceptable behaviour. These social norms are upheld by socialising agents such as parents, peers, schools and the media. If these socialising agents are all sending out the same messages about how to behave, then the impact of these messages on children and young people cannot be ignored.

"There are lots of social influences on gender role. Two is the minimum you need to know about, and here we've covered two which we think you will find most interesting – schools and media."

THE INFLUENCE OF SCHOOLS ON GENDER ROLE

Throughout their school life children may find themselves treated differently according to their sex. Gender stereotypes may be confirmed by teachers in the way they praise and punish their pupils. Sex-typed behaviour may also be supported by the way classes and the curriculum are organised and through the use of teaching resources.

Expectations of gender role and expected differences in sex-typed behaviour may significantly affect the way a teacher responds to a child. Huston's research (1983) supports this claim as it was found that in primary schools girls received less disapproval than boys even though their behaviour was equally disruptive. This may be a reflection of the assumption that boys are more likely to demonstrate disruptive behaviour than girls unless they are strictly controlled. School systems generally reward conformity and non-disruptive behaviour – qualities that are characteristically associated with females. Fagot (1984) observed teachers reinforcing quiet play in young children of both sexes and thus promoting this as the acceptable way to behave. Huston (1983), however, also points out that teachers reinforce academic behaviour, praising children who are on task and punishing disruptive behaviour regardless of sex. They also tend to ignore classroom behaviour that is atypical of sex. So, girls can be assertive learners and boys can be quiet and passive (thus displaying characteristic learning styles of the opposite sex), as long as it is not disruptive. Whilst passive behaviour from children in a classroom may make a teacher's job easier, male sex attributes are consistent with the role of active, assertive learner – behaviour that is in conflict with preferred classroom conduct (Voivodas, 1983).

The power of the teacher in influencing gender stereotypes was demonstrated in a study by Serbin et al (1979). There were two parts to Serbin's study: one which observed teachers confirming gender stereotypes and a second designed for teachers to challenge the stereotypes. In the first part of the study, nine female pre-school teachers were asked to introduce a new toy each day to a class of 3–4-year-old children. They were observed asking children to demonstrate the new toy to the rest of the class. The toys were categorised into those considered to be for boys, those for girls or neutral. The researchers found that, to demonstrate the fishing set, teachers called upon the boys more often than the girls. In demonstration of the sewing set some teachers called upon more girls but other teachers, perhaps aware that they were being observed, were more even in their choice of child. In the second part of the study, sets of toys including trucks and dolls were introduced to the classes of 3–4-year-olds. In the first condition the teacher introduced the toys in a stereotypical way, e.g. "We can pretend we are mummies washing the baby" and "Daddies can go to work in the truck". In the second condition, non-stereotypical introductions were made, containing references to both sexes. The children played with the toys according to the introductions made by the teacher. Boys were more likely to play with the trucks and girls with the dolls if this was the expectation given in the introduction; but no significant differences in toy choice were found between boys and girls if the toys were introduced in a non-stereotypical way. This shows how influential teachers can be in either confirming or challenging gender stereotypes.

In responding to differences in boys' and girls' behaviour, teachers may direct what they teach, and the methods they use, to the benefit of boys. Clarricoates (1978) found that teachers chose topics that would hold the attention of the boys. The girls were expected to behave, so that the boys could be the focus of the teacher's attention: therefore lessons become androcentric. Boys in Clarricoates' study were deemed to be more brilliant, profound and interesting, though the girls were described as easier to control. Stanworth (1981) found that high school teachers could identify the boys in their classes by name shortly after the start of the academic year and could describe their individual characteristics. Girls' names, on the other hand, were not readily recalled and it took longer for the girls to become identified as individuals by the teacher. Teachers certainly seemed to get to know the boys in their class sooner than the girls – though whether this was a conscious decision on the part of the teacher, or whether it was the actions of the boys themselves that made them more noticeable, is difficult to say. Direct observations of boys in the classroom demonstrated that they received more verbal attention from the teacher than did the girls. Boys are asked more challenging and complex questions and receive more criticism and praise than the girls (Sadker et al, 1984). Sabar and Levin (1987) studied a group of talented high school students who volunteered to take part in a science enrichment course. The boys dominated discussions while the girls took a back seat: however, the achievement of both sexes was equal.

> **ASK AN EXAMINER**
>
> *"Androcentric is a common term: don't be afraid of using it yourself. It refers to taking the male point of view. The opposite is gynocentric, which is taking the female view, but this is much less frequently used. Doesn't that tell you something about how androcentric things are!"*

In a study by BenTsvi-Mayer et al (1989) 300 teachers and student teachers of pupils under 12 years of age were asked to nominate their most prominent pupils. They were asked to consider ability, achievement, behaviour and the amount of time the child dominated the teacher's thoughts. Boys were more prominent than girls in most

categories and though boys were cited as having more frequent discipline problems this did not detract from the overall picture of boys as high achievers. Girls were considered to be successful in Hebrew and in possession of outstanding social skills which were deemed 'natural' for their sex. Boys were generally perceived as the 'best' students and described as having the most potential, especially in maths. Girls were described more in terms of what they had 'accomplished' rather than what they had 'achieved'. The researchers do point out, however, that the study was conducted in Israel where Judaism is very much male-oriented, and worship and study of the religion often excludes women. There is also much emphasis on national security, and the 'military male' may be regarded as being special, even as early as his school days. Despite these cultural concerns, the researchers still conclude that a teacher's influence on their pupils' development is widely accepted. If boys are the focus of teachers' attention and girls are peripheral, this may lead to the confirmation of sex stereotypes that could distort children's perception of themselves and of the opposite sex.

Research by Yee and Eccles (1988) draws attention to the powerful influence of parents on children when it comes to both subject choice and belief in their abilities. Children's self-concept of their ability in maths, and their level of confidence in numeracy, was more directly related to their parents' beliefs about their aptitude for the subject than to evidence from the child's past achievement. Parents, even more than teachers, held sex-differentiated views about their sons' and daughters' aptitude for maths. The parents of 48 children aged 11–14 of high and low ability in maths completed a questionnaire about their perceptions of their child's ability. They were also questioned about their child's effort and reasons for success or lack of success in maths. When rated by their parents as successful in maths, boys were deemed to be talented, and girls to have worked hard, to achieve good results. Parents generally thought that maths was harder for girls and that enrolment on high level maths courses was less important for girls than for boys. A more recent study by Tenenbaum et al (2008) supports the importance of the parent in directing children towards particular subjects at school. The focus of her research was in trying to explain why in the United States 75% of people engaged professionally in science are men. Her study included observations of parent–child interaction during visits to museums or the cinema, or whilst out shopping.

The results were striking. Fathers were much more likely to use complicated terms in helping their sons understand scientific concepts compared with the more basic explanations they gave to their daughters. Mothers showed little difference in the way they spoke to their children, regardless of sex. Tenenbaum et al concluded that this gender difference in the fathers' explanations could account for the uneven distribution of males and females in science. The powerful influence of the parent as a socialising agent must be considered, as the seeds of gender stereotypes could be sown long before the child enters school. Their experience of school may serve to reinforce the already established stereotypes and if school does try to challenge their concept of gender the attempts may be met with strong resistance.

"Although the influence of parents on gender stereotypes is not considered here in full, this research serves to show how difficult it is to separate the influences of socialising agents on gender stereotypes. In some instances they work together to reinforce gender messages."

Influences on children at school may be more subtle than those direct messages given out by teachers. The resources used in teaching – such as textbooks, audio-visual materials and more recently educational computer programs – can also play a part in amplifying pre-existing gender stereotypes. In a study conducted in the UK, Littleton (1998) researched the use of computers in schools, focusing particularly on the programming 'style'. He claims that the increased use of computers in school could place girls at a disadvantage in comparison with boys. His research highlighted boys and male teachers as more frequent users of computers than girls and female teachers.

Girls also tended to report less positive attitudes towards the use of computers than boys. Turkle and Papert (1990) suggest that there are cognitive 'style' differences between males and females that could affect the way they approach a task on the computer. Boys tend to prefer programs that are more formal and analytical, compared with girls, whose approach is more open-ended and exploratory. It may be that the software developed for learning in schools follows the preferred masculine style, particularly if those involved in the software design are themselves male. Littleton et al (1998) put this to the test by designing two different versions of a problem-solving task on the computer. The demands of the task were the same: the key difference was in the characters manipulated by the children, which were either 'pirates' or 'honey bears'. A group of 24 boys and 24 girls aged between 11 and 12 were tested on the problem-solving task. The boys' performance was not affected by the version of the task they were given but the girls' performance was much improved in the 'honey bears' version. This version was free from stereotypical masculine elements. The characters had no specific gender and the transport in the game was less 'mechanical', with rowing boats, balloons and ponies as opposed to cars, planes and ships. The researchers concluded that by making superficial changes to educational computer software, girls' performance on computer-based tasks can improve to equal that of the boys.

"The study by Littleton et al is a really useful one. We've presented it here in the context of schools, but of course since it is focusing on bias in media (computer software) it can also be used when discussing the influence of media on gender roles! Whilst 'media' is often interpreted as meaning TV, television is only one medium. Be sure to broaden your thinking of media to include all forms of mass communication – magazines, computers, radio, billboards."

THE INFLUENCE OF THE MEDIA ON GENDER ROLES

Many different forms of communication can come under the collective heading of 'media'. These include books, magazines, newspapers, television and radio. In recent times our access to these varied forms of communication has grown and they are all now an accepted part of daily life. The advent of television in particular has provided a new medium with which to communicate with children and the research into the impact of television on children's social development is extensive. Eysenck (1996) claims that children aged between 4 and 11 years watch on average three hours of television each day. Content analysis of the programmes viewed by children suggests that males and females are often presented in traditional roles, with men outnumbering women 2:1 or 3:1 in most television shows. Huston et al (1990) found large individual differences among younger age children, stating that some 3–5-year-olds watched as much as 75 hours of television over a one week period while some watch none at all. Individual viewing patterns remained stable over a two year period, indicating that television viewing habits established in childhood can be long-lasting.

It is interesting to consider the gender-role differences that there may be between children who watch a lot of television and those who have never had access to this form of communication. A study conducted in Canada took the opportunity to study the impact of the introduction of television in a town which previously had no television reception. The town which was labelled 'Notel' was compared with two other towns labelled 'Unitel' which had access to one television channel and 'Multitel' with access to four channels. The children of each town were asked to rate how appropriate or frequent certain actions were for boys and girls their own age, to determine their attitudes to gender role. At the start of the study the children with access to television were more stereotyped in their responses. Two years later the study was repeated during which time 'Notel' gained access to one television channel. Gender-role stereotyping in 'Notel' had increased, particularly amongst the boys – who, it would seem, had more readily absorbed the gender stereotypical messages generated by the television. What is not clear from this study, however, is what programmes the children were watching over the two year period.

Katz (1979) agrees that the development of children's gender role may be affected by watching television but considers the analysis of the types of television watched by the children to be more informative. Commercial television such as cartoons and advertisements may contain more gender stereotypical information than educational television programmes. Manstead and McCulloch (1981) found that in television advertisements men were often the voice-over and the source of information about products, with women presented as the users of products. Children exposed to this kind of information whist watching television for entertainment may demonstrate stronger gender stereotypes than children whose viewing mainly consists of educational programmes. A study conducted by Levy (1989) assessed the impact of different types of programmes on gender roles in 3–5-year-olds. The relationship between the type of television preferred by children and their concept of gender role differed for boys and girls. In the sample of children who preferred to watch commercial television the boys demonstrated more knowledge about gender-role stereotypes than the girls. Explicit attempts by educational television to convey messages of equality between the sexes had more impact on the girls than on the boys. The girls in this sample had processed the information generated by the programmes and showed more flexibility in their gender-roles. Levy's findings only highlight a relationship between the types of television viewed and the impact on stereotypical beliefs. We cannot then conclude that television is the cause of gender stereotypes. It may be that children who have already developed gender-role stereotypes turn to the type of television that confirms their views.

In an attempt to understand how much children are influenced by what they see on television Wober (1987) explored children's perceptions of male and female occupations. The children were a sample of 334 members of a national UK viewing panel aged between 5 and 12 years. They were asked about the occupations carried out by male and female television characters as well as their own career aspirations. Typical jobs carried out by women on television included 'serving customers in a shop', 'taking care of children', and 'typing in an office'. Male television characters were seen 'working machinery', 'piloting aeroplanes' and 'repairing electrical machinery'. The children's own career aspirations demonstrated clear links to those they had witnessed on the television. In a similar study conducted in the US, Thompson and Zerbinos (1997) questioned 89 children aged from 4 to 9 years old about the cartoons they watched. The researchers wanted to know about the frequency of cartoon watching, favourite characters and descriptions of the male and female characters in the cartoons. The children were also asked about the kinds of jobs they would like to do as adults. Most cartoon characters were perceived in stereotypical ways, with boys described as violent and active and girls as domesticated and preoccupied with their appearance. Children who noticed more gender stereotypical behaviour in the cartoon characters were more likely to report more stereotypical career aspirations. It is difficult to demonstrate the effect that media representation of males and females has on the development of gender roles in young children. The effects of the media may be just one factor in their socialisation process. Certainly the adolescent viewer uses far more subtle criteria for judging the influence of television characters. Duck (1990) found that teenagers chose media figures they would 'most like to be like' based on their own characteristics. A 14-year-old girl with a high self-esteem chose Meryl Streep and said that she admired her as a woman who "isn't worried what people think". A 15-year-old boy assessed as having a low self-esteem chose a character from a fantasy game because "I like the way he seems not to have any feelings".

For young children, access to the media is most likely to come from television as programmes are designed specifically to appeal to their level of understanding. As they mature and their cognitive ability grows they gain wider access to other forms of media such as magazines, cinema and radio. The graph below shows the circulation figures for popular teen magazines – with the most popular, *Sugar*, reaching a readership of 190,000 in June 2007. The figures demonstrate the wide influence that this form of media has.

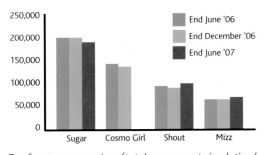

Top four teen magazines (total average net circulation/ distribution), ABCs Report, August 2007.

Peirce (1993) considered teenage magazines aimed at adolescent girls as a powerful socialisation force. She studied the magazines *Seventeen* and *Teen*, with circulations of over one million each in the United States. She carried out a content analysis of stereotypical portrayals of women in the short stories in the magazines, particularly focusing on stories in which reliance on others was necessary for the female's identity and survival. Over 100 stories were analysed and in 62% of them the

female lead character depended upon someone else to solve her problems and show her the error of her thinking. In 43% of the stories the conflict involved boys. In a story in *Seventeen*, a girl who has just found a boyfriend is quoted as saying "Now I was someone with a future", clearly showing that her identity was defined by the acquisition of the 'right type of boyfriend'. One problem with research like this, according to Peirce, is that it doesn't tell us what effect these stereotypical portrayals are having on teenage girls. Are they causing or contributing to stereotypical behaviour? Content analysis is useful in analysing and monitoring changes in messages that are being delivered through the media but it cannot answer questions about cause and effect. The prevalence of stereotypical images in the media also makes it difficult to isolate the effects of one particular medium. Peirce turns to dependency theory to help answer questions about the impact of teenage magazines on gender roles. She concludes that teenage girls are dependent on teen magazines for information that is relevant to their lives. Dependency on this source of information can be clearly seen in the popularity of these magazines. Teenage girls are still being socialised in the ways of the world and are therefore not yet secure in their social realities. This makes them more receptive to the stereotypical messages that the magazines convey.

Another form of media which has become increasingly popular with young people over recent times is the video game, with some characters such as Tomb Raider's Lara Croft becoming youth icons. Research into the impact of video games on socialisation is rare though one study attempted a content analysis of gaming magazines to discover the differences in the way that men and women are portrayed in the games. Dill and Thill (2007) found that generally females were underrepresented in video games and that when they did appear they were most commonly depicted as sex objects: 80% of the female characters rated by the researchers fell into this category. Female characters were sometimes portrayed in ways that countered the accepted stereotypical female role of helpless victim or sex object. These were female characters that demonstrated high levels of aggression – although in 39% of females assessed, the aggression was combined with being scantily clad so they appeared tough and sexy at the same time. Male characters were almost exclusively portrayed as powerful aggressors and shown greater respect than the female characters. A typical image from a game magazine is of a muscular male with a hostile

DEPENDENCY THEORY (DE FLEUR AND BALL-ROKEACH, 1982)

We depend upon the media for a wide variety of information. Levels of dependency vary and are influenced by the individual's social reality. Social realities are constructed over time and are the product of the way a person is socialised by environmental forces. If social realities are insecure then people may be more receptive to the information presented by the media. The media provide us with information to help us understand the world: this in turn helps us to gain an understanding of ourselves, as we are able to compare our behaviour with others'. Media dependency is determined by our need for information, our ability to get the information elsewhere and our level of interest in a subject. The greater the media dependency the more likely we are to change our thoughts, feelings and actions based upon its messages. When people have an adequate social reality, and the messages given out by the media are not linked to dependency, then those messages will have little impact on the way an individual behaves.

facial expression posing with a gun in a glamour style shot. Dill and Thill also found that young people did not have to be gamers to be aware of the impact of games as some have been made into films, and adverts for games appear in magazines and on the television. A survey of 17–19-year-old college students confirmed the awareness of male characters as aggressive and female characters as sex objects even amongst non-gamers. Video game characters are becoming increasingly life-like and gaming is now the top online activity for children and adolescents. According to reports from Dill and Thill, 63% of people in America over the age of 6 years play video games. With video games predicted as the fastest growing form of entertainment in the next five years, it will become increasingly important to understand their impact as agents of socialisation.

An understanding of the powerful influence that the media has on the development of gender roles in children and adolescents has led to the instigation of projects aimed at improving children's gender-role attitudes. One such project in the US was known as 'Freestyle' and was the result of collaboration between researchers, educationalists and television producers. The idea was to produce an instructive television series of 13 episodes designed to expand career awareness in children aged between 9 and 12. The programmes were a series of short stories depicting characters in non-traditional roles. Attitude questionnaires given to the children before and after viewing highlighted a shift in thinking. Boys expressed greater acceptance of girls playing basketball and football and being involved in mechanical activities; and girls themselves expressed more of an interest in these activities. The children's perceptions of male and female roles became less stereotyped and they became more accepting of boys carrying out traditional female tasks such as caring for young children and helping around the house.

It is difficult to assess the long-term impact of projects like 'Freestyle': however, longitudinal analysis of the portrayal of men and women in the media does seem to reveal a decrease in polarisation and less extreme gender stereotyping. A content analysis of the obituaries of male and female managers was conducted by Kirchler (1992). She compared the obituaries published in 1974, 1980 and 1986 in three daily newspapers in Germany. She found that in 1974 the male managers were described as intelligent, knowledgeable, entrepreneurs who were experts in their field. Female managers on the other hand were described as adorable, likeable, superiors. The 1986 obituaries, when they described male managers, employed adjectives similar to those that had been used for males 12 years previously; but women were now more likely to be described as courageous and committed – although still not as being knowledgeable, experts or entrepreneurs. Research shows, however, that the behaviour of male and female managers is very similar and, when asked directly, work colleagues did not report differences in working for a male or female leader (Neubauer, 1990; Passaver, 1992). It can be assumed therefore that the obituaries described perceived rather than actual personality traits and that they were a representation of the gender-role stereotypes held at the time.

CROSS-CULTURAL STUDIES OF GENDER ROLE

'Culture' encompasses the knowledge, beliefs and values shared by a society that are passed down the generations through imitation and communication. Ideas of appropriate behaviour for males and females vary across cultures to a degree, although most societies have a system based upon division between the sexes, particularly with regard to labour. Differences that are universal and persistent are often considered to indicate biological differences between the sexes. Cultural differences in gender roles that arise from cultural comparisons could reflect areas of gender behaviour that are flexible and therefore culturally determined. In an attempt to understand which aspects of gender role are biological and which are a response to cultural influences, researchers often look to studies of traditional cultures and compare them with modern industrialised societies. Traditional cultures offer a picture of life that reflects the way humans lived in the past without the clutter of modern living.

Extensive research has been conducted on the Ache of Paraguay who until recently lived a traditional lifestyle as foragers (Hill and Hurtado, 1989). Their existence was very much hand-to-mouth and therefore 25–35% of their time was devoted to hunting and foraging. This activity included everyone in the group: both men and women had a role to play and it is here where we can see more traditional divisions of labour. Men lead the foraging trip carrying their bows and arrows and the women and children follow on behind carrying the family possessions. Some men walk with their wives and carry small children on their shoulders. After about an hour of walking, the men and women separate, with the men moving forward at a faster pace hunting for game, and the women following behind foraging for fruit and insects as they go. The Ache share food throughout the group and sharing behaviour is highly valued in both men and women. Women who share vegetables are praised and children are taught that stinginess is the worst trait any person can have. All hunters regardless of their status give their kills to be divided amongst the group and almost never eat from their own kill. Division of labour amongst the Ache does reflect traditional gender roles, with men hunting and women involved in light work and child care, but both sexes work less when other more important needs arise. Men spend less time hunting when they have children to take care of (Hill et al, 1985). The emphasis on sharing amongst the Ache also extended to group decisions, with adults of both sexes having input with no designated leader – although one or two powerful men were sometimes referred to as leaders when the need arose. It is interesting to contrast this former way of life with the current existence of the Ache: more recently they have been living in reservations with elected chiefs, who have only ever been men. It could be argued that this change has only occurred since their contact with the West and that it is the result of the influence that Western culture has had upon them.

Ache man hunting.

Occupational roles may be one area where flexibility in gender roles can be observed. In Western culture the role of physician is one that is traditionally held in high regard and is stereotypically a male occupation. However, in the former Soviet Union 77% of doctors are female (Riska, 2001). On the face of it these statistics may indicate a non-stereotypical gender role for women in Russia but this is not actually the case. Riska points out that in Russia industrial employment is regarded as more important economically and politically than healthcare, so men are traditionally employed in the higher status roles in industry, leaving the lower status healthcare roles to the women.

Another unusual case of role reversal can be seen on the island of Margarita off the coast of Venezuela, where women exhibit high levels of physical aggression (Cook, 1992). They engage in ferocious physical fighting with other women and occasionally with men but their status in all other respects is traditional and they have little formal power. Environmental conditions determine their behaviour as the women are often left by the men to fend for themselves and their children in a harsh environment. High levels of aggression help them to survive and have become an accepted part of the female gender role.

Both these cases highlight cultural differences in accepted roles for women but also indicate underlying similarities in the status of the women. The research also emphasises the need, when studying gender roles, not only to observe what other cultures do but also to understand the way that they think. Some of the most influential research on culture and gender was conducted by the famous anthropologist Margaret Mead in the 1930s. Mead lived amongst three tribes in New Guinea and reported on what she interpreted as gender role

MARGARET MEAD

Margaret Mead

Mead described the cultures of three pre-industrialised societies in New Guinea; the Arapesh, Mundugumor and Tchambuli tribes. The Arapesh were described as having gender roles that were similar for both men and women with child care a shared responsibility and all individuals exerting emotional, cooperative and non-assertive behaviours. In contrast both the men and women of the Mundugumor tribe adopted a masculine role and were aggressive and insensitive. In the Tchambuli people gender roles were reversed with men displaying artistic traits and social sensitivity, showing concern for others and staying at home to look after the children. The women were assertive, practical and handled the business affairs. Mead concluded from this that gender roles seem to be neither universal nor biological. The main problem with Mead's work was her inability to leave behind her own cultural interpretations, which coloured her observations. She has also been criticised for ignoring evidence that did not fit in with her expectations and there are thought to be many contradictions in her work. It is generally accepted nowadays that the flaws in her research are such that it cannot be used to draw firm conclusions about the nature of cross-cultural differences in gender roles.

reversals amongst the men and women of the tribes. Mead's research is often quoted as 'classic', yet subsequent re-analysis of her work has revealed that it is extremely flawed in its methodology and interpretation.

This issue of difficulty in interpreting findings from cross-cultural studies has also been confronted in a study by Sugihara et al (1999) who attempted to measure masculinity and femininity in the Japanese culture. The researchers tested 265 college students using the Japanese version of the BSRI (Bem Sex Role Inventory) devised in America. The expectation was that the study would reflect traditional gender roles in Japan with high masculinity scores for the men and high femininity scores for the women. Men did score higher on behaviour such as assertiveness, athleticism, and ambition; but on leadership, risk-taking, aggression and love of children the scores for men and women were equal. Overall there were no significant differences between genders on the masculinity-femininity scale of the BSRI: in fact both men and women scored higher on the femininity scale than on the masculinity scale. The findings seemed to reflect diminishing gender-role differences between men and women and led the researchers to question how this result could have occurred. One possible explanation could come from the process of translation of the scale from English to Japanese. Previous research has shown that literal translation of questionnaires and scales into the language of a target culture is not always possible due to the frequent lack of words with the same meaning. However, translation of the BSRI in the present study

was carried out from English to Japanese and back to English again with 93% reliability. Even if equivalent words are available their exact meaning may not be the same. Desirable masculine and feminine traits in the Japanese culture are different from those in the United States. Japanese men describe their ideal woman as gentle and quiet with an inner strength. The ideal man in Japanese culture is also seen as having internal rather than physical strength. It would seem that the Japanese are expected to possess both masculine and feminine qualities, which may have affected the outcome of the results. A similar problem arose for Kaschak and Sharratt (1983) when trying to apply the American version of the BSRI to gender roles in South America. They found that only half the items on the BSRI represented masculinity and femininity in Costa Rica and the other half were not characteristics appropriate to that culture.

Sugihara et al (2002) responded to the findings of their original study by developing a Japanese Gender Role Index (JGRI) that would reflect culturally appropriate male and female characteristics. For over 2,000 years the Japanese culture has placed emphasis on harmony, inner strength and the maintenance of a hierarchical system with male dominance over women and children. Women in Japanese history, although subordinate, still had a right to inherit property and position and were expected to demonstrate the same bravery and loyalty as men. Japanese men were traditionally expected to be accomplished in literature and the arts. In more recent times in Japan these values have been maintained, with men working and women staying at home. However, the Japanese woman is given complete power and control of the home, including finances and decision making, so the man can totally devote himself to work. This could explain why even when given a culturally specific scale of masculinity and femininity, it was found that both men and women possessed an equal number of masculine and feminine characteristics. These minimal gender-role differences may not reflect the traditions of the past: they could also be attributed to current developments in providing equal access to education for women in Japan and the increasing number of women entering the workforce.

Some interesting differences between gender roles in Japan and the US were also highlighted by Sugihara et al's (2002) research. Behaviour such as assertiveness and independence were valued as masculine traits in America but in Japan these individualist behaviours were not seen as socially desirable for either gender. Instead, both men and women were expected to show conformity, obedience and kindness – values traditionally associated with femininity in the West. These findings run parallel to data from a study comparing Chinese and American gender roles (Chia et al, 1994). Chinese women preferred masculine, dominant males to a lesser degree than women in the US. The ideal Chinese man is not the 'macho' type but is accomplished in art, music and military skills.

Intelligence and learning

NIGEL HOLT

You are expected in the examination to show both the skills of knowledge and understanding and the skills of analysis and evaluation in relation to the topic Intelligence and learning.

Where opportunities for their effective use arise, you will need to demonstrate an appreciation of issues and debates. These include the nature/nurture debate, ethical issues in research, free-will/determinism, reductionism, gender and culture bias, and the use of animals in research.

You will also need to demonstrate an understanding of How Science Works. You can do this through the effective use of studies in your answer (as description or evaluation) or where appropriate by evaluating methodology and findings.

WHAT YOU NEED TO KNOW

THEORIES OF INTELLIGENCE

- Theories of intelligence, including psychometric and information processing approaches
- Gardner's theory of multiple intelligences

ANIMAL LEARNING AND INTELLIGENCE

- The nature of simple learning (classical and operant conditioning) and its role in the behaviour of non-human animals
- Evidence for intelligence in non-human animals, e.g. self-recognition, social learning, deception

EVOLUTION OF INTELLIGENCE

- Evolutionary factors in the development of human intelligence, e.g. ecological demands, social complexity, brain size
- The role of genetic and environmental factors associated with intelligence test performance, including the influence of culture

THEORIES OF INTELLIGENCE

What is intelligence? Unfortunately, it is not easy to define and in a hundred years of debate and research, psychologists have failed to reach a consensus. It probably refers to the differences in the ways that people are able to solve problems, think logically, use language, understand concepts, learn, demonstrate skills, integrate ideas, achieve personal goals, and a multitude of other things. What it means to be intelligent can depend on who you are and where you live. For instance, in Western cultures, intelligence is usually measured in terms of ability to gain qualifications, pass examinations and hold down jobs with high levels of esteem. In some other cultures, being intelligent may be measured in terms of ability to hunt, how long a diver can hold his or her breath, or whether someone can communicate with spirits. People's idea of intelligence even varies historically, with views of intelligence having changed radically over time.

Intelligence is not a solid entity that can be weighed and packaged. However you describe it and wherever you come from, it is clear that intelligence is something that is invented by your culture. Psychologists refer to it as a 'socially constructed' concept, which means that it is something that, although it doesn't physically exist, is accepted as part of a culture. The concept has attracted considerable controversy – over how to define it, how to measure it, and even whether it

should be measured at all. Passer et al (2009) give a working definition of intelligence, at least from a Western perspective, as:

"The ability to acquire knowledge, to think and reason effectively, and to deal adaptively with the environment".

PSYCHOMETRIC THEORIES

The psychometric approach to measuring intelligence is concerned with identifying what it is that makes us perform differently on different tasks, and how we might measure it.

The psychometric theories of intelligence attempt to identify how intellect, or mental ability, is shaped, or made-up. Mental abilities are what we measure as intelligence. The task for the psychometric approach is to identify these mental abilities and then find ways to measure them reliably. The problem is that we do not know how many different mental abilities there are. Some psychometric approaches identify very few; some identify many more.

"You won't be asked about a particular theory in the exam – it will be a more general question on psychometric theory. Several different and distinct psychometric theories have been presented here in order to give you plenty to write about!"

DEFINITIONS OF INTELLIGENCE

"Viewed narrowly, there seem to be almost as many definitions of intelligence as there were experts asked to define it." So said Robert Sternberg, and indeed, it would be hard to disagree with him. Below are just a fraction of the many hundreds of definitions which give a taste of the breadth and diversity of the intelligence debate in psychology.

"An intelligence is the ability to solve problems, or to create products, that are valued within one or more cultural settings." *H. Gardner*

"The ability to carry on abstract thinking." *L. M. Terman*

"Intelligence is a general factor that runs through all types of performance." *A. Jensen*

"A global concept that involves an individual's ability to act purposefully, think rationally, and deal effectively with the environment." *D. Wechsler*

"...the term intelligence designates a complexly interrelated assemblage of functions, no one of which is completely or accurately known to man..." *R. M. Yerkes and A. W. Yerkes*

"...the cognitive ability to learn from experience, to reason well, to remember important information, and to cope with the demands of daily living." *R. Sternberg*

"Intelligence is what is measured by intelligence tests." *E. Boring*

SPEARMAN'S PSYCHOMETRIC THEORY

Charles Spearman (1923) investigated the correlation between test results in different academic areas. He noticed that English and Maths scores in schools were usually very highly positively correlated, and suggested that performance on intellectual tasks depended on a general mental capacity which he referred to as 'the g-factor'. Spearman said that it was g that provided the overall, general level of your intelligence and it did not depend on any training you might have had in a particular subject. g provides your 'core level' of intelligence. Your ability in a subject is due in part to g and in part to your ability to learn that subject – what Spearman referred to as the s-factor. Even today, g is thought to be the most important measure of what we know as intelligence.

Evaluation of Spearman's theory

» According to Schmidt and Hunter (2004), measurements of g are good predictors of job success. This means that there is a positive correlation between g level and how successful you will be at your job. In fact, g is a better predictor of job success than ability at job-specific skills! It seems that it doesn't matter if you are particularly good at welding if you want to be a metal worker: your g level is what's important, as a high g level means that you are in a good position to learn these new skills once in the job.

» Kuncel et al (2004) conducted a meta-analysis that looked at studies investigating success in education and success in working life. A large number of papers (127) were analysed. It was found that g level was highly correlated with success in both education and work, suggesting that g is a good predictor of general success in both areas.

» The level of g is closely related to our ability to process information. Jensen (1998) suggests that g is much more than an abstract, difficult to identify concept. He says that it may well have a physiological basis, which would support Spearman's idea that our underlying level of g (general intelligence) is inherited.

» Spearman's theories were based on observations of correlation data. His conclusion that there was a single underlying level of general intelligence is based on measurements that show that people's scores on different types of tasks tend to be highly correlated with one another. A high correlation does not by any means indicate a perfect correlation, nor does it prove a causal link. This means that although scores on one test may be similar to scores on another test, other factors, rather than a single level of intelligence, may well influence the scores.

» It is clear from studies of crystallised and fluid intelligence that g can be divided, at least into these two sub-levels. Evidence in support of Cattell and Horn's psychometric models of intelligence strongly support this point.

» It has been argued by many theorists in this area that intelligence is far too complex to be reduced to one or two factors. The alternative psychometric models have all indicated that g should be divided up in some way to account for this complexity.

THURSTONE'S PSYCHOMETRIC THEORY

L.L. Thurstone said that intelligence should be thought of as a range of primary mental abilities. He said that intelligence should be measured not as a single factor (g) but as seven separate and independent mental abilities in which individuals differed.

Ability	Definition
SPACE - S	Ability to visualise items and mentally manipulate them
VERBAL COMPREHENSION - V	Ability to define and understand words
WORD FLUENCY - W	Ability to produce words quickly
NUMBER - N	Ability to solve mathematical problems
PERCEPTION - P	Ability to see similarities and differences between things
MEMORY - M	The ability to remember and recall things
REASONING - R	The ability to use rules to deal with problems

1. Space

The ability to visualise relationships between items. Thurstone said that one mental ability was the ability to deal with items in space. For instance, being able to imagine an object and rotate it in your mind to another orientation is easier for some people than others. Those who have this ability are said to score highly on this mental ability. For instance, do the blocks on the right match those on the left? To carry out the task you have to mentally rotate and manipulate one set of blocks to see if you can make it match the other.

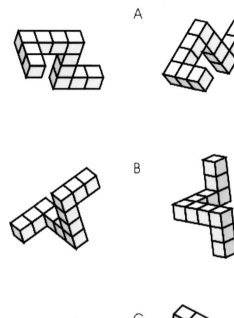

2. Verbal comprehension

The ability to gather information from what you read. Thurstone designed tests that required participants to read a passage of text and answer 'true or false' questions about it.

Here's an example.

College opens at 8am for breakfast in the café, which must be ordered before 8.30. Lunch is served after 4th period, beginning at 11.45 and ending at 2.00. Dinner can be ordered at lunchtime to be served at 4.30. Students can bring guests but they must ask permission 24 hours in advance.

1) You can order lunch at 9:45am if you wish.

True False Can't Say

2) Guests cannot be accommodated at breakfast time.

True False Can't Say

3) Dinner can be ordered at 11.45

True False Can't Say

3. Word Fluency

Thurstone said that our ability with words was one of his mental abilities. Participants would be

tested on word tasks, including speed with identifying words and making rhymes. Here are three examples:

Say as many words as you can beginning with the letter S in 60 seconds.

Say as many words as you can that rhyme with the word 'trap' in 60 seconds.

Identify as many vegetables as you can in 60 seconds.

4. Number

These tests examined ability to carry out mathematical tasks quickly and accurately. Participants would be given a page of relatively simple mathematical tasks and asked to carry out as many of them as possible in a given time.

5. Perception

In these tasks, Thurstone investigated the accuracy with which people could identify odd things in images, perhaps things that did not belong in a picture, or differences and similarities between pictures.

6. Memory

A good memory is often regarded as indicating high levels of intelligence. Thurstone identified memory as one of his mental abilities. These tests were designed to investigate how well people could remember something by 'rote'. This means learning a passage of text and repeating it word for word. Those with a good memory score higher on this type of task.

7. Reasoning

Finally, Thurstone identified skill at reasoning as a mental ability. Can you identify, or 'induce' rules, when faced with information or evidence? For instance:

What letter comes next in the following sequence?

a c e g i __

What number comes next in the following sequence?

5 6 11 17 28 __

Evaluation of Thurstone's theory

» For Mayer (2000), the concept of separate mental abilities is extremely useful in targeting areas for improvement. For instance, if we can identify 'number skill' as a mental ability then we can target training to help improve it if we find it is low. Without knowledge of specific strengths and weaknesses, such as those which Thurstone identified, education and training would be much harder to structure and target.

» Guilford (1967) agrees with Thurstone that identifying intelligence as a single factor (g) is too simplistic and underestimates the complexity of intelligence. Like Thurstone, Guilford argues that g should be divided into sub-categories of mental ability.

» In a meta-analysis of over 460 sets of results from different tests, Caroll (1993) provides support for Thurstone's concept of several mental abilities underlying intellectual tasks. In fact, Caroll went further, indicating that mental abilities could be split into three levels: *general mental abilities* (equivalent to Spearman's g), *broad abilities* (where Thurstone's abilities are included) and *narrow abilities*, where specific skills for certain tasks are included. Carroll called this his '3-striatum psychometric model'.

» Even though Guilford agrees with Thurstone that g is better divided into different mental abilities, he says that there are far more than the seven identified by Thurstone. In fact, his 1982 research article indicates that there are as many as 120. It seems that Thurstone's theory may be too simplistic.

» Thurstone's mental abilities were decided upon by using a mathematical technique called factor analysis, which is basically a long series of correlation calculations. Because of this, Thurstone's theory can be criticised for relying on correlation evidence that suggests a link between things that might all be described as 'spatial, verbal, mathematical etc'. A link does not mean that they are all influenced by the same things: it simply means that they happen to be linked or correlated in some way, and Thurstone does not tell us how.

CATTELL AND HORN'S PSYCHOMETRIC THEORY

Raymond Cattell and John Horn developed Spearman's idea of g. In their theory g is split into two factors, described as different but related parts of our intelligence. Cattell and Horn identified them as 'crystallised' and 'fluid' intelligence.

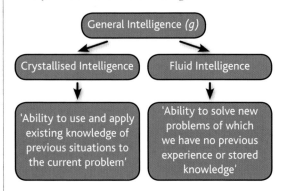

Crystallised *intelligence* (or gC) is the ability to apply what you already know to a new situation. In order to solve new tasks successfully we must retrieve information we already have about how best to carry out the task. Masunaga (2000) says that experts have high levels of crystallised intelligence. Expertise is a very difficult thing to define or identify, but we know it when we see it. An expert is someone who approaches a problem and knows the best way to tackle it. This is because they are very good at retrieving information about past experiences, and applying previously-learned methods and techniques to new situations. An expert computer programmer, for instance, will be able to draw on all their experience to quickly develop a working computer program, whereas a novice programmer would take much longer, having to consult books and web pages to gain the knowledge required to carry out the task.

If we experience a completely new problem, how do we go about solving it? When we do not have any experience of a problem-situation then crystallised intelligence is of no use to us. We must adapt what we already know to fit the new task. This is called *fluid intelligence* (or gF). Adaptation involves

TOWER OF HANOI – A GOOD MEASURE OF FLUID INTELLIGENCE

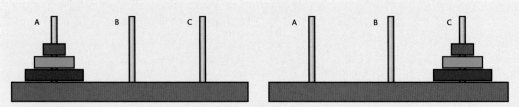

This is the 'Tower of Hanoi' problem. The start position is in the top panel, with the three disks on the left. The task is to move the three disks into the position shown in the bottom panel. You may only move one disk at a time, and you cannot place a larger disk on top of a smaller one. It is possible in nine moves.

careful thinking and reasoning, and it is reasoning that those with high levels of fluid intelligence are particularly good at. For instance, consider the Tower of Hanoi task. If you have never seen it before, the Tower of Hanoi requires careful reasoning. Applying these skills to a new, or even abstract problem (a theoretical problem that may only exist in your imagination) is the basis for fluid intelligence.

Evaluation of Cattell and Horn's theory

» According to Weinert and Hany (2003) there is evidence that, as we get older, crystallised intelligence improves and remains quite stable, but fluid intelligence tends to decline as we enter later adulthood. The fact that two separate abilities tend to behave differently as we age is evidence that there are different categories of intelligence.

» Some types of task correlate strongly with measures of fluid intelligence, and some with measures of crystallised intelligence. This suggests that the two really are different from one another, supporting Cattell and Horn's distinction (Kline, 1998).

» Geary (2005) suggests that fluid intelligence and crystallised intelligence actually use different parts of the brain, further suggesting that they are separate entities. Crystallised intelligence seems to be a function of brain systems involving the hippocampus, a structure in the brain that has long been associated with storage of long-term memories. Fluid intelligence appears to involve the use of brain systems more associated with attention and short-term memory, such as parts of the frontal cortex and the cingulated gyrus.

» Undheim (2008) took a second look at evidence that had previously been used to support the concept of crystallised and fluid intelligence. The data from this original research was re-analysed using a different mathematical technique. In addition to this, a very large new study of over 5,000 participants was instigated. The results of the research indicated that Cattell and Horn's distinction between crystallised and fluid intelligence could not be supported. Instead, Undheim indicates that splitting general intelligence into these two parts is too simplistic, and since neither is very well defined by Cattell and Horn anyway, both would be better further divided up.

» Brody (2000) says that far from being distinct and different, crystallised and fluid intelligence sometimes correlate with each other at rates in excess of 0.5. For psychological data this is a high positive correlation. Some have argued that this closeness suggests that they are not really distinct types of intelligence at all, but two aspects of the same thing.

» Some psychologists consider working memory and gF to be closely related. Working memory is a well-established concept in psychology and refers to that part of the memory system which temporarily stores and uses information. Research by Jaeggi et al (2008) suggests that exercising working memory can help and even improve gF. What is interesting about this particular study is that, whilst research has established that direct practice on intelligence test-type material can improve gF, this is the first to demonstrate that training on an entirely different task can do the same. They gave participants visual and auditory training tasks designed in such a way that they would not get any easier with practice, i.e. they would remain demanding for working memory. They found that success on intelligence tests measuring gF was positively related to the amount of training – the more training, the greater the gF improvement. Jaeggi et al have shown that not only can fluid intelligence be improved through training, but this applies regardless of the starting point, so that people of very low or very high fluid intelligence are equally trainable. This contradicts the more traditional psychometric view that regards intelligence as a largely fixed commodity.

INFORMATION PROCESSING THEORIES

Information processing theories examine the mental activities people engage in when solving problems. Rather than the content of intelligence, which is the concern of psychometric theories, the emphasis here is on common cognitive processes, i.e. on how people solve problems rather than what is being measured or what the score is.

"Your exam question won't mention Sternberg by name – it will ask for an 'information processing theory'. Be sure that you understand that Sternberg's theory is information processing theory and give a good account it. You also need to know two information processing theories – you can use Gardner's theory (see later) in this case, but make sure you emphasise the information processing part of it."

STERNBERG'S TRIARCHIC THEORY

For Sternberg (2007), intelligent behaviour is about adapting successfully to changing environmental conditions. Behaviours may therefore be more or less intelligent according to the context in which they occur. For instance, a top computer programmer might be considered intelligent in Western culture because of their ability to solve particular problems which are important in our culture. However, this 'intelligence' would count for nothing if we were lost deep in a tropical jungle. Here, a local inhabitant who had no experience of a computer but who could successfully forage for food would be more 'intelligent'.

TYPES OF INTELLECTUAL COMPETENCE

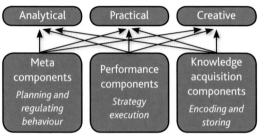

UNDERLYING COGNITIVE PROCESSES

For Sternberg, intelligent behaviour is basically the interplay of the *context* in which the behaviour occurs, the *prior experiences* brought to bear on a particular task, and the *cognitive processes* required by the task. Sternberg splits our intelligence system into two parts: *intellectual competence* and *underlying cognitive processes*. Each of these parts is itself divided into three sections.

"A picture tells a thousand words, apparently. There is nothing to say that you cannot draw diagrams in your exam if they help your explanation. Learning to draw a diagram can be a great way to remember things. Even if you don't use it in the exam, a quick sketch on some rough paper can really help."

Types of intellectual competence

Sternberg claims that there are three different intellectual competences. In order to develop intelligence we should target all three of these areas and schooling systems should be designed to focus on each of the three if the aim is to develop a person's intellectual ability.

Analytical Intelligence: This is the sort of intelligence that tests like the IQ test and WAIS (Wechsler Adult Intelligence Scale) are good at measuring. Good analytical intelligence is shown by the ability to solve problems by using strategies that manipulate the elements of a problem.

Practical Intelligence: This type of intelligence provides us with the ability to deal with everyday life. It is the kind that allows us to time-manage ourselves, organise our lives and in some cases the lives of others.

Creative Intelligence: When we encounter a new problem of a type or form not previously experienced, thinking creatively about how to solve it is extremely useful. Creative intelligence is the set of mental abilities that allows us this flexibility to deal with new or unique problems.

Underlying cognitive processes

Sternberg says that the different types of intellectual competence (analytical, practical, creative) are supported and provided for by three separate cognitive systems. Each of these cognitive systems has input into each of the intellectual abilities.

Metacomponents: These are skills that we use to plan and organise what it is that we are going to do. Included here are general problem-solving skills, such as formulating predictions and hypotheses about what might happen if we tried something. Sternberg says that it is these metacomponents that provide the general differences we see in intelligence levels in a population. Those with strong abilities here will show higher levels of general intelligence.

Performance components: These are the skills we use when we are actually carrying out the task. Performance components seek strategies for carrying out the task from metacomponents and apply them to the current task – and where relevant, information from past experience, provided by the knowledge acquisition components, is built in. Performance components also interpret what is happening during the task and adjust our performance accordingly.

Knowledge acquisition components: We could think of this cognitive process as our 'learning from experience' component. Here we hold memories of tackling problems and tasks in the past, providing the information where relevant to the current task where it is dealt with by the performance components. The knowledge acquisition components also allow us to store information about how we dealt with the current task and what happened, adding to our store of knowledge to be used next time.

Evaluation of Sternberg's information processing approach

» A study of Brazilian street children showed that they were extremely good at the sort of mathematics they needed in their everyday lives, perhaps for gambling, or calculating the change when selling small items. This is despite their extremely poor performance at mathematics in school. For Sternberg (2004), this is support for the triarchic theory's idea that practical experience is not necessarily related to academic performance, and so forms a separate part of intellectual competence.

» Kenyan children were tested on their abilities in academic tasks and their knowledge of natural medical treatments for illnesses. A good knowledge of herbal properties is extremely important for survival, and so is a very practical skill. Sternberg (2001) found no correlation between academic ability and this practical, medical knowledge. He even showed that the two were often negatively correlated, which suggests that as academic ability increases, practical medical ability decreases and vice versa. This is evidence that practical ability should be regarded as a separate intellectual competence.

» A study by Sternberg (1985) found that older people solved problems differently from younger people. This, says Sternberg, is evidence that the younger people had not yet developed the planning and problem-solving skills that the adults had. In other words, the younger people's metacomponents were different from those of the older people – evidence for differences in the underlying cognitive processes.

» Sternberg's theory says that the three types of intellectual competence are distinct and different from one another. Caroll (1993) says that performance on tasks that require each type of intellectual competence show some correlation. This suggests that the three may well be part of a common intelligence system measured by IQ. The three types of intellectual competence may therefore not be as separate as triarchic theory suggests.

» Gottfredson (2003) challenges the claim of triarchic theory that practical intelligence is different from general or academic intelligence. He says that the evidence for this is poor. Only certain aspects of the many studies carried out to investigate the difference between practical intelligence and g are used to support the theory, and so the evidence for a difference is exaggerated.

» According to Carson et al (2003), creativity comes from a high IQ. The higher the IQ the more creative the person. This suggests that it is not appropriate to think of creative intelligence as completely different from IQ, as the triarchic theory suggests.

"Although each theory has been evaluated separately here, you can also employ other theories as evaluation by using them as alternative explanations. Not only does this give you more material to work with, but can also be a very effective way to evaluate a theory – e.g. how does this theory measure up to other theories?"

GARDNER'S THEORY OF MULTIPLE INTELLIGENCES

Whilst psychometric theories focus on varieties of intellectual abilities, Gardner (2000) proposed that there are multiple intelligences. This idea that there are separate intelligences comes from his early observations of people who might, through brain damage for example, lose ability in one particular area but have other preserved abilities. He also noted that some people tend to excel in one or two things but have no other particularly developed abilities: for example people with savant syndrome have poor language and communication skills but have exceptional skills in a particular ability, such as art or mathematics.

"You need to learn Gardner's theory – you could be asked a question on it in the exam. Make sure that, as a minimum, you learn the logic of his approach and can remember and say something about as many of his 'multiple intelligences' as possible."

In order for an ability to be included as an intelligence several criteria have to be satisfied:

1. **The potential for brain damage to affect this ability in isolation from others.**

   For example, language abilities can be selectively damaged or spared by strokes.

2. **The existence of individuals with exceptional skills in these areas, e.g. savants and prodigies**.

   This enables us to see particular intelligences in relative isolation.

3. **The existence of the ability in experimental psychological tasks**.

   Tasks can be devised which can isolate the particular skills in the intelligences and determine how they are related.

4. **The ability should be measurable**.

   Tests can be developed to assess which skills have common underlying factors and which do not.

5. **Abilities should be identifiably different from others by having a distinct developmental history with an end 'expert' performance standard**.

   The skills of someone like a top athlete and the steps taken to attain this expertise can be examined.

6. **Evolutionary plausibility**.

   Forms of the particular intelligences can be seen in other species, for example spatial skills in birds.

7. **Propensity for encoding in a symbol system**.

   Codes such as language and mathematics reflect important aspects of the intelligences.

8. **At least one identifiable core operation**.

   A core operation is a basic information processing mechanism in the brain. Core operations include:

Linguistic:	syntax, phonology, semantics, pragmatics
Musical:	pitch, rhythm, timbre
Logical-mathematical:	number, categorisation, relations
Spatial:	accurate mental visualisation, mental transformation of images
Bodily-kinaesthetic:	control of one's own body, control in handling objects
Interpersonal:	awareness of others' feelings, emotions, goals, motivations
Intrapersonal:	awareness of one's own feelings, emotions, goals, motivations
Naturalistic:	recognition and classification of objects in the environment

"In his description Gardner makes it clear that he has developed another information processing theory. This is important! You are expected to know two information processing theories – you have Sternberg and Gardner presented here. Remember to emphasise the information processing aspects of Gardner's theory, and remember that as well as having an essay on information processing theories you could be asked a question just on Gardner's multiple intelligences!"

According to Gardner, there are at least eight separate and relatively independent kinds of intelligence which relate to the core operations. Whilst all brain-unimpaired people possess these intelligences, each person has them in a unique combination.

1. Linguistic intelligence

Those with high levels of linguistic intelligence show abilities with all aspects of language. This includes the written forms of language as well as spoken forms. Linguistically intelligent people could be, for example, great public speakers, such as Winston Churchill, or Barack Obama. Also in this group would be authors and poets, who work with forming words into sentences that make sense. These might include J.K. Rowling and William Shakespeare. Linguistic intelligence is also needed by other people for whose work language is important. Lawyers and solicitors, for instance, must use language skilfully if they are to be successful.

2. Logical-mathematical intelligence

Logical-mathematical intelligence is the ability to detect patterns, think logically and reason deductively. This is the type of intelligence shown by mathematicians and scientists.

3. Visuospatial intelligence

Those with high levels of visuospatial intelligence are good at imagining, designing and working on three-dimensional things such as buildings and sculptures. They are skilled at working with both large and small spaces. This is the type of intel-

	Intelligence Type	Description	Example
1	Linguistic	Ability with spoken and written language	The writer, William Shakespeare
2	Logical-mathematical	Reasoning logically, mathematically and scientifically	The physicist, Albert Einstein
3	Visuospatial	Solving spatial skills such as building and designing things	The architect, Frank Lloyd Wright
4	Musical	Perception of musical qualities such as rhythm, and an ability to understand music	The musican, Mozart
5	Bodily-Kinaesthetic	Using one's own body to solve problems	The footballer, Wayne Rooney
6	Interpersonal	The ability to understand *other* people's thoughts, intentions, motivations and desires	The great leader, Gandhi
7	Naturalistic	Identifying and understanding information that occurs in the natural world	The naturalist, Charles Darwin
8	Intrapersonal	The ability to understand *our own* thoughts, intentions and motivations	All of us strive for this!

ligence you might find in architects and garden designers.

4. Musical intelligence

Those with great musical intelligence are good at all or different aspects of expression. These might include composition, performance, recording and producing music. This need not be the type of music you hear played by orchestras in the world's grandest opera houses. Yes, Mozart and Tchaikovsky clearly had great musical intelligence, but so too do today's great musicians and performers.

5. Bodily-kinaesthetic intelligence

This is the type of intelligence associated with solving problems by using all or part of our own bodies. Our kinaesthetic sense is used to detect our bodily position, and great knowledge and control of this sets some people apart from others. Great gymnasts and dancers clearly have this type of intelligence, but so too do others who show great dexterity in their jobs. These might include watch makers and surgeons, for whom careful control of movements is extremely important.

6. Interpersonal intelligence

This type of intelligence is concerned with understandings of other people's motivations and intentions. Those with interpersonal intelligence make great work-mates, and often good managers, who are highly skilled at working with people and getting the very best out of them. They are also good negotiators and counsellors, who listen carefully and can make accurate decisions about a

situation. The great politicians all show high levels of interpersonal intelligence.

7. Intrapersonal intelligence

This is the capacity to understand ourselves. Good intrapersonal intelligence allows us knowledge and understanding of our weaknesses and strengths, fears and limits. We know how to deal with our frustrations, motivations and emotions. This is just the type of information we need to be able to run our lives successfully.

8. Naturalistic intelligence

Those who are good at identifying items in nature are said to have good naturalistic intelligence. Zoologists, game-wardens, hunters, those who fish, metereologists and weather watchers could all be said to have good naturalistic intelligence.

Gardner's theory allows us to say that the intelligence of traditionally brilliant people, like Marie Curie and Albert Einstein, may be comparable with that shown by others, with great abilities in areas we may not, until now, have regarded as indicating intelligence. These might include the undeniable sporting skills of Tiger Woods, the artistic cooking flair of Jamie Oliver and the huge musical talent of Amy Winehouse. The intelligence needed to survive on the street, or live successfully on the wrong side of the law, as a thief or drug-dealer, might also be added. Indeed, the list of intelligences continues to grow, as Gardner (2004) has proposed two more: *mental searchlight intelligence* (an ability which allows people to scan widely and take in and utilise lots of information quickly); and *laser intelligence* (an ability to focus on and become expert at very specific things such as science).

Evaluation of Gardner's Multiple Intelligences theory

» Gardner (2000) claims that the different types of intelligence are controlled and organised by different but interacting parts of the brain. Observations of brain damaged individuals certainly support the idea that very specific particular abilities can be lost. However, this is not evidence that they correspond to Gardner's intelligences, nor have all Gardner's intelligences been indisputably shown to be under the control of distinct brain systems.

» Small numbers of people who have autistic spectrum disorders (known by most people as 'autistics') have a form of autism that shows itself in a person's possession of great skills in one area or another. These people are called savants, and they may show enormous skill at drawing from memory, having seen an image for a few minutes at most, or an unbelievable musical ability for instance. Gardner (1983) said that savants were evidence of his multiple intelligence theory, as a very large proportion of savants have artistic or musical abilities, but severely impaired social intelligence. This suggests the existence of different types of intelligence.

» Aspects of multiple intelligence theory have been widely used in education. *Project Spectrum* however has gone one step further and adopted the concept of multiple intelligences wholesale. Project Spectrum was a long-term project developing an alternative approach to the curriculum for preschool and early primary education, based on the concept of multiple intelligences. The kinds of teaching and assessment children are exposed to are far more varied than in the traditional curriculum. For example, assessments might take place as children play with stimulating materials, so rather than answer abstract questions, children demonstrate their competence by doing things. Materials used in the classroom reflect the various intelligences, so that things like singing and performance become important activities, as do practical activities such as assembling things and observable problem-solving tasks. So multiple intelligence theory is being applied, and, it is claimed, with some success.

» Concerns have however been expressed about the use of this theory in education. There may be too much focus on what children do well at the expense of putting work into areas of weakness. For example, whether or not linguistic intelligence is recognised as a natural strength, something like reading is still an essential life skill which has to be mastered.

» For White (1997), the definitions of the different intelligences are insufficiently clear. Gardner himself says that there is often a form of 'judgement' involved in deciding on how to separate the intelligences. This is clearly subjective and so the theory may lack reliability, as one person's judgement may not be the same as another's.

» Critics of Gardner suggest that none of the intelligence types, other than the first three, should really be regarded as intelligences at all, but would be better considered as 'skills' or 'talents'. Only the first three intelligences can be reliably measured, and this is by using traditional IQ tests (Passer et al, 2009).

» Waterhouse (2006) however makes a more direct attack on Gardner's theory. She points out that despite the widespread acceptance of the multiple intelligence concept, the theory lacks adequate research support for it to be adopted for educational use. Furthermore, regardless of Gardner's assertions that the theory was developed from an evolutionary perspective and that the core operations were embedded in neuroscience, there are no cognitive psychologists, evolutionary psychologists or neuroscientists actively engaged in research aimed at validating the various intelligences. The clear suggestion is that scientists do not accept the scientific claims of the theory.

Wayne Rooney, someone who demonstrates bodily-kinaesthetic intelligence.

ANIMAL LEARNING AND INTELLIGENCE

Whilst evolution determines a great deal of an animal's behaviour, behaviour can also result from an animal's experience in its environment. In order to respond effectively to their natural environments appropriately and effectively, non-human animals must be able to learn and adapt. Our understanding of how animals learn and how that learning influences their behaviour has been greatly enhanced by the theories of classical and operant conditioning.

CLASSICAL CONDITIONING

Classical conditioning was discovered by Russian physiologist Ivan Pavlov. Pavlov noticed that experimental dogs in his laboratory were responsive to the sound of their food being delivered. They would become excited at hearing the footsteps of the technician who normally brought their food and begin to salivate. Recognising that this was not a natural response, since salivation is a reflexive response to food, not to the researcher, he concluded that the dogs had made a link, or association, between the sound of the footsteps and the food. Based on this observation and subsequent experiments, he developed a method of demonstrating how new relationships between stimuli were learned. This is now known as Pavlov's paradigm.

The first step involved presenting dogs with food, in response to which Pavlov's dogs salivated. This natural reflexive behaviour Pavlov called the *unconditioned response (UR)*. A UR is caused by a naturally occurring stimulus, which he called an *unconditioned stimulus (US)*. It is, for example, an automatic natural reflex (unconditioned response) for a dog to salivate to food.

"This is a good diagram to learn. If you have to describe classical conditioning in the exam you can get a lot of marks by just drawing this (accurately!) and describing what's going on."

Shortly before each time the food (US) was presented, Pavlov rang a bell. Dogs do not salivate to the sound of bells therefore it is called the *neutral stimulus (NS)*. After several pairings of the US and NS, conditioning was tested by presenting the sound of the bell (NS) alone.

Pavlov found that the dogs would eventually salivate to the sound of the bell alone – they had learned a new association between the sound of a bell and food. The bell had become a *conditioned stimulus (CS)*, and the salivation to its sound a *conditioned response (CR)*. Pavlov called the learning process 'conditioning'. He said that regularly experiencing one stimulus in the presence of another stimulus would eventually lead to the animal being conditioned to respond to both stimuli in the same way.

Pavlov further found that presenting the conditioned stimulus (the bell) repeatedly without any food made the link weaken and eventually disappear. He called this *extinction*. Another interesting phenomenon associated with classical conditioning is *spontaneous recovery*. After extinction, the new learning can appear to be lost. However, the conditioned response may return spontaneously at some later time. The conditioned response is,

Before conditioning

| Unconditioned Stimulus (US) food | → | Unconditioned Response (UR) salivation |

During conditioning

| Neutral Stimulus (NS) bell |

↓

| Unconditioned Stimulus (US) food | → | Unconditioned Response (UR) salivation |

After conditioning

| Conditioned Stimulus (CS) bell | → | Conditioned Response (CR) salivation |

Pavlov's paradigm

however, weaker than it had been before extinction. The fact that an animal may experience spontaneous recovery suggests that the relationship between the CR and the US is still present in the animal even though the animal has not shown it in some time. This means that the animal must, somehow, have suppressed the relationship. This suppression is called *inhibition*.

Timing is terribly important in classical conditioning. If the US is not presented at the same time as, or very near to, the CS then an animal may not learn the link between the two events. To use his research as an example, had Pavlov not rung the bell very close to the time that food was presented, the dogs would not have learnt the relationship. He called this the *law of temporal contiguity*. There are different types of temporal contiguity:

Forward conditioning: The bell is presented just before and during food presentation, producing very strong learning.

Backward conditioning: The bell is presented during and just after food presentation, producing weak learning.

Simultaneous conditioning: The bell and the food are presented at the same time, producing very strong learning.

Trace conditioning: The bell is rung and stopped before the food is presented, producing weak learning.

Pavlov found that any stimuli resembling the conditioned stimulus could generate the same conditioned response. The more similar the stimulus was to the real CS, the more likely it was to bring about the CR. This is called *generalisation* – the CS-CR relationship could be generalised to similar but different stimuli. Pavlov also showed that animals could distinguish between the genuine CS and other stimuli which were similar but different. He called this *discrimination*.

THE ROLE OF CLASSICAL CONDITIONING IN THE BEHAVIOUR OF NON-HUMAN ANIMALS

Classical conditioning can be seen in the behaviour of wild animals, as well as of laboratory animals such as Pavlov's dogs. It can most easily be observed in foraging behaviour. For instance, the ability to discriminate between plants and animals that can or cannot be eaten will clearly give an animal survival advantages. Blue tit foraging serves as a good example of this. This bird is small and has a high metabolism so it has to eat very regularly to stay alive. Since its main diet is caterpillars, it must be able to discriminate between caterpillars which can be eaten safely (nearly all of them), and those that should be avoided because they are toxic and would make the bird sick (those with bright red or yellow markings). Failure to discriminate in this way would cause the bird a lot of problems!

TASTE AVERSION IN COYOTES AND WOLVES

One type of classical conditioning is called *taste aversion conditioning*. This is where animals learn to avoid certain foods because past encounters with the food resulted in illness or discomfort. Garcia et al (1977) made use of this in their study of the wild foraging behaviour of coyotes and wolves.

The researchers wrapped mutton in the raw skin of a sheep and left it out for wolves and coyotes to eat. The mutton had been injected with lithium chloride, an odourless substance which would make anything that ate it feel ill. Next, the animals were led towards live sheep, which would not make them ill if eaten. If the coyotes and wolves had been conditioned by the poisonous mutton they would not approach the sheep, believing that they would make them ill. If however the poisonous mutton had had no long-lasting effects on their learning they would approach the sheep as normal.

Garcia et al found that both coyotes and wolves did not attack the sheep. The coyotes smelled the sheep and turned away almost immediately. The wolves did approach and catch sheep at first, but on contact with the animal they released them and withdrew.

It was concluded that the relationship between conditioned stimulus and conditioned response was evident in the wild as it had been in the laboratory. In this case the conditioned stimulus was the smell and taste of the sheep (mutton) and sheep skin. The conditioned response was the feeling of illness. This confirms that animals can learn these relationships, and that doing so can protect them from illness and even death.

"It is an argument in support of classical conditioning that it can be seen to occur in the natural wild behaviour of animals, so any of this material can be used to positively evaluate the theory."

That classical conditioning is important in the behaviour of animals is a very straightforward observation to make. An electric fence is put around a field to deter cows from crossing. Although it looks a flimsy blockade to a large advancing cow, it works very well, because of classical conditioning. A cow touches the wire and receives a shock. It now associates the fence with something unpleasant and avoids future contact. A similar tactic is used by some golf courses to prevent rabbits getting onto the greens and tearing them up in their search for roots! Some bird seeds are sold covered in pepper in order to deter squirrels. Why would this work? Squirrels hate pepper: having encountered the 'doctored' seed in the bird feeder, they associate pepper with the food source, and will soon learn to avoid first the food, then the bird feeder altogether. Birds are not affected by this – they can't detect pepper so will continue feeding.

The relationship between food and illness is a very important one. Eating food that makes an animal ill can have catastrophic consequences. A weak animal is vulnerable to attack, and illness will leave the animal open to predators. In times of scarcity, when food is hard to find, the food and illness relationship is even more direct. Put simply, one bad meal can literally kill an animal. It is well known that rats will eat a small piece of an unknown food substance to see if it makes them ill before consuming a larger more satisfying portion.

EVALUATION OF CLASSICAL CONDITIONING

Classical conditioning is a relatively old theory, having been identified originally by Pavlov around the beginning of the 20th century. The theory has stimulated a great deal of research since then, some of it supporting the theory, some of it not.

The research of Hollis (1984) provides an example of how classical conditioning can be seen in the behaviour of a wide range of animal species. He produced conditioned behaviour in the gourami fish. When faced with another male fish, male gourami show aggressive behaviour. When a red light was paired with the arrival of another male

fish the gourami eventually became aggressive when the light came on, regardless of whether or not another male was present. This is evidence that wild animals are readily prepared to learn by classical conditioning. Hollis (1990) extended his earlier work, showing that gourami could be trained to respond less aggressively when they anticipated the arrival of a female fish with which they might mate. Pairing a red light with the presentation of a female fish eventually resulted in less aggressive behaviour at the presentation of the red light alone. This is evidence, says Hollis, of the flexibility of classical conditioning in the learning of a range of behaviours.

Pavlovian classical conditioning does however have its limitations. Some of the best evidence for this comes from studies of taste aversion. In one study, Garcia and Koelling (1966) gave two groups of rats sweetened water to drink. After tasting the sweetened water, one group of rats was made sick by exposure to X-rays and the other group received an electric shock. This is the classical conditioning stage – according to Pavlovian conditioning both groups of rats should now associate the sweetened water with sickness and avoid it in future. However, this was not the case. Garcia and Koelling found that when again presented with the chance to drink sweetened water, only the X-rayed group avoided it – the shocked rats happily drank it. This occurred because the taste of sweetened water became a conditioned stimulus (CS) when it was associated with a biologically relevant event (US) like sickness. Wild rats depend on taste to select food: therefore they may be biologically predisposed to make an association between taste and sickness. Taste did not become a CS when associated with shock because taste is not biologically relevant to shock-produced pain.

This 'Garcian' conditioning differs in several respects from the more traditional Pavlovian conditioning, and clearly indicates that the latter theory has certain important limitations and requires revision:

One trial learning: Taste aversion studies show that it is possible for animals to learn relationships between a stimulus and a response in one single trial. This is contrary to the theory of classical conditioning that suggests that a number of pairings of the NS and US are needed for a conditioned response to develop.

Extinction: In classical conditioning, the unconditioned stimulus eventually extinguishes if the NS and US are never again paired.

However, taste aversions are very hard to extinguish, and with taste stimuli, the NS/US relationship holds very strongly for a long time even though the pairing is not repeated.

Contiguity: Pavlovian classical conditioning says that short intervals are needed between the presentation of the NS and US for conditioning to take place. This is not the case in taste aversion studies. There is a long delay between taste and becoming sick from X-ray overdose but the relationship is still learned.

Studies like that of Garcia and Koelling suggest that animals readily learn to associate taste with sickness because it is related to their natural means of selecting food. This is supported by studies which have shown that animals which do not select food by taste have difficulty learning an association between taste and sickness. For example, birds select food by sight rather than taste so while they readily learn to identify sickness-producing food on the basis of how it looks, they do not readily learn to do so on the basis of taste (Wilcoxon et al, 1971).

It seems that what may be classically conditioned is a reflection of an animal's evolutionary adaption to their natural environment. This directly contradicts the traditional Pavlovian conditioning view that the laws of learning are the same for all species in all situations. This built-in bias rather supports the alternative ethological view that animals adapt their learning ability to suit their particular environments.

Ethologists argue that to truly understand an animal's behaviour, the animal has to be studied in its natural environment. For this reason ethologists have long been critical of laboratory-based research into animal behaviour, such as conditioning studies. The tasks required of animals in these studies do not arise naturally but are elicited by the artificial laboratory environment. Such studies also use a very limited range of animals, typically the rat or pigeon. This has given rise to distorted and false views about animal behaviour, such as the belief that the laws of classical conditioning apply equally to all species.

OPERANT CONDITIONING

In classical conditioning, Pavlov showed that dogs could learn to associate the sound of a bell with the delivery of their food. They learned that the sound of the bell meant that food would be delivered, and so salivated, not at the food itself, but rather, to the sound of the bell. This salivating is an elicited response.

In classical conditioning, learning happens to an animal – it doesn't have to do anything for learning to occur. It is essentially a passive, involuntary learning. This clearly does not explain all animal learning. Sometimes, an animal's own behaviour determines whether it will learn or not – in other words, an animal does something then learns from the consequences of its actions. The theory of operant conditioning was proposed by B.F. Skinner (1940) in order to explain this different type of learning. Skinner based his theory on the earlier work of Thorndike.

Thorndike's 'Law of Effect'

In 1911, Edward Thorndike developed a cage-like apparatus he called a 'puzzle box'. In his research, he placed a hungry cat inside the puzzle box, which could be opened by pressing a lever or pulling on a string. The important thing here is that the cat was hungry. Thorndike placed food just put of reach through the bars of the box. The cat tried its best to get to the food, scratching and digging at the walls and the bars of the puzzle box. Thorndike showed that eventually the cat learned how to escape, by pushing the lever or pulling on the string, enabling it to reach the food. As the research continued, Thorndike noticed that the cat became faster and faster at escaping, clearly showing that they had learned how to escape, by operating the opening mechanism. He called this 'instrumental learning', adding that the animal was not actually gaining any great insight into their problem, but instead they were applying a 'trial and error' based system, where they tried something and if it worked they tried it again. He called this the *law of effect*, which means that if an action has positive consequences it will be more likely to be repeated in the future, and if an action has annoying or frustrating consequences it will be less likely to recur in the future.

Skinner's box

Building on Thorndike's earlier work, Skinner described operant conditioning as a type of learning in which behaviour is influenced by the consequences that follow it. For instance, a cat in a puzzle box will push a lever if the consequences are that it is allowed to escape and eat the food outside the box. The lever-pushing is encouraged because of the pleasant consequences that follow it.

Skinner developed a piece of apparatus called a *conditioning chamber* (it later became more commonly known as a Skinner box).

Skinner box.

In effect, the box is an easy to clean chamber containing a feeding shoot, a lever and possibly a light and a buzzer. Hungry rats are placed in the chamber and their behaviour observed and recorded. It is in the nature of a hungry rat to engage in exploration of the cage. Eventually, it will accidentally press the lever. This lever press results in the appearance of a food pellet. The rat quickly associates the lever with food, and learns that as a consequence of its behaviour (lever press) something pleasant will happen (food will be dispensed). The rat will now happily press the lever whenever it wants food – it has been conditioned.

Reinforcement

One of the key concepts in operant conditioning is *reinforcement*. A reinforcer is anything that increases the likelihood of a behaviour occurring again. In the case of the Skinner box, food is the reinforcer for lever pressing. (Reinforcements that result in positive consequences, like getting a food reward, are known as *positive reinforcers*.) Whilst this demonstrates that behaviours can be encouraged by rewarding them, the converse is also the case. Behaviours that go unrewarded or are met by unpleasant consequences are less likely to recur. This is called *punishment*.

He showed this experimentally by providing a mild electric shock to the rat through the floor of the Skinner box if it pressed the lever. He found that the negative consequence (the shock) meant that the behaviour (lever pressing) became less and less regular. If you have had pets you will know that negative consequences for unwanted behaviour can often discourage the animal. For instance, a puppy can be discouraged from using your nice new sofa as a chew-toy simply by raising your voice. The tone of the voice is experienced as unpleasant for the puppy and so it learns that its naughtiness must stop or its new owner will continue to shout.

Negative reinforcement describes a situation where a behaviour is encouraged that makes an unpleasant consequence less likely. For instance, rats can learn that if they push a lever when a red light comes on they will not receive an electric shock. The rat learns to produce the lever-pressing behaviour in response to the light – not for food, but to avoid the negative consequences of their not pressing the lever.

Operant conditioning also distinguishes between *primary* and *secondary* reinforcers. Primary reinforcers are naturally occurring things like water, comfort, warmth and food: when presented as consequences for behaviour, they are particularly strong encouragements for the repetition of that behaviour. A secondary reinforcer is not naturally occurring, but is associated with the primary reinforcers. For example, if a clicking sound is heard by the rat in a Skinner box when it presses the lever, the rat will learn to start pressing the lever when it hears the clicking sound. In this example, the clicking sound is not directly related to a reward, but is associated to a primary reinforcer by the lever pressing.

Many of the phenomena associated with classical conditioning also apply to operant conditioning. *Generalisation* occurs when animals make responses which resemble the original reinforced response. For instance, a rat may be conditioned to push a lever every time it hears a buzzer. It may, however, produce the same response (but less often) to the sound of a different buzzer. *Discrimination* occurs when an animal is able to distinguish a behaviour that will bring about a reward from another behaviour that won't. If a response is never again reinforced then *extinction* will occur – that is, the learned response will gradually fade.

Behaviour shaping

Once simple behaviours are learned through positive and negative reinforcement, more complex behaviours could be encouraged by combining them, a process Skinner called *behaviour shaping*. Shaping starts with a reinforcement of any behaviour which resembles the desired behaviour. The process of generalisation means that an animal is not just more likely to repeat this behaviour, but similar behaviours also. When a behaviour appears that resembles the one that is wanted, that too is reinforced. The animal is basically having its behaviour shaped in successive approximations towards the desired behaviour. Ultimately, the animal's behaviour will not resemble that which it started with. Quite complex behaviours can result from behaviour shaping. Indeed, it could be argued that relatively few animal behaviours are the result of a single reinforcement but rather due to a reinforcement history.

Schedules of reinforcement

In operant conditioning the researcher does not have to reward or punish the animal every time it produces the behaviour under investigation, a lever press for example. They may decide to provide consequences for the behaviour every time the behaviour happens, or they may decide to present consequences every tenth time, for instance. These are called *schedules of reinforcement*. A *continuous schedule* is when an animal is reinforced every time they produce the desired behaviour. *Partial schedules* on the other hand are when the animal is reinforced only occasionally. There are a number of different types of partial schedules:

Type of schedule	Description
Fixed ratio schedules	The reinforcer is presented after a fixed number of responses. For instance, an animal will receive food on every 10th occasion.
Variable ratio schedules	The reinforcer is presented on an average number of responses. For instance, the animal will receive food *on average* every 10 presses. Sometimes it will have to press more, sometimes less, before food is delivered – but it will average 10 presses.
Fixed interval schedules	The reinforcer is presented after a set amount of time has passed. For instance, food will be presented 30 seconds after a lever press.
Variable interval schedules	The reinforcer is presented after an average amount of time. For instance, food may be presented, on average, 30 seconds after a lever press. Sometimes the animal will have to wait longer, sometimes less, before food is delivered, but the average will be 30 seconds.

Schedules of reinforcement.

Researchers have found that speed of learning and speed of extinction can depend on the schedule of reinforcement used. Partial reinforcement for example produces faster and stronger learning that continuous reinforcement. Variable interval schedules produce particularly persistent behaviours since the animal doesn't know when it is going to be rewarded: it only understands that at some point it will be. Behaviour (e.g. lever pressing) with this schedule is stronger than with fixed ratio, where an animal will quickly learn what to expect in terms of reinforcement and will more quickly cease the learned behaviour (e.g. lever pressing) after a certain number of lever presses without reinforcement.

THE ROLE OF OPERANT CONDITIONING IN THE BEHAVIOUR OF NON-HUMAN ANIMALS

The ability to adapt their behaviour to their environment and learn by experiences granted by operant conditioning provides an animal with a great evolutionary advantage. Changing behaviour to suit different conditions might be described as a form of intelligence, and if it helps the animal to survive then the animal is more likely to reproduce. This means that its genes are passed onto the next generation.

Much of the research on operant conditioning has been carried out in carefully controlled laboratories. Some may say that this means that the research lacks ecological validity, and that the relationships between the observed behaviours and the consequences of those behaviours may not happen in uncontrolled natural conditions. However, there is observational research to show that the principles of operant conditioning really are evident in wild animal behaviour. One of the most famous of these studies was from West and King (1988) who found that female cowbirds influence the outcome of male song development.

EVALUATION OF OPERANT CONDITIONING

Operant conditioning is a well-established theory which has attracted a great deal of research and debate since its inception in the 1940s.

There is ample evidence that operant conditioning is an important part of the behavioural repertoire of wild animals. West and King's research with cowbirds was a clear demonstration of how birds might alter their song patterns in response to a mating display from a female. Fuji (2002) showed that the laboratory-based operant conditioning principle applied directly to the behaviour of wild animals, by placing a version of the Skinner box out-of-doors. He found that wild pigeons could

THE SONG OF THE COWBIRD

Cowbirds are insect eating birds resident in North America. They are called cowbirds because they congregate around herds of cattle that disturb insects as they move, thus providing a moving restaurant for the birds.

Cowbirds are described as brood parasites, which means that the adult female lays her eggs in the nest of another species of bird. A brood parasite common to this country is the cuckoo. The principle for both birds is the same. The original egg is removed from the nest and the new egg put in its place. Once hatched the fledgling cowbird is fed by the original owner of the nest.

One consequences of being brought up by an adult bird of another species is that the infant cowbird does not hear the song of an adult cowbird while developing. West and King (1988) used this fact in their investigation of the type of song the cowbirds eventually sang.

The researchers identified two groups of cowbirds, geographically separated. Each group had a slightly different song or 'accent'. Females in one group preferred males with one accent; females in the other group preferred males with another accent. West and King reared male cowbirds in isolation, which meant that they never heard the song of another cowbird during their development. They compared the songs of males in each of the two different geographical groups with the songs of the males reared in isolation. West and King found that the song of the birds reared in isolation was much richer and more complex than the song of either of the two other groups of birds that had developed naturally in the wild.

West and King concluded that because they have never heard an adult cowbird as an infant the song of the 'isolation' birds has elements of both 'accents'. As they develop and join a particular group, these birds learn that females 'respond' only to a certain type of song when choosing a mate. The female response is a form of dance that involves a specific wing movement. The male birds learn that producing a particular kind of song can encourage this wing movement, which they hope will lead to their being accepted as a mate. This ultimately is what happens. West and King concluded that this was evidence of operant conditioning in the wild. In terms of operant conditioning, the wing movement is reinforcing the adjustment of the male song.

be conditioned in just the same way as laboratory animals.

The principles are not restricted to birds. Morrison (1988) reports that dolphins have been trained, using operant conditioning, to guard and patrol the sea surrounding US nuclear submarine bases on the lookout for intruders that may attack from beneath the sea. Passer et al (2008) indicate that dolphins were also used to patrol around US ships in the Vietnam war. Brembs (2003) has shown operant conditioning in invertebrates, namely aplysia (the sea slug), and Holden et al (2003) report the use of operant conditioning to shape the behaviour of rhinoceroses at ZSL Whipsnade Zoo. The aim in this case was to make the animals more manageable and easier to access for health and husbandry reasons through behaviour shaping. They report that, by this means, many more health assessments – such as eye and mouth inspections, ultrasounds, and blood samples – can be carried out without causing the stress of capture or anaesthetic. One rhinoceros was trained to have its nails filed by placing its foot on a block.

A rhinoceros at Whipsnade presenting its foot for inspection.

Operant conditioning says that it is the consequence of a behaviour that determines whether it will happen more or less in the future. Research with pigeons has suggested that this may not be the case. Pecking is a pigeon's natural response to food. They peck at the ground whenever they see food, collecting some of it as they go. However, Mackintosh (1981) says that pigeons taught to peck at an illuminated disk in reward for food will peck at the disk once it is lit even if no food is given. This suggests that the consequence of the pecking does not matter to them – their behaviour is the same if they get food as it is if they do not. The pigeons are in effect demonstrating classical rather than operant conditioning: the implication of this is that many behaviours ascribed to operant conditioning may in fact be due to classical conditioning.

Operant conditioning does not involve learning arbitrary associations between stimulus and response – an animal's biology places constraints on what can be learned. The reinforcer and response must somehow be related, for learning to occur quickly and easily. These are called *response-behaviour constraints*. Examples of these can be seen in escape and avoidance learning. In *escape learning*, an animal learns a response that will allow it to escape from something unpleasant, for example an electric shock. Research shows that a pigeon will learn faster if the required escape response is wing flapping rather than pecking. This is because a pigeon's natural response to danger (like an electric shock) is to flap its wings, so it will learn more quickly to escape if the relevant response is a natural defensive reaction. With *reward learning*, an animal acquires a response that is reinforced by food. A pigeon for example will more readily learn something if it is allowed to peck, to get a food reward, rather than to flap its wings. This is because pecking is part of the pigeon's natural eating activity, and there is a direct behavioural link between pecking and eating.

Further evidence for biological limits on operant conditioning comes from research which has demonstrated *instinctive drift*, or *misbehaviour*. Animal trainers have found that, instead of learning the desired behaviour, an animal will occasionally 'misbehave' and learn something closer to one of its instinctual behaviours. Breland and Breland (1961) tried to train raccoons to pick up large coins and place them in a piggy bank as part of an advertisement for a bank. Problems occurred however when the raccoons picked up the coins – they would hold and rub them in a 'miserly' fashion, quite the opposite to the image the bank was wanting to portray. This behaviour is similar to food washing behaviour found in wild raccoons. It seems that the learned responses competed with instinctive ones; natural evolutionary behaviours appear to take precedence over learned ones. The researchers observed similar problems training other animals, for example pigs.

The examples of response-behaviour constraints and instinctual drift show that the laws of operant conditioning do not apply to all situations equally. As with classical conditioning, the ethological view that learning reflects an animal's evolutionary adaption to the demands of their own natural environment seems to hold true.

INSIGHT AND COGNITIVE LEARNING: PROBLEMS FOR CLASSICAL AND OPERANT CONDITIONING

ASK AN EXAMINER

"Both classical and operant conditioning are approaches in psychology which focus on learning behaviour rather than cognition. What this means is that anything which demonstrates the importance of cognition in learning can be used as a criticism of both. We have two examples of learning involving cognition here, so they can be used to criticise classical and operant conditioning equally."

In 1925, Wolfgang Kohler carried out a series of classic experiments with chimpanzees. He was interested in seeing how the animals solved complicated problems without any instruction. One animal, called Sultan, performed extremely well. The problem presented to Sultan was as follows. Food was suspended out of Sultan's reach. In the room were some bamboo poles, and boxes upon which the animals could stand. Sultan successfully managed to balance the boxes on top of one another, climb to the top of the stack, and use a stick to reach the food suspended above his head. Solving the problem required no conditioning training of any kind. Kohler referred to this as *insight* or *discovery learning*. It cannot be explained by either classical or operant conditioning and appears to be a result of cognition.

Insight learning is not confined to primates like chimpanzees. Weir et al (2002) have reported the amazing behaviour of a female Caledonian crow called Betty. In order to retrieve food, Betty made a hook by bending a piece of wire which she then used to get at food from deep at the bottom of a pipe. What's most interesting here is that, whilst Caledonian crows use twigs as tools in the wild, Betty had no experience of bendable materials before the research was carried out!

Having bent a piece of metal into a hook shape, Betty fishes out the food.

Studies by Edward Tolman in the 1930s showed that rats could develop a mental map which they could use when running mazes. This was in contrast to the dominant psychological view of the day which held that learning was a result of observable and measurable conditioning processes. Tolman and Honzik (1930) demonstrated this with maze learning in rats. They timed rats through the maze until the end where food was available. When they could go straight to the food without error they were considered to have learned the maze. One group of rats was given food as a reward (a group learning by operant conditioning – the food being the reinforcer for maze learning). This group was completing the maze without error by day 17. A second group of rats was not given any reward at all but was placed in the maze for as much time as the first group. As would be predicted by operant conditioning theory, the absence of reinforcement meant that the second group showed no particular improvement in maze learning. The third group was placed in the maze in the same way as the second group, except that on day 10 a food reward was introduced, as with the first group. Within a couple of days the rats in this third group were performing as well as those in the first group. This rapid learning should not have happened, according to operant conditioning theory, as the third group of rats would have begun learning from the point of reinforcement (and would have taken about the same time to learn as the first group). Tolman (1948) explained that the rats were displaying *latent learning*. This third group of rats had been learning the maze during the first ten days in the absence of any reinforcement. They had formed a 'mental map' of the maze during this time, so that when they were motivated to get to the end of the maze by food they could use this hidden (or latent) learning. Latent learning suggests the use of cognition by animals, in direct contradiction to the principles of classical and operant conditioning.

TELLING THE DIFFERENCE BETWEEN CLASSICAL AND OPERANT CONDITIONING

The differences between classical and operant conditioning can be reduced to three main things – timing, elicited/emitted behaviours, and different associations. They can be remembered with the acronym TED.

1. Timing (T)

In classical conditioning the stimulus is followed directly by the response. It is the stimulus that triggers the response. For instance, Pavlov's bell comes first and triggers the dog's salivation. In operant conditioning the reinforcer or punisher happens *after* the conditioned behaviour. For instance a rat in a Skinner box must produce the desired behaviour (lever pushing) before it receives its associated stimulus (some food).

2. Elicited or emitted behaviours (E)

Classical conditioning works with automatic, reflexive behaviours, e.g. dogs salivate not by choice, but automatically. These are called *elicited behaviours*. Operant conditioning works by the animal making a choice to produce a behaviour, e.g. rats do not reflexively push a lever, they do it by choice. These are called *emitted behaviours*.

3. Different associations (D)

In classical conditioning, the animal learns to associate one stimulus with another. Pavlov's dogs, for instance, associated the sound of a bell with food. In operant conditioning animals associate a behaviour with a consequence for that behaviour. For instance, when rewarding an animal, a lever push will be followed by food. The animal learns to associate pushing the lever with pleasant consequences.

EVIDENCE FOR INTELLIGENCE IN NON-HUMAN ANIMALS

Most of us have experiences of animals behaving in a way that makes us certain that they have shown intelligence. Cats can learn to open doors to get at food, and dogs can do tricks. Dolphins have been used by the US navy for many years to patrol waters around their ships on the lookout for attacks from beneath the sea. Other animals provide vital services for those with sensory problems. Guide dogs are a common sight in our towns, and dogs are also trained to help those with other problems such as hearing difficulties, by identifying telephones, door bells and, perhaps more importantly, smoke alarms. Whilst these may appear to be intelligent behaviours, psychologists have traditionally been a little cautious in attributing such behaviours to 'intelligence'.

The problem that we experience when we try to identify evidence of intelligence in animals is very similar to the difficulty of identifying intelligence in humans. It is not absolutely clear what intelligence is, and so identifying it in animals is not at all simple.

ASK AN EXAMINER

"The debate about whether or not animals have 'intelligence' in the way humans do is very wide ranging. There are lots of different ways of addressing the debate, but in this section we have organised it as three separate lines of argument – whether or not animals show self-recognition, social learning, or theory of mind."

Since animals can't be tested like humans, the research in this area has concentrated on identifying animal behaviours which might indicate intelligence, based on what we recognise in ourselves as intelligent. Many kinds of behaviours fall into this category, but here we will restrict our consideration to just a few.

SELF-RECOGNITION AS EVIDENCE OF INTELLIGENCE

When you look in the mirror you recognise the person looking back at you. This is self-recognition, and is considered a high-level cognitive ability and as such a behaviour indicating intelligence. This ability to recognise one's own reflection is so part of our nature that we simply don't notice or question it. It is not however common to all animals. Cats and dogs show very little interest in their reflections, and whilst some animals respond vigorously to mirror images of themselves, it is because they believe they are looking at another individual. Budgerigars will happily chirp for hours at a supposed other budgerigar in the mirror, and Siamese fighting fish will attack their reflection as though it were another fish. There is some evidence, however, that certain animals behave in similar ways to humans when confronted by their reflection in a mirror. The first systematic studies of mirror self-recognition were conducted on chimpanzees by Gordon Gallup in the early 1970s.

GALLUP'S RED MARK TEST

Gallup (1970) wanted to see if animals (in this case chimpanzees) were able to show self-recognition. If they were, it would be evidence of a relatively high level of cognitive ability, shown only until that point by humans.

Chimpanzees were placed in front of mirrors and soon became accustomed to the reflection, using the mirrors to investigate parts of their own bodies (this is called self-directed behaviour). This in itself was very interesting and suggested awareness, but Gallup took the research further. The chimpanzees were placed under light anaesthesia and had a small red dot marked on their forehead. Once recovered from the anaesthesia, the animals were placed in front of a mirror. Gallup found that the chimpanzees touched the mark on their own forehead, not the reflection, much more in a mirror-present condition than in a mirror-absent condition. This suggested to Gallup that the animals were capable of self-recognition. In order to identify and touch the red spot, the animal must be self-aware, and must know that the image in the mirror is its own reflection.

Gallup found that after an extended period in front of a mirror, chimpanzees ceased to respond to the image as though it were a conspecific (i.e. a member of its own species) and began to use the mirror as a guide to performing self-directed behaviour, such as picking teeth, blowing bubbles and manipulating food on its lips. For Gallup, it was reasonable to interpret this as evidence of self-recognition, but he needed a more objective test. He therefore developed the mark test, whereby a chimp would have a red mark unobtrusively placed on a part of the body which could only be seen in a mirror. Gallup could then observe the response of the animal to the newly acquired mark.

For Gallup (1977), experience with a mirror does not induce self-recognition behaviour, but rather the mirror allows the animal to engage in a behaviour which is part of its inherent cognitive capacity. Animals which do not show mirror recognition fail because they lack a sense of their own identities.

Gallup's research with chimpanzees has been supported by other studies using similar procedures. Swartz and Evans (1991) however, have shown that not all chimpanzees show self-recognition. They conducted a test using the red mark procedure on 11 chimpanzees. In line with previous research they expected their animals to demonstrate evidence of self-recognition. However, although several chimpanzees used the mirror to direct behaviour, only one passed the mark test by touching the mark previously placed on their forehead during routine anaesthesia. Eliminating the likelihood that procedural issues explain the differences between these and previous findings, Swartz and Evans explain the failure of most their chimpanzees to pass the mark test as being due to individual differences among chimpanzees. What the nature of this individual difference is, however, remains unclear. According to Povinelli et al (2000), failure in these mark tests is quite common, with about 25% failure in young adults and considerably more in young and aging individuals.

Hayes (1998), however, identified methodological problems with the procedure developed by Gallup. Hayes says that such research is flawed because the baseline, non-mirror condition was presented first in all occasions, with the mirror and dot condition coming second every time. Hayes says that the animals would be naturally more active in the second condition simply because they had recovered more from the effects of the anaesthetic. This means that the results could be biased

because of this order effect. Hayes points out that the evidence that any non-human animals, including primates, use mirrors to investigate their own bodies is very limited. It is not clear, for example, if some of the mark touching really is what it appears to be, given that chimpanzees in any case engage in a great deal of head touching behaviour. It is also unclear why some animals show self-awareness and some do not, and it need not be to do with intelligence at all. Hayes argues that even if an animal does use a mirror to investigate their own bodies, and even if they do identify the spot in the reflection as being on their own head, it is a huge leap to say that this means that the animal has a concept of 'self' or is expressing 'self-awareness'.

"Commenting on methodological problems with any piece of research can be a good way of gaining marks. Make sure to pick out meaningful and obvious problems though – try to avoid being trivial and speculative."

Whilst a range of animals show self-directed behaviour in front of a mirror, until recently the only species to have clearly demonstrated self-recognition using the mark procedure was humans (after approximately 2 years of age), chimpanzees, bonobos, and orang-utans. There is no evidence of self-recognition in monkeys, nor (curiously and uniquely among the great apes) gorillas. More recent research, however, suggests that self-recognition may be more widespread in the animal world than people like Gallup would have us believe.

Previous research with elephants showed that they interact with mirrors in ways which suggest self-recognition, but they do not pass the red-spot test. Plotnik et al (2006) point out that this research used small mirrors that were kept at a distance and out of reach. They hypothesised that self-recognition may exist in elephants, since like other animals where self-recognition skills have been indicated, they too live in socially complex groups. They put a large mirror in the exercise yard belonging to three female Asian elephants. All the elephants were seen to interact with the mirrored images, inspecting their mouths and making repetitive body movements. Each elephant was marked with visible paint on the forehead and also received a colourless mark as a control for odour and tactile cues. One elephant (named Happy) crossed to the mirror immediately after being released into the yard and for several minutes showed clear evidence of touching the visible but not sham mark. Whilst the other two elephants failed the mark test, Plotnik et al point out that this is consistent with other research, for example with chimpanzees, which show that not all animals succeed in such tests. Another reason for the failures might be that elephants are not very concerned about appearance. Unlike chimpanzees who spend a great deal of time grooming, elephants 'substrate groom' with dirt, suggesting that small marks on their body are unimportant to them.

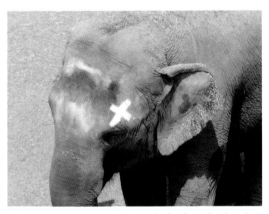

Happy the elephant with her mark clearly on her head.

Research by Prior et al (2008) provided the first evidence that mirror self-recognition is not restricted to mammals, by subjecting magpies to the mark test. The birds were marked with either a red, yellow or black mark (the black mark, being almost invisible against the black feathers, was a control against tactile cues and also eliminated the need for anaesthesia). Each bird was tested with each colour mark and also as a baseline measure without a mark in front of a mirror twice. Out of five magpies tested, two birds showed evidence of mark-directed behaviour, with the birds removing the mark in all the colour conditions. Activity aimed at the black mark was low or absent. Prior et al point out that this research calls into question the role of the neocortex in self-recognition. This brain region is the most evolutionarily recent: it exists only in mammals and has been thought crucial for self-recognition skills.

Self-recognition skills have also now been found in pigeons. Toda et al (2008) found that pigeons could discriminate between a filmed 'reflection' of themselves in real time and a recorded delayed 'reflection'. The pigeons also seemed able to tell when the image reflected their own movements and when it did not. They could discriminate between images of their own movements after a 5 – 7 second delay and images of movements that were not their own. According to Toda et al, this demonstrates a higher cognitive ability than that shown by 3-year-old humans, who struggle to recognise their own images after a two-second delay. This research shows that the ability to show such intelligent behaviour as self-recognition is not limited to more highly evolved animals like primates.

A magpie with a yellow mark below its beak (Prior et al, 2008).

SOCIAL LEARNING AS EVIDENCE OF INTELLIGENCE

Whilst social learning is well-established as a form of human learning (e.g. Bandura, 1969), there is a good deal of evidence that other animal species too can learn in this way.

For example, there are often differences in the behaviours of animal groups that cannot be attributed to genetics. Whiten et al (1999) investigated troops of chimpanzees living around a river on the Ivory Coast in Africa. They found that those animals living on the west bank of the river used stones to crack open nuts for food, whereas those living on the east bank did not. Since the animals on each bank are genetically the same, and since nuts and stones are found on each bank of the river, the different behaviour must be to do with learning. Whiten et al (1999) also observed chimpanzees using long thin sticks and blades of grass to catch ants and termites. What's most interesting is that chimpanzees in different areas used different types of tools for the job, and used the tools slightly differently. A group in Tanzania, for instance, would hold the stick in a certain way, but a group on the Ivory Coast would hold the stick differently. Other chimpanzees in Senegal would take great care to prepare the stick by removing the bark, whereas chimpanzees elsewhere would not. These inter-group differences must come about because of different learning processes.

Some forms of learning reflect *species-specific behaviour* that is genetically pre-determined: for example, birds instinctively know how to build a particular kind of nest, a skill shared by all birds of the same species. They are not necessarily good at it however, and have to practise to get it right. This is especially true of birds that build complex nests. For example, adult weaver birds (cousins of the sparrow living in Africa) build very elaborate nests, and whilst immature weaver birds have the instinct to build nests, they don't have the skill and are quite hopeless at it. *Trial and error learning* on the other hand is a flexible form of learning based on conditioning. Whilst it has the advantage of enabling animals to adjust to changing environments, it has costs. For example, it involves an animal learning from the negative consequences of an act, which can be costly to an organism.

Whether an animal copies the behaviour of another animal can depend on the situation in which the behaviour occurs. For instance, if an animal is watching the behavour of another animal they may not copy that behaviour unless they are standing right next to them. This a process called *local enhancement*. Lorenz (1935) showed that ducks in a pen will not use a hole to escape unless they are very close to another duck using it. Just seeing a duck moving through the hole is not enough to learn the behaviour. Another example comes from Fisher and Hinde (1949). Tits have been known to puncture milk bottle tops to get at milk. This behaviour spread quickly across the country after the introduction of doorstep milk delivery. The learning was in part facilitated by seeing other birds near milk bottles. These behaviours are often considered examples of social learning, though it has been argued that they lack evidence of higher level mental skills and are not therefore good evidence for intelligence.

It has been pointed out, however, that there are some forms of social learning which indicate intelligence. This form of social learning clearly indicates that an animal is closely observing others, is creating a mental representation of the event, and depending on the consequences for the observed animal or available opportunity, may reproduce the observed behaviour at some point in the future. It can be seen that this kind of 'higher' learning has clear survival value: it has all the advantages of trial-and-error learning but without the costs. For example, observing the behaviour

of others allows an animal to learn from both the successes and failures of other animals around them, without personal risk. This social learning is considered intelligent behaviour because – unlike species-specific, trial-and-error learning and local enhancement – learning in this way is purposive and reflexive and requires some degree of conceptual ability.

An example of this kind of higher-level social learning can be seen in several kinds of behaviours, such as *teaching*. Teaching involves one animal modifying the behaviour of another (usually a conspecific) for no obvious immediate benefit. Where a benefit is evident it is usually because it involves an adult teaching something to one of its young, when the benefit can be seen to be more long-term in increasing the fitness of a family member. Behaviour which might be interpreted as *teaching* has been observed in the actions of a number of animals, especially predators, where adults appear to provide opportunities deliberately for their young to learn to hunt and kill. Teaching behaviour is prevalent, however, amongst primates, especially apes. There are many observations, for example, of chimpanzee tutoring. Boesch (1991) noted many examples of adult chimpanzees carefully cracking nuts with two stones and teaching this skill to their young. Rapaport and Ruiz-Miranda (2002) demonstrate that tutoring may be much more common amongst lower primates, such as monkeys, than once thought. They reported examples of tutoring in wild golden lion tamarinds. The adult monkeys would give out food calls, to which only their immature offspring responded. The young were then directed to the location of hidden food. These events occurred at a time the young were learning to forage, but doing so poorly. Rapaport and Ruiz-Miranda suggest that the adults were helping the young to master the skill of capturing hidden prey by drawing their attention to situations conducive to learning.

Another form of higher-level social learning is *imitation*. Imitation can be described as the copying of a new behaviour through observation. For Thorndike(1898), imitation was "learning to do an act by seeing it done". There are different forms of imitation and some appear to involve little or no cognition, such as contagion and mimicry. A *mimic* is something that appears to be like something else. A number of different animals imitate the appearance of other animals – for instance, the viceroy butterfly mimics the appearance of the monarch butterfly. This is because the viceroy

SOCIAL LEARNING IN JAPANESE MACAQUE

The Japanese macaque (also known as the Japanese Snow Monkey) is found throughout Japan. The Snow Monkey lives socially, often in a troop of up to 30 other animals. What's really interesting about Snow Monkeys is that they invent new behaviours and pass them on to the rest of the troop by imitation. Suzuki (1963) reports that one of the troop being studied, Mukabili, waded into a hot spring to retrieve some beans that had been thrown for her by keepers. The springs were nice and warm, and the climate in the mountains was extremely cold. Mukabili found that she liked it in the hot water, and returned again and again. Her behaviour was eventually copied by the rest of the troop. The pleasant hot water does not improve the survival of the monkeys, but it clearly gives them pleasure.

Another study took place with a separate troop of snow monkeys who lived near a beach elsewhere in Japan. In order to encourage the monkey out of the forest and into the open where they could be watched, researchers threw food onto the beach. One young monkey, Imo, in a apparent moment of 'insight', spontaneously began to wash his food in the sea to remove sand. Within a short period, over 80% of the monkeys in the troop between 2 and 7 years old were also washing their food. Only 18% of monkeys aged over 8 years imitated this food washing behaviour. This age difference was considered important evidence for social learning – younger monkeys interact much more than older ones, so they had many more opportunities to observe this food-washing behaviour (Kawai, 1965).

Such conclusions have been criticised however. The learning may have been due to local enhancement rather than higher forms of social learning. The washing behaviour of some monkeys may have drawn the attention of others not to the food washing behaviour as such but to the food *and* the water, leading other monkeys to discover food washing for themselves. It has also been suggested that food washing may have been operantly conditioned by the observers, since this behaviour was given more attention and food was ultimately thrown deliberately to observe food washing. Thus, this behaviour was being positively reinforced.

is edible but the monarch is not: imitation thus gives the viceroy a survival advantage, as a predator would mistake the viceroy for a monarch and not eat it. *Contagion* occurs when one animal's behaviour stimulates the same already learned behaviour in another animal. For example, when one baboon in a troop begins to groom another it is not unusual to see this catch on so that soon most of the troop is grooming. None are *learning* to groom in this case.

Other forms of imitation, however, appear altogether more 'intelligent'. One of the earliest and best known studies of imitation in animals was conducted on Japanese macaques in the 1960s. This series of studies was also particularly important because, after being integrated into the behaviour of monkeys in the troop, the new learning appeared to be culturally transmitted to the next generation so that new macaques also engaged in behaviours similar to the adults in the troop, as though it were a very naturally occurring part of their behavioural repertoire.

THEORY OF MIND AS EVIDENCE OF INTELLIGENCE

A very important indicator of intelligent behaviour is theory of mind. This is the understanding that other people have thoughts and emotions different from one's own. This is a very human ability, so deeply ingrained that it is rarely brought to our attention as a particular trait or skill – it is just 'how we are'. Many behaviours indicate that an individual has theory of mind, but a key behaviour is deception. In order for one animal to deceive deliberately, it has to have an understanding of what another animal knows or doesn't know, it would have to be able to imagine how it would like another animal to think or behave following deception, and it would have to devise a means of deception successfully bridging these two points. These are clearly highly complex cognitive skills, whereby there is deliberate manipulation of belief states. If it can be demonstrated that one animal can *intentionally* deceive another it would be good evidence of intelligence.

Dishonesty appears to be very common in the animal world. For example, the viceroy butterfly mimics the appearance of the monarch butterfly. This is because the viceroy is edible, but the monarch is not, predators would mistake the viceroy for a monarch and not eat it. The shrike will use alarm calls to warn other shrikes of danger from predators, but will also use alarm calls to scare other shrikes away from food. Another bird, the

THE DECEITFUL GROOMER

Kummer (1982) reports the case of a female hamadryas baboon who clearly wanted to groom a sub-adult male – something that would never be tolerated by the dominant male. The baboon took 20 minutes to shift her position gradually, inch by inch, closer to her grooming target. From his position, the dominant male would only have been able to see the back of the female's head – not her arms nor the bent-over sub-adult male enjoying a grooming from this flirtatious female baboon. Is this behaviour simply the result of her learning that grooming out in the open would attract the ire of the dominant baboon? Or is it that she knew that she could manipulate his beliefs and acted intentionally to deceive him?

green plover is a ground-nesting bird which, when a predator approaches, hops around pretending to have a broken wing, thereby drawing the attention of the predator away from their nest. It has been argued, however, that this kind of deception is *functional*, in that the animals do not 'know' they are being deceptive but are engaging in a fairly mindless adaptive behaviour that has evolved as a result of selection pressures.

Research suggests nevertheless that some behaviours, such as predator distraction in plovers, are more than just unplanned instinctual responses. Ristau (1991) carried out a series of studies with plovers which suggested that the birds may be capable of thinking in simple rational terms about their behaviour. Feigning an injury is after all a risky behaviour, in which the adult bird exposes itself to risk from predation and wasted energy. In one study, Ristau had two distinctively dressed human 'intruders' walk past incubating plovers – one would look directly at the nest as he passed, and the other turn to look in the opposite direction. The plovers reacted more strongly to the intruder who looked directly at their nests. Furthermore, on subsequent intrusions the birds appeared to adjust their behaviours according to which intruder they recognised approaching. The birds appeared to have an understanding of the intruder's intentions. This is further supported by the observation that the behaviour of displaying birds is not stereotyped but is adjusted according to particular situations. They watch the intruder intently, adjusting their display, judging the degree of threat and balancing personal risk with behaviour required to draw the intruder away. It is possible of course that this deceptive behaviour is still functional, and requires little or no mental representation at all.

Some animals, however, appear to engage in a form of deception which involves the more cognitively complex intentional deception. Behaviours such

as these are widely reported in the behaviour of both captive primates and their wild counterparts. What appears to be intentional deception was demonstrated in a laboratory study by Woodruff and Premack (1979). Chimpanzees were allowed to see a trainer hiding food under one of two containers. The task for the chimpanzee was to be able to discriminate between two trainers – one was the 'cooperative' trainer and the other was the 'competitive' trainer. If the animal pointed to the correct container when the cooperative trainer was there it would get the food. If it did so with the competitive trainer however, the food would go to the trainer and the opportunity to gain the food would be lost. In order to get the food then, the chimpanzee had to be honest with the cooperative trainer whilst deceiving the competitive one, and indeed this is what was observed. Chimpanzees showed a tendency to direct the competitive trainer to the wrong container, thus preserving the food so they could point to the correct container with the cooperative trainer present. Some chimpanzees could do this with both trainers present. On the face of it, it seems that the chimpanzees were demonstrating an understanding that the trainers would act on their false information, thus indicating theory of mind. However, there is reason to be cautious about jumping to this conclusion. A great deal of training was needed before the chimpanzees started to apparently deceive the competitive trainer. This would have provided ample opportunity for the animals to learn appropriate responses through conditioning. It is difficult therefore to be sure that complex mental processes were operating in this case.

Intentional deception appears common in wild primates. Indeed, it has been suggested that theory of mind evolved because of the social interactions within the kinds of close-knit groups seen in primates. Linden (2000) reports the case of chimpanzee double deception in Tanzania's

Gombe Stream Reserve. The reserve contained several feeding stations which could be opened by remote control. One chimpanzee happened to have the good fortune to be alone when one of the nearby feeding stations opened. When it noticed that a dominant chimpanzee had moved within view it closed the box and behaved nonchalantly as though nothing had happened, until the chimp had passed. However, this first chimpanzee was also to be undone, since this event had been witnessed by another dominant chimpanzee who hid out of sight nearby. When the first dominant chimpanzee had gone, the second dominant animal came out of hiding to take the food from the 'lucky' first chimpanzee.

The general suggestion from research into animal deception is that animals do indeed communicate inaccurate information or deliberately avoid communicating information. Whilst this behaviour often appears to involve conscious intent, especially in primates, the fact that such behaviours can also be explained in non-mentalistic conditioning terms means that the debate about whether or not animals demonstrate theory of mind through deception is still ongoing.

EVOLUTION OF INTELLIGENCE

Why are we humans as intelligent as we are? It is true to say that many non-human animals can show extraordinary abilities. Chimpanzees have been shown to be able to express themselves with some sign language, and dolphins are widely regarded as intelligent non-human animals – but it is fair to say that in the animal world humans are clearly right at the top of the intelligence tree. How we achieved this level of intelligence can be explained in terms of evolution theory.

> **ASK AN EXAMINER**
>
> *"There are many ways of explaining why humans evolved high levels of intelligence: some of them appear contradictory and some of them complementary. In all likelihood, there is more than one factor influencing the evolution of intelligence. Here we present just three explanations: brain size, ecological demands, and social complexity."*

EVOLUTION BY NATURAL SELECTION

The basic premise of evolution theory is rather simple and elegant. Animals produce many more young than could possibly survive. Offspring are often very slightly different from either parent, and these variations (or mutations) sometimes enable animals to cope better with environmental demands and reach maturity. The ones that do reach adulthood are the strongest of their generation and when they breed they pass the characteristics that helped them survive to their young. Those with traits that help them survive are more likely to reproduce themselves (i.e. they are selected out by the process of evolution for their fitness), and so the cycle continues. As many generations go by, the traits that have aided survival and reproductive fitness are passed on and become widespread in the population. Such a process involves changes to both physiology and behaviour, so that the end result can be an animal that bears little resemblance to its ancestors.

EVOLUTIONARY FACTORS IN THE DEVELOPMENT OF HUMAN INTELLIGENCE

BRAIN SIZE

The key difference between humans and other animals is our highly evolved brain. There are major evolutionary costs involved in having a larger brain, however. Large brains use up a higher proportion of an individual's energy. Humans use 22% of their energy sustaining the brain compared with only 8% in chimpanzees. This means that humans need a constant supply of nutrition, to generate the energy needed. Large expansion in the human brain size occurred about two million years ago and coincided with the introduction of significant amounts of meat into our diet. A steady supply of meat would have produced a rich source of nourishment for our early ancestors. There are also potential risks to humans in giving birth to large-brained offspring. The longest axis of the human foetus's head only just fits the widest axis of the female birth canal, so the baby has to rotate its head during birth. The potential risks in this manoeuvre are that the umbilical cord can become wrapped around the baby's neck and restrict the airways. The rotation of the foetus's head also results in the baby being born face down. This is different from what happens with any other primates, and means that the mother is unable to see if the baby's airways are obstructed.

EINSTEIN'S BRAIN

Witelson et al (1999) provide us with in-depth and fascinating insight into the brain of Einstein. Their research provides evidence for increased size and density in areas of the brain related to particular skills and abilities. In 'The exceptional brain of Albert Einstein' they explain how his brain was removed after his death in 1955 and preserved. They go on to indicate how investigations of Einstein's brain showed that it was, surprisingly perhaps, no larger than a 'normal' human brain, and in fact, it was smaller in some regions than similarly aged brains. However, further investigation showed that some parts of the brain were indeed larger compared with the same areas in other brains. In particular the parietal lobe was larger and extremely densely packed with neurons (brain cells) and glials (support cells), which support the activity of neurons, by providing nutrients. If you look at the cortex of the human brain you will find many folds and gaps called fissures. Einstein's parietal lobes were so rich with neurons and glials that these fissures were tightly packed, not something we normally see in the brain. You may not be terribly surprised to hear that the parietal lobes are responsible for mathematical thinking among other things, just what Einstein was so good at!

Another consequence of having a large brain is that the infant is born after only a nine month gestation period and is relatively immature at birth compared with other primates. This level of immaturity means that human babies require a much longer and more intense period of parental investment than other primates. The helplessness of the baby during this time makes it more vulnerable and impacts on the parents as they have to spend more time with the baby and therefore less time procuring resources to support the family. Given the costs involved in having a large brain, it is reasonable to assume from an evolutionary point of view that the benefits and advantages of a larger brain for the survival of the species must outweigh the costs, otherwise a larger brain would not have evolved.

Evolution tells us that if there is an advantage to something it will be developed and passed from generation to generation. Intelligence is no different. If there is an evolutionary advantage to being intelligent, then the more intelligent we are, the greater will be our chance of survival and so the more likely we will be to be able to reproduce and pass on our genes to the next generation.

The relationship between intelligence and brain size has been the focus of much research. It seems to make sense that the larger the brain, the more intelligent the human. Recent developments in technology have allowed research into the measurement of brain size using magnetic resonance imaging (MRI) scans. A meta-analysis conducted by McDaniel (2005) aimed to provide support for the idea that more intelligent people have larger brains. Using data from 37 samples involving 1,530 people the researcher found a positive correlation between brain size and intelligence. Intelligence was measured using standard IQ tests and it was confirmed that the bigger the brain the higher the intelligence.

THE ENCEPHALISATION QUOTIENT (EQ)

Humans have evolved uniquely 'large' brains. 'Large' does not mean biggest (that belongs to the sperm whale which has a 9 kg brain compared to the 1.3 kg human brain). 'Large' here means relative to body size. The relative size of a brain is indicated by its encephalisation quotient (EQ). This is calculated by dividing the actual brain mass by its expected brain mass (based on body mass). EQ's higher than 1 indicate animals with higher than expected brain size. Humans, with an EQ of 7, have by far the highest measure – this is three times the size than would be expected of a primate our size. Our closest animal relative, the chimpanzee, has an EQ of 2.5. Whilst there are different ways of calculating EQ's, humans always score highest. Interestingly, EQ scores don't seem to be terribly reliable for some very large animals. For example, large whales such as the blue whale and humpback whale have very low EQ's, barely above 0.1, yet these are not considered unintelligent animals.

It is thought that this increase in EQ began about five million years ago when the evolutionary branch that led to modern humans split from that leading to present-day apes. The most dramatic human brain growth occurred in the last 2.5 million years. It has been suggested that the current human EQ was probably established some 100,000 years ago.

It's not just the general size of the brain that we need to consider when we think of brain size in relation to intelligence. Healy et al (2004) have looked into a very interesting debate in science. This concerns the theory that the natural history of a species can provide us with evidence for why animals show different abilities. More than this, they describe an area of research called 'neuroecology' that suggests that different parts of the brain have developed specifically because they are needed more and more as evolution progresses. Indeed, areas of the brain such as the cerebral cortex and the frontal lobes do appear to have changed in size over the course of our evolution (Kolb and Whishaw, 2005).

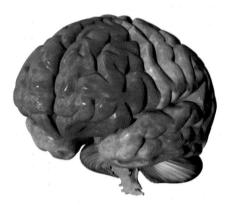

Purple areas are the frontal lobes. The outermost surface of the brain (about 5mm thick) is the cerebral cortex.

The cerebral cortex is the most highly evolved part of the brain. It allows us to understand, think and problem-solve, and gives us the intellectual skills that make humans unique in the animal world. The frontal lobes are regarded as the area of the brain that really differentiates us from the rest of the animal kingdom, however. In fact, Krasnegor et al (1997) say that human evolution can be thought of as the era of the frontal lobe. To put it in perspective, our frontal lobes constitute about 30% of our brain. The nearest to humans in that regard is the chimpanzee, with frontal lobes taking up about 17%. A cat's brain is about 3% frontal lobe, and a dog's is about 7%. Damage to the frontal lobes can be extremely debilitating, resulting in such things as a loss of intellectual abilities like planning and organising.

Evaluation of the relationship between brain size and intelligence

So far we have learned that the size of our brains increased as we evolved. What is not clear is whether it is this increased brain size that allowed us to evolve or whether it was evolution that provided us with larger brains. It turns out that it is even less clear than that. While it is certainly the case that we have larger brains than we used to, there is by no means a perfect positive correlation between brain size and where we are in evolution. Kolb and Whishaw (1995) show that the brain size of neanderthal man was actually larger than ours, even though they were not nearly as intellectually and socially advanced as we are now.

When we measure the IQs of men and women we find that they are almost identical. However, when we measure the brain sizes of men and women we discover that men have larger brains. If the relationship between brain size and intelligence was as simple as saying that larger brains meant higher intelligence we would expect the larger brained males to have larger IQs and this is clearly not the case.

It may not be the actual physical *size* of the brain that contributes to intelligence. It could be more to do with the *density* of cells in the cortex – more neurons mean more brain power. As we saw earlier, part of Einstein's brain was extremely densely packed with neurons and supporting glials, even though overall his brain was no larger than other people's brains. There is now agreement amongst psychologists and neuroscientists that it is not the size of the brain that is the issue in intelligence – it is the efficiency of function that is important. Part of the evidence for this comes from research that looks at how the brain consumes and expends energy. Research by Haier et al (1993) shows that more intelligent people's brains consume and expend less energy when solving problems than less intelligent people's brains. They used PET scans (Positron Emission Tomography) to look at how brains performed when individuals were carrying out problem-solving tasks. They found that the highly intelligent brains consumed less glucose (used as energy by the brain) than the low intelligence brains.

It appears that our brains have indeed grown in size as we have evolved. It is also clear that we have become more able and more intelligent. There is, then, a positive correlation between increased intelligence and increased brain size.

ECOLOGICAL THEORY

One of the key selection pressures that promoted the development of intelligence may have been efficiency in food gathering. However, providing a diet that is varied and rich in nutrients requires a degree of cognitive ability. The primate needs to be able to remember the foods that were nutritious and not harmful and recall where to find them. This requires memory for the best foraging sites. Related to this would be a cognitive map of the terrain – which is related to good spatial skills and an ability to know which direction to go in and how to find the way home. These skills would also benefit individuals when hunting. The ability to be a successful hunter requires a great deal of skill in understanding and anticipating the movements of your prey. It also demands forethought and planning and the coordination of the movements of a team. Thus those who were most intelligent may have made better hunters and were therefore more likely to be successful in sustaining their species and surviving.

It follows that the more intelligent we are, the more likely we will be able to make efficient use of our ecology and so survive. Intelligence, then, provides us with the means to efficiently adapt to and use our environment. Our use of tools and invention of different types of tools for different jobs will have begun from a requirement to survive. Inventing and using a tool requires the ability to invent the *right* tool for the task. To develop efficient ways of using tools in hunting, killing, farming, cooking and a myriad of other things requires intelligence. The incredible advances in the evolution of our species came as humans began to use tools, pretty much at the same time as our brain was reorganising for the redevelopment of important areas responsible for abilities like spatial-awareness and emotion. The larger reorganised brain, coupled with the simple dexterity and basic tool use, was a recipe for advancement. Eventually, the ability to make and use tools became an important part of survival. Those without the intelligence and the ability to apply it lacked an evolutionary advantage. Better tool use allowed for more efficient gathering, and hunting, and eventually rudimentary farming. Better quality food provided those with the means to get it with the ability to raise more and healthier children, who could then be taught their parents' skills, which would survive and be built upon from generation to generation.

Evaluation of the ecological theory

The skills involved in successful hunting and foraging exist in other species with smaller brains and lower intelligence. Lions are extremely skilled hunters but lack the intelligence of humans. Chimpanzees can seek out a special plant to cure worm infections and they can also recall the location of stones selected for their particular usefulness in cracking nuts (Boesch and Boesch, 1984).

Other animals have shown tool use. Certain chimpanzees for instance, have used tools in the form of thin sticks which they manipulate to retrieve insects from deep inside termite mounds. Relatively speaking, however, this is nowhere near the level of sophistication achieved by humans in the invention and application of tools.

Freeman and Heron (1998) describe how humans may have begun this invention by using one stone to shape another stone into a point for use as a knife or as a spear head. Scientists have discovered human-like bones in areas where animal bones have been found showing the marks of tools. These bones date from approximately 2.5 million years ago and provide important evidence about our evolution. Freeman and Heron go on to indicate that tool making arose when our ancestors moved away from living in trees, to bipedal (two legged) locomotion on the ground. Walking upright freed up our hands and allowed for the eventual development of the opposable thumb. This physical characteristic gives primates a degree of dexterity required for fine motor skills and is necessary for the creation of even the simplest stone axes. Archeologists describe the ancestor that first showed this thumb joint as *homo habilis*, which translates as handy man. Although the invention of these simple tools seems to indicate a breakthrough in intelligence, it took over two million years before tools became more sophisticated and varied. This is too late to explain the development of intelligence, which has been increasing for over three million years.

SOCIAL THEORY

The role of social complexity in the evolution of intelligence is directly related to the size of the brain. The social world of the human can be diverse. We have different types of relationships with different people. We inhabit different roles at different times of our lives, and indeed different times of the day. There are evolutionary advantages to being part of a social group. Survival is enhanced by the resources that can be procured by a group, compared with an individual; and greater protection is provided by living in larger groups. Group living also provides more opportunities for sharing knowledge and valuable information that may be important for survival.

Related to the idea that social complexity plays a very important role in the evolution of intelligence

MACHIAVELLIAN INTELLIGENCE IN SAKI MONKEYS

Evidence of tactical deception in primates comes from research by Byrne and Whiten (1990). They gathered 253 accounts of tactical deception in primates from a variety of researchers. Intentional deception was found most often in great apes, suggesting that they are able to understand the mental states of others. Their actions included concealing objects from another, ignoring and feigning lack of interest in an object to distract others' attention from the desired object, and distracting others to gain advantage. In one particular account of Saki monkeys a male is observed chewing a small twig. A female approaches and tries several times to grab the twig from the male but without success. The female appears to give up and starts to groom the male's forearm – the one not holding the twig. After a few moments she grabs the twig and runs off with it. We can see here how the female uses tactical deception to feign lack of interest in the twig, thus lulling the male into a false sense of security whilst all along she is plotting to steal the twig.

is the requirement for humans to develop cooperative relationships. Hogan (1953) says that the need to be in a social group with others is extremely important in the survival of the human species. Living together cooperatively provides more chance of reproduction, sharing of duties of care for young; and an increased chance of survival through such things as self-defence. The need to belong to a group is so great that people must be careful to avoid rejection. In fact, Baumeister and Tice (1990) indicate that the fear of rejection may itself be something that has evolved specifically to help people avoid losing their place in the social group.

Harcourt (1992) says that it is only certain animals that form relationships with others in their social group because they will be useful later in their lives. Most such relationships are formed for short-term gain, such as copulation, food or immediate safety. You will not be surprised, either, that only certain primates form the type of alliances that will be useful to them at a later stage – and these include baboons and, yes, humans. Successfully managing social exchanges and relationships presents an intellectual challenge. Primate intelligence has evolved to respond to this challenge. Humphrey (1976) points out that keeping a balance in group living between manipulating others for personal gain and maintaining the cohesion of the group requires subtle cognitive skills. An example of intelligent behaviour can be seen in the instance of reciprocal altruism. This can be summed up by the phrase 'you scratch my back and I'll scratch yours'. Doing a favour for somebody often means that they will return that favour. Grooming provides us with an example of this in the primate world. Grooming is undertaken for more than just hygiene purposes. Research shows that primates who spend a lot of time grooming one another are also more likely to defend each other against threat of attack. The act of grooming seems to be the basis for a closer social bond.

Reciprocal relationships can be mutually beneficial but they are also vulnerable to deception and cheating. Apes and humans are adept at tactical deception and can deliberately deceive in order to achieve a goal. This is known as *Machiavellian intelligence*. Once an individual develops the motivation to deceive others for personal gain he is at a considerable advantage over the rest of his species. Other members of the species are now under pressure to develop skills to detect deception and cheating. Those that can detect cheats and non-cheats will emerge as the fittest. Trivers (1985) suggests that this cycle will continue, creating subtle forms of cheating with even more subtle forms of detection. It can be seen how this cycle of deception and counter-deception brought about a huge growth in intelligence. The development of memory is a good example. An individual needs to recall how others behaved in previous situations and how they themselves responded, in order that they can maintain their own deception or prepare to outwit cheats.

Evaluation of social theory

There is evidence to suggest that the size of the brain is directly related to the size of the social group a species is part of (Dunbar, 1993). This is called the 'social brain hypothesis'. The size of the group we can be part of is called 'Dunbar's number'. For humans, it turns out that the number is about 150. This means that for humans, our social group is restricted by the size of our brains to about 150 individuals with whom we can engage in sensible social relationships.

SOME EXAMPLES OF WASON SELECTION TASKS

1. You are shown a set of four cards placed on a table, each of which has a number on one side and a colour on the other side. The visible faces of the cards show 5, 2, yellow and brown.

   Which of these cards must be turned over to show that if a card displays an even number on one face, then its opposite face must show a primary colour?

2. Teenagers who don't have their own cars usually end up borrowing their parents' cars. In return for the privilege of borrowing the car, the Goldsteins have given their kids the rule,

   "If you borrow my car, then you have to fill up the tank with fuel."

   Of course, teenagers are sometimes careless and irresponsible. You are interested in seeing whether any of the Goldstein teenagers broke this rule.

   These cards represent four of the Goldstein teenagers. Each card represents one teenager. One side of the card tells whether or not a teenager has borrowed the parents' car on a particular day, and the other side tells whether or not that teenager filled up the tank with fuel on that day.

   Which of the following cards would you definitely need to turn over to see if any of these teenagers are breaking their parents' rule:

   "If you borrow my car, then you have to fill up the tank with fuel."

   Don't turn over any more cards than are absolutely necessary.

A positive correlation has been found between the size of the neocortex and the prevalence of tactical deception in primates (Byrne, 1995). The neocortex is the outer covering of the brain whose functions include thought processing, problem solving, memory and language. In humans the neocortex is far larger than the other two main parts of the brain (the brainstem, governing instinctive behaviour; and the limbic system, governing emotional behaviour). In primates it has been found that the larger the neocortex, the greater is the ability to deceive.

Evidence for human skill in managing social exchanges and detecting cheats is provided by Cosmides and Tooby (1992). They used Wason selection tasks to test how well people performed in a series of problems designed to test logical reasoning. Some of the tasks were abstract problems and others were set within a social context. Cosmides and Tooby found that people were far more adept at solving the social problems, getting these right about 75% of the time, compared with no more than 10% success for the abstract problems. This suggests that humans are much better at performing mental tasks when they relate to social exchange and the violation of social rules.

Ridley (1993) argues that neither ecological nor social theory stands up on its own as an explanation for the evolution of human intelligence. He suggests that sexual selection explains human intelligence as this idea incorporates both ecological and social theories. Individuals of a species who are most successful at attracting mates will leave more copies of their genes for future generations. Humans who were most intelligent were more successful at attracting mates as they may be better at presenting themselves in more attractive ways and at outwitting the competition. More intelligent individuals may also be better hunters and this makes them more attractive to the opposite sex in terms of providing resources and supporting offspring. Thus these intelligent, devious hunters will pass on their genes to their offspring and an intelligent species evolves.

THE ROLE OF GENETIC AND ENVIRONMENTAL FACTORS ASSOCIATED WITH INTELLIGENCE TEST PERFORMANCE

There is good evidence to suggest that our level of intelligence – and therefore our performance on intelligence tests – is, to some extent, inherited.

MEASURING INTELLIGENCE

The idea of measuring intelligence using tests began with the work of the French psychologist Alfred Binet in the late 19th century. He focused on showing that children were of high enough ability to be educated in school. Binet asked teachers to indicate what intellectual problems children at different ages typically experienced. He then worked out tests that identified these problems. From this he was able to say whether or not a child was performing at the level expected for his age. This idea was extended into the intelligence quotient (IQ), devised later in the early 20th century by Wilhelm Stern.

Stern said that a person with exactly the intelligence level you would expect for their age would have an IQ of 100. Those with intelligence levels higher than would be expected for their age would have IQs higher than 100, those less intelligent than would be expected would have lower IQs. Stern described the age at which a child was performing in terms of intelligence as their 'mental' age.

The IQ is calculated using the following formula.

$$IQ = \frac{MENTAL\ AGE}{CHRONOLOGICAL\ AGE} \times 100$$

For example, a child with a chronological (actual) age of 10 years, and a 'mental age' of 10 would have an IQ of 100, a child of 10 with a 'mental age' of 12 would have an IQ of 120, and so on.

The legacy of Binet and Stern is very evident today, since the tests designed for parts of the original IQ asessments, whilst having been modified and added to, are still being used in one form or another. These days intelligence is measured using a lengthy series of tests that measure a range of abilities, including abilities with words, numbers, general knowledge, spatial tasks and different 'puzzle-like' challenges that measure how good we are at solving different types of problems. The best known and most widely used of these is the Weschler Adult Intelligence Scale (or WAIS for short).

Spearman's g for instance is often considered as our inherited level of intelligence. Some gene defects certainly do have a direct effect on intelligence: for example Down's syndrome and PKU are both due to chromosomal abnormalities, and both have significant effects on intellectual growth. The human genome project that has identified all of the genes in human DNA has allowed us to look carefully at all of our genetic structure. However, whilst currently a number of possible genes for intelligence have been identified, rather than intelligence being monogenic (i.e. caused by a single gene) it seems very likely that several genes will interact in some way in the formation of our genetically inherited level of intelligence (Posthuma and DeGeus, 2006).

Debate in psychology has moved in recent decades away from whether intelligence is genetic to a discussion of the relative contribution of genes and environment in intelligence test performance. One way to approach the question of the relative contribution of genetics has been to measure and compare the intelligence of genetically related individuals. Studies of this type have generally shown that the more closely related people are, the more similarly they perform on tests of intelligence. A meta-analysis of 111 studies by Bouchard and McGue (1981) found that whilst correlation

coefficients became stronger as family resemblance increased, there was also clear evidence that both genetic and environmental factors make important contributions to intelligence. For example, there should be no correlation at all for unrelated persons reared together (such as two adopted children) if intelligence was genetic, but there is a coefficient of 0.20. This suggests that there is an environmental influence.

Relationship	IQ test correlation
Identical twins reared together	0.86
Identical twins reared apart	0.72
Non-identical twins reared together	0.60
Parent with child reared at home	0.50
Siblings reared together	0.47
Siblings reared apart	0.24
Unrelated persons reared together	0.20
Adoptive parent and adopted child	0.19
Cousins	0.15

IQ test correlations of related individuals.
Adapted from Bouchard and McGue (1981).

The problem, however, is separating the effects of nature and nurture, as family members not only share genes but also share similar environments and lifestyles. One way of reducing this problem has been to look at intelligence in twins. Identical, or monozygotic (MZ), twins have 100% of their genes in common, but share the same environment. Non-identical, or dizygotic (DZ) twins are no more similar than any other sibling (they share 50% of their genes) but share the same environment. What this means is that the principal difference between MZ and DZ twins is their genetic similarity, and so if MZ twins are more similar in their intelligence test scores than DZ twins, this must be some indication of the genetic contribution. The very strong correlation between MZ twins of 0.86 is good evidence of a genetic contribution. However, since the IQs are not perfectly correlated, some role for environmental influence is indicated. The fact that there is only a slight change in the correlations of MZ twins when they are reared apart, however, suggests that a changed environment has had relatively small impact on what is clearly a strong genetic influence.

Wilson (1986) points out that further evidence for environmental influence on intelligence comes from studying the continuity of intelligence over time. Intelligence for both fraternal and identical twins are highly correlated during infancy and early childhood. However, whilst with increasing age the correlation for MZ twins becomes stronger, it tends to decline in DZ twins. The early high correlation is, according to Wilson, due to passive environmental factors, such as very similar environmental experiences created by parents: that is, twins seek out similar experiences that suit their genes. Passer et al (2009) say that the influence of genetics on intelligence does not stop with the initial genetic blueprint, but continues to exert an influence in often subtle ways. For example, MZ twins continue to be similar because of greater 'niche picking'. This means that as we grow older we make choices to live and work in places that suit us, that are in some way compatible with our genetic makeup. Thus, even though the environment does influence our performance on intelligence tests, it is our genetics that helped us choose that environment in the first place.

Another approach to assessing the role of genes is to look at the similarity of adopted children to both their biological and adoptive parents. Plomin et al (1985) have shown that genes play an important role in that children tend to resemble their natural parents more than their adoptive ones. There are great difficulties in interpreting this kind of evidence however. For example, adopted children are not placed at random, but often go into families that resemble the one from which they came. Therefore, just because children are reared apart from their biological parents does not mean that they cease to share environmental influences. Research suggests, however, that quite dramatic changes in intelligence test performance can be achieved by permanently changing the child's environment. Adoption studies have shown that moving a child from an impoverished to an enriched environment can produce long-lasting gains in intelligence of up to 25 IQ points (Capron and Duyme, 1989). This is demonstrated in a classic study by Skodak and Skeels (1949). They followed the progress of 100 children born to retarded parents who were adopted before the age of 6 months. The mothers were mostly from low socio-economic backgrounds, but the children were adopted into homes that were above average both economically and educationally. They found that the IQs of these children were above average throughout childhood and adolescence, and substantially above those of their biological parents. This reflects the contribution of an enriching

EARLY INTERVENTION PROGRAMMES

In some countries, particularly Western countries, early intervention programmes such as the American 'Head Start' have been set up to try to ensure that young people, particularly those from disadvantaged backgrounds, get the best chance they can, and do not drop out of schooling at a later age. The programme does have its detractors, however. McKey et al (1985) showed that although the intentions were good, those from the 'Head Start' group showed no greater ability than those from a normal schooling background within two years of joining a regular high school. It seems that the environment outside school, as well as genetic factors, influenced their ability to perform academically.

Many more intervention programmes have been tried, some with much greater success. The most recent is the 'Sure Start' programme in the UK. This is focused on 0–3-year-olds from poor and disadvantaged backgrounds and is showing some very promising results. The mothers of the children report that home life is better and more settled for the children on the programme. Melhuish et al (2007) reported that the results were still a little unclear, but that they indicate that both children and parents are beginning to feel the benefit of the extra help.

environment to measures of intelligence. The complex interaction of environment and heredity can be seen in the finding that children whose mothers had higher IQs benefited most from the adoption than those of mothers with lower IQs.

Schiff and Lewontin (1986) claim that even though our genetics may well have a great deal to do with our performance on intelligence tests, our environments also have an important influence. Several aspects of home life are associated with intelligence performance. For example, Bradley and Caldwell (1984) suggest that factors such as the amount of time parents spend with children, and the amount of toys, reading materials and such like available to the child, are consistently correlated with intelligence. According to Laosa (1982) several behaviours by mothers play a causal role in the development of intelligence, such as reading and problem solving with their children, and providing a model of behaviour. Ceci and Williams (1997) suggest that IQ is increased by schooling. Those that do not attend show reliably lower performance on intelligence tests than those who attend school. That intelligence scores are

good predictors of school success should come as no surprise, since tests were designed for this very purpose. Indeed, the abilities assessed by IQ tests, such as reading and writing, are targeted and nurtured by education. Our socio-economic status refers to the social environment in which we live, resulting from income. Typically, those of higher socio-economic status have more books in their houses, and are more able academically. They generally eat better food and live in nicer neighbourhoods with less crime and violence and a greater feeling of safety. Lubinski (2004) estimates a correlation of 0.4 between IQ and socio-economic status. This means that the higher the socio-economic status, the higher the IQ.

It has also been suggested that the influence of environment can be *transgenerational*. This means that even before conception, environment has had an influence. For example, if a women suffers from ill-health or struggles in a challenging environment during pregnancy, her foetus suffers too. If the foetus is female then the eggs which will provide her own children (which are by now formed) will be adversely affected. In effect, the next generation is

CULTURAL DIFFERENCES IN MENTAL ABILITIES

Cultural differences in mental abilities were demonstrated by Lesser et al (1965). They tested the intelligence of 3,200 6- and 7-year-old black, Jewish, Chinese and Puerto Rican children in the child's dominant language. They assessed spatial, verbal, number, and reasoning abilities. They found that, whilst Chinese children were assessed as most intelligent and Puerto Rican the least, the four groups differed in their relative competence in the separate abilities tested.

Order → ↓		1	2	3	4
1	Chinese	Spatial	Number	Reasoning	Verbal
2	Jews	Verbal	Number	Reasoning	Spatial
3	Blacks	Verbal	Reasoning	Spatial	Number
4	Puerto Rican	Spatial	Number	Reasoning	Verbal

Order of test scores from highest to lowest (adapted from Aiken, 1971).

These results are not due to socio-economic class, as the same pattern of results was found when this was taken into account. Furthermore, Lesser retested 208 (65%) of the original children five years later and found that 56% of them could be correctly classified in the appropriate ethnic group based only on their ability scores (Lesser, 1976). A follow-up study by Sodolsky and Lesser (1967) in another city, Boston, showed similar patterns in the abilities of Chinese and black children. Sikei and Meyers (1969) on the other hand found that the intelligence test scores of ethnic groups in their study did not significantly differ overall. They tested 4-year-old white and black children and found they only differed in scores of verbal comprehension, pointing to the importance of language in intelligence testing. They suggest that this finding may be explained by the children's age, in that they had not had sufficient exposure to their culture to adopt its typical patterns of thinking and behaving. The research of Sikei and Meyers however is contradicted by many other studies which have found distinct intellectual profiles for cultural groups. It seems that there is disagreement about the nature of a cultural difference in intellectual ability, and whether, indeed, there is such a difference. Factors such as sensitivity of the tests used, age and culture of the participants tested, as well as potential cultural bias in the tests themselves, are all potential confounding variables.

being affected by the grandmother's environmental experience.

Further evidence for the effects of the environment on intelligence comes from efforts to enhance the environments of children in some way, such as with early intervention programmes. A famous example of such a programme is Head Start. Studies which have followed the progress of children who attended this programme show they have greater improvements in IQ than those who did not attend. This appears to be the case only in the short-term however, as by the time the child is in the later years of schooling this advantage disappears. This does not mean to say that such programmes do not have many benefits other than improving intelligence – they have been found to improve attitudes to school and academic achievement, and to improve attendance and dropout rates (Seitz et al, 1985).

THE INFLUENCE OF CULTURE ON INTELLIGENCE TEST PERFORMANCE

The issue of culture and intelligence is a sensitive one, since statements along the lines that one national, racial or cultural group differs from another in intelligence test performance are open to use and abuse for political purposes. For example, immigrants to the United States in the 1920s were tested by psychologists who found that Scandinavian and German immigrants had higher average intelligence test scores than other immigrant groups. On the basis of this testing, some groups were even labelled 'feeble-minded'. Based on these test results some individuals at the time argued for laws restricting the immigration to the US of people who were not from Northern and Western Europe.

"You may be asked a question specifically on the influence of culture so make sure that you prepare adequately for it! "

A frequent criticism of intelligence testing is that the tests themselves are *culturally specific*. People living in different cultures often demonstrate unique intellectual skills. For example, Inuit people of the Arctic region have particularly well-developed visuo-spatial skills, probably associated with a hunter-gatherer lifestyle where such abilities are highly advantageous. As a result, these people are more adept at certain skills. In other cultures, the patterns of intellectual ability favoured more

closely resemble those that are advantageous in formal schooling. The kinds of cognitive skills developed by schooling, such as following directions, considering several alternative responses, using mnemonic strategies, and time-limited testing, are all also the kinds of skills which will enable people to do well on intelligence tests. In fact, education may be the most important variable affecting intelligence test scores, since it influences performance on just about every facet of intelligence tested. This may mean that intelligence tests are biased towards measuring the intelligence of particular populations, so if they are used with anyone outside this group of people the results may not be trustworthy.

"Since it is also an environmental factor, culture can be applied to the issue covered earlier of whether intelligence is due to genes or environment."

Vernon (1979) outlines a number of problems, listed below, in testing intelligence cross-culturally. Without taking these problems into account, any comparison of intelligence test performance is likely to be too simplistic to be meaningful since the problems are sufficiently significant to mean that the results of testing are unlikely to reflect the intelligence of those being tested.

1. Many cultures are simply unfamiliar with intelligence testing. They lack sufficient motivation or interest and often don't take the process seriously. Vernon (1979) notes that there is often excitement or anxiety about the tester, especially when the tester is of a different race.

2. Some test items do not make sense to people from other cultures. Warburton (1951) reports the case of Gurkhas who did not understand the notion of fitting the right shaped peg into the matched-shape hole and simply used force to fit the pegs into any space they could. Using pictures or diagrams appears straightforward enough until you realise that different cultures respond to pictures in different ways. Deregowski (1989) points out that the way in which people perceive the world depends on where in the world they live. For instance, some cultures are not used to interpreting two-dimensional drawings as three-dimensional scenes, since such images are not part of their normal experience.

3. An important factor affecting test performance is any handicap caused by poor nutrition and medical care. This is quite unusual in wealthier countries which develop these tests, but in poorer non-Western countries such problems are quite common.

4. Many environmental factors which are important influences on intelligence test scores vary considerably across cultures. Such factors include lack of interest in formal education, reduced stimulation through lack of travel, television, books etc., little schooling. These problems are relatively uncommon in the West but likely to affect many people living in non-Western countries.

In producing culture-fair tests, some attempts might be made to alter intelligence tests to make the items more meaningful (for example, changing 'blackbird' to 'vulture' for an African test), and to make the instructions and purpose of the test clearer. However, even then the test would lack validity. Validity might be achieved in the Western original test through, for example, predictive validity, where test scores are correlated with future performance in some area. This is going to be difficult if not impossible to achieve in many cultures. Another problem lies with test *norms*. For instance, IQ tests compare the person's performance with what might be expected of the person, known as the 'norm'. These 'norms' are calculated by testing many different kinds of people and averaging their score. The problem is that the people tested, in calculating the norms, may not be from the same culture as the person on whom the test is next to be used. For instance, the person being tested may be an African man, living and working in his home country of Zimbabwe, and the people used to calculate the norms may have been inhabitants of the South-East of England. This means that comparing scores to these norms may not be fair. What is the norm for one cultural group may not be the same for a different group of people. To improve the fairness of the test, a whole new set of norms would have to be calculated. Traditional intelligence tests then might not be culturally fair, either in how they are constructed or in how they are administered.

It has been argued that there is a test bias in traditional IQ tests since the content is not necessarily familiar to children from some social or cultural backgrounds. For instance, what is clever or admired in one culture may not be described as clever in another. An ability to identify herbs and plants that can help heal an open would is extremely important in some poor countries, whereas most people in affluent societies can visit a hospital for help from someone with medical training.

It has proved virtually impossible to design a test of intelligence without introducing some degree of cultural bias (Sternberg, 2008). Notwithstanding the problems with validity and norms already mentioned, the process involves more than just translating a test from one language to another, since the concepts used in the test are a source of bias. Many intelligence tests rely heavily on vocabulary. The WAIS for instance has an entire component that tests 'verbal IQ'. This kind of test bias was recognised by psychologist Robert L. Williams in the 1970s. He developed an IQ test based on the language and experience of African Americans in order to demonstrate racial and cultural biases in testing: his culturally-specific test is called the Black Intelligence Test of Cultural Homogeneity (BITCH). This was a 100 item multiple choice test consisting of vocabulary selected from the Dictionary of American Regional English. This dictionary contains hundreds of words used mainly by African Americans (although it is worth noting that language like this quickly goes in and out of fashion and can eventually cross cultural boundaries). For example, 'bad' means excellent, 'bro' means brother, 'ace' means close friend, and 'hincty' means high class.

EXAMPLE OF A BITCH TEST ITEM

Blood is... (a) a vampire
(b) a dependent individual
(c) an injured person
(d) a brother of colour

The language used in the test would be more familiar to African Americans than to most whites, and indeed Williams found that African Americans performed better on the BITCH test than whites. Williams points out that the difficulties faced by white people doing this test are comparable with the difficulties of black African Americans doing traditional IQ tests. It seems that the importance of language bias is clearly demonstrated when you encounter a test based on norms different from your own.

One approach to overcoming cultural bias has been to avoid using language and instead design tests which use images that do not require rules

THE FLYNN EFFECT

In the 1990s, James Flynn discovered that, over the last 60 years, IQs have increased, and that this trend seems to be the case in all cultures where data exists. For example, people in the UK score, on average, 28 points higher on IQ tests now than they did in 1942. This phenomenon has become known as the 'the Flynn Effect'.

According to Neisser (1998), this increase in measured intelligence, like the increase in physical size that has occurred over the years, may be to do with better nutrition and hence better health. Whilst this has undoubtedly contributed to the IQ improvements, many psychologists doubt that it could account entirely for the dramatic changes.

It is also suggested that because our environments are so much more complex than they used to be, our intelligence has had to develop to keep pace. Studies by Bradmetz and Mathy (2006) in France for example, show increases over generations in the IQs of children. They say that this is because of the use of technology and media helping with verbal reasoning skills, which are then scored higher in tests of intelligence. Likewise, technologies such as computers, and visual learning strategies in education have meant that people score better on visuo-spatial skills, too. However, this could not account for changes across cultures where such influences have been minimal at best

For many children, education has improved and children stay in school for longer, and this could explain the Flynn Effect since most of the skills assessed by traditional IQ tests are 'school' skills. However, this does not explain the improvements in cultures where schooling has not changed so dramatically.

From generation to generation IQs are improving, yet explaining the Flynn Effect is complex. Since it is not likely that genes are responsible for this improvement in intelligence (the pace of change has been far too fast to be explained by genetic mechanisms), the Flynn Effect is clearly something to do with our environment.

embedded in a particular culture to be understood. A set of tasks just like this was designed by Raven in 1963, and called *Raven Progressive Matrices*. These include tests that require people to reason and consider the relationships between geometric shapes. It is argued that carrying out tasks like this does not require culturally-specific knowledge. Jensen (1998) has shown that performance on the Raven (as it is known) correlates very strongly with intelligence scores on traditional tests such as the Wechsler Adult Intelligence Scale (WAIS). This shows that the Raven and the WAIS are measuring more or less the same thing, but the Raven does it in a way that is not specific to any particular culture.

However, even though the Raven is assumed to contain minimal cultural bias, it has been argued that it is virtually impossible to design a test of intelligence without introducing *some* form of bias. Because of these problems in test design, many psychologists consider that cross-cultural comparisons of intelligence are impossible. Such efforts may also be meaningless, given that different cultures place their own values on the skills of their people. Kline (1991) questions the purpose of cross-cultural comparisons anyway, since there are fundamental problems with the endeavour . Even if it were possible, it is likely to be the case that some people will take advantage of any findings showing a difference, for their own political purposes. In Klein's view, an attempt to find cultural differences "…adds nothing to theoretical understanding or to social or educational practice".

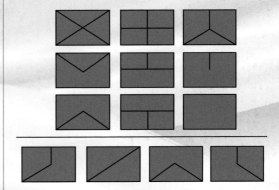

The Ravens Progressive Matrix consists of tasks like this. Which one of the four shapes below the line should be used to fill the lower right box above the line? The answer is the third from the left.

Cognition and development

NIGEL HOLT

You are expected in the examination to show both the skills of knowledge and understanding and the skills of analysis and evaluation in relation to the topic Cognition and development.

Where opportunities for their effective use arise, you will need to demonstrate an appreciation of issues and debates. These include the nature/nurture debate, ethical issues in research, free-will/determinism, reductionism, gender and culture bias, and the use of animals in research.

You will also need to demonstrate an understanding of How Science Works. You can do this through the effective use of studies in your answer (as description or evaluation) or where appropriate by evaluating methodology and findings.

WHAT YOU NEED TO KNOW

DEVELOPMENT OF THINKING

- Theories of cognitive development, including Piaget, Vygotsky and Bruner
- The applications of these theories to education

DEVELOPMENT OF MORAL UNDERSTANDING

- Theories of moral understanding (Kohlberg) and/or prosocial reasoning (Eisenberg)

DEVELOPMENT OF SOCIAL COGNITION

- Development of the child's sense of self, including theory of mind (Baron-Cohen)
- Development of children's understanding of others, including perspective-taking (Selman)
- Biological explanations of social cognition, including the role of the mirror neuron system

THE DEVELOPMENT OF THINKING

The mental skills we need to allow us to process information about the world around us are called cognitive skills. Cognitive psychology focuses on mental processes such as thinking, remembering, language and problem solving. Cognitive-developmental psychologists are interested in the development of these skills and how they are organised at each stage of development from birth. A number of very influential theories have been put forward to explain intellectual development: the most comprehensive account is that of Jean Piaget, whose theory we turn to first.

"Whilst there are a number of different theories of how we develop our cognitive abilities, it's worth pointing out that none of these theories is wrong and none may be regarded as entirely correct. They are just theories, with their own strengths and weaknesses. So what makes one theory better than another? The answer is always to be found in the amount and quality of evidence a theory has in its favour. Even then one may not be regarded as 'better' than another, just as different!"

THEORIES OF COGNITIVE DEVELOPMENT – PIAGET

Jean Piaget was an extremely influential developmental scientist, interested in how children think and how this ability develops. His research was based on his great skills of observation and he pioneered many of the techniques of watching and measuring abilities that developmental psychologists use to this day.

Piaget said that children necessarily thought in ways that are less sophisticated or complex than adults, reflecting their experience of the world. It is because they have less knowledge and experience that children think in a different way from adults. Cognitive development for Piaget is a process of adaptation to an expanding world, requiring formulation of new rules and mental structures in order to organise knowledge, to reason and solve problems.

CONSTRUCTED KNOWLEDGE

Piaget set out to investigate how it was that children developed their understanding of the world around them. What's fundamental about Piaget's theory is that he believed that the child *constructed* their knowledge of the world by actively interacting with it. The child is thought of as an explorer, finding their way through the world and developing as they do. Thus Piaget believed that the child actively investigated their world and through this interaction they learned how it responded to them and how they might respond to it. The intention of all this exploration is to allow the child to change or adapt so that they can cope with the requirements of the world. For example, consider watching a child play with building bricks. Their play may result in their building of a tower or a house of some kind. In this way the child is learning how to manipulate objects to resemble other objects that they might then use in their play. They are adapting themselves and the world around them, developing an understanding of how things work in the world.

The concept of *schema* is extremely important in Piaget's explanation of cognitive development. A schema (plural schemata) is best described as a 'collection of ideas', and we have schemata for a vast number of things. For instance, when we need to find something in our room, we hunt for it. Piaget would say that we are using our 'hunting for things' schema. When we make a cup of tea we follow a kind of routine. Piaget would say that we are enacting our 'making a cup of tea' schema. These are very different examples, but they illustrate a very important point. A schema can mean some collection of actions, or an understanding of how something, like looking for things, is carried out. How we learn these schemata is absolutely central to Piaget's description of how we develop cognitively.

Assimilation occurs when we link new information to an existing schema. For instance, a baby may watch people as they look in at her in the cot. She may see that they smile at her. She may assimilate this smiling action into her 'that seems like an important action' schema. What she does with this new information is irrelevant: the key point is that the new information has been assimilated. It has been identified as 'potentially important'. Note also that we are quite choosy about what we decide to assimilate. We could not possibly take in all the information around us, so being able to assimilate things, or absorb things into our existing knowledge structure, is very useful.

Accommodation is the act of changing a schema to fit the new information you have assimilated to it. For instance, a child may have a schema for 'bird' and as a result refer to every bird as the same object. It can assimilate new knowledge about 'bird' as it encounters more and more birds – some are bigger than others, they vary in colour,

and they make different sounds, but basically a bird is a bird. However, after encountering an ostrich or a penguin the child is going to have to adjust its bird schema to accommodate this new information about birds – some birds don't fly and some don't even look like birds.

As long as a child is simply enlarging its schemata through assimilation it is in a state of mental balance called *equilibrium*. Accommodation, however, involves adapting schemata to new events and information, something which causes some kind of mental discomfort, which Piaget called *disequilibrium*. Because disequilibrium is uncomfortable we are motivated to come to terms with the new information as soon as possible. The movement from equilibrium to disequilibrium and back again is called *equilibration*. Piaget thought that the child was constantly in a state of equilibration, changing and developing schemata.

PIAGET AND INHELDER (1952) – THE THREE MOUNTAINS TASK

The three mountains apparatus.

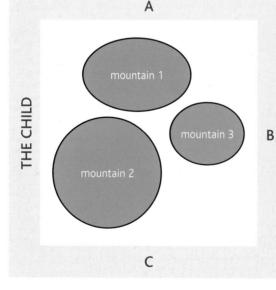

In this task, the child must say what the doll is able to see, from different positions. In order to do this correctly, the child must be able to 'put themselves in the doll's shoes'. On the mountains might be small objects, such as a model house or a model tower. At different positions around the table, the house or tower may become visible, depending on the position of the larger mountains. In other words, what the doll and child are able to see depends on where they are seated.

The experimenter can ask the child: "What does the doll see when seated at position A, or B, or C?". In each case, the perspective of the doll changes. The child is asked simply to draw the view from the perspective of the doll in each case. To complete the task successfully the child must be able to imagine what the mountains look like from the doll's position. Piaget found that children in the pre-operational stage were not able to complete this task satisfactorily. He concluded that this meant that the child was exhibiting 'egocentrism', an inability to see things from others' viewpoints.

PIAGET'S STAGES OF COGNITIVE DEVELOPMENT

Piaget said that children's intellectual abilities develop in stages. These stages are universal – by this Piaget meant that all children pass through each stage of development. In addition to this, Piaget described the stages as invariant, which means that each child passes through each stage in the same order. Each stage is slightly different from the rest, and is characterised by the appearance of different intellectual abilities.

Sensorimotor stage (Birth to 18 months)

This stage is called sensorimotor because the child's thinking mainly involves sensing and doing – hearing, seeing, moving, touching etc. Younger children in this stage of development (up to about 8 months) are unable, according to Piaget, to understand that things out of sight, perhaps behind or under other things, still exist. Understanding that just because something is hidden by something else does not mean that it has ceased to exist is called *object permanence*. After 8 months, children begin to understand that objects in the environment exist whether or not the infant perceives them.

Pre-operational stage (18 months to 6 years)

During the sensorimotor stage a child is limited to sensory and behavioural schemata. The acquisition of language during the pre-operational stage, however, allows a child to *think* about information – a skill which characterises the next stage of development. Piaget called the process of thinking through an action, rather than performing an action, an *operation*. The pre-operational stage is so called because the child has not yet mastered this kind of symbolic thinking.

Piaget said that, when in the pre-operational stage, the child is *egocentric*, that is, they tend to see the world only from their own viewpoint. For example, a young child has difficulty understanding why it is she has to share her toy train or refrain from hitting another child with it. Piaget used the three mountains task to investigate the phenomenon. In the three mountains task, a child is required to see a mountain scene from the perspective of a doll. If asked to select the doll's view from a choice of photos or draw what the doll sees, pre-operational children have great difficulty.

"Developmental psychology lends itself to observational studies. Remind yourself of the different kinds of observation and the pros and cons associated with each. You are bound to get a chance to evaluate developmental studies – and commenting on their methodology, which will more often than not be an observation, is a good way to gain marks in the exam."

Animism is a phenomenon closely linked to egocentrism. It refers to the tendency to attribute life like characteristics to inanimate objects such as toys and other man-made items. For instance, a toy might be described as 'shy' or 'naughty' by the pre-operational child. Drawings of inanimate objects, such as houses, clouds or the sun will often feature smiling mouths and eyes.

Children in the pre-operational stage lack the ability to conserve. *Conservation* is the understanding that even though the appearance of something can change, the amount of substance there remains the same. For instance, modelling clay can be rolled into a sausage shape. Taking the sausage shape and remodelling it into a ball does not change the amount of modelling clay. The pre-operational child is unable to understand that the amount has not been changed. For Piaget, children are concentrating on one aspect of a situation, or *centring*, in this case what the clay looks like. Children are in effect having difficulty *decentring* – that is, considering more than one aspect of a situation at a time.

SOME EXAMPLES OF CONSERVATION

Put simply, conservation is the understanding that, even though the appearance of something may change, its basic properties remain the same.

Conservation of Volume

A child is shown two identical glasses holding equal amounts of water and is asked, "Which has more water, or are they both the same?" The contents of one glass are then poured into a taller and narrower one. The question is repeated and the pre-operational child indicates that the taller thinner glass has more liquid.

(a) Initial equality

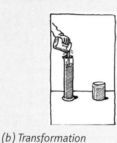

(b) Transformation

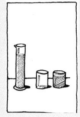

(c) Which glass has more juice

Conservation of Number

Two identical rows of seven counters are laid out, closely spaced together. Pointing to the rows, the child is asked "Which row has more counters, or are they both the same?" Then one row is rearranged, spreading the counters out so that the row appears longer. The question is repeated and the pre-operational child answers that the bottom row has more counters.

Conservation of Mass

Two equal amounts of clay are rolled out into two balls. The child is asked "Which has more clay, or are they both the same?" One is rolled out into a sausage shape and the child is asked the question again. The pre-operational child suggests that the sausage-shaped piece has more clay.

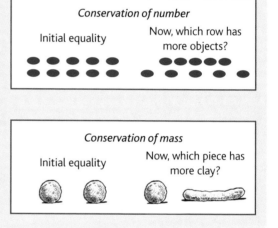

Conservation of number

Initial equality — Now, which row has more objects?

Conservation of mass

Initial equality — Now, which piece has more clay?

> ### ASK AN EXAMINER
>
> "It's very possible that you may need to answer a question on one or more of the theories in this section. Remember, an alternative theory can be used as effective evaluation. For instance, Vygotsky, whose theory we will discover next, can be used as an evaluation of Piaget and vice versa. Just identify and make clear how they are similar or how they are different."

Concrete operational stage (6 years to 12 years)

This stage is called the 'concrete operational' stage because the child develops solid, logical rules about how the world works. The concrete operational child becomes able to conserve as they learn to 'decentre'. So for example, in a conservation of volume task, when the contents of a short fat glass are poured into a tall thin glass the concrete operational child is able to think about the shape of the glasses as well as the level of the liquid. Concrete operations involve children knowing that other people do not necessarily share their own thoughts and feelings, and children now are capable of increasingly complex forms of logical thinking. For example, they understand the principle of *reversibility*, which means that the child begins to understand that what they have just done in the world can be undone or reversed. They are also able to see that doing something in one direction can be the same as doing it in another direction, as in 2 x 4 is the same as 4 x 2. The child in this stage also learns to use *inductive logic*. This is using information we already know and applying it to other situations. For instance, a child who eats lots of sweets and then feels sick, will eventually learn that eating too much makes them feel sick. The principle learned from the original eating and feeling sick incident is applied to the general principle of eating too much.

Formal operational stage (12 years onwards)

Whereas the concrete operational child likes to think in terms of rules, e.g. *what is*, the formal operational child is able to think in more complex terms, e.g. about *what might be*. Situations no longer have to be experienced as in the earlier stage, they can now be imagined. Abstract and hypothetical thinking is now possible to test and solve problems and think about concepts with no concrete reality. So for example numbers can be replaced by abstract symbols and the adolescent can solve algebraic problems, and they can debate such issues as "Is there a god?". Formal operational thinking allows us to consider several hypotheses simultaneously, and to use this ability to solve problems systematically. Because of this ability to think in abstract and hypothetical ways, for example how the world could be better, idealistic, political and ethical thinking emerges during this stage. This kind of idealistic thinking sometimes lacks a sense of realism, so that adolescents, especially, have difficulty seeing or accepting the practical limitations inherent in their views. Piaget called this kind of thinking *formal operational egocentrism*.

RESEARCH INTO PIAGET'S THEORY

Object permanence

Baillargeon and DeVos (1991) investigated Piaget's claims that children younger than 8 months did not understand the idea of object permanence. In their research, they investigated the abilities of 3.5 and 4.5-month-old infants and found that, contrary to Piaget's claim, even very young children had object permanence. This seems to suggest that how a study is carried out is crucial to whether or not a child understands object permanence.

Conservation

A similar criticism applies to how Piaget tested children's conservation skills. McGarrigle and Donaldson (1974) showed that making the conservation task relevant to a child's level of understanding could allow children much younger than predicted by Piaget to solve conservation tasks.

More recent research has criticised their Naughty Teddy experiment however. Moore and Frye (1986) have said that the teddy itself may have been so exciting and distracting that the children may not have even noticed that the counters had been transformed. This might explain their correct response to the question. However, there is evidence from Light et al (1976) to support the Naughty Teddy experiment. They showed that whether children were able to show conservation of number or not in a task like this depended on

---

OBJECT PERMANENCE IN VERY YOUNG CHILDREN

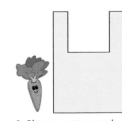

Stage 1: *Short carrot moved behind the screen*

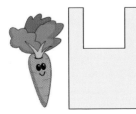

Stage 2: *Tall carrot moved behind the screen*

Baillargeon and DeVos (1991) felt that very young children may understand object permanence but look as though they don't because they are unable to maintain their attention on the task. They developed an apparatus where young children could be shown an impossible situation. The researchers knew from previous findings that young children maintained attention on a task longer if it contained something surprising or seemingly impossible. A screen was designed with a 'notch' in the top.

In stage 1, the short carrot is moved behind the screen from the left and reappears on the right. In stage 2 the tall carrot is moved similarly, but because it is tall, it appears through the 'notch' in the screen as it passes from left to right. In a third, impossible stage, the tall carrot began to move from left to right but did not appear, as expected, through the notch in the screen.

Baillargeon and DeVos found that the infants in the experiment looked for much longer in the third impossible stage than in either of the other stages once the carrot reappeared from behind the screen. They concluded that the infants did understand that the carrot, even though out of sight, was still there – the infants' response showed that they were puzzled when the tall carrot did not appear through the notch. They were able to show object permanence after all, even at 3.5 months of age. This is evidence that Piaget's earlier claim that object permanence was not possible until 8 months was incorrect.

THE NAUGHTY TEDDY STUDY

McGarrigle and Donaldson (1974) showed that changing the way that a conservation task is presented so that younger children could understand what was being asked of them enabled children to solve conservation problems at a younger age than Piaget said.

 As with Piaget, the children in the experiment were asked if the number of counters in each row was the same. All children tested answered correctly, that it was.

Next, the second row of counters was deliberately, and carefully, adjusted by the researcher.

When they now asked if the numbers of counters in each row were the same, the researchers found similar results to Piaget. Children younger than 6 years old were unable to answer correctly, indicating that they were unable to conserve 'number'.

 Finally, McGarrigle and Donaldson employed the services of 'Naughty Teddy'. The counters were returned to the original, matching rows, and the children told to watch out for Naughty Teddy as he often messed up the experiment. Soon after this an experimenter moved a teddy through the experiment, across the table, moving the counters as the experimenter had done previously.

Children were again asked if the number of counters in each row was the same. This time much younger children were able to respond correctly. In fact, the researchers showed that children as young as 4 were able to respond correctly, and so were able to conserve after all. The researchers concluded that Piaget was wrong, younger children can conserve in the right situation – it is the context in which the task is carried out that matters.

whether the change to the counters was seen as deliberate in some way. If it was seen as deliberate, then children were more likely to say that there had been a change in number; if the change was seen as accidental, as with Naughty Teddy, then they were more likely to give the correct response, that the number had not changed. Eames et al (1990) have replicated the Naughty Teddy experiment, and have found very similar results, further supporting McGarrigle and Donaldson's research findings.

> **ASK AN EXAMINER**
>
> "Replication of research findings is very important. If research can be replicated, as Eames et al (1990) replicated the findings of McGarrigle and Donaldson's original Naughty Teddy work, then we can say that the research gains in validity and reliability."

EVALUATING PIAGET'S THEORY OF COGNITIVE DEVELOPMENT

1. Piaget said that we all move through all the stages, and that we do so in the same order. However, there is evidence that not everyone reaches, for instance, the formal operations stage. In fact, Dasen (1994) has estimated that relatively few adults (only 1 in 3) ever reach the formal operations stage at all, and Huit and Hummel (1998) say that it is actually only about a third in industrialised Western cultures. Elsewhere it is even lower, indicating a cultural difference in the way people develop. Bradetz (1999) carried out some research with 62 15-year-old children. He tested them with a number of different Piaget-like tasks and found that only one of the children had reached the formal operational stage. Piaget's theory predicts that the majority of these children should be in that stage, which is clearly not the case.

2. Much of Piaget's original research was carried out with his own children, the rest with a small number of children from relatively wealthy, well-educated backgrounds. These families will have valued the intellectual skills under investigation by Piaget, and so would have helped their children to develop them. In addition to this, Piaget was part of a Western intellectual culture and was looking for certain abilities and skills. Matsumoto and Hull (1994) say that other cultures may not look for the same

skills in the development of intellectual abilities, favouring more practical or interpersonal skills. Piaget's theory does not consider the possibility of different types of cognitive abilities developing differently in different cultures. His original research can be said to be ethnocentric.

3. Piaget said that a process of maturation dictated that we pass through the stages at the same time or age. However, we know that very young children can be taught relatively complex skills. McGarrigle and Donaldson (1974) showed with Naughty Teddy that young children can conserve for instance if the task is presented carefully and in a way that helps the child understand what is happening. Baillargeon and DeVos (1991) went on to show that object permanence was possible at a younger age than Piaget had noted.

4. Larivee et al (2000) say that Piaget's theory of cognitive development is an over-simplification. They say that cognitive development is much more complex and should not be reduced to a relatively straight forward theory of stages like this. Many psychologists, such as Siegler (1996) and Karmiloff-Smith (1992) feel that saying that all children pass through the same stages at similar ages and all in the same order is greatly over-simplifying the process of intellectual development. Karmiloff-Smith (1992), for instance, has argued that development through a particular stage is extremely variable. Some children develop some concepts and ideas in one way and at one point in the stage, and some develop completely differently.

ASK AN EXAMINER

"You don't just have to learn the theory, you have to learn about how the theory has been applied to education. This goes for all three theories of cognitive development that you have to learn."

THEORIES OF COGNITIVE DEVELOPMENT – VYGOTSKY

Like Piaget, Vygotsky believed that cognitive development occurred in stages, with a different style of thinking characterising each stage. However, in contrast to Piaget's idea of the child as a naïve scientist independently exploring their environment, Vygotsky placed a strong emphasis on the role of culture and social interaction. For this reason

Vygotsky's theory is often referred to as a *sociocultural* theory. Culture here means all the knowledge and understanding we have around us, for example in libraries, on the internet, through media and through word-of-mouth. Since it is our culture that holds all the knowledge available to us, it is this that prescribes what children learn. The richer the culture, and the greater the knowledge store within our culture, the greater the potential for our cognitive development.

Vygotsky believed that children were born with basic cognitive abilities and that these abilities are developed and changed into more complex cognitive abilities through informal and formal interactions with those around them who convey the knowledge of a culture. These higher, more complex cognitive abilities are necessary in order to contribute to society, for example to art and science, and so can be thought of as the 'tools' of a culture.

For Vygotsky then, social activity was key to understanding cognitive development. Language is our means of communicating this cultural knowledge, and so Vygotsky felt that language was extremely important in our development. Vygotsky indicates that certain types of cognitive development will take place at certain periods in the child's life. These age ranges begin with infancy and end with adolescence. The really important feature here is how language is used.

Pre-intellectual speech: 0–3 years:

Vygotsky says that, before 2 years of age, language is completely separate from thinking. During the first year, children learn primarily through conditioning, much like lower animals. The child gradually comes to use language, but only in a very basic way, since they do not understand the symbolic nature of language. They learn to use language to express very simple feelings and thought processes, and in an attempt to control the behaviours of others around them. Speech at this stage is regarded as social speech.

Egocentric speech: 3–7 years:

By the time a child reaches 3 years of age they are beginning to use language in their problem solving. This is a sort of egocentric, or inner speech, where the child often talks out loud to themselves when solving problems. The child may talk to themselves while playing with building blocks for instance. This type of speech is an outward expression of their thinking, and is called *monologue*, where the child provides a sort of running commentary on his or her own actions. Vygotsky also noticed that when 3–7-year-olds play with others,they do not necessarily use speech as would older children or adults. Instead, groups of children of this age engage in a group or collective monologue of sorts. Vygotsky said that speech is now being used not just for communication but also for thinking.

Inner speech: 7 years onward:

Here the child learns to use language more effectively to understand the culture around them. Children stop talking to themselves when solving problems. Their speech continues silently, says Vygotsky, and is now inner speech. It is these inner conversations that help the child organise their problem solving. Vygotsky said that inner speech was different from the kind of language used in communication; it has begun to take on a very important role in that it is influencing the way we think. This inner speech can be thought of as an inner monologue.

Vygotsky said that there was a close link between language, as the controller of access to cultural influences, and the thought process. He argued that, while developing their skills with language, children pass through a number of stages of the development of 'concepts' such as 'long', 'thin', 'big', 'heavy' and so on. These are Vygotsky's four stages of concept formation. He investigated this himself in one of his few systematic explorations of his theory. Children were handed wooden blocks. Each block was given a nonsense label,

not relating to the shape of the block at all. For instance, when blocks were tall and square, Vygotsky may have described them as 'ZAT'. The nonsense labels were given consistently, so whenever a tall square block was handed to the child the same nonsense label, ZAT, was used. The task was for children to use their understanding of concepts to work out what each nonsense label meant.

Stage 1: Vague syncretic stage

In this stage the child shows little or no understanding of concepts. They approach problems largely by trial and error and are not systematic at all in their efforts.

Stage 2: Complexes stage

In this stage children begin to use non-random strategies, but they are not successful in discovering the concepts.

Stage 3: Potential concept stage

Children begin to use systematic strategies. However, they are limited in this stage to focusing on only one feature of the blocks – for instance, the shape, or the weight.

Stage 4: Mature concept stage

Children use systematic strategies to identify the concepts correctly.

Vygotsky concluded that in stage 3 children had difficulty in forming concepts because they became focused on only one feature of the object, and could not widen their perspective to other features. In stage 4, the correct concept is formed

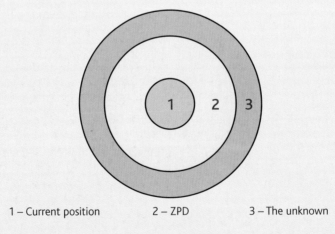

ZONE OF PROXIMAL DEVELOPMENT (ZPD)

1 – Current position   2 – ZPD   3 – The unknown

The child sits at the centre of the zone, with the current level of ability. In the diagram, this is position 1. Surrounding the current position is the zone itself: in the diagram this is area 2. This indicates the region through which the child must move in order to develop intellectually. Surrounding this region is area 3, the unknown. This indicates the intellectual abilities currently out of reach. Area 3 will form the next zone of proximal development once the child has moved through the current zone.

because the child becomes able to see more than one feature of the object.

Vygotsky emphasised the importance of collaboration and group work. He said that cooperative working is important in the development and utilisation of these language skills. If tasks are designed carefully, the success of the group becomes important as well as the success and development of those in the group. The development of one of the group member also adds to the development of the other group members.

THE ZONE OF PROXIMAL DEVELOPMENT (ZPD)

Vygotsky said that the *zone of proximal development* is the distance between the child's current intellectual ability and their potential intellectual ability. In order to develop, the child must move through this zone. For instance, a child who is able to add up building blocks has the potential to understand that adding is a concept that can apply to many things. Currently though, they only understand that adding one more building block makes more building blocks. There is a distance, intellectually, between their wider understanding of the concept of adding and the position in which they currently find themselves.

Vygotsky says that the role of instruction is central to helping the child move through the ZPD. Carefully watching and engaging with the learner, and reacting to their strengths and weaknesses, can help the child develop by moving them out of their comfortable current position and into the ZPD. While in the ZPD the child may need some help and support as they become more able to use their new knowledge and abilities. Supporting the child in this way is known as scaffolding (Wood et al, 1976). It is this support, or 'scaffold', that allows the child to develop to their full potential. Once the child has moved into the ZPD, and has become able to stand alone, it becomes their 'current position' and they are faced with a new ZPD to pass through. The child enters the ZPD, is scaffolded until they can support themselves on their own, they reach their potential, and the process begins again.

RESEARCH INTO VYGOTSKY'S THEORY

Ramachandran and Hubbard (2003) reported that language can influence the way we think about things. Their research was concerned with a phenomenon called synaesthesia, whereby people experience objects that they see in the world as a smell or a sound. They report the case of Esmerelda Jones, who experiences the colour blue whenever she hears the musical note C sharp. She uses this skill to colour code piano keys, which helps her remember and play music and musical scales. Ramachandran and Hubbard explain that it is not just people like Esmeralda Jones who show this type of ability. They show that the way in which language is used, and the names we give things, can influence the way all of us think.

In their research they used two different shapes, one smooth and curvy like shape 1 and one jagged and pointy like shape 2.

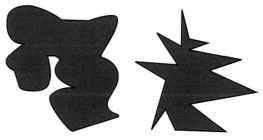

shape 1   *shape 2*

They asked participants which of the shapes was a 'bouba' and which was a 'kiki'. Of course, the names for the shapes were entirely invented, either could have been a kiki or a bouba. They found that 98% of participants said that shape 1 was the 'bouba' and shape 2 was the 'kiki' even though none of the participants had ever seen the shape, or heard the possible names for the shapes before. We all, then, have a bias to associate certain sounds with certain shapes.

Ramachandran and Hubbard say that this is because humans learn to associate certain sounds with certain shapes as they develop, and so the language we use can significantly influence how we think about the world around us. Ramachandran and Hubbard have also shown that the areas that deal with visual stimuli and speech are both at the back of the brain. They say that both of these areas are capable of making the same area in the front of the brain activate. This part of the brain, in the motor area, is concerned with the activity of speaking. They say that this is evidence that our understanding of the world around us and language are very closely linked.

The zone of proximal development and scaffolding

McNaugton and Leyland (1990) investigated Vygotsky's theory of the zone of development and how assistance while in the ZPD influenced later performance. In their research they chose to investigate jigsaws, a common activity that any children engage in, and with which parents, as helpers, often join in.

McNaughton and Leyland observed children completing jigsaws with the help of mothers and noted the level of difficulty that could be achieved. They carefully observed the mothers' helping behaviour during this part of the research. In the next session the children returned and worked on jigsaws on their own. The jigsaw solving ability when alone was lower for most children than when they were aided. The ability to complete jigsaws on their own was their current ability and the ability that they reached with their parents was their potential ability. This is evidence that with assistance children can indeed perform at a level above that which they might achieve on their own.

The observations of the mothers' helping behaviour carried out in the first stage of the research, where children were assisted in their jigsaw completion, were analysed. McNaughton noticed that the amount of helping behaviour the mothers gave was directly related to the difficulty of the jigsaw.

> When the jigsaws were extremely difficult, and beyond the ZPD of the child, the helping behaviour was focused on completing the jigsaw rather than helping the child complete the jigsaw.

> When the jigsaw was very easy indeed and below the ZPD of the child, the helping behaviour was directed mainly at making sure the child focused their attention on the task.

> When the jigsaw was within the ZPD of the child, and neither too hard nor too simple, the helping behaviour was focused on helping the child solve the puzzle themselves.

McNaughton and Leyland concluded that parents realised that when the task was too difficult there was no point in helping the child as it was clearly beyond their potential ability. Similarly, when the task was too easy the child became distracted very easily, and so helping with the task was not necessary, instead their role was to keep the child focused on the task. When the jigsaw was within the ZPD, and within reach of the child's capabilities, the mother helped the child by sharing their understanding of how the task might be completed. McNaughton and Leyland concluded that scaffolding activity was dependent on the perceived difficulty of the task.

EVALUATING VYGOTSKY'S THEORY OF COGNITIVE DEVELOPMENT

Vygotsky's ideas have been very positively received by educators who have provided support for his ideas. Some, however, have identified problems with the theory.

1. Vygotsky's theory does not always allow for individual differences in the way people learn. For instance, he indicates that group working is beneficial as it helps those engaging in it to share ideas and develop together. Research into group working generally agrees that this is the case, but there is some evidence that not everyone benefits from this approach. Blaye et al (1991) investigated the performance of children working in pairs on a problem-solving task based on a computer game. Whereas they found that those who worked in pairs benefited in some ways, at least 30% of those who worked alone performed just as well. We can conclude that group working may be beneficial for a large number of us, but it is not necessary for all of us to perform to the best of our abilities. In addition to this, group working discourages some qualities that some may feel are beneficial in an educational environment. Bennett and Dunne (1991) say that group working discourages competitiveness, even though it is largely beneficial, encouraging logical thinking. If it is the intention of an educator to generate some form of competition in the classroom, perhaps as an encouragement to improve effort and grades, then group working will not necessarily help in this aim.

2. Vygotsky's emphasis on the importance of social factors is very attractive to educators and to society in general as it highlights the importance of society in the development of children's cognitive skills. Accessing these social factors requires an ability with language and the opportunity to interact with social knowledge, through access to materials or through conversations with peers, educators and caregivers. However, some, including Piaget, feel that this is an overemphasis, and social factors are not as important in cognitive development as Vygotsky indicated. Instead, they indicate the importance of self-discovery and experimentation with the world as the key

to cognitive development, not necessarily the interaction with others.

3. The role of the teacher is extremely important in Vygotsky's theory of cognitive development. A child passing into and through the zone of proximal development can be supported and challenged by an educator, who can act as a scaffold until the child is able to progress unaided. In this way a teacher can help a child reach their cognitive potential. On the other hand the followers of Piaget's ideas would say that this is an overemphasis on the importance of social interaction and particularly the intervention of the teacher in the learning process. In interacting in this way we are stifling discovery learning and potentially negatively influencing the cognitive development of the child. In addition to this, scaffolding can be a very difficult skill indeed. Each child will need a different level of support at different stages and with different tasks. It takes a highly skilled and flexible educator to maintain this focus, especially in a large class of children. This may be possible when only one child is instructed at any one time, but even then maintaining flexibility and just the right amount of support can be difficult, as can knowing when it is appropriate to remove the support and allow the child to continue unaided. Expecting this level of skill and focus in an educational environment may be regarded by some as unrealistic.

THEORIES OF COGNITIVE DEVELOPMENT – BRUNER

Like Vygotsky, Josef Bruner identified social context as vital in the development of cognitive abilities. His theory also has some similarities with Piaget's in that he too believed that we learn by assimilation and accommodation. He also believed that the child learned best by personal discovery, as did Piaget. In this way Bruner draws on the two other major thinkers in the field, Piaget and Vygotsky, in developing his influential theory.

Bruner said that childrens ability to solve problems and show an accurate understanding of the world depends on how they think about their surroundings. Bruner says that children have three modes of thinking about or representing the world: enactive, iconic and symbolic modes.

1. Enactive mode (0–18 months)
Thinking, during this stage of development, involves the child acting out or performing physical actions. Here the emphasis is on doing things, so thinking is basically a motor action. The knowledge that we acquire during this stage is entirely dependent on what we are able to do physically.

2. Iconic mode (18 months to 6 or 7 years)
Bruner said that this form of representation begins to appear at about 1 year of age. In the iconic mode, the child thinks about the world in terms of mental images. Being able to hold images in the mind allows children to draw and paint, something that they take a great deal of enjoyment in doing at this stage. Being able to think in the iconic mode allows children to represent their understanding of the world, but it does not allow the child to solve complex problems. That requires a symbolic representation.

3. Symbolic mode (6–7 years onwards)
In the symbolic mode, Bruner says that the child thinks about the world in terms of symbols. In this case the symbols are things like words, numbers and musical representations of things. These symbols can now be used for problem solving. For instance the child may write the word 'mummy' to refer to their mother, or the number 2 to refer to two apples. The word and the number are symbols that represent the objects. Language and other kinds of symbol such as numbers and music can now be used in thinking about problems. This is the basis of thinking logically.

Bruner developed Vygotsky's earlier theory of the zone of proximal development and the concept of scaffolding. He believed that a child's cognitive development could be helped and encouraged. To do this, an educator should watch the child carefully, identifying where they struggle or fail. When this happens they should intervene and support the child. Bruner says that this sort of intervention is necessary for successful cognitive development.

The role of language is very important in Bruner's theory and is most obviously seen in the description of the symbolic representation of the world. Language allows the child to think in terms of symbols, and in the abstract. For example, the child is able to use language to think about concepts such as justice, and fairness. These ideas are called abstract concepts as they do not have a physical structure and cannot be 'pictured'.

To investigate the role of language, Bruner took Piaget's conservation of liquid task, where the contents of a short fat glass can be poured into a tall thin glass. In his research he covered the top quarter of the glass into which the liquid was poured with a screen. This meant that children were unable to see the level of the liquid in the second glass. Thus, they were unable to use the iconic mode in to complete the task as they could not compare a mental image of what was present with what they could see once the liquid had been transferred. In his task, Bruner used three glasses – a short fat one, an even shorter and fatter one and an extremely short and extremely fat one. In each case liquid could be transferred between the glasses in front of children, but the screen over the glasses meant that they were unable to see the level of the liquid in each glass.

He found that with the screen in place, half of the four-year-olds and almost all of the 5–7-year-olds showed that they were able to conserve – that is to say, they knew that the amount of liquid remained the same after every transformation (pouring from one glass to another). However, after the screen was removed, the 4-year-olds stopped conserving. Being able to see the level of the liquid meant that

they were no longer able to answer the question correctly. The 5–7-year-olds continued to answer the question correctly.

Bruner concluded that the 4-year-olds were using an iconic representation to solve the problem. They simply compared the level of the water in the current glass with their mental representation of the level of the water in the previous glass. The levels were different and so the amount of liquid must have changed. However, the 5- and 7-year-olds were completing the task using the symbolic mode, which allowed them to conserve because verbalising the answer with the screen in place allowed them to think symbolically when the screen had been removed. Bruner said that it was the act of saying the correct answer with the screen in place that allowed them to complete the task successfully once it had been removed. Bruner concluded that verbalising the answer had forced them to use the symbolic mode and that this was

DEVELOPING SYMBOLIC THOUGHT

A study by Bruner and Kenney (1966) tested 5-year-old, 6-year-old and 7-year-old children, each child being presented with the same two tasks. Nine glasses of varying sizes were arranged in a particular pattern on a 3x3 matrix (see picture A). In the *reproduction* task, the children described the pattern, then the glasses were removed from the matrix and jumbled. The children were required to replace them in their original pattern. This task required an iconic mode of thought, as it just involved reproducing a visual image. In the *transposition* task, the children again described the pattern of glasses, but after they were removed and jumbled the children had to rearrange the glasses as in a mirror image (picture B). This task required symbolic thought, because the children could not just copy a mental picture but had to use reason to reverse the pattern.

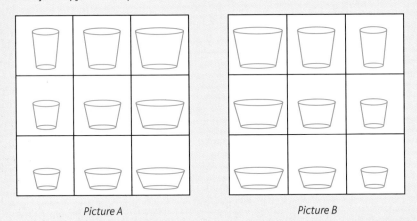

Picture A   *Picture B*

The results showed that most children over the age of 5 were able to complete the reproduction task successfully, and so demonstrated iconic thinking. However, very few children under the age of 7 were able to complete the transposition task, whereas most who were 7 could complete both tasks successfully, showing that 7-year-olds were able to think both iconically and symbolically.

Bruner and Kenney concluded that the result supports the theory that children become able to use a symbolic mode of representation at around 7 years of age. This mode allows children to generate rules such as 'the fat one goes on the left, the thin one on the right and the medium sized one in the middle', the kind of thinking needed to solve this problem.

evidence that language was extremely important in problem solving and cognitive development.

EVALUATING BRUNER'S THEORY OF COGNITIVE DEVELOPMENT

Bruner's theory has been extremely usefully applied to education and training. Bruner's theory is informative in a number of ways, not only in suggesting how the educator might approach the practice of teaching itself, but also in helping us understand how society should think about education. Bruner says that the purpose of education is to help and guide people to be able to think intuitively and freely.

"This is a good point to remind you to use other theories as part of your evaluation! What is similar and what is different between Bruner and Piaget and Vygotsky? Similarities show support, differences indicate a possible criticism."

There is a lot of research to support Bruner's idea that children are capable of different types of mental representation as they get older. Bruner and Kenney (1966) for example demonstrated differences in the thinking of 5, 6 and 7-year-old children.

APPLICATION OF THESE THEORIES TO EDUCATION

APPLYING PIAGET'S THEORY TO EDUCATION

Piaget's theories have been applied widely in education. His theory is about how children develop their understanding of the world and how they learn concepts, about how they learn to think and reason. These skills are essential in life and are at the very heart of education. In the 1960s the British Government commissioned the Plowden report that strongly recommended that Piaget's ideas be applied in our schools. Although the popularity of his theory has fluctuated somewhat since, it can be reasonably claimed that Piaget's thinking has influenced all of us. His theory can be applied in our understanding of what children are able to learn at different stages in their development. This has become known as stage-specific instruction. He has also been influential in the techniques used in the classroom. Piaget said that children learn best by self-discovery of information. This is described as 'discovery learning' and is evident in many of the world's education systems.

What children are able to learn – stage-specific instruction

Piaget's theory is a stage theory. It identifies different stages of development and the cognitive skills children have in each. Knowing this is extremely useful to the educator, as lessons and instruction can be shaped to the stage the students are currently passing through. This is called *stage-specific instruction*. We might think of this as the child's *readiness* to learn. When they are in the right stage, they are ready to learn new skills. Activities can then be developed to encourage the development of these new skills, facilitated by the teacher. Depending on the stage the students are in, the educator might:

» Provide toys and props and set children tasks to solve with them.

» Encourage problem solving in groups where weaker students can be encouraged and driven on by more able students.

» Develop problems whose solution requires students to use stage-appropriate logic and reasoning.

"If you are asked a question on the application of a theory to education, be prepared to have to evaluate this application too. We've provided plenty of material here to help you with this, so no excuses!"

Evaluating stage-specific instruction: Ojose reports research from Burns and Silbey (2000) who also support stage-specific instruction, indicating that children learn best when activities are carefully designed to match their stage of development. However, Brainerd (1983) investigated readiness to learn and concluded that Piaget had underestimated the ability of children to master tasks. Brainerd took 4-year-olds, and carefully instructed them on tasks that related to the concrete operational stage. Piaget said that concrete operational skills were not possible until 7 years of age at the earliest. Brainerd showed that even 4-year-olds could perform these tasks well. This suggests that stage-specific instruction is a good general rule, but that does not mean that it is necessary, as teaching children skills from stages above theirs is possible.

Egan and Kauchak (2000) say that whereas representing an idea in one way to one child may be helpful, it may not be helpful to all children in the same stage. This indicates that while stage-specific instruction may well be a useful tool for some children, the teacher must be careful to be able to differentiate, or change their methods, where necessary, so as to benefit as many children as possible.

How we should teach children – discovery learning

Piaget's discovery learning approach is very different from the more traditional teacher-centred approach to learning. In the past, children were thought of as receivers of information, as passive listeners who sat at desks while the teacher instructed them. In Piaget's theory the child can be thought of as a scientist or an explorer, and so the experience of learning is one of discovery rather than one of being a passive recipient. The experience of finding their way through the world allows children to develop their intellectual abilities by doing what they are naturally inclined to do – testing ideas and learning from the results. Knowing this is very helpful to the educator. If we know that the child learns best through *self-discovery*, as Piaget indicates, then teaching material and instruction can be organised appropriately.

What's important here is that the child must be encouraged to find things out for themselves through discovery. Bryant (1984) says that to some extent, he is surprised that educators are interested in Piaget's work at all, since Piaget did not really think educators were very important. Educators often see their role as that of someone with knowledge, who tells students to do things and how to do them. Piaget said that this was pointless: educators should facilitate the child's own learning, rather than instruct.

Piaget also tells us that children learn and develop through accommodation and assimilation. To do this, the child passes through a state of disequilibrium and must organise their learning and knowledge, and question their existing schemata so as to achieve equilibrium. The instructor can assist in this process by challenging the child, placing them into the state of disequilibrium. In order to get back into equilibrium the child must challenge their existing schemata, and in doing so they develop intellectually. Teachers can encourage the state of disequilibrium by challenging what a child thinks to be true, or asking questions that they may struggle a little to answer.

"Another way to evaluate the application of a theory, of course, is to look critically at the theory itself! If the theory is flawed, so may be the application. This applies to all three theories and their applications."

Evaluating discovery learning: Cross-cultural research indicates that Piaget's discovery learning may not be universally appropriate. Asian children do very well indeed in school and in general their academic achievement is much better than that of all other cultures. Asian education systems do not, generally, use a discovery learning approach, favouring instead a more traditional schooling instruction method.

Stigler et al (1987) defend this component of Piaget's theory from the cross-cultural criticism identified above. They say that comparing Western education systems with Asian education systems can be very misleading. For instance, the time spent teaching mathematics in schools in Taiwan was found to be approximately twice as much as it was in American schools . It seems it may not only be the way in which children are taught that matters; it could also be the amount of time they are taught that plays a role. Those who claim that Asian is better than Western education simply because they do not use Piaget's discovery learning approach are not considering the other factor – time spent teaching – that could account for the difference.

Meadows (1994) points out that discovery learning is useful, but it largely ignores the added benefit a teacher can give in a more traditional 'tutorial' type of education. This agrees with Brainerd (1983) who is of the opinion that discovery learning is generally much less effective than the more traditional education style adopted more often these days in Asian countries.

De Jong and Van Joolinen (1998) say that discovery learning in computer-based environments is very important indeed. They concluded in their review of the available literature on the subject that discovery learning could be very effective when children and young adults were required to solve computer-based problems. They also point out that the effectiveness of discovery learning can be reduced when the learners encounter problems or difficulties in their explorations as they move forwards, learning more and more complicated things. The researchers say that it is here that there is a role for an instructor. Instructional support should be given when needed to help the learner develop their learning when they reach a difficult problem or step in their discovery learning. This supports Piaget's ideas of helping children into a stage of disequilibrium. A computer-training environment like this might be developed with some difficult learning obstacles along the way. When they meet these difficult stages, children would struggle a little, and enter disequilibrium. Their existing schemata of how to continue to the next point are now doubted, and the educator can help them carefully assimilate the new information.

APPLYING VYGOTSKY'S THEORY TO EDUCATION

Vygotsky's theories have now been applied to education, his thinking adding a great deal to the process of teaching and learning. The concept of the zone of proximal development and the related idea of scaffolding have clear applications to the classroom or indeed any environment where a child is learning with the support of an older brother or sister, a parent, or their teacher or lecturer.

Scaffolding in education

Scaffolding means that the educator, or caregiver, need not wait until the child appears ready to learn or move on intellectually. The child can be supported in their instability as they enter the ZPD. This support, or 'scaffold', eventually allows them to work alone.

Olson and Pratt (2000) say that the type of instruction given during scaffolding should be just slightly beyond the level that the child can achieve alone. If the support is far beyond the current capabilities of the child they will not be able to continue alone once the support is removed. Mothers in McNaughton and Leyland's jigsaw study appeared to know this intuitively, deciding that assisting the child on tasks beyond their reach was not appropriate, and opting instead to help the child complete the jigsaw quickly, rather than engage in any instruction. Bransford et al (2000) say that the scaffolding process has six stages:

STAGE	EXPLANATION
1. Motivate	Get the child's interest
2. Simplify	Make the task more manageable
3. Maintain focus	Keep the child focused on the task
4. Point out performance	Clearly identify the difference between the child's performance and the desired level of performance
5. Reduce frustration	Provide a supportive environment, helping the child to avoid becoming frustrated
6. Demonstrate	Clearly demonstrate to the child how they should be performing.

If we follow these stages in an education setting, a child can be helped through their ZPD. It is very important that the instructor should be flexible, and react when it seems the child may become frustrated. It is also important that the instructor is skilled enough to be able to simplify tasks and show the child exactly what is expected of them. In short, the process requires careful and thoughtful application of skills on the part of the instructor.

Corner et al (1997) investigated the importance of the quality of scaffolding. In their study, 2-year-old children were supported in their problem solving activities by their fathers. In each case, the researchers rated the quality of the scaffolding they observed. They showed that scaffolding did indeed help the child learn, but that the quality of the scaffolding was very important in the child's intellectual development. They found in a follow-up study that the children who had received better scaffolding continued to improve more than children who had received less focused scaffolding. This has implications for education in that it highlights the importance of the type of support the educator gives. It also shows that good teaching strategies and good scaffolding can have a longer lasting impact on the cognitive performance of the child than less well-organised attempts to help the child.

The importance of language in education

The importance of the type of language used during scaffolding has been shown in a number of studies. Scaffolding certainly seems to be effective, but using different kinds of language at different stages in the process and at different ages is also very important. Vygotsky's theory of the development of pre-intellectual, egocentric and inner speech tells us that language is used differently at different stages. Egocentric speech, for instance, is a very important stage in cognitive development as it marks the point at which speech is being used not just as a means of communication, as it would have been in the pre-intellectual child. Instead, the speech is moving to a place where it is being used as a means of solving problems and rapidly developing cognitive abilities. Research has also shown that children do indeed use different kinds of language during cognitive development. Behrend et al (1992) observed children carefully as they solved problems in the classroom. When they saw lip-movements, but heard no speech they concluded that the child was engaging in inner speech. These children were seen to perform better that those children who did not use inner speech.

Berk (1994) investigated children in mathematics classes and found that many of them (60%) talked to themselves while solving problems. Her observations allowed her to conclude that the child would perform the tasks much better if these 'conversations' contained information relevant to the problem. We can conclude from this that the speech helped the child focus on the task in hand, as Vygotsky had said. The implications of this finding are clear. Making sure a young child is silent in class may be detrimental to their performance if they are not yet able to engage in inner speech. Berk went on to investigate children's activities with building blocks and found that they began in their problem solving speaking out loud, but as they grew in confidence, their self-monologues became shorter and fewer, eventually disappearing altogether. This supports Vygotsky's theory that children move from external monologues to internal speech as they progress cognitively. An understanding of how children use language and what this signifies in terms of their intellectual abilities is clearly important and useful to the educator.

The way in which parents talk to their children can influence their understanding of concepts and ideas that are often difficult to grasp. Tennenbaum et al (2008) investigated how parents talk to their children about science and scientific concepts. The research, using 52 boys and girls, was carried out in the United States, and investigated why it is that over 75% of people engaged professionally in science are men. At the beginning of the study, parents rated how good their child was at science,

and how much they enjoyed it, and no difference was found on either measure between girls and boys. The conversations of both children and parents were then observed in a number of different activities, both 'scientific' – perhaps a visit to a museum of some kind – and 'non-scientific' – perhaps shopping or a visit to the cinema. The results were quite striking. Fathers were much more likely to use more complicated terms in helping their sons understand scientific concepts than they were in helping their daughters to do the same thing. Mothers, on the other hand showed no, or little, difference in the ways in which they spoke to their children, whether male or female. Tennenbaum et al concluded that this 'gender' difference in the fathers' explanations could account for why far fewer women are engaged in science later in life. This shows that hearing more complex explanations helped the child to understand the ideas being discussed. Vygotsky would say that the boys' understanding of science was scaffolded and supported by the language used by the father during the development of their understanding of science, whereas the girls' understanding was not supported in the same way. The implications of this are clear. Paying close attention to the language we use during a child's development can have significant implications later in their lives. In this case, the huge imbalance in the number of men and women working in science may be explained, in part, by their earlier developmental experiences of learning about the subject.

Group working in education

Vygotsky said that working together was an important part of learning. He called this *collaborative learning* and said it gave an opportunity for children to use their language skills to talk to one another and develop their ideas and concepts. There is evidence to suggest that group working is beneficial to the majority of students. Gokhale (1995) showed that collaborative learning certainly helps students at university gain an understanding of 'critical thinking'. In her research she compared the performance of students who worked individually with those who worked collaboratively. All students were given a lecture, and handed a worksheet. Half were told to work on the sheet alone, and half worked collaboratively in groups. Finally, all were tested on their understanding of the topics covered on the sheet, which included some quite difficult problems involving critical thinking skills. The results were clear. Those that worked collaboratively performed much better than those who worked individually. On top of this, those in the collaborative group felt that their experience of working with others helped them gain a better understanding and stimulated their thinking.

Group working encourages and maintains motivation. Nichols (1996) compared cooperative group working with the more traditional methods of using whiteboards to instruct the students from the front of the classroom. In their research, 81 students from a high school in America were assigned to one of three geometry class groups:

» **Group 1:** nine weeks of group working followed by 9 weeks of traditional teaching

» **Group 2:** nine weeks of traditional teaching followed by nine weeks of group working

» **Group 3:** 18 weeks of traditional teaching (a control group).

The researchers compared the motivation of the students throughout the research. The students in groups 1 and 2, who had worked cooperatively for half of the time, were significantly more motivated than those in group 3. They also showed that the highest levels of motivation were found during periods of group working. This suggests that group work at least provides students with the motivation to learn, if nothing else.

Neilsen (2006) reviewed research into the effectiveness of group work and concluded that it was highly beneficial. She says that group working encourages the sharing of knowledge, which can be beneficial to the development of the understanding of others. She also says that group working provides those in the group with access to a wider range of possible solutions to problems, further developing their understanding and approaches to problem solving.

APPLICATION OF BRUNER'S THEORY TO EDUCATION

Bruner's research draws heavily on the theories of both Piaget and Vygotsky. As such, many of the applications of those theories to education are relevant here. For instance, Bruner is a firm advocate of scaffolding as a technique for helping a child learn. Gradually removing the scaffold as the child moves on in ability and confidence is important in both Vygotsky's and Bruner's theories.

The spiral curriculum

Bruner's major innovation and impact on education comes from his theory of the spiral curriculum. With a traditional curriculum, subjects are taught in large 'chunks', to everyone at the same time, before moving on to something new. With a spiral curriculum, however, subjects are broken down into smaller chunks which are repeatedly revisited, each time at a slightly more complex level. This allows learning to progress in a way which suits individual learners, and provides challenge and opportunities to master skills. For Bruner, this approach also reflects how we naturally learn.

The role of the instructor engaging in the spiral curriculum is very important. Bruner says that the instruction must be *honest*. By this he means that the instructor should return around the spiral to earlier basic ideas and concepts until it is absolutely clear that the child understands them. Doing this at increasing levels of difficulty ensures that the learning can progress on a solid foundation. In many ways, the spiral curriculum can be seen as careful scaffolding.

DiBiasio et al (1999) compared a regular curriculum approach to teaching with a spiral curriculum, using a group of chemistry students. They had the students work on projects which had no end point, meaning that once one problem was solved the students continued to the next, slightly more complicated problem. The researchers found that the best way to help students progress was to return over and over again to earlier solved problems until the students were certain that they understood the solution before moving onwards and upwards in complexity. This spiral curriculum approach was most successful in improving students' understanding of the most complex concepts being taught. The researchers also said that this approach was very successful in developing the students' interest in the subject, their teamwork skills, their confidence and their motivation to continue, all extremely important aspects of applying Bruner's theory to education. Whysong et al (2008) report similar success with a spiral curriculum for teaching ethics to university students.

Reciprocal teaching and learning

Reciprocal teaching is a method developed by Palinscar and Brown (1984) employing techniques with similarities to the principles of the spiral curriculum. It is particularly useful for understanding written text. First, the method makes good use of small group collaborative learning. The teacher and a group of students all read through the text to be understood together. Next, one of the group identified as the 'discussion leader', perhaps the teacher, or perhaps one of the students, summarises what they have just read. A discussion follows, and group members say whether they agree with the discussion leader's summary and why. Next, they may re-read the passage as a group, and then continue with the discussion until the group are satisfied with their understanding. This summary, discussion, question asking, and re-reading route to understanding also bears a resemblance to the general properties of Bruner's spiral curriculum, where material is returned to over and over again until it is fully understood.

Marston et al (1995) compared reciprocal teaching with other methods. In their research they looked at how well students learn using computer-assisted learning materials, traditional direct instruction (where the teacher directs learning from the front of the class), and reciprocal learning. Their results showed that reciprocal learning was more beneficial, improving comprehension and understanding better than the other teaching methods used. This is supported by Klinger and Vaughn (1996) who found that such a reciprocal learning approach helped bilingual students to better understand English text.

Motivation to learn

Bruner says that if we understand why a child wants to learn then we are better placed to help them do so. As the child gets older, the motive for learning may be to get good marks, and this may drive their learning. However, at a younger age their motive for engaging in the learning process may be that they want to have fun. What is most important is that the child feels that they are participating in their education rather than just receiving instruction, since this is the best way to ensure they are motivated. In 1966, Bruner himself said:

> To instruct someone...is not a matter of getting him to commit results to mind. Rather, it is to teach him to participate in the process that makes possible the establishment of knowledge. We teach a subject not to produce little living libraries on that subject, but rather to get a student to think mathematically for himself, to consider matters as an historian does, to take part in the process of knowledge-getting. Knowing is a process not a product.

Brophy (1987) says that motivation to learn is something developed through the general experience students have of learning and dealing with new information. Having the correct environment to generate this experience, both in school and at home, is critical. Brophy encourages us to see education not simply as the domain of school, but also of home life. Brophy argues that when children are raised to be confident in their

learning, then when in school they will be able to engage with learning confidently. This confidence is important in another aspect of Bruner's theory, intuitive thinking.

Intuitive thinking

Experts may leap straight from a problem to a solution without any lengthy logical thinking. They often do this because they have a 'feeling' or a 'hunch' that they should proceed in a certain direction to solve the problem. This feeling is called *intuition*. After they have engaged with the problem, and often solved it quickly with very little fuss, the expert may think back on the solution they applied and decided whether it was useful or not. Through this engaging with an intuitive 'hunch' and evaluating the effectiveness of the solution the expert learns and develops their knowledge.

Bruner said that we should encourage and develop this sort of intuitive thinking wherever possible. It is more important that learners have an intuitive understanding of something than a detailed knowledge of the methods required to complete the problem and how they work. For instance, Bruner said that a detailed knowledge of mathematics is less important than an intuitive knowledge of what to do with numbers. He said that students develop intuition better if they see their educators and teachers behaving intuitively. For instance, students will be encouraged to think intuitively themselves if they have a teacher who is happy to answer questions from students intuitively. The teacher who carefully analyses the question, thinking through it carefully and in detail before arriving at an answer, is less likely to encourage intuitive thinking in her class. This intuitive answering can be thought of as 'intelligent guessing' at the answer and Bruner said that guessing in this way, and becoming more confident at acting on intuition, should be encouraged. It serves not only to develop expert-like problem-solving skills, but it also builds self-confidence and an increased willingness to take risks in problem solving. During this development the child may feel a little unsure of themselves, and so would benefit from some 'scaffold-like' support, but will soon be able to stand alone and answer quickly, confidently and most important of all, intuitively.

DEVELOPMENT OF MORAL UNDERSTANDING

How is it that you know that you should not steal things, and that it is not acceptable to punch people? Whether you engage in these behaviours or not is irrelevant really: you still know that in our society it is wrong to steal and it is not acceptable to engage in violent behaviour. Knowing this means that you have some moral understanding. How children come to learn right from wrong, to empathise with other people, and to feel guilty, has attracted the interest of many developmental psychologists, with perhaps the work of Lawrence Kohlberg being the foremost theory.

KOHLBERG'S THEORY OF MORAL UNDERSTANDING

Building on an earlier description of moral understanding developed by Piaget, Kohlberg argued that moral development is closely related to cognitive development. The methodology used by Kohlberg to investigate moral development was to present stories that described a moral dilemma to young subjects and ask them what they would do. One of the most famous of these moral dilemmas was the story of Heinz.

Kohlberg presented children with Heinz's dilemma and questioned them afterwards, asking, for example, should Heinz steal the drug? Why? Which is worse, letting someone die or stealing? Why? What does the value of life mean to you? Is there a good reason for a husband to steal if he doesn't love his wife? Would it be as right to steal for a stranger as to steal for his wife? If Heinz is caught, should he be sent to prison? If Heinz is caught and brought to trial, should the judge sentence him? Why? What is the responsibility of the judge to society in this case?

Kohlberg was not so much interested in whether the children felt that the husband was correct in stealing the drug or not: what really interested him was why the children came to the conclusions they did. From their responses, Kohlberg was able to develop his theory of moral development. He said that moral understanding progressed through three levels, each with two stages; pre-conventional morality, conventional morality and finally post-conventional morality.

Level 1: Pre-conventional morality

In stage 1 the child makes moral decisions depending on whether they are punished or not for their behaviour. Quite simply, if they are punished, the behaviour must be wrong; if they are rewarded for something the behaviour must not be wrong. The authority figure is totally external to them, be it their mother or father, or even the police.

In stage 2 the child makes decisions purely in their own immediate interest and for personal gratification. If it's good it feels nice; if it is not it feels bad. Here the child also begins to understand the notion of fairness, and the idea of making an agreement or deal.

Level 2: Conventional morality

In stage 3 the child begins to make moral decisions based on the norms of some group to which the child belongs. For instance, if it is normal in their family to behave in a certain way then it must be acceptable. It is in this stage that the child begins to develop an internal understanding of the norms of their group. The group or family to which they belong becomes important here and they begin to understand the notion of being 'good' and not 'naughty' simply because it is what they are supposed to do.

In stage 4 the child begins to make moral judgements based on whether the person meant to do something or not. Here they begin to shift their ideas of morality from their small group or family to the community at large. They begin to

HEINZ'S DILEMMA

In Europe, a woman was near death from a special kind of cancer. There was one drug that the doctors thought might save her. It was a form of radium that a druggist in the same town had recently discovered. The drug was expensive to make, but the druggist was charging ten times what the drug cost him to make. He paid $200 for the radium and charged $2,000 for a small dose of the drug. The sick woman's husband, Heinz, went to everyone he knew to borrow the money, but he could only get together about $1,000 which is half of what it cost. He told the druggist that his wife was dying and asked him to sell it cheaper or let him pay later. But the druggist said: "No, I discovered the drug and I'm going to make money from it." So Heinz got desperate and broke into the man's store to steal the drug for his wife. Should the husband have done that?

understand that it is wrong to break laws, and that people should do what is expected of them (e.g. go to school or work).

Level 3: Post-conventional morality

In stage 5 the person moves on again. They begin to understand that they should behave so that the maximum good is achieved for as many people as possible. They understand that some people think something may be right or correct, but others may think something else may be right or correct. The idea of laws becomes clear to the child, but they understand that laws may be changed if necessary. They also understand that certain things, such as freedom or the right to life, are issues that should be constant and upheld at all times.

In stage 6 the person becomes able to apply their own ethical standards. They can decide which laws are appropriate to them and which not. They use their conscience to decide whether to break laws or not. This is advanced morality where the person becomes able to express their opinions and stance on different issues. Kohlberg himself said that moral dilemmas, such as the Heinz dilemma, were not useful in distinguishing between stages 5 and 6. For instance, the answers a stage 5 person

might give to the Heinz dilemma would be the same in stage 6. The technique is not sensitive enough or appropriate for identifying the ethical standards that characterise stage 6. Kohlberg said that very few people actually reach stage 6. It is here that people begin to truly understand the concepts of human rights, that people really are equal, that we should respect human dignity and that all have the right to justice. These are universal principles that are greater, said Kohlberg, than the norms we accept in our societies that tell us how we are supposed and allowed to behave.

Typical answers to the Heinz dilemma at each stage of moral development are given in the table on page 23. You can see that the type of moral reasoning at each stage becomes increasingly complex.

Kohlberg's theory of moral development is closely linked to Piaget's theory of cognitive development. Each stage in moral development identified by Kohlberg requires a different level of reasoning and thought. For instance, to be able to think morally at level 3, a person must have developed at least as far as Piaget's formal operational stage, as it requires reasoning with difficult abstract principles

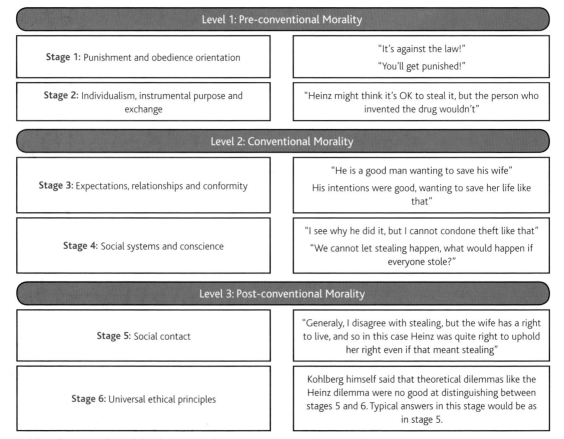

Kohlberg's stages of moral development and typical responses to the Heinz dilemma at each stage.

and concepts such as fairness, justice and human rights. However, Kohlberg points out that it is not enough just to have developed cognitively. Just because someone is able to reason with abstract principles, as they would be in the formal operational stage, this does not necessarily mean that they will be able to reason morally at level 3. In other words, cognitive development is a necessary, but not sufficient, condition to allow moral reasoning to happen.

Piaget's concept of disequilibrium is also relevant in Kohlberg's theory of moral development. A child making a decision at stage 1 may become uncomfortable or unsure of their response when they realise that others around them at higher levels disagree with their decisions. This disagreement between the child and others may make the child aware that there are alternative options and approaches that can be taken. It is here that the child enters disequilibrium. Working hard to attain equilibrium by understanding others' moral decisions helps the child move on within the stage and attain the next stage, and ultimately the next level of moral reasoning.

EVALUATING KOHLBERG'S THEORY OF MORAL UNDERSTANDING

1. Colby et al (1983) carried out a longitudinal study over 27 years. They tested male participants six times each during the period, and found support for Kohlberg's theory that we all pass through the stages of moral development in the same order. This is further supported by research revealing similar developmental trends in morality (e.g. Colby and Kohlberg, 1986).

2. Edwards (1980) suggests that the stages are universal, and relate to all cultures – there is 'invariant progression': people appear to move through the stages in the same order in different cultures. A meta-analysis of 53 studies by Eckensberger (1983) appeared to provide support for this idea of universal and invariant progression.

3. Gilligan (1982) has said that Kohlberg's research is gender biased. A good deal of the longitudinal research is carried out on men but the criticism goes deeper than that. Gilligan said that Kohlberg's theory was based on morality from a male perspective. Men, she says, identify morality in terms of rules, and rights. This is a formal view of morality. Gilligan says that women have a different form of morality, related more to ethics and care. For

this reason Kohlberg's theory does not relate to women as well as it does to men.

4. Gilligan (1982) says that the dilemmas used in Kohlberg's research, such as the Heinz dilemma, were artificial. She showed that people questioned about real-life situations employed a different sort of moral reasoning. She says that in different situations people may apply different moral judgements and that Kohlberg's theory does not allow for this sort of flexibility. Research by Conley et al (1997) using real-life examples appears to support this view. They found that understanding the types of moral decisions people make is not as straightforward as either Kohlberg or Gilligan claim. For instance, participants who had had particularly bad symptoms when they had experienced a sexually transmitted disease responded differently to moral dilemmas from those whose symptoms had not been as severe. This suggests that it is not enough to say that it is the 'reality' of the dilemmas that matters most: rather it is the often subtle individual differences such as past experience that need to be taken into consideration when understanding moral decisions.

5. Simpson (1974) says that Kohlberg's theory is based on Western thinking, ideas and philosophy and does not really relate to non-Western ideas of morality and justice. For this reason, people outside the West may not progress fully through Kohlberg's stages but may stop at stage 3, before the influence of the social system becomes important. That is not to say that these people don't continue developing morally, it just means that Kohlberg's theory may not be sensitive enough to identify quite how the morality is developing. For instance, Ferguson et al (1991) showed that Nigerian children exhibited different kinds of moral reasoning from Northern Irish children and concluded that this was because Nigerian children were more likely to have been brought up to be less questioning and more obedient than Northern Irish children. Similarly, Harkness et al (1981) carried out research using Kohlberg's dilemmas with rural African men of the Kipsigis society. They found that the elders from these traditional societies scored a little higher than the non-elders, but that none scored higher than stage 4. The researchers say that this may be because the moral emphasis in these rural, traditional societies is different. Unlike the West, emphasis is on the person's role in

MORAL REASONING AND SEXUALLY TRANSMITTED DISEASE

"Ah, Mr Bond, I've been expecting you..."

Conley et al (1997) were interested in investigating whether moral judgements based on hypothetical dilemmas might be different from moral judgements based on real-life dilemmas.

Fifty nine participants were recruited to take part in the study. 30 of them (12 men and 18 women) had previously had a sexually transmitted disease, in this case genital herpes. The other 29 participants (fifteen men and fourteen women) had never had the disease. Each participant was presented with four dilemmas. In two dilemmas the characters had a decision to make relating to real-life situations about sexually transmitted diseases. Of the other two dilemmas, one related to a difficult moral decision regarding euthanasia (assisted killing of someone who may be ill); and the other related to the decision a man must make when he recognises another man, now a useful member of society, as being an escaped prisoner.

The two dilemmas relating to sexually transmitted disease are:

1. Mary is deciding whether or not to have sex with Jack and inform him of something she has until now kept from him. She has had genital herpes for three years but currently has no symptoms. She wonders whether she should take the chance of spreading the disease to him.

2. Sally wants to have sex with John, her new sexual partner, without using a condom. John is trying to decide whether to risk an adverse reaction from her if he suggests that they can have sex, but they should use a condom.

In dilemma 2 neither Jack nor Sally is known to have a sexually transmitted disease, but the dilemma does make it seem this may be a possibility. In each case, participants were asked how the characters in the dilemmas should proceed. Each participant was interviewed about each dilemma. Later, the interviews were rated by different researchers to identify which type of moral reasoning was displayed in each case. The different ratings for each researcher were compared and any discrepancies discussed and resolved.

The results showed that a familiarity with the dilemma did influence the types of moral decisions made, but that the relationship was by no means clear. It was not as simple as to say that those who had experienced a sexually transmitted disease made a certain type of moral decision; and those who had not, made a different type of moral decision. A range of moral reasoning was found throughout the participants. The researchers concluded that whilst there is support for Kohlberg's theory here, Gilligan's criticism of Kohlberg is legitimate and real-life dilemmas do make a difference to moral decision making.

their community. This suggests that Kohlberg's stages are of limited use when discussing the morality of non-Western societies.

ASK AN EXAMINER

"Kohlberg's theory bears some similarities in structure to Eisenberg's, but does not regard empathy and emotion as being important in moral judgements. Take care not to confuse the two theories."

EISENBERG'S THEORY OF PROSOCIAL REASONING

An alternative theory to Kohlberg's theory of moral understanding is Eisenberg's theory of prosocial reasoning. Nancy Eisenberg agrees with Kohlberg, that moral development runs closely with cognitive development. Eisenberg's theory adds to the earlier work of Kohlberg rather than completely replacing it. Eisenberg feels that people make emotional decisions, and the way they are feeling emotionally can influence their moral judgement and so her theory allows for a greater emotional input into moral development than does Kohlberg's. Her theory is described as a theory of prosocial reasoning because it describes how people develop an understanding of what is helpful to others around us.

Empathy is extremely important in her theory. Empathy is the ability to share and understand the feelings of others. Some of us are more empathic than others, but it seems natural to be able to understand how other people are feeling. Children's play may be a very useful way of developing the skills of empathy. Pretending to be other people, and taking on different roles, may well be extremely good training for understanding how and why other people feel the way that they do.

Eisenberg (1982) identifies five levels of prosocial reasoning, each linked to a particular age at which the child becomes able to reason slightly differently.

Level 1

This is the hedonistic level. Hedonism is the act of selfish, self-oriented pleasurable behaviour. The enjoyment of others is not important to a hedonist, so hedonism could be described as a very self-centred and selfish way of thinking. The child in the hedonistic stage is only interested in self-gratification and so will only really show pro-social behaviour if it gains them some form of personal benefit.

Level 2

This is the needs-oriented level. In this level the child understands that others have needs, and will sometimes consider them in their behaviour. However, at this level, the child shows very little, if any, evidence of sympathy for others. And whereas many of us would feel guilty if we did something wrong, the needs-oriented child shoes little or no guilt at all.

Level 3

This is the approval-oriented level. It is here that the child really begins to behave prosocially, but only if they are rewarded in some way by the approval of others. For instance, a young child may help their little brother to do something, but only if their little brother or their caregiver displays some kind of approval following their action. At this level the child begins to show that they understand what is, and what is not, appropriate.

Level 4

Here the child starts to show sympathy for others, and guilt when they have done wrong. They also begin to demonstrate an understanding of principles. There is evidence of self-reflection so that a child considers whether its actions would produce positive feelings or guilt. They also start to understand the idea of values and duties. They have a duty to behave in a certain way, and they may value kind or good behaviour. Later there is also a transitional level between this and the next stage.

Level 5

The last level is the strongly internalised level. Here the belief structure forms part of the person.

LEVEL OF PROSOCIAL REASONING	SCHOOL AGE	DESCRIPTION
1. Hedonistic	Infant and some primary	Most likely to be prosocial for own personal benefit.
2. Needs oriented	Primary and some infant	Some consideration of others, but not really evidence of feeling guilty or sympathetic.
3. Approval oriented	Primary and some secondary	Understands what is appropriate behaviour, but most likely to be prosocial in return for praise or approval from others.
4a. Self-reflective-empathic 4b. Transitional	Secondary and some primary	Sympathy for others and guilt when having done wrong is evident. Some understanding of the concept of principled behaviour, values and duty.
5. Strongly internalised	Some secondary, some primary	The person's self-respect becomes bound up with internalised principles of right and wrong in different circumstances.

The person's principles become part of them, part of what makes them tick if you like. It is these principles that provide the person with a feeling of self-respect. If they behave in this way, which is true to themselves, and to their own principles, then they will not feel bad about themselves.

EVALUATING EISENBERG'S THEORY OF PROSOCIAL REASONING

Eisenberg conducted a good deal of research herself using dilemmas in a similar way to Kohlberg. However, her dilemmas were very focused on identifying where the child may see a conflict or a disagreement between their own needs and the requirements of others.

1. Eisenberg (1995) reports the results of a longitudinal study that confirm her 'levels of prosocial reasoning' theory. Eisenberg used dilemmas in this study to identify the level each participant was in. The study followed participants from 4 years of age up to teen age, and found that the type of moral reasoning they used changed as they grew older.

2. Eisenberg et al (2002) extended their 1995 study which had shown that prosocial reasoning develops with age. Using the same methodology she continued to follow her participants as they grew from adolescence into adulthood. The results showed that we continue to develop prosocial reasoning even into adulthood. The researchers showed that the type of prosocial reasoning shown in adulthood was strongly correlated with friends' and family's judgements of the person's personality as a child and whether the person showed empathy towards others while growing up. It seems that the type of prosocial reasoning we show when we are adults is closely related to the way in which we develop our understanding of morality at a young age. This suggests that it could be a sensible idea to develop children's understanding of prosocial reasoning while in school, as this will influence their ability to reason prosocially as adults. Ultimately, this can influence the society in which we live.

3. In other research, Eisenberg found similar patterns of development in different countries, including Germany, Poland and Italy. She found that prosocial reasoning changes with age similarly in similar ways in different Western cultures. These data are different, however, from those found with Israeli children living in a communal Kibbutz system, whose emphasis is on fairness and shared values. That research (Eisenberg, 1986) found very little needs-oriented reasoning at all, suggesting that culture has an influence on the development of moral reasoning.

4. Eisenberg introduces empathy as an important component of her theory but uses dilemmas in her investigations in a similar way to Kohlberg. The dilemmas used by Eisenberg and Kohlberg may be perceived as artificial and so not related to the lives of the participants. Moral and prosocial judgements based on artificial dilemmas like this may themselves then be artificial, and not at all the type of decision that a person may make in real life. Because of this the research might be accused of lacking ecological

THE DEVELOPMENT OF PROSOCIAL REASONING

Eisenberg et al (1995) wanted to see how prosocial reasoning changed as children grew older. The research was constructed in part to investigate the validity of Eisenberg's theory of prosocial reasoning. A longitudinal study was carried out whereby the prosocial reasoning of a group of children was measured every 2 years for 14 years. The study began when the children were 2 years old, and followed them into their late teens. Moral dilemmas were presented to the children and their responses assessed for their level of prosocial reasoning. The dilemmas required the children to indicate how they might behave when someone may need help when hurt, or other situations requiring them to do good. Each were scored for hedonistic level and for needs-oriented level, 16 being the highest possible score.

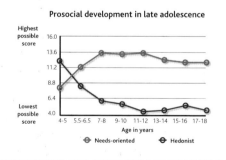

Notice from the graph that as participants get older, their scores for needs-oriented prosocial reasoning go up until they are about 11 but their scores for hedonistic prosocial reasoning reduce. This data supports Eisenberg's theory of prosocial reasoning, as when people aged they developed different forms of prosocial reasoning.

Redrawn from Eisenberg et al (1995)

INFLUENCES ON MORAL REASONING

According to Rest and Narvaez (1991) our moral decision making, and whether we choose to behave in certain ways, is not only to do with the level of moral reasoning we are in. They identify three important factors that influence how people will respond to moral issues.

1. Moral sensitivity

A person can only make a moral decision about something if they think that there is a moral issue at stake. It doesn't really matter what level of moral development a person is in if they can't identify a situation as requiring a moral decision.

2. Moral motivation

If we are not motivated to act morally then we are not likely to do so. Where something makes the moral conflict higher (perhaps when there is a cost to our acting morally) moral motivation begins to influence our moral decisions more. For instance, if we see that a situation requires us to make a moral decision, but the costs of the decision are too high (perhaps it may be dangerous or expensive in another way to intervene in a situation), then we are less likely to act morally.

3. Moral strength

Carrying through a moral decision, and sticking to what we think is right, can require a degree of strength and certainty in ourselves.

---

validity. If the decisions made by participants do not relate to real life then a theory based on those decisions is valid only for artificial dilemmas, not real life situations.

5. Miller et al (1990) found evidence that questions the universal applicability of Eisenberg's theory. In their research they found that Hindu children and adults in India felt a moral obligation to help people who needed help, be they strangers, friends or family, whether their need for help is serious or mild. American children, on the other hand, felt that the decision to help someone when the need was mild was a choice rather than a moral obligation. This is a cross-cultural difference and suggests that Eisenberg's theory is not necessarily universally applicable.

6. It is not always possible to predict how a person will respond from the level of moral or prosocial reasoning they are in, as Eisenberg might suggest. Rest and Narvaez (1991) say that whether someone behaves morally depends on a number of factors, including moral sensitivity, moral motivation and moral strength.

"Sometimes the same, or a similar evaluation point is relevant for two different theories. The work of Rest and Narvaez is an example. It can be used as an evaluation of Kohlberg's or Eisenberg's theory. Both identify levels of moral development, and so both can be evaluated similarly on that point."

DEVELOPMENT OF SOCIAL COGNITION

According to Allport (1985) social cognition is an approach to social psychology which attempts "to understand and explain how the thoughts, feelings, and behaviour of individuals are influenced by the actual, imagined, or implied presence of others". Social cognition, then, is concerned with the knowledge that individuals acquire about themselves and others and how this influences thinking and behaviour. A crucial difference between social cognition and non-social cognition (such as more traditional cognitive research into memory, thinking and language) is that social cognition focusing on how we think about the social world around us. In other words, social cognition is to do with *social* thinking. Social thinking, and therefore behaviour, according to this approach is not determined by simple learned responses and reinforcements, but is a reflection of internal mental representations of the world. Two people can experience exactly the same event (i.e. they have the same cognitions) yet perceive the event completely differently. This tells us that people interpret objective reality in subjective ways and, according to the social cognitive approach, these interpretations are influenced by social experience and knowledge.

ETHICS   NATURE/NURTURE   GENDER   CULTURE   DETERMINISM   REDUCTIONISM

DEVELOPMENT OF THE CHILD'S SENSE OF SELF

Over the time that you have known your best friend you have formed ideas and impressions about them. You have an idea of what they like to do, what they like to eat, their favourite kinds of films and music. You have formed an impression of their personality and this gives you an idea of how they might behave in different situations. In exactly the same way, we form an impression of ourselves. A sense of self includes ideas and beliefs about who we are as individuals (this is referred to as our *self-concept*), and about our self-worth (referred to as *self-esteem*). Our understanding of the self is linked to the particular role we are playing at any one time. Markus and Whurf (1987) point out that we have many different views of the self, depending on what role we are playing. We all have multiple roles in society, for example as students, sons, daughters and perhaps even mothers or fathers.

The self-concept then can be thought of as everything that you know about yourself. This includes the knowledge of your own opinions, desires, ambitions, feelings, ideas and attitudes to others and to things. We are not born with this understanding however: it develops over time. Indeed, it could be considered something that is part of our life-span development since we never really stop learning about ourselves. Since the self is an expression of our individuality, the development of the self can be considered a process of individuation.

SELF-CONCEPT AND SELF-AWARENESS

One very important developmental task for an infant in the first couple of years of life is to learn that they are separate and distinct from other objects and people in their environment. By the age of 2 the child begins to understand who they are and about their place in the world. They have learned that things and people around us can influence us, just as we ourselves are capable of influencing the world. A child is showing evidence of becoming 'self-aware'. The development of self-awareness has been investigated by Lewis and Brooks-Gunn (1978). They found that infants were able to recognise themselves in a mirror by the time they were 2 years old, which for them was evidence of self-awareness. Their findings were supported by more recent research from Bullock and Lutkenhaus (1990) who concluded that children could recognise their own photographs by about 21 months to 2 years of age.

In further research, Lewis and Brooks-Gunn (1979) found that children's awareness of their own face as a reflection depended on whether movement cues were present that depended on their own movements. In other words, what was required for children to identify the spot on their own nose was if the child recognised that the mirror image moved at the same time that they did. They filmed children and showed them the films of themselves at a later date. They found that more children recognised their own images from the moving films than from a still photograph. The researchers say that real self-recognition truly shows itself when a child can recognise themselves from a still, unmoving image. This is supported by Bullock and Lutkenhaus (1990) who measured self-awareness as a child's ability to recognise themselves from a photograph. They suggest that self-awareness begins to develop at about 15 months but is developed in about 75% of children aged between 21 and 24 months.

Research of this kind has led to the suggestion that self-recognition is linked to developing cognitions about the face. Neilson et al (2006), however, showed that this is not the case. They found that toddlers seated in high chairs who had a mark surreptitiously placed on a leg would search for the mark on themselves when given the opportunity to view the mark in a mirror. Clearly, the development of self recognition involves recognising other parts of the body too.

Povinelli et al (1996) suggest that a mirror test does not provide evidence of the complete development of a sense of self. They showed children a video of themselves being surreptitiously marked on their head by a researcher three minutes earlier. Although children typically pass the mirror test at 2 years of age, only children around 4 years responded to the video by reaching for the mark on their head. Povinelli et al explain this by suggesting that success on a mirror task indicates recognition of a *present* self, whilst success on the video task represents a developmental change to a more sophisticated *temporally extended* sense of self. Suddendorf et al (2006) point out however that the performance of older children in the video condition was still quite poor, with only 62% of 30–42-month-old children passing the test. This indicates that there is something inherently difficult for children in self-recognition tasks involving video feedback. The researchers identify a

THE RED SPOT TEST AND SELF-AWARENESS

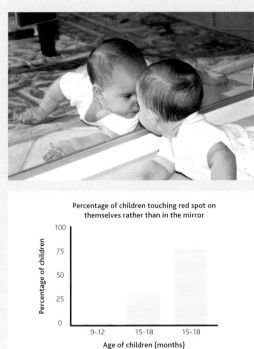

Percentage of children touching red spot on themselves rather than in the mirror

Percentage of children (y-axis: 0, 25, 50, 75, 100)

Age of children (months) (x-axis: 9-12, 15-18, 15-18)

Lewis and Brooks-Gunn (1978) designed a technique which they believed demonstrated the development of self-awareness, which basically involved placing infants between 9 and 24 months of age in front of a mirror and observing their behaviour.

Stage 1: The baby is simply placed in front of the mirror and their behaviour is noted. This behaviour depends on the age of the child, but generally, very young children between 9 and 12 months will look at their own reflection. They may try and touch it in some way, or pull faces at it.

Stage 2: The researcher pretends to wipe the baby's face with a cloth, but instead puts a small red rouge dot on their nose. On removing the cloth the researchers again observe how the infant behaves in front of the mirror. If the baby tries to touch the spot on their own nose rather than the nose in the mirror then the child is showing self-awareness.

The results indicate that between 9 and 12 months, infants display no real ability to identify the spot on their own nose from the reflection. This shows that they do not understand that the reflection is them. By 21 to 24 months most children touch their own nose once they see the reflected red spot. This suggests that their concept of self-awareness has developed.

number of features of video presentation that may be producing the greater difficulty that children have with tasks in this medium. For example, video images tend to be smaller. Videos and mirror images also differ in symmetry – for example, when the right arm is moved a video image shows the opposite arm moving, while a mirror shows the corresponding arm.

Suddendorf et al (2006) went on to test 24-month-old, 30-month-old and 36-month-old children using a traditional mirror test and using a live video feed of the child's face which mimicked a mirror image (i.e. the image was equal-size and of the correct orientation). In order to control for any effects of TV familiarity (children by this age will have interacted with TVs and have expectations of such an experience – e.g. TV does not provide immediate here-and-now feedback), video was back-projected onto a screen. They found that the youngest children had more difficulty completing the video task. Older children, however, managed the task well every time. It is possible that this difference was due to the fact that, unlike a mirror task, eye contact is not possible to the same degree and quality in a video task. To investigate the possibility that eye contact in a mirror image is the crucial factor underlying self-recognition, they

repeated the study but this time with a red mark on the leg rather than the nose. Images and reflections of the children's legs were presented to them and the researchers found that again the children found the video version harder than the mirror version. Whatever was causing the poorer performance was something much more subtle than video image size and symmetry. These findings also contradict the claims of other researchers who suggest that children are able to recognise themselves in mirrors and video feedback equally by 24 months of age (e.g. Miyazaki and Hiraki, 2006).

Suddendorf et al suggest that their findings may be further examples of a 'video deficit'. A growing body of evidence suggests that toddlers perform more poorly on a range of tasks when material is presented via video. This phenomenon has yet to be fully explained, though it has been suggested it is due to younger children being more sensitive to the subtle social cues missing in video. As a child grows older these cues become less important and 'video deficit' disappears. Findings of research by Demir and Skouteris (2008) raise the possibility that Miyazaki and Hiraki may be right in their assertion. They gave self-recognition tests to children aged 24 to 30 months and found that, as with Suddendorf et al, whilst the children succeeded in a traditional test mirror test, they failed in a live video feed test. However, more than half the children who failed the video test showed self-recognition after video-training. It appears that practice, which presumably compensates for some of the deficiencies of video presentation, reduces video deficit in self-recognition tasks.

SELF-ESTEEM

How a child is rewarded during childhood is important in the development of their self-esteem.

Recognising a child's successes during their development and not behaving negatively towards them all the time can help them develop positive self-esteem. For instance, reward and encouragement from their mother or caregiver may make them feel good, which might lead the child to begin to develop a positive feeling about themselves. Those with high positive self-esteem feel that their actions are positive, and received by others in the way they mean them to be. They feel that others think positively about them and that they are more able to achieve their goals. Conversely, those with negative self-esteem feel bad about themselves: they feel that they are not valued by those around them and that their activities are not well received. This negative feeling may be encouraged during

development if achievements and successes are not sufficiently identified or encouraged.

Self-esteem can have a significant effect on a person's life, as Coopersmith (1967) showed. His longitudinal research followed boys aged between 9 and 10 for 15 years and found that low-self-esteem can influence academic performance and also personal success and happiness. He also showed that a child treated negatively during development can acquire a reduced feeling of self-worth. His research suggests that the role of parents is extremely important in the development of our self-concept. Coopersmith also said that factors like intelligence, and our perception of our own intelligence, can influence our self-esteem, as can our popularity. Those of us who feel we are intelligent are more likely to feel positively about ourselves than those of us who feel that we are less intelligent. Similarly, the more popular amongst us will show more positive self-esteem than the less popular.

Sears (1970) found similar results to Coopersmith, showing that even if one parent behaved positively towards a daughter she would benefit in terms of feeling more positive about herself. More recent research from Hoelter and Harper (1987) agrees,

TRENDS IN THE DEVELOPMENT OF SELF

AGE	SCHOOL AGE
9–12 months	The relationships between the child's actions and their consequences is central in the development of the self. Here the child learns the relationship between actions and reactions, and how they can affect the world around them.
15–18 months	The child begins to recognise themselves in mirrors and photographs.
2.5–6 years	The self begins to realise that they can be properly in control of their physical achievements (such as being able to build something) and their cognitive achievements (being clever enough to work through a problem). They realise that others may not see the world as they do and that they may actually have information about things that they know, but others may not. At this age, the actions of others are generally put down to 'intent' meaning that if something happens it is thought that someone necessarily meant it to happen, which is, of course not always the case. Sometimes things just happen by accident.
6–9 years	The child begins to realise that they are responsible for and can control their achievements in the social world, not just the physical and cognitive areas. They begin to regard themselves in terms of how others think of them, and how they compare to others around them. The child begins to display the concept of self-esteem, and they begin to understand that other people are able to think about how and what they themselves are thinking.
10–13 years	The child's social roles become vital in how they understand their self-concept. How they respond to the world around them becomes central here. The child becomes able to use their own opinions for evaluating their own behaviour – they do not need to be told that something is naughty or good, they can decide whether something is good or naughty themselves. The child is now able to take in their perspective of the world and consider others' perspectives of the world at the same time.
13–17 years	Here the young person begins to develop principles and values. Importantly, they begin to recognise the broader impact of their and other people's actions on society in general.

LONG-TERM EFFECTS OF EARLY EXPERIENCE ON SELF-ESTEEM

Coopersmith (1967) investigated how feelings of self-esteem were related to different aspects of a person's life, including their success in a number of areas such as academia and personal life.

In the research, 9 and 10-year-olds filled out a questionnaire which allowed Coopersmith to identify how the children felt about themselves, their school life, their friends and their family. In addition to this, their teachers completed questionnaires which required them to rate the boys in terms of their motivation to succeed, their academic abilities, how they responded to teachers and how they behaved with their friends. Coopersmith also had the boys' parents complete similar questionnaires. After the children had finished their school years, Coopersmith returned to see how they had done.

Coopersmith found that, at 10 years old, boys with high self-esteem were more likely to be popular, have more friends and show greater motivation in school. Those with low self-esteem were less likely to be popular, to try hard, or to have a large group of friends. When they had completed their schooling, Coopersmith found that those with high self-esteem were more likely to have achieved well than those with low-self esteem. On top of this, those with higher self-esteem were more likely to get higher status jobs or university places. Interestingly, Coopersmith discovered a positive correlation between positive ratings of self-esteem they gave themselves and the reports that parents gave of treating the child positively. This suggests that positive self-esteem is related in some way to being treated positively by parents during development. Coopersmith also found that those with low self-esteem grew up to be unhappier, to feel more isolated and less confident than those with high self-esteem.

showing that adolescents who reported that they felt supported by their parents showed higher levels of self-esteem. Felsen and Zielinski (1989) report similar but subtly different findings. They say that the relationship between parents' attitude towards the child and the resulting feeling of self-esteem works in both directions. By this they mean that children who feel positive about themselves are more likely to be treated positively by their parents. This suggests that a little encouragement from a parent can go a long way as it potentially has a big effect, making the child feel more positive about themselves, and in turn making the parent more likely to respond more positively to the child and so on.

The influence of peers on self-esteem

It's not just our family that influences how we feel about ourselves and our behaviour. Those with whom we mix outside our homes can have a great impact upon us: in particular our peers can have a strong influence on how positively we feel about ourselves. Bosacki et al (2007) carried out a survey of over 7,000 teenagers. In their research they had participants complete a self-report questionnaire that required them to answer questions relating to a number of issues including self-esteem, peer

THE INFLUENCE OF PEERS ON SELF-ESTEEM

In this research, Thompson et al (2007) investigated the extent to which adolescent girls were influenced by their peers. This group of adolescents are often on the receiving end of very hurtful and negative comments from their peers, and so often report feelings of negative self-worth. 325 girls, of between 14 and 17 years old, took part in the research. Self-esteem was calculated using a psychological test. Each participant also completed a number of other tests designed to assess how important they felt peers regarded body shape and size, how important they felt their friends' opinions were, and how much they perceived themselves as being teased because of their weight and appearance. In addition to these measurements, the participants also completed questionnaires that assessed their satisfaction with their own bodies, and how much pressure they had been under from their peers to diet.

The results were striking. Peer attitude was found to be a significant influence on the participants' estimations of body dissatisfaction, drive for thinness and incidence of bulimia, as well as their measures of self-esteem. The researchers concluded that the overweight girls in the research were significantly influenced in a number of different ways by their peers. Their self-esteem was negatively affected, their body image was damaged and they were more likely to engage in unhealthy activities such as crash-dieting and bulimia than their peers. The research also showed that the participants were less likely to engage in discussions about weight with their peers, perhaps because they were aware that they might be criticised and so their self-esteem would be further damaged. It can be concluded from this research that many aspects of self-concept, in particular self-image and self-esteem, can be influenced by our peers.

relationships, popularity and family relationships. They found that self-esteem was closely related to peer relationships and feelings of depression. The more positively a person felt about themselves the more likely they were to have positive peer relationships and the less likely they were to suffer from depression. This is supported by Reynolds (2008). She carried out questionnaire research over a five day period with 11-year-olds. Participants were asked to complete questionnaires, at home before each day at school, that allowed her to measure their mood and levels of self-esteem. Then, when they returned home, she had them complete the questionnaire again, and in addition to this, they were required to report any events of significance that happened in the school day. The results were very clear. Those children that experienced problems with peers in the school day, perhaps in terms of arguments and disagreements, experienced a fall in their self-esteem, and a worsening of their overall mood. This research allows us to conclude that our relationships with peers can affect how positively we feel about ourselves. Thompson et al (2007) showed that the influence of peers can be extremely wide ranging and can have an impact on a number of aspects of a person's self-concept, including their self-esteem and their body image.

THE INFLUENCE OF SOCIETY AND CULTURE ON SELF CONCEPT

Like other aspects of cognition and development, we can expect culture to have a significant influence on the development of a child's sense of self. For instance, Western society, and increasingly the rest of the world, has placed a premium on thinness as being attractive. This is a cultural norm and our attitudes to cultural norms like this can influence how positively we feel about ourselves – if we are not thin, and do not care at all about the cultural pressure to be thin, then a positive self-image is certainly possible. However, if we are concerned about the cultural norm, then we may feel less positive about our self-image, and so our self-esteem and overall self-concept may suffer as a result. In this way, social norms can influence the distinctions we may perceive between our self-image and our ideal self (what we would like to be). The larger the gap between the two, the less positively we may feel about ourselves.

Bochner (1994) investigated differences in self-concept between those from individualist societies and those from collectivist societies. In his research he compared Australian and English

people with people from Malaysia. He asked each person to complete ten statements that began with the words 'I am…'. Each set of responses was assessed in terms of whether they were idiocentric, allocentric or group self-references. An idiocentric self-reference is one that concentrates on a person's own ways or opinions. For instance 'I am generous' is idiocentric as it refers directly to the person themselves. An allocentric statement is one which refers to others. For instance, and allocentric statement might be 'I am my mother's son', Finally a group-focused self-reference is one which refers to community, such as 'I am a useful member of society'. Bochner found that those from the individualistic societies (Australia and England) were much more likely to make more idiocentric statements, and fewer group and allocentric statements, than those from the collectivist society (Malaysia). For Bochner, this means that we should think of self-concept as being directly related to the type of culture in which we live. For example, if we live in an individualistic culture we are more likely to have a self-concept reflecting individualist values.

"Individualist and collectivist culture are terms which crop up regularly in psychology, so it is worth being acquainted with what they mean. Basically, Western (individualist) cultures tend to emphasise the rights, goals and attitudes of the individual. Non-Western (collectivist) cultures on the other hand tend to emphasise the group and the duties of individuals towards groups."

The Shona community of Zimbabwe are a largely agricultural society. The men often work as blacksmiths, and the women weave beautiful and useful baskets. This is a traditional society, with a traditional religion based around a belief in spirits. Mpofu (1994) looked at how these people regarded their self-concept and found some unusual results. He collected data from 210 students from a Shona background and found them to have, generally speaking, an individualist self-concept, based around self-sufficiency and the importance of the individual. However, he found a difference between the men and women participants, in that the women, while still forming an individualistic self-concept, tended to make more collectivist, 'group and society' oriented comments, whereas the men were quite clearly individualistically focused. The results suggest that even though the participants had decided to study rather than maintain their traditional, Shona life full-time, the traditional differentiation of male and female roles had still influenced their self-concepts. This is evidence that the culture from which we come can influence how we think of ourselves.

THEORY OF MIND

ASK AN EXAMINER

"Whilst you could talk about theory of mind in a general question on the development of a sense of self, be clear that you could get an exam question just on theory of mind."

If you thump someone on the arm you know that it will hurt. You don't have to experience it yourself. Similarly, if you watch someone put their house keys on the kitchen table and then they are moved, by someone else, into another room, you know that the person will look for their keys on the kitchen table first then complain that someone has moved them. You do not think automatically that the person will look in the other room for the keys first – after all, how would they know that they had been moved?

Knowledge of how someone will behave, or should behave, in a given situation is called having a 'theory of mind'. According to Wilde et al (2005), " 'Theory of mind' is the phrase researchers use to refer to children's understanding of people as mental beings, who have beliefs, desires, emotions, and intentions, and whose actions and interactions can be interpreted and explained by taking account of these mental states." Our theory of mind, then, allows us to understand other people from their perspective. This social cognitive ability allows us to interact fully with the world around us. Without it even the simplest of social interactions can be very difficult indeed.

One way of investigating theory of mind is by using a 'false-belief' problem. The example of the keys on the kitchen table is a practical illustration of a false-belief problem that many of us experience on a daily basis. Correctly solving a false-belief problem requires the ability to see the situation from another's point of view and understand what causes the person to have this point of view. Wimmer and Perner (1983) designed a procedure to test how we develop this understanding

that has become known as the Sally–Anne task. The task progresses in five steps:

The Sally–Anne Task

Step 1: Sally and Anne are introduced to the participant.

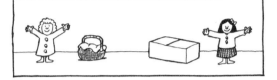

Step 2: Sally places a marble into her basket in full view of Anne.

Step 3: Sally leaves the room.

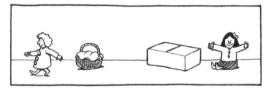

Step 4: Anne takes the marble from the basket and moves it into the box.

Step 5: Sally returns. The participant is asked "Where will Sally look for her marble?"

Wimmer and Perner noticed that when children aged between 2 and 3 were asked, they said that Sally would look in the box for the marble even though Sally could not possibly have known that Anne had moved it. This is because 2–3-year-olds believe that Sally has the same knowledge they do. Since they know where the marble is, they assume that Sally does too. If the same question is asked of a 4-year-old, they will probably say that Sally will look in the basket, where she had originally left the marble. This is because they know that Sally had not seen Anne move the marble and so she will not know she should look in the box. According to Wimmer and Perner (1983), 4-year-olds can complete the task because they understand Sally's 'mind' whereas the 2–3-year-olds do not. Wellman et al (2001) conducted a meta analysis of 178 studies and found that, regardless of variations in task (such as with materials, instruction, testing conditions, culture and social class) success in false-belief tasks starts around 4 or 5 years.

It has been suggested that the development of a theory of mind is part of a broader range of cognitive developmental changes that occurs around the same time. Examples of this would be the understanding that people, rather than inanimate objects, have thoughts and feelings (thus replacing animism); and the ability to view situations from another person's point of view (replacing egocentrism). Quite how children develop a theory of mind remains unclear, however. One crucial factor appears to be the development of language. Milligan et al (2007) did a meta-analysis of 104 studies which had looked at the relationship between theory of mind and language, using false-belief tasks. From a total sample size of almost 9,000 children, they found a significant positive relationship between false-belief understanding and children's general language ability.

Whilst there appears to be a strong link between linguistic ability and theory of mind, the exact role of language is as yet unknown. Charman et al (2002) suggest that the importance of language might explain why girls demonstrate higher skills on false-belief tasks than boys, since girls are on average more advanced linguistically than same-age boys, especially in the more affective components of language. This supports research by Ruffman et al (1999) who found that parenting style has an influence on theory of mind. They suggest that false-belief understanding is helped by responses of mothers which require infants to reflect on the feelings of others. This supports previous research which shows that how parents talk about emotion influences emotional understanding in children (e.g. Denham et al, 1994).

According to Meins et al (1998), success on theory of mind tasks is related to quality of attachment. In their longitudinal study they found that secure attachment at 11 or 13 months of age was related to better false-belief understanding at 49 months, and enhanced performance on two further false-belief tasks at 61 months. They put this down to securely attached children having mothers who treat them as individuals with their own mental states, something Meins et al referred to as 'maternal mind-mindedness'. This however remains unproven, as there is no clear evidence yet that this is what mothers of securely attached children actually do or, even if such a child-rearing orientation exists, whether it encourages better performance on false-belief tasks.

Although developed by Wimmer and Perner in 1984, the most famous use of the Sally–Anne task was by Baron-Cohen et al (1983) who used the task in his investigation of theory of mind in children with autism, a developmental problem in which the child is often described as being distant or withdrawn. Baron-Cohen has said that autistic children cannot complete the Sally–Anne false-belief task whereas non-autistic children of their age can.

Baron-Cohen et al (1983) set up the Sally–Anne task as described earlier. In his research he had three groups of children. Group 1 had all been diagnosed with Autistic Spectrum Disorder (ASD), which means that they all suffered with the symptoms of autism. Group 2 was a group of children who were of the same ages as those in group 1, but who were not suffering with any disorders at all. Group 3 was a third group of children, also age-matched to the other groups, but this time the children all had Down's syndrome. Down's syndrome is a disorder where individuals have particular physical features and also have reduced cognitive abilities. Before the test took place, the IQ of groups 1 and 3 was measured, and was found to be, on average, 82 for the ASD group and 64 for the Down's syndrome group. Each child was presented with the Sally–Anne task. In order to complete the test successfully, each student must say correctly where Sally will look for the marble. Of course, the correct answer is "the basket" where she had left it. "Where will Sally look?" is the *belief* question and correctly answering it is evidence, said Baron-Cohen et al, for an understanding of others' beliefs or states of mind.

The results are shown in the histogram.

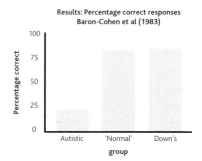

Results: Percentage correct responses Baron-Cohen et al (1983)

The results showed that 85% of those in group 2 (those with no disability) and 86% of those in group 3 (those with Down's syndrome) completed the task correctly. However, those in group 1 (those with autism) had difficulty with the task, with only 20% answering correctly.

Baron-Cohen et al concluded that those with autism, even though they had measured levels of intelligence comparable to the Down's syndrome group, performed badly because they were unable to understand what Sally might be thinking. This means that the autistic group were unable to express a theory of mind, and it is this that distinguishes them from those without autism. The inability to complete the task successfully was not, then, anything to do with a difficulty with intelligence: it was, instead, a much more subtle difference of social cognition that meant that autistic children could not complete the task successfully.

EVALUATING THEORY OF MIND

1. Calaghan et al (2005) looked at whether children from different cultures respond differently to false-belief tasks. In their research they identify a number of difficulties with previous research that has investigated false-belief task performance in different countries. Up until Calaghan et al's research, cross-cultural research had used a range of different false-belief type tasks which had been carefully designed to be relevant to the cultures in which they had been used. Calaghan et al felt that for a true cross-cultural test the same task should be used in different cultures, and so they designed a single task and used it in Canada, Peru, India, Samoa and Thailand. They found that the age at which participants were able to understand the concept of false-belief was the same at around 5 years in each culture. This suggests that false-belief is a concept that can be applied cross-culturally.

Previous research had found that the understanding of false-belief differed a little between cultures, but Calaghan et al say that this was because previous methodology was flawed, as it used different tasks in different countries and so the results of the different tasks were not a fair comparison.

2. According to McAlistair and Peterson (2006) brothers and sisters may have an influence on younger children's understanding of theory of mind as shown through their performance on false belief tasks. Their research was longitudinal and followed 63 Australian children for 14 months. First of all, the researchers measured the children's abilities on false-belief tasks and calculated their understanding of theory of mind from the results. Then, they retested the children 14 months later. The results showed that having one or two older brothers or sisters significantly improved a child's measure of theory of mind. Even when ages and the economic situation of the family are taken into consideration the influence of having brothers and sisters was significant. The researchers suggest that this may be due to the requirement of those with brothers and sisters to interact socially more often and on different levels than those without. The research suggests that our family environment influences our understanding of theory of mind.

3. Hogrefe et al (1986) used the 'Smarties task' to investigate theory of mind and showed that it appeared between 3 and 4 years of age. This agrees with the age suggested by the results of the false-belief tasks. In this false-belief task, knowing that a tube of Smarties actually contains pencils can be used by those with a theory of mind to understand that others who have not seen the contents of the tube would think it contained Smarties. Showing 3-year-olds the pencils inside the tube led

THE SMARTIES TASK

Hogrefe et al (1986) showed children a tube of Smarties, and then asked "What do you think is in the tube?". Three-year-olds and 4-year-olds both say "Smarties!". When the tube is opened it contains pencils. Next, the children are asked "What do you think your friend will think is in the Smarties tube?" The 4-year-olds all say "Smarties" but the 3-year-olds are unable to imagine that their friends would know anything different from themselves, and since they know the tube contains pencils they answer that their friends too will think that the tube contains pencils. The researchers concluded that this means that the 3-year-olds could not express a theory of mind, whereas the 4-year-olds understood that their friends would not know that the Smarties tube contained pencils and would think, as had they, that the tube would contain exactly what it was supposed to, Smarties.

them to believe that everyone must know that the tube contains pencils simply because they know that it does. This means that they do not have a theory of mind. Four-year-olds on the other hand understood that others may think differently, and would think, naturally, that a Smartie tube contained Smarties.

Measuring theory of mind using false-belief tasks such as the Smarties task or the Sally–Anne task has been criticised.

A child's ability to complete a false-belief task correctly may be nothing at all to do with their having developed a theory of mind: it may, instead, be to do with their developing another, more general skill. It could be that they just understand the question better because their ability with language has improved. The older they get, the better they are with language. Younger children, with poorer language skills, happen to be poor at false-belief tasks; older children, with better skills, are better at them. It may be that their improved skill as they age is simply because they better understand the task itself (Lewis and Osborne, 1990).

Some researchers argue that the false-belief tasks over estimate the age at which theory of mind appears. Onishi and Baillargeon (2005) claim that even 15-month-old infants, who cannot speak, show surprise when they witness a person searching for a moved object and actually find it is there. In their research a 15-month-old baby was seated beside a table, upon which were a green and a red box. The child watched as an actor repeatedly took a toy, hid it under a box and retrieved it from the box. The actor did this over and over again. Then, in sight of the child, but seemingly out of sight of the actor, the toy was moved to the other box. Now, the actor 'did not know' where the toy was.

The amount of time the infant spent looking at each box was measured in each trial. The longer the child spent looking at a box was taken as meaning that the child expected the actor to look in that box for the toy. The results showed that the 15-month-old children spent reliably longer looking at the box in which they expected the actor to look, even though it may not contain the toy. So, when the toy was moved without the actor knowing, the child looked at the box that they expected the actor to look in, where it had originally been. Even though they knew the toy was not there, they understood, shown through the amount of time they spent looking at it, that the actor would expect the toy to be where they had left it. This suggests that the child was able to understand

what the actor expected to be the case, and this, say the researchers, is evidence of a theory of mind. The researchers go on to say that the task does not require the child to have any ability with language, whereas traditional false-belief tasks such as the Sally–Anne and Smarties tasks require verbal skills. They say that if tested correctly even very young children can show a theory of mind; and that the reason previous research has shown theory of mind as developing later, by the age of 4, is that the tasks are related to the development of language, not just the development of a theory of mind.

> **ASK AN EXAMINER**
>
> "Onishi and Baillargeon (2005) and Lewis and Osborne (1990) both say that false-belief tasks such as the Smarties task are not good measures of theory of mind as they are heavily dependent on language skills. If a task does not measure what it says it measures, in this case theory of mind, its validity is questioned. This 'language' criticism is really a question of task validity. You can use this as evaluation of theory of mind tasks in your examination."

DEVELOPMENT OF CHILDREN'S UNDERSTANDING OF OTHERS

The development of a theory of mind is a step towards the ultimate social goal of being able to understand those around us and interact with them successfully. Another step is to understand that others have different feelings and experiences, or *perspectives*. According to Robert Selman, an ability to take on the perspective of others is absolutely vital on a number of different levels. If we are to help others, then being able to take their perspective can be extremely beneficial. If it is required that we work as a member of a team to solve a problem, then a knowledge of the perspectives of the other team members would be enormously useful. When we engage in competition with others, then having an idea of competitors' perspectives could be put to our advantage. This ability to take the view of others is a sophisticated adult skill which contrasts with a child's difficulty in imagining what someone else may be thinking or feeling.

SELMAN'S THEORY OF PERSPECTIVE-TAKING

According to Selman (1976), perspective-taking is an important aspect of social development that

RESEARCHING PERSPECTIVE-TAKING

Selman investigated perspective-taking by using stories. The different characters in the story each had a different perspective on what was going on. Here's a famous example adapted from Selman and Byrne (1974).

"Holly is 8 years old and likes to climb trees. In fact, she is the best tree-climber around. One day, while climbing a tree she falls from the bottom branch, but does not hurt herself. Her father sees her fall and is upset. He asks her to promise never to climb trees again. Holly promises. Later in the day Holly meets up with her friends and they all meet up with Sean. Sean's kitten is stuck up a tree and cannot get down. Unless they do something straightaway the kitten may fall. Holly is the only one who can climb trees well enough to reach the kitten and get it down but she remembers her promise to her father."

After telling the story to a group of children, Selman asked them the following questions.

1.   Does Holly know how Sean feels about the kitten?

2.   Does Sean know why Holly cannot decide whether or not to climb the tree?

3.   What does Holly think her father with think of her if he finds out?

4.   Does Holly think her father will understand why she climbed the tree?

In answering questions about the story the participants needed to consider the story from the perspective of the people in the question. For example, to answer how Sean feels about the kitten the participants need to think about the story from Sean's perspective. Selman and Byrne found that the answers participants gave to these questions varied largely with age. The answers of the very youngest participants for instance indicated to the researchers that they were completely incapable of understanding how Sean may have felt about the kitten. These participants could not take Sean's perspective. As the age of the participants increased, Selman and Byrne found that the ability to understand a situation from the perspective of others also increased. This formed the basis of their attempt to chart the development of perspective-taking.

takes time to emerge. Understanding develops through an invariant sequence of stages, each characterised by a particular way of thinking. Changes in perspective-taking occur because of an interaction between children's cognitive development and their experiences with the environment. Selman investigated perspective-taking with stories, or dilemmas, similar in some ways to those used by Kohlberg and Eisenberg and found that, as we grow from about 3 years old to teenage, we steadily develop an ability to perceive the world from the perspective of others. This means that very young, pre-school children are unable to understand how someone else may feel in a given situation, but teenagers are able to understand how in different situations another person may feel happy or sad, angry or elated. Selman's research led him to his theory that the development of perspective-taking progresses through five levels. You'll find them in the table on page 284.

ASK AN EXAMINER

"Take a look at Selman's levels of perspective-taking. Now look at Eisenberg's levels of prosocial reasoning. You should see some interesting similarities! When two theories agree with each other we have a good opportunity for evaluation. Selman's levels are supported by the Eisenberg's, and vice versa."

Level 0 – Egocentric perspective-taking

Selman said that those at level 0 cannot take others' perspectives. He describes this level as 'egocentric', using the term in much the same way as Piaget did. The perspective of the student is entirely self-centred: they are unable to step into someone else's shoes and see the world from another person's perspective.

Level 1 – Subjective perspective-taking

When they reach school age, Selman said that young people begin to realise that those around them can hold different opinions, thoughts and perspectives from their own. Whereas older people realise that these perspectives can be very different and the judgement of how people think can be quite complicated, the level 1 child's understanding of these differences is quite simplistic. For instance, they may understand that another child feels happy or sad while they themselves may not, but that is about the limit of their capabilities.

Level 2 – Reciprocal, second-person perspective-taking

At this level, perspective-taking is becoming more complex. The level 2 person is able to understand that other people may have quite different opinions about things than they do. They begin to understand that people may act in a certain way not because they want to but because they should.

SELMAN'S LEVELS OF PERSPECTIVE-TAKING

Level 0 – Egocentric
Incapable of taking others perspectives. Do not realise that other people do not have their own opinions. (Infant and primary school)

Level 1 – Subjective
Realise that others may have different opinions and thoughts than them. Not yet well understood. (Most primary school students)

Level 2 – Reciprocal (Second-person)
Understand that others may have different opinions that may disagree with theirs. They understand that someone may act in one way but think differently in a way that may not match their actions, and that sometimes people do things they did not mean to do. (Most older primary students)

Level 3 – Mutual (Third-person)
Can see things from their own, and others perspectives, and can also understand the perspective of a third person who may be looking in on the actions of their own two-person relationships with another person. The need to satisfy themselves and others is understood, and so the need for cooperation and compromise is understood. (Secondary school, and older primary students)

Level 4 – Societal (Symbolic)
Understand that past=events influence people opinions and actions and therefore people's personalities. A basic understanding that people may act 'unconsciously' i.e. that they may not be aware of why they act as they do. (Most secondary, some older primary students)

In other words, people may feel differently from what their behaviours indicate. They know that sometimes people may try to hide they way they feel about something, masking their true opinions for some reason or another, perhaps to lie to someone, or to avoid hurting others' feelings.

Level 3 – Mutual, third-person perspective-taking

The person at level three begins to understand that it is often necessary to satisfy the needs of both themselves and the people around them. In order to do this, it is important to develop relationships built on cooperation and trust to achieve a mutually satisfactory goal. It is around this time that students begin to form stronger friendship bonds built around these principles. The level 3 person becomes able to see the relationships they have with others from the perspective of an outsider, or third person.

Level 4 – Symbolic, societal perspective-taking

This is where perspective-taking is based on the true nature of human behaviour in all its subtlety and complexity. Here the person is able to see how the environment, the upbringing and experiences influence others' behaviours. They are able to say that someone behaves in the way that they do because their experiences of life have taught them that this is how to behave. The level 4 person is also able to see that people may not always be aware of the way in which they are behaving and that it may annoy or upset people around them.

EVALUATING SELMAN'S THEORY OF PERSPECTIVE-TAKING

1. Selman's theory finds support in a number of areas, not least in its similarity to Eisenberg's important theory. Notably, both theorists regard the development of prosocial reasoning and levels of perspective-taking as taking a similar course, both in the things people are able to do at each stage and in the ages at which they pass through each stage.

2. Selman's theory exploring the development of understanding of the perspectives of others has been hugely influential in recent years, and has been applied in many different settings. These have included its use in the treatment of those who have social difficulties; and in the classroom, where better teaching can be achieved by seeing things from the perspectives of students.

Selman's theory is extremely valuable in therapy (Kinney, 1999). His descriptions of perspective-taking can be very helpful in understanding why young children behave in the way that they do and how their behaviour develops as they learn how to understand the perspectives of those around them. This is very useful, for instance, when a child is suffering from a psychological trauma of some kind. There is no point in a therapist encouraging a younger child to take another person's perspective if they are developmentally unable to do so. Similarly, Selman tells us that older children are able to take the perspectives of others, and can be encouraged to do so. This can allow the therapist to help the older child understand how their actions may have affected those around them, something which may be useful if a child is battling with behavioural difficulties.

Selman's theory is also relevant educationally (O'Keefe and Johnston, 1989). Educators can employ his theory in their understanding of how children's thinking progresses as they get older. This can help them design their lessons and lectures to use the child's abilities with perspective-taking to understand ideas and concepts. For instance, a teacher who wants to discuss how people in different roles and in opposing countries behaved during World War II may develop their teaching to make use of Selman's theory of perspective-taking. The older students may benefit greatly from carefully directed questions about how others felt and for what reason, but the younger students at the lower levels may have great difficulty with this and the teacher would need to take another direction in the classroom.

3. Järvelä and Häkkinen (2000) have used Selman's perspective-taking theory as part of their analysis of modern communication methods, in particular the use of the internet as a communication tool. Using a web-based communication system, (for example, a type of the popular 'messenger' software), may indeed involve perspective-taking skills, but the researchers suggest that Selman's stages may not apply in situations like this. These types of communication methods are described as 'asynchronous' because a person communicating with another in this way must wait for them to respond before they themselves reply. This is different from face-to-face communication, where interruptions are regular, and there are important body language signals which indicate feelings. They argue that the *social distance* between those communicating is increased in these asynchronous situations, meaning that information usually available from social interaction is reduced, including information that helps people take the perspective of others. Selman's theory may, then, be seen as context dependent, applying more in some situations than others. In the case of asynchronous electronic communication – for example messenger and SMS services – Selman's theory may not apply quite as effec-

tively as it might if the two people were having a more traditional face-to-face communication.

4. While perspective-taking theory may be useful in the education of younger children, according to Harmon-Jones (2005) it can also be misleading. For instance, a child may behave in a certain way not because they are at a particular level of perspective-taking, but because they are doing their very best to cope with a difficult situation. For instance, if a child experiences prejudice and aggression from people around them, the result may be mistrust and a feeling of suspicion of others. This will then influence how they appear to behave around others, and will affect, in turn, people's judgements of their perspective-taking skills. It is not that they are unable to take perspectives: it is just that their experience is such that they are very careful in their judgements of others. Harmon-Jones indicates that cultural influences, such as racism and other forms of prejudice, should be taken into account in the assessment of a child's perspective-taking abilities.

5. Recent work on how people communicate has found evidence that Selman's stages may not be relevant in all situations. Other thinkers, including Vartanian (2002), say that we may not be able to predict the type of perspective-taking behaviour shown by all children from his theory. If a young person does not take someone's perspective, this is not necessarily because they are unable to do so. Harmon-Jones (2002) goes on to indicate that cultural factors should be considered in our understanding of the perspective-taking skills of children, a factor not considered by Selman.

Vartanian (2002) writes that adolescents often think that others are observing and evaluating them. This is called the 'imaginary audience'. One would think that Selman's model of perspective-taking might suggest why adolescents believe in this imaginary audience, but research shows there is no correlation at all between the existence of the imaginary audience and the level of perspective-taking that the person is in. In other words, Selman's model does not predict the imaginary audience behaviour, even though one might think that it should, since the concept of the imaginary audience is tied closely with our understanding of the perspectives and attitudes of those around us, as is Selman's theory.

6. Österman et al (1997) carried out cross-cultural research investigating how children from

different countries solve disputes between one another. 'Conflict resolution' can be achieved in a number of ways when two people, or two groups of people, have an argument. One side may back down perhaps, or the two groups may arrive at an agreement of some kind. Österman et al wanted to see if the way in which children from Finland, Israel, Italy and Poland approached disputes could tell us something about perspective-taking.

The conflict resolving behaviour of over 2,000 children was observed, and the findings generally agreed with Selman's theory. However, some important cross-cultural differences were found. For example, Israeli and Finnish children tended to be more constructive in their resolutions than Italians, preferring to discuss more, to try and find solutions. This suggests that just because people appear not to take the perspectives of others, this does not mean that they cannot – it may just mean that experience and culture has taught them that taking the perspective of others is not the best way to approach a problem. The researchers also found a marked difference between the behaviour of males and females. Females showed more sensitivity to the perspectives of others than did males and in all cases were more willing to use this information in their conflict resolving activity. This, said the researchers, may have been because generally, young females have better verbal skills than young males and can express themselves better. It may also be that the less physically strong females preferred a non-physical resolution as well as the widely accepted societal norms that young women should not engage in violence, whereas it is more acceptable for a male to do so. Whilst Österman et al's research broadly supports Selman's theory, it clearly indicates that we must consider cultural differences and gender when concluding why people appear to take the perspectives of others.

BIOLOGICAL EXPLANATIONS OF SOCIAL COGNITION

In psychology, different perspectives are often offered as explanations of the same phenomenon. The psychological perspective in our understanding of social cognition has a great deal of research behind it, and has generated many well-respected theories and explanations. More recently research, however, has generated biological explanations for some aspects of social cognition.

That the brain is specialised for dealing with social cognitions is not a new idea. For example, it has been known for some time that damage to certain parts of the brain can alter a person's personality and aspects of self-awareness. Anosognosia, for example, is a symptom where there is an apparent lack of awareness of the physical or mental impairments caused by brain damage. At the extreme this might involve an anosognosic denying a physical problem such as paralysis, or a visual anosognosic denying they are blind. It has been understood that damage to the frontal lobes either through accident or surgery can result in quite dramatic changes to personality and self-concept. However, probably the most important discoveries about the biological origins of social cognition were very recent ones concerning the origins of what are known as mirror neurons.

"You are expected to know about biological explanations for social cognition, and mirror neuron research offers the best. Learn about how mirror neurons work, what this means for things like theory of mind and self, and be prepared to evaluate the research. It is bound to come up as an exam question occasionally!"

THE ROLE OF THE MIRROR NEURON SYSTEM

In the 1980s, Giacomo Rizzolatti and colleagues were concerned with investigating the parts of the brain that allowed monkeys to control hand and mouth movements. They had placed electrodes into the brain, recording the activity of single neurons when the monkey performed actions such as reaching out for, or licking at, food. Quite unexpectedly, the researchers one day noticed that when they arrived at the lab eating an ice cream, unusual brain activity was recorded in the monkey. Every time the monkey saw a researcher take a lick of the ice cream, the neuron in the monkey from which they were recording appeared to activate. Further investigations found that when, for example, the monkey saw a researcher picking up a peanut to hand to the monkey, neurons would activate that were the same neurons which would activate when the monkey itself picked up the peanut. The researchers concluded that the neuron from which they were recording seemed to show activity when the monkey performed an action themselves or when they perceived others performing the same action. They had identified the mirror neuron.

It is this reciprocal nature of the mirror neuron which makes it extremely exciting to those interested in social cognition. Most neurons fire when they receive information, or when they generate information for the person to produce as an action. Mirror neurons do both. They fire when a particular action is generated by the person, and also when the same action is perceived as happening in another person. What this means is that a particular activity is coded as having happened in another person, or as having been produced by the person owning the neuron. If we have a cell in our brain that fires when we smile, and also fires when we see someone else smile, we immediately have the biological evidence that someone has produced the same behaviour as we have. This is a chance for scientists to investigate at a biological level how we learn to imitate behaviour or how we learn to understand what another person means when they do something.

Research suggests that mirror neurons may be quite widespread throughout the brain and not just for activities that can be seen. Gazzola et al (2006) have performed research that shows that some mirror neurons in the macaque monkey are active when the monkey produces a certain sound during an activity, and also when the monkey hears the sound being produced by someone or something else. Research from Bangert et al (2006) has taken this research further and linked it to human activity. In their research they investigated the brain activity of musicians and non-musicians. They found that similar sites of musicians' brains were active when playing or listening to music being played, whereas in non-musicians, playing and listening to music generated activity in different areas of the brain.

MIRROR NEURONS AND THEORY OF MIND

Mirror neuron sites have been found in different parts of the brain, including part of the frontal lobe. The implications of these recent findings are extremely exciting for the understanding of theory of mind, how people feel empathy for others, as well as enabling us to better understand people with disorders such as autism, who are unable to access these skills.

Keyssers and Gazzola (2006) have suggested that theory of mind skills are are provided by a kind of feedback mechanism in the brain. If we see others behaving in a certain way, then we are able to understand their state of mind because our brain takes in the information we are experiencing and stimulates some form of understanding of our own bodily state that would generate the same feelings in us. Thus, we know how people are feeling because we know how *we* would feel in the same situation. It is possible that mirror neurons allow us to make the link between what others are experiencing and how this would make *us* feel. In this way the discovery of mirror neurons allows us an answer to how we link what we see with how it should make us feel. It is possible then, that those without a theory of mind are missing mirror neurons, or at least the mirror neurons are not operating correctly. Galesse and Goldman (1998) have described mirror neurons as a possible part of a 'mind reading' system. By this they mean that the neurons may well provide us with the ability to understand the minds of others. This, of course, is a description of a theory of mind. Some developmental psychologists have said, however, that the mirror neuron does not explain everything about theory of mind. Autism, for instance, has been described as a social problem *characterised* by lack of theory of mind. However, having the basis for a skill, and gaining the skill itself, especially one

MIRROR NEURONS IN MUSICIANS

| Pianists listening | Pianists playing | Non-musicians listening | Non-musicians playing |

The images here are fMRI scans of the brains of musicians and non-musicians. fMRI is a way of recording both the structure and activity of the brain, in near real-time. The bright coloured areas in the picture are where the brains are active. If you compare the brains when musicians are listening and playing you can see that the activity is in similar places. If you compare the activity in the brains of non-musicians when listening and playing you can see that the activity is in different places. This shows that there are parts of the brain that respond to doing something yourself as well as experiencing others doing activities (Bangert et al, 2006).

as subtle and complicated as a theory of mind, are two very different things. Mirror neurons may well be necessary for us to gain a theory of mind, but they are by no means enough to provide us with a theory of mind. Just because we have the equipment to be able to do something does not mean that we will be able to do it. We need all sorts of other input too, and a problem such as autism is much too complicated to be explained in terms of a lack of mirror neurons. Many things can influence whether we perceive the emotions, feelings and intentions of those around us. Our experiences growing up, for instance, may help us to be more sensitive to others' feelings than some people. Both nature and nurture play a role (Carpenter and Neilsen, 2008).

MIRROR NEURONS AND MORAL UNDERSTANDING

Grayling (2008) has said that the existence of mirror neurons in all of us suggests that morality and moral understanding is, at least in part, innate. Mirror neurons allow us to empathise and recognise moral behaviour in others, and provide the conditions at a biological level for repeating this behaviour ourselves, experiences which subsequently become part of our knowledge of the world. Whilst a mirror neuron system provides us with the prerequisite hard-wiring for an understanding of morality, this obviously does not mean that we will inevitably behave morally, or understand the subtleties of some moral decisions. We must of course consider the role of our upbringing in developing our ability to reason morally and prosocially. On their own, mirror neurons are not a sufficient explanation, but taken together with careful nurturing experiences they form part of the social cognition system which allows us to develop moral understanding.

RESEARCH INTO THE MIRROR NEURON SYSTEM

1. Wicker (2003) took fMRI scans of participants shown films of people wrinkling up their faces as if disgusted by a terrible smell. Next, they imaged the same people's brains while they sniffed a chemical that smelled a little like rotten butter. They found that the same part of the brain was active when they watched the film and when they smelled the chemical. This shows that the same part of the brain, a mirror neuron, fired when the rotten smell was experienced, as well as when someone else was seen to be experiencing a rotten smell of some kind. This is evidence for the existence of mirror neurons that allows us to engage in quite complicated imitation involving various sensory processes.

2. Glaser et al (2003) looked at how the brains of expert dancers respond when watching other experts dance. Two groups of dancers took part in their research. The first group were expert ballet dancers from the Royal Ballet school in London. The second group were experts in a Brazilian form of martial art called capoeira. Crucially, capoeira is very much like a dance, and is extremely difficult to master. However ballet and capoeira are easy to distinguish and require different movements. Each dancer was shown short films of ballet or capoeira dancers while lying perfectly still in a functional MRI scanner. The results showed that the parts of the brain associated with mirror neurons were most active when dancers watched the type of dance in which they themselves were expert. Ballet dancers showed more brain activity when watching ballet than when watching capoeira and vice versa. This means that even when not producing the movements themselves, the dancers' brain response depended on whether they were watching something that they themselves were expert in or not. The researchers say that the implications of this are very important. If injured, a dancer may be able to maintain a level of skill or experience partly by watching others dance. We can extend this to other skilled activities such as sport. An injured sports person may be able to recover their abilities faster if, during injury, they maintain the link between their skilled activity and brain activity by watching others perform on film.

3. Watching a film of someone being touched lightly on the leg generates brain activity in exactly the same place as actually being touched in that place (Keyssers et al, 2004). Evidence, say the researchers, for mirror neurons linked to touch. This means that we are able to understand how someone else feels when they are touched. This is very important in a social world where touch is so very important in showing care and an emotional response to those around us.

4. Evidence suggests that there is a common 'pathway' for disgust, be it imagined, read, tasted, smelled or watched. Jabbi et al (2008) showed that watching a disgusted face, smelling or tasting a substance that causes the person to be disgusted and also reading or imagining stories that made them feel

disgusted caused activity in the same part of the brain. This suggests that the mirror neuron could allow us to code the same emotions if generated in any number of ways.

5. Molnar-Szakacs et al (2007) have shown that there are mirror neuron sites that respond to activities produced by ourselves and produced by others from our own culture, but that they do not respond when the activities are performed by someone of a different culture. In their research they recorded the brain activity of American participants watching an American and a Nicaraguan actor make different hand gestures. These gestures were the kinds of movements the American participants would have been familiar with, The brains of the participants were also recorded as they themselves produced the hand gestures. The results showed that the American participants' brains were more active when they watched the American actor performing than when they watched the Nicaraguan actor performing. The researchers concluded that a person's ethnicity and culture are both important in influencing the activity of the brain. They go on to say that this could be biological evidence of how mirror neurons help us shape the culture in which we live, helping us process the traditions and norms of our particular culture by making us more sensitive to our own culture than others.

EVALUATION

While the evidence for mirror neurons certainly is strong and growing, some researchers, such as Dinstein and colleagues, urge caution. They themselves are actively researching the neurons, but say that fMRI techniques and the experimental techniques used by researchers may not be accurate enough to allow them to identify the neurons from surrounding cells in the brain that are also active at the same time.

1. In humans, making participants imitate the behaviour of others while being scanned by fMRI has formed a good deal of the research. Dinstein et al (2007) have suggested that the importance of mirror neurons may have been exaggerate using this technique as very large areas of the brain show activity each time under fMRI and it is difficult to assume that individual neurons are causing this activity. It may be that a whole host of neurons are activated, and it could be that the mirroring of performed and seen activity is provided by a bank of neurons, not just a single mirror neuron. The original work identifying mirror

neurons in monkeys used a technique of direct recording from the neuron itself. They say that the activity seen in the brain during these experiments may be due to the activity of these other neurons performing other cognitive roles, and not the mirror neurons at all.

2. Some researchers doubt whether the research on mirror neurons in monkeys can be applied directly to humans. Turella et al (2007) looked at the existing research data identifying mirror neurons in monkeys and compared this with the data claiming the existence of similar mirror neurons in humans. They have found very little evidence that the two compare. This could mean that different animals have different mirror neuron systems, and the function of this system in one species might be quite different from its function in another. This may be a good example of how generalising between species is dangerous, as the evidence for a mirror neuron system, or 'circuit' as they describe it, in humans is weak at best.

3. Nielsen and Carpenter (2008) urge caution in drawing too many conclusions about the functions of mirror neurons. To say that the mirror neuron allows us to imitate others and understand their minds is a gross oversimplification of an extremely complex human behaviour. Imitation begins directly after birth and babies only imitate certain types of behaviour. They will only imitate if the adult behaves towards them appropriately and whether they imitate or not depends on a range of social, developmental and environmental factors. A whole host of issues such as the temperament of the baby, the context, the current mood of the baby, the behaviour of the adult, and many factors influencing the relationship of the adult to the child, must be considered. This complexity should not and cannot, say Nielsen and Carpenter, be reduced to the activity of particular neurons.

ASK AN EXAMINER

"Whenever you come across explanations which argue that biology offers a thorough explanation you have the opportunity to bring in 'approaches' comment relating to nature/nature, reductionism, and determinism. Here is a great opportunity to earn marks: don't miss it."

Psychopathology

GARETH GRIFFITHS

WHAT YOU NEED TO KNOW

You will be expected to:

- Demonstrate knowledge and understanding of ONE of the following disorders:
  - » Schizophrenia
  - » Depression
  - » Anxiety disorders – phobia
  - » Anxiety disorders – obsessive compulsive disorder
- Apply knowledge and understanding of classification and diagnosis to the chosen disorder

For the chosen disorder you should be familiar with the following:

- Clinical characteristics
- Issues surrounding the classification and diagnosis, including reliability and validity
- Biological explanations for the disorder
- Psychological explanations for the disorder
- Biological therapies for the disorder, including their evaluation in terms of appropriateness and effectiveness
- Psychological therapies for the disorder, including their evaluation in terms of appropriateness and effectiveness

SCHIZOPHRENIA

CLINICAL CHARACTERISTICS OF SCHIZOPHRENIA

Schizophrenia is a severe, debilitating *psychotic* disorder. People with this condition lose touch with reality, have difficulty expressing themselves in a way which is appropriate to the real world, and fail to realise they have a problem.

Crow (1980) made a distinction between two types of schizophrenia: Type I syndrome and Type 2 syndrome:

Type 1	Type 2
Characterised by *positive symptoms*. By this we mean that something is added to the sufferer's personality. An example might be visual or auditory hallucinations or delusions of grandeur.	Characterised by *negative symptoms*. By this we mean that something is taken away from the sufferer's personality. An example might be a loss of appropriate emotion or poverty of speech.

Schizophrenia is defined by disturbances in the form and content of thought, perception, emotion, sense of self, social relationships, and psychomotor behaviour. Schizophrenics often display some minor physical abnormalities and subtle motor, social, or cognitive impairments which do not necessarily place individuals outside normal functioning. After the onset of the full syndrome, with the appearance of both positive symptoms, such as delusions and hallucinations, and negative symptoms, such as impaired cognition, volition, and emotion), substantial functional deterioration in terms of work, interpersonal relationships, or self-care usually occurs. This deterioration especially applies to the first five to ten years after onset, after which the deterioration reaches a plateau and fails to become any worse.

According to the diagnostic manual DSM-IV, the criteria for a diagnosis of schizophrenia include:

1. *Characteristic symptoms*: Two or more of the following, each present for much of the time during a one-month period (or less, if symptoms lessen with treatment).

   » Delusions

   » Hallucinations

   » Disorganised speech, which is a manifestation of formal thought disorder

   » Grossly disorganised behaviour (e.g. dressing inappropriately, crying frequently) or catatonic behaviour (movement disorder such as rigidity or waxy flexibility)

SUBTYPES OF SCHIZOPHRENIA

Once psychiatrists accepted the distinction made between the group of disorders called schizophrenia, it soon became apparent that there were different subtypes of schizophrenia. These have been identified by the classification manuals in use in psychiatry today.

The main subtypes are:

1. *Paranoid schizophrenia* – this is characterised by the presence of delusions or auditory hallucinations.

2. *Disorganised schizophrenia (hebephrenic schizophrenia)* – a sufferer of this subtype will display the stereotypical symptoms of someone with schizophrenia. This person will have difficulty responding appropriately to the real world and their behaviour will be disorganised and unpredictable, as will their speech. They often also show what is called 'flat affect', that is, a person showing no emotion at all; or inappropriate affect, i.e. inappropriate emotion (laughing at a funeral for example).

3. *Catatonic schizophrenia* – sufferers experience severe disturbance of motor functioning. This might manifest itself in complete immobility or even excessive motor activity.

4. *Undifferentiated schizophrenia* – this subtype covers sufferers who don't neatly fit into any of the other subtypes. These sufferers might not have enough symptoms to fit clearly into one of the other categories.

5. *Residual schizophrenia* – this is used to describe the condition of a person who has suffered at least one attack of schizophrenic symptoms, but in whom there is a lack of positive symptoms within the past 12 months. There may be evidence of negative symptoms however. This subtype of schizophrenia is often regarded as the transitional stage between full schizophrenia and a diagnosis of schizophrenia in remission.

» Negative symptoms – affective flattening (lack or decline in emotional response), alogia (lack of or decline in speech), or avolition (lack of or decline in motivation).

Regardless of the number of symptoms a person displays, the one which above all others qualifies them as suffering from schizophrenia is the existence of hallucinations. The speech disorganisation criterion only matters if it is severe enough to impair communication.

2. *Social/occupational dysfunction*: For a significant portion of the time since the onset of the disturbance, one or more major areas of functioning such as work, interpersonal relations, or self-care, are markedly below the level achieved prior to the onset.

3. *Duration*: Continuous signs of the disturbance persist for at least six months. This six-month period must include at least one month of symptoms (or less, if symptoms have remitted with treatment).

"Be prepared to describe the clinical characteristics of schizophrenia in an exam. You don't need loads of detail – the question won't be worth many marks if asked and you can get them all with a short but accurate response."

The onset of schizophrenia most commonly occurs in mid to late adolescence, but it does range from mid to late adolescence through early adulthood. Its prevalence is said to be about 1% in the population (i.e. one person out of every one hundred will suffer from schizophrenia): however, common sense seems to tell us that this figure is probably an over estimate. Further studies into how common schizophrenia is suggest that it is significantly lower than this. A meta-analysis by Saha et al (2005) using over 200 studies carried out in 46 different nations suggests that the likelihood of someone developing schizophrenia is about 4 per 1,000, that is 0.4%. This study also found that there were no differences between the prevalence of sufferers in urban or rural areas or between genders. This has been disputed by many psychologists, who have proposed that schizophrenia is a lot more common in urban areas and also in areas of a lower socio-economic status (Srole et al, 1962).

ISSUES SURROUNDING THE CLASSIFICATION AND DIAGNOSIS OF SCHIZOPHRENIA

"You will have studied and discussed issues surrounding the definitions of abnormality at AS level and so you should be aware of some of the problems and pitfalls associated with the process of defining what is normal and what is abnormal."

The classification of mental disorders started with Emil Kraepelin. It was he who first started to see similarities in the symptoms of the patients he was treating, and to group them into some of the disorders that we recognise to this day. For example, he was the first to group together patients suffering from "dementia praecox" (early dementia) in a set of symptoms that we now regard as being schizophrenic. Due to the foundations laid in the late 19th century by pioneers like Kraepelin we now have much more sophisticated ways of diagnosing mental disorders. These modern systems are constantly evolving to include new discoveries. The main tools used for the diagnosis of mental disorders that we have now are called the DSM-IV criteria. This stands for the Diagnostic and Statistical Manual of Mental Disorders. IV means it's the 4th edition, published in 1994. The DSM is produced by the American Psychiatric Association and is the diagnostic tool most widely used in the psychiatric institutions around the world. Another of the commonly used diagnostic tools is the section relating to mental disorders in the International Statistical Classification of Diseases and Related Health Problems (most commonly known by the abbreviation ICD) which is produced by the World Health Organisation. The ICD is currently in its 10th edition (ICD – 10). There is very little difference between the two methods of diagnosis and they are often used alongside each other: however, it may be that the ICD is used in a wider variety of countries.

Classifying disorders into groups and types makes it easier for problems to be identified. Diagnosing a mental disorder is almost always done using the DSM-IV and the ICD – 10 as it is a fast and easy way to break down the symptoms, treatments and prognoses of disorders. Informing a colleague that someone suffers from schizophrenia conveys a vast amount of information in a very short space of time because of the shared understanding provided by using the same diagnostic tool. However, there is a risk in using this professional 'jargon', so that explaining a particular disorder to a sufferer or loved one becomes difficult and can result in confusion and anxiety.

The main issues surrounding the diagnosis of mental disorders centre on the reliability and validity of the diagnoses. When we talk about the reliability of the diagnostic tools we generally mean inter-rater reliability: this concerns the extent to which two or more diagnosticians would arrive at the same conclusions when faced with exactly the same individual. Many mental health professionals have raised concerns about the reliability of the diagnosis of mental disorders in our society and studies have shown that inter-rater reliability is actually quite low. In a now famous study, Beck et al (1961) looked at the inter-rater reliability between two psychiatrists when considering the cases of 154 patients. It was found that inter-rater reliability was as low as 54%, meaning their diagnoses only agreed with each other for 54% of the 154 individuals.

"You need to know about reliability and validity of classification and diagnosis – make sure you learn about them and mention them in any examination answer on classification and diagnosis."

There may have been a number of reasons for this. For example, it seems that in many of the 154 cases, the patients gave different information to the two diagnosticians. This illustrates how difficult it is to gain information from patients much of the time. It is true that diagnosticians will have the medical records of patients available to them: however, a true diagnosis can never really be made until the patient is clinically interviewed. This means that the health professional will be relying on retrospective data, given by a person whose ability to recall much relevant information is unpredictable – and who may even be exaggerating the truth or blatantly lying!

It was originally hoped that the use of diagnostic tools could provide mental health professionals with a standardised method of recognising mental disorders, so that the individual biases and personalities of practitioners would not have an effect on the diagnosis. This hasn't proved to be entirely the case unfortunately. It seems that, however clearly the symptoms of schizophrenia are set out, the behaviour of an individual is always open to some interpretation. One person could interpret a certain action in one way while another person could view it in an entirely different manner, i.e. the process is *subjective*. The most famous, and most illuminating study into the reliability, validity and subjectivity of the classification of schizophrenia was carried out by Rosenhan et al (1972). They found that 'normal' people could get themselves diagnosed with schizophrenia and admitted to

ON BEING SANE IN INSANE PLACES

Rosenhan et al 1972 recruited eight individuals whom they called "pseudo-patients". These individuals were healthy and had varied lifestyles but all of them worked with or knew the researchers in some capacity. The goal of the pseudo-patients was to get themselves admitted to psychiatric hospital on the basis of their fake schizophrenic symptoms. They were to do this by going to their allocated hospital and meeting with a psychiatrist. They were then told to report to the psychiatrist a false name and address that they had been given. The only truthful details they could give about themselves were details of their actual medical history. They were told to report to the psychiatrist only one symptom, that they had been hearing a rather undistinguishable voice that said only single words like "thud", "empty" and "hollow". They were also told that if they were admitted, they should, from that point on, act "normally" and report to the psychiatrists that they didn't hear the voices anymore.

All pseudo-patients were admitted to the psychiatric hospitals, all but one being diagnosed as suffering schizophrenia (the other diagnosed with a mood disorder) and none was suspected by the staff at the institutions of being a fake patient. Indeed, the actual patients in the hospital were much better at detecting these fake patients; around a third of the patients reported that they thought these pseudo-patients were actually sane and were "faking". All pseudo-patients were eventually discharged from their institutions as "schizophrenics in remission" after a stay of between 7 and 52 days.

A lot of the behaviour that the psychiatrists observed in the pseudo-patients would be considered quite normal in most situations. However, in the context of a psychiatric hospital, this behaviour seemed to be misinterpreted. For example, one pseudo-patient kept notes on their experiences and this was interpreted as pathological "writing behaviour" by the staff in that institution.

psychiatric hospitals merely by claiming that they heard voices. In a follow-up study, the researchers checked the reliability of psychiatric diagnosis by warning a hospital that they could expect pseudo-patients over a three-month period. Forty one patients were suspected of being fakes during this time, and 19 of those individuals had been diag-nosed by two members of staff. In fact, there were no pseudo-patients.

Clinicians have a tendency to put those suffering a mental illness into a category and fail to recognise that there are varying degrees to which that person may be experiencing that disorder. It is tempting for us to label a person as a 'sufferer of schizophre-nia' while not really knowing the extent to which they are suffering that condition and how much it is affecting their life. This is another example of the problem of subjectivity. It is usually left to the skill of the individual health professional to decide which behaviours constitute a symptom and which do not. Thus the beliefs and biases of some might mean the unnecessary labelling of mil-lions of people as suffers of a mental disorder. For instance it is hard to know where to draw the line between what constitutes a mild schizophrenic symptom and and what is a (perhaps uncharac-teristic) mood swing. This can be seen in the fact that most cases of schizophrenia are diagnosed at a relatively late stage, the disorder having grown pro-gressively worse over a period of time. Sometimes the disorder must reach a particular level of sever-ity before it can be recognised with confidence as a mental health issue.

Another problem arises with the recognition of schizophrenia as a condition distinct from other mental health problems. For example, the bounda-ries between schizophrenia and mood disorders such as depression are often very blurred, since they share many symptoms – and the matter is further complicated by the observation that depression is often co-morbid (i.e. it often seems to occur together) with schizophrenia. While the DSM and ICD classify the various mental disorders into groups and certainly aid in diagnosing schizo-phrenia, the diagnosis of disorders is ultimately left to the individual psychiatrist or psychologist. These manuals are just 'diagnostic tools' and the real work is carried out by the mental health pro-fessional. This leaves the diagnosis of the various disorders open to a great deal of criticism.

Another point that seems especially relevant in today's economic climate is the limited time and resources that are available to many professionals working in the National Health Service. It is clear

that diagnoses are often made by professionals who are rushed, and preoccupied with admitting only the most serious cases in order to safeguard the resources of the institutions they are working for. Meehl (1977) suggests that mental health professionals should be able to count on the total reliability of the diagnostic tools they have at their disposal if they:

» paid close attention to medical records;

» were serious about the process of diagnosis;

» took account of the very thorough descriptions presented by the major classificatory systems;

» considered all the evidence presented to them.

In a perfect world, all these things might happen, but as already stated, it is just not possible in today's health system, with its emphasis on seeing as many patients as possible.

The issue of validity has already been mentioned in relation to the diagnosis of mental disorders. When we question the validity of diagnoses, we are asking about the extent that our system of clas-sification and diagnosis is reflecting the true nature of the problems the patient is suffering; the prog-nosis (the course that the disorder is expected to take); and how great a positive effect the proposed treatments will actually have.

Some commentators have highlighted the extent to which many disorders described in the diagnos-tic manuals actually overlap. There seems to be a growing trend in clinical psychology to diagnose patients as suffering from 'co-morbid' disorders (i.e. as mentioned earlier, disorders that often seem to occur together). It may be that many individu-als do not neatly fit into the categories that have been created. Instead of acknowledging that the methods by which diagnostic decisions are arrived at are lacking validity, clinicians diagnose two separate disorders.

There is huge debate surrounding the issue of 'labelling' when it comes to classifying and diag-nosing mental disorders. Diagnosing someone with a disorder means that we are labelling them, and these labels are extremely hard to remove. Someone who has suffered from schizophrenia may always have the label 'schizophrenic' applied to them, even if they haven't experienced a symptom in a long time. This is somewhat the case with all mental disorders in that a person who has suffered a mental disorder has to disclose that information in situations such as job interviews, or they could face formal action. For example, an employee who had failed to disclose such information at interview could be fired. Unlike the experience of having had influenza for instance, the label of 'schizophrenic' stays with a person. Because we have little understanding of the causes of schizophrenia, our treatments for it are not always effective and sufferers of schizophrenia risk carrying the stigma of their condition for the rest of their lives. According to modern psychiatric methods for the classification of mental disorders, you do not 'recover' from schizophrenia and there is no 'cure'. Sufferers who haven't experienced any of the symptoms associated with any of the 'positive' schizophrenic categories but do experience some negative symptoms are said to be suffering 'residual schizophrenia' which is often the transitional stage between full-blown schizophrenia and 'schizophrenia in remission'. So once diagnosed with this disorder a person will never really escape the label: even if they don't experience another symptom they will be regarded as a 'schizophrenic in remission' and are doomed to carry the burden of this label for the rest of their lives.

One of the biggest controversies of recent times in relation to the diagnosis and classification of mental disorders surrounds the issue of cultural relativism. Sections of the newer versions of the DSM and ICD attempt to highlight and deal with the issue of cultural differences between subcultures within our societies, and between different cultures around the world. Davison and Neale (1994) explain that in Asian cultures, a person experiencing some emotional turmoil is praised and rewarded if they show no expression of their emotions. In certain Arabic cultures however, the outpouring of public emotion is understood and often encouraged. Without this knowledge, an individual displaying overt emotional behaviour in a Western culture might be regarded as abnormal in that context.

To diagnose a mental disorder, some interaction between a health professional and the potential patient must take place. This raises another problem in terms of culture. The clinician might not speak the same language as the person they are attempting to diagnose and therefore any interaction between clinician and patient should be done using a translator: otherwise the patient and diagnostician risk experiencing a serious lack of understanding because of these language difficulties. The term 'lost in translation' is very appropriate in this situation. The symptoms of mental illness are very rarely so clear that no discussion with the sufferer is necessary, and therefore the sufferer will need to be able to describe their symptoms in as much detail as possible. If an individual's symptoms are not being described sufficiently clearly, there is a danger of a misdiagnosis – and this can lead to inappropriate treatment or no treatment at all.

Although the criteria for the classification and diagnosis of mental disorders have been set out quite comprehensively, it may well be that certain criteria used to classify some disorders are incorrect. The DSM and ICD have very similar approaches to the classification and diagnosis of schizophrenia, agreeing on the symptoms and characteristics. However, Schneider (1959) proposed a different approach to the diagnosis of schizophrenia. Schizophrenia shares many symptoms with other psychotic disorders. In order to distinguish schizophrenia from those other conditions, he argued that the fact that a person has a particular symptom should not be regarded as being as important as the content of that symptom. It was the nature of the symptom that would determine whether a person was schizophrenic. For example, he studied the types of hallucinations that sufferers of schizophrenia would be afflicted with, arriving at a number of what he called "first-rank symptoms" which he could use to distinguish schizophrenia from other types of psychosis. These "first-rank symptoms" included thought insertion and thought broadcast, hearing voices and delusional perceptions. However, this approach has been criticised by some for being too stringent, on the grounds that that any one of these symptoms could indicate that a person is suffering from schizophrenia.

A further complication with schizophrenia is that an individual cannot be diagnosed with the condition if an existing mood disorder or a pervasive developmental disorder has been diagnosed in the past or if the person is suffering from one of those disorders at present. It may also be the case that such symptoms are brought about as a result of another medical condition or the abuse of illegal drugs or other medications. Organic problems such as brain tumours can also produce schizophrenic-like symptoms, so this possibility has to be ruled out during diagnosis since the prognosis and treatment in this case is different.

CAUSES OF SCHIZOPHRENIA

BIOLOGICAL EXPLANATIONS

"You need to know about at least two biological explanations for schizophrenia, and to be able to evaluate each of them."

GENETIC EXPLANATIONS

It is highly likely that schizophrenia is transmitted from parents to children via their genes, since research has consistently indicated that the risk of developing schizophrenia in families where there is already someone with the disorder is greater than the 1% naturally occurring rate in the general population. This fact is not sufficient in itself to prove that schizophrenia is genetic, as children of schizophrenic parents don't just share some of their genes, they usually share the same environment too.

It is very difficult to separate the influence of genes and environment. One attempt has involved looking at the history of schizophrenia within families to see if the risk of particular members getting the disorder varies according to the amount of genes they share. Gottesman and Shields (1972) examined the medical records of 57 schizophrenic twins studied between 1948 and 1964. About 23 of the twins were found to be identical (monozygotic, or MZ) and about 34 non-identical (dizygotic, or DZ). If one of the pair had schizophrenia and the other did not, then that non-schizophrenic twin was followed and assessed for at least the next 13 years to see if schizophrenia developed later in their lives. It was found that if an MZ twin had schizophrenia, the likelihood that their identical twin would also develop it was about 42%. If a DZ twin had schizophrenia, the chance that their non-identical twin would then develop it was a great deal less, at about 9%.

Gottesman (1991) went on to review over 40 other studies that had carried out investigations similar to that of Gottesman and Shields in 1972. On the whole, the studies found similar results, with the average concordance of schizophrenia in MZ twins coming to 48%, and the average concordance of schizophrenia in DZ twins coming to 17%.

Relationship		Concordance (%)
unrelated	General population	1
	Spouse	2
3rd degree relative	First cousin	2
2nd degree relative	Uncle/aunt	2
	Nephew/niece	4
	Grandchild	5
	Half-sibling	6
1st degree relative	Sibling	9
	Non-identical twin (DZ)	17
	Identical twin (MZ)	48

Adapted from Gottesman (1991).

This MZ/DZ difference is an indicator of genetic contribution. MZ twins are 100% genetically the same, whilst DZ twins share 50% of their genes, like any other siblings born apart. Assuming that the upbringing of DZs and MZs is very similar (i.e. there is no significant difference in the environments of DZ twins and MZ twins), then the only difference in these twin pairs is the degree to which they share genes with their sibling. The difference in the concordance rates (17% versus 48%) must therefore reflect the genetic contribution to schizophrenia.

In an attempt to separate the effects of genes and environment, some researchers have turned to adoption studies. This approach enables researchers to look at the rates of schizophrenia in children born to schizophrenic parents but reared by adoptive families without the disorder. In these situations, if schizophrenia was genetic one might expect the rate of schizophrenia in adopted children to resemble their biological rather than adoptive parents. Kety et al (1988), studied 5,483 Danish children who were adopted between 1923 and 1947. More adoptees who were separated from a schizophrenic biological parent developed schizophrenia or a related disorder than did control adoptees (32% versus 18%, respectively). Furthermore, children born to non-schizophrenic parents but raised by a schizophrenic parent did not show rates of schizophrenia above those predicted for the general population. These findings have been replicated by other studies – for example, by Kendler et al (1994) and Kety et al

(1994), and clearly suggest a genetic contribution to schizophrenia.

Evaluation of genetic explanations

Whilst some psychologists claim that evidence supports the hypothesis that schizophrenia has a biological basis and that this biological basis is genetic, other psychologists continue to be unconvinced by the evidence. They argue that in cases where MZ twins both have schizophrenia, it may not actually be because they share genes, but rather because they share very similar experiences of the outside world. They are more likely to be dressed the same, treated and reacted to in the same manner, have similar friends and go similar places, and it may be that these experiences, and not the genetic similarities, are the cause of the shared disorder.

There is evidence to suggest some kind of genetic involvement in the development of schizophrenia, for example the chance of an identical twin of a schizophrenic acquiring the condition is much higher than the likelihood of a member of the general population developing it. However, what that link is and how it works is something that scientists are yet to discover. It does seem, however, that schizophrenia is not entirely genetic. If it was, the MZ twins would have a concordance rate of 100%, since they are genetically identical. Whilst Gottesman's concordance rate of 48% is impressively high, it is far from 100%. Gottesman's data also clearly points to environmental influences in the development of the disorder. He shows that the concordance rate for siblings is 9%, whilst that for DZ twins is 17%, yet siblings are no more genetically similar than DZ twins. The doubling of risk in DZ twins must therefore indicate that something in their shared upbringing is increasing the risk of their developing schizophrenia.

Whilst adoption studies provide strong evidence for a genetic component to schizophrenia, one must approach firm conclusions based on this data with some caution. Adoption agencies will very often adopt out children to families with very similar backgrounds and lives, and as Kamin (1977) points out, they are often even adopted out to members of the same family. This means that individual twins reared apart may not be experiencing such dissimilar environments after all.

Another problem with twin and adoption studies is that, in the early days of adoption research, there was no fool-proof way of testing whether twins were really identical or non-identical. It may well be the case that many of the twins identified as identical were in fact non-identical. Not only this, but twin studies do not always use the same diagnostic tools, so that it is not entirely clear what is being compared in these studies. Also, twins are relatively rare in the general population and so is schizophrenia – it is very unusual indeed to find twins with schizophrenia. This means that researchers are using very small samples of participants.

Although genetic influences on the causes of schizophrenia are reasonably strong, identifying the biological location of the cause of schizophrenia has proved problematic. No subtype of schizophrenia has been found to be passed on to offspring in a logical fashion, the way it should if the cause was purely genetic, as is the case with other types of genetic disorders such as cystic fibrosis. It is likely that there are multiple, potentially interacting genes with small effects that add up to the debilitating disorder that we know as schizophrenia (Miyamoto et al, 2003).

An interesting finding highlighted by Heston (1970) suggested the possibility that a person may have a predisposition to develop some kind of mental disorder if they have an identical twin that suffers schizophrenia, but that the disorder the twin suffers doesn't have to be schizophrenia. It was found that if one MZ twin has schizophrenia there is a probability of about 90% that the other will have 'some sort' of mental disorder, but not necessarily schizophrenia.

NEUROCHEMICAL EXPLANATIONS

The Dopamine Hypothesis

The most widely accepted explanation of schizophrenia is the dopamine hypothesis (Snyder, 1976). This states that over-production of a neurotransmitter called dopamine is responsible for the symptoms of schizophrenia. The theory was proposed after observations of the effects of leisure drugs like LSD (lysergic acid diethalymide) and amphetamine, both of which enhance the activity of dopamine in the brain. Sometimes, an overdose of drugs produces symptoms almost indistinguishable from schizophrenia. An overdose of amphetamines for example can produce something called amphetamine psychosis.

Dopamine-containing neurones are concentrated in the basal ganglia and frontal cortex. These areas are concerned with the initiation and control of movements, and degeneration of the dopamine system in these areas produces Parkinson's disease. Drugs which are used to treat Parkinson's disease also point to a role for dopamine. The disease is treated with a dopamine replacement called L-Dopa, which has the effect of increasing dopamine levels. The consequences of too much L-Dopa can be schizophrenic-like symptoms.

Evaluation of dopamine hypothesis

Evidence for the dopamine hypothesis comes from research into drugs that influence dopamine levels in the brain. In healthy patients, these drugs induce effects similar to Parkinson's disease and research has indicated that Parkinson's disease is the result of a lack of dopamine in an area of the brain called the basal ganglia. Amphetamines seem to increase the level of dopamine in the brain and research has shown that giving amphetamines to sufferers of schizophrenia often worsens their symptoms.

A problem with studies carried out into levels of dopamine and schizophrenia is that they are carried out 'post-mortem'. Because of this we can't say if the increase in dopamine is a cause or effect of schizophrenia. Efforts have been made to study dopamine in living schizophrenic patients using PET scans (positron emission tomography). These scans attach a tiny radioactive molecule to a

naturally occurring substance in the body, usually glucose. When the glucose is used in the body, it takes the radioactive substance with it and a machine which measures and locates the radioactivity can map out the parts of the body and brain that seem to be experiencing the most use at any particular time. Gelder et al (1989) stated that while a lot of evidence suggests that dopamine is an important aspect of how antipsychotic drugs work, there is not much support for the notion that overproduction of dopamine is the sole cause of this psychotic disorder. PET scans allow us to study how dopamine works in the brain of living patients, but the evidence relating to its function in the development of schizophrenia is as yet inconclusive.

There are further problems with the dopamine hypothesis. Drugs that affect levels of dopamine do not benefit all sufferers. Whilst many people recover fully after medication with dopamine-based drugs, others only partially respond and others still show few or no positive effects. It may be that drugs work differently according to the type of schizophrenia shown. It has been suggested that drugs which reduce levels of dopamine may

---

SCHIZOPHRENIA AND DRUG USE

There has been growing evidence to suggest that exposure to certain recreational drugs, especially at a time when the human brain is not fully developed, can lead to the development of schizophrenia. One such illegal drug that has attracted a great deal of research in this regard is cannabis. With experience of this drug being relatively common in the UK, it is possible that cases of schizophrenia, exacerbated by cannabis, are set to rise. A survey of 3,075 university students from 10 UK universities found that about 60% had some experience with cannabis; nearly 25% had tried it more than once or twice and 20% of students reported regular (weekly or more frequent) use (Webb et al, 1996). Experience with cannabis had usually started at school, and other surveys have shown that 30–40% of 15–16-year-olds have tried it (Miller and Plant, 1996).

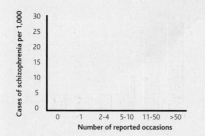

Cannabis consumption at age 18 and later risk of schizophrenia.

Andreasson et al (1987) studied young Swedish men who took part in national service: this is the system whereby individuals are legally bound to serve in the Swedish army for at least one year. A survey of these Swedish conscripts asked about their use of cannabis. It was found that those who had been regular users of cannabis were six times more likely to develop schizophrenia than non-users. The survey also showed that those who had reported using cannabis on more than 50 occasions were the most likely to develop the illness.

Murray (2004) reviewed evidence that related to whether the use of cannabis actually caused schizophrenia. His meta-analysis produced three main findings. Firstly, the use of cannabis seems to result in a two-fold increase in the risk of developing schizophrenia later in life. Secondly, if cannabis is a cause of schizophrenia, then its eradication would result in a possible reduction in the number of people developing schizophrenia by 8%. Lastly it was proposed that cannabis use was probably not in itself an adequate explanation of a cause. Whilst it is probably a contributory factor in some cases, for most experts it is more likely that a complex interaction of factors leads to schizophrenia. Murray went on to state that discouraging and educating individuals about the dangers of cannabis use could prevent an increase in the incidence of drug-related schizophrenia – although it must be remembered that the nature of a direct causal link between cannabis use and schizophrenia has yet to be established.

effectively reduce the positive symptoms of type 1 schizophrenia, but they do very little for the negative symptoms of type 2 schizophrenia.

Whilst amphetamines increase the levels of dopamine in the brain they also increase the levels of other neurotransmitters, so it is not possible to state with certainty that it must be the increase in dopamine that causes the schizophrenic-type symptoms observed. It is also the case that some people do not respond with schizophrenic-like symptoms to amphetamines and L-Dopa. It seems that whilst dopamine is implicated, it would be an oversimplification to claim that dopamine causes schizophrenia.

NEUROANATOMICAL EXPLANATIONS

Scans have consistently shown structural abnormalities in the brains of schizophrenics. These differences seem to centre on the size of parts of the brain called ventricles: these are naturally occurring spaces within the brain containing cerebrospinal fluid. It has been proposed by many researchers that these ventricles appear to be larger in sufferers of schizophrenia. Torrey (2002) has proposed that, on average, the ventricles of sufferers are around 15% larger than the ventricles of non-schizophrenics. This is especially the case for people who suffer from type 2 schizophrenia. It is not the enlarged ventricles as such which cause schizophrenia, but the loss of brain tissue that would have occupied the space. In fact Lambert and Kinsey (2005) did research this area and found that the reason for the enlarged ventricles in the brains of sufferers could be their apparently smaller frontal and temporal lobes, and also abnormal blood flow to certain parts of the brain.

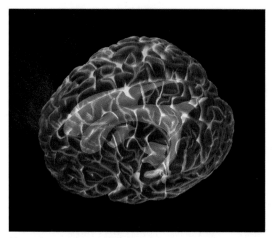

The red areas show ventricles of the brain.

Ho et al (2004) studied the relationship between the size of these ventricles and the development

of schizophrenia. It was found that, when compared to a control group of participants who did not suffer schizophrenia and had no history of schizophrenia in the family, people who did suffer from schizophrenia were more likely to have larger ventricles. Also, their brains were more likely to produce increased quantities of cerebrospinal fluid, possibly contributing to the larger sizes of the ventricles. The researchers followed their participants over several years and found that the larger the ventricles became in the brains of sufferers, the less likely it was that their symptoms would ease and become more manageable.

Another study carried out by Hata et al (2003) indicated a significant positive correlation between minor brain anomalies in the area of the lateral ventricles in early adolescents and the subsequent onset of schizophrenia. It seems that the larger the lateral ventricles were, the more likely these teenagers were to develop schizophrenia in late adolescence.

The term hypofrontality is often mentioned in relation to schizophrenia. Hypofrontality means that the frontal lobes have less brain tissue than is normal, resulting in reduced activity. Molina et al (2005) found that hypofrontality was an important sign of later development of schizophrenia. They compared a number of individuals with hypofrontality to a number of individuals without it and found that significantly more individuals who had hypofrontality went on to develop schizophrenia than their non-hypofrontality group.

Evaluation of neuroanatomical explanations

There is a cause-and-effect problem with neuroanatomical explanations. It is difficult to say whether the differences in the neuroanatomical structures of sufferers of schizophrenia cause the condition, or whether having schizophrenia causes the changes in the brain.

There is also a lot of conflicting research relating to whether these brain abnormalities are a consistent occurrence in the brains of schizophrenia sufferers. Whilst research has indicated a relationship between minor brain anomalies and the development of schizophrenia, many brain areas have been implicated and many studies have failed to replicate previous findings. Fundamentally, humans do not have brains which are exactly the same from one person to the next – brains naturally vary in size and weight and shape. It is for example not easy to measure ventricle enlargement accurately, and in any case there are no set criteria for what constitutes enlargement. Ventricles enlarge naturally with age, and are usually larger in male brains anyway. Often, physiological measures such as ventricle size and hypofrontality are 'averaged', which leads to an underestimation of individual difference.

Research by Highley et al (1999) states that different brain anomalies occur in different parts of the brains of male and female sufferers. Many researchers have also shown that brain anomalies are more pronounced in the brains of males sufferers than they are in those of female sufferers. This wouldn't necessarily support the idea that abnormal development in one specific part of the brain is the cause of schizophrenia.

PSYCHOLOGICAL EXPLANATIONS

"You need to know about at least two psychological explanations for schizophrenia, and to be able to evaluate each of them."

PSYCHODYNAMIC EXPLANATION

According to traditional psychodynamic explanations, schizophrenia is caused by a problem with an ego defence mechanism called regression. Freud's theory of personality states that we have three components in our personality – the Id, the Ego and the Superego – which we develop during different stages of our life. As a newborn baby we just have the part of our personality called the Id which is focused solely on getting what it wants and fulfilling our very basic urges. As we grow up we develop an Ego, which is our understanding of the rules of society, and our Superego, which is our sense of right and wrong. Freud believed that if a child is raised by cold or uncaring parents, their Ego will attempt to protect them from the trauma this causes. To do this it employs the defence mechanism of regression, which is when a person psychologically reverts to a past stage in their development, usually what Freud called the "Oral Stage" which occurs in the first year of life, where the focus of all a person's attention was on themselves and satisfying their own basic desires. However, a person brought up in a cold and uncaring environment will have a weak Ego, and so, in dealing with the huge demands placed on it by employing its defence mechanisms, the Ego shatters, leaving the Id in charge of the sufferer's personality. In psychodynamic terminology,

this is known as primary narcissism as a person becomes totally focused on themselves, to such an extent that they lose all touch with reality: they are unable to distinguish between themselves and others and between their needs, desires and fantasies. Freud saw the symptoms of thought disorder, withdrawal from society and inability to communicate as evidence of a self-centred focus. The auditory and visual hallucinations were the result of the sufferer's attempts to regain some contact with the real world and of being unable to distinguish between life and their basic desires and fantasies.

Family systems theory

In another psychodynamic explanation, Fromm-Reichman (1948) proposed that schizophrenia was caused by "schizophrenogenic families", and in particular a schizophrenogenic mother (a mother who causes schizophrenia). These mothers, she suggested, seem to convey conflicting messages to the child. They are cold and distant but dominating and severe. They were often rejecting of the child but still demanded that the child show emotional expression and were dependent on the mother at all times. It was this atmosphere of needing and wanting the affection from the child, but at the same time, deriding the child and even punishing them for showing it, that was typical of a schizophrenogenic relationship.

For Fromm-Reichman, there seemed to be a link between schizophrenogenic families and those with high emotional tension, many secrets, close alliances and conspiracies. Fromm-Reichman showed these types of families to be very much different from 'normal' families in a number of ways. They showed very vague patterns of communication between members of the family. Also they had very high levels of conflict and lacked the abilities to arrive at resolutions.

Brown et al (1966) focused on one aspect of the theory proposed by Fromm-Reichman, and that was the emotion expressed within the family of a schizophrenic sufferer. They conducted a nine-month follow-up study of schizophrenic patients who had returned to their family homes after being discharged from hospitals. They interviewed the various family members that the patients would be living with on their return home and divided these families into two groups – high expressed emotion (high EE) and low expressed emotion (low EE). At the end of the nine-month period Brown et al wanted to see if there was a difference in the number of patients that had relapsed during this time between the high EE and low EE groups. The difference was significant. In the nine months following their return home, 10% of the patients returning to low EE homes had relapsed. In the high EE group of families, 58% had relapsed. Subsequent studies have also found very similar data. Vaughn and Leff (1976) for example found that high EE in families was linked to high rates of relapse in recovering patients (51% relapse in high EE families, 13% relapse in low EE families).

Evaluation of psychodynamic explanation

The development of biological approaches to the explanation and treatment of schizophrenia has meant that those that are psychodynamic have become far less fashionable. Alternative psychological views, such as cognitive ones, also contributed to this fall in popularity.

The androcentric nature of Freud's theories, heaping much of the blame on the mothers of schizophrenics, has attracted considerable criticism. A great deal of research has found that the parents of the vast majority of schizophrenic sufferers are not cold and uncaring, as Freud described them, but sensitive and caring individuals, scared and devastated by their child's illness.

Another criticism that has been applied to the psychodynamic theory of schizophrenia relates to the therapies that have been established to try and cure individuals of this disorder. Presumably, if psychodynamic theory can explain why schizophrenia has occurred, it can propose a way to cure it. So far, there have been no real breakthroughs with sufferers of schizophrenia who have undergone psychodynamic therapy.

A problem with family systems is that we cannot infer a cause and effect relationship between the behaviour of the family and the presence of a schizophrenic child. The data gained from research into this will almost always be retrospective and therefore it is difficult to draw conclusions relating to the accuracy and reliability of the information. It may also be the case that the disturbed behaviour in the family is not the cause of a child developing schizophrenia, but rather that the disturbed behaviour in the family is the result of the family having a schizophrenic in their midst.

Brown's theory of expressed emotion is not as popular as it once was, as an explanation for schizophrenia. It may well be that these high EE families contain higher numbers of schizophrenic sufferers: however, it is unlikely that this is the only cause. A number of studies have found that some individuals with schizophrenia relapse even when kept from their families – therefore, this can't be the only cause of their disorder. In the mid-1970s, the focus began to move from families *causing* schizophrenia to ways in which the *course* of schizophrenia could be affected by families. Indeed, it is becoming more popular to consider family as a contributory factor, and not a cause. It is this view of high EE as a contributory factor which has led psychologists to look at high EE in relation to its effect on relapse rates and not just to focus on whether it is the cause of schizophrenia.

Fromm-Reichmann's theory of the schizophrenogenic mother has gained little support over the years and it seems evident that most individuals who suffer schizophrenia do not have the types of mothers that Fromm-Reichmann suggested were the cause of this disorder. In fact, it appears that research has failed to support the notion of a schizophrenogenic mother. Waring and Ricks (1995) actually found that the mothers of the vast majority of schizophrenics are much more commonly shy, withdrawn and suffering from anxiety.

COGNITIVE EXPLANATION

Whilst a number of different cognitive explanations have been put forward, they all have in common the idea that schizophrenia is caused by disorganised and disordered thinking.

One of the most important general cognitive theories of schizophrenia is the attention deficit theory. According to Frith (1979), schizophrenia is the result of a faulty attention system. Preconscious thought (i.e. thought that occurs without awareness) contains huge quantities of information from our senses that would normally be filtered, leaving only a small amount to enter into conscious thought. Schizophrenia may be the result of a breakdown of this filtering process, resulting in an overload. It is this that gives rise to cognitive abnormality. For example, thoughts that would usually be filtered out as irrelevant or unimportant are now interpreted in conscious awareness as more significant than they really are. Because there is a problem with attention, schizophrenics have difficulty focusing on anything for any period of time, giving the impression of disordered thought. For Frith, this accounts for the positive symptoms of schizophrenia, such as delusions, auditory hallucinations and disorganised speech.

According to Bentall (1994), schizophrenics have deficits and biases in how they process information. There is an attentional bias towards stimuli of a threatening and emotional nature, so that stimuli associated with violence, pain etc. receive automatic and subconscious priority in processing. This can be seen in how schizophrenics perform on emotional stroop tests. If 'colour' words like 'red' and 'green' are substituted for emotional words such as 'death' and 'laugh', it generally takes a schizophrenic longer to name the colour of the ink in which the emotional word is printed than is needed by non-schizophrenics. This is because the meaning of the word receives automatic subconscious processing, and because the word meaning receives a disproportionate amount of attention the naming of the ink colour is interfered with. This kind of attentional bias causes many of the positive symptoms. For example, paranoid delusions may be caused by an individual misinterpreting an event as threatening due to the exaggerated amount of processing it receives (someone cutting a cake with a knife, for instance).

Evaluation of cognitive explanation

According to Frith (1992), cognitive deficits are caused by abnormalities in those areas of the brain that use dopamine, especially the neural pathways that connect the prefrontal cortex to the hippocampus. He showed that schizophrenics have reduced cerebral blood flow to these areas (indicating reduced brain activity) during certain cognitive tasks.

There is some support for Bentall's cognitive processing bias theory. For example, research has shown that schizophrenics are more sensitive than normal control participants in judging whether a photograph showing painful electric shock being administered to someone is genuine or involves an

actor. It has been suggested that this sensitivity is due to the stimuli receiving greater processing.

One might predict that if schizophrenics have an attentional problem then they would have difficulty doing tasks than require focused attention. However, schizophrenics do not seem to be any easier to distract than normal, when engaged on cognitive tasks (McKenna, 1994). One very important aspect of this cognitive theory therefore lacks experimental support. Indeed, McKay et al (1996) point out that a lack of such support has resulted in the attention deficit theory being abandoned by most researchers. Most cognitive research now focuses on explaining specific symptoms of schizophrenia rather than the disorder as a whole, although as yet there is no widely accepted cognitive explanation of any particular schizophrenic symptom.

Schizophrenics clearly have disordered thoughts, but it is debatable whether this is a cause of the disorder or a symptom of it. This means that it is not clear whether cognitive deficits cause schizophrenia (and the associated physiological changes), or whether the cognitive deficits are an effect of other causes, such as neurochemical changes.

Whilst cognitive theories appear to explain many of the positive symptoms of schizophrenia satisfactorily, they don't adequately explain negative symptoms.

BEHAVIOURAL EXPLANATION

Behavioural explanations propose that schizophrenia is a learned response to certain environmental events. Liberman (1982) believed that most of us learn to respond and react in socially acceptable ways to appropriate stimuli – for example, most of us will learn to smile in a situation that makes us happy. This behaviour is positively reinforced or rewarded by role models or other adults as they give us attention and smile back. Liberman believed that, for whatever reason, the families or the important role models in the lives of young, future schizophrenia sufferers, don't reinforce their appropriate behaviour towards social stimuli, and so they disregard these stimuli. Instead, they begin to notice less socially relevant stimuli and they react towards these instead. Their responses are seen as being bizarre by most people in society and so they are often told off or punished for this behaviour, but instead of making the behaviour stop, the punishment or disapproval acts as some form of reinforcement. As many people have experienced, children often behave in naughty or inappropriate ways because they know they will get negative attention from an adult. Even though this attention is in the form of the child being told off, it's still attention and it's often more than the child will receive in other situations. Once this pattern of behaviour is learned, it is very difficult to reverse and so this bizarre behaviour carries on into adulthood and becomes much more apparent in a more mature environment. Behaviourists believe that this bizarre behaviour can account for the symptoms that are observed in sufferers of schizophrenia.

Evaluation of behavioural explanation

There has been inconsistent support for this theory of schizophrenia. One of the main criticisms of this theory has been that if a person can learn to become schizophrenic, then by the same processes they should be able to learn to undo the process and become 'normal'. There have been many attempts to use the behaviourist approach to ease the symptoms of schizophrenia, but few reports of any significant positive effects.

Belcher (1988) has shown that ignoring the bizarre responses of schizophrenic sufferers and reinforcing their socially acceptable behaviours by the use of food, attention, etc., does increase the number of appropriate social interactions and responses of schizophrenics. It does not however cure the problem.

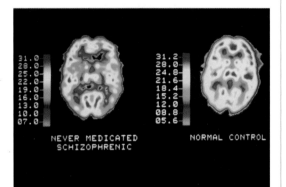

PET scans of a normal (right) and schizophrenic human brain. Each image shows an axial section (horizontal slice) of the brain. PET (positron emission tomography) scans show the distribution of a radioactively labelled substance introduced into the body. They reflect the function of particular tissues more than their structure, and are used to help diagnose a number of mental disorders, including schizophrenia. In this scan red shows areas of high activity, and blue or purple areas of low activity. The schizophrenic brain shows a distinctive pattern. This clearly indicates that there are biological as well as psychological contributions to schizophrenia.

THERAPIES FOR SCHIZOPHRENIA

BIOLOGICAL THERAPIES

"You need to know about at least two biological therapies for schizophrenia, and to be able to evaluate each of them in terms of their effectiveness and appropriateness – be sure to learn this distinction and demonstrate your understanding of these ideas in the exam."

DRUG THERAPY

The vast majority of people who suffer from schizophrenia will follow some kind of drug therapy to try to alleviate their symptoms. Antipsychotic drugs (also called neuroleptics) were first discovered in the 1950s when it was found that drugs given to hospital patients to calm their anxiety prior to surgery also calmed the positive symptoms of schizophrenic sufferers. These drugs, which contained phenothiazine, were soon commonly used to control schizophrenic symptoms. Subsequent research established that phenothiazine alleviated the positive symptoms of schizophrenia by acting on the neurochemical dopamine in the brain. Most modern antipsychotic drugs work by blocking the effects of dopamine.

The different antipsychotic drugs in use to treat schizophrenia are divided into three categories:

typical/conventional antipsychotics (e.g. chlorpromazine, which is a phenothiazine, the oldest type of antipsychotic); less typical/conventional antipsychotics (e.g. pimozide, which have effects on some particular aspect of psychotic behaviour and are often seen as a last resort if other drugs have failed); atypical antipsychotics (e.g. risperidone, which are the newest form of antipsychotics and seem to be the most effective over a broader range of psychotic symptoms and which, according to recent research, appear to have a lower risk of relapse and fewer side effects).

Appropriateness of drugs as a treatment for schizophrenia

It has been claimed that drug therapy for schizophrenia treats the symptoms of the disorder, and not the cause. A useful comparison to make is between antipsychotic drugs taken for schizophrenia and an antibiotic drug like penicillin, used to treat an infection. While an antibiotic seeks out and kills the infectious organism that is causing an illness, an antipsychotic drug cannot seek out and kill/change the cause of schizophrenia. This is because we don't really know what the cause of schizophrenia is, so the best we can do is to help reduce the effects of the illness. Drug therapy for schizophrenia has thus been likened to putting a cold flannel on someone's head when they have a fever.

Some sufferers treated in this way are also liable to relapse after the course of drugs has been discontinued. The result is that many schizophrenics will probably need antipsychotic medication for the rest of their lives. As with other drugs, once a person's body gets used to them, it starts to compensate and change, therefore dependency becomes an issue. As a consequence, higher and higher doses will then be needed to get the same results and effects, and the consequences of skipping medication can become magnified.

There are some serious side effects related to antispychotic drugs. Between 20% and 25% of sufferers who take these drugs will suffer from some form of disordered motor movements like tremors and involuntary tics. These and other symptoms are the reason why many sufferers (approximately 50%) stop taking such drugs within the first year. However, the newer forms of antipsychotic drugs (atypical antipsychotics) have been found to be more effective, while at the same time decreasing the number and severity of side effects, and therefore sufferers taking these atypical antipsychotics are more likely to persevere with their medication.

Another problem is that not all sufferers will respond in the same way to antipsychotics. Around 30% of sufferers who take them will not respond favourably. Antipsychotics also only seem to help with the positive symptoms of schizophrenia. The negative symptoms thus need to be addressed with other drugs or with psychological forms of treatment.

Effectiveness

It is clear that, for most sufferers, antipsychotic drugs successfully calm the effects of schizophrenia, and that for many they provide a cure from the disorder. Silverman et al (1987) stated that antipsychotics not only reduce the symptoms of schizophrenia but also have beneficial side effects for some people in increasing levels of attention and information processing.

Chlorpromazine is probably the most widely used antipsychotic and was first used on schizophrenia patients in 1952 by Delay and Deniker. They reported a reduction in the symptoms of schizophrenia displayed by their patients soon after administration. Despite all their shortcomings, antipsychotic drugs such as chlorpromazine appear to be the single most effective treatment for schizophrenia that we have at our disposal today (May et al, 1981). Chlorpromazine has been found to be even more effective than the phenothiazines, helping approximately 80–85% of schizophrenics as compared to the 60–75% helped by phenothiazine (Kane, 1992).

PSYCHOSURGERY

Psychosurgery involves damaging the brain in order to bring about behavioural changes. The first use of psychosurgery to treat schizophrenia came in the 1930s with attempts to sever the connection between the frontal lobes and the rest of the brain. The patients so treated were calmer and displayed none of the symptoms of the disorder of schizophrenia: however, they were sluggish and apathetic and had no real quality of life. At the time, before the advantages that came with the introduction of antipsychotic drugs, this was seen as a revolutionary treatment for people who were previously considered incurable.

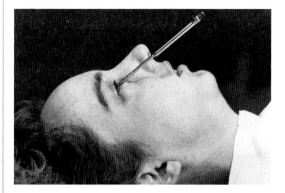

Whilst early efforts involved a surgical procedure, more 'efficient' methods were soon developed to sever frontal lobe connections. The 'ice-pick' lobotomy involved an instrument very similar to an ice pick being inserted under the upper eye-lid and hammered up into the brain through the orbital socket followed by a rotation to sever connections. Many more patients could now be 'cured' of schizophrenia, with some psychiatrists boasting that they could treat a dozen patients in a single morning. The exact figure is not known, but it is estimated that some 18,000 lobotomies were performed in the United States alone between 1939 and 1951.

By the 1970s the use of frontal lobe lobotomies for schizophrenia had all but died out due to the introduction of effective drug therapies. Some countries carried on with operations until the 1980s. Between 1980 and 1986, 32 lobotomies were performed in France, and around 15 each year in the UK. Some are still carried out in this country and also in certain states in the USA, although usually only in very exceptional circumstances.

Appropriateness of psychosurgery in the treatment of schizophrenia

Studies using MRI scans have actually shown that there is abnormal functioning in the frontal lobes of the brain in schizophrenia sufferers, and therefore, it may be that some kind of psychosurgery that reduces the functioning of the frontal lobe may actually help to control the symptoms of some sufferers. However, whether such a drastic step as deliberately damaging the brain can ever be justified is a matter of debate. Indeed, psychosurgery is virtually unknown in any but the most serious cases. Where it does occur it is because no other form of treatment has worked to reduce the suffering.

A very serious problem with this method of treatment is that it is totally irreversible. Once it has been carried out, it cannot be undone, meaning that the side effects are permanent. Indeed, whilst there are many reasons for a drop in popularity of psychosurgery, one contributing factor was the often serious nature of its side effects. Major loss of memory, emotional disturbance, loss of creativity, personality change, lack of social inhibition and other serious problems have been recorded. In some unfortunate patients, the side effects of surgery became more of a problem than the original condition, so for these, treatment was no treatment at all.

Effectiveness

Research into psychosurgery reported that between 1942 and 1954, 41% of patients who underwent such procedures 'recovered' or "greatly improved", 28% were "minimally improved", 25% showed "no change", 4% had died, and 2% were made worse. (Tooth and Newton, 1961).

Some psychologists have taken issue with findings like those cited above, however. These issues generally surround the definition of the term 'recovered'. It seems that Tooth and Newton use the term 'recovered' in the same way that we would use the term 'cured', but this term is wholly inappropriate when discussing the effects of psychosurgery on sufferers of schizophrenia. It has been said that psychosurgery does not 'cure' sufferers, but it can often reduce their symptoms in the same way that drinking alcohol 'cures' anxiety and stress, and maybe we should think about psychosurgery affecting the symptoms of schizophrenia in the same way as a person suffering from anxiety might be affected by being permanently drunk.

PSYCHOLOGICAL THERAPIES

"You need to know about at least two psychological therapies for schizophrenia, and to be able to evaluate each of them in terms of their effectiveness and appropriateness – be sure to learn this distinction and demonstrate your understanding of these terms in the exam."

BEHAVIOUR THERAPY

Because of the seriousness of schizophrenia, it has been proposed by many psychologists that to use some form of psychological therapy to treat this disorder would be quite ineffective, and to a large extent this is the case. However, behavioural therapy has been used in conjunction with other types of treatment like drug therapy, to help sufferers with their behaviour and facilitate their return to society, or even just allow them to function in an institutional setting.

One of the most frequently used methods is called the token economy, which works according to basic operant conditioning principles. In the first stages of the treatment, schizophrenia sufferers would be rewarded for not displaying any behaviour that would be considered strange or bizarre, then, as the treatment progresses, they are rewarded for performing actions which society would consider 'normal'. Such behaviours might include making their bed, combing their hair or washing, etc. They are positively reinforced for their 'normal' behaviour with 'tokens' which would allow them to watch a film, or buy special types of food like chocolate, sleep in a private room or listen to music.

This process was first investigated by Ayllon and Azrin (1968) when they studied a whole wing of a mental institution to assess how this technique worked in practice. Forty five female patients were involved and they were rewarded for not showing any psychotic behaviour and also for performing what were considered to be helping or 'normal' actions, by being given plastic tokens that they could exchange for some of the benefits already mentioned.

Appropriateness of behaviour therapy in the treatment of schizophrenia

Token economies have proven useful to many institutions where, in past times, schizophrenics would be isolated and confined in order to exercise control. Using token economy has allowed patients in such institutions more freedom and independence, which has helped the therapeutic process considerably.

The fact remains however that this therapy isn't really dealing with the causes of schizophrenia. A person being treated with this therapy isn't being treated with a view to their eventually being free of the disorder. Paul and Lentz (1977) point out that whilst this type of therapy does seem to have an effect on the behaviour of schizophrenics, even its strongest proponents are careful not to make any claims about their patients being 'cured'. Token economy is fundamentally a technique of managing behaviour. As it is a form of manipulation, the ethics of treating patients in this way have been questioned.

Effectiveness

Paul and Lentz (1977) looked at the effectiveness of token economy compared to other forms of therapy. Patients suffering from chronic schizophrenia were put into one of three groups, either a *learning group* (in which the patients operated around a token economy system); a *milieu therapy group* (in which the patients were treated morally, asked their opinions, made democratic decisions and were praised for their good behaviour); or lastly a group in which the patients were treated as they normally would be in a general mental institution. Around 90% of all patients were receiving drug treatment at the start of the research. However, by the end of the research four and a half years later, the number of patients in the group undergoing the 'general mental institution treatment' who were receiving drug therapy rose to 100%. In the milieu therapy group it dropped to 18%, whilst in the token economy group it fell to 11%. Members from all groups had been allowed to return to communities with supervision. However, the token economy group did significantly better in the community than any of the other

patients. These findings indicate positive results from receiving token economy therapy.

Ayllon and Azrin (1968) found that this method of token economy significantly reduced the bizarre behaviour displayed by many of the patients while also significantly increasing their helping behaviour and 'normal' behaviour. A study by Gripp and Magaro (1971) found that the symptoms of patients with schizophrenia treated using the token economy method improved significantly more than patients who were treated using methods traditionally employed in similar wards. Gershone et al (1977) also compared token economy treated schizophrenic sufferers to traditionally treated sufferers and found that they spent more time doing activities, less time in bed and made fewer disturbing comments to other patients on the ward.

COGNITIVE-BEHAVIOURAL THERAPY

Cognitive-behavioural therapy (CBT) is a therapy which aims to address and change a sufferer's dysfunctional emotions, thought processes (cognitions) and the subsequent behaviours that result. CBT uses theories proposed by the behaviourist approach and also the cognitive approach. While behaviourist therapies like systematic desensitisation and the token economy seemed to be having some success in treating some forms of mental disorder, they failed to make a big impact on other areas. For example, behaviourist therapies like token economy had little effect on schizophrenia. This may be because the behavioural approach tended to overlook the influence of a person's cognitions and thought processes in the development of many psychological problems. According to Meichenbaum (1977) the majority of mental disorders are the product of abnormal thoughts and feelings. Since our behaviour is largely the product of our thoughts and feelings, it would be logical to find a way of adapting or changing these thoughts and feelings so that the subsequent behaviour is affected for the better also.

There are a number of forms of CBT, one of the most common being Rational-Emotive Therapy first proposed by Albert Ellis in 1962. This therapy states that dysfunctional behaviour and emotional distress is the result of irrational thoughts. Ellis stated that irrational thoughts lead to an irrational "internal dialogue", and that this will go on to produce irrational behaviour and so these should be replaced with more rational thoughts and cognitions. A later and now more widespread therapy was developed by Aaron Beck. This proposes that mental disorders are primarily due to *errors of logic* and therefore addressing these will have an effect on behaviour. These forms of CBT aim to help schizophrenics challenge their illogical thinking and unusual explanations for their own feelings. The goal is to strengthen a sufferer's logical reasoning skills, thus providing an alternative to the often bizarre psychotic thoughts and feelings.

CBT often tries to deal with the interpretation of the hallucinations of sufferers, as they are often seen as threatening in some way. These hallucinations are then reacted to and it might be this misinterpretation and subsequent reaction that reinforces the hallucinations, making them more frequent. CBT attempts to challenge a sufferer's interpretation of the hallucinations and to propose alternative explanations for them, also helping the sufferer to understand how these hallucinations may have developed as a result of their experiences of everyday life. A more recent development in cognitive-behavioural therapy, of particular use in schizophrenia, is coping strategy enhancement (CSE). This therapy aims to help schizophrenics cope better with their psychotic symptoms. The therapist works with the schizophrenic to develop ways of managing symptoms, targeting specific symptoms such as auditory hallucinations.

Appropriateness of cognitive-behavioural therapy in the treatment of schizophrenia

Many clinical psychologists have criticised the use of CBT in the treatment of individuals with psychotic disorders such as schizophrenia as a psychotic disorder is generally characterised by a lack of coherent thinking and a person's lack of insight into their condition (they don't realise they have a problem). Cognitive therapies were, therefore, thought to be an inappropriate way of treating psychotic disorders and schizophrenia in particular.

The growth in support for a biological basis of schizophrenia has led clinicians to question the appropriateness of cognitive therapies even further, culminating in the various theories suggesting that an excess in the production of dopamine is responsible for many of the symptoms experienced by schizophrenia sufferers.

CBT might be of particular value as a therapy working alongside others, such as drug therapy. Drugs reduce the positive symptoms, allowing the sufferer to engage more fully with the psychological therapy.

Morrison et al (2003) believe that CBT can effectively be adapted to challenge the dysfunctional beliefs that sufferers experience and that it could therefore reduce their symptoms and distress, possibly leading to a lasting decrease in the symptoms associated with schizophrenia.

Garrett (2008) described successfully using CBT to change a patient's mind about taking the antipsychotic drugs she was prescribed and therefore reducing her symptoms in that way.

Effectiveness

Zimmermann et al (2005) found that CBT was effective in that it was better at treating the positive symptoms of schizophrenia than having no treatment at all. They also proposed that the effect of this treatment was relatively long-lasting and could help sufferers for up to 12 months.

Another area in which CBT seems to be useful is in recognising, and therefore counteracting, a possible relapse of symptoms. Often, stressors can cause a relapse in sufferers of schizophrenia. CBT helps a person recognise the stressors, recognise that their reaction to the stressor is inappropriate and therefore hold back a relapse of schizophrenic symptoms. A study by Turkington et al (1998) found that CBT was effective in treating the symptoms of schizophrenia in the short-term, and also occasionally in the long-term. Sensky et al (2000) found that it was effective in reducing the symptoms of schizophrenia even nine months after the treatment had been stopped. Other studies have not been so promising though. Tarrier et al (2000) found no real benefits of CBT a year after CBT treatment was stopped, and even less after two years.

Zimmermann et al (2005) found that while CBT may not help all subtypes of schizophrenia and all sufferers equally, there does seem to be a place for CBT when helping with the auditory and visual hallucinations that sufferers experience; and it particularly helps in reducing the distress and negative emotions experienced by individuals who suffer these hallucinations.

A review of the overall benefits of CBT in treating schizophrenia was carried out by Kopelowicz and Liberman (1998). They found that CBT moderately improved the symptoms of schizophrenia in 50% to 60% of sufferers, but only when it was used in conjunction with drug therapy. The relapse rate was moderate and the treatment was deemed to be moderately expensive.

PSYCHODYNAMIC THERAPY

Freud had very little to do with psychotic disorders (where a person loses touch with reality): his work was mainly focused on neurotic disorders (where a person keeps hold of their contact with reality). The 'talking cure' – what psychologists have called psychoanalysis – was never really meant to be used for schizophrenic sufferers and Freud never really advocated its use for people with any kind of psychotic disorder as he thought that the essence of their condition made a personal relationship, essential for development in psychoanalysis, impossible. However, subsequent psychoanalysts have adapted the treatment so that it might be used when dealing with those suffering from schizophrenia and some therapists have even claimed to have had some success.

The people mainly responsible for the use of psychodynamic theory with sufferers of schizophrenia were Sullivan and Pratt in the 1920s. It was Sullivan's belief that schizophrenia was a way of returning, or regressing, to an early childhood in terms of cognition and communication. He proposed that schizophrenia was often accompanied by a stressful event that a person who had developed a weak ego couldn't cope with. This person who is unable to cope with the changes in their life regresses to childhood – a period in which they had no responsibility and their situation held very little stress.

Sullivan's therapy sought to achieve an insight into the influence that their past experiences have had on their current condition. They are also encouraged to learn the adult form of communication essential for normal living so that they are able to clearly express the effect of their past. A very gradual relationship is developed, one which is safe and doesn't threaten the sufferer in any way. Initially, the psychoanalyst will not even make eye contact or talk to the sufferer face to face, preferring instead to do so whilst by their side.

Appropriateness of psychodynamic therapies in the treatment of schizophrenia

One of the cornerstones of psychodynamic therapies is the theory that a patient can only be 'cured' when they have gained sufficient 'insight' into their condition. As schizophrenia is a psychosis and this type of disorder is characterised by a lack of personal insight (they don't realise they have a problem), psychodynamic therapists therefore could never really claim to have 'cured' sufferers using this means of therapy.

It has been proposed by psychologists that the people who were undergoing the psychodynamic treatment that these early psychoanalysts were offering, may not have had schizophrenia at all, and that the diagnosis of schizophrenia was, at one time, a kind of umbrella term that many psychiatrists would use to cover all manner of mental disorders. Many of the people who were treated by Sullivan and Pratt would not have been diagnosed with schizophrenia if they had been assessed using today's criteria.

Effectiveness

There is very little research to suggest that this type of therapy works with schizophrenia. Whilst Sullivan and Pratt report very successful results in their work with schizophrenics using their psychoanalytical technique, it is not possible to corroborate these claims.

Drake and Sederer (1986) looked at the effectiveness of a range of different therapies, of which psychoanalysis was one, and found that therapies which involved a close client-therapist relationship, age regression and high levels of emotionality actually worsened a sufferer's symptoms, often leading them to become hospitalised for significantly longer periods. Stanton et al (1984) also reported very little effect on schizophrenic sufferers through the use of psychoanalysis.

In a study which looked at a number of patients who had been diagnosed with schizophrenia, discharged from a mental institution in New York between 1963 and 1976, Stone (1986) reported that there was a significant lack of improvement in any of the schizophrenics who had undergone this form of therapy. It was further observed that their gaining an insight into their condition was often a worsening factor. The suggestion was that intruding into the mind of a sufferer of a serious and chronic psychotic disorder could do more harm than good.

DEPRESSION

We all think we know what depression is, and maybe even think we've suffered from it at some time. However, the distress that most of us have experienced is not depression in the clinical sense. Clinical depression seriously impairs everyday functioning. According to the diagnostic manuals DSM-IV and ICD – 10, depression is classified as a disorder in which a disturbance in the individual's mood is the main symptom. The two types of mood disorder included in the DSM-IV are *major depressive disorder* and *bipolar I disorder*. The former is used to describe people who have depressed moods, whilst those who suffer with the latter have cycles of depression and mania. These two types have different causes, courses and treatments. Generally, when people talk of depression they are referring to the more common major depressive disorder (MDD), and so this particular form of depression is the focus of the remainder of this chapter.

"There are several different types of depression – you aren't meant to know them all. A good understanding of just one kind is all that is necessary: you will notice here that we focus on major depressive disorder."

CLINICAL CHARACTERISTICS OF DEPRESSION

The symptoms of MDD can be divided into different categories:

Cognitive Symptoms include such issues as: *low self-esteem, guilt, self-dislike, loss of libido, negative thoughts, suicidal thoughts, poor memory and a lack of ability to think or concentrate.*

Behavioural Symptoms include: *decrease in sexual activity, loss of appetite, disordered sleep patterns, poor care of self and others and also suicide attempts.*

Physical Symptoms include: *loss of weight, loss of energy, aches and pains, sleep disturbances and menstrual change.*

Emotional Symptoms include: *sadness, irritability and apathy (a lack of interest or pleasure in activities).*

According to DSM-IV, for a diagnosis of depression to be made, at least five of the following symptoms

have to be present in the sufferer during a two week period. These symptoms must represent a behaviour which is significantly different from previous behaviour and at least one symptom has to be a depressed mood or a loss of interest or pleasure. The symptoms also should not be explicable in terms of recent loss or be associated with a general medical condition.

» Depressed mood most of the day, nearly every day, as indicated by either subjective report (e.g. feels sad or empty) or observation made by others (e.g. appears tearful). (In children and adolescents, this symptom may be expressed as an irritable mood.)

» Markedly diminished interest or pleasure in all, or almost all, activities most of the day, nearly every day.

» Significant weight loss when not dieting or weight gain or decrease or increase in appetite nearly every day.

» Insomnia (inability to sleep) or hypersomnia (a desire to sleep all the time) nearly every day.

» Psychomotor agitation (erratic physical movement, twitches maybe) or retardation (lack of any movement) nearly every day.

» Fatigue or loss of energy nearly every day.

» Feelings of worthlessness or excessive or inappropriate guilt nearly every day.

» Diminished ability to think or concentrate, or indecisiveness, nearly every day.

» Recurrent thoughts of death (not just fear of dying); recurrent suicidal ideation without a specific plan; or a suicide attempt or a specific plan for committing suicide.

"Be prepared to describe the clinical characteristics of depression in an exam. You don't need loads of detail – the question won't be worth many marks if asked and you can get them all with a short but accurate response."

MDD is by far the most common mental health problem. It is now believed that depression accounts for approximately a third of all visits to a GP in the UK (Singleton et al, 2001). Rates of

5.2% to 17.1% in the general population have been suggested. Angst (1999) stated that 1 in 20 people in the Western world will suffer from MDD at some point in their lives. It is also more common in women than men, although the reasons for this have attracted considerable debate. Depression can occur at any age but is most common between 20 and 50 years. Recent research however has shown an increase in the occurrence of depression in under 20s. Rates of recorded depression have been steadily climbing over the past 90 years, but there have been many theories relating to why this might be the case. It may be that depression is becoming more common due to adverse environmental or physiological factors. However, it might equally be that depression has always been occurring across the world at the rate it is today, and that, because it is becoming more acceptable and being understood to a greater extent, it is now being diagnosed more often. This in turn could be because sufferers are not afraid to visit a doctor about their psychological issues, and doctors themselves are becoming better at spotting real psychological problems.

ISSUES SURROUNDING THE CLASSIFICATION AND DIAGNOSIS OF DEPRESSION

"You will have studied and discussed a number of the issues surrounding the definitions of abnormality at AS level and so you should be aware of some of the problems and pitfalls that are associated with the process of defining what is normal and what is abnormal."

The classification of mental disorders started with Emil Kraepelin. It was he who first started to see similarities in the symptoms of the patients he was treating, and to group them into some of the disorders that we recognise to this day. For example, he was the first to group together patients suffering from "dementia praecox" (early dementia) in a set of symptoms that we now regard as being schizophrenic. Due to the foundations laid in the late 19th century by pioneers like Kraepelin we now have much more sophisticated ways of diagnosing mental disorders. These modern systems are constantly evolving to include new discoveries. The main tools used for the diagnosis of mental disorders that we have now are called the DSM-IV criteria. This stands for the Diagnostic and Statistical Manual of Mental Disorders. IV means it's the 4th edition, published in 1994. The DSM is produced by the American Psychiatric Association

WHY MORE FEMALE THAN MALE DEPRESSION?

It is the case that more females seem to suffer from MDD than males. Researchers have made many different attempts to explain this. Some believe that women simply encounter a lot more stress in their lives and therefore are much more likely to develop what is known as reactive depression (i.e. caused by some environmental event). It is true that women are still subject to a certain amount of discrimination in their everyday lives. Social norms expect them to look after their homes, as well as, often, holding down a job. In many spheres they are still paid less for doing the same jobs as males; and women continue often to be overlooked for certain jobs because many employers are afraid of their female workers becoming pregnant and thus being entitled to paid maternity leave.

Other theories state that it may be that women think about problems and go over issues in their minds more than males. It may be that women are more likely to 'ruminate' over issues and problems whereas males will quickly forget them.

It may be that the changes women go through during puberty are a lot more stressful than the changes experienced by men. The differences between a woman's pre-pubescent body and her post-pubescent body are extreme in terms of appearance and in terms of hormonal and other internal changes.

Finally, although it has also been proposed that there is no real difference in the number of women and men who suffer from depression, it appears that, while women are likely to seek help for this disorder, men will only rarely do so. Thus, many men who have depression never seek help for it and so they are never included in the statistics.

and is the diagnostic tool most widely used in the psychiatric institutions around the world. Another of the commonly used diagnostic tools is the section relating to mental disorders in the International Statistical Classification of Diseases and Related Health Problems (most commonly known by the abbreviation ICD) which is produced by the World Health Organisation. The ICD is currently in its 10th edition (ICD – 10). There is very little difference between the two methods of diagnosis and they are often used alongside each other: however, it may be that the ICD is used in a wider variety of countries.

Classifying disorders into groups and types makes it easier for problems to be identified. Diagnosing a mental disorder is almost always done using the DSM-IV and the ICD – 10 as it is a fast and easy way to break down symptoms, treatments and prognoses of disorders. Informing a colleague that someone suffers from MDD conveys a vast amount of information in a very short space of time because of the shared understanding provided by using the same diagnostic tool. However, there is a risk in using this professional 'jargon', in that explaining a particular disorder to a sufferer or loved one becomes difficult and can result in confusion and anxiety.

It was originally hoped that the use of diagnostic tools could provide mental health professionals with a standardised method of recognising mental disorders, so that the individual biases and personalities of practitioners would not have an effect on the diagnosis. This hasn't proved to be entirely the case, unfortunately. It seems that, however clearly the symptoms of depression are set out, the behaviour of an individual is always open to some interpretation. One diagnostician could view a certain action in one way while another could interpret it in an entirely different manner.

It is the case that, as with other illnesses, we have a tendency to put those suffering a mental illness into a category and fail to recognise that there are varying degrees to which that person may be experiencing that disorder. It is tempting for us to label a person as a 'sufferer of depression' while not really knowing the extent to which they are suffering and how much it is affecting their life. This is particularly a problem with depression, where many of the symptoms in the DSM criteria could be experienced by someone who is very unhappy, rather than clinically depressed.

Consequently, the process of deciding what are abnormal disorders and what are not is also quite subjective: it is usually left to the skill of the health professional to decide. Thus, the beliefs and biases of some might mean the labelling of millions of people as suffering from a mental disorder. A good example of this stems from when it was considered that homosexuality was a mental disorder and that homosexuals needed some form of treatment to 'cure' them. The views of society today are vastly different from those of the medical professionals who advocated such an idea less than 40 years ago and indeed it was as early as 1973 that it was decided that homosexuality should no longer be classified in this way.

The main issues surrounding the diagnosis of mental disorders centre on the reliability and validity of the diagnoses. When we talk about the reliability of the diagnostic tools we generally mean inter-rater reliability: this concerns the extent to which two or more diagnosticians would arrive at the same conclusions when faced with exactly the same individual. Many mental health professionals have raised concerns about the reliability of the diagnosis of mental disorders in our society and studies have shown that inter-rater reliability is actually quite low. In a now famous study, Beck et al (1961) looked at the inter-rater reliability between two psychiatrists when considering the cases of 154 patients. It was found that inter-rater reliability was as low as 54%, meaning their diagnoses only agreed with each other for 54% of the 154 individuals.

There may have been a number of reasons for this. For example, it seems that in many of the 154 cases, the patients gave different information to the two diagnosticians. This illustrates how difficult it is to gain information from patients much of the time. It is true that diagnosticians will have the medical records of patients available to them: however, a true diagnosis can never really be made until the patient is clinically interviewed. This means that the health professional will be relying on retrospective data, given by a person whose ability to recall much relevant information is unpredictable – and who may even be exaggerating the truth or blatantly lying!

"You need to know about reliability and validity of classification and diagnosis – make sure you learn about them and mention them in any examination answer on classification and diagnosis."

Another point that seems especially relevant in today's economic climate is the limited time and resources that are available to many professionals working in the National Health Service. It is clear that diagnoses are often made by professionals who are rushed, and preoccupied with admitting only the most serious cases in order to safeguard the resources of the institutions they are working for. Meehl (1977) suggests that mental health professionals should be able to count on the total reliability of the diagnostic tools they have at their disposal if they:

» paid close attention to medical records;

» were serious about the process of diagnosis;

» took account of the very thorough descriptions presented by the major classificatory systems;

» considered all the evidence presented to them.

In a perfect world, all these things might happen, but as already stated, it is just not possible in today's health system, with its emphasis on seeing as many patients as possible.

The issue of validity has already been mentioned in relation to the diagnosis of mental disorders. When we question the validity of diagnoses, we are asking about the extent that our system of classification and diagnosis is reflecting the true nature of the problems the patient is suffering; the prognosis (the course that the disorder is expected to take); and how great a positive effect the proposed treatments will actually have.

Some commentators have highlighted the extent to which many disorders described in the diagnostic manuals actually overlap. There seems to be a growing trend in clinical psychology to diagnose patients as suffering from 'co-morbid' disorders (i.e. disorders that often seem to occur together). It may be that many individuals do not neatly fit into one or other of the categories that have been created. Instead of acknowledging that the methods by which diagnostic decisions are arrived at are lacking validity, clinicians diagnose two separate disorders. Kessler et al (1996) found that the chances of someone with a form of MDD suffering from another anxiety disorder is about 58%. They also found that the chances of someone with MDD suffering from any other disorder at all is about 74%.

Co-morbid disorders	Percentage of people also suffering with depression
Generalised anxiety disorder	17%
Agoraphobia	16%
Specific phobia	24%
Social phobia	27%
Panic disorder	10%
Post-traumatic stress disorder	19.5%

There are many types of depression in the two classification systems, and it can be difficult for those making the diagnosis to tell the difference between them, especially when they are working under pressure. Indeed, it has been shown that as many as 25% of people with depression have more than one kind of depression at the same time (known as "double depression").

There is huge debate surrounding the issue of 'labelling' when it comes to classifying and diagnosing mental disorders. Diagnosing someone with a disorder means that we are labelling them, and these labels are extremely hard to remove. Someone who has suffered from depression may always have the label 'depressed' applied to them, even if they haven't suffered a symptom in a long time. This is somewhat the case with all mental disorders, in that a person who has suffered a mental disorder has to disclose that information in situations such as job interviews, or they could face formal action. For example, an employee who had failed to disclose such information could be fired. Unlike the experience of having had influenza, for instance, the label of 'depressive' stays with a person.

One of the biggest controversies of recent times in relation to the diagnosis and classification of mental disorders surrounds the issue of cultural relativism. Sections of the newer versions of the DSM and ICD attempt to highlight and deal with the issue of cultural differences between subcultures within our societies, and between different cultures around the world. Davison and Neale (1994) explain that in Asian cultures, a person experiencing some emotional turmoil is praised and rewarded if they show no expression of their emotions. In certain Arabic cultures however, the outpouring of public emotion is understood and often encouraged. Without this knowledge, an individual displaying overt emotional behaviour in a Western culture might be regarded as abnormal in that context.

To diagnose a mental disorder, some interaction between a health professional and the potential patient must take place. This raises another problem in terms of culture. The clinician might not speak the same language as the person they are attempting to diagnose and therefore any interaction between clinician and patient should be done using a translator: otherwise the patient and diagnostician risk experiencing a serious lack of understanding because of these language difficulties. The term 'lost in translation' is very appropriate in this situation. The symptoms of mental illness are very rarely so clear that no discussion with the sufferer is necessary and therefore the sufferer will need to be able to describe their symptoms in as much detail as possible. If an individual's symptoms are not being described sufficiently clearly, there is a danger of a misdiagnosis – and this can lead to inappropriate treatment or no treatment at all.

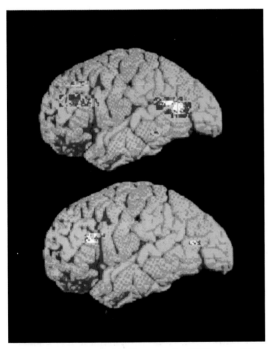

Coloured Positron Emission Tomography (PET) scan of the brains of a depressed patient and healthy patient. The left-side of the brain is seen, in external view. Colour-coded regions in red/yellow depict areas of low brain activity. At top, the depressed brain contains large areas in the prefrontal cortex (at left) and parieto-temporal (at right) with low activity. At bottom, the healthy brain treated for depression shows metabolic activity and blood flow has resumed in these affected areas. This clearly suggests a biological contribution to depression.

CAUSES OF DEPRESSION

BIOLOGICAL EXPLANATIONS

"You need to know about at least two biological explanations for depression, and to be able to evaluate each of them."

GENETIC EXPLANATIONS

Psychologists are divided as to whether depression is something that can be passed on via our genes or whether the reasons for depression are more psychological. Research on the heredity of depression within families shows that some individuals are more likely to develop the disorder than others. If you have a parent or sibling who has had clinical depression, you may be 1.5 to 3 times more likely to develop the condition than those who do not have a close relative with the condition. This suggests that there may be some kind of genetic factor in the cause for depression.

Several studies using twin data have tended to confirm this. If there is a genetic component to depression, the identical (monozygotic) twin of a depressed person will have a higher chance of developing depression than a non-identical (dizygotic) twin of such a person. McGuffin et al (1996) found that the chances of one identical twin developing depression if their twin has the disorder is about 46%: if the twins were non-identical, the chance was roughly 20%. Thus, we can see that genes do appear to play a part in the development of depression.

Scientists have recently isolated a gene that starves the brain of serotonin. The neurotransmitter serotonin is important in mood regulation and low levels in the brain have long been associated with depression. Therefore a gene which is responsible for decreasing levels of serotonin could be linked to the causes of depression. This mutant gene has been found to be ten times more likely to occur in depressed patients than in non-depressed controls (Caron and Zhang, 2005). Patients with the mutant gene did not respond to anti-depressant drugs designed to increase levels of serotonin. This suggests that the gene may be an underlying factor in a small group of depressed patients who do not respond to drug treatments. Amongst the patients identified with the mutant gene, in the above study, 65% had a family history of mental illness, thus offering further support for the existence of a genetic factor in depression.

There has been some progress with genetic marker studies. These look for genes which are commonly associated with depression, and which may point the way to identifying actual depressive genes, or other factors which have a causal link with depression. Individuals with heart disease are twice as likely to experience clinical depression compared with the general population. A recent study by McCaffery et al (2009) concluded that there may be a genetic explanation for this. The genes in question are related to the vascular system, suggesting that the health of this system – which includes the body's network of blood vessels, arteries and veins – may be a predictor of depression in individuals with heart disease.

Evaluation of genetic explanations

Genes can not be the only influence on whether depression develops. If they were, then the identical twin of a person who already suffers depression would definitely develop it also – i.e. the relationship would be 100%. Kendler et al (1993) showed that the chance of a child of someone who suffers depression also developing the disorder was only just higher than the chances of the general population. This suggests that genes and familial inheritance are not as important in the development of depression as many thought.

Another study by Kendler et al (2006) indicated that genes seem to be more influential in the development of females' depression than they do in males' depression. Their study was carried out on 15,493 pairs of male/female twins identified from the Swedish Twin Registry. Kendler et al discovered that the heritability of depression was significantly higher in the females than it was for the males.

It is quite conceivable that patients with heart disease would be more likely to suffer also from depression. To be diagnosed with heart disease can have serious implications for a person's lifestyle and possibly their work and income. Patients may also be told that their prognosis is poor and that there is little chance of improvement or recovery. Given the possible effects that the diagnosis of heart disease could have, it is not surprising that people so diagnosed have a greater tendency to experience depression also. The researchers did note that depression often set in soon after the first experience of heart problems.

NEUROCHEMICAL EXPLANATIONS

Psychologists have established beyond reasonable doubt that levels of certain biochemicals in the body can seriously affect a person's moods. Recreational drugs are taken by many individuals because of the effect they have on their moods, and these drugs actually work by altering the levels of certain biochemicals in the body and brain. Knowing this, many researchers proposed that if increasing these biochemicals can improve mood, then decreasing them can cause depressive symptoms. It is very possible then that low levels of these substances could be a contributory factor in the development of depressive disorder.

The catecholamine hypothesis

One of the most famous of neurochemical theories was proposed by Joseph Schildkraut in the 1960s. It was named the "catecholamine hypothesis" as he proposed that a low level of noradrenaline, one type of catecholamine, was the main cause of depression.

The link between noradrenaline and depression was established by accident as long ago as the 1950s. A number of drug trials were being carried out at this time to explore the effectiveness of certain drugs to lower blood pressure. One such drug was reserpine which, as well as reducing blood pressure, also lowered noradrenaline. It was observed that participants whose noradrenaline levels were lowered seemed to develop periods of acute depression. It was assumed that this was due to the reduced level of the neurotransmitter noradrenaline. Researchers then set about attempting to create a drug which would increase the amount of noradrenaline in the brain and, it was hoped, reduce the symptoms of depression.

Evaluation of the catecholamine hypothesis

There is a great deal of research that supports the catecholamine hypothesis. However, much research also contradicts Schildkraut's hypothesis. Certainly, while there does seem to be a relationship between low levels of noradrenaline and MDD, levels of noradrenaline do not affect the moods of everyone in the same way, if they affect them at all. This variability can be further seen in sufferers of depression who are prescribed drugs which increase the levels of noradrenaline in the body, but have little effect on the depressive disorder.

Noradrenaline re-uptake inhibitors (NRIs) block the re-uptake of noradrenaline, in order to enhance its activity in the brain's neurons. This makes more noradrenaline available to the brain and therefore, if a low level of noradrenaline is responsible for depression, this should lessen the symptoms. Versiani et al (1999) compared the effect of noradrenaline re-uptake inhibitors, which increase the amount of noradrenaline in the brain, to placebos in a double blind study. It was found that the NRIs were much more effective in alleviating the symptoms of depression, while there was also a much lower risk of relapse than there was with the placebo (22% relapse on NRIs, 56% with the placebo).

Elkin et al (1996) reviewed a comprehensive study that examined the effects of imipramine, a drug which provides the brain with higher levels of noradrenaline. It was found that, compared with psychological therapies and placebos, it had a much greater effect on the symptoms of depression in severe cases.

It has been difficult to say for sure whether the catecholamine hypothesis holds the key to the disorder of depression. There is a lot of research which suggests that low catecholamine production, especially noradrenaline, is linked to depression. However, studies show that in some depressed patients there is evidence that no depletion of noradrenaline is occurring. Furthermore, studies suggest it may be that not all sufferers of depression experience a lower level of noradrenaline, as some forms of depression may well be reactive, (i.e. due to events and stressors in the environment), and these types of depression seem to show no decrease in the levels of noradrenaline. However, the individuals who seem to be genetically predisposed to depression commonly show this pattern of a reduction in noradrenaline. It may be that different types of depression are caused by physiologically different processes. This suggestion may have a knock-on effect regarding the treatment of these types of depression. Schatzberg and Schildkraut (2000) proposed that the use of anti-depressants that increase the levels of noradrenaline would not be effective in many cases of reactive depression.

The serotonin hypothesis

The most widely supported neurochemical theory centres on the neurotransmitter serotonin. This theory was first proposed during trials of tricyclic drugs which were originally devised to calm the symptoms of the disorder of schizophrenia in the

1950s. It was found that they often encouraged an episode of 'mania' which was quite disastrous in schizophrenic patients. However, scientists started to wonder what effect these drugs might have on patients who were depressed. The first trials of the drugs seemed to be successful and they have been used for this purpose in one form or another ever since.

The serotonin hypothesis suggests that depression is caused by a low level of this neurotransmitter. Scientists know that serotonin has a huge effect on mood, and levels of serotonin in the brain are associated with aggression (Caspi et al, 2002). Methylenedioxymethamphetamine or MDMA (the drug Ecstacy) is said to have an euphoric effect on a person's mood: this works by increasing the amount of serotonin released by neurons in the brain. We can see that serotonin does affect our moods quite dramatically so it would be logical to assume that a problem with our body's ability to regulate our levels of serotonin could lead to some kind of mood disturbance, possibly depression.

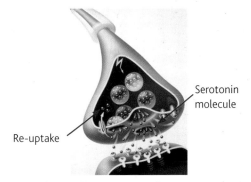

Diagram showing the transmission of serotonin across a synapse. Whilst normally this chemical is reabsorbed by the transmitting neuron (re-uptake), tricyclic drugs prevent this resulting in more serotonin remaining in the synapse.

Tricyclic drugs work by preventing the re-uptake of serotonin into a synapse, therefore allowing more of it to be available to be received by the receptor. Advances in science have included progress in the area of serotonin re-uptake inhibitors and now we have selective serotonin re-uptake inhibitors (SSRIs), such as Prozac, which focus only on serotonin and no other neurotransmitter.

Evaluation of the serotonin hypothesis

Tricyclic drugs seem to help many sufferers of depression and these drugs work by increasing the levels of serotonin in the brain. Other drugs which increase the levels of serotonin in the brain can also have a significant effect on mood. This strongly implicates serotonin in depression.

It might be the case that these drugs have little more than an acute placebo effect. A study by Kirsch et al (2002) found that the effect of anti-depressants and placebos was "negligible". Studies that have examined the effects of anti-depressants, placebos and also regular exercise have found that exercise is significantly more effective at reducing the effects of depression than are anti-depressants.

In 2005, anti-depressants became the most pre-scribed drug in the United States, causing more debate over the issue. Some doctors believe this is a positive sign that people are finally seeking help for their issues. Others disagree, saying that this shows that people are becoming too dependent on anti-depressants.

NEUROENDOCRINE THEORIES OF DEPRESSION

A great deal of modern research into depression has focused on the area of the neuroendocrine system, and in particular, certain hormones which are produced in response to stress. The pathways that are responsible for our stress responses are the HPA (hypothalamic pituitary adrenal) system and the sympathomedullary pathway. The sympathomedullary pathway is responsible for our short-term immediate stress response, with the HPA being responsible for our longer lasting, more chronic responses to stress. It is the HPA axis that scientists seem to be interested in, concerning its relationship to the chronic stress response and eventual depression.

"It would be useful to remind yourself of the body's response to stress that you covered at AS level. It will help your understanding here."

According to Pariante (2007), there is substantial research to suggest that depression is characterised by an over activity of the hypothalamic-pituitary-adrenal system. Pariante also claims that an under-standing of stress is essential to our understanding of depression and so any treatment of depression has to address the issues surrounding chronic stress also.

The process behind the proposed effect of stress hormones on mood and depression centres around what is known as corticotrophin-releasing hormone (CRH). This is released from the hypothalamus when stress is encountered. This CRH then reaches the pituitary gland which, in response to the presence of CRH, releases adreno-corticotrophic hormone (ACTH): when this arrives at the adrenal cortex, it activates the release of corticosteroids – most importantly, cortisol, which is a type of glucocorticoid.

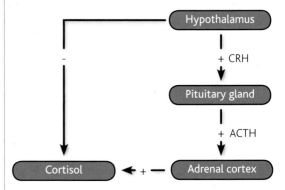

One function of the hypothalamus in the HPA system is to monitor levels of cortisol in the blood. When cortisol reaches a certain level the hypothalamus reduces its influence on the pituitary gland, slowing down the stress response. When cortisol falls below a certain level, the hypothalamus can if need be stimulate more activity in the pituitary gland. In effect, cortisol is acting as a negative feedback loop, causing the slowing of the stress response.

Brief periods of controllable stress involving the HPA are good for us. In fact, they are often associated with arousal and excitement. However, over-activation of this system can make us vulnerable to a range of illnesses, including mood disorders. It is suggested that, in depressed people, there is hyperactivity of the HPA axis, caused by hyperactive CRH neurons in the hypothalamus. In effect, in such people the hypothalamus continuously stimulates the pituitary, regardless of the amount of cortisol in the blood.

It has been shown that depression-type symptoms can be induced in animals in a laboratory setting by injecting CRH into a certain area of the brain (Bao et al, 2008). It has also been found that people with a condition called Cushing's syndrome, who are treated by a procedure that increases levels of glucocorticoid hormones, frequently experience periods of depression. Furthermore, Bao et al (2008) believe that they can account for the gender differences in depression rates by reference to the different hormones produced by males and females. They state that while the female hormone oestrogen can stimulate the production of CRH, male hormones (androgens) suppress the production of CRH.

SEASONAL AFFECTIVE DISORDER (SAD)

Seasonal affective disorder is characterised by the occurrence of bouts of depression in the winter time or during extended periods of dark and cold. This depression is seasonal in nature, so that it generally lifts during the spring and summer. A diagnosis of SAD was first proposed by Rosenthal (1984). He later outlined the symptoms of SAD, indicating that they seem to include a depressed mood, a significant increase in sleeping and tiredness, significant lack of energy, a craving for carbohydrate-rich foods and often, weight gain. The condition seems mainly to affect those who live in more temperate, or moderate, climates and research has suggested that it occurs in around 1% to 3% of the populations of countries.

Theories have centred on the hormone melatonin as the culprit for the cause of this disorder. Melatonin is a hormone which is released during the hours of darkness, and which seems to have a 'slowing' effect on the body, increasing feelings of tiredness and decreasing energy levels. Studies have shown that a lack of exposure to light can increase levels of this hormone in the body, possibly contributing to the symptoms of SAD (Wetterberg, 1999).

Melatonin is secreted by our pineal gland and has an important role in our sleep–waking patterns. This secretion is encouraged by the response to light detected by a part of the brain called the Suprachiasmic nucleus (SCN). It has been found that in some people the SCN triggers the release of melatonin even when no light is present. Thus it is possible that in sufferers of SAD, there is an oversensitive SCN, causing the release of melatonin in response to very slight changes in light. This is further supported by studies that have shown that treating sufferers with artificial light therapy, in which they are exposed to high levels of artificial ultraviolet light, can alleviate the symptoms considerably (Gitlin, 2002).

Some psychologists propose that early exposure to cortisol, even as early as exposure in the womb, can have an effect on specific neurone strength and production. Bennett (2008) stated that exposure to stress and the hormones that accompany a stress response can lead to regression (or loss) of synapses in an area of the brain called the prefrontal cortex. This process can often result in a malfunctioning of brain cells and can increase the activity of the HPA stress pathway, leading to an increase in the production of corticosteroids and cortisol. In turn, this can cause further regression of synapses and further malfunction of the HPA pathway, and so on. This view fits in with research which shows that the prefrontal cortex does not function normally in depressed people. Drevets (1998) stated that depression is associated with significantly lower levels of activation of the prefrontal cortex and used PET scans to support this statement.

Davidson et al (2002) indicated that there were several areas in the brain which seem to be functioning abnormally in sufferers of depression. One of the areas they highlighted was the hippocampus. The hippocampus seems to have a strong influence on the amount of adrenocorticotrophic hormone (ACTH) that humans produce; and the levels of ACTH have a direct effect on the individual's levels of cortisol. Brown et al (2004) found that patients who receive corticosteroid therapy (which increases the levels of corticosteroids) have smaller hippocampal volumes and a higher rate of depression, indicating that the hippocampus and related hormones may have some effect on depression.

It has been proposed that it may not be the direct effect of cortisol and CRH that is the true cause of depression, but that the abnormal release of cortisol and CRH might enlarge the adrenal glands. This increase in the levels of cortisol, it is argued, may result in a decrease in the production of serotonin and hence the proposition is that this decrease in the levels of serotonin is the real culprit for depressive symptoms (Roy et al, 1987).

Evolutionary theorists have also offered an explanation for why depression and the production of stress hormones could be linked. They believe that depression is an adaptive response to stress; it is nature's way of ensuring that inferior animals do not mate with superior animals of their species. For example, the male lion that has been defeated by a stronger male might enter a state that we recognise as including the symptoms of depression. This happens in order to prevent the animal from attempting to pursue unobtainable goals; to signal inferiority; and to stop aggressive behaviour from stronger, more dominant animals.

Evaluation of the neuroendocrine hypothesis

A great deal of research suggests that this theory has some application to an explanation of depression. It has been shown that effective antidepressants actually decrease the levels of CRH in sufferers. However, these findings should be treated with care, as it is difficult to assess whether the decrease in CRH is due to the direct effects of the anti-depressants, and that this is what causes a decrease in depression; or whether the anti-depressants cause the decrease in depression and it is the decrease in depression that is the cause of the decrease in CRH.

Similarly, it isn't possible to conclude whether an increase in cortisol or CRH or any abnormality in the HPA pathway is the cause of depression – as it could be that the depression is the cause of the abnormal functioning of the HPA axis, and the abnormally high production of CRH and cortisol.

Research has suggested that, with conditions whose treatment results in increased levels of glucocorticoids, (as is the case for Cushing's syndrome, mentioned earlier) the patient often experiences periods of depression. This theory would suggest that a person given treatment that reduces the levels of glucocorticoids should not experience depressive symptoms. However, there is opposite evidence from disorders in which the treatment does lower the levels of glucocorticoids, such as Addison's disease: it seems that a large proportion of patients receiving this treatment do actually experience symptoms of depression. Pariante (2007) stated that this seems to be "a cruel effort of nature to tease us". Abnormally high levels of glucocorticoids seem to be related to depression, as do low levels of glucocorticoids.

PSYCHOLOGICAL EXPLANATIONS

"You need to know about at least two psychological explanations for depression, and to be able to evaluate each of them."

COGNITIVE-BEHAVIOURAL EXPLANATION

"Learned helplessness" was first proposed by Seligman (1974). Originally a behavioural theory, it explains how people who experience constant failures in life can begin to feel that it is impossible to avoid them and therefore don't even try to – i.e. they learn to become helpless. Later versions of the theory took on more cognitive dimensions. Seligman first encountered this phenomenon by accident while studying the effects of inescapable electric shocks on dogs and their ability to learn. He forced dogs to experience electric shocks in an electrified cage and then observed the dogs in a situation in which they were put in a cage which allowed them to escape electric shock by jumping a short partition wall. Having learned to avoid electric shocks, the dogs were then faced with unavoidable electric shocks. Seligman found that the response of these dogs was to 'give up', make no further effort to escape, and simply sit and receive more shocks. Although this study was carried out on dogs, it does seem to relate to human behaviour, in that depressed humans also seem to be in a state of 'helplessness'.

It was also found that people who have developed this style of faulty thinking are unable to solve problems or get themselves out of the negative situation they are in when faced with problems in the future.

Further studies into learned helplessness have led to the inclusion of more explicit cognitive processes, especially the role of attribution. When we discuss attribution we are talking about who or what a person blames for a certain event. According to Abramson et al (1978), depressed people have three *attributional styles*.

> Firstly, they saw the dimension of *internal-external* attribution. An internal attribution means that the person blames themselves; an external one means that the person blames some other factor or cause.

> The second dimension relates to whether the cause of the failure is *stable* or *unstable*. If a person fails an exam, and assumes that they will always fail their exams, they make a stable attribution. If the cause is seen as a 'one-off' and unlikely to happen again, this is an unstable attribution. A person might fail their exam the first time but they will think, "I was having a bad day; it won't happen next time."

> Lastly, there is the dimension of a *global* or *specific* cause. Attributing a global cause means that a failure in one specific aspect of someone's life will be interpreted as a failure of their life in general, including a failure of all things they attempt in the future! Conversely, a person makes a specific attribution if they ascribe failure to the circumstances of a specific instance. They realise that their failure is only applicable to that particular situation and that it bears no relation to any other aspect of their life: for example, failing a driving test will not mean that a person is going to fail their psychology A2 exam!

Abramson et al proposed that a person who has a personality where they attribute failure to internal, stable and global factors will be the most likely to develop a state of learned helplessness and the subsequent depression likely to accompany it.

Evaluation of cognitive-behavioural explanation

The theory of learned helplessness was proposed after studying the effects of inescapable electric shocks on dogs. The problem with any study that has been carried out using animals is that we are unable to readily generalise these findings to humans. Humans have complex conscious thoughts while animals (as far as we know) don't, so it is impossible to state that humans would react in exactly the same way as animals do, in a similar situation.

Although the above point may well be accurate, studies have attempted to explore the effects of learned helplessness on humans. Hiroto and Seligman (1975) attempted to study learned helplessness in humans by putting them in a similar situation to the dogs in Seligman's (1974) study, except that they replaced the electric shocks with an extremely loud noise. Participants were put in a situation in which they were subjected to an uncontrollable and unexpected loud noise. Like the dogs, they were then put in a situation in which they could actually stop the loud noises by performing a particular task that would require some kind of problem solving. It was found that a group of individuals who had been subjected to the uncontrollable and unexpected loud noise condition took a lot longer to stop the noises in a second condition (where they could stop the noise by carrying out a problem-solving task) than a control group of participants who hadn't experienced the loud, uncontrollable and unexpected noise condition.

The learned helplessness theory of depression has been modified further by Abramson et al (1989). They emphasise the importance of the stable/ unstable and global/specific dimensions. They state that a person who has a strong tendency to attribute events to stable, global factors is likely to experience what they called "learned hopelessness". This is characterised by a feeling that nothing a person does, now or ever, will have an effect on the outcome of their life: it is having this type of personality that Abramson et al believe will eventually lead to depression.

PSYCHODYNAMIC EXPLANATION

There are many psychodynamic theories of depression, but they all have in common the view that the disorder is caused by a combination of unconscious forces and early childhood experiences. Freud's original theory relating to depression stated that the seed of depression was sown very early in a person's life, during the "oral stage" of psychosexual development, which occurs during the first year of a child's life. His view was that during this stage, a child relies on their caregiver to satisfy their needs, via oral stimulation. If a person is more than sufficiently gratified at this stage, this may lead to their becoming excessively dependent on other people in order to maintain their levels of self-esteem. If the person they depend upon is then taken away from them due to death, separation or simply a withdrawal of affection, the child attempts to get the affection and attention back by "introjecting" the personality (i.e. taking on the personality) of the parent whose affection they have lost. Freud also hypothesised that deep in our unconsciousness, unknown to us, are feelings of hatred and negativity towards the people we love: therefore, people who have taken on the personality of a loved one in that way begin to hate themselves. This develops into a cycle of self-abuse and self-blame and eventually can transform into depression.

Evaluation of psychodynamic explanation

As with most psychodynamic theories, this one has been criticised as being unscientific. It is merely the opinion of one man who proposed his theories nearly one hundred years ago. The theory was proposed using a sample that had poor population validity in that Freud predominantly studied middle-class, middle-aged, Viennese women. This is hardly a representative population.

Because these theories are so unscientific they don't easily lend themselves to scientific investigation, and therefore, it is very difficult to test them. This relates to a danger with Freud's theories in that they are what psychologists call 'unfalsifiable'. They can be neither proved nor disproved. In the case of Freud's theory of depression, he could propose that a person has been deprived of affection as a child, or even abused. If the client has no recollection of such occurrences a psychoanalyst could then give the argument that those memories have been repressed or that the client is in denial. There is no way to prove or disprove whether these processes are taking place.

Whilst there is evidence that some depressed people have experienced a loss of a parent (e.g. Bifulco et al, 1987), not all children who lose their parents through death, separation, etc. become depressed. This suggests that this theory may not be the only reason that people develop depression.

COGNITIVE EXPLANATION

> ASK AN EXAMINER
>
> *"The cognitive approach offers the most widely accepted psychological explanation of depression, and it also led to the development of the most successful psychological therapy. Make sure you know about the cognitive approach – it shows that you have a good level of understanding."*

The psychologists that propose a cognitive cause for depression believe that people experience this disorder because of the negative ways in which they think about events that occur in their lives. There are a number of cognitive theories but the most famous was proposed by Aaron Beck in 1967. This theory states that a negative outlook on life can lead to the symptoms of depression, and this negative outlook is the product of what he called a negative "cognitive triad" and "errors in logic".

The triad consists of negative thoughts of the self, thoughts of the present world and thoughts of the future. These components of the cognitive triad interact to influence the normal cognitive processes that we would use to shape our understanding of the world and our behavioural reactions to it. According to Beck, the cognitive triad of a depressed person would be very much different from that of a non-depressed person, and these differences in the way they think cause them to experience depression. For example, depressed people tend to view themselves, their environment, and the future in a negative, pessimistic light. As a result, depressed people tend to misinterpret facts in negative ways and blame themselves for any misfortune that occurs. This negative thinking and judgement style functions as a negative bias: it makes it easy for depressed people to see situations as being much worse than they really are, and increases the risk that such people will develop depressive symptoms in response to stressful situations.

"Errors in logic" contribute to this negative cognitive triad. People who suffer depression will often distort or exaggerate problems and the causes of these problems. This occurs when a sufferer focuses on some negative aspect of a situation while ignoring other, more positive information relating to the event. A number of different logical errors cause this to happen. Firstly, a person may indulge in what Beck calls *arbitrary inference*. This means that a sufferer is likely to jump to conclusions about why the event that has occurred has happened to them. In doing so they will use very little information, meaningless information or erroneous (wrong) information. Another error of logic that Beck referred to was *overgeneralisation*, meaning that sufferers of depression will often make vast, sweeping judgements about themselves based on a tiny event or occurrence. Beck also said that there was *magnification* and *minimisation* in faulty depressed thinking. Magnification could be best described by the term 'making a mountain out of a molehill', whereby a person might blow something out of all proportion. Minimisation is the tendency to under emphasise positive events. Beck also believed that sufferers of depression indulge in what he called *personalisation*. This occurs when a person feels they are to blame for certain events that have occurred in the lives of others.

In addition to cognitive distortions and biases, depressed thinking is also influenced by *negative schemata*. These are core negative beliefs, usually developed in early childhood, which are triggered when an individual encounters a situation which resembles that in which the schema was developed. So for example, many adults respond to situations with 'I can't do that' not because they really can't, but because the situation activates a schema, developed as a consequence of failure much earlier in life, of being inept.

Evaluation of cognitive explanation

There has been a huge amount of research surrounding the cognitive theories of depression and generally, they have arrived at quite a positive conclusion. For example, Reynolds and Salkovskis (1992) found that sufferers of depression do tend to indulge in a great deal more negative thinking than individuals who don't suffer from depression. They also experience a higher number and frequency of *intrusive negative thoughts* than individuals who don't suffer depression.

Evans et al (2005) completed a review of the cognitions of many sufferers of depression and found support for Beck's views of depression and the *negative cognitive triad* and the maladaptive views and cognitions that sufferers of depression hold. They also found that the more of these maladaptive cognitions that the sufferer holds, the more serious is their depression. Hammen and Krantz (1976) asked a group of depressed females and a group of females not suffering from depression to read paragraphs of situations in which females were encountering certain difficult or stressful situations. The women suffering from depression made significantly more errors in logic in their interpretations of the situations than the women who were not suffering from depression.

Whilst research has indeed been quite supportive of the cognitive approach to depression, the cognitive approach isn't really a totally comprehensive explanation. It shows that negative thinking and depression are very closely linked but it fails to outline whether these negative thoughts and cognitions are the cause of depression, or are merely the result of depression. It could be that another factor is responsible for the onset of depression and the negative cognitions are a result of the altered mood. For example, it could be that a neurochemical imbalance is affecting the way that the depressed person thinks.

THERAPIES FOR DEPRESSION

BIOLOGICAL THERAPIES

"You need to know about at least two biological therapies for depression, and to be able to evaluate each of them in terms of their effectiveness and appropriateness – be sure to learn this distinction and demonstrate your understanding of these ideas in the exam."

DRUG THERAPY

Anti-depressants are the main form of treatment in the Western world to control the symptoms of depression. They come in many forms. The first types of anti-depressants were known as *tricyclics*. They work by inhibiting the re-uptake of certain neurotransmitters like serotonin and noradrenaline in the brain. To explain how this works, try to picture what happens when a person breathes. When we breathe out we exhale carbon dioxide, some of which escapes our mouths and nostrils, but some of which we breathe back in. Our brain cells work a little like this: when they breathe out, they exhale certain neurotransmitters like serotonin and noradrenaline, each of which pass on a certain message to the next neurone, but they also breathe back in and just as we inhale some of the carbon dioxide we've breathed out, they inhale some of the neurotransmitters they breathed out. What tricyclic drugs do is stop the neurons breathing in (or re-uptaking) serotonin and noradrenaline: thus, more of these neurotransmitters are available to pass to the next neurone and the relevant messages passed on by these neurotransmitters are intensified.

Another class of anti-depressant drugs are called monoamine oxidase inhibitors (MAOIs). When they were first tested they were found to induce manic episodes in people by increasing the levels of serotonin, dopamine and noradrenaline in the brain. This was attributed to the effects that MAOIs have on these neurotransmitters. They work because they inhibit the production of monoamine oxidase which is an enzyme naturally produced by the human body in order to break down neurotransmitters. As these MAOIs stop monoamine oxidase being produced, there are not enough of them present to break down those neurotransmitters and so they stay in the sufferer's body for a greater length of time and therefore they have a greater effect.

Since the development of tricyclics and MAOIs there has been further progress in drug therapy: one such has been the development of Selective Serotonin Re-uptake Inhibitors (SSRIs). These work in much the same way as tricyclics; however, they target the re-uptake of serotonin only and therefore they have fewer side effects. They are also less likely to result in overdose or the sometimes fatal reactions that MAOIs and tricyclics have when combined with certain alcoholic drinks like red wine.

Appropriateness of drug therapy in the treatment of depression

The development of anti-depressant drugs was a revelation when they first appeared. They were thought of as a cheap, quick and easy alternative to the lengthy and expensive process of psychological therapy. However, it is becoming clear now that perhaps their very nature, in that they are very cheap, quick and easy, is their downfall. They are becoming over prescribed and merely treat the symptoms of depression while the cause of the depression survives.

It seems that one of the main problems of drugs as a treatment for depression is that scientists don't always understand why they work. There are many theories relating to how they increase levels of available serotonin or noradrenaline: however, until the exact neurochemical cause of depression is known, drugs will never be more than a preventative 'shot in the dark', chosen on the basis of a best guess in relation to why a person is suffering.

Another point relates to the fact that the effects of the drugs might not be the reason that sufferers' depression is eased. Further research into the effectiveness of tricyclic drugs has found that although these drugs are designed to increase the amount of serotonin in the brain, and they do so very effectively, this only lasts for the first several days after taking the drug, after which, the levels in the body return to normal. It has been found that tricyclic, and other anti-depressant drugs, tend to take between 7 and 14 days to begin to have an effect on a sufferer. It is likely that, by this time, the levels of serotonin in a person's body are back to what they were originally – which suggests that they couldn't possibly be having an anti-depressant effect on the sufferer.

As with all drugs, there is a huge problem with side effects. Common side effects of anti-depressants have been weight gain, anxiety, drowsiness, sexual dysfunction, among many others. Closely related to the problem of side effects is that of dependency. Most drug companies who develop and sell these drugs will state that there is no question of physiological dependency. What these companies don't state, however, is that there is likely to be a certain amount of psychological dependency (i.e. the person *thinks* they need the drugs). It is also the case that while it seems there is little evidence of physiological dependency, the body is still changed by taking the drugs, adapting to the presence of different levels of chemicals. Therefore, a person will need higher and higher doses of the anti-depressant to achieve the original effect of the drug.

Often, doctors will over-prescribe anti-depressants, making them a treatment which could be described as using 'a sledgehammer to crack a nut'. By this we mean that, in cases of mild to moderate depression, disrupting a delicate and well-balanced system with orally-taken chemicals on a long-term basis is always going to create problems.

Effectiveness

A large-scale study that compared the effects of cognitive therapy, interpersonal therapy, pharmacotherapy (drugs) and placebos was carried out in 1977 by the National Institute of Mental Health. Elkin et al (1996) outlined some of the most relevant findings in their review of the subject in 1996. They stated that they believed that this study showed that, on the whole, the use of drugs (imipramine in this case) was quicker than cognitive therapy, interpersonal therapy or the placebo and had an effect on those following this line of therapy within the first few weeks. However, it was also the case that the participants who had seen a significantly greater reduction in their depression symptoms were those who were suffering from severe MDD. Those who were suffering only mild depressive symptoms fared little better on the anti-depressants than the participants who were undergoing the other therapies, or even those taking a placebo.

Science is also questioning whether anti-depressants have much of an effect on sufferers at all. An interesting study was carried out in Canada by Moncrieff (2007) which led her to conclude the following:

I suggest that the term "anti-depressant" is a misnomer. The small advantage that anti-depressants have over placebos in RCTs (randomised control trials) is easily accounted for by non-specific psychological and pharmacologic effects. Other evidence does not confirm that anti-depressants have a clinically significant effect. We have no reason to suppose that any drugs can reverse the diverse problems that are labelled as depression. We need to emphasise other ways of responding to people who seek help from psychiatrists when they are distressed. The quest for the magic bullet for depression may be a wild goose chase.

Further research has shown that a healthy lifestyle, eating healthily and exercising, is just as effective in controlling the symptoms of depression as any anti-depressant drug.

ELECTRO CONVULSIVE THERAPY (ECT)

There are few topics as controversial in psychology as the use of electroconvulsive therapy in sufferers of mental disorders; and few issues polarise opinions in this way. The history of ECT is filled with accusations of barbarity and the treatment has often been labelled inhumane. While many believe it to be an amazing marvel of modern scientific treatment for mental illness, others see it as little more than unscientific cruelty.

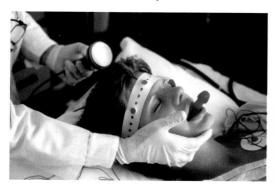

ECT has as its origins in observation in the 1930s that individuals with epilepsy do not seem to suffer mental illnesses. The conclusion was drawn that seizures somehow made epileptics immune to mental disorders. Logically therefore, by creating a seizure similar to an epileptic seizure, in a sufferer of a mental disorder, their symptoms could be alleviated or even cured. This treatment was first devised to treat individuals suffering from schizophrenia, but it seemed to have little or no effect. What the scientists did find though was that individuals who suffered schizophrenia co-morbid with depression showed improvement in their depression even though their schizophrenia symptoms remained.

The idea behind ECT was proposed by a Hungarian doctor called Meduna who induced seizures by the administration of the chemicals camfour or metraxol. The use of electricity to induce seizures in humans was first proposed by two Italian neurologists, Cerletti and Bini. They had been experimenting with the use of electric shocks to induce seizures in animals before this point. The technique has undergone many developments and is no longer as crude as it was when Cerletti and Bini first used it in 1937 to attempt to treat certain mental disorders. The technique involves a therapist purposely administering an electric shock to one side or hemisphere of a patient's brain via electrodes attached to the temples. The shock lasts less than a second and has a strength of about 800 milliamps (a TV, microwave and vacuum cleaner need a current of about 4 amps) and forces the patient to experience a seizure similar to that of an epileptic seizure. If a unilateral shock is administered (i.e. to one side of the brain), it is usually applied to the right hand side, to minimise any loss of language memory as the left hemisphere of our brain generally controls language. In order to make the procedure safer the patient is also anaesthetised, given a muscle relaxant (to ensure the patient doesn't break bones, tear tissue or tendons or dislocate limbs during the seizure) and a rubber gum shield is placed in the mouth to stop the patient biting their tongue off.

ECT used to be common, but since the development of safer drugs it has become less popular. In 1999, 11,340 patients received ECT treatment in England alone; 41% of these patients were over 65 years of age and 15% were given ECT without their consent (Johnstone, 2003). The patient can receive about six treatments, but with no more than two or three a week. ECT is generally used unilaterally nowadays (as this is usually the most effective with fewest side effects) and is employed in very severe cases of depression where drugs have not had an effect.

Appropriateness of ECT in the treatment of depression

One of the biggest problems with ECT is that it can result in some short-term memory loss after the treatment. If a bilateral shock is administered, this memory loss can include elements of language and so it can sometimes be very damaging to the patient. Rogers et al (1993) state that about one third of patients receiving ECT report the experience as "distressing" and say that they have experienced significant memory loss as a result of their treatment.

It is not entirely clear how ECT works. It is thought to improve symptoms by affecting neuro-transmitters in the brain, especially serotonin and noradrenaline. However, there is no convincing evidence that ECT causes damage to the brain. In fact, evidence suggests that ECT can be beneficial to brain cells, which has led to the suggestion that ECT might work by actually delaying or even reversing the damaging effects to the brain of depressive illness. Healy (1998) stated that there is no real evidence that ECT has any effect on the widely accepted primary causes of depression and "there is no known lowering of serotonin in depression". Some critics of ECT point out that it seems extremely unscientific to use a method of treatment of which so little is understood.

There are ethical concerns surrounding ECT. Johnston (1999) states that "it is not justifiable to give people something that harms their brains and gives them an epileptic fit". Many people have likened ECT to hitting a television when the picture isn't perfect, and have questioned whether it could be doing more harm than good. Another ethical issue concerns informed consent. This should be given by the patient prior to treatment, but the extent to which a severely depressed person is able to give informed consent is debatable.

An aspect of this treatment that seems most positive is that ECT seems to have fast acting effects. For those who suffer depression to the extent that they want to harm themselves, waiting six to eight weeks for drugs to take effect isn't always an option. Because of this, it has been proposed that ECT has saved many lives.

Effectiveness

It is estimated that 50–70% of severely depressed patients initially benefit from ECT, but further medical treatment is sometimes required, as treatment with ECT is often not sufficient to permanently 'cure' the symptoms of depression. Greenblatt et al (1964) reported that ECT is effective in eight out of ten cases of depression. However, the sources of the data gained by Greenblatt and colleagues have been questioned as they did not provide any information about the data on which these conclusions are based.

A study by Buchan et al (1992) has been reported to be one of the most comprehensive accounts of the effectiveness of ECT to date. They studied the effects of 'real' ECT with something psychologists call 'sham' or placebo ECT (this occurs when the patient has exactly the same experience as real ECT, including muscle relaxant and anaesthetic but is not given the electric shock). They found that ECT did have some beneficial effects, but only on sufferers of depression who had accompanying delusions, which is quite rare in depressives. For the 'average' depressed person, according to Buchan et al, ECT has few benefits.

Rey and Walter (1997) claim that up to 70% of patients with severe depression get relief with ECT. On the other hand, Schwartz (1995) says that 85% of those who are initially helped by ECT relapse, so any benefits can be short-lived. This is supported by Breggin (1997) who found that ECT may have some benefits to certain patients, but that these benefits do not generally last for more than four weeks.

However it works, the research does actually indicate that ECT is successful for some individuals with depression, although it is often the last resort. When regular treatments like drugs don't have an effect on sufferers of depression, this might be the only course of action to take. For a small number of cases then, ECT remains a useful therapeutic tool.

PSYCHOLOGICAL THERAPIES

"You need to know about at least two psychological therapies for depression, and to be able to evaluate each of them in terms of their effectiveness and appropriateness – be sure to learn this distinction and demonstrate your understanding of these terms in the exam."

COGNITIVE-BEHAVIOURAL THERAPY

Cognitive-behavioural therapy (CBT) aims to address and change a sufferer's dysfunctional emotions, thought processes (cognitions) and the behaviours that result. CBT uses theories proposed by the behaviourist approach and also the cognitive approach. While behaviourist therapies like systematic desensitisation and the token economy seemed to be having a degree of success in treating some forms of mental disorder, they failed to make a big impact on other areas. For example, behaviourist therapies had little or no effect on the disorder of MDD. This may be because the behavioural approach tended to overlook the influence of a person's cognitions and thought processes in the development of many psychological problems. According to Meichenbaum (1977) most mental disorders are the product of abnormal thoughts and feelings. Since our behaviour is largely the product of our thoughts and feelings, it would be logical to find a way of adapting or changing these thoughts and feelings so that our subsequent behaviour is affected for the better also.

There are a number of forms of CBT, one of the most common being Rational-Emotive Therapy, first proposed by Albert Ellis in 1962. This therapy states that dysfunctional behaviour and emotional distress is the result of irrational thoughts. Ellis stated that irrational thoughts lead to an irrational "internal dialogue", and that this will go on to produce irrational behaviour and so these should be replaced with more rational thoughts and cognitions. A later and now more widespread therapy was developed by Aaron Beck. This proposes that mental disorders are primarily due to *errors of logic* and therefore addressing these will have an effect on behaviour.

Beck's therapy, in common with other cognitive-behavioural approaches, is relatively brief, usually lasting no more than about 20 sessions. CBT generally begins by examining the thought processes that someone who suffers from a mental disorder is experiencing. Many individuals have certain emotionally self-defeating beliefs such as "I must be excellent at absolutely everything, otherwise I am worthless!" After some of these cognitions are uncovered, they are then challenged and addressed. For example, in the case of the previous statement "I must be excellent at absolutely everything, otherwise I am worthless!" the individual will be challenged to explain *why* not excelling at everything makes them a worthless person. A person will be required to practise certain optimistic statements which challenge their present cognitions and over time these challenges result in a person's cognitions changing, leading to a change in their dysfunctional behaviour.

Appropriateness of CBT in the treatment of depression

CBT is not an overnight cure. It might take months to have any success in treating a person's depression, and so a person needs to weigh up the costs and the benefits before beginning their treatment. An important aspect of this cost-benefit analysis is the motivation that a sufferer has to get better. As CBT often takes time to make any sort of improvement, the sufferer has to ask themselves if they have the motivation to start and continue with the treatment. A symptom of depression is a total lack of motivation and goal orientated behaviour, and so a sufferer may not feel that they want to embark on such a treatment.

As we mentioned above, CBT is a treatment that takes place over a length of time. As well as the emotional costs and benefits, financial costs and benefits need to be considered. The treatment is not as cost-effective as many others, such as anti-depressants, and whilst it is becoming more common, it is not always available free on the NHS.

Unlike some other forms of treatment, CBT has no real side effects or withdrawal symptoms, and causes no real physical change in a person. Thus, there are no issues of dependency or tolerance, as there are in drug treatments. Therefore, when a person feels as if they don't need any more treatment, they can, if they like, stop treatment immediately, although this is discouraged. With drug treatment, on the other hand, the physical effects are well documented, meaning a person would be unable to stop that course of treatment with immediate effect and would have to be 'weaned' off anti-depressants gradually.

Unlike anti-depressants or ECT, CBT doesn't just deal with the symptoms of depression but with the actual cause. It can make a real change in a person's outlook and behaviour and therefore it helps them deal with the problems they face every day, enabling them to adapt to stressful situations and problems in a way that drugs and ECT could never achieve.

Effectiveness

Many studies, including one by Rush et al (1977), have shown that CBT is at least as effective at treating depression as anti-depressants. Other studies have demonstrated that CBT is significantly superior to anti-depressant drug treatments, especially over periods of more than a year (Blackburn and Moorhead, 2000).

Derubeis et al (2005) studied three groups of participants who were all sufferers of depression. Group one were treated with CBT, group two were treated with anti-depressants and group three were designated the placebo group (they were given a pill that did nothing). After 8 weeks the researchers found an improvement in 43% of the CBT group and an improvement of 50% in the anti-depressant group while only 25% of the placebo group experienced an improvement. Furthermore, they found that these improvements were maintained over the next 16 weeks.

One of the problems of treating depression with anti-depressants is that the relapse rate is quite high. It has been estimated that 50% of people who are helped by medication experience depression again within two years. CBT seems to have a long-term benefit however, with relatively low rates of relapse (Hensley et al, 2004).

Evans et al (1992) found that CBT was at least as effective as anti-depressant drugs in the treatment of depression and in preventing a relapse in sufferers over a two-year period. However, the most effective method of treatment according to Kupfer and Frank (2001) is a combination of CBT and anti-depressants.

PSYCHOANALYTIC THERAPY

Psychoanalytic therapy was developed by Freud in the late 1800s. The aim of the therapy is to bring to consciousness repressed wishes and painful memories from childhood, in the process making the client aware of the unconscious causes for their symptoms. This should make the person cope better with their inner conflicts. The process of therapy involves the client working with a therapist in the safety and security of a consulting room to uncover repressed memories. Several techniques are used for this:

Free association

This involves the client talking openly without holding anything back. The ego will attempt to censor what is said by using ego defence mechanisms. It is hoped that a free flow of thoughts and feelings will allow previously unconscious thoughts to slip through.

Dream analysis

This is where dreams related by the client are interpreted. For Freud, dream content could have meaning since it is through dreams that unconscious thoughts are expressed more freely. He suggested that the manifest content of dreams (that is, the literal dream events as reported) often concealed a latent content (the actual meaning of the dream). The important aspects of a dream do not appear literally then but in a symbolical form. The therapist works with the client to interpret the significance of the dreams.

Word association

Whilst in a relaxed state, the client listens to a list of words spoken one at a time by the therapist and has to reply with whatever comes to mind. The hope is that the client responds occasionally with unexpected words and associations, hesitations and silences. These might indicate important unconscious processes which can then be explored by the therapist.

Appropriateness of psychodynamic therapy in the treatment of depression

Psychodynamic therapy is expensive and takes place over a long period of time. Some key clinical characteristics of depression such as a sense of helplessness, low motivation, self-esteem and apathy make it very unlikely that a depressed person would 'last the course'. Since psychoanalysis depends for its success on the client wanting to know where their illness has come from, a depressed person who has little or no interest in the causes of their problem is unlikely to benefit from analysis.

Concerns have been expressed about the appropriateness of using psychodynamic therapy with depressed individuals. Because depressed people tend towards dependency on others, the nature of the client/therapist relationship (which some critics comment is one of dependency) may be unsuitable and foster further (perhaps inappropriate) dependency.

Effectiveness

It has been claimed that the likelihood of recovering from a mental disorder is less with psychoanalytic treatment than without. In a classic critique of psychoanalytic therapy, Eysenck (1952) gathered evidence from outcome studies which showed that people on a waiting list for therapy were more likely to recover spontaneously from their symptoms than those actually receiving treatment. He compared the results of 24 studies, to see if psychoanalysis was more likely than other forms of therapy to result in positive mental health changes. He found that whilst patients did recover with psychoanalysis, the rate was comparable to that experienced without treatment, and that psychoanalysis was less effective than behavioural therapies. For Eysenck, the conclusion was quite clear – psychoanalysis does not work. It has since been suggested however that Eysenck was rather selective in the choice and analysis of his data. Bergin (1971) re-examined Eysenck's data and reached the opposite conclusion – whilst some people do indeed spontaneously recover without treatment (as they are prone to do with many illnesses), psychoanalysis was over twice as effective as no treatment at all.

According to Grünbaum (1993), any apparent benefits of psychoanalysis are the result of unintended placebo effects. Basically, it is the action of being treated itself that results in improvement, not actually *what* the psychoanalyst does, that leads to improvement. The reason why psychoanalysis might lead to a 'cure' is that the client is in a powerful relationship with the therapist. Part of the power of a therapist is that they can never be wrong: for example, should the patient challenge the therapist then their challenging behaviour could be interpreted as just another symptom of their disorder. This means that the client is under strong pressure to conform to the therapist's expectations. Grünbaum also points out that the very earliest evidence for effectiveness of psychoanalysis is flawed. Freud himself only ever presented 12 case studies of psychoanalysis for public scrutiny, and none of these was fully evaluated in terms of outcomes and benefits to the client.

Traditional forms of psychoanalysis have not generally been considered effective treatments for depression. However, research into the success of more modern forms of the therapy has been more positive in this regard. Elkin et al (1989) for example found that a more modern form of psychoanalysis called interpersonal psychodynamic therapy (IPT) compared favourably to cognitive-behavioural therapy. Leichsenring (2001) conducted a meta-analysis to compare the effectiveness of short-term psychodynamic psychotherapy (STPP) and CBT. Only studies with more than 13 therapy sessions were included (as this was considered the point at which this form of therapy starts to show beneficial effects). Leichsenring found no significant difference in the effectiveness of these two methods for treating depression.

ANXIETY DISORDERS – PHOBIA

Phobia belongs to the family of disorders known as anxiety disorder. Other types of anxiety disorder include generalised anxiety disorder, obsessive compulsive disorder, panic disorder and post-traumatic stress disorder, and these share many of their symptoms with phobia.

"Phobia is one of a number of disorders which all have something in common – anxiety. We've included a general bit of background on anxiety disorders to help put phobic disorder into some kind of context."

The DSM-IV and ICD – 10 are diagnostic manuals used by clinicians that contain lists of symptoms and behaviour pertaining to a wide range of psychological disorders. A number of anxiety disorders are outlined and classified. In general, anxiety disorders are characterised by the experience of pathological or abnormal fear or anxiety. They are among the most common forms of mental disorder experienced in Western culture, with a large number of sufferers in the UK and America. Kessler et al (2005) proposed that around 18% of individuals living in America will experience some form of anxiety disorder in their lifetime. Fear, stress and anxiety are all very healthy, useful and common feelings in humans and animals. However, when we lose control of these feelings it can have a serious impact on our lives. Anxiety disorders are classified as *neuroses*: these are a large group of disorders that cause intense distress. They are characterised by a patient's insight into their problem (they know their actions are not healthy), and generally involve feelings of unrealistic anxiety.

THE CLINICAL CHARACTERISTICS OF PHOBIAS

The term phobia (from the ancient Greek 'phobos', meaning fear) is used a lot in everyday language. People complain of a phobia of spiders or wasps, or of speaking in public. There is a difference however between being really scared of something and having a phobia of it. A fear turns into a phobia when a person's life and routine is affected by overwhelming anxiety that disrupts their everyday normal functioning. A phobia can be defined as "an excessive, unreasonable, persistent fear triggered by a specific object or situation" (Neale, 2008). Phobias may be expressed as a fear of certain situations, activities, things, or people. The main characteristic of a phobia is that it is totally irrational: in other words there is no need to be afraid of the object or situation which the sufferer fears. Phobias cause an intense fear response that is persistent and rarely disappears without treatment. Another serious symptom that accompanies this disorder is the excessive and unreasonable desire to avoid the feared subject or

ANXIETY DISORDERS	
DISORDER	**DESCRIPTION**
Generalised anxiety disorder	Persistent worry/anxiety about minor things, to the extent that a person's life is disrupted by their behaviour.
Phobias (including specific phobias and social phobias)	Intense and irrational fear of an object or situation.
Obsessive compulsive disorder	Anxiety-provoking thoughts that are uncontrollable and persistent, followed by certain rituals or behaviours that a person has to perform in order to satisfy their feelings of anxiety.
Panic disorder	Sudden attack of many different anxiety based symptoms like palpitations, shortness of breath, nausea. These can be referred to as panic attacks..
Post-traumatic stress disorder	An extreme response to a traumatic event which provokes anxiety, avoidance of situations and objects, and a numbing of emotion. It has been called many things over the years from 'shell shock' to 'battle fatigue'.

Some of the common anxiety disorders and their main symptoms.

situation. It is estimated that about 6% to 7 % of the population suffer from phobias. Some are not so disruptive that a person can't get on with life in a relatively normal way. Others however are very disabling.

"Be prepared to describe the clinical characteriscs of phobia in an exam. You don't need loads of detail – the question won't be worth many marks if asked and you can get them all with a short but accurate response."

According to DSM-IV, there are three main types of phobia: specific phobias, social phobias and agoraphobia.

1. **Specific phobias** are intense and irrational fears of particular objects or situations. They are often divided into four categories:

    Natural environment type (a fear of something naturally occurring in the environment like water or heights)

    Animal type (a commonly occurring phobia – for example the fear of spiders)

    Situational type (a fear of particular situations or events: for example many people have a fear of flying)

    Medical type (fear of medical procedures and illnesses – for example blood-injection-injury phobia).

The fear of spiders (or arachnophobia) is an example of a specific phobia.

2. **Social phobia** is the irrational fear of performing some kind of action in the presence of others. Being nervous in front of others is quite normal and doesn't necessarily indicate a social phobia. Some people with this phobia however will have an irrational fear about performing the most mundane tasks in front of other people, things that most others would not think twice about doing. These actions might include using public transport, eating and drinking – all causing so much anxiety that these actions are avoided at all costs. Most sufferers fear only specific social situations, although those with what is known as generalised social phobia have this irrational fear of most social encounters.

3. **Agoraphobia** is an intense and irrational fear of being incapacitated by a panic attack in a situation where escape would be difficult or embarrassing, or where help would be unavailable. As a result of this fear, sufferers avoid public and unfamiliar places. In extreme cases, they confine themselves to a 'safe place', typically their home. Although the least frequent of the three classes of the condition, agoraphobia is the most commonly seen by clinical psychologists since it has such a debilitating effect on the life of the sufferer and their family.

ISSUES SURROUNDING THE CLASSIFICATION AND DIAGNOSIS OF PHOBIA

"You will have studied and discussed issues surrounding the definitions of abnormality at AS level and so you should be aware of some of the problems and pitfalls that are associated with the process of defining what is normal and what is abnormal. "

The classification of mental disorders started with Emil Kraepelin. It was he who first started to see similarities in the symptoms of the patients he was treating, and to group them into some of the disorders that we recognise to this day. For example, he was the first to group together patients suffering from "dementia praecox" (early dementia) in a set of symptoms that we now regard as being schizophrenic. Due to the foundations laid in the late 19th century by pioneers like Kraepelin we now have much more sophisticated ways of diagnosing mental disorders. These modern systems are constantly evolving to include new discoveries. The main tools used for the diagnosis of mental disorders that we have now are called the DSM-IV criteria. This stands for the Diagnostic and Statistical Manual of Mental Disorders. IV means it's the 4th edition, published in 1994. The DSM is produced by the American Psychiatric Association and is the diagnostic tool most widely used in the psychiatric institutions around the world. Another of the commonly used diagnostic tools is the section relating to mental disorders in the International Statistical Classification of Diseases and Related Health Problems (most commonly known by the abbreviation ICD) which is produced by the World Health Organisation. The ICD is currently in its 10th edition (ICD – 10). There is very little difference between the two methods of diagnosis and they are often used alongside each other: however, it may be that the ICD is used in a wider variety of countries.

Classifying disorders into groups and types makes it easier for problems to be identified. Diagnosing a mental disorder is almost always done using the DSM-IV and the ICD – 10 as it is a fast and easy way to break down symptoms, treatments and prognoses of disorders. Informing a colleague that someone suffers from phobia conveys a vast amount of information in a very short space of time because of the shared understanding provided by using the same diagnostic tool. However, there is a risk in using this professional 'jargon', in that explaining a particular disorder to a sufferer or loved one becomes difficult and can result in confusion and anxiety.

It was originally hoped that the use of diagnostic tools could provide mental health professionals with a standardised method of recognising mental disorders so that the individual biases and personalities of practitioners would not have an effect on the diagnosis. This hasn't proved to be entirely the case unfortunately. It seems that, however clearly the symptoms of phobias are set out, an individual's behaviour is always open to some interpretation. One person could view a certain action in one way while another person could interpret it in an entirely different manner.

It is the case that, as with other illnesses, we have a tendency to put those suffering a mental illness into a category and fail to recognise that there are varying degrees to which a person may be experiencing that disorder. It is tempting to label a person as a 'sufferer of phobic disorder' or a 'sufferer of agoraphobia' while not really knowing the extent to which they are suffering that phobia and how much it is affecting their life. Consequently, the process of deciding what are abnormal disorders and what are not is also quite subjective: it is usually left to the acumen of the individual health professional to decide. Thus the beliefs and biases of some might mean the unnecessary labelling of millions of people as suffering from a mental disorder. For instance it is hard to know where to draw the line between what is a rational fear and what is irrational, and more specifically what is a fear and what is a true phobia. A child with a phobia of dogs may be seen as far more rational than a grown man with a phobia of buttons. Although the child may display extreme anxiety when in the presence of dogs, the fact that the dog may pose a threat to the child cannot be dismissed. While the DSM and ICD classify the various mental disorders into groups, and assist in diagnosing phobias, the diagnosis is ultimately left to the individual psychiatrist or clinical psychologist. These manuals are just 'diagnostic tools' and the real work is carried out by the psychiatrist. This leaves the diagnosis of the various disorders open to a great deal of criticism.

"You need to know about reliability and validity of classification and diagnosis – make sure you learn about them and mention them in any examination answer on classification and diagnosis."

The main issues surrounding the diagnosis of mental disorders centre on the reliability and validity of the diagnoses. When we talk about the reliability of the diagnostic tools we generally mean inter-rater reliability: this concerns the extent to which two or more diagnosticians would arrive at the same conclusions when faced with exactly the same individual. Many mental health professionals have raised concerns about the reliability of the diagnosis of mental disorders in our society and studies have shown that inter-rater reliability is actually quite low. In a now famous study, Beck et al (1961) looked at the inter-rater reliability between two psychiatrists when considering the cases of 154 patients. It was found that inter-rater reliability was as low as 54%, meaning their diagnoses only agreed with each other for 54% of the 154 individuals.

There may have been many different reasons for this. For example, it seems that in many of the 154 cases, the patients gave different information to the two diagnosticians. This illustrates how difficult it is to gain information from patients much of the time. It is true that diagnosticians will have the medical records of patients available to them: however, a true diagnosis can never really be made until the patient is clinically interviewed. This means that health professional will be relying on retrospective data, given by a person whose ability to recall much relevant information is unpredictable – and who may even be exaggerating the truth or blatantly lying!

Another point that seems especially relevant in today's economic climate is the limited time and resources that are available to many professionals working in the National Health Service. It is clear that diagnoses are often made by professionals who are rushed, and preoccupied with admitting only the most serious cases in order to safeguard the resources of the institutions they are working for. Meehl (1977) suggests that mental health professionals should be able to count on the total reliability of the diagnostic tools they have at their disposal if they:

» paid close attention to medical records;

» were serious about the process of diagnosis;

» took account of the very thorough descriptions presented by the major classificatory systems;

» considered all the evidence presented to them.

In a perfect world, all these things might happen, but as already stated, it is just not possible in today's health system, with an emphasis on seeing as many patients as possible.

The issue of validity has already been mentioned in relation to the diagnosis of mental disorders. When we question the validity of diagnoses, we are asking about the extent to which our system of classification and diagnosis is reflecting the true nature of the problems the patient is suffering; the prognosis (the course that the disorder is expected to take); and the extent to which the proposed treatments will be successful. Some commentators have highlighted the amount that many disorders described in the diagnostic manuals actually overlap. There seems to be a growing trend in clinical psychology to diagnose patients as suffering from 'co-morbid' disorders (i.e. disorders that often seem to occur together). It may be that many individuals do not neatly fit into the categories that have been created. Instead of acknowledging that the methods by which diagnostic decisions are arrived at are lacking validity, clinicians diagnose two separate disorders.

Defining anxiety disorders may seem straightforward, and in a way it is. They are a type of what psychologists call neurotic disorders. These are characterised by the fact that sufferers keep a hold on reality: thus they realise that they have a problem, and that their behaviour isn't productive or helpful to them or anyone else. A feature of anxiety disorders, however, is high co-morbidity, so that a person will often suffer from more than one such disorder at the same time. This is probably because the symptoms for all anxiety disorders are very similar, in that they all involve the physical symptoms of heightened anxiety, like a racing heartbeat, high blood pressure, sweating, nausea, etc. Also, there are similar cognitive factors that may be identified as being the cause, or part of the cause, of many different anxiety disorders. For example, a feeling that a person has a loss of control of a particular situation could be the cause of panic disorder, a phobia or generalised anxiety disorder.

There is huge debate surrounding the issue of 'labelling' when it comes to classifying and diagnosing mental disorders. Diagnosing someone with a disorder means that we are labelling them, and these labels are extremely hard to remove. For example, someone who has suffered from agoraphobia will always have the label of 'agoraphobic', even if they haven't suffered a symptom in a long time. This is the case to some degree with all mental disorders, in that a person who has suffered such a disorder at any time has to disclose that information in situations like job applications, or they could face formal action. For example, an employee who had not disclosed this information at interview could be dismissed. Unlike the experience of having had influenza for instance, a label such as 'agoraphobic' stays with a person.

One of the biggest controversies of recent times in relation to the diagnosis and classification of mental disorders surrounds the issue of cultural relativism. Sections of the newer versions of the DSM and ICD attempt to highlight and deal with the issue of differences between subcultures within our societies and between different cultures around the world. Davison and Neale (1994) explain that in Asian cultures, a person experiencing some emotional turmoil is praised and rewarded if they show no expression of their emotions. In certain Arabic cultures however, the outpouring of public emotion is understood and often encouraged. Without this knowledge, an individual displaying overt emotional behaviour in a Western culture might be regarded as abnormal in that context.

To diagnose a mental disorder, some interaction between a health professional and the potential patient must take place. This raises another problem in terms of culture. The clinician might not speak the same language as the person they are attempting to diagnose and therefore any interaction between clinician and patient should be done using a translator: otherwise the patient and diagnostician risk experiencing a serious lack of understanding because of these language difficulties. The term 'lost in translation' is very appropriate in this situation. The symptoms of mental illness are very rarely so clear that no discussion with the sufferer is necessary and therefore the sufferer will need to be able to describe their symptoms in as much detail as possible. If an individual's symptoms are not being described sufficiently clearly, there is a danger of a misdiagnosis – and this can lead to inappropriate treatment or no treatment at all.

CAUSES OF PHOBIA

BIOLOGICAL EXPLANATIONS

"*You need to know about at least two biological explanations for phobia, and to be able to evaluate each of them.*"

GENETIC EXPLANATIONS

One way to investigate whether phobias are genetic in origin is to study their incidence in identical twins. Since identical twins are genetically the same, when one twin shows the phobia then logically, if it is entirely genetic, the other twin should have the phobia too. Kendler et al (1992) found that genetically identical (or monozygotic) twins are much more likely to both have a specific phobia than non-genetically identical or dizygotic twins. This suggests that there is some genetic factor involved in the development of phobia. It has been found that identical twins that are reared apart, in different families and environments, sometimes develop the same phobias – for example, one pair independently becoming claustrophobic (Eckert et al, 1981).

Family studies have also been conducted. Fyer et al (1995) for example found that the incidence of a first degree relative of someone with a social or specific phobia also having the same phobia was a lot higher than could be expected by chance in the general population.

Some of the best evidence for genetic involvement comes from the study of blood-injection-injury phobia. The normal physiological response to a fearful situation involves activation of the autonomic nervous system, experienced as such things as increased heart rate and blood pressure. Blood pressure cannot be allowed to rise as this would be dangerous to the organism, so the *sinoaortic baroreflex arc* acts to counteract this. The baroreflex is a natural mechanism which the body uses to compensate for sudden increases in blood pressure. Activation of this baroreflex lowers blood pressure. A strong response causes low blood pressure in the head, resulting in a *vasovagal syncope* (or 'swoon'). The interesting thing about vasovagal syncope is that the tendency to overcompensate seems to be inherited. The phobia itself develops over the possibility of having this 'fainting' response in situations which we are naturally inclined to respond to with increased blood pressure – those involving gore and possible personal injury. Öst (1992) argues that this disorder is strongly familial. In examining families of people with blood-injection-injury phobia he found that, in 25 blood phobics, 64% had at least one first-degree relative (i.e. parent or sibling) with blood phobia. This is much higher than the occurrence of a blood-injection-injury phobia in the general population (around 3% to 4%). Öst suggests that, in addition to inheriting a strong vasovagal response that makes them susceptible to fainting, the patients with blood phobia also inherit a biological vulnerability to experiencing anxiety (e.g., perhaps they have inherited autonomic lability – that is, their arousal levels are susceptible to rapid change).

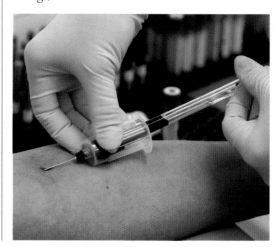

There is a theory that states that a particular genetic trait called inhibition (similar to shyness) makes it more likely that a phobia will be passed on to a person's offspring. Kagan and Snidman (1990) showed that some children as young as 4 months old were more likely than others to cry when they were exposed to certain toys or other stimuli. Further support comes from a study by Rosenbaum et al (1991). They hypothesised that young offspring of parents with panic disorder and agoraphobia were more likely to display inhibition (i.e. to show high stress reactions and withdrawal) in unfamiliar or challenging situations. A longitudinal study was conducted in children from the age of 21 months to 7 years. Some of these children were identified as inhibited, and others that were considered 'normal' were used as the control. Psychiatric assessments were carried out on parents and siblings of all the children. The parents of the children categorised as inhibited were twice as likely to demonstrate symptoms of anxiety disorders and social phobia compared with the parents of the control group. It could be this inherited inhibition that may influence the later development of phobias. This was supported by the work of Biederman et al (1990) who found that infants who displayed this trait of inhibition were more than five times more likely to develop a phobia than children who were considered 'uninhibited'.

Evaluation of genetic explanations

Most family studies show that the relatives of those with phobias are more likely to suffer phobias compared with relatives of non-phobic controls. However, there are methodological problems with family studies. The main problem is that in most instances family members share the same environment and so therefore could have learned the behaviour. Whilst twin studies offer more reliable data to test the genetic hypothesis, unfortunately very few have been conducted. The lack of research effort may be an indication that there is very little support for the genetic transmittance of anxiety disorders.

Kendler et al (1992) interviewed 722 female twins with a lifetime history of phobia. They found that MZ twins had significantly lower rates of agoraphobia than DZ twins, which goes against the genetic theory. This may demonstrate the 'buffering' effect of the close emotional bond between MZ twins.

Social inhibition may well be inherited: however, it is also possible that it could be the result of exposure to certain stimuli or chemicals whilst in the uterus or even in the environment after being born.

Although there does seem to be a genetic influence in relation to certain phobias, it can not be concluded that the genetic influence is the only cause of these phobias, as when a study is carried out on families, genes are not the only thing that the individuals in the study have in common. They will also have their environments in common as they will, more than likely, have been raised in the same house and shared similar experiences.

With blood-injection-injury phobia, whilst an over-reactive baroreflex mechanism might provide conditions for a predisposition towards acquiring the phobia, other conditions have also to be in place for the phobia to develop. For example, the sufferer must probably at first encounter a gore scenario (in reality or film) during which the association between this stimulus and the unpleasantness of fainting is made. It seems that, to cause blood-injection-injury phobia, a complex interaction must occur between behavioural and biological factors. It can probably be brought on by an overactive vasovagal reaction due to a particularly sensitive baroreflex mechanism, but can also be the result of conditioning factors. Also, there are many people with severe syncope reaction tendencies who do not develop phobias, and likewise people who develop the phobia when they have little or no fainting reaction.

NEUROANATOMICAL EXPLANATION

These explanations state that phobias are due to areas in the brain that function differently in some people. These areas may have more or fewer neurons or be structurally different in other ways, or may be more or less active than other areas.

Recent research also indicates that an area of the limbic system in the brain seems to be implicated in the formation of phobic reactions. Psychologists have known for a long time that the amygdala seems to be responsible for emotional, fearful and stressful responses, and especially associations made between the environment and emotions in humans. It may be that malfunction in this part of the brain is particularly responsible for the formation of phobias.

Neuroscientists are also finding that other biological factors may also be involved in phobias, such as greater blood flow and metabolism in the right than in the left hemisphere of the brain. Kagan and Snidman (2000) proposed that 20% of children are born with a temperament that predisposes them to overreact in unfamiliar situations as infants. This fearful reaction continues through childhood and by adolescence a third will have developed serious social anxiety. The researchers found that these adolescents were more likely to have one or more of the following biological features: a more reactive cardiovascular system; more activity in the right cortical region of the brain than the left; and a narrower facial skeleton.

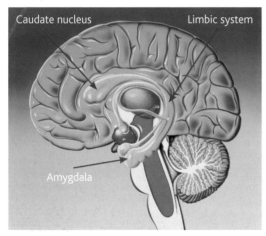

Diagram of the cross-section of the brain showing the limbic system.

Evaluation of neuroanatomical explanation

In phobia, there is support for a role of limbic structures (the limbic system is a more 'basic' part of our brain in evolutionary terms, responsible for behaviours we share with lower animal species, especially the animal instincts like our fight or flight response). Rauch et al (1995) used positron emission tomography (PET) to examine cerebral blood flow in response to specific phobias. They found that there was an increased amount of blood flow to areas of the brain known as paralimbic structures. This suggests that these structures may play a part in the function and development of phobias. Also, Fredrikson et al (1995) used PET scans to compare brain reactions in phobic and non-phobic participants. They found that an area of the brain commonly associated with phobias and other anxiety disorders, the basal ganglia, was not activated more by phobic stimulation. However, the thalamus always reacted to phobic, but not aversive or neutral, stimulation. They concluded that the thalamus could be implicated in the phobia reaction. Not all research has produced data to support this, however. Similar research carried out by Mountz et al (1989) found that there was no real significant difference in cerebral blood flow in individuals with a phobia in a calm state or

a phobic state and there were no real differences between the cerebral blood flows of phobic and non-phobic participants.

Another part of the brain that research has indicated may influence the development of phobias is the orbitofrontal cortex (OFC). Research by Schienle et al (2007) showed that changes were observed in the activity in the medial (middle) part of the OFC before and after a person with a specific phobia underwent a course of cognitive-behavioural therapy to reduce their phobia. They suggested that this indicates that the OFC plays a part in the appraisal of the phobia object or situation as being a threat.

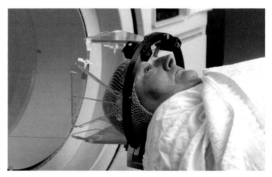

Patient about to undergo a brain scan.

ASK AN EXAMINER

"Remember, you can use alternative psychological explanations as evaluation of biological explanations!"

NEUROCHEMICAL EXPLANATIONS

There may be areas in the brain that are more or less active, or levels of neurotransmitters that are higher or lower, in the brains of phobics compared with other individuals. There are several factors which indicate that there may be a neurochemical cause of phobia, or neurochemicals may at least contribute to them. Stein (1998) found that individuals who display the symptoms of a phobia seem to have abnormal levels of the neurotransmitters serotonin and dopamine. This may be related to the increased numbers of serotonin and dopamine pathways in the limbic system.

Individuals who suffer from phobias also seem to have low levels of a neurotransmitter called gamma aminobutyric acid (GABA) which seems to act like a natural calming agent in the brain, reducing brain activity and lessening physiological arousal. The fact that sufferers of phobias have less GABA in their systems might increase their physiological arousal, and this may in turn cause these individuals to be more reactive to anxiety-provoking objects or situations, making them more likely to develop a phobia.

Evaluation of neurochemical explanations

The fact that symptoms of phobia can be alleviated using drug therapy suggests that there is indeed at least a contribution of neurochemistry in phobia. Drugs which increase levels of GABA or mimic its effects in the brain are successful anxiolytics (anxiety-reducing drugs) for some people.

That serotonin and dopamine are involved in phobia is demonstrated by the result of inhibiting the production of monoamine oxidase, which is an enzyme that breaks down serotonin and dopamine molecules in the brain. As serotonin and dopamine levels increase in consequence of drugs which have this effect, symptoms of phobia often reduce.

PREPAREDNESS THEORY

It has been suggested that there is an innate predisposition to anxiety. Many people have phobias concerning spiders, enclosed spaces, rats, height etc. which pose no real threat to life. Few people however have phobias about travelling at fast speeds in a car, which does pose a realistic threat to life. Preparedness theory proposes that humans have been 'prepared' to be fearful of things which in our distant past were of significant danger. Evolution may have favoured 'anxious genes' as anxiety may have increased our distant ancestors' chance of survival.

We are more likely to be afraid of some animals than others.

Another interesting point to make is that a phobia of cars is virtually non-existent, and yet, almost everyone has experienced or witnessed a car accident in which someone has been injured. Seligman (1971) stated that it may be that people are inherently "prepared" to learn certain phobias. For millions of years people who quickly learned to avoid snakes, heights, and lightning probably had a good chance to survive and to pass their genes on to their offspring. We have not had enough

time to evolve a tendency to fear cars and guns, even though they are far more dangerous to our survival in modern society.

Evaluation of preparedness theory

Seligman (1971) found that people were a lot more likely to develop phobias to certain stimuli than others. He tried to condition a fear in participants by showing them a photo of a spider or a snake and accompanied this with an electric shock. He found that only three or four repetitions of this procedure would condition a fear of these stimuli in a person. However, he also tried to establish a fear of flowers in the same way and found that it was a lot harder to condition this fear in participants. He argued that whilst humans are 'prepared' for learning associations, this does not apply to all stimuli equally. This may be because we have a biological predisposition to develop phobias for things of whose nature we are uncertain.

This is supported by Merckelbach et al (2005) who found that fear of an animal was associated with its unpredictability of movement.

Preparedness theory is supported by Bennett-Levy and Marteau (1984). They point out that not all animals are equally likely to cause phobias. They asked people to rate each of 29 animals according to its perceived ugliness, perceived harmfulness, and how afraid they were of it. They found that fear was strongly correlated with the appearance of the animal – the more different they were from humans the more they were feared. This they suggest is the innate basis for a predisposition to fear certain animals. Disgust may be another basis for fear. Davey et al (1998) studied animal fears in people from seven different countries (Western and Eastern) and found that there were significant similarities is responses to animals, especially in disgust ratings.

PSYCHOLOGICAL EXPLANATIONS

"You need to know about at least two psychological explanations for phobia, and to be able to evaluate each of them."

BEHAVIOURAL EXPLANATIONS

The behavioural approach explains both the acquisition and continuation of phobia through the processes of classical and operant conditioning.

Classical conditioning is learning by association. An individual experiences the pairing of a previously neutral object with a negative experience of fear and anxiety. For example a child with no previous fear of dogs gets bitten by a dog and from then on associates dogs with fear and pain. Due to the process of generalisation, the child is not just afraid of the dog that bit her but shows fear of all dogs.

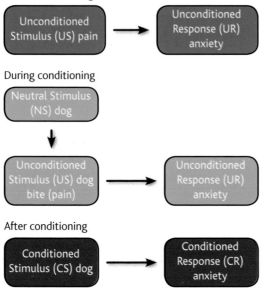

Before conditioning

Unconditioned Stimulus (US) pain → Unconditioned Response (UR) anxiety

During conditioning

Neutral Stimulus (NS) dog ↓ Unconditioned Stimulus (US) dog bite (pain) → Unconditioned Response (UR) anxiety

After conditioning

Conditioned Stimulus (CS) dog → Conditioned Response (CR) anxiety

Diagram demonstrating classical conditioning of a phobia of dogs.

Due to the fact that an emotion is being conditioned rather than a behaviour, the conditioned response is often referred to as a conditioned emotional response (CER). Whilst classical conditioning explains the acquisition of a CER, it is operant conditioning which now maintains the phobia through negative reinforcement. Avoidance of the feared object or situation results in a lessening of anxiety, which is rewarding. This increases the likelihood of engaging in this anxiety-reducing behaviour again. In the example of the association created between a dog and fear, the possibility of encountering a dog is anxiety-provoking: avoiding dogs or the possibility of encountering dogs reduces this anxiety, thereby reinforcing this behaviour.

If you need a reminder, a more detailed description of the principles of classical conditioning can be found in the Intelligence and Learning chapter elsewhere in this book.

The first demonstration that phobias can be learned through classical conditioning was by John Watson and Rosalie Rayner in 1920. They used the pairing of a white rat and a frightening loud noise to condition a phobia of rats in an infant. After just a few pairings with an aversive noise, the toddler developed behaviours which Watson and Raynor interpreted as phobic.

Evaluation of behavioural explanations

Whilst learning theories can partially account for how fears might develop, they are not able to explain all aspects of phobia. It is not clear from learning theories why some phobias are more readily acquired than others. Seligman's work

WATSON AND RAYNER (1920) – THE STUDY OF 'LITTLE ALBERT'

Albert was a 'normal' child of about 11 months of age when John Watson asked the child's mother (who was his secretary) if she would be willing to allow him and his colleague, Rosalie Rayner, to carry out a study using Albert as a participant. The mother didn't really know the true extent of the experiment that would be carried out on her first born son and so she agreed. The study would attempt to condition a phobia in Albert using the principles of classical conditioning; and once the phobia had been conditioned, Watson would use the same classical conditioning principles to 'cure' Albert of the phobia.

The study required Albert to sit on a mat while Watson and Rayner approached him with various objects that initially had no effect on Albert, apart from a desire to play with these exciting objects. These included things like a dog, a monkey, fire, and most importantly, a white rat.

Albert had no fear of any of these objects at the start of the experiment, but that was about to change. Watson and Rayner wanted Albert to begin to associate the appearance of the white rat with a fear response. They did this by hitting two metal bars together behind Albert's back every time the rat appeared and approached Albert. This sudden loud noise was enough to frighten little Albert and he soon learned that this noise and the subsequent fear only seemed to occur when the little white rat appeared. Therefore, Albert began to associate the fear response with the little white rat and soon became afraid of the animal – he had been classically conditioned to fear the rat. Albert not only feared the rat, but he *generalised* his fear to other similar objects. He started to develop a fear of things that resembled the rat, like cotton wool, and other furry white animals.

demonstrates the idea of preparedness. That is the readiness with which phobias of some objects can be learned, compared with others. He found it easier to condition a phobia of snakes or spiders than of flowers. Preparedness theory suggests that this is because snakes and spiders posed a threat to humans during our evolutionary past and we evolved to recognise them as a threat to our survival now. This also explains why phobias of heights and fire are more common than phobias of cars. According to learning theory, car phobia should be common in the Western world where cars present a huge danger. Many people have experienced being in a collision but this very rarely results in a lasting phobia of cars or driving. Preparedness theory argues that this is because we have not evolved to respond with lasting fear as cars are a recent development in our history and did not pose a threat to our survival when we lived as hunter-gatherers.

Research carried out by Kleinknecht (1982) points to another reason why some phobias are more common than others. It may be the case that we have many safe experiences with cars and tools, using them nearly every day without many negative outcomes, and these positive or neutral experiences may outweigh any bad ones. We tend not to have many experiences with snakes or spiders and those we do have are more likely to be negative or anxiety provoking.

Other research also suggests that phobias can not be explained sufficiently by using the learning theory approach. Öst & Hugdahl (1981) have stated that nearly half of all people with phobias have never really had an anxious experience with the object of their fear, and some have never had an experience with the object of their phobia at all. It may be that we hear about a negative experience that someone has had, like getting injured by a snake, and we become afraid as a result of that information. This strongly implies a cognitive role in the development of some phobias, an idea which is not accounted for by traditional learning theories.

Research by Mineka (1985) has led her to suggest that learning theories are not enough on their own to explain phobias. She believes that people develop phobias of things that are unpredictable or that we cannot control. An example of this is brontophobia (an irrational fear of lightning). A person afraid of lightning will probably not be afraid of an electrical appliance or electrical socket, even though accidents with these kill a lot more people than lightning. It is also the case that a person with brontophobia is unlikely to have experienced or heard about anyone they know being struck by lightning and killed. Stories of people who have had accidents with electrical appliances and sockets are quite common though. Mineka (1985) suggests that it is the uncertainty and unpredictability of lightning that we are predisposed to fear, whereas the danger of an electrical socket is quite controlled and harnessed.

THE SOCIAL LEARNING THEORY EXPLANATION OF PHOBIAS

Many psychologists believe that phobias tend to develop as a result of vicarious learning (learning simply from watching others) and vicarious reinforcement, which means that we observe the consequences of actions and behaviour and those consequences will determine whether we attempt similar actions or behaviours in the future.

This approach has been applied to many mental disorders, but it seems an especially appropriate explanation for the development of phobias. A child might observe their parent's fear reaction to a particular object or situation and may itself learn, vicariously, to fear this object. A baby which has never seen a snake before will look to its mother for information about how to respond to this novel object. If the mother's reaction is passive and neutral the baby will play with the snake and show no fear. If, however, the mother displays anxiety and snatches the baby away the baby learns from her reaction that a snake is an object of danger and will not attempt to play with it and may even display fear of snakes in the future. This effect will be more pronounced, depending upon the gender of both the role model and the observer. Somerville et al (1980) studied the effect of the gender of the model and found that an attractive role model of the opposite sex was more likely to be modelled than an attractive role model of the same sex.

Evaluation of social learning theory

Hoffman et al (1995) studied individuals with a social phobia and used self-reports to assess what it was about a social situation that had made them develop the phobia they had. When asked whether they had had some kind of vicarious learning experience associated with their phobia, most people said they had not.

Mineka et al (1984) studied the effects of vicarious learning in rhesus monkeys. Monkeys with a fear of snakes were observed by their offspring interacting fearfully with toy and real snakes. After six sessions, the reactions of the offspring were virtually identical to the reactions of their parents. After six months, the phobia was still just as strong in these young monkeys.

As with other learning theories, the social learning theory cannot fully explain why a person develops a certain phobia. As Hoffman et al (1995) stated above, many individuals with phobias don't ever report a 'modelling' incident in which they observe the phobic reactions of another to the focus of their irrational fear. Conversely, not all people who do witness a situation in which a 'model' has a phobic or fearful reaction to a particular situation or object go on to develop a phobia of that situation or object.

Merckelbach et al (1991) used a research resource called the Phobic Origin Questionnaire (developed by Öst & Hugdahl, 1981). They examined the extent to which 42 individuals with a severe spider phobia attributed their phobia to conditioning experiences or modelling experiences. Modelling experiences were most often reported, with 71% of the participants recalling such an incident, and 57% a conditioning experience. It was found, however, that individuals who had reported a conditioning background felt less extreme cognitive symptoms when confronted with the phobic stimulus than patients with a modelling experience.

"Notice that preparedness theory is very 'flexible' and can be used in many different ways. Learning this theory and research into it allows you to talk about preparedness theory itself, and to use it to evaluate both biological and learning theories, and as evidence for the stress-diathesis model (covered later in this chapter)."

COGNITIVE EXPLANATIONS OF PHOBIAS

The cognitive view of phobias states that a phobia develops due to faulty thinking processes and that these faulty thinking processes are linked to a focus on negative stimuli and negative events related to the phobia object or situation. This then leads to the sufferer tending to believe that these negative events are more likely to occur in the future when facing the phobia object or situation.

There seem to be a great number of cognitive factors involved with the development of phobias. Individuals with a phobia seem to be subject to excessive negative information processing biases when they make predictions about future situations in which they may encounter the situation or object of which they have their irrational fear. For example, a person who has a phobia of spiders may predict that, if faced with one, it may chase and bite them. It is also the case that individuals with a phobia seem to rate negatively their ability to deal with or control a situation in which they are faced with their phobia.

This tendency for some people to focus on a negative event occurring again in the future is what Beck (1967) called a cognitive "error in logic".

SOCIAL LEARNING OF FEAR IN MONKEYS

Monkeys raised in captivity who had never been exposed to the dangers of the wild were exposed by Cook and Mineka (1990) to four different 'toys' closely resembling either a snake, a rabbit, a crocodile or a flower. Initially, the monkeys showed very little fear of any of these toys. The next step was to show the monkeys video footage, edited so that it presented an image of either a snake, rabbit, crocodile or flower, followed by footage of an adult monkey responding fearfully and giving a distress call. After this was shown to the laboratory-reared rhesus monkeys, they were, again, exposed to the same 'toys' resembling the snake, rabbit, crocodile or flower. Cook and Mineka found that watching the video of the adult's fear response in relation to the snake or the crocodile resulted in something called vicarious learning (learning through observation of others). There was no such vicarious learning demonstrated in relation to the rabbit and flower though. The researchers reasoned that this was because we have evolved a biological predisposition to develop a fear or phobia of certain dangerous objects that our ancestors might have been exposed to long ago and that when the laboratory-reared monkeys observed the video of the adult responding fearfully to the snake or the crocodile, this was enough to activate this dormant fear.

This occurs when a person who suffers from a phobia wrongly believes that every time they encounter the object or situation they are afraid of, something terrible will happen to them. This is clearly wrong as we are unlikely to be bitten by every dog that we encounter, but it is an error of logic that a person with a phobia of dogs would experience.

Leading psychologists like Ellis (1962) and Beck (1963) state that cognitive errors such as thoughts of catastrophic events, and irrational beliefs relating to phobic objects, contribute to a person's fear of certain objects and situations. A common catastrophic thought and irrational belief of someone suffering a spider phobia might relate to a fear that spiders are going to chase them, crawl on them and possibly bite them. Beck et al (1985) also found that people with phobias tend to be more concerned with their anxiety when they are faced with their phobia than they are with the actual object of their phobia. It seems that the initial anxiety experienced when facing a phobia object may be misinterpreted by the sufferer as a warning that something terrible is going to happen, and it is this fear of their anxiety response that sufferers of phobias are really afraid of. Consequently, this creates a vicious circle with the sufferer experiencing more and more fear. Reactions to objects which elicit a phobic response are recognised by sufferers as being irrational and so at least part of the cognitive process which analyses these objects and situations is working appropriately.

Evaluation of cognitive explanations

Di Nardo et al (1988) studied a group of people who were experiencing a severe and debilitating phobia of dogs (cynophobia), and also a group of people who had no particular phobias at all. From extensive interviews with all the participants it was discovered that 50% of those suffering from cynophobia had had some kind of negative and traumatic experience with a dog in their childhood. Whether the other 50% of the people with cynophobia had experienced a similar event and couldn't recall it, or had even repressed it, is unknown. The interesting finding was that 50% of the participants who had no phobias at all also reported that they had experienced some traumatic event concerning a dog in their childhood. Interviews with those who did have cynophobia suggested that the reason that the sufferers who had had a traumatic experience with a dog in their childhood developed their phobia was that they had focused on the likelihood of that kind of event happening again; whereas the participants who had experienced a traumatic event associated with a dog and didn't develop a phobia hadn't focused on that possibility.

Tomarken (1989) presented snake phobics and non-phobics a series of slides, some of which were of neutral objects (e.g. trees) and some of which were of snakes. Afterwards, all the participants were asked how many snakes, trees etc. they had been shown. The researchers found that phobic people tended to overestimate the number of snakes. This is good evidence for the role of distorted thinking in phobia.

A study by Ohman and Soares (1994) however found that conscious cognitive processing is not necessary for a phobic response. A fear response can be experienced by a person with a specific phobia without that sufferer being aware that they have been exposed to the object they are afraid of. In their study, participants who had a spider or snake phobia were shown pictures of their phobia objects for a fraction of a second, so quickly that they had no time to consciously recognise the object. After the picture of the phobia object had been shown to the participants for 30 milliseconds, a picture of a neutral stimulus consisting of some pattern was shown. Because of the extremely short length of time that the phobia object was shown before the patterned stimulus was displayed, the participants did not recognise that they had processed a picture of their phobic object.

CULTURAL RELATIVISM

The issue of cultural relativism is important in relation to phobias. Most of the phobias that humans experience will be influenced by the cultures we live in. For example, Kleinman (1988) has pointed out that agoraphobia is significantly more common in Western cultures (North America and Europe) than in others. Another phobia that seems to be culture-bound (seems to exist in only one culture) is a condition apparently specific to Japan called taijin kyofusho. This is an irrational fear of offending or harming other people through a person's poor social behaviour. This isn't like a social phobia, in that a person does not have an irrational fear of embarrassing themselves: the irrational fear associated with this disorder is that the sufferer's behaviour will cause others embarrassment. This may be related to the collectivist culture that is prevalent in Japan, whereby society promotes working with others and the achievement of the group, not the individual.

However, tests of their physiological responses (heart rate, blood pressure, brain activity, galvanic skin response) showed that they were undergoing some increase of anxiety at the time the pictures of the phobia objects were shown.

THE DIATHESIS-STRESS MODEL

This theory tries to bridge the gap between biological and environmental causes of phobias. It states that a person may have a biological predisposition to develop a phobia, but that this predisposition may never develop into the phobia itself, unless something in the environment triggers it. This trigger could be in the form of exposure to the object or situation, or may be in the form of observational learning – watching another person display a fear response to a particular object or situation.

A number of psychologists, such as Cook and Mineka (1990), have attempted to explain why so many of us may have a phobia about spiders or snakes, when the vast majority of us will never come into contact with a spider or a snake that could ever be dangerous to a human; and yet phobias of cars, knives and guns are extremely rare, despite the fact that these kill many times more humans than spiders and snakes. It is the opinion of these psychologists that a predisposition to develop certain phobias has evolved in humans and other animals over hundreds of thousands of years. There was a time when humans, or the ancestors of the human race, were in contact with very venomous spiders and snakes, and to be bitten by one of them would mean certain death as there were no hospitals or anti-venoms at that stage in pre-history. Thus, this fear has evolved in us as it serves a purpose, or to put it another way, it has an adaptive value and this fear might have saved many lives as it would provoke a flight response in our ancestors, taking them out of harm's way. However, Cook and Mineka demonstrated that this phobia has to be triggered by an event in the environment before it can start to have an effect. They therefore demonstrate the importance of an interaction of biological predispositions and environmental triggers in the formation of phobias.

"The diathesis-stress model is good to know about, as it bridges an apparent gap between psychology and biology. It says that explanations for mental illness need not be one or the other but can be a combination of both biological and psychological factors. Indeed, this is what most researchers nowadays think."

THERAPIES FOR PHOBIA

BIOLOGICAL THERAPIES

"You need to know about two biological therapies for phobia, and be able to evaluate them. The way to do that here is to consider two or more kinds of anxiolytics (anti-anxiety drugs) used to treat phobia."

DRUG THERAPY

Anxiolytics are a common form of treatment of phobias. Early types of anxiolytics used to treat anxiety disorders and phobias were called barbiturates. However, in the 1950s these were widely cast aside as they were found to be extremely addictive and there was an unacceptably high risk of a lethal overdose, and new types of anxiolytics were uncovered. The two classes of drugs that took over from barbiturates were propanediols and benzodiazepines. These are widely used today to treat a number of different anxiety disorders, however, benzodiazepines are not used extensively to treat phobias as they only seem to have benefits in the short-term.

Benzodiazepines work by increasing amounts of a neurochemical called gamma aminobutyric acid (GABA) which is our body's way of reducing physiological activity. We produce this when we need to calm our physiological responses and brain activity. Benzodiazepines increase the effectiveness of GABA by mimicking its form and tricking brain cells into thinking important parts of the brain are indicating that their brain cells should be less active than they currently are.

A class of anti-depressant drugs called monoamine oxidase inhibitors (MOAIs) are also used in the treatment of phobias and these seem to fare better than benzodiazepines for some in phobia treatment. They work by inhibiting the production of monoamine oxidase, which is an enzyme naturally produced by the human body in order to break down the neurotransmitters serotonin, dopamine and noradrenaline. As these MOAIs stop monoamine oxidase being produced, there are insufficient amounts of it present to break down these neurotransmitters which as a consequence stay in the sufferer's body for a greater length of time, having a greater positive effect on the sufferer.

To diminish the anxiety related to social phobia, particularly for individuals who have to perform on stage or make speeches to large audiences doctors also prescribe beta-blockers. These work directly on the central nervous system to enhance feelings of calm by reducing heart rate and blood pressure. They block the effect of adrenaline on a person's natural fight or flight response. These drugs are fast acting and can relieve symptoms from an hour and a half after taking them.

Appropriateness of drug therapy in the treatment of phobias

As with all drugs, there is a huge problem with side effects of anxiolytics. Common side effects have been drowsiness, fatigue and ataxia (problems with coordination). There are also some less common side effects such as constipation, incontinence, urinary retention, dysarthria (a slurring of the speech), blurred vision, diplopia (double vision), hypotension (consistently low blood pressure), nausea, dry mouth, skin rash, tremor.

All drugs risk side effects, but some more than others have to be treated with great care. A big problem with monoamine oxidase inhibitors is that an overdose may occur or that fatal reactions may be suffered when combined with certain alcoholic drinks like red wine.

The development of drugs was a revelation when they first appeared, as they were thought of as a cheap, quick and easy alternative to the lengthy and expensive process of psychological therapy. However, it is becoming clear now that perhaps their very nature, in that they are very cheap, quick and easy, is their downfall. They are becoming overprescribed and merely treat the symptoms of phobias while the cause of the phobia remains.

It seems that one of the main problems of drugs as a treatment for phobias is that scientists don't always fully understand why they work. There are many theories relating to how they increase levels of available serotonin or noradrenaline. However, until the exact cause of a phobia is known, the selection of a particular drug will never be more than a preventative 'shot in the dark', a best guess at why a person is suffering with a phobia.

Most companies who develop and sell these drugs will state that there is no question of physiological dependency. What these companies don't state is that there is likely to be a certain amount of psychological dependency (i.e. the person thinks they need the drugs). There is a great deal of evidence to suggest that taking barbiturates, monoamine oxidase inhibitors and benzodiazepines can lead to a physiological dependency: the body is changed by taking the drugs, adapting to the presence of different levels of chemicals, and leading a person to need higher and higher doses of the drug to achieve its original effect.

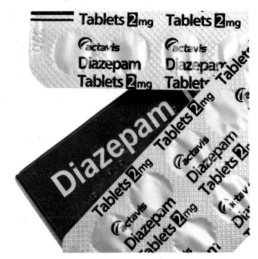

Benzodiazipines are very effective in reducing brain activity and consequently they do reduce the anxiety experienced in phobic situations. However, they are not always an appropriate treatment for phobias.

Effectiveness

Gelernter et al (1991) compared the effectiveness of benzodiazepines (a commonly used anxiolytic) and monoamine oxidase inhibitors (MAOIs) and found, oddly, that the MAOIs were more effective in treating social phobias than benzodiazepines.

Stronger axiolytics such as alprazolam have fared marginally better than their weaker benzodiazepine cousins, with an improvement in 50% of sufferers who have taken alprazolam to combat their social phobia, but again, there is a very high rate of relapse and the side effects, such as short-term memory loss, can be debilitating.

The minor anxiolytics like benzodiazepines may not be effective for long-term treatment as they would need to be taken in high doses during a phobic reaction. This would be accompanied by a feeling of drowsiness and fatigue and as the effects of these drugs wear off, the anxiety experienced would return, maybe, even stronger.

As mentioned previously, MAOIs seem to be more effective at treating phobic reactions than some anxiolytics. Heimberg et al (1998) found that MAOIs were successful in treating phobias in 60% to 80% of cases; and that drugs were just as good as psychological therapies such as cognitive-behavioural therapy – and in certain areas, were even better. A major problem with MAOIs has been that they can have very serious side effects such as hypertension (continuous high blood pressure) and stroke, when they are taken alongside certain food and drink (e.g. red wine).

An issue with the effectiveness of drugs as a treatment for phobias is that some may work for certain types of phobias but not for others. For example, Seligman (1994) reviewed many different studies that have examined the effectiveness of drugs on phobias and found that while MAOIs have a success rate of about 50% to 80% for social phobias, they were little better than placebos when treating specific phobias.

A study by Furmark et al (2002) compared the effectiveness of an anti-anxiety drug called citalopram with that of cognitive-behavioural therapy, in the treatment of social phobia. Eighteen individuals with social phobia were assessed using a PET scan to measure brain activity whilst taking part in a public speaking task. The participants were matched for sex, age and severity of phobia and then randomly allocated to three groups. The first group were treated using citalopram, the second group were given cognitive-behavioural therapy and the third group were told they were on a waiting list. The third group acted as a control. After nine weeks the effectiveness of the treatments was measured in two ways – a repeat PET scan and a self-report questionnaire. Participants were also questioned one year later to assess rates of relapse. There were significant improvements in both the citalopram and CBT groups and very little change in those on the waiting list. Improvements were accompanied by reduced activity in the amygdala and other areas of the brain associated with social anxiety. Those participants who showed the greatest reduction in brain activity after nine weeks also reported greater clinical improvement in their social phobia a year later.

"You may already have noticed that some studies and theories can be used in several ways. The study by Furmark et al (2002) is one of those – it can also be used to evaluate the effectiveness of cognitive-behavioural therapy as well as drug therapy."

The fast-acting effect of beta-blockers means that they can be used successfully on individuals in anticipation of a social event or performance. Taylor (1995) found them effective in managing anxiety in musicians and public speakers. They reduce stress because people do not need to worry about public speaking events that may be coming up in the future – they know they can do it after the first event supported by beta-blockers. This can have the knock-on effect of improving confidence so that drugs may not be needed to support them in future events.

PSYCHOLOGICAL THERAPIES

"You need to know about at least two psychological therapies for phobia, and to be able to evaluate each of them in terms of their effectiveness and appropriateness – be sure to learn this distinction and demonstrate your understanding of these terms in the exam."

SYSTEMATIC DESENSITISATION

Many therapies have been developed from the principles of the behavioural approach but they are all based on the same idea: if behaviour can be learned through classical and operant conditioning it can also be unlearned using the same processes. One of the most successful therapies is systematic desensitisation. The therapy uses the principles of classical conditioning and is designed to reduce anxiety, so its most successful application is in the treatment of phobias.

The basic idea is to expose a phobia sufferer gradually to the object of their phobia, in an attempt to reduce their anxiety. The first stage of the process of systematic desensitisation is to learn relaxation techniques such as breathing exercises and muscle control. Once these skills have been learned, the individual must learn to use them to react to and overcome anxious situations. The next step in this process is to construct and establish what is called an anxiety hierarchy. This is a set of situations which the sufferer sees as provoking responses ranging from mild anxiety to extreme anxiety. The individual will then be exposed to these situations, starting with the least anxiety-provoking, initially by imagining themselves in those situations, then using their relaxation skills to reduce any anxiety they feel. Once the hierarchy of fear has been successfully imagined after a number of sessions, the therapy may progress to actually physically experiencing these situations and, again, using relaxation skills to reduce any anxiety. It is hoped that, eventually, an individual will learn to cope and overcome the fear in each step of the hierarchy, which will lead to overcoming the highest level of fear in the hierarchy.

Appropriateness of systematic desensitisation in the treatment of phobia

Rothbaum et al (2002) compared the effectiveness of a standard exposure treatment to one which used virtual reality in treating people with a fear of flying. They found the techniques to be similar in effectiveness, with eight out of fifteen virtual reality and ten out of fifteen standard exposure clients accepting an invitation to take a post-treatment flight. This is supported by Choy et al (2007). They carried out a meta-analysis of studies designed to treat phobias using a number of variations on systematic desensitisation. They compared studies using systematic desensitisation through the imagination, in real-life situations and using virtual reality. They found that different methods of systematic desensitisation have their positive and negative points when applied to different phobias. For example, using virtual reality methods in systematic desensitisation for height or flying phobias is reasonably successful, but for specific animal phobias or social phobias, it seems less so.

Choy et al (2007) also highlighted the issues surrounding the appropriateness of *in vivo* systematic desensitisation – that is, systematically exposing sufferers to their phobias in real life. It seems that using this type of therapy to treat phobias results in a very high level of discontinuation from participants due to the levels of stress involved. Discontinuation of a treatment part way through may actually do more harm than good. Individuals have been exposed to the object of their phobia and experienced high levels of anxiety thus reinforcing their already existing fear. This is supported by Barlow and Durand (1989). They suggest that subjecting some sufferers of phobias to systematic desensitisation, especially in the early stages of their treatment, can actually make their phobia worse.

Systematic desensitisation may be more appropriate for certain specific phobias as there are possibly different underlying reasons for the development of agoraphobia or social phobias. For example, it may be that the reason for a person's social phobia

is their poor social skills, and that by learning some new and more effective social skills, they will experience an improvement in their phobia.

The underlying reason behind agoraphobia is often thought to be its co-morbidity with panic disorder. A person who suffers agoraphobia will normally have some experience of having a panic attack in public and there is a view that the agoraphobia develops as a result of the individual's fear of having another panic attack in public and of being unable to control the anxiety or get any help. Therefore, systematic desensitisation may not have the desired effect on this phobia.

Effectiveness

The therapy of systematic desensitisation is considered by the majority of clinical psychologists to achieve the most positive results in the treatment of certain phobias.

Research by McGrath et al (1990) arrived at the conclusion that systematic desensitisation was successful in 75% of the phobic sufferers that they treated with this therapy. However, in a study carried out by Menzies and Clarke (1993), although systematic desensitisation was found to be superior to having no therapy in the treatment of phobias, there was not as great an improvement.

Psychologists like Wolfe (2005) have consistently found that systematic desensitisation helps individuals who are suffering from a phobia and the key to the success in overcoming these fears seems to be the eventual, actual contact with the object or situation of which the individual has the irrational fear.

The research of Craske and Barlow (1993) found that, even though many psychologists consider systematic desensitisation to be inappropriate for agoraphobia, there was an improvement made in 50% to 80% of participants in the studies they reviewed. However, most of these improvements were very slight and there was a high relapse rate, with 50% of sufferers relapsing within a month of completing treatment.

COGNITIVE-BEHAVIOURAL THERAPY

Cognitive-behavioural therapy (CBT) aims to address and change a sufferer's dysfunctional emotions, thought processes (cognitions) and subsequent behaviours. CBT uses theories proposed by the behaviourist approach and also the cognitive approach. While behaviourist therapies like systematic desensitisation seemed to be having a degree of success in treating some forms of phobia, they have little effect on others, such as agoraphobia. The cognitive psychologists believed that this was because the behaviourist view of mental disorders seemed to overlook, or in some cases completely ignore, the influence of a person's cognitions and thought processes in the development of many psychological problems. According to Meichenbaum (1977) the majority of mental disorders are the product of abnormal thoughts and feelings. Since our behaviour is largely the product of our thoughts and feelings, it would be logical to find a way of adapting or changing these thoughts and feelings so that the subsequent behaviour is affected for the better also.

Defining what we mean by cognitive-behavioural therapy is quite problematic and this has plagued CBT since its early years. There are many forms of CBT, one of the most common being rational-emotive therapy, first proposed by Albert Ellis in 1962. This therapy states that dysfunctional behaviour and emotional distress is the result of irrational thoughts. In very simple terms, it means that a person is almost told to "pull themselves together"! Ellis stated that irrational thoughts lead to an irrational "internal dialogue" – that is, talking to yourself. This will go on to produce irrational behaviour and so the approach taken by this form of CBT is that these thoughts and cognitions should be replaced with more rational ones, resulting in rational behaviour. Later approaches and therapies have been produced by psychologists like Donald Meichenbaum and Aaron Beck who proposed that mental disorders are primarily due to errors of logic, and therefore addressing these will have an effect on behaviour.

CBT generally begins by examining the thought processes that a sufferer of a mental disorder is experiencing and beginning to understand the problem they are experiencing. Ellis would propose that many individuals suffering from a mental disorder have certain emotionally self-defeating beliefs such as "I must be excellent at absolutely everything, otherwise I am worthless." After some of these cognitions are uncovered, they are then challenged and addressed. For example, in the case of the statement "I must be excellent at absolutely everything, otherwise I am worthless" the individual will be challenged to explain *why* not excelling at everything makes them a worthless person. A person will be required to practise certain optimistic statements which challenge their present cognitions: over time these challenges result in a person's cognitions changing, resulting in a change to their dysfunctional behaviour.

Appropriateness of CBT in the treatment of phobia

Therapies that use a cognitive approach have been questioned by many psychologists. Critics of the cognitive approach state that one of the defining characteristics of a phobia is that a sufferer has 'insight' into their condition – that is, they know that their fear is irrational. A cognitive therapy would generally try to address a person's cognitions about the danger of a phobia object, in that it would try to change the sufferer's appraisal of the object as being dangerous. However, as a sufferer generally acknowledges that the fear of their phobia object is irrational, they would already understand this – yet they still seem to have a fear of the object (Turner et al, 1992).

CBT requires a degree of commitment from the individual suffering from a phobia. Treatment often involves weekly sessions over months, with homework given at each session and follow-up treatment required for up to a year. Therefore, a person needs to weigh up the costs against the benefits before beginning their treatment. An important aspect of this cost–benefit analysis is the motivation that a sufferer has towards getting better. As CBT will often take months, the sufferer has to ask themselves if they have the motivation to start and continue with the treatment. Whether the phobia object is something that the sufferer is likely to face on a daily basis or is something that has an effect on their lives every day will influence a person's motivation to go ahead with CBT. Another important aspect is financial cost, as CBT is not as cost-effective as many other kinds of treatment such as anxiolytics.

Unlike other forms of treatment, CBT has no real side effects or withdrawal symptoms, and causes no real physical change in a person – so there are no dependency or tolerance issues as there are in drug treatments. Therefore, when a person feels that they don't need any more treatment they can, if they wish, stop treatment immediately, although this is discouraged. With drug treatments, on the other hand, the physical effects are well documented, meaning a person would be unable to stop such a course of treatment with immediate effect and would have to be 'weaned' off the treatment gradually.

Unlike drug therapy, CBT doesn't just deal with the symptoms of depression but with the actual cause. It makes a real change in a person's outlook and behaviour and therefore it helps them deal with the problems they face every day, enabling them to adapt to stressful situations and problems in a way that drugs could never achieve.

Effectiveness

Ellis (2005) has observed some success when treating phobias with his version of cognitive-behavioural therapy, rational-emotive therapy. Cowan and Brunero (1997) have suggested that rational-emotive therapy can at least bring moderate relief to individuals suffering from a phobia.

Wallach et al (2009) showed that CBT for some phobias can be successful when carried out "virtually" – that is, using virtual stimulus when a person is required to practise the skills and new cognitions that they have developed during therapy. In treatment of social phobia the individual wears a virtual reality helmet that creates the illusion of standing in front of an audience. The phobic is gradually exposed to more testing experiences, to practise coping in different situations. They begin with a small attentive audience and build towards audiences ranging from those who look bored and don't listen to those who walk out or even throw things at the speaker. This helps to develop coping skills that can be applied in the future. Wallach claims that it is important to recognise that a complete absence of anxiety in a public speaking situation is unnatural. Phobics are taught that performance can be enhanced with a little anxiety and that they cannot expect to be completely devoid of anxious thoughts. One of the biggest positive aspects that virtual CBT had over normal CBT was that while there were quite a high number of individuals who discontinued CBT, there were 50% fewer individuals discontinuing the virtual CBT. Da Costa et al (2008) carried out a similar study using individuals who had a phobia of flying and found that CBT, paired with a virtual reality environment in which to practise newly developed skills and cognitions, was superior to other forms of therapy in reducing phobic responses to flying.

Schienle et al (2009) used functional magnetic resonance imaging (fMRI) to investigate the long-term effects of CBT on individuals who had been suffering from a phobia of spiders. Ten participants who had shown positive effects from CBT took part in a follow-up investigation. The participants were compared to eight non-phobic females and were presented with the same pictures depicting spiders or having a neutral content, which they had viewed six months earlier. The participants' self-report and behaviour indicated a positive long-term clinical improvement. According to the fMRI scans, cognitive-behavioural therapy also seemed to have a lasting effect on medial orbit-ofrontal cortex (OFC) activity which seems to be involved in emotion-related learning, especially in the representation of positive stimulus-outcome associations.

ANXIETY DISORDERS – OBSESSIVE COMPULSIVE DISORDER

Obsessive compulsive disorder (OCD) belongs to the family of disorders known as anxiety disorder. Other types of anxiety disorder include generalised anxiety disorder, phobic disorder, panic disorder and post-traumatic stress disorder, and these share many of their symptoms with OCD.

"OCD is one of a number of disorders which all have something in common – anxiety. We've included a general bit of background on anxiety disorders to help put obsessive compulsive disorder into some kind of context."

'Obsessive' and 'compulsive' are words that are commonly used in our culture to describe someone who's a perfectionist, extremely neat and tidy, who doesn't like clutter and mess. While this description does apply to some people who have OCD characterised by a need for things to be tidy and in order, it doesn't really represent most of the individuals that we label with this debilitating disorder.

"Be prepared to describe the clinical characteristics of OCD in an exam. You don't need loads of detail – the question won't be worth many marks if asked and you can get them all with a short but accurate response."

How many of you *have to* avoid walking over a drain? Or maybe you *have to* salute a magpie if you see one. We all have our little harmless rituals: some are quite common, others less so. Do you have any rituals or behaviour that you have to perform in certain situations? What do you think will happen if you don't perform these actions? Are you afraid something bad will occur to you or someone you love? These recurrent thoughts that you have to do something because failing to do so would mean that something bad is going to happen are what we would call 'obsessive', and the behaviours that we feel we have to perform in order to stop these obsessions are called 'compulsions' – hence the term 'obsessive compulsive disorder'.

ANXIETY DISORDERS

DISORDER	DESCRIPTION
Generalised anxiety disorder	Persistent worry/anxiety about minor things, to the extent that a person's life is disrupted by their behaviour.
Phobias (including specific phobias and social phobias)	Intense and irrational fear of an object or situation.
Obsessive compulsive disorder	Anxiety-provoking thoughts that are uncontrollable and persistent, followed by certain rituals or behaviours that a person has to perform in order to satisfy their feelings of anxiety.
Panic disorder	Sudden attack of many different anxiety based symptoms like palpitations, shortness of breath, nausea. These can be referred to as panic attacks.
Post-traumatic stress disorder	An extreme response to a traumatic event which provokes anxiety, avoidance of situations and objects, and a numbing of emotion. It has been called many things over the years from 'shell shock' to 'battle fatigue'.

Some of the common anxiety disorders and their main symptoms.

CLINICAL CHARACTERISTICS OF OCD

The DSM-IV and ICD – 10 are diagnostic manuals used by clinicians that contain lists of symptoms and behaviour pertaining to a wide range of psychological disorders. A number of anxiety disorders are outlined and classified. In general, anxiety disorders are characterised by the experience of pathological or abnormal fear or anxiety. They are among the most common forms of mental disorder experienced in Western culture, with a large number of sufferers in the UK and America. Kessler et al (2005) proposed that around 18% of individuals living in America will experience some form of anxiety disorder in their lifetime. Fear, stress and anxiety are all very healthy, useful and common feelings in humans and animals. However, when we lose control of these feelings it can have a serious impact on our lives. Anxiety disorders are classified as *neuroses*: these are a large group of disorders that cause intense distress. They are characterised by a patient's insight into their problem (they know their actions are not healthy), and generally involve feelings of unrealistic anxiety.

The DSM states that for a person to suffer with OCD, they must have either obsessions, compulsions, or both. The DSM lists the following as symptoms of obsessions and compulsions:

Obsessions

» Recurrent and persistent thoughts, impulses, or images that are experienced at some time during a disturbance; and which are intrusive and cause marked anxiety or distress.

» The thoughts, impulses, or images are not simply excessive worries about real-life problems.

» The person attempts to ignore or suppress such thoughts, impulses, or images, or to neutralise them with some other thought or action.

» The person recognises that the obsessional thoughts, impulses, or images are a product of his or her own mind, and are not based in reality.

Compulsions

» Repetitive behaviours (e.g. hand washing, moving items into order) or mental acts (counting, repeating words, etc.) that the person feels driven to perform in response to an obsession, or according to rules that must be applied rigidly.

» The behaviours or mental acts are aimed at preventing or reducing distress or preventing some dreaded event or situation: however, these behaviours or mental acts are not actually connected to the issue, or they are excessive.

Another factor in OCD is that the patient must have an insight into their problem: in other words, they must realise that the symptoms they are displaying are unhealthy and that they need to seek help for them. The obsessions and compulsions must also be distressing, and must be disrupting the everyday life of the sufferer to such an extent that they have to devote a large amount of time to them during the course of an episode. The onset of OCD can often be triggered by a certain period

CASE STUDY OF AN OCD SUFFERER

Ben has been suffering from OCD for about six months. He feels his OCD is now affecting his life to such an extent that it is causing him to become depressed and suicidal. Ben has to leave his home at least two hours before any appointment that he may have, because of his obsessions and compulsions relating to checking that his house has been locked and the lights switched off. He states that his initial obsessions are intrusive and recurrent thoughts that if he doesn't check every door and window and light, something bad is going to happen to him. Maybe someone will get in and lie in wait for him at night. Maybe the electricity feeding the light will somehow cause a fire. Because of this, Ben has to perform certain actions or rituals – the compulsive aspect of OCD. These actions include the repeated checks of every door and window at least nine or ten times before he will actually leave the house, and even then he will leave the house with a certain anxiety that he has missed something.

SOME COMMON OBSESSIONS AND COMPULSIONS

COMMON OBSESSIONS	COMMON COMPULSIONS
Contamination. Obsession with germs and dirt, etc.	Excessive washing of hands, clothes, etc.
Indirectly harming self or others, e.g. person might think that something terrible will happen to them or their family if they don't lock every door in the house	Repeating behaviours, ritualistic behaviour, checking behaviour
Forbidden, sexual thoughts and/or urges	Counting to self or even out loud
A need for order and excessive tidiness	Ordering and arranging objects
Imagining losing control and/or acting aggressively	Praying excessively, talking to oneself

of stress or trauma. Kringlen (1970) found that OCD was usually triggered by some major stress-provoking event such as pregnancy or pressures at work. OCD often occurs at the same time as certain other disorders – i.e. they are what psychologists call 'co-morbid'. Rachman and Hodson (1980) stated that OCD was often co-morbid with depression, while Austin et al (1990) found that it was also commonly co-morbid with panic disorder (frequent panic attacks) and phobias.

It is common for the first signs of OCD to show themselves in adolescence and the result is often a gradual build-up to full-blown OCD, often some years down the line. The risk of the average person developing OCD is about 2.5%, but rates vary according to different psychologists and also depending on individual differences. For example, Stein et al (1997) stated that women are more likely to become sufferers than men. Most cultures seem to demonstrate some form of OCD, although the way in which this OCD is demonstrated differs. For example, a study by Fontenelle et al (2004) found that females were a lot more likely to become sufferers, but that their obsessions and compulsions were different according to the countries in which they lived. In Middle Eastern sufferers, obsessions and compulsions were a lot more likely to involve religion, while in Europe and North America, this was less likely to be the case.

It could be that many cases of OCD actually go undiagnosed as many people with the disorder don't actually seek help for it. Kessler et al (1999) proposed that as few as 40% of sufferers will actually seek help for their disorder. This may be due to embarrassment or the stigma attached to mental illness and OCD in particular.

ISSUES SURROUNDING THE CLASSIFICATION AND DIAGNOSIS OF OCD

ASK AN EXAMINER

"You will have studied and discussed issues surrounding the definitions of abnormality at AS level and so you should be aware of some of the problems and pitfalls that are associated with the process of defining what is normal and what is abnormal."

The classification of mental disorders started with Emil Kraepelin. It was he who first started to see similarities in the symptoms of the patients he was treating, and to group them into some of the disorders that we recognise to this day. For example, he was the first to group together patients suffering from "dementia praecox" (early dementia) in a set of symptoms that we now regard as being schizophrenic. Due to the foundations laid in the late 19th century by pioneers like Kraepelin we now have much more sophisticated ways of diagnosing mental disorders. These modern systems are constantly evolving to include new discoveries. The main tools used for the diagnosis of mental disorders that we have now are called the DSM-IV criteria. This stands for the Diagnostic and Statistical Manual of Mental Disorders. IV means it's the 4th edition, published in 1994. The DSM is produced by the American Psychiatric Association and is the diagnostic tool most widely used in the psychiatric institutions around the world. Another of the commonly used diagnostic tools is the section relating to mental disorders in the International Statistical Classification of Diseases and Related Health Problems (most commonly known by the abbreviation ICD) which is produced by the

World Health Organisation. The ICD is currently in its 10th edition (ICD – 10). There is very little difference between the two methods of diagnosis and they are often used alongside each other: however, it may be that the ICD is used in a wider variety of countries.

Classifying disorders into groups and types makes it easier for problems to be identified. Diagnosing a mental disorder is almost always done using the DSM-IV and the ICD – 10 as it is a fast and easy way to break down symptoms, treatments and prognoses of disorders. Informing a colleague that someone suffers from OCD conveys a vast amount of information in a very short space of time because of the shared understanding provided by using the same diagnostic tool. However, there is a risk in using this professional 'jargon', in that explaining a particular disorder to a sufferer or loved one becomes difficult and can result in confusion and anxiety.

It was originally hoped that the use of diagnostic tools could provide mental health professionals with a standardised method of recognising mental disorders so that the individual biases and personalities of practitioners would not have an effect on the diagnosis. This hasn't proved to be entirely the case, unfortunately. It seems that, however clearly the symptoms of OCD are set out, the behaviour of an individual is always open to some interpretation. One person could view a certain action in one way while another could interpret it in an entirely different manner.

Classification then refers to the systematic grouping the symptoms of mental disorders into categories on the basis of similarities and relationships between them. It is also the case that, as with other illnesses, we have a tendency to put those suffering a mental illness into a category and fail to recognise that there are varying degrees to which that person may be experiencing a disorder. It is tempting for us to label a person as obsessive while not really knowing the extent to which they are suffering and how much it is affecting their life. Consequently, the process of deciding what are abnormal disorders and what are not is also quite subjective: it is usually left to the acumen of the individual health professional to decide. Thus, the beliefs and biases of some might mean the unnecessary labelling of millions of people as suffering from a mental disorder. For instance, it is hard to know where to draw the line between what is 'house proud' and what is 'obsessive' behaviour when it comes to cleaning. While the

DSM and ICD classify the various mental disorders into groups and assist in diagnosing obsession, the diagnosis is ultimately an individual matter. These manuals are just 'diagnostic tools' and the real work is carried out by the health professional. This leaves the diagnosis of the various disorders open to a great deal of criticism.

The main issues surrounding the diagnosis of mental disorders centre on the reliability and validity of the diagnoses. When we talk about the reliability of the diagnostic tools we generally mean inter-rater reliability: this concerns the extent to which two or more diagnosticians would arrive at the same conclusions when faced with exactly the same individual. Many mental health professionals have raised concerns about the reliability of the diagnosis of mental disorders in our society and studies have shown that inter-rater reliability is actually quite low. In a now famous study, Beck et al (1961) looked at the inter-rater reliability between two psychiatrists when considering the cases of 154 patients. It was found that inter-rater reliability was as low as 54%, meaning their diagnoses only agreed with each other for 54% of the 154 individuals.

There may have been a number of reasons for this. For example, it seems that in many of the 154 cases, the patients gave different information to the two diagnosticians. This illustrates how difficult it is to gain information from patients much of the time. It is true that diagnosticians will have the medical records of patients available to them: however, a true diagnosis can never really be made until the patient is clinically interviewed. This means that the health professional will be relying on retrospective data, given by a person whose ability to recall much relevant information is unpredictable – and who may even be exaggerating the truth or blatantly lying!

Another point that seems especially relevant in today's economic climate is the limited time and resources that are available to many professionals working in the National Health Service. It is clear that diagnoses are often made by professionals who are rushed, and preoccupied with admitting only the most serious cases in order to safeguard the resources of the institutions they are working for. Meehl (1977) suggests that mental health professionals should be able to count on the total reliability of the diagnostic tools they have at their disposal if they:

» paid close attention to medical records;

» were serious about the process of diagnosis;

» took account of the very thorough descriptions presented by the major classificatory systems;

» considered all the evidence presented to them.

In a perfect world, all these things might happen, but as already stated, it is just not possible in today's health system, with an emphasis on seeing as many patients as possible.

"You need to know about reliability and validity of classification and diagnosis – make sure you learn about them and mention them in any examination answer on classification and diagnosis."

The issue of validity has already been mentioned in relation to the diagnosis of mental disorders. When we question the validity of diagnoses, we are asking about the extent to which our system of classification and diagnosis is reflecting the true nature of the problems the patient is suffering; the prognosis (the course that the disorder is expected to take); and the extent to which the proposed treatments will actually have a positive effect.

Some commentators have highlighted the extent that many disorders described in the diagnostic manuals actually overlap. There seems to be a growing trend in clinical psychology to diagnose patients as suffering from co-morbid disorders. It may be that many individuals do not neatly fit into the categories that have been created. Instead of acknowledging that the methods by which diagnostic decisions are arrived at are lacking validity, clinicians diagnose two separate disorders. Defining anxiety disorders may seem straightforward,

and in a way it is. They are a type of what psychologists call neurotic disorders. These are characterised by that fact that sufferers keep their hold of reality: thus they realise that they have a problem, and that their behaviour isn't productive or helpful to them or anyone else. A feature of anxiety disorders, however, is high co-morbidity, so that a person will often suffer from more than one anxiety disorder at the same time. This is probably because the symptoms for all anxiety disorders are very similar in that they all involve the physical symptoms of heightened anxiety, like a racing heartbeat, high blood pressure, sweating, nausea, etc. Also, there are similar cognitive factors that may be identified as being the cause, or part of the cause, of many different anxiety disorders. For example, a feeling that a person has a loss of control in a particular situation could be the cause of panic disorder, a phobia or generalised anxiety disorder.

There is huge debate surrounding the issue of 'labelling' when it comes to classifying and diagnosing mental disorders. Diagnosing someone with a disorder means that we are labelling them, and these labels are extremely hard to remove. Someone who has suffered from OCD will always have the label of 'obsessive', even if they haven't experienced a symptom in a long time. This is somewhat the case with all mental disorders, in that a person who has suffered such a disorder has to disclose the fact in situations like job interviews, or they could face formal action. For instance, an employee who had not revealed such information in a job interview could be fired. Unlike the experience of having had influenza for example, the label of 'OCD sufferer' stays with a person.

One of the biggest controversies of recent times in relation to the diagnosis and classification of mental disorders surrounds the issue of cultural relativism. Sections of the newer versions of the DSM and ICD attempt to highlight and deal with the issue of cultural differences between subcultures within our societies, and between different cultures around the world. Davison and Neale (1994) explain that in Asian cultures, a person experiencing some emotional turmoil is praised and rewarded if they show no expression of their emotions. In certain Arabic cultures however, the outpouring of public emotion is understood and often encouraged. Without this knowledge, an individual displaying overt emotional behaviour in a Western culture might be regarded as abnormal in that context.

To diagnose a mental disorder, some interaction between a health professional and the potential patient must take place. This raises another problem in terms of culture. The clinician might not speak the same language as the person they are attempting to diagnose and therefore any interaction between clinician and patient should be done using a translator: otherwise the patient and diagnostician risk experiencing a serious lack of understanding because of these language difficulties. The term 'lost in translation' is very appropriate in this situation. The symptoms of mental illness are very rarely so clear that no discussion with the sufferer is necessary and therefore the sufferer will need to be able to describe their symptoms in as much detail as possible. If an individual's symptoms are not being described sufficiently clearly, there is a danger of a misdiagnosis – and this can lead to inappropriate treatment or no treatment at all.

CAUSES OF OCD

BIOLOGICAL EXPLANATIONS

"You need to know about at least two biological explanations for OCD, and to be able to evaluate each of them."

NEUROANATOMICAL EXPLANATIONS

Jenike (1986) found that there may be a relationship between the onset of some forms of OCD and brain damage caused by a virus, encephalitis or even brain tumours. It is often proposed that this brain damage might result in a problem in short-term memory and that it can have a chain reaction, in that often a person will doubt that they've performed a certain task or behaviour. This is a common characteristic in sufferers of OCD and may explain the reason for the repetitious behaviour they often exhibit.

An interesting study was carried out by Rauch et al (1994) who studied PET scans of the brain activity of OCD sufferers when faced with the object of their obsessions and compulsions. For example, a person with a cleaning obsession and compulsion was shown something dirty, and then their brain activity was observed using the PET scan to see which parts were the most active. It was found that the frontal lobes and an area called the basal ganglia seemed to be more active when shown their objects of compulsion than in non-sufferers.

According to Rapoport (1990), OCD is specifically a problem of the basal ganglia. Basal ganglia is the name given to a series of interconnected brain structures running in a loop from the front of the brain (in particular the orbital frontal cortex) through a series of structures deeper in the brain including the striatum, globus pallidus and thalamus and back again to the cortex. Indeed, neuroimaging studies have shown increased activity in these areas in OCD sufferers. Problems with the basal ganglia have been associated with other compulsive-type behaviours in other disorders such as Tourette's syndrome. This is a mental disorder characterised by seemingly compulsive vocal and motor (physical movement) tics. In fact the same system of brain structures has been implicated in the cause of both OCD and Tourette's. It has been noted by Rauch and Jenike (1993) that sufferers of Tourette's syndrome often suffer from OCD as well (the conditions are co-morbid).

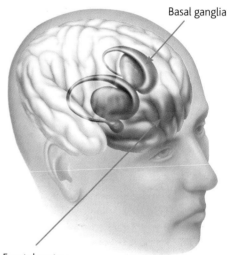

Diagram showing some of the brain structures implicated in the cause of OCD.

A crucial link between OCD and the basal ganglia is that the basal ganglia are involved in the formation of habits. Animal studies have shown that habitual responses appear to be stored as memories in the striatum. It may be that there are changes to the cortical-striatal communication pathways in OCD sufferers, causing a dysfunction in the initiation and control of repetitive behaviour. It may be that there are imbalances between several parts of the basal ganglia. Saxena et al (1998) for instance suggests that several basal ganglia structures together form a 'control system' that regulates projections to the thalamus and frontal cortex. A failure in this basal ganglia control system means that habitual and routine-like motor responses are not inhibited. Damage in the frontal cortex might also contribute to OCD since this part of the brain is involved in selecting, controlling and inhibiting behaviour.

Evaluation of neuroanatomical explanations

There is support for the idea that OCD has a biological basis. A case study of a young boy who collapsed with a brain haemorrhage at the age of 8 was reported by Rapoport (1990). It suggests that OCD may indeed be caused by abnormal brain functioning due to trauma. Rapoport stated that after the boy had survived brain surgery, he was plagued by an obsession and compulsion related to the number 7. Rapoport (1990) also reviewed an epidemic that occurred in Europe from 1916 to 1918 called the "the great sleeping sickness". This was a widespread contraction of a viral brain infection across the countries of Europe during this period. Records of the time find that there was also a rise in the number of cases of OCD, following this epidemic. This might be because the viral infection caused some damage or brain abnormality that contributed to the development of OCD.

Baxter et al (2000) questioned whether the abnormal brain activity in regions of the brains of sufferers was the cause or consequence of the disorder. They found that treating the disorder with drugs or psychological therapies "normalised" the activity of several brain structures associated with OCD. This makes it unclear whether it is the abnormal activity causing the OCD or vice versa.

Many studies have highlighted differences in the brain functioning of OCD sufferers by using PET scans. Cottraux and Gerard (1998) and Gehring et al (2000) conducted two such studies that found that a region in the brain called the cortical-striatal-thalamic circuit seems to have differing activity levels in those suffering OCD. MacGuire et al (1994) provided support for this as the cause of OCD. The researchers submitted sufferers to PET scans and, while they were undergoing these scans, showed them items which would trigger their obsessional thoughts. They found that the cortical-striatal-thalamic circuit did indeed show an increase in activity during the viewing of obsession-related images, suggesting that these brain structures do have some influence on the symptoms of OCD. A problem with this theory and the accompanying studies that attempt to support or refute this idea is that while a lot of research finds an increase of activity in this area, other studies show a decrease (Berthir et al, 1996).

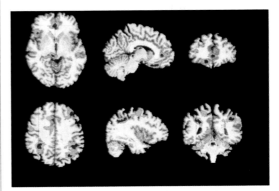

Coloured Positron Emission Tomography (PET) scans of a human brain, showing active areas in obsessive compulsive disorder. The brain is sectioned axially (left), sagittally (centre), coronally (at right). In this patient, positive correlations (activity increases as symptoms get stronger) are in the top row, seen coloured in the left orbital region, prefrontal, left frontal gyri and thalamus. Negative correlation (activity decreasing as symptoms strengthen) are in the bottom row in the right frontal gyrus and parietal regions. Active areas coloured red/yellow show blood flow detected by a radioactive tracer.

NEUROCHEMICAL EXPLANATIONS

Neurochemical theories have largely focused on the neurotransmitter serotonin. Research has examined the effects of drugs that increase the amount of serotonin available in the brain and their effects on the symptoms of OCD. Two classes of drugs that increase the amounts of serotonin available to the brain are tricyclic drugs and selective serotonin re-uptake inhibitors (SSRIs). OCD is commonly co-morbid with depression, and it is often the case that when sufferers of depression and OCD are given drug treatments which increase the amount of serotonin available in the brain, the symptoms of OCD also seem to ease. This has led many researchers to theorise that it is a lack of serotonin that possibly causes OCD. Research results, however, are quite varied. For example, many studies have found that supplying drugs which increase the levels of serotonin in a person's system actually makes the symptoms of OCD worse (Hollander et al, 1992).

Other neurochemical theories have proposed that OCD is possibly related to an abnormality in neurotransmitter systems that are linked to the serotonin systems. Therefore, it isn't lack of serotonin that is the cause of the OCD – and so increasing serotonin isn't going to improve the symptoms of OCD. Drugs which affect the serotonin neurotransmitter system may seem to be effective in treating OCD because they will have a knock-on effect on the system that is linked to the serotonin levels, rather than a direct effect on serotonin itself.

Evaluation of neurochemical explanations

One area of interest that has pointed to a possible cause of OCD has been the use of drug therapy for sufferers of the disorder. Murphy et al (1996) have studied the effects of SSRIs which increase the amount of serotonin in the brain. Murphy et al found these drugs to be successful in treating the symptoms of obsessions and compulsions in individuals with OCD. The reason these drugs affect the disorder is not clear, but some researchers have theorised that it is due to the drugs decreasing the amount of serotonin receptor sites on neurons and therefore, decreasing the activity of serotonin.

The exact function of neurotransmitters in the development of OCD is far from clear and there seems to be a great deal of contradictory research. Bastani et al (1990) produced findings that conflicted with those of Murphy et al (1996) as they found that increasing the amount of serotonin in the brain in many sufferers of OCD actually made their symptoms worse.

Whether there are improvements or not through treatments which attempt to change the neurochemical imbalances of a sufferer's brain, the treatment of OCD using drug therapy generally ends with relapse after the medication is stopped. This may indicate that neurochemical imbalances may be only partially to blame for the symptoms of OCD (DeVeaugh-Geiss et al, 1992).

"Remember, you can use alternative psychological explanations as evaluation of biological explanations!"

GENETIC EXPLANATIONS

Researchers have looked at the possibility that OCD is genetically inherited and have used research with twins and family studies to explore this. No research has managed to pinpoint a particular gene that may be responsible for the obsessions and compulsions seen in sufferers of OCD, but a great deal of research does tend to suggest that genes play a role in the development of this disorder.

OCD tends to run in families and research has shown that several generations of a family can experience anxiety that is alleviated through repetitive behaviour. Close relatives of OCD sufferers are nine times more likely to also be diagnosed with OCD (Arbor, 2006). Recent research indicates a role for a particular gene that seems to be associated with OCD, although it cannot be said that the presence of this gene causes OCD. The role of the identified gene is to help regulate the flow of a substance called glutamate. Variations in the gene may lead to alterations in the flow of glutamate to the brain that could increase the chances of an individual developing OCD. Brain imaging and spinal fluid studies have shown differences in the glutamate system between OCD patients and healthy volunteers, indicating that the flow of glutamate to the brain could be a contributory factor (Arnold et al, 2006).

A high concordance rate has been found for OCD in monozygotic (identical) twins. Research by Rasmussen and Tsuang (1986) found 65% of monozygotic twins in a sample of 20 pairs where both twins were diagnosed with OCD. These statistics offer support for the genetic component in OCD. Carey and Gottesman (1981) compared OCD in monozygotic and dizygotic (non-identical) twins. They found that the MZ twins were 87% concordant for OCD compared with 47% for the DZ twins. Allen et al (1995) found that there was a strong likelihood that if one member of a pair of identical twins develops a disorder related to OCD, then their identical twin was more likely to develop OCD than a member of the general population. This indicates the possibility of a genetic link for OCD.

Families of OCD sufferers have also been studied to establish a genetic link for the disorder. A study of 46 children and adolescents with OCD revealed that 17% of the parents also suffered from the disorder (Lenane et al 1990). In a later study Leonard et al (1992) found 13% of first degree relatives of child and adolescent OCD sufferers also met the DSM criteria for OCD. Bellodi et al (1992) noted that in children who suffered from OCD before the age of 14 the likelihood of relatives also having OCD was 8.8%. In children who were diagnosed with OCD at a later age, the likelihood was lower, at 3.2%. This shows that there is a greater prevalence of OCD in families when the onset of the disorder is early. These statistics are still high compared with the chances of suffering from OCD in the general population which is about 1.5%.

Evaluation of genetic explanations

Caution must be exercised in using twin studies as not all studies use set criteria to diagnose OCD in twins or to establish the level of genetic link between twins. Genetic testing should be carried out to ascertain whether sets of MZ twins are actually identical – this confusion is more common than you might think. The study by Tsuang (1986) used only MZ twins but did not compare the sample with DZ twins to clarify the strength of the genetic component. The twin study by Carey and Gottesman (1981) addressed this issue by using both identical and non-identical twins as a comparison. Their research was very thorough in that they drew their twin sample for the Maudsley Twin Register – a reliable source of information on twins that would have established their genetic relationship. Each twin pair was diagnosed at the psychiatric unit of their local hospital and followed up by personal interview and further assessment of their psychiatric status.

Another problem in interpreting the findings of twin studies comes from the lack of standardisation of diagnostic criteria used across different studies. This makes it difficult to compare the set of statistics from one study with the findings of another if they are basing their diagnosis of OCD on different sets of criteria. A further limitation is the lack of 'blindness' used in diagnosing the twins. Researchers evaluating OCD in the second twin would have been aware of the diagnosis of OCD in the first twin. This could lead to bias and misinterpretation of symptoms in the second twin.

McKeen and Murray (1987) stated that it seems to be the case that there is a strong genetic/familial link for all anxiety disorders and that first degree relatives of sufferers of OCD are much more likely than members of the general population to develop an anxiety disorder. Lambert and Kinsley (2005) stated that the likelihood of an identical twin developing OCD if their twin has the disorder is about 53%, while in non-identical twins the chances of the twin of a sufferer also developing the disorder is about 23%. This, as with other statistics, suggests that while there does seem to be a genetic component to the development of OCD, it can not be the only cause of the disorder. There would have to be a 100% concordance for OCD in identical twins for researchers to claim categorically that there is a genetic cause for OCD.

It is very difficult to separate genetic and environmental influences on behaviour. Even where genetic links have been shown in identical twins reared apart it is still the case that adoption agencies will very often hope to place children for adoption with families with very similar backgrounds and lives. In cases where each twin is placed into a separate family they still tend to be reared similarly – and often, they are even adopted by members of the same family (Kamin, 1977).

Another interesting finding is that in the cases where a child and parent have OCD, it doesn't necessarily follow that the child will have the same type of OCD as the parent has. For example, a father may have obsessive/compulsive behaviour and thoughts which force him to check the doors and windows in his house, while his daughter, who also has OCD, might have obsessions and compulsions which are entirely different: maybe she is excessively tidy and has obsessions and compulsions that force her to wash her hands 50 times a day. This may seem to suggest that the cause of OCD is actually biological – as, if the child were learning their obsessions and compulsions from their parents, it should follow that they would learn the same obsessions and compulsions. The fact that they often don't might indicate that they have inherited a genetic predisposition to have obsessions and compulsions but that the object of these hasn't yet been established.

Many of the family studies conducted before 1990 are difficult to interpret because of lack of control samples and differences in the diagnostic criteria applied to OCD. In an attempt to reduce bias in diagnosis of the OCD sufferers, later studies used structured interviews conducted by interviewers who were blind to the aim of the research. In many more recent studies of psychiatric disorders, family history and medical records are used alongside structured interviews, in order to make as accurate a diagnosis as possible. Many OCD sufferers are secretive about their disorder and have a tendency to hide symptoms, so it is possible that a true picture of the extent of a sufferer's symptoms cannot be gained by using direct interviews only.

PSYCHOLOGICAL EXPLANATIONS

"You need to know about at least two psychological explanations for OCD, and to be able to evaluate each of them."

BEHAVIOURAL EXPLANATIONS

Psychologists who adopt a behaviourist, or learning theory, approach propose that sufferers of OCD stumble on their obsessions and compulsions quite by accident. For example, it may be that you are in a state of fear, anxiety or stress due to an incident that has occurred. Whilst in this state you then go to wash your hands and, quite coincidentally, during that time, your fear, anxiety and stress seems to lift. Such feelings do not last forever, and so there is bound to be a time when they will reduce. A learning theory approach states that if a behaviour that a person is carrying out coincides with this reduction in fear, anxiety or stress, then that behaviour will become associated with that reduction of those feelings. Even though these two things happen together purely coincidentally, through classical conditioning they become associated. This association will make it more likely that a sufferer will repeat their behaviour during future times of anxiety, fear or stress. This approach suggests that the obsessions and compulsions that are characteristic of OCD are learned responses that have been reinforced by their consequences.

Negative reinforcement may be able to explain why a person continues to practise compulsive behaviour. When the sufferer performs their compulsions they will experience a reduction in fear or anxiety as a result of their behaviour. It is this reduction in fear that reinforces their future compulsions in response to any obsessive thoughts they may have, and makes it more likely that the sufferer will perform the same behaviour if they encounter the same obsessive thoughts in the future. These compulsive behaviours then could be reducing the anxiety caused by the obsessional thoughts of the sufferer.

> **ASK AN EXAMINER**
>
> *"If you need a reminder, a more detailed description of the principles of classical conditioning can be found in the Intelligence and Learning chapter elsewhere in this book."*

Evaluation of behavioural explanations

The behavioural theory has been praised for its ability to explain how OCD is maintained through the process of negative reinforcement. Some support for this idea comes from Hodson and Rachman (1972) who studied 12 individuals with OCD who had obsessions with dirt and being clean. They also had the compulsion of washing their hands an inordinate number of times during the day. The brain activity of these sufferers was recorded during a period of time in which they were exposed to the object of their obsessions, dirt and "contaminated" objects. It was found that anxiety, measured using brain activity, was greatly reduced when the sufferers carried out their compulsive behaviour of washing their hands. This suggests a cycle of negative reinforcement in response to compulsive behaviour and can at least partially explain the reinforcing aspect of the compulsions in response to their obsessions. Despite the learning theory's ability to explain how OCD is maintained, it is unable to explain, fully, how the disorder develops in the first place. It cannot explain exactly how the obsessional thought processes first develop in the minds of sufferers.

It also seems that the anxiety-reducing value of the compulsions is very different from sufferer to sufferer and depends on the form of the sufferer's obsessions and compulsions. For example, Rachman and Hodgson (1980) reported that sufferers with a cleaning compulsion were able to lessen their anxiety by hand washing, but sufferers with a checking compulsion were less able to reduce their anxiety through their compulsion of checking locks and windows, etc.

PSYCHODYNAMIC EXPLANATIONS

A psychodynamic approach to OCD regards the obsessions experienced by sufferers as being the result of normally unconscious id impulses. In most people, these id impulses are kept in our unconscious, hidden away from our conscious thought and are therefore unable to harm us and make us aware of the extent of our deepest darkest urges. In some people the unconscious impulses are not kept in their unconscious but are played out in their conscious minds. These are the basis of the obsessions that OCD sufferers experience. Usually, in a healthy psyche, an inappropriate id impulse is intercepted by the ego and this component of our personality then makes use of defence mechanisms to appease the id impulse and block the true nature of the impulse from our conscious thoughts. Often, this defence mechanism is something Freud called "undoing", whereby a person will think about something or behave in a certain way that their unconscious mind thinks will undo the impulse that they have experienced. In the OCD sufferer, this impulse is not unconscious and neither are the related thoughts and behaviours, or compulsions. Because of this, the "undoing" defence mechanism has to be carried out in real life.

The reason these impulses escape the unconscious is said to relate back to the anal stage of Freud's psychosexual development. In this stage, Freud stated that infants gain pleasure from being able to control and release their faeces. Freud believed that this stage occurs around the second year of an infant's life. The important part of this stage of psychosexual development was toilet training. Freud believed that if a child entered into this stage and was too harshly toilet trained in that they were not given enough independence, or they were harshly punished for failing to use the toilet in the correct manner, then the child could develop an intense unconscious anger, and aggressive id impulses. This can lead to the child unconsciously rebelling against the wishes of the parents to toilet train the child and the child may become messy, dirtying themselves and generally being a lot more destructive. If the harsh training continues, and includes even stricter punishments and harsh sanctions for the child's messy and unconsciously destructive behaviour, the child will feel embarrassed and dirty. These initial feelings of disgust in their dirtiness or aggressive impulses could be the beginning of a sufferer's obsessions; the compulsions are then the result of the ego and its "undoing" defence mechanism.

Evaluation of psychodynamic explanations

Freud's ideas, and the psychodynamic approach in general, are usually met with a great deal of scepticism in modern psychology. Not even all psychodynamic theorists agree with Freud's original ideas. For example, Erikson (1963) stated that it may not be the case that the aggressive impulses that have been highlighted by Freud as a characteristic of OCD are a result of poor toilet training in the anal stage of development. It may be that the aggressive impulses Freud speaks of are rooted in a serious sense of insecurity.

Adler (1931) proposed a psychodynamic view which had a slightly different approach to the origins of OCD. Adler's view was that OCD results from a childhood feeling of incompetence which is due to excessively domineering or excessively doting parents. This makes a child develop an unconscious inferiority complex and their obsessions and subsequent compulsions are the child's way of attempting to gain some control and boost their self-esteem.

Most psychodynamic theorists, nevertheless, do agree with Freud's opinion that OCD would be accompanied by strong aggressive impulses. Fitz (1990) however, during a review of the research carried out into the area of the psychodynamic approach and OCD, came to the conclusion that there is no clear evidence to support the psychodynamic explanation for the development of OCD.

Attempts to treat OCD using psychodynamic methods have also been largely unsuccessful, according to Bram and Björgvinsson (2004), and if this is the case, it is unlikely that psychodynamic theories behind the development of OCD hold much water either.

THERAPIES FOR OCD

BIOLOGICAL THERAPIES

ASK AN EXAMINER

"You need to know about two biological therapies for OCD and be able to evaluate them. The way to do that here is to consider two or more kinds of drug used to treat the symptoms of OCD. Remember to focus on the appropriateness and effectiveness of drug therapies for this disorder."

DRUG THERAPY

The most common biological treatment for OCD is the use of tricyclic and selective serotonin re-uptake inhibitor (SSRI) drugs. These drugs increase the amount of serotonin available to the brain. Whilst they are usually prescribed to treat depression, studies have shown that in some cases these drugs also reduce the symptoms of OCD.

Certain anxiolytic (anxiety-reducing) drugs are also used to treat the anxiety that accompanies OCD. In particular, clinicians employ a type of anxiolytic called *benzodiazepines* – which work by increasing the effectiveness of a neurochemical called gamma aminobutyric acid (GABA) which is our body's way of reducing physiological activity. We produce this neurochemical when we need to calm our physiological responses and brain activity. Benzodiazepines increase the effectiveness of GABA by mimicking its form and tricking brain cells into thinking important parts of the brain are indicating that their cells should be less active than they currently are.

These drugs are very effective in reducing brain activity and consequently, they do reduce the anxiety experienced by sufferers of OCD during their periods of obsessional thought.

Another form of anxiolytic drug that can be used to treat the anxiety associated with OCD is *beta-blockers*. These work by blocking the amount of adrenaline, noradrenaline and corticosteroids that are released into the body by the adrenal glands during times of stress or anxiety. Beta-blockers reduce the activity of the *autonomic nervous system* and therefore, the physiological effects of the anxiety caused by the obsessions experienced by a sufferer of OCD. The heart rate and breathing are slowed, so the person feels calmer.

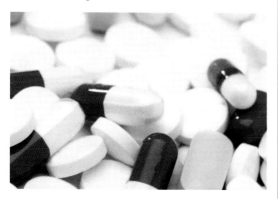

Appropriateness of drug therapy in the treatment of OCD

The treatment of OCD with tricyclics and SSRIs has provided some positive results. The Clomipramine Collaborative Study Group (1991) has researched the use of tricyclics and SSRIs in the treatment of OCD and has found these drugs to be effective in the treatment of this disorder in double blind tests carried out using them in comparison with placebos.

Drugs which treat OCD are problematic in that they treat the symptoms of the disorder but, as there is no real consensus about the actual cause of OCD, they can't ever really provide a 'cure': the most they can do is to treat the symptoms and manage them. The development of drugs was a revelation when they first appeared as they were thought of as a cheap, quick and easy alternative to the lengthy and expensive process of psychological therapy. However, it is becoming clear now that perhaps their very nature, in that they are very cheap, quick and easy, is their downfall. They are becoming over prescribed and merely treat the symptoms of OCD, while the cause of the condition survives.

Relapse, in cases in which tricyclics and SSRIs are initially successful in treating the symptoms of OCD, is extremely high (Koran et al, 2002). This was a factor highlighted in research carried out by McDonough (2003) who studied sufferers of OCD who had been following a course of drug therapy and who had discontinued their therapy.

There are problems when using drugs to treat OCD in that they can cause a great number of side effects. Some common side effects of tricyclics are dry mouth, memory problems, blurred vision and hyperthermia (prolonged raised body temperature). For SSRIs the side effects can include anhedonia (an inability to find pleasure in normally pleasurable things), apathy, nausea, headaches, and many more. Common side effects of anxiolytics have been drowsiness, fatigue and ataxia (problems with coordination). There are also some less common side effects such as constipation, incontinence, urinary retention, dysarthria (a slurring of the speech), blurred vision, diplopia (double vision), hypotension (consistently low blood pressure), nausea, dry mouth, skin rash, and tremor.

It seems that one of the main problems of drugs as a treatment for OCD is that scientists don't really know why they work. There are many theories relating to how they increase levels of available serotonin or noradrenaline. However, until the exact cause of OCD is known, drugs will never be more than a preventative shot in the dark, a best guess at why a person is suffering. Delgado and Moreno (1998) state that there is no consensus view on the function of serotonin and other neurotransmitters in the cause of OCD and that therefore, drugs which increase these chemicals should be avoided when treating this disorder.

Most companies who develop and sell these drugs will state that there is no question of physiological dependency. What these companies don't state is that there is likely to be a certain amount of psychological dependency (i.e. the person *thinks* they need the drugs). There is a great deal of evidence to suggest that taking drugs can lead to a physiological dependency – i.e. the body is changed by taking the drugs, adapting to the presence of different levels of chemicals, and leading a person to need higher and higher doses of the drug to achieve its original effect.

Effectiveness

Hohagen et al (1998) found that tricyclic antidepressants do seem to have an effect on the symptoms of OCD. However, this effect only seems to be present when the OCD is co-morbid with depression.

Many psychologists now see psychological treatments as being a lot more effective than drug treatments of OCD. Greist (1998) outlined a psychological treatment called *Exposure and Ritual Prevention Therapy (ERPT)* and compared its effectiveness to that of drug treatments. It was found by Greist that ERPT was just as effective a treatment for OCD as drugs were. However, since ERPT is not accompanied by the side effects, risk of dependency and tolerance that treatment with drugs brings, then this treatment should always be preferred.

A wide range of anti-depressants have actually been found to have a positive effect on the symptoms of OCD (Steketee and Barlow, 2004). The drugs most commonly prescribed to treat OCD have been serotonin re-uptake inhibitors, a class of drugs similar to SSRIs (selective serotonin re-uptake inhibitors). The difference between these drugs is that while SSRIs are very particular about the neurotransmitters and receptors in the brain cells they affect, SRIs are slightly less selective, having an effect, not just on serotonin, but on other neurotransmitters and receptors also. Mundo et al (2000) found treatment of OCD sufferers with SRIs led to a 50% reduction of symptoms. However, it was the case that these sufferers still experienced some symptoms, despite their reduction.

Whilst SSRIs and tricyclics are not always successful if used on their own, studies have found that employing a combination of SSRIs and tricyclics can often be effective.

Some clinical psychologists believe that the best form of treatment that we have at our disposal today is the use of drugs, and in particular, a SRI called clomipramine. Rauche and Jenike (1998) found that when OCD sufferers take this drug, their obsessions reduce considerably and their compulsions are far more easily resisted. Foa and Kozak (1993) stated that between 50% and 60% of sufferers of OCD will benefit from treatment with clomipramine. However, this does mean that a large number of patients will not benefit from treatment with clomipramine, and even those who are treated and improve are very rarely totally cured.

The combination of psychological and drug therapies has not really been shown to be any more successful than either therapy on its own, but treatment with drugs definitely seems to be more effective than having no treatment at all (Leonard, 1998).

PSYCHOLOGICAL THERAPIES

"You need to know about at least two psychological therapies for OCD, and to be able to evaluate each of them in terms of their effectiveness and appropriateness – be sure to learn this distinction and demonstrate your understanding of these terms in the exam."

EXPOSURE AND RITUAL PREVENTION (ERP) THERAPY

Exposure and Ritual Prevention therapy (also known as Exposure and Response Prevention therapy) is a form of behaviour therapy, similar to systematic desensitisation. Systematic desensitisation was a therapy developed by Joseph Wolpe, which uses the principles of classical conditioning developed by Ivan Pavlov to expose a sufferer of OCD to the object of their obsessions and compulsions gradually, in an attempt to reduce their anxiety.

Like systematic desensitisation, the first stage of the process is to learn relaxation skills which will successfully control mild fear and anxiety responses to situations which cause the sufferer the anxiety associated with their obsessional thoughts. Once these skills have been learned, the sufferer must learn to use them to react to and overcome anxious situations. The next step in this process is to construct something similar to what Wolpe called a "hierarchy of fear", and that is, *graded exposure* to the situations and thoughts that accompany their OCD. These are a set of situations which the sufferer sees as provoking responses ranging from mild anxiety to extreme anxiety. The individual will then be exposed to these situations, starting with those causing the least anxiety, initially by imaging themselves in those situations, then using their relaxation skills to reduce any anxiety they feel. Once the process of graded exposure has been successfully employed after a number of sessions, the therapy may progress to actually physically experiencing these situations and, again, using the sufferer's relaxation skills to reduce any anxiety felt in these situations. It is hoped that, eventually, an individual will learn to cope and overcome the fear in each step of the hierarchy, which will lead to overcoming the last and most anxiety-provoking step of the graded exposure hierarchy.

Appropriateness of (ERP) in the treatment of OCD

ERP is quite a difficult treatment for sufferers of OCD to join as they are forced to face their most anxiety-provoking situations. Sufferers often feel unable to expose themselves to the situations that trigger their anxieties and unable to resist acting out their compulsions. Wilhelm (2000) found that as many as 30% of OCD sufferers who begin ERP drop out of therapy before completing their treatment.

Abramowitz (2006) pointed out that while the success of ERP has been impressive, the procedures used are far from perfect, as a substantial amount of sufferers of OCD will either refuse treatment, drop out prematurely, or fail to benefit.

The process of ERP has been seen as one of the most appropriate methods for treating OCD as it is a highly flexible therapy that can be adapted to group therapy, self-help therapy, family therapy and computer-guided therapy (Fischer et al, 1999).

Effectiveness

Abramowitz et al (2005) stated that ERP was probably one of the most promising developments in the treatment of OCD that clinical psychology has discovered in modern years. However, it does need some research and some further work. The researchers found that ERP and cognitive therapy are more effective than having no treatment at all. However, while ERP seems to be more effective than cognitive therapies, more people seem to drop out of ERP and therefore, it is responsible for helping fewer people, even though it is more effective in those people it treats.

Two psychologists from the University of Sydney in Australia have identified a flaw in treatment with ERP, during a review of studies exploring the effectiveness of ERP on OCD. Starcevic and Brakoulias (2008) wanted to explore whether different sub types of OCD, related to the types of obsessions and compulsions experienced, were more or less responsive to ERP. They found that sub types in which the symptoms include overt compulsions (compulsions that others can see) were generally associated with a relatively good response to ERP,

and this therapy was found to be have a significantly greater rate of success than that achieved by drug therapy. For example, washing/cleaning and checking compulsions tend to respond better to ERP than to drug treatment. However, in the majority of the studies, hoarding and pure obsessions (the subtype characterised by sexual or religious obsessions and absence of overt compulsions) have been associated with poor response to ERP, but were also associated with poor response to drug therapy.

According to Barlow and Durand (1995), subjecting some sufferers of OCD to ERP (and thereby the source of their anxiety), especially in the early stages of a treatment based around systematic desensitisation, can actually amplify their symptoms.

Whittal et al (2008) reported significant improvements in OCD sufferers who were treated with ERP. It was found that 50% of the sufferers who actually completed the course of ERP were eventually rated as "recovered" two years after the completion of the therapy, while only 10% were regarded as "relapsed".

Finally, a very positive account of the contribution made by ERP to the therapy of OCD was given by Abramowitz (2006) who stated that:

> the psychological treatment of obsessive-compulsive disorder (OCD) with exposure and response prevention (ERP) methods is one of the great success stories in the field of mental health. Within the span of about 20 years, the prognosis for individuals with OCD has changed from poor to very good as a result of the development of ERP.

COGNITIVE-BEHAVIOURAL THERAPY

Cognitive-behavioural therapy (CBT) is a therapy which aims to address and change a sufferer's dysfunctional emotions, thought processes (cognitions) and the behaviours that these will result in. CBT uses theories proposed by the behaviourist approach and also the cognitive approach. Cognitive psychologists believe that the behaviourist view of mental disorders seemed to overlook, or in some cases completely ignore, the influence of a person's cognitions and thought processes in the development of many psychological problems. According to Meichenbaum (1977) the majority of mental disorders are the product of abnormal cognitions. Since our behaviour is largely the product of these, it would be logical to find a way of adapting or changing these thoughts and feelings so that the subsequent behaviour is affected for the better also.

Defining what we mean by cognitive-behavioural therapy is quite problematic and this has plagued CBT since its early years. There are many forms of CBT, one of the most common being *Rational-Emotive Therapy*, first proposed by Albert Ellis in 1962. This therapy states that dysfunctional behaviour and emotional distress is the result of irrational thoughts. In very simple terms, it means that a person is almost told to "pull themselves together"! Ellis stated that irrational thoughts lead to an irrational "internal dialogue" – that is, talking to yourself. This will go on to produce irrational behaviour and so these irrational thoughts and cognitions should be replaced with more rational ones.

Later approaches and therapies have been produced by psychologists like Donald Meichenbaum and Aaron Beck who proposed that mental disorders are primarily due to *errors of logic* and that therefore, addressing these will have an effect on behaviour.

CBT generally begins by examining the thought processes that a sufferer of a mental disorder is experiencing and to try to begin to understand what the problem they are experiencing is. Ellis would propose that many individuals suffering from a mental disorder have certain emotionally self-defeating beliefs such as "I must switch this light on and off 23 times, otherwise something terrible will happen to me or my family!" After some of these cognitions are uncovered, they are challenged and addressed. For example, in the case of the statement "I must switch this light on and off 23 times, otherwise something terrible will happen to me or my family!" the individual will be challenged to explain *why* not switching the light on and off 23 times will result in something terrible happening to them or their family. A person will be required to practise certain optimistic

statements which challenge their present cognitions: over time these challenges result in a person's cognitions changing, resulting in a change to their dysfunctional behaviour.

Some of the most common dysfunctional beliefs that occur with OCD are:

» **Responsibility appraisals** where a sufferer may see themselves as being solely responsible for the prevention of negative outcomes resulting in harm to themselves or ones they love

» **The over-importance of thoughts** where a sufferer may feel that having a particular thought about performing a certain action is like actually performing that action (e.g. thinking about someone dying might actually lead to their death!)

» **Exaggerated perception of threat** where a sufferer may have an exaggerated, irrational belief in the likelihood of harmful outcomes occurring.

To treat OCD using a CBT approach, each of these dysfunctional beliefs should be addressed, as follows:

» A sufferer will be educated to see that intrusive thoughts are relatively normal and that thinking about a behaviour is not the same as carrying it out

» CBT will focus on a sufferer's assessment of potential risks. They will work through the possibilities of their outcomes and assess the likelihood of those outcomes occurring

» Sufferers will then have what CBT calls 'homework': they would be given exercises to practise their new more functional beliefs and to disprove their old dysfunctional beliefs.

Appropriateness of CBT in the treatment of OCD

Therapies that use a cognitive approach have been questioned by many psychologists. They state that one of the defining characteristics of a neurosis like OCD is that a sufferer has 'insight' into their condition – that is, they know that their behaviour is irrational. A cognitive therapy would generally try to address a person's cognitions about the irrational nature of the obsessions and compulsions, in that it would try to change the sufferer's appraisal of those obsessions and compulsions as being dangerous in some way. However, as a sufferer generally acknowledges that their obsessions and compulsions are irrational, they would already understand this, yet they still seem to have their obsessions and compulsions (Turner et al, 1992).

Unlike other forms of treatment, CBT has no real side effects or withdrawal symptoms, and causes no real physical change in a person – and so there are no issues of dependency or tolerance issues as there are in drug treatments. Therefore, when a person feels that they don't need any more treatment they can, if they want to, stop treatment immediately, although this is discouraged. With drug treatments, on the other hand, the physical effects are well documented, meaning a person would be unable to stop such a course of treatment with immediate effect and would have to be 'weaned' off the treatment gradually.

Other psychological therapies like ERP are quite difficult for sufferers of OCD to join as such therapies force them to face their most anxiety-provoking situations. Sufferers often feel unable to expose themselves to the situations that trigger their anxieties and unable to stop acting out their compulsions. Wilhelm (2000) found that as many as 30% of OCD sufferers who begin ERP drop out of therapy before completing their treatment.

CBT requires a degree of commitment from the individual suffering from OCD. Treatment often involves weekly sessions over months, with homework given at each session and follow-up treatment required for up to a year. Therefore, a person needs to weigh up the costs against the benefits before beginning their treatment. An important aspect of this cost–benefit analysis is the motivation that a sufferer has towards getting better. As CBT will often take months, the sufferer has to ask themselves if they have the motivation to start and continue with the treatment. Another important aspect is financial cost, as CBT is not as cost-effective as many other kinds of treatment such as anxiolytics.

Unlike drug therapy, CBT doesn't just deal with the symptoms of OCD but with the actual cause. It makes a real change in a person's outlook and behaviour and therefore it helps them deal with the problems they face every day, enabling them to adapt to stressful situations and problems in a way that drugs could never achieve.

Effectiveness

DeRubeis and Crits-Christoph (1998) have carried out research that suggests that CBT approaches to the treatment of OCD are just as effective as other psychological therapies at reducing the symptoms of the condition.

Hoffman and Smits (2008) conducted an extensive meta-analysis of the use of CBT for sufferers of anxiety disorders. Their analysis utilised 27 methodologically sound studies on this subject. They found that the biggest positive effects of CBT were seen in the treatment of obsessive compulsive disorder, but that all anxiety disorders could benefit from treatment using CBT.

CBT has been shown to be successful in treating OCD where other treatments have failed. A study conducted by Tundo et al (2007) found that in sufferers who had been resistant to drug therapy in relation to OCD, 42% were either "much improved" or "very much improved" after a period of treatment using a CBT approach.

CBT seems also to have employed modern technology to lessen the amount of time spent with a therapist and therefore, cost to the sufferer. "BTsteps" is a computer guided way of delivering cognitive-behavioural therapy. Its effectiveness was studied by Tumur et al (2007). They compared therapist-led CBT with the computer-led CBT and found that, although the therapist-led CBT was more effective overall, the computer-led CBT was effective with sufferers who were already making significant improvements, even after the therapy was discontinued.

Blanco et al (2006) compared the effectiveness of CBT and drug treatment for OCD and concluded that, overall, CBT provided sufferers with serious cases of OCD the biggest improvement as measured by the Global Assessment of Functioning Scale, which indicates how well a person with a mental disorder is able to function in society.

Media psychology

ROB LEWIS

You are expected to develop knowledge, understanding and critical thinking in relation to the topic Media psychology.

This includes applying knowledge and understanding of research methods, approaches, issues and debates where appropriate. You must also show an appreciation of the relationship between research, policy and practices in applying psychology in everyday life.

WHAT YOU NEED TO KNOW

MEDIA INFLUENCES ON SOCIAL BEHAVIOUR
- Explanations of media influences on pro- and anti-social behaviour
- The effects of video games and computers on young people

PERSUASION, ATTITUDE AND CHANGE
- Persuasion and attitude change, including Hovland-Yale and Elaboration Likelihood models
- The influence of attitudes on decision making, including roles of cognitive consistency/dissonance and self-perception
- Explanations for the effectiveness of television in persuasion

THE PSYCHOLOGY OF 'CELEBRITY'
- The attraction of 'celebrity', including social psychological and evolutionary explanations
- Research into intense fandom, e.g. celebrity worship, stalking

EXPLANATIONS OF MEDIA INFLUENCES ON PRO- AND ANTI-SOCIAL BEHAVIOUR

It has been estimated that by the age of 18 a child born today will spend more time watching a television screen than in any single activity other than sleep; and television, it has been argued, has changed our lives more than any other single technological innovation in the 20th century. Television 60 years ago was still very much in its infancy and relatively unknown. Now, it is ubiquitous, to be found all over the world. Children spend more cumulative time watching TV than going to school. It is not surprising therefore that some people have questioned the effects of exposure to such media on young people and indeed on society as a whole. Rideout et al (2003) found that about 80% of parents surveyed said that their children under 6 years of age imitated what they saw on television. Interestingly, it was also reported that the children copied more pro-social than aggressive behaviours (87% to 47% among 4 to 6-year-olds).

Whilst it is the major source of information, TV is not the only medium which could be argued to influence behaviour. We are exposed to many forms of media, including print media (magazines, newspapers and books), music (including lyrics), and most recently and perhaps most pervasively, video games (computer and console games).

EXPLANATIONS OF MEDIA INFLUENCE ON ANTI-SOCIAL BEHAVIOUR

In everyday language, 'anti-social behaviour' refers to "…virtually any intimidating or threatening activity that scares you or damages your quality of life", and includes things like yobbishness, littering, and rowdy and noisy behaviour (The Home Office, 2009). Whilst this certainly constitutes anti-social behaviour, psychologists have generally taken a more narrow view of anti-social behaviour, focusing mainly on aggressive behaviour.

There has been considerable controversy in the last few decades over the question of whether exposure to anti-social media influences the tendency

of viewers to behave anti-socially themselves. The debate has centred around whether any effects are short-term or long-term, whether specific types of media have a particular influence, and what the underlying psychological mechanisms of any influence might be.

Television has been the major focus of discussion and research, mainly because the medium plays such a central role in everyone's life (although recently video games and computers have attracted the attention of psychologists). The growth of television and its influence on society can be estimated by considering that, in 1970, UK households had three television stations to chose from (BBC1, BBC2 and ITV) All of these ended their programming before midnight, and offered little or no daytime TV. The situation had changed very little until the 1980s when Channel 4 was introduced. It is estimated that in 1980, only 5% of households owned a video recorder. The introduction of TV has revolutionised the experience of television, so that there are now hundreds of channels available 24/7.

Studies have established beyond doubt that violence and aggression are widely present in television programmes. Influential research by Smith and Donnerstein (1998) involved an analysis of the content of television programmes. They quote survey data showing that adolescents between 12 and 17 years in the US watch around 20 hours of TV a week, with 2 to 11-year-olds spending an average of 22 hours a week watching TV. (These figures will almost certainly have risen since the late 1990s). Their content analysis revealed television programming as having an overwhelmingly anti-social content.

61	% of TV programmes containing violence
4	% of TV programmes with an anti-violence theme
44	% of violent behaviours on TV committed by an attractive role model
75	% of violent TV scenes where there is no punishment for or condemnation of violence
40	% of TV programmes featuring 'bad' characters never punished for their aggression
43	% of violent TV scenes involving humour

Adapted from Smith and Donnerstein (1998).

There is a growing consensus among psychologists that television has an unhealthy influence on social behaviour. Huesmann et al (2003) reported the findings of a longitudinal study into media influence on anti-social behaviour. Adults who had been exposed to violent TV 15 years previously were measured on levels of physical aggression. Controlling for socio-economic status, IQ, parental education and initial levels of aggressiveness, they found a strong positive correlation between the two measures. This was consistent with previous findings by other researchers. To put the strength of this correlation into context, Bushman and Anderson (2001) point out that this television/aggression correlation is larger than the one between exposure to lead and children's IQ, and is nearly as large as the one between smoking and lung cancer.

It should be remembered in any debate about media effects that these effects are only one of many factors potentially influencing anti-social and aggressive behaviour. It may be that the major influence of media content is in those already prone to aggressive tendencies. For example, it exacerbates aggressive tendencies in those who are already exposed to real-life anti-social behaviour within the family, or who have pre-existing neuro-physiological abnormalities.

OBSERVATIONAL LEARNING AND IMITATION

A great deal of human behaviour is influenced by the observation of how others behave. We use what we see other people doing not only to learn new things but also to regulate our own behaviour. According to social learning theory, people (but especially young children) will readily imitate models. Social learning theory predicts that whilst people can learn from whoever they observe, the likelihood of an individual acquiring the observed behaviour themselves is increased if the model possesses certain qualities. For instance, if the model is similar or attractive to the observer; if the observer identifies with the model in some way; if the context in which the behaviour is observed is realistic; and if the model is rewarded for their behaviour.

"This is the most widely used explanation for the effects of anti-social media. Having an understanding of social learning theory is very useful – it crops up in many chapters of this book."

Observational learning is readily seen in children because they are rapidly learning new motor and social skills, but this kind of learning continues throughout life, perhaps becoming harder to see because the learning is often more abstract. For example, whilst specific overt behaviours might be learned from models especially when young, later as an individual matures this learning more frequently takes the form of social schemata, or scripts. These are sets of 'rules', often quite complex, about understanding and dealing with different situations. Schemata not only guide our behaviour but also influence how we interpret what we experience. Research has shown that observational learning is not necessarily conscious or intentional but can be automatic and unconscious, even at the more complex social schema level.

In a classic series of experiments, Bandura et al (1963) investigated the circumstances under which children would learn to imitate an aggressive model. Although this was not a study on the effects of media as such, some of the experiments the researchers undertook appear to have direct bearing on media effects. One study involved children being mildly frustrated by being taken away from a room full of toys. Some of these children then watched a filmed sequence on TV of an adult hitting a bobo doll (an inflatable upright punchbag). Afterwards the children were put back into a playroom containing a bobo doll amongst a range of other toys. Observers behind a one-way mirror recorded more imitative behaviours in these children than in other children who had been removed from the toy room but not shown the TV film. Other studies showed that children could learn as easily from a cartoon figure as from a human adult. Research also shows that such influences can occur very early in life. It has been shown that children as young as 1-year-old can imitate behaviours seen on a television screen (Barr et al, 2007). The implications of these studies are quite clear – children readily imitate aggressive behaviour observed in models seen in film.

Although the effect on behaviour can sometimes be relatively short-lived, some research suggests that exposure to media can have long-term consequences – newly observed and imitated behaviour can become incorporated into a more long-term repertoire of behaviours. In a bobo doll study conducted by Hicks (1968), children were shown to be able to reproduce the aggressive behaviour six to eight months later.

Whilst such experiments have been criticised for their artificiality (i.e. they lack external validity in

BANDURA'S BOBO DOLL STUDY

"If you want to know more about this study you will find it explained in greater detail in both the aggression and gender chapter of this book."

Bandura et al (1963) compared the extent to which children would imitate real-life, filmed and cartoon models. Nursery school children of both sexes were exposed to one of three scenes of aggression towards a bobo doll (an inflatable punchbag):

1. Real person in the same room as the child

2. Real person on film

3. Film of a person dressed in cartoon cat outfit in a cartoon setting.

Bandura et al found that children in all three conditions were more likely to imitate aggressive models than children in a control group who were not shown an aggressive scene. Especially pertinent, given the likely television choices of this age group, was the fact that the cartoon film was just as likely to promote imitation as the two conditions involving real models.

that the studies are experimental and don't reflect behaviour outside this setting), many other studies have confirmed the general findings. For example, Steuer et al (1971) showed nursery school children either violent or non-violent TV programmes during their school breaks and then observed their later playground behaviour. They found more aggressiveness in children who had viewed the violent TV.

EXCITATION-TRANSFER

According to Zillman (1969), media messages can create a generalised emotional arousal which can influence any behaviour which an individual engages in while the arousal lasts. In effect, arousal in one emotional state can transfer to and intensify a subsequent emotional state, so that even non-aggressive but arousing media can trigger increased aggressive behaviour.

Excitation-transfer is demonstrated in a study by Donnerstein and Berkowitz (1981). They had male university students watch a film containing sex and violence, a non-violent sex film, or a film which contained neither sex nor violence. In a later experiment the men were given an opportunity to retaliate against a woman who had angered them earlier, by giving her electric shocks. Those men who had viewed the violent sex film gave the woman more intense electric shocks that those who had watched the other films. The researchers suggest that these findings indicate that sexually stimulating media with a violent content can make men more prone to physically assaulting females who provoke them.

TV AND AROUSAL

A number of different characteristics of TV programmes have been found to be arousing. Sport has been found to be particularly arousing, as has very funny comedy and suspenseful drama. This is possibly because the three types share a degree of uncertainty – excitement from a sporting event comes from not knowing whether your team will win; and from a drama because of twists and turns in the plot. In addition, these programme types tend to encourage involvement. For example, identifying with a sports team or central character in a drama is likely to get viewers involved more in what they are watching. It is perhaps not surprising that the type of TV which produces the most arousal is that which contains explicit sexual content. Research shows that the type of TV producing the least arousal are nature programmes. In fact, according to Zillman (1974), watching a nature film can have the effect of reducing arousal below baseline levels. It is worth remembering, though, when this research was conducted. Nature programmes have changed since the early 1970s. Nowadays, nature programmes are often made to be exciting and dramatic, for example containing much more fighting and death. A sign of the times?

Excitation-transfer effects can occur with any kind of media activity with arousing properties, including news media, television, films and video games. Whilst this explanation appears restricted to short-term effects of media, there is some suggestion that excitation-transfer can have long-term consequences. For instance, if a person is frequently exposed to anti-social media followed by anger-provoking events then this experience may feed into their self-image and influence future attitudes and behaviour. Indeed, research suggests that such a process can be remarkably fast, with Uhlmann and Swanson (2004) showing that after as little as ten minutes playing a violent video game people can come to see themselves differently, associating themselves with having aggressive traits.

EMOTIONAL DESENSITISATION

This explanation basically says that people who watch a lot of anti-social media cease to respond with as much unpleasant emotional arousal as they did originally. Whilst a negative emotional reaction to a violent act usually reduces the likelihood of engaging in violence (that is, it has an inhibitory effect), arousal diminishes with each repeated exposure, which means that aggression becomes less inhibited.

There is a great deal of research to support this view. For example, Drabman and Thomas (1974) demonstrated that children who viewed a violent film showed a less emotional response to and therefore a greater tolerance of subsequent violent scenes. This is supported by Linz et al (1989) who found that repeated exposure to violent pornography reduced the likelihood of their participants labelling similar new material as violent or pornographic. It is not clear however whether such findings show long-term effects or how they reflect the cumulative effects of long-term exposure to anti-social media.

These studies investigate the effects of media violence on physical aggression, but there is also evidence to suggest that such exposure can influence anti-social thoughts and emotions. For example, Drabman and Thomas (1975) suggest that exposure to media violence can encourage a sense of indifference in those who subsequently witness aggressive acts. They found that young children shown a violent film clip were slower to call for help when they saw other children fighting than those who had watched a neutral film. It seems that seeing the violent clip had made the children more tolerant of violence. Studies with university-aged participants show similar findings. After

viewing violent film segments, people have been shown to be more accepting of physical aggression, and more likely to have hostile thoughts and emotions. This effect may be magnified after prolonged exposure. Zillman and Weaver (1999) for instance had male and female university students view either four violent or four non-violent feature films on consecutive days. The day after the last film, participants took part in what they thought was an unrelated task, but one which was really designed to assess hostile behaviour. More hostility was shown by those males and females who had previously watched the violent films.

COGNITIVE PRIMING

Cognitive priming refers to the idea that aggressive cues can trigger aggressive feelings and thoughts. According to this theory, aggressive thoughts and feelings can trigger other such thoughts and feelings associated in memory.

A study by Josephson (1987) appeared to demonstrate cognitive priming. It involved exposing 396 7 to 9-year-old boys to either a violent or non-violent film. Later, impartial observers were asked to rate the instances of aggressive behaviour in the boys during games of hockey. More aggressive behaviour, such as tripping, kneeing, shoving, and pulling hair, was seen in the boys who had witnessed the violent film.

Cognitive priming is not restricted to filmed media. In one of the most controlled studies of its kind, Anderson et al (2003) found that songs with violent lyrics increase aggression-related thoughts. They gave their participants either violent or non-violent songs to listen to. Afterwards, participants were given a variety of psychological assessments measuring aggressive thoughts and feelings. In order to ensure that the results were not affected by genre, song length, artist, or comprehensibility, the researchers used a clearly violent song and a non-violent song by the same group. They also accounted for potential gender effects, and a personality test indicated any pre-existing hostile tendencies. Results showed that violent songs led to more aggressive interpretation of ambiguous words (e.g. "rock"); increased the relative speed with which people read aggressive versus non-aggressive words; and increased the amount of aggressive word completions (e.g. "h_t" was more likely to be completed as 'hit' than 'hat'). These effects were independent of personality traits and gender. It has been argued however that listeners, especially younger ones, do not perceive the song lyrics in the same way as adults (or adult researchers who closely examine the lyrics!). If lyrics are to have the negative effects that some researchers claim, then they must be understood by the audience, and there is some evidence that this may not be the case. Rosenbaum and Prinsky (1987) for example found that when their college-aged participants were asked to rate 35 popular groups or performers according to the extent to which they sang about sex, they overwhelmingly reported that love rather than sex was the theme. According to Desmond (1987) only about one third of young listeners can accurately describe the meanings of popular songs.

Studies examining the influence of violent songs have returned mixed results, with some showing a significant effect on attitude and behaviour and some not. This may be due to confounding variables in research design. For example, having listened to songs varying in genre (rap or heavy metal) and lyric content (murder, suicide, or neutral), participants in a study by Ballard and Coates (1995) showed no measurable changes in mood, including anger. The problem with this study however was that the performances sometimes made the lyrics nearly incomprehensible. Another major confounding variable is that the music and lyrics may have quite different impacts and the individual may be responding to one more than the other. For example, the lyrics may be aggressive and misogynistic but a person responds to the accompanying music which might be relaxing.

INDIVIDUAL DIFFERENCE AS A MODERATOR

Whilst almost everyone is or has been exposed to media, exposure varies considerably depending on a person's age, family viewing habits, and family socio-economic status. Even then, not everyone is influenced by it to the same degree, suggesting that characteristics of the viewer may influence the impact or the way that people react to and interpret media.

Pre-existing tendencies

According to Anderson et al (2003), the children at greatest risk of influence from anti-social media are those that already have anti-social characteristics. It seems that some individuals are predisposed to be more influenced by what they experience in the media than others. It may be that this is because they more readily relate to and are attracted by violent characters. The notion of reciprocal determinism suggests that different types of individuals seek different types of media which they are then influenced by. This

is supported by research on adolescents and their use of violent media (e.g. Slater et al, 2003).

One of the most influential controlled studies on the effects of media violence was conducted by Leyens et al (1975). They assigned boys living in separate cottages at a correctional centre in Belgium to watch either violent or non-violent films each night for five nights. The boys were then observed each evening for a period of time following the movies and were rated for levels of aggression – for example frequency of hitting, slapping, choking and kicking other boys. It was found that boys who had seen the violent films engaged in significantly more aggressive acts. Moreover, the researchers noted that the effects were not evenly spread, so that the greatest influence was seen in boys who had been rated as initially more aggressive. These findings are supported by a similar field experiment at an institution for juvenile offenders in the US. Exposure to violent films resulted in reports of increased physical and verbal attacks (Parke et al, 1977).

Age

Research consistently shows that the influence of media is greatest with younger children. For example, Eron et al (1972) tested children at 8 at 19 years and found a greater influence of media in the young child. On the other hand, Johnson et al (2002) found a greater effect of television on people aged 30 than on those aged 22 or 16. One complicating factor affecting comparison of ages is that different measures of aggression are often used with different age groups. For example, effects on children are often measured by their aggressive behaviours, whilst it is aggressive thoughts and attitudes that are more often assessed in adults. In a meta-analysis of 217 studies which had investigated the effects of television violence, Paik and Comstock (1994) found that these effects appeared to vary with age, with the greatest effect being in children under 6 years old. Worryingly, given the viewing preferences of this age group, the type of television which had the strongest effect on aggression was animated and fantasy violence.

Gender

It seems that the greatest evidence of a gender difference appears in the oldest research. More recent investigations show very little or no gender difference. This may be due to changes in society, where female aggression has become increasingly more acceptable. It may also be due to increasing amounts of female aggression in the media – for example the iconic figure of Lara Croft. In all probability, gender differences will continue to narrow. One area in which research consistently shows a gender difference is in the kinds of aggression displayed. For example, in males early exposure to aggressive media is related to later direct physical aggression; whilst in females early media experience is related to later indirect aggression (Huesmann et al, 2003).

EXPLANATIONS OF MEDIA INFLUENCE ON PRO-SOCIAL BEHAVIOUR

The emphasis of most research on the influence of media has been on its potential negative effects. Whilst violent and anti-social content appears to fill much of the media, there are many examples of media having pro-social effects. The term pro-social encompasses a wide range of behaviours – for example, cooperation, helping, sympathy and empathy. According to Rushton (1979), something pro-social is "that which is desirable and which in some way benefits another person or society at large".

The potential good of television was recognised many years ago in the late 1950s in the US. By 1959 there were 45 educational television channels in America operated by either universities, education authorities or the community. These were averaging five-day airtime, nine hours a day.

By the mid-1960s such television programming became mainstream with the establishment of the Children's Television Workshop. Whilst it produced a number of popular programmes for the US market, by far the most successful was *Sesame Street*. This television show aimed to provide preschool children at home something that would both entertain them and foster intellectual and cultural development. It is still broadcast today, and has been the focus of research.

SOCIAL MODELLING

Some of the earliest research investigating the effects of pro-social media looked at the issue of whether exposure to appropriate social models might affect the likelihood of engaging in pro-social acts. The logic applied was that social learning processes which are helpful in explaining the influence of anti-social media should apply equally to the learning of pro-social behaviour.

An example of this research is Sprafkin et al (1975). They allowed some 6-year-olds to watch an episode of *Lassie* in which there was a scene of a puppy rescue, while some others watched an episode without a rescue scene, and a third group watched an episode of *The Brady Bunch*. Afterwards, all the children played a prize-winning game during which they came into contact with a group of apparently distressed whining puppies. Those who had viewed the *Lassie* rescue spent more time trying to comfort the puppies than the other children, even though doing so would interfere with winning. For Sprafkin et al, this was evidence that experiencing helpful media models can create a social norm which encourages pro-social behaviour.

EMPATHY

Empathy is the ability to feel an emotion as it is experienced by someone else. A person's empathic skills develop over time, and start at about the age of 18 months. At first, empathy is egocentric, but by the age of 3 a child is starting to respond to the

HOW PRO-SOCIAL IS TV?

Pro-social acts are more common in television programmes than might be imagined. Smith et al (2006) carried out a large-scale study in which they analysed the content of over 2,000 entertainment shows randomly selected from a week of programming on 18 US TV channels. Nearly three-quarters of all programmes contained at least one pro-social act, whilst approximately 50% of programmes contained anti-social acts. On average, viewers would have been exposed to three pro-social acts an hour. Pro-social acts were found to be more common in children's shows. Further research however shows that whilst children are more likely to encounter pro-social than anti-social acts on TV, anti-social behaviours were more *concentrated*. This increases the impact of exposure to this type of media, which already has the advantage over pro-social media in that it is more explicit and immediate.

feelings of others in a more genuinely empathic way.

Research suggests that the extent to which pro-social media influences a child's behaviour is dependent at least in part on the extent to which they feel that they share experiences with media characters. Empathy is an important factor underlying the extent to which a person identifies with a media character, and the kinds of pro-social behaviour engaged in by the character can be a strong marker guiding the subsequent behaviour of the observer. Because empathy is a developmental skill, this effect is least with very young children.

Children readily identify with characters they encounter on-screen, and can develop quite close attachments to them, especially at pre-school age. According to Yancey et al (2002), this fondness for media characters can persist into adolescence. In their study, nearly 40% of teenagers questioned named a media figure as a role model – similar to the figure for a parent or relative. Duck (1990) found that teenagers chose media figures they would "most like to be like" based on their own characteristics. A 14-year-old girl with a high self-esteem chose Meryl Streep and described her admiration for this character as a woman who "isn't worried what people think". A 15-year-old boy assessed as having a low self-esteem chose a character from a fantasy game because "I like the way he seems not to have any feelings."

PARENTAL INFLUENCE

Parents play a crucial role in how media affects their children. Parents can both enhance the effects of the media and also reduce risks involved in exposure to certain media content. Singer and Singer (1998) suggest that parents who watch programmes containing pro-social behaviour can enhance their child's understanding by for example explaining and discussing the moral content. This serves to reinforce the pro-social message, which is often essential if younger children are to understand it. Coates and Hartup (1969) for example found that 4-year-old children learned and recalled more of a model's behaviour when an adult helped by verbally labelling the model's behaviour than through observation alone.

Pro-social morals in television and film are generally much harder for children to understand than violent acts. Pro-social situations typically have more dialogue and less action, and have plots that are more challenging to follow and comprehend. This is exemplified in a study by McKenna and Ossoff (1998). They asked children aged 4 to 10 years about the moral messages contained in an episode of *Mighty Morphin Power Rangers*. Whilst most of the children understood that there was a lesson to be learned from the programme, only the 8 to 10-year-olds were able to identify it. Younger children tended to focus on the fighting more than the message. If parents help children to think more critically about what they are watching, the impact of anti-social media content can be reduced and the impact of pro-social messages can be maximised.

THE GENERAL LEARNING MODEL (GLM)

The GLM (Buckley and Anderson, 2006) proposes that learning from media involves a complex interaction of personal and situational variables. It describes a continuous cycle of interaction between the environment and a person. Behaviour is primarily influenced by two things: *personal variables* and *situational variables*. Personal variables include consistent attitudes, beliefs, previous experience, emotions, behavioural tendencies etc. that a person brings to a situation. Examples of such variables that might influence a personal response to pro-social media include personal history of media exposure, comprehension of content, age and ability level, and personality. From the category of situational variables, examples affecting the influence of pro-social media include aspects of the media itself (e.g. the interest and excitement it generates) and the nature of the current exposure.

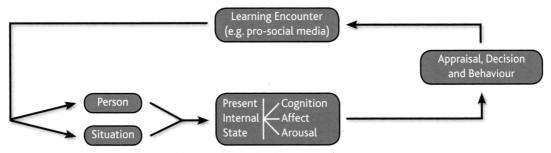

The general learning model (adapted from Buckley and Anderson, 2006).

Personal and situational variables influence three types of internal state: cognitions, affect and arousal. *Cognitions* include things such as thoughts, attributions, schemata and attitudes. So for example, seeing a pro-social media scene might increase pro-social thoughts and trigger pro-social behaviour. Personal and situational variables might also influence *affect* (i.e. mood and emotion), which then later influences behaviour. For example, mood can increase the processing of information that is affectively similar (called mood-congruent cognition), or there may be mood-dependent effects, where people pay more attention to information that matches their mood. Too much *arousal* can inhibit new learning, whilst too little arousal can lead to boredom and result in little attention being paid to the media. These three variables are highly interconnected. For example, the way we feel (affect) influences cognition (how we think); and our arousal levels can influence both how we think and feel.

> *"The GLM suggests that pro-social media should foster pro-social behaviour, and likewise exposure to anti-social media can have negative consequences. You can use this theory to explain media influences of pro- and anti-social behaviour!"*

These three variables – cognition, affect and arousal – in turn influence appraisal and decision processes that lead ultimately to behaviour. Each cycle of the GLM can be seen as one learning trial. With more cycles, the behaviour becomes more well-learned and part of the knowledge base so that the learning is more readily activated and used in later situations.

This theory is supported in a study by Greitemeyer (2009) on the effects of pro-social lyrics in songs. In a series of studies, participants were exposed to songs and then tested for changes in cognition, affect and thought. For instance, in one study participants listen to either pro-social or neutral songs and found that they tended to complete word-fragments with more pro-social words. For Greitemeyer, having listened to songs with a pro-social content affected the internal state of participants and increased the accessibility of pro-social thoughts, as outlined by GLM. Exposure to pro-social media in the form of song lyrics appeared to foster pro-social tendencies in the way predicted by GLM. Greitemeyer points out however that this study only tests short-term consequences of pro-social media and more research is needed to test if GLM also explains long-term changes.

THE EFFECTS OF VIDEO GAMES AND COMPUTERS ON YOUNG PEOPLE

Video gaming is now the world's largest entertainment medium. Video and computer games sales are a multi-billion pound market, with the gaming industry grossing greater revenues than both the movie and music industries. Many children now have game players in their bedrooms, and gaming is becoming the leisure activity of choice for many young people. In a representative sample of US teens, Lenhart et al (2008) found that 94% of girls and 99% of boys played video games.

According to Stone and Gentile (2008), video games can have quite specific effects along five dimensions, as can be seen in the following table.

Dimension	Effects
Amount	Appears most related to displacement effects, such as poorer performance at school and obesity due to less activity.
Content	Effects are specific to the content of the game: e.g. reading games improve reading and aggressive games increase aggression.
Context	Effects of content may be changed by context of game play, e.g. the social contexts of MMO (massively multi-player on-line) games where people interact in virtual environments.
Structure	Effects are influenced by how the game is structured: e.g. games that require constant scanning of the screen improve visual attention skills.
Mechanics	Related to the mechanical devices used, so the greatest effects will be seen when the devices are most 'real', e.g. playing a shooting game with a pistol rather than a keyboard.

Dimensions and effects of video games, adapted from Stone and Gentile (2008).

THE EFFECTS OF VIDEO GAMES AND COMPUTERS ON AGGRESSIVE BEHAVIOUR

Early studies of the effects of video game violence showed little indication of negative effects on behaviour. However, video games have changed considerably since the early eighties – compared to what we see in today's games, their violent content was quite mild. Modern games allow greater interaction so that players can become a part of the narrative, and are much more violent. Players can become immersed in a virtual reality with the ability to manipulate a realistic audio-visual environment. Some psychologists have expressed fears that young people who play such games excessively may come to see the line between fantasy and reality blurred.

Gentile et al (2007) report that 70% of 8 to 16-year-olds questioned claimed to play M-rated games ('M' for 'Mature'), whilst 61% said that they owned such games. When asked to name their favourite game, 50% named an M-rated game. As for parental involvement, 44% of respondents said that they bought M-rated games themselves, with 56% saying that a parent was with them the last time they did this. Only 27% said that a parent had ever stopped them from getting a game because of its content.

Findings from more recent research into video games are generally in line with those from research into televised violence. Anderson et al

(2007) had 161 9 to 12-year-old children play either violent or non-violent video games for 20 minutes. After this, the children were given another computer game to play which allowed them to select the degree of punishment to deliver to an opponent (e.g. a blast of noise). They found that children who had played violent video games previously tended to deliver stronger punishments than those who had played a non-violent game. It is perhaps interesting to note that the 'violent' games used in this study were rated 'E' (for 'Everyone') or 'T' (for 'Teen'). Anderson et al then looked into the long-term effects of playing violent video games and found that the amount of violent game-playing at the start of the study predicted the degree of increased aggressive behaviour and hostile feelings five months later.

Grüsser et al (2007) investigated whether *excessive* gaming was related to aggressive attitudes and behaviour. They recruited 7,069 gamers to take part through an on-line gaming magazine. Nearly 12% of the participants could be considered 'pathological gamers' – that is, their game playing satisfied criteria for addictive behaviour. Responses to a questionnaire indicated only weak evidence for a link between excessive gaming and aggression. The study however did not differentiate the kinds of games played by excessive gamers.

According to Peng et al (2008) violent video games might have a particular effect on people who already have aggressive personalities. They had forty participants play two popular violent computer games for the first time – *The Godfather*, (where they played as a gangster) and *True Crime: Streets of LA* (where they played as a violent police officer). Both games involved the characters in violent acts, such as punching, kicking and using weapons. Some of this play was captured for content analysis. Several weeks before the study took place participants were given a questionnaire to measure their levels of aggression. It was found that participants with higher physical-aggressive personality scores from the questionnaire engaged in more frequent violence when playing the games. This study has important implications. It might be that people with aggressive predispositions are particularly attracted to such games, or that playing a game in a more violent way might have greater effects on later aggressive thoughts and actions.

Are people with aggressive predispositions particularly attracted to violent video games?

THE POSITIVE EFFECTS OF VIDEO GAMES AND COMPUTERS

De-Lin Sun et al (2008) point out that it is difficult to measure the effects of excessive game playing because players suffer the negative consequences and the benefits from playing at the same time. They suggest that the positive effects of game playing may last longer than those that are negative. Computer gaming has been found to improve a range of cognitive skills, such as visuo-spatial and attentional skills. Sims and Mayer (2002) found that players of the game *Tetris* had improved spatial skills of the kind required by the game. Evidence from Karni and Sagi et al (2003) shows that such cognitive experiences can lead to long-term changes in the brain.

"Video games and computers are not all bad! If you are asked to write about this in the exam, you can if you wish take a more positive view than is normally taken. However, as with most things, a balanced view is usually best."

Indeed, despite research warning of the dangers of video games for encouraging anti-social behaviour, it would be an overstatement to say that the effects of video games and computers are all negative. Video games have been shown to have potential benefits for pro-social behaviour. Gentile et al (2009) conducted three studies in three countries with three age groups, to test whether video games in which characters help each other increased both short-term and long-term pro-social behaviour. Findings from the US part of the study, involving 161 college students, showed that those who were randomly assigned to play pro-social games behaved more helpfully towards another student in a later task than those who played violent games. It appears that pro-social gaming can also have prolonged effects. In a sample of Japanese 10 to 17-year-olds, pro-social game playing was related to pro-social behaviour over a three to four month period. Gentile et al suggest that since games can have both positive and negative effects, parents should monitor their children's game playing to ensure that games with maximum benefits are played.

It has been claimed that obesity is a global epidemic where, in the US alone, 15% of children aged 6 to 11 years are chronically overweight. Low activity levels and a lot of screen time are widely recognised as major contributors to this obesity. Children and their parents however are highly resistant to relinquishing screen entertainment, so the problem is not going to go away. Some video games promote physical activity so might be a way of reversing the effects of a sedentary lifestyle caused in part by increased time in front of a screen. Lannigham-Foster et al (2006) found that, whilst watching TV and playing traditional computer games expended similar amounts of energy, energy expenditure trebled with active video games. This is supported by Mellecker at al (2008), who compared heart rate and calorie expenditure in children while playing an active bowling game, an active running game, a seated bowling game, and during rest. Compared to the resting condition, they found 39% more calories were burned during the seated game, 98% more in active bowling, and 451% more (equivalent to 3.9 more calories a minute) on the running game. This clearly indicates a benefit in calorie expenditure for active game playing. They point out that the four-fold increase in energy expenditure during active game playing might compensate for weight gain caused by sedentary entertainment choices. As such, it could help prevent young people from becoming overweight.

Whilst video games like *Wii Sports*, *Dance Dance Revolution* and *Guitar Hero* offer ways of getting people more active, it has been argued that they are not a replacement for more traditional forms of exercise. Graves et al (2009) compared the energy expenditure in adolescents whilst playing four computer games – a sedentary Xbox 360 game and three active Wii Sports games. They found that, whilst playing an active game used 51% more energy than a sedentary one, this was nowhere near as much energy as playing the sport for real. For example, it has been estimated that whilst playing virtual games of tennis will burn off calories, actually playing tennis will burn off four times as many. It is recommended that young people engage in an hour of moderate to vigorous activity each day (Sproston and Primatesta, 2003), and clearly active gaming is not going to provide anything like that. One advantage of virtual games of sport however is that they can develop confidence in people in something they might not ordinarily try, by improving coordination skills and rule knowledge, which in turn might encourage them to try the real thing.

THE SOCIAL EFFECTS OF VIDEO GAMES AND COMPUTERS

According to Padilla-Walker et al (2009), the use of video games leads to poorer relationships with family and friends. In a survey of 813 university students they found that as the amount of time playing video games went up, the quality of relationships with parents and peers went down. In order to play video games, young people remove themselves from social settings, or it may be that they are already struggling with relationships and have turned to video games-playing as an escape or an alternative way to spend time. This supports previous research by Nie and Erbring (2000) who found that more time on the internet meant less time socialising with family and friends both in person and over the telephone.

A recently recognised problem associated with internet use is 'internet addiction'. Typically, people show a psychological dependence on the internet and devote so much time to surfing that family, friends and employers suffer (Young, 1998). Research has found that high internet use can be related to reductions in psychological well-being. In a two-year study of internet users, Harman (1998) found that heavy users spent a reduced amount of time with family and friends, and this increased their feelings of loneliness. The fact that much on-line activity appeared to be social, in that it involved chat-rooms and e-mail, did not seem to have a positive influence.

Some psychologists however are revising earlier concerns about the effects of the internet on adolescents, and are suggesting that its benefits outweigh any negative effects. According to Valkenburg and Peter (2009), as media use changes, so its outcomes also change. They propose two main reasons for this shift. The first has to do with the volume of internet adoption. For instance, Mesch reported in 2001 that only 11% of adolescents were on-line, whilst now the vast majority of adolescents in Western countries have access. For the most part, adolescents use this technology to nurture existing relationships rather than to create new ones. Secondly, communication technologies have improved considerably. User-friendly technologies such as Instant Messaging and networking sites like MySpace and Facebook have encouraged adolescents to communicate with others. It is estimated that 88% of adolescents use Instant Messaging to communicate with friends.

According to Valkenburg and Peter, these social effects of the internet can be explained by their

SAFER CHILDREN IN A DIGITAL WORLD: THE BYRON REVIEW

In 2007 the UK Government commissioned a review by psychologist Dr Tanya Byron into the risks faced by children of exposure to inappropriate material in video games and on the internet. The review points out that whilst the internet and video games are popular and offer opportunities for play and learning, they also come with threats from exposure to easily accessible harmful and inappropriate material. Dr Byron suggests that there is a 'generational digital divide'. On the one hand there is the technological confidence of children; and on the other there are parents ill-equipped to manage the risk to children. The review makes a number of recommendations:

● All computers sold in the UK should come with good quality easy-to-use pre-installed parental control software. This also applies to games consoles, which should have parental controls to stop children playing games intended for older age groups.

● Current games ratings standards should be reformed to make them clearer to understand. For example, they should include specific warning about content.

● A new UK Council for Child Internet Safety should be set up.

● The control of user-generated material should be improved to ensure that inappropriate material never gets on-line.

● Social networking websites should be made safer by requiring them to adhere to a code of practice.

internet-enhanced self-disclosure hypothesis. This says that the internet enhances self-disclosure, and self-disclosure is a key contributor to relationship formation. Reduced visual, auditory and social status cues in internet communication encourage self-disclosure in adolescents who, because of their age, are often self-conscious and shy. Finally, the theory also predicts that the improved quality of internet relationships has added benefits of acting as a buffer against stressors in adolescence.

> *"People don't just use computers to play video games. Demonstrate a broader understanding of the issues by including material on internet communication in your examination answer."*

ASK AN EXAMINER

PERSUASION, ATTITUDE AND CHANGE

There are many different ways of defining 'attitude', but the most common definition says that it is a rather enduring assessment of people, objects and ideas. Traditionally, an attitude is considered to have three components: *cognitive*, which equates to our thoughts and beliefs about the person, object or idea; *affective*, which is the evaluative component relating to how positive or negative we feel about our attitudes; and *behavioural*, which relates to how we act as a result of the cognitive and affective components. All three components are inter-related: so for example if someone has a positive attitude towards a football club, then they *believe* that the football club is great, they may *feel* passionately about 'their' team, and they *act* to support their team, by going to see them play, wearing the team jersey etc.

A common objective of media such as news, political broadcasts, infomercials and advertising is to implant information into the minds of the audience, in the hope (if not expectation) that it will change attitudes. The principal reason for changing an attitude is that attitudes are related to behaviours: therefore the belief is that a changed attitude might also result in a change in behaviour. We are exposed to a great deal of information every day which attempts to do just this – persuade us to abandon one attitude in favour of another.

"What you really need is an understanding of how attitudes are changed. Two well-known theories are presented here – don't just learn to remember them, but learn to apply them. Think of an advert – how does this model explain its persuasiveness? Practise this skill and you will soon have a sound grasp of this topic!"

PERSUASION AND ATTITUDE CHANGE

Persuasion can be described as the process of changing attitudes. The pioneering work on how attitudes could be changed through persuasive communication was conducted in the 1950s and 1960s by Carl Hovland and colleagues at Yale University in the United States.

HOVLAND-YALE MODEL OF PERSUASION

The Hovland-Yale model of persuasive communication says that attitude change only occurs if a message is *learned* and therefore *remembered*. In order for this to occur, the recipient must first pay *attention* to the message, and *understand* what it is that is being communicated. Even then, persuasion is not guaranteed, as whether or not the message is accepted and acted upon will depend on how motivated the individual is to do so.

"You'll notice that we have given you examples of the Hovland-Yale model in action – this is the kind of understanding you need. Don't just learn to describe the model – learn to use it."

The Hovland-Yale model suggests that a number of factors influence the persuasiveness of a message:

Source

This variable refers to *who* communicates the message. One aspect of source found to be important is the credibility of the communicator. A credible source has its maximum influence immediately following the communication. Without any further reminders about the source, the impact of the source diminishes over time. Messages are most persuasive when they come from sources that are regarded as highly credible because they are

thought to have relevant experience, to be expert and trustworthy. Persuasiveness is increased if an expert appears to be presenting the truth in an unbiased way. The message can be made to appear more trustworthy and persuasive if it seems that the source is supporting a message contrary to their own self-interests – for instance the "I'm not doing myself any favours telling you this, but…" approach.

Another important aspect of source is attractiveness. As receivers we are more likely to be persuaded by a source whom we find physically attractive, likable and similar to us. It is no coincidence that advertisers spend a great deal of money hiring attractive and likable celebrities to help sell products.

Some advertisers employ important sounding scientific terms in marketing their product, often used by 'experts' such as scientists; or products are endorsed by an attractive and 'trustworthy' celebrity.

Message

This variable refers to *what* is being communicated. A rational and reasoned message is one way to persuade an audience of a particular point of view. However, such approaches may not always result in people paying close attention, so other ways are often used to grab attention and focus it on the main message. One way to make a message more effective is to make an emotional appeal, in particular to the emotion of *fear*. Many television adverts depict horrifying consequences of certain behaviours in an attempt to dissuade viewers, for example, from drinking and driving. It seems that messages that arouse fear in recipients can produce a sense of insecurity and a motivation to reduce the fear, which can result in compliance with the message.

The relationship between persuasion and fear is not straightforward however. Rogers and Mewborn (1976) showed that fear messages which argue that something threatening will occur unless preventative measures are taken are only persuasive to the extent that those measures are understood by the recipient as effective. In other words, fear messages only work to the extent that a solution is also provided. Research also shows that if a message arouses too much fear then some members of the audience may be so occupied by their own emotions that they pay less attention to the content of the communication (McGuire, 1969). It seems that messages that evoke moderate fear are most persuasive, especially if they are perceived to contain effective and feasible instructions to reduce threat.

Some media messages appeal to fear by showing what could happen if a certain behaviour continues. However, if people feel they can do nothing about the threat they are unlikely to change their behaviour. This may be the case with safe driving campaigns, which have been running for many years. These may not work on those drivers who feel that cars will always kill someone and the only solution is to stop driving – which of course they are not going to do.

Recipient
This factor refers to the people *to whom* the message is sent. A number of recipient attributes appear to have a bearing on the effectiveness of a message, for example the intelligence of the recipient. People who are intelligent are more likely to comprehend and retain a message, improving the likelihood of attitude change. However, this higher intelligence is likely to increase understanding of the message and perhaps make the recipient more critical of its content, thereby reducing likelihood of attitude change. It may even be that more intelligent people are less swayed by a message because they are more confident in the attitude they already have. Similar processes have been found to apply to other recipient attributes like self-esteem. For example, Nisbett and Gordon (1967) found that people with high self-esteem were more likely to be swayed by complex but substantiated statements than were people with medium self-esteem, who were more swayed by easy to understand but unsubstantiated statements.

It is important then that the message matches the audience, and this may involve sending different messages to different audiences.

Channel
This factor refers to *how* the message is sent, and refers to the fact that communication must occur through some kind of medium, such as radio, television, written word or even face-to-face. The most powerful mass medium in undoubtedly television, which overtook radio in the 1950s. The reason for this is that the medium is readily accessible and messages incorporate both sound and vision. Mass media messages have their greatest influence, however, when they are combined with what appears to be personal communication. Appeals which seem to be personally directed are particularly persuasive since research shows that personal communication has the most immediate impact on attitudes and behaviour.

ELABORATION LIKELIHOOD MODEL
The elaboration likelihood model (ELM) attempts to explain the processes that lead to persuasion (Petty and Cacioppo, 1983). The term *elaboration* refers to the extent to which people think about arguments contained in persuasive messages. According to ELM there are two modes of thinking that lead to attitude change following exposure

to a persuasive message – the *central route* and *peripheral route* to persuasion. Persuasion which occurs through a central route is said to be more long lasting than changes which occur through a peripheral one.

The central route

Central route thinking means that a recipient of a message is engaged in effortful cognitive processing, so that there is thoughtful consideration of the message. The central route involves a focus on the core of the argument, and the use of prior knowledge and experience to assess and elaborate information. Because this mode of thinking involves more effortful thought, messages taking a central route can produce more permanent changes in attitude.

Central route processing involves the recipient taking an active part in the process: it can only occur when the recipient has both the motivation and ability to think about the message. Without interest in the topic of the message the recipient is not going to be motivated to engage with it.

Factors like personal relevance and message source influence this motivation. So for example, the more personally relevant a message is, the more likely a recipient is to attend to and process it. The ability of the recipient to think, and hence understand the message, determines the extent of processing and subsequent motivation. When messages are therefore aimed at reasonably well-informed people, a central route may be more successful (e.g. arguments to do with quality).

The peripheral route

Less mental effort is required with the peripheral processing route to persuasion, so people are swayed by more superficial things. Change occurring through this route is likely only to be temporary. The likelihood of elaboration is low here, with individuals not thinking much about message content. Instead, they use non-content, or 'peripheral' cues to inform their attitudes. These peripheral cues may take many forms, but typically they include things like the attractiveness, likability or expertise of the messenger, emotional reactions etc.

For people who are too involved in a message, who are in a heightened mood, or are distracted, a message through the peripheral route may be more successful (e.g. by using dialogue which appears sympathetic to the recipient's position; or by adopting an attractive presentation). Also this route is more effective for ill-informed recipients.

Whether someone takes a central or peripheral route to persuasion is determined by a number of factors which influence the likelihood of persuasion, such as the motivation and ability of an individual to process information and the nature of the message. The elaboration likelihood model suggests that attitudes changed through a central route are more likely to result in permanent or long lasting change than those modified through a peripheral route (Petty et al, 1986). A really persuasive message then is one which, by using cues like personal relevance, interest, fear etc. motivates people to take a central route.

In terms of persuasiveness, arguments along the central route are limited by their quality – because people are able and often willing to think about the content, then the message has to be convincing. The peripheral route however allows for much more creativity, where arguments involving deception, manipulation and innuendo are much more likely to be successful, even if they are quite weak. Wegner et al (1981) showed that, regardless of what the target of a message does in defence, innuendo can incriminate and devalue and have an impact long after the actual message has been forgotten.

The ELM and persuasive advertising

According to Lien (2001) a number of factors have been found to influence the ability and motivation of individuals to think about and therefore be persuaded by advertising messages.

1. Message repetition

The more times a recipient encounters a message the more opportunities there are to examine the argument. This kind of elaboration will lead to a more favourable attitude as long as the repetition avoids producing a strong sense of boredom, so easy-to-process messages are best in this regard. The effects of repetition are not the same for all aspects of an attitude however. Whilst repetition

THE PERIPHERAL ROUTE AND THE MERE EXPOSURE EFFECT

The effectiveness of peripheral cues is often explained in terms of non-cognitive processes, a well-known example being the 'mere exposure' effect. The frequency with which the recipient is exposed to a message has a major impact on the effectiveness of that message. Research by Zajonc (1968) showed that increasing frequency of exposure to a stimulus results in more positive feelings about it. This is called the 'mere exposure' effect, and it seems to apply to even quite meaningless stimuli. For example, Zajonc varied the number of times participants were exposed to Chinese characters and found that they expressed greatest liking for those they had seen the most.

Advertisers use this mere exposure effect by repeatedly exposing their product to the target market. The idea is that, without even having tried it, people will come to like the product. Familiarity appears to breed liking, but only up to a point. Research has shown that too much exposure can result in the opposite effect, where people start to have negative feelings. A simple example of this is when you first hear a song – you might like it and for some time sing along. After a while however you can become fed up with it and have quite the opposite feelings about it. The trick is then to manage the exposure of a message so that it has maximum positive impact. This is why advertisers regularly change their campaigns and manufacturers change their branding, as a constant bombardment may have the opposite of the desired effect.

can increase elaboration because of familiarity, it can also be the case that people can tire of the advert, especially its affective component. For example, an advert on behalf of an animal charity might produce a strong emotional reaction at first but viewers can quickly become indifferent to it, and even come to react against it, such as by switching channels. The potential negative consequences of repetition can be avoided however, and persuasiveness improved. One way to do this is by having a high impact advert that has limited repetition. Another way that persuasiveness is improved is with partial advert repetition, where there are varied or partial adverts for the same product.

2. Prior knowledge

The way that people process information is influenced by what they already know of the product. The more knowledge that someone brings to a message the more they will be able to think about the message content. For people with such prior knowledge, more detailed processing of information tends to occur when there is some discrepancy in the advert, for example when the content doesn't seem to make sense, or doesn't match what we know of the brand. People with low or no knowledge benefit more from messages that can be processed literally.

NEW – LARGER PACK!

In the 1980s, M&M's sold in the US were re-launched with new packaging printed with the claim "New – larger pack". This was quite true – however, the pack contained fewer M&M's than the original. After many complaints, the new design was dropped.

Lammers (2000) investigated the impact of this deception on consumers, using the ELM as a basis for explaining any effects. Forty undergraduate students took part in what they were told was a study into 'candy preferences'. The participants were assessed for attitude towards M&M's (termed 'involvement') using the Personal Involvement Inventory. Afterwards they were shown either the deceptive M&M packaging (where they were informed of the deception) or the original M&M packaging, and asked to indicate on a scale of 0% to 100% the likelihood they would purchase M&M's within the next 30 days.

Lammers found that deceived participants assessed low in involvement rated their intention to purchase lower than participants assessed as highly involved. He argued that people who are highly involved with the product were more likely to disregard package deception since they consider such peripheral things as secondary to the central values of M&M's – e.g. they taste good. On the other hand, lowly involved people would be more susceptible to peripheral cues like package deception than to the central ones and therefore would be less likely to discount package deception when considering future purchases.

This has implications for those involved in marketing who may be tempted to deceive similarly. Most consumers purchase goods under low-involvement conditions – for them to find out they were victims of a deception could carry considerable costs.

RESISTANCE TO PERSUASION

Once you understand the various strategies employed by persuasive messages you will see that there are various ways to resist being persuaded. Indeed, many attempts to persuade actually fail, either from a conscious effort on the part of the listener or, more often than not, through subtle unconscious processes.

Counterargument

When we hear a persuasive message, perhaps from an advertiser or salesperson, we silently counterargue to ourselves – e.g. is the product really that good? Do I really need it? Thus by concentrating on our own counterargument we are paying less attention to the message and are less likely to be persuaded by it. To overcome this, what the advert or salesperson needs to do is distract you and reduce your counterargument, for example by giving you more than one argument to attend to, perhaps one visual and one verbal.

Reactance

When a message appears to limit choice and freedom we often respond with reactance, which is a preference for the restricted action. For this reason a media message which says 'Please dispose of litter carefully' may be more successful than one which says 'Don't drop litter!'. We can prepare ourselves to resist persuasion through reactance by getting into the habit of using self-statements which stimulate our reactance tendencies, such as "According to whom!", "I won't be dictated to!".

Forewarning

People are more likely to resist a persuasive message if they are warned about it in advance. So, in terms of television commercials for example, we are more likely to resist the sales message if we remind ourselves that it is an advertisement whose purpose is to encourage us to buy a product rather than a selfless piece of entertainment.

3. Self-referencing

Research shows that elaboration is best when recipients can relate information to themselves. This is because thinking about themselves increases the likelihood of linking new information to existing knowledge, something which is well established as a principle for improving memory. However, it seems that self-referencing only has an effect on the persuasiveness of an advert when the recipient has the motivation to attend to it – we are unlikely to think about adverts that don't interest us.

4. Arousal

Evidence suggests that increases in arousal are related to reductions in our capacity to process and retain information. Because less capacity is available, complex central arguments become less influential. Recipients in these circumstances tend to focus on simpler central arguments or less demanding peripheral information.

5. Media type

Advertising exists in the entire range of media. Television adverts present information through a number of senses, and because of this, influence people whether or not they are seeking the message in the advert. They can be used to encourage processing through either the central or peripheral route. According to the *information processing parsimony hypothesis* (Holbrook, 1978), because consumers like to minimise cognitive effort, they are unlikely to read something that isn't of interest to them. This means that printed adverts have more limited opportunities to influence – consumers can more easily choose to ignore them than say TV adverts, where there is sound and vision.

THE INFLUENCE OF ATTITUDES ON DECISION MAKING

Attitudes don't readily change – once an attitude is formed, it is relatively permanent and maintained across different situations. Whilst an individual's attitudes bear some resemblance to their behaviours, they do not perfectly predict them. For example, you might prefer not to have sugar in your coffee (an attitude) but you might drink a cup of coffee with sugar to be polite (the behaviour). For the most part however, this kind of attitude discrepant behaviour is not the norm and, all things considered, we tend to act in ways which reflect our attitudes. Attitudes do change however, and several theories have been proposed to explain the underlying psychological processes. Two of the most famous are cognitive dissonance theory and self-perception theory.

"You just need to be aware of how these two famous theories – cognitive dissonance and self-perception – explain how a change in attitude can lead to a change in behaviour."

COGNITIVE DISSONANCE THEORY

Cognitive dissonance theory attempts to explain why people may become motivated to change attitudes. Developed by Festinger (1957), the theory makes three assumptions about human cognition:

» People have a need for cognitive consistency.

» People experience psychological discomfort when there is cognitive inconsistency.

» People are motivated by psychological discomfort to resolve the inconsistency and restore balance.

When there is a mismatch between two or more cognitions, a disharmony (or dissonance) is produced. Because people have a natural tendency to prefer and maintain consistency, so this psychologically uncomfortable state creates a drive to reduce the discomfort. The desire to reduce dissonance is for Festinger a fundamental *need* in human beings, and we are highly motivated to reduce unpleasant feelings produced by it. He suggested three ways to eliminate dissonance:

» Reduce the importance of dissonant cognitions (e.g. a smoker is faced with information telling her that smoking is bad for her health but thinks hey, life is full of risks she could be hit by a bus when crossing the road).

» Add more consonant (or consistent) cognitions so that they outweigh the dissonant ones (e.g. the smoker thinks that although smoking might be bad for her health, the relaxation and enjoyment she gets from smoking is worth it).

» Change the dissonant cognitions so that they are no longer inconsistent (e.g. the smoker could give up smoking).

Cognitive dissonance has implications for those wishing to change attitudes, through the media for example. Because we don't like dissonance, once we have established a firm attitude we become more likely to give attention to media messages that are consistent with this attitude, and less likely to engage willingly with media messages that are inconsistent with our attitudes. For example, someone who is a vegetarian is unlikely to seek out television programmes extolling the virtues of a carnivorous diet. This kind of selective exposure has an impact on attempts at persuasion through mass communication, such as media advertising. Cognitive dissonance may therefore be an underlying factor in patterns of media selection – Bryant and Zillman (1984) suggest that people actively engage (or disengage) with media in an attempt to limit their exposure to media information that is inconsistent with their attitudes or beliefs. This is not always the case, however. According to Frey (1986), in cases where a person feels that information is easily refutable they may actually choose to expose themselves to inconsistent information. For example, someone with a very clear political conviction may decide to watch a party political broadcast from an opposing party.

In times of natural disaster, fundraising organisations frequently use mass media in their appeals for donations to help crisis relief. These campaigns often use graphic images and tales of suffering. Waters (2009) suggests that the use of such material creates a dissonance in individuals who view them. According to Festinger's theory, in these situations people would be motivated to reduce this psychological discomfort. Waters investigated the responses to appeals for help for the December 2004 tsunami relief effort. He surveyed a sample of donors and non-donors and found that donors were individuals who were more likely than non-donors to experience dissonance in response to mass media appeals, and he suggests that it was this that led them to contribute. He also found that those individuals experiencing increased dissonance after initial news of the tsunami reduced

I MUST LIKE IT, I'M DOING IT!

A classic study by Festinger and Carlsmith (1959) demonstrated cognitive dissonance theory. Participants were individually given very dull and repetitive tasks to perform for an hour, and paid either $1 or $20. Having completed the tasks, each participant was asked to introduce the task to the next participant, telling them that the procedure was fun and exciting (clearly a lie). The researchers afterwards measured their attitude to the task, and found that those paid only $1 had a more positive attitude towards the task than those paid $20. It was suggested that this counter-intuitive finding was due to the effects of cognitive dissonance. The participants paid $20 experienced consonant cognitions – that they did not have to change any attitude, since they were paid $20 to say something inconsistent with their attitude (that the task was fun and exciting rather than dull and boring). The $1 participants however experienced dissonant cognitions. They could not explain away their behaviour (i.e. lying) in the same way the $20 participants had, so reduced dissonance by changing their attitude – the task wasn't that bad after all!

DISSONANCE OR SELF-PERCEPTION?

Although the underlying processes are different, both cognitive dissonance theory and self-perception theory readily explain attitude change. Traditionally, social psychologists have considered them to be separate and competing theories (this is perhaps not surprising given that Bem presented self-perception as an alternative to cognitive dissonance theory!) According to Fazio et al (1976) however, the two theories are actually complementary and, properly applied, both are correct. They claim that cognitive dissonance theory better explains the impact of attitude-incongruent behaviour on attitudes. These are behaviours that lie outside a person's 'latitude of acceptance', i.e. those that go beyond a person's most preferred position. Such changes should lead to dissonance, which motivates attitude change. Self-perception on the other hand better explains attitude-congruent behaviour. This is behaviour that falls within a person's 'latitude of acceptance', i.e. behaviours that are only a little different from the preferred position. In this situation, there is no dissonance to motivate changing attitude, so Fazio et al suggest that in these cases, self-perception might be a more appropriate explanation.

the amount of news they watched, read or listened to. It appears that they were avoiding certain media in order to reduce their dissonance. One implication of these findings is that appeals for aid must be imaginative and proactive in their use of media, given that even sympathetic donors avoid news to further reduce dissonance. Repeated footage of a disaster is unlikely to have a lasting positive effect on donations, and perhaps other types of appeal which do not produce such dissonance might also be useful.

An image of the after-effects of the 2004 tsunami.

SELF-PERCEPTION THEORY

According to Bem (1965), people come to understand themselves by making inferences based on their own observations of their behaviour. Self-perception can be seen to influence attitudes since, once we have engaged in a behaviour, we observe that we must therefore have an attitude in favour of that action. For example, if you select one brand of cereal over another then you infer that you have done so because you prefer that brand to the other (that is, you have a more positive attitude towards it). This is not so different from how we might approach other people's behaviour, in that we watch how they behave and from that observation attribute certain attitudes. For example, if we observe someone avoiding eating meat we assume

that they must have a certain attitude towards it, i.e. they are probably vegetarian. Observations of our own behaviour don't necessarily lead to changes in attitude of course, and this is accepted by self-perception theory. Sometimes we behave in ways which strongly contradict an existing attitude, without making any apparent or significant change in attitude. It seems that self-perception best explains change when we have rather weak or inconsequential attitudes, or when there are situations in which we are not quite sure what attitude to have. Whilst cognitive dissonance theory assumes that we must be motivated to change our attitude, no negative state is required with self-perception theory. Using our own behaviour to infer attitudes is a natural and automatic process requiring no external cue.

Self-perception then involves making inferences about our own behaviour based on our own observations of it, and this process offers an alternative explanation for the findings of Festinger and Carlsmith (1959). Whereas dissonance theory says that $1 participants changed their attitudes to the task to reduce the dissonance caused by lying, self-perception theory predicts that having been paid $1 to lie, participants looked to themselves. Since $1 does not justify the behaviour, they really must have enjoyed the task after all.

EXPLANATIONS FOR THE EFFECTIVENESS OF TELEVISION IN PERSUASION

Television has a major influence on how we think and behave. We learn many things through TV about which we have little or no direct experience. Television attempts to entertain and it seeks to inform; and although it undoubtedly exerts a powerful influence, not all television explicitly attempts to *persuade*. Public information broadcasts are one example of attempts through television to change the behaviour of viewers, such as those warning against drink-driving and those encouraging safe sex. Another is the Party Political Broadcast, in which political parties attempt to make the case for a vote in their favour. The most obvious example of attempts to persuade, however, are the very frequent television commercial advertisements. These adverts are attempts by businesses to influence the consumer behaviour of viewers. Huge amounts of money are spent on television advertising: in 2007 over £2.4 billion was spent on ITV1, Channel 4, S4C and Five alone. Indeed, many companies spend the bulk of their marketing money on television advertising, with slots during popular programmes costing astonishing amounts. For example, the rate for a 30-second commercial advert during the 2009 American Football Superbowl final was around $3 million, and that doesn't include the considerable cost of producing the ad. Probably the greatest influence of television however is the subtle effects it can have over time, resulting in drastically changed social and personal attitudes. Television has changed the way we view our lives and the world around us and it is to this kind of influence we turn first, before looking in more detail at explicit attempts to persuade through commercial advertising.

Uses and gratifications theory

One approach to understanding the persuasiveness of television is by appreciating the needs that are satisfied by it, and how television goes about gratifying these needs. This kind of approach has been called the *uses and gratifications* approach. McQuail (1972) for example claims that the reasons people view television are:

1. To escape the boredom of everyday life.
2. To have something to talk about with others.
3. To compare the content of the programmes with their own experiences.
4. To keep in touch with world events.

Katz et al (1973) asked television viewers to explain what they get out of various media and how media gratified their needs. They broadly found support for McQuail's categories, but also found that different media satisfied specific needs. For example, people read newspapers for information about world events, and read books for escape. Television however satisfied the most diverse needs, to some extent encompassing those satisfied by all other media.

Cultivation theory

It has been suggested that media cultivates beliefs and perceptions about the world (Gerbner et al, 1980). The more that someone is exposed to certain media messages then the more likely it is

A CONTENT ANALYSIS OF MUSIC VIDEOS

Listening to music undoubtedly has benefits, such as reducing anxiety, bringing different subcultures together, and providing information about society, social roles, and behaviour. But it may also serve to cultivate attitudes about the world. However, concerns have been raised over the possibility that music might have undesirable consequences too.

The phenomenal rise of the music video as a form of entertainment began in 1981 with the introduction of MTV in the US, and the music video's popularity quickly spread around the world. In the decades since the advent of MTV, music videos, like lyrics, have become more explicit in both message and content. It has been argued that a combination of lyrics and imagery has a greater influence on the audience than lyrics alone, and there is some suggestion that exposure to such material has a significant cultivation effect.

Rich et al (1998) trained eight college students aged 17 to 24 years to analyse music videos for violent content. The videos were acquired by recording afternoon and weekend broadcasts from the four most popular music video networks: Black Entertainment Television, Country Music Television, Music Television (MTV), and Video Hits-1. Seventy six (or 15%) of the 518 videos examined contained one or more acts of overt personal violence. The 76 violent videos had an average of six violent acts for each two to three minute segment – a total of 462 stabbings, shootings, kickings, and punchings. Males and females were victimised equally, although where the aggressor could be clearly identified it was male 78% of the time.

One study indicating a cultivation effect of exposure to such material was conducted by Wester et al (1997). They gave male participants music to listen to with different styles of content: sexually violent; the same music without the lyrics; sexually violent lyrics without music; or no music/lyrics. It was noted that those exposed to violent lyrics viewed their relationships with women as more hostile.

that they will come to perceive the world in a way that resembles them, even if those messages are distorted or unrealistic. So for example, someone who watches television containing the anti-social message that the world is a violent and threatening place will come to see the world in this way. The same principle applies to heavy viewing of pro-social media, or indeed any message. Gerbner and colleagues referred to this process as *mainstreaming*. They also suggest that an associated process called *resonance* significantly boosts cultivation. This occurs when media content is congruent with actual or perceived reality, so that the media message is 'double dosed'. For example, the first media message 'dose' is that women who are heavy media users think that the world contains much more violence than it actually does. The second 'dose' comes from their experience that an awful lot of this violence is directed towards women. In actuality, violence is not common and men are much more likely to be victims than women. The media message however 'resonates' with these heavy female viewers, making them more fearful that light viewers.

There is considerable evidence for cultivation effects of media. Morgan (1989) found that that many heavy TV viewers have opinions about race that reflect their TV viewing. Hughes (1980) found that heavy TV viewers who watched violent programming came to see the world as a more mean and threatening place. The cultivation theory applies to all age groups, although since children and teenagers rely more on media for knowledge about the world, it could be said that this age group is particularly vulnerable to the effects of media content.

Hansen and Hansen (1990) suggest that music videos can affect aggressive thinking and attitudes and have a cultivation effect. They showed university students rock music videos which had either anti-social themes or themes that were deemed neutral. They found that the students who were shown the videos with anti-social themes were subsequently much more accepting of anti-social behaviour. Johnson et al (1995) investigated the effects of exposure to rap music videos on young African-American males. Compared to participants in non-violent or no-video conditions, participants exposed to such videos displayed greater acceptance of the use of violence; indicated a higher likelihood that they would engage in violence; and expressed greater acceptance of the use of violence against a woman.

An ideal way to research cultivation effects would be to compare the levels of anti-social behaviour before and after the introduction of a particular medium. A comparison could then be made between the levels of anti-social behaviour and this would give some indication of its impact. Some studies have attempted this kind of historical analysis, but the results must be treated with caution because of the very many uncontrolled variables involved. Because of television was not introduced to all societies at the same time, some researchers have taken the opportunity to investigate the effects of TV on communities just as they are being introduced to this medium. For example, Williams (1986) found that in one Canadian community in which television had only recently been introduced, the levels of aggression in children increased much more than in two other comparable communities without television. However, as only the total amount of television watched was measured, it is not possible to draw conclusions about the influence of any particular content. Centerwall (1992) for example compared crime rates before and after the introduction of television in the US, Canada and South Africa. He concluded that interpersonal violence had increased as a result of the frequent portrayal of violence on television.

Media/viewer relationships are extremely complex and as such cultivation theory has difficulty explaining the effects of mixed media messages or the varying influences of particular genres. Questions about cause and effect also arise – people may view particular media because they are already sympathetic to the content, in which case the media has not, as such, cultivated the beliefs.

TELEVISION ADVERTISING

Explaining the effectiveness of television adverts is difficult and complex since there are so many influences on human behaviour to account for. A great deal of money is spent on researching factors which influence persuasiveness, as the stakes are very high. Good or poor advertising can make or break a product or even a company.

"OK, we've said this before but let's say it again in case you haven't got the message – learn to apply this stuff! Learn what advertisers are doing so that you can apply your knowledge in the exam!"

The effectiveness of TV advertising can broadly be summarised in terms of the influence of television adverts on behaviour and cognition. These are not necessarily separate issues of course, since behaviour directly affects cognition, and vice versa. However, attempts to persuade can often be seen to focus on one more than another.

Persuasion through the behavioural route

One of the most common techniques used by advertisers is *classical conditioning*. Advertisers present images and stories which create a positive feeling in the viewer. The expectation is that by repeatedly presenting this positive stimulus with their product, the two things will become associated and thus influence purchasing choice. For example, an advert for a washing powder might attempt to create good, positive feelings by using images of blue skies, fields of buttercups and fresh air. The hope is that when we are wandering supermarket aisles, these feelings will be triggered by seeing the product, increasing the likelihood of our selecting it before competing products.

Advertisers employ a variety of techniques to encourage such associations, including the use of novel or well-liked tunes, and celebrities who might already produce the kind of response in viewers which the advertisers would like associated

with their product. Just like Pavlov trained his dogs to salivate to the sound of a bell, advertisers want consumers to respond with positive feelings at the sight of their product.

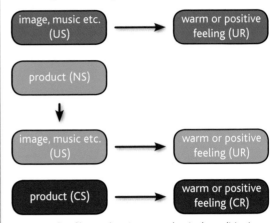

An example of how advertisers use classical conditioning.

Advertisers also use the principles of *social learning theory* in their efforts to persuade. For example, they often show celebrities modelling their product. The hope is that by seeing someone we admire or aspire to be like with a product, we will desire the product ourselves in order to be like the model. This process of *imitation* applies to all age groups – what changes over a lifetime is not the process of imitation but our susceptibility to being impressed by models, and the kind of model

DEAR SANTA...

There is a general consensus amongst researchers that commercials intended for children have the desired effect of influencing them in the direction of wanting the product advertised. The success of the advertisers, however, comes at a price – increased parent–child conflict, especially in younger children, and pressure on parents which often results in them spending beyond their means. There is a difference however in wanting a product and actually asking for it. Sheikh and Moleski (1977) point out that in their study, even though 90% of the children said that an advert would result in a child wanting the product, children would only be willing to ask for it 60% of the time. Of course, a crucial factor here is who exactly is being asked. The annual ritual of children offering a wish list to Santa presumably lessens constraints on asking, since an important trait of this mythical figure is to make unlikely things come true.

Pine and Nash (2002) looked at the effects of television adverting on young children below 7 years of age. They point out that some psychologists have argued that such young children are immune to the persuasive effects of television advertising because of their relatively poor recall skills. Others have argued that children of this age, not having very highly developed critical faculties, are particularly vulnerable to persuasive messages. Pine and Nash analysed the content of letters to Father Christmas and assessed the television habits of 83 children between 4.8 and 6.5 years of age. They found that children who watched more commercial TV tended to ask for greater numbers of items from Father Christmas. However, almost 90% of the branded toys that the children would have seen advertised did not feature in the letters, suggesting that brand name recall is poor in this age group. They also provided evidence that adverts influence children to become consumers at a very early age. A matched group of Swedish children asked for significantly fewer items than the English children. There is a ban on advertising to children under 12 in Sweden.

we aspire to be like. As social learning theory predicts, the impact of the model varies according to such things as prestige, credibility and attractiveness. This means that we are more likely to be influenced by a Formula 1 driver being used in a car advert than a television chef; and likewise a television chef is more likely to be a convincing model selling kitchen utensils than cars. Models vary in the degree to which they possess desirable characteristics: it is not enough then just to have a famous face selling a product: the famous face has to fit, for maximum persuasive influence.

Persuasion through the cognitive route

In order for persuasive information to be consciously processed, we must focus our *attention* on the core message. Advertisers want people to concentrate mental activity on their message – they want our attention. The problem for those who wish to persuade however is that attention is *selective*. We don't tend to attend to every stimulus we encounter, but we tend to pick and choose what it is we invest mental effort into. One major task of advertisers then is to understand what it is that attracts our attention, and use these factors to their own advantage to manipulate viewers. Needless to say perhaps, things are not that straightforward. For example, it is well established by cognitive psychologists that not all information needs to be attended to at a conscious level to be remembered, as it can be *pre-attentively* processed. Shapiro et al (1997) for instance found that their participants were more likely to chose a brand when it had been previously presented pre-attentively, even though they had no memory of having seen the brand before.

Many factors influence whether or not we attend to information in television adverts. Among them are those presented here:

Relevance – If viewers are not very interested in the product then they tend to pay more attention to contextual information than the product itself. This means that it sometimes benefits advertisers to make sure that their product is the thing that stands out, not the scenery or clothing, or some other background factor.

Affect – Attention needs to be drawn to pleasant information, since research shows that this increases attention and thereby improves product memory. Unpleasant stimuli can also attract attention however, and can be used to good effect, especially when we can't easily avoid the stimuli. For example, adverts with irritating

soundtracks can be remarkably effective ways for advertisers to raise public awareness of their product.

Surprise – It is part of human nature to attend to stimuli that are unusual or surprising. No doubt, this had survival advantages in our evolutionary past, and this can be used to good effect by advertisers: although a sense of surprise is short-lived, a memory for the event can linger for a long time.

Salience – The larger and more unavoidable a message is, the more likely we are to process its content.

Prominence – The order in which adverts make their appearance can also be important. 'Pioneer' adverts (those which use an image or technique for the first time – for example, having a gorilla playing a set of drums) may be more successful in grabbing attention during the initial stages of the advertising campaign, before other advertisers catch on and are tempted to emulate the success with the same approach.

Research suggests that how people *perceive* television adverts has a direct influence on their responses to them. Factors such as visual and aural cues have been extensively investigated.

Visual cues – Colour appears to be a very important visual cue in adverts. Gorn et al (1977) for example found that people preferred adverts which used pastel colours because they contributed to a feeling of relaxation. Rich-tone colours were preferred because of their stimulation, and produced feelings of excitement. It seems that advertisers need to pay attention to their use of colour, so that the feeling the advert produces in viewers matches the image they wish to create for the product.

Visual images are also extensively used in adverts, since these require less mental effort to process and are relatively easy to remember and associate with the product. Their use can vary considerably, for example the use of a particular logo or product wrapping. One of the most common uses however is seen in adverts aimed at children, with the use of cartoon figures and imaginary characters such as a 'monster' to sell a cereal. The advantage of non-verbal images in this case is that even pre-verbal children can express a preference for a product when shopping with a parent!

Aural cues – Research has mainly focused on the effects of music on television adverts. Whilst background music can have a positive effect, it can also have a negative one. The key for advertisers is finding the right music for the market they are targeting. After all, it doesn't matter if adults find a jingle and song annoying and avoid the advert if the (target) adolescent market is attracted to it. As a rule of thumb, familiar music works well because product information is being linked to already existing knowledge (linking new information to existing memories is a well-established memory aid), and catchy tunes are easily remembered and readily associated with a product.

The goal of advertising is to persuade the viewer to take one form of action (i.e. their preferred one) over another, and central to this is the formation of a *long-term memory* which will influence future behaviour in the desired direction. Advertisers then are interested in persuading us by creating strong, clear and positive memories of their message. Memories for adverts are formed in different ways. For example, we may remember information specifically about the brand; we may remember information about the product; or we may remember affective information – how we feel about the advert, for instance.

Research shows that adverts are prone to *competitive interference*: that is, memories for adverts can be affected by exposure to other adverts, especially ones selling similar products. Burke and Srull (1988) found that not even repetition of an advert could improve memory for an advertised product when there is this kind of memory interference effect. The effect however appears to be mostly limited to memory for unfamiliar products. Kent and Allen (1994) found that there were no interference effects for already familiar products when they were exposed to competition from other familiar and unfamiliar ones. Competitive interference then seems to be a problem particular to unfamiliar brands and products. This implies that advertisers for products aiming to compete with established lines need to do something special with their advertisements to improve the chance that they will be remembered.

Repetition is often used by individuals to commit something to memory, so perhaps it is not surprising to find that it is also used by advertisers to aid memory for their products. Repetition is especially effective when the goal of the advertiser is simply to get the viewer to remember. To consider this

a successful technique, the approach has to be matched carefully to the goals of the campaign – the 'mere exposure' effect only works up to a point where exposure fatigue can result in diminishing returns. This is why advertisers attempt to improve product memory by varying how they advertise the product. Unnava and Burnkrant (1991) found that people would remember an unfamiliar brand or product more if the advert was varied, rather than the same one being used repeatedly. Given the regularity with which advertisers change the way they advertise the same product, this appears to be a message that has got through.

McGuire's theory

Based on the principles of the Hovland-Yale model, McGuire (1969) argues that an effective advertisement is one that has successfully passed through several stages of a decision-making process, or 'decision tree'. 'Success' means that the end result of this process is that a consumer buys the product. At each of the decision-making stages (or 'branches') a person is faced with a 'yes/no' decision. A 'yes' takes the person to the next stage, whilst a 'no' at any point means that the advertisement has failed. The role of the advertiser is, at each stage, to maximise the likelihood of a 'yes' decision.

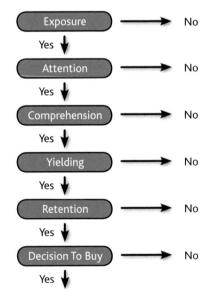

Exposure

Only those exposed to an advert can possibly be influenced by it. Therefore everything possible must be done to ensure maximum exposure and to be certain that the target audience sees the advert. This is why, when 'channel-hopping', the same advert can be seen on different channels, and why adverts for specific products are screened at particular times of day.

Attention

Even in those exposed to the advert, only some will pay attention. People often use commercial breaks to go to the bathroom or make a cup of tea. Advertisers have to use tricks and devices to make their advert as attractive as possible so that people keep watching – spectacular special effects, music and sound, comedy, surprise, sequential and 'mystery' ads (where it is not always clear what is being sold) are all frequently used.

Comprehension

It is important that the advert is constructed in such a way that viewers clearly understand the message. Is this product bigger than another? Does it smell nice? Are the benefits of using the product clear? At this stage, knowing what is being said is more important than belief in the message.

Yielding

This stage refers to the viewer agreeing with the message – they have to believe it. Some viewers of course may question the ad further before they yield: for example they might respond sceptically to a claim for a product as the "biggest ever!" Biggest ever *what* exactly? Whilst some viewers will believe the claim of a message, others may need a little more convincing.

Retention and decision to buy

This decision stage might occur some time after exposure, since very often viewers are not in a position to buy at the time of the advert (although within-store televisions are increasingly being used). Even though a viewer has comprehended and yielded, the viewer has to remember the message. Advertisers and manufacturers use techniques like package design and in-store position of the product to aid retention and recall. Other factors are also important, such as product price and again a range of techniques is used to influence the decision to buy – for example by relying on our natural ability to be fooled by number. The *actual* difference between £2.99 and £3.00 is less than the difference *perceived* by the customer, and multi-buys always *seem* more of a bargain than they actually are.

"McGuire's theory is a really straightforward way of explaining how television advertisers are attempting to persuade viewers. Now you can start to apply psychology when you watch those TV ads!"

THE PSYCHOLOGY OF 'CELEBRITY'

"What is fame? The advantage of being known by people of whom you yourself know nothing, and for whom you care as little."

Lord Byron, poet 1788–1824

Although 'celebrity' has nowadays become almost synonymous with 'famous' and 'star' (just take a look at the use of the terms in the average day's television schedules), Giles (2000) makes a distinction between 'celebrity' and the somewhat more prestigious though abused term 'famous'. For Giles, being famous means to be deserving of attention and recognition because of some significant personal achievement and impact on the world. 'Celebrity', on the other hand, is a much more modern phenomenon. The word derives from the French 'célèbre' meaning 'well known', and indeed celebrities are known for nothing in particular other than being 'known'. What constitutes 'celebrity' has certainly changed, more so in recent times with the massive growth in popularity of reality television. The desire for celebrity status has changed drastically too. In a 2008 survey, over a quarter of children stated that they wanted to be a celebrity when they grew up, with three of the top five career choices named by children involving celebrity status. Famous footballer, actress and pop star topped the children's list, with the nearest non-celebrity career aspirations being teacher and vet.

THE ATTRACTION OF CELEBRITY

It would not be an exaggeration to say that society appears obsessed with the muli-million pound celebrity industry. Many people seem either very attracted to the idea of being a celebrity, or interested in the vagaries of celebrity lifestyles. Shelves are piled high with magazines which are either completely devoted to celebrity (such publications account for a third of all news-stand sales), or which allocate significant chunks of content to it. Many television programmes like *The X Factor* and *Britain's Got Talent* promise those who aspire to it the hope of a shortcut to celebrity status. Boone and Lomore (2001) point out that 90% of the people they surveyed confessed to having been attracted to a celebrity at some point in their lives, with 75% indicating that they had had 'strong attachments' to one or more celebrities. The effects of this obsession are pernicious and one can only

388 | A2 PSYCHOLOGY: THE STUDENT'S TEXTBOOK

speculate at the long-term consequences. In a 2006 poll for National Kids' Day, children under 10 rated being a celebrity as their "very best thing in the world". Second came good looks, and third came being rich. For the second year running, God came tenth. In another National Kids' Day survey, this time in 2008, when children were asked "Who is the most famous person in the world?" TV presenter Simon Cowell came top, with God and the Queen second and third respectively.

It is perhaps not hard to see why many psychologists are interested in knowing why celebrity is so important to us. Answering the question, however, is actually a very difficult, complex process. Many of the emerging issues do not appear amenable to experimental psychology, belonging as they do to explanations at a more social level where sociological and anthropological perspectives might be more useful. Psychological research, however, is providing some very important insights into the attraction of celebrity.

SOCIAL PSYCHOLOGICAL EXPLANATIONS FOR THE ATTRACTION OF CELEBRITY

"The rise of celebrity culture has been rapid, and only relatively recently has psychology risen to the challenge of trying to explain its attraction. Two explanations are summarised here, offering contrasting social psychological approaches to understanding the attraction of celebrity."

Parasocial interaction

The term 'parasocial interaction' was introduced by Horton and Wohl (1956) to describe the responses of people to entertainment characters whom they feel they know but have never met. They pointed out that many people in the media address viewers more or less directly, and that people often respond as though the media person was there in front of them. Over time, some form of parasocial relationship can develop between viewers and media characters, something which increases the importance of the media character in the viewer's life. Parasocial relationships appear relatively normal in that they do not seem to be related to any particular problem personal traits, such as chronic loneliness, low self-esteem and neuroticism. People with well-developed social abilities can have strong parasocial relationships. Indeed, research shows that parasocial relationships are like real ones in many ways. Factors which influence a positive and enjoyable real relationship also apply to parasocial ones. In a similar fashion to real-life relationships, the attractiveness and similarity of the media character seem to be important. Admiration is also a factor, since celebrities often possess character traits which other non-celebrities would like to have too. Parasocial relationships are psychologically real to those that are experiencing them (Derrick et al, 2007).

Having parasocial relationships with celebrities may not be all bad, and for many people it may be a positive thing. People who are shy might find parasocial relationships attractive because their needs for social interaction are being met at least in part by the parasocial interaction. Parasocial relationships are relatively 'safe'. There is little or no risk of face-to-face contact and rejection, for example. People who have problems creating and maintaining real relationships might turn to parasocial ones as safe alternatives. For some, this may only be a temporary situation, with parasocial relationships helping people through particularly difficult times. Derrick et al (2008) suggest that parasocial relationships can allow people with low self-esteem to see themselves more positively. They showed that people with low self-esteem saw their favourite celebrity as very similar to their ideal self. Crucially, when primed to think about this celebrity prior to assessment, low self-esteem people saw themselves more similar to their ideal selves. This effect did not occur when they were primed by thinking about a close relationship partner. It seems that, for some people, parasocial relationships can have enhancing effects that are lacking in real-life relationships.

The formation of parasocial relationships may be particularly important during adolescence, a time when individuals are searching for identity. During this time, young people can become intensely attached to media figures, whose morals and values become very influential. Giles and Maltby (2004) point out that during this time when young people are growing more independent, media figures can become more important role models than parents.

Religiosity

Schumaker (2003) points out that there seems to be an association between the decline of organised religion and fascination with celebrity. As levels of religiousness reduce in society, the tendency towards celebrity worship increases. He quotes a

Barry Manilow fan as saying: "It's the same sort of thing people get out of religion. They obviously get something from God and Barry is the same sort of thing. He helps me get through life". It has been argued that humans have a fundamental need to worship. Indeed, indications of ritual and worship are found in the earliest evidence of human life. In a society that is becoming ever more secular, this need to worship is being displaced onto celebrities.

Whilst celebrities are viewed with a devotion and reverence resembling religious worship by some of their fans (Giles, 2000), research has not supported a direct link between positive attitudes to celebrity and tendency to religious fervour. Maltby et al (2002) compared scores on the Celebrity Attitude Scale with a variety of religiosity measures and found a modest negative correlation of –0.2. As religiosity increased, tendencies towards celebrity worship decreased Another study by Maltby (2004), this time using different measures of religiosity, again found a negative correlation (but a stronger one). It seems that whilst celebrity worship superficially resembles religious worship, there are probably different (as yet unidentified) underlying psychological processes in operation.

According to Houran et al (2005), non-religious people are more interested than religious people in celebrity culture. For these people, the worship of celebrity fulfils the same function as a church does for believers. Jindra (1994) asserted that *Star Trek* fandom had strong affinities with a religious-type movement. Through interviews with fans ('Trekkies') and participant observation at fan conventions, Jindra came to the conclusion that whilst *Star Trek* does not fit the more strict criterion for a religion that it must have a deity, it does however appear to have the features of a quasi-religion. It has organisation, dogma, a recruitment system, and a 'canon'. *Star Trek* fandom seems to be serving the same purpose for devotees as any other civil religion. Neither is this an isolated case. Another well established example of media/religiosity link relates to the science fiction film *Star Wars*. First mentioned in the 1977 movie *Star Wars IV: A New Hope*, Jediism has become a worldwide phenomenon. Influenced by Daoist, Shinto and Buddhist teachings, Jediism has many things in common with more traditional organised religions, such as ethics, monastic practices, and spirituality. In the 2001 UK Census, 390,127 people stated their religion as Jedi. This placed it ahead of Sikhism, Judaism, and Buddhism, although these figures are claimed to be part of a hoax rather than

a true reflection of religious belief (for example, the geographical dispersion of Jedi belief seemed to coincide with university towns).

The UK Church of Jediism.

Social comparison theory

According to Festinger (1954), people have a need to evaluate their own opinions and abilities. Since questions that we ask about ourselves cannot be answered objectively, we instead socially construct answers. In search of information, we turn to what other people say and observe how other people behave. For example, if a student wants to know how good they are at a particular subject, they compare themselves to other students. This is a realistic comparison to similar others and gives the person making the comparison at least a sense of an accurate perception of where they stand. People don't always make these kinds of comparisons, however. If we want to feel better about ourselves we might be motivated to make comparisons to people who are most likely to yield a favourable outcome – for example to someone who is not as skilled or adept as we are. This is a *downward comparison* (i.e. a comparison to someone worse off). On the other hand, comparisons might be made with those we aspire to be like, and these are called *upward comparisons*. Into this category fall celebrities, who to different degrees present idealised images of self and are influential behavioural role models. The extent to which people base their own beliefs and opinions on those of others varies considerably and depends on a number of factors, such as existing self-image and self-esteem, and age. Adolescence for example is a time during which individuals are particularly prone to social comparison processes since it is during this time that they are forming their own adult identity and developing a sense of independence.

Negative body image and low self-esteem have been attributed to upward comparisons, especially with media containing, as it does, images of celebrities with unrealistic physical attributes (Wilcox and Laird, 2000). This body dissatisfaction caused by upward comparison has also been blamed for increases in eating disorders. For instance, Shorter et al (2008) assessed eating problems in female students by using the Eating Attitudes Test and compared the result to a measure of the difference between how they perceived their bodies and how they perceived the body of a favourite celebrity. They found that the greater the gap in the body comparisons, the more likely a person was to have disordered eating attitudes. It seems from this study that some women are motivated to engage in disordered eating to close the gap between how they perceive themselves and the standard set by the celebrity. Social comparison with celebrities may apply to many more contexts however. Jones (2001) found that adolescent boys and girls tended to use celebrities, rather than peers, for social comparison of physical attractiveness. Chan and Prendergast (2007) suggest that social comparison processes involving celebrity lead to greater materialism. Adolescents who compare their possessions with those of media celebrities come to believe that material possessions are important and related to happiness and success. For Chan and Prendergast then, upward comparisons with celebrity can encourage materialistic aspirations.

EVOLUTIONARY EXPLANATIONS FOR THE ATTRACTION OF CELEBRITY

Evolution theory assumes that any behaviour which appears widespread or universal today must once have served a useful survival purpose. Natural evolutionary pressures which have shaped our physical features also exert their influence on such things as thought and social behaviour. Entertainment is one such universal feature of human behaviour which has resulted from such pressures. All human cultures have forms of art and some means of entertainment, and almost certainly contain individuals recognised as having some talent in these areas. There are a number of approaches to explaining the attraction of celebrity from an evolutionary perspective.

"It is typical that evolutionary psychology offers more than one explanation for something, and celebrity is no exception. Several are offered here, all appearing a little different from each other. Remember – behaviour can evolve for more than one reason so it isn't necessarily a matter of choosing between them."

Entertainment as play theory

According to Vorderer (2001), since entertainment experiences have a great deal in common with play experience, entertainment could be considered a form of play. Logically, since play has an evolutionary function, therefore so must entertainment.

Play is a behaviour observed in many species, indicating that the behaviour itself is much older than the modern human species, *homo erectus*. The fact that it is so widespread also suggests that it must serve some important function. In terms of evolution, play in early humans may have been nothing more than incidental behavioural responses, governed by specifically evolved circuits in the brain, whose function was to engage the organism in exercise to encourage physical development and also to practise skills which would be needed as adults. Play served a useful purpose then, preparing an animal for hunting, fighting and mating. As cognitive systems evolved, many species were freed from a strictly behavioural function for play. Cognition enables internal representations of events and the mental manipulation of behavioural routines. One consequence is that play ceased to become tied to actual events and enactments. Animals with developed cognition can imagine situations, and the more highly developed the cognitive abilities the more abstract and creative these mental representations of play become. At the top of the evolutionary tree are human beings, where the need for play to serve basic biological functions is reduced, but in whom cognitive capacities have evolved far beyond those of other animals.

There is archeological evidence which indicates that our ancestors employed a form of media for entertainment purposes as long as 40,000 to 50,000 years ago, with carving and rock art. This early art suggests that these people were able to create narratives and plots, and therefore the basic elements for the development of more sophisticated media entertainment were in place. The advantage of being able to represent storylines in the form of art was that it took the pressure off the cognitive system to store all this information, so it was now freed up to devote even more mental resources to imagination and creativity.

Leisure time theory

According to Zillman (2000), between 200,000 and 600,000 years ago human development had reached a point where subsistence needs were more easily met and our species could be a little less vigilant in our threat detection. This was achieved by, for example, more efficient hunting in groups and the increased use of tools. A key change however was the domestication of fire. Mastery of fire provided comfort in the cold, a deterrent for predators, and a means to cook more nourishing food. The result of these developments was an increase in leisure time. This spare time may at first have been used for religious and ceremonial purposes. Over thousands of years, however, increasing amounts of leisure time were put to ever more creative use by our evolving cognitive system. This gave rise to entertainment and culture. As mastery of the environment has improved over the last 40,000 years, so humans have had ever more time to devote to entertainment. Indeed, it can even be seen in modern times that cultures which have the most developed forms of media entertainment are those who have to labour least to satisfy basic daily needs. The attraction to celebrity therefore is the result of having a brain whose capacity has evolved beyond that needed to satisfy survival needs.

Ornamental mind theory

According to Fisher's sexy 'runaway' sexual selection theory, females will choose males to mate with based on the characteristics they find most attractive. Both this male trait and the preference of the female will then be passed onto the next generation. This means that they both become fixed in the gene pool of a species, the increasingly attractive male trait being selected by more females attracted to it. It is important to note here that this male trait might have no adaptive value and be nothing more than an accessory desirable to females.

Miller (2000) suggests that this kind of sexual selection underlies the evolution of creative intelligence. In effect, the male brain is a sexual ornament used to attract females. Females are inclined by their biology to select males who are the most interesting and entertaining of a group. It could be argued that the attraction of celebrity is one consequence of these sexual selection processes. The fact that over two thirds of the readership of celebrity gossip magazines are female might be seen as support for this notion.

The ornamental mind theory says then that through a process of runaway sexual selection the human mind has ended up as a fitness indicator. The theory basically says that the human mind is designed so as to entertain other minds during courtship. Whereas in modern times we can rely on forms of entertainment such as cinema and concerts to assist with impressing and wooing potential partners, our ancestors did not have this facility. Just as is the case today, to prove boring when trying to attract a partner invited failure. A creative and entertaining mind therefore can have benefits in the courtship game (Miller, 2000). Thus celebrity is attractive because the traits which have allowed individuals to achieve this status – for example creativity, exhibitionism, entertainment value – are those which evolution has singled out as fitness indicators. We want to be celebrities therefore because celebrity brings with it a reproductive advantage.

Gossip theory

It has been suggested that fascination with celebrities arises because they are a rich source of gossip. The term 'gossip' usually refers to the act of exchanging information about someone who is not present. It is something which appears universal in the human species – wherever they might live in the world, people appear to love talking about other people. For McAndrew (2008), gossip is just another aspect of social behaviour that is adaptive. Our very early ancestors lived in much smaller and more isolated social groups than we do now, so that every face they saw was almost certainly a familiar one. It paid in those times to know what was happening in the wider social group. It was important to keep track of alliances and relationships, and those who posed potential threats. It was also important to have a concern about social status, since in smaller social groups those with status have power that can exert a more direct influence on an individual's well-being. Gossip carries information that is potentially useful, and having this information might allow one person to gain an advantage over another. Shared secrets also help to bond social groups together. Gossip also gives those individuals without status or power a sense of involvement and influence over events. It paid to be socially successful in this environment, and gossip was one route to this. Ultimately, knowledge about who is doing what and with whom could help to ensure survival, and those who were best at gossiping would have a survival advantage. Whilst society has changed dramatically since the times of our early ancestors, our 'hard-wiring' hasn't. Humans still have this innate tendency to gossip, and whilst we do gossip (quite prolifically so) about people we have direct knowledge of, celebrities also provide an ideal vehicle for this basic instinct. Celebrities might be an attractive target for gossip because they are perceived to have a high status – based on wealth, success, admiration and the attention they receive from others. The media provides plenty of information to fuel this gossiping, with television shows, newspapers and magazines full of the latest news on what people are wearing, latest affairs, and personal trials and tribulations.

Dunbar (1996) takes a slightly different angle on celebrity gossip. He suggests that gossip evolved in humans to serve the same purpose as grooming in primates. Primates don't groom each other entirely for health reasons. Time is spent grooming which could, if grooming had no purpose, be spent foraging or mating. It is a route to social communication and helps to bond social groups together. Dunbar estimates that as much as two thirds of all human communication consists of gossip. Celebrity is attractive because it is a source of gossip which is very useful in strengthening social relationships.

RESEARCH INTO INTENSE FANDOM

That celebrities attract fans is a given fact – it is a part of the natural history of celebrity that there is a fan base of some size or other. Whilst most people have opinions, and like or dislike celebrities to some degree or other, being a 'fan' is a little more than this. 'Fan' after all is short for 'fanatic', a definition of which is "a person whose enthusiasm and zeal for something is extreme or beyond normal limits" (Collins Concise English Dictionary).

CELEBRITY WORSHIP

The extent to which a person is a fan of celebrity can be considered to vary along a continuum, at the one end being a passing interest and at the other an intense worship. Most fan worship is middling on this continuum and amounts to little more than could be described as a strong interest. For example, a fan of a pop group may develop a collection of memorabilia, buy all the CDs, go to concerts, and keep up with current news by checking out websites. Their life otherwise goes on as normal, with their fandom and day-to-day living separate. Other fans have a significant preoccupation with their celebrity, and their fandom takes up a lot of time, energy and money, but nonetheless they function normally. Some fans however approach the extreme end of the continuum. For them, their fandom encroaches on day-to-day life, sometimes substantially so. Their life appears completely preoccupied with celebrity, and their behaviour could be described as obsessional. The term 'celebrity worship' is used to describe this obsessive behaviour pattern.

Individual differences in celebrity worship have been assessed using the Celebrity Attitude Scale (CAS). Developed by Maltby et al (2002), this measures three dimensions of celebrity worship:

Entertainment-social: fans are attracted to celebrities because of their entertainment value and because it serves social functions (e.g. talking to friends). (Items in the scale such as 'My friends and I like to discuss what my favourite celebrity has done' relate to this dimension.)

Intense-personal: fans develop strong and intensive and compulsive feelings about their favourite celebrity, bordering on the obsessional. (Items in the scale such as 'I have frequent thoughts about my celebrity, even when I don't want to' relate to this dimension.)

Borderline-pathological: fans develop uncontrollable fantasies and behaviours relating to their favourite celebrity. This is the most extreme form of celebrity worship. (Items in the scale such as 'If I were lucky enough to meet my favourite celebrity, and he/she asked me to do something illegal as a favour I would probably do it' relate to this dimension.)

McCutcheon et al (2003) surveyed 600 participants and found that 20% fell into the first category, and followed celebs for entertainment value. Another 10% fell into the second category, feeling that they had a 'special bond' with the celebrity. Less that 1% were considered borderline-pathological. The differences between intense-personal and borderline-pathological celebrity worship are significant. Whilst the former type of relationship is a passive one, in that the fan does not really expect to interact with the celebrity, people in the borderline-pathological category actually believe themselves to be in a relationship with the celebrity and have a focus on how this may develop in the future. Houran et al (2005) used the term 'erotomania' to describe some extreme types of celebrity worship. Erotomania is a disorder whereby a person has the delusion that another person (in this context a celebrity) secretly has feelings for them.

Maltby et al (2005) suggest that celebrity worship is associated with poor body image. They surveyed 229 adolescents, 183 university students, and 289 adults using the CAS and assessments of body image. They found a strong association between intense-personal celebrity worship and body image, but only in female adolescents. It seems that some adolescent females have particularly strong parasocial relationships with media figures whose body shapes they admire. The relationship between celebrity worship and body image seems to disappear in early adulthood. This supports previous research suggesting that the most important psychological influence of media during adolescence is in the development of parasocial relationships (Giles, 2002). This research also supports research which links exposure to the media with eating disorders (e.g. Harrison, 1994).

Whilst for some people parasocial relationships might be beneficial, reducing sense of loneliness and isolation, for others such relationships could become addictive and get in the way of more productive 'real' relationships. In a minority of people, this can develop into an obsessional interest in people in the media. McCutcheon et al (2002) proposed the *absorption-addiction hypothesis* to explain how parasocial relationships can become abnormal, so that individuals become obsessed with one or more celebrities. They proposed that some people become embroiled in such parasocial relationships because they have deficits in their own personal identities. Absorption is an attempt to establish identity and achieve a sense of fulfilment. This absorption has addictive qualities so that individuals engage in more extreme behaviours to sustain satisfaction with the relationship.

For Schumaker (2003), some kinds of fan worship are examples of an intense *celebrity worship syndrome*. Whilst it is not a clinically recognised problem, he describes this syndrome as an obsessive addiction disorder affecting both males and females equally. Those most seriously afflicted with celebrity worship syndrome become solitary, anti-social, impulsive and highly delusional. Such people can believe for example that 'their' celebrity has a particular interest in them, and values their opinion and guidance. Schumaker reports the case of one celebrity worship syndrome sufferer who, on hearing that her idol had become engaged, slashed her neck, arms and legs, explaining that: "She's going to change him if he gets married and I am not going to live with that".

STALKING

Some researchers consider stalking to be an example of celebrity worship taken to the extreme. Stalking is a potentially dangerous obsession, described as behaviour focused on a particular individual which is intrusive or unwanted, and which creates fear in the recipient. Although anyone can be a victim of stalking, and indeed most stalking in society does not involve fans and their celebrities, it is the stalking of celebrities that most often makes the news.

According to Meloy (1999) stalking can be considered either 'private' or 'public'. In private stalking, there has been a previous relationship between the stalker and the victim. Public stalking however is a more predatory form of stalking in which the target is a public figure, such as a celebrity. There is no single explanation for why some individuals stalk, but research is beginning to identify a number of factors which predispose certain individuals to engage in this intrusive behaviour.

Attachment theory of stalking

Attachment theory maintains that attachments developed in infancy remain relatively stable over a lifetime, and that the kinds of emotional bonds formed early in life between a child and parent are reflected later in life in the nature of adult-to-adult bonds. This occurs because a child develops an internal working model of relationships – that is, a set of expectations about relationships which stays with the person throughout life. Whilst early stable attachments lead to healthy development into and through adulthood, there is a growing body of research suggesting that early attachment problems can lead social and emotional problems later in adulthood. Hazan and Shaver (1987) for example found that adult romantic relationship patterns resembled childhood attachments. People with secure attachments in childhood tended to form secure relationships with their adult partners, and those who experienced insecure attachments tended to feel less secure with their adult partners.

Based on Bowlby's theory of an internal working model, Bartholemew (1990) developed a theory which describes four types of adult attachment: secure, preoccupied, dismissing and fearful. According to Meloy (1992), stalkers most closely resemble the preoccupied attachment pattern. For Kienlen (1998), the motivations of stalkers differ according to the kind of insecure attachment they have:

The *'preoccupied' stalker* – someone who has a poor self-image and constantly seeks approval from others. Stalking results from some kind of real or imagined rejection and is an attempt to restore a positive sense of self.

The *'fearful' stalker* – someone who has a poor self-image but sees others as unsupportive and unreliable. Stalking is a result of a cycle of wanting someone to help boost self-image but rejecting them because of a lack of trust. Stalking is a way of boosting this negative self-image.

The *'dismissing' stalker* – remains distant and aloof from others in order to maintain an inflated self-image. When relationships break up this person may stalk out of revenge for what they perceive as mistreatment.

There is a growing body of research to support the idea that stalking is related to disturbed attachment patterns. In an analysis of the criminal records of 25 stalkers in a Missouri jail Kienlen et al (1997) found that the majority had experienced childhood attachment disruptions and had lost important personal relationships six months prior to starting their stalking behaviour. For instance, 48% had experienced the breaking up of a marriage, and 28% the potential loss of a child (e.g. through a custody dispute). Furthermore, Lewis et al (2001) compared the psychological characteristics of stalkers to a control group and found that stalkers have traits typical of insecure attachment,

I'M YOUR GREATEST FAN...EXAMPLES OF CELEBRITY STALKERS

Steven Spielberg

More than one in four of the 1.4 million annual US stalking victims are men, and despite the impression left by the media, few male victims are pursued by females who have been spurned – 90% are stalked by other men. Film director Spielberg was one such victim. He was stalked for two months by 31-year-old body builder Jonathan Norman. He hatched a plot to invade Spielberg's home in order to rape him in front of his family, and was arrested outside Spielberg's house with a 'rape kit', including duct tape, handcuffs and a utility knife. Norman was found guilty and, because of previous convictions, was sentenced to 25 years in prison under 'three strikes' laws.

Brad Pitt

Aspiring actress Athena Rolando was arrested in 2000 after having broken into the actor's home in Los Angeles. She had been there for ten hours and was discovered dressed in his clothes. She was carrying a book on witchcraft and a note to Pitt and, even after her arrest, she sent the actor chocolates and flowers. Rolando was placed on probation for three years, required to stay at least 100 yards from Brad Pitt and undergo psychological counselling.

Madonna

In May 1995, Robert Hoskins, 38, scaled the walls of Madonna's Hollywood Hills estate and left notes on her door threatening to kill her if she didn't marry him. On another visit he was shot and injured by one of her bodyguards. Whilst in prison awaiting trial, Hoskins filled his cell with graffiti, such as 'I love Madonna', 'Madonna Love Me', and 'The Madonna Stalker'. When confronted about the graffiti, Hoskins claimed that Madonna wrote it and when he got out of jail he was "going to slice the lying bitches' throat from ear to ear". Hoskins was found guilty of stalking, making threats and assault on a bodyguard, and was sentenced to a minimum of ten years in prison.

Catherine Zeta-Jones

Dawnette Knight subjected Catherine Zeta-Jones to a series of 19 threatening letters as the result of an obsession with her husband, Michael Douglas. Believing that Zeta-Jones was an opportunist who only married Douglas for his money, one of Knight's letters was a vow to slice Zeta-Jones up and feed her to the dogs. After her arrest, she wrote a letter of apology to Zeta-Jones in which she confessed to being "a confused young woman infatuated with Michael Douglas". She was charged with stalking and 24 counts of making criminal threats, and was sentenced to 3 years in prison as well as a 10-year restraining order barring Knight from contact with Zeta-Jones and her family.

such as ambivalence towards others they were in a close relationship with, inadequate interpersonal attachment, and emotional instability.

McCutcheon et al (2006) investigated whether childhood insecure attachment is associated with attachment to celebrities and tendencies to condone celebrity stalking. They measured childhood attachment, the tendency to condone celebrity stalking and celebrity worship in 299 university students. They found that those who were measured as having an insecure childhood attachment were more likely to excuse celebrity stalking. McCutcheon et al hypothesise that one aspect of the relationship difficulties that adults with insecure childhood attachments have is a greater likelihood to form parasocial relationships. This is a typical relationship between celebrity and fan. Such relationships might appeal to insecurely attached adults because it is relatively safe. Because the relationship is not 'real', there are few demands made, and the risk of rejection is low as long as no attempt is made to seek contact with the celebrity. It should be remembered however that, rather than being a direct cause of stalking, a disordered attachment is a predisposing factor, i.e. it only increases the risk of this happening.

Testimony continues at the Santa Claus stalking trial.

Relational goal pursuit theory of stalking

This theory is based on the assumption that people want to engage in relationships because they are desirable, and because they are desirable people acquire goals to possess certain kinds of relationships with others. As with any goal, when the goal is thwarted people often engage in extra effort to achieve it. If the effort needed to achieve the goal is greater than its value then it is abandoned in favour of an alternative one. Applied to stalking, this theory says that people who engage in the obsessional pursuit of a relationship that is rejected by the other person tend to magnify the importance of their relationship goal. This leads to thoughts and feelings which serve to further fuel their efforts.

The nature of goals and goal-setting is central to an understanding of relational goal pursuit theory. Goals are structured hierarchically, so that lower-order goals are often necessary in achieving higher-order goals. It is easy to discard lower-order goals, whereas higher-order goals are more deep-rooted. For example, a lower-order goal might be to eat a particular breakfast cereal to achieve a higher-order goal of good health and a particular body shape. The goal of eating the cereal can be readily abandoned in favour of some other strategy, but it would not be so easy to abandon the more ingrained higher-order goal.

Some people come to view lower-order goals as more important than they really are because of the way they *link* lower-order goals to higher-order goals, for instance, when they see success in the lower-order goals as essential to the attainment of a higher-order goal (McIntosh, 1976). It might be that people become stalkers because they come to believe that happiness (higher-order goal) depends on accomplishment of goals such as being in a particular kind of relationship (lower-order goal). In this way, the relationship now takes on an exaggerated importance and is pursued in the face of all kinds of resistance and obstacles.

Applied to celebrity stalking, fans seeking connection with a celebrity link this lower-order goal with a higher-order one, for example improved self-worth. When the goal is blocked, rumination occurs (McIntosh et al, 1995). This is where the fan constantly thinks about the unmet goal, the thoughts becoming more and more intrusive and unpleasant, for example exaggerating the consequences of goal failure. These negative thoughts are accompanied by negative feelings which cause further rumination. Excessive pursuit behaviours are rationalised; negative consequences are not recognised; and the fan further exaggerates their ability to attain what they desire – a relationship with the celebrity (Cupach and Spitzberg, 2004).

The psychology of addictive behaviour

CLAIRE WILLIAMS AND NIGEL HOLT

You are expected to develop knowledge, understanding and critical thinking in relation to the topic of Addictive behaviour.

This includes applying knowledge and understanding of research methods, approaches, issues and debates where appropriate. You must also show an appreciation of the relationship between research, policy and practices in applying psychology in every day life.

WHAT YOU NEED TO KNOW

MODELS OF ADDICTIVE BEHAVIOUR

- Biological, cognitive and learning models of addiction, including explanations for initiation, maintenance and relapse
- Explanations for specific addictions, including smoking and gambling

FACTORS AFFECTING ADDICTIVE BEHAVIOUR

- Vulnerability to addiction including self-esteem, attributions for addiction and social context of addiction
- The role of media in addictive behaviour

REDUCING ADDICTIVE BEHAVIOUR

- Models of prevention, including theory of reasoned action and theory of planned behaviour
- Types of intervention, including biological, psychological, public health interventions and legislation, and their effectiveness

THE PSYCHOLOGY OF ADDICTIVE BEHAVIOUR

INTRODUCTION

The term 'addiction' derives from the Latin word 'addicere', meaning 'to sentence'. Just as someone might be sentenced to prison, so too might the person be sentenced to an addiction. In recent years the term 'addiction' has come to refer to a range of behaviours associated not only with alcohol and drug dependence but also with food, exercise, gambling and even relationships with others.

Addiction has become a very serious social problem that afflicts many millions of people and touches the lives of everyone they know. Take a look around the area where you live. You will quickly see how available many of the facilities for addictive behaviour are. These include bookmakers, where gambling is possible on any number of events – ranging from football results, through horse racing to things that you might not expect, such as whether it will snow on Christmas Day. The National Lottery has provided an easy way to gamble, with many people buying far more than one ticket on each occasion. Other establishments that may well attract people with addictions include newsagents (where tobacco, containing nicotine – one of the most addictive substances known – can be easily bought), or off-licences, pubs and supermarkets that can provide access to cheap alcohol. Access to drugs may be a little harder to see, but it is clear that the use of illegal drugs is very widespread indeed. Research published in 2002 found that, within the UK alone, around 1 in 3 of the adult population had taken an illegal drug at some time, with 12% of adults reporting use in the last year. For 18–24-year-olds, the corresponding figures were 50% and 29% respectively (Drugscope, 2002).

"You need to know about two adddictive behaviours in particular. Whilst there are opportunities to talk about others, make sure that you really know about smoking and gambling."

DIAGNOSING ADDICTION – SMOKING

Smoking is a form of drug addiction, the active component of tobacco being nicotine. The most recent edition of the Diagnostic and Statistical Manual (DSM-IV-R) refers to drug dependence as:

"a cluster of cognitive, behavioural, and physiological symptoms indicating that the individual continues use of the substance despite significant substance-related problems".

The criteria used within DSM-IV-R to identify dependence on a substance include the following:

» the individual develops tolerance: much larger doses of drug are needed to achieve a given effect

» efforts by the individual to reduce or control his/her substance use are unsuccessful

» the substance is often taken in larger amounts or over a longer period than the individual intended

» the individual devotes a lot of time to making sure he/she has access to the substance

» and important social, occupational, or recreational activities are reduced or given up as a result of substance use.

Tobacco dependence is more prevalent than dependence on any other substance of abuse (Anthony et al, 1994). The popularity of tobacco spread rapidly from Columbus's trading with the native American Indians in the 16th century. It did not take long for sailors and merchants to imitate the smoking of rolled leaves of tobacco and to experience, as the Indians did, the increased craving for it.

The threat to health that smoking poses has been documented convincingly throughout the world since the mid-1960s. Among the medical problems associated with, and almost certainly caused or made worse by, long-term cigarette smoking are lung cancer, emphysema, cancer of the larynx and oesophagus, and a number of cardiovascular diseases.

One of the many statistics on the health hazards of smoking is the estimate that 30–35-year-olds, smoking two packs a day (that's 40 or more cigarettes), have a mortality rate twice that of non-smokers. Further, it has been predicted that by 2020 tobacco will have become the largest single health problem worldwide, causing approximately 8.4 million deaths annually (Murray and Lopez, 1997). Despite this wealth of evidence, the number of people that quit remains low even though there are several medical treatments available to help users give up the habit (Haas et al, 2004).

DIAGNOSING ADDICTION – GAMBLING

It was not until 1980 that the DSM defined a gambling disorder – called pathological gambling (PG). To be diagnosed with PG a person must meet at least five of the following criteria:

» is preoccupied with gambling (e.g., preoccupied with reliving past gambling experiences, or planning the next venture, or thinking of ways to get money with which to gamble)

» needs to gamble with increasing amounts of money in order to achieve the desired excitement

» has made repeated unsuccessful efforts to control, cut back, or stop gambling

» is restless or irritable when attempting to cut down or stop gambling

» gambles as a way of escaping from problems or of relieving a dysphoric mood (e.g., feelings of helplessness, guilt, anxiety, depression)

» after losing money gambling, often returns another day in order to get even ('chasing' one's losses)

» lies to family members, therapist, or others to conceal the extent of involvement with gambling

» has committed illegal acts, such as forgery, fraud, theft, or embezzlement, in order to finance gambling

» has jeopardised or lost a significant relationship, job, or educational or career opportunity because of gambling

» relies on others to provide money to relieve a desperate financial situation caused by gambling.

It's very clear from these criteria that pathological gambling really can be understood to be an addiction comparable in many ways to the addictions with which we are, perhaps, more familiar. Gambling is a very common recreational behaviour. A large number of adults gamble, and most do so without encountering any significant psychological problems. Nonetheless, gambling problems have been estimated as affecting as many as 5% of the adult population – with certain groups such as young adults, people with mental health disorders and those in prison having much higher rates (Shaffer et al, 1999). Given the increased availability of legalised gambling and its popularity over the past few decades, more research on the health impacts of specific levels of gambling behaviour is now being undertaken.

MODELS OF ADDICTIVE BEHAVIOUR

There are a number of biological and psychological explanations for addiction. Each of these explanations takes a different view of how addictions to, for example, smoking or gambling are initiated, how they are maintained and how addicts often relapse into their addictions. In the following sections we will examine biological, cognitive and social learning models that attempt to explain addictions to smoking and gambling. It is important to note, however, that addictions are complex behaviours that rarely have their origins in a single explanation. Any reasonable understanding of an addiction requires a broad multi-disciplinary approach, involving a combination of biological, psychological and social explanations.

THE BIOLOGICAL MODEL

The *physical dependence theory* suggests that people become addicted because doing without the item or behaviour to which they are addicted is so unpleasant. An important concept associated with physical dependence theory is 'tolerance'. As a person continues to smoke he/she becomes *tolerant*, and needs to engage in the activity more and more to maintain the positive feeling it gives. Stopping the activity may well result in unpleasant side effects of *withdrawal*.

*"Warning! You need to know about the **biological** model of addiction and how it is applied to initiation, maintenance and relapse for both smoking and gambling. Unless you are organised (like this chapter is organised!) you could get confused. So, first we explain what the biological model is, then we apply it to initiation, maintenance and relapse of smoking; and then to initiation, maintenance and relapse of gambling."*

Withdrawal is where a person stops engaging in his/her addictive behaviour and experiences a range of unpleasant physical symptoms which can include shaking, sweating and other aches and pains. Other physical symptoms may include an increased heart rate and raised blood pressure. More serious withdrawal symptoms could also include hallucinations, bouts of confusion and even seizures.

The process of withdrawal from the addictive behaviour is called *detoxification*, and can be carried out with or without the support of a number of specialist organisations and facilities. This support can be psychological and encouraging, but it may also be medical. If a person is experiencing the more serious withdrawal symptoms, including visual hallucinations and seizures, then medical support may well be required.

The process of detoxification frequently takes place in a rehabilitation clinic, often shortened to 'rehab'. It is true to say that detoxification, withdrawal and rehab are most associated with the type of addictive behaviours we see commonly covered by the media, particularly people's (usually celebrities') dependence on alcohol and other drugs. However, other very common addictions – such as those to nicotine and gambling – can also generate withdrawal symptoms; and those suffering an addiction to these behaviours may well benefit from the skilled support rehab is able to offer.

"*Remember, this is* psychology in action. *You may need to apply your knowledge in the exam rather than write an essay, so don't just learn this stuff rote-like, really try to understand how psychology is being applied. It is something you are going to have to do yourself.*"

According to the *positive reward theory,* addiction occurs because the feelings we get from engaging in the activity, be it smoking or gambling, are perceived to be so pleasant and rewarding. Many smokers will tell you that their first experience of smoking is not pleasant at all. In fact the first experience of inhaling hot smoke from a cigarette often causes people to choke and cough, or worse! Gambling, however, often generates an almost immediate feeling of excitement and a fast, some might say 'safe', buzz.

Consider the experiences felt by someone placing a small bet on a horse race. As the race approaches the gambler may sense an increased heart rate, a slow, but noticeable quickening of the breath and finally a surge of adrenaline. Gamblers will tell you that this feeling of excitement is extremely compelling, just as those who engage in dangerous sports,

such as base jumping or cliff diving, will confirm that their activity generates a natural 'high'.

Even if the excitement is followed by disappointment when the chosen horse does not win, the gambler has still been rewarded with the feeling of excitement associated with the bet, and the anticipation and event of the race itself. Engaging in the activity has provided a positive reward; and this, as the theory of operant conditioning predicts, will make it more likely that the behaviour will occur again.

ANIMALS DO IT TOO

THE HARDEST PART IS ADMITTING YOU HAVE A PROBLEM.

It's worth noting before we go on that although we are concerned mainly with addictive behaviours such as smoking and gambling by humans, self-administration of addictive substances by wild animals is well documented. For example, elephants and other animals have been observed becoming repeatedly intoxicated by eating the fruit of the marula tree; baboons consume tobacco in the wild; and intoxicating mushrooms are eaten by cattle, reindeer and rabbits. These observations suggest that addictive behaviour is widespread amongst many animals, not just humans.

SMOKING – THE BIOLOGICAL MODEL

Initiation

Forshaw (2002) indicates that the initiation of smoking behaviour may well be driven by a combination of pressures, including biological, social, cultural and environmental pressures. For some people, smoking is a pleasurable accompaniment to their relaxing activities, often in the pub with friends, or in other social groups. For others it is a necessary aid to coping with challenging and stressful situations. There is, however, evidence that the reason people take up smoking in the first place may well be something to do with their genetics. For example, Lerman et al (1999) have shown that people with a particular gene are less likely to take up smoking than those without it. The gene, called SLC6A3-9, works in the dopamine system. Dopamine will be discussed in more detail later in this chapter.

Maintenance

Whatever the reason for starting smoking, the reason for continuing the behaviour, according to the biological model, is *chemical addiction*. Quite why smokers become addicted can be explained in this model by the role nicotine plays. There is clear evidence that the nicotine within tobacco is an extremely addictive drug producing significant changes in how our brain functions.

Nicotine regulation model

Shachter (1977) asserts that the physical dependence theory is relevant to smokers. In the nicotine regulation model, he argues that smokers continue to smoke to maintain nicotine in the body at a level high enough to avoid any negative withdrawal symptoms. In his research he compared how many cigarettes different smokers needed to consume each week. Some of his participants were given cigarettes with a low nicotine content, and some, cigarettes with a high nicotine content. Those with the low nicotine cigarettes smoked more than those with the high nicotine cigarettes, just as would be predicted by the nicotine regulation model. The higher nicotine content allowed smokers to reach the level of nicotine required with fewer cigarettes. The result was clearest with heavy smokers: they smoked, on average, 25% more low-nicotine cigarettes than high nicotine cigarettes.

The reward system

Earlier, we mentioned that Lerman et al (1999) showed that those carrying a particular gene were less likely to take up smoking, and we noted that this gene worked in the dopamine system in the brain. Sabol et al (1999) went on to show that this gene (SLC6A3-9) was extremely important in enhancing people's ability to stop smoking, and that those not carrying it were more likely to

remain as smokers, maintaining their addictive smoking behaviour.

Dopamine is a naturally occurring chemical in the brain. It is a neurotransmitter responsible for communication in different parts of the brain, including the so-called reward system. Biologically, nicotine has been shown to increase dopamine release within the brain reward system, therefore providing us with a positive feeling. Maintaining addictive smoking behaviour continues to provide the smoker with this positive feeling. Injections of drugs that block the action of dopamine in the brain have been shown to reduce the reward nicotine provides. Animal research by Corigall and Coen (1991) showed that it is possible to train rats to self-administer nicotine through implants directly into the reward centres of their brain, to provide themselves with positive feelings. Injecting the rats with a drug that prevents dopamine release decreases this nicotine self-administration.

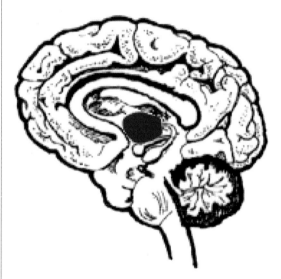

The reward centre in the brain.

It has also been found that nicotine enhances the reward value of other stimuli. You can think of nicotine as an amplifier, making the reward gained from other things that much greater. Self-stimulation procedures can be used to show this. A small electrical stimulation of the brain's reward centres can generate a positive feeling, and research has shown that rats can be trained to self-administer these small electrical charges. Nicotine has been shown to enhance the reward value of such electrical stimulation. This means that rats who receive nicotine need lower electrical stimulation to experience the same level of reward (Harrison et al, 2002). When the exposure to nicotine is stopped, and the rats experience withdrawal, the self-stimulation increases. This indicates that the rats require higher current intensities to perceive the stimulation as rewarding when not exposed to nicotine (Epping-Jordan et al, 1998). It follows that people maintain their addictive smoking behaviour because it makes other behaviours seem that much more enjoyable. If smoking were stopped, other activities would need to be that much more exciting to compensate for the removal of the nicotine.

Relapse

As mentioned earlier, a physical dependence on a drug such as nicotine can mean a quite high tolerance. Stopping long-term use of smoking at high tolerance levels can result in severe withdrawal symptoms. It is clear that the unpleasant feelings of withdrawal can be avoided if the person relapses and resumes the addictive behaviour.

Lerman et al (2007) have shown that smokers who are deprived of nicotine during withdrawal show increased activity in certain parts of their brain. In their study, Lerman et al used a scanner to measure blood flow in the brain. They tested regular smokers just after a cigarette, and then after a single night where the smokers abstained from their habit. The results showed that after the night without smoking there was an increased blood flow to parts of the brain concerned with attention, memory and also reward. They concluded that these parts of the brain become particularly active when the person is craving a cigarette. The researchers also suggested that some people are more prone than others to cravings because of changes in brain chemistry. This research is useful in knowing what it is that encourages an ex-smoker to relapse, and why some people are more likely to relapse than others.

GAMBLING – THE BIOLOGICAL MODEL

Initiation

As with smoking, quite why people take up gambling in the first place is likely to be explained in terms of a combination of social, environmental and also biological factors. The biological explanation of the initiation of problem gambling behaviour is closely tied to the physical response gambling generates in the body of those that gamble. This can be explained in terms of the positive reward theory. As we described earlier, a bet can be followed by a period of anticipation where the body responds and prepares itself for the event with an increased heart rate, and a flow

of adrenaline. Adrenaline is part of the natural fight-or-flight response of the body, and release of this hormone is a normal and healthy reaction to an acute stressor. However, there is considerable evidence that the burst of energy associated with its release is highly addictive. This positive reward of adrenaline need not come only from an anticipation of a race, or event upon which the person has placed money. An immediate response can come from something as simple as placing money into a slot machine. So, the initiation of a gambling addiction is directly related to this positive reward of an adrenaline 'rush' which occurs with gambling behaviour. For a gambler, to gain the positive feeling again is very easy – it is enough simply to place another bet, or slide another coin into the fruit machine.

Bergh et al (1997) say that there is a link between pathological gambling, the reward system, genetics and impulsive behaviour. Comings et al (1996) for example showed that there is evidence from genetic studies that pathological gamblers are more likely to carry a gene called D2A1 than those who do not engage in this problem behaviour. On this basis, it could well be that some people are born more likely to become problem gamblers than others.

There is also interesting evidence from Rugle and Melamed (1993). They showed that electroencephalogram (EEG) patterns of problem gamblers were similar to those of children with attention deficit hyperactivity disorder. This suggests that those with a gambling problem show similar brain activity to children who have trouble controlling their attention and behaviour. All of this research suggests a possible biological basis, or at least a biological weakness, as being responsible for initiating addictive gambling behaviour.

Maintenance

Several studies have provided evidence for similarities between problem gambling and other addictions such as smoking. Wray and Dickerson (1981) reported that gamblers who are prevented from gambling often report changes that resemble withdrawal symptoms. Although these symptoms may not be as intense as those following sustained smoking behaviour, they are still withdrawal symptoms, and as such they are highly influential in determining whether a gambler maintains his/her behaviour. Avoiding withdrawal symptoms is simple: keep gambling and they will not appear. Similarly, Orford et al (1996) compared alcoholics and problem gamblers. The two groups reported similar levels of perceived strength of addictions, even though problem gamblers reported less intense withdrawal and less dependence.

Some investigations have examined how brain activities differ in individuals with a gambling addiction compared to those without. One study used functional magnetic resonance imaging (fMRI) which shows how blood flow in the brain changes when people experience different emotions and stimuli. Potenza et al (2003) investigated urge or craving states in men diagnosed with pathological gambling disorder. When viewing gambling tapes, and just before they began to feel an emotional response, the gamblers showed different blood flow in their brains when compared to non-gamblers These differences were not observed during viewing of videotapes with happy or sad situations, so it must have been something to do with the fact that the tapes were concerned with gambling. An addiction to gambling could have something to do with an inability to control behaviour. The results of Potenza et al are consistent with those from studies of people who lack control in other behavioural areas, including aggression (New et al, 2002) and decision making (Bechara, 2003). It seems likely, then, that the parts of the brain responsible for dealing with control of decision making are involved in addictive gambling behaviour.

Relapse

Just as with other addictive behaviours such as smoking, relapse into gambling behaviour can be explained from a biological perspective. We have already seen that those with gambling addictions experience similar, if milder, withdrawal symptoms to those felt by people addicted to drugs such as nicotine. In many ways, it is easy to stop the withdrawal symptoms by re-engaging in the addictive behaviour. If, once the behaviour is stopped, the gambler feels anxious, experiences an increased heart rate and raised blood pressure and even mild tremors and sweating, then placing a bet may remove these withdrawal feelings.

Ciarrochi et al (1987) note another point that is relevant here. Those addicted to gambling often have other problems such as addictions to alcohol or even shopping. It has been reported that, when giving up gambling, people may switch attention to another of their addictive behaviours. Similarly, when that behaviour becomes too much of a problem in their lives, they may switch back to gambling, as a means of maintaining the positive

feelings received from engaging in one or other of the addictive behaviours.

THE COGNITIVE MODEL

Cognition is thinking. The cognitive model, then, indicates that people initiate and maintain addictive behaviour, and may relapse into that behaviour, because of the way they think. According to Beck et al (2001), the cognitive model of addiction indicates that addicts find themselves in a 'vicious circle', as shown in the diagram below.

Low Mood → Using (smoking or gambling)

Financial, Medical, Social Problems

*"Warning! You need to know about the **cognitive** model of addiction and how it is applied to initiation, maintenance and relapse for both smoking and gambling. Unless you are organised (like this chapter is organised!) you could get confused. So, first we explain what the cognitive model is, then we apply it to initiation, maintenance and relapse of smoking; and then to initiation, maintenance and relapse of gambling."*

A low mood can be relieved by engaging in the addictive behaviour. This in turn leads to financial, social or medical problems which in turn lead to low mood, and the circle begins all over again.

There are three important issues that help to clarify cognitive explanations of smoking and gambling. These are coping, expectancy, and self-efficacy.

COPING

A key idea in the cognitive model of addiction is that people engage in addictive behaviours to cope with stress in their lives. In terms of addiction, coping is thought to fulfil three major functions.

1. *Mood regulation.* Addictive behaviours can be used to increase positive mood and reduce negative mood.

2. *Performance enhancement.* The addictive behaviour may make the person feel alert or more able to perform certain tasks.

3. *Distraction.* The behaviour may serve to distract the addict from less pleasant life experiences.

Quite how these functions operate depends on the addictive behaviour.

EXPECTANCY

The concept of expectancy has received a great deal of attention with respect to addiction. For example, significant expectation effects have been found to be associated with why and how often we engage in an addictive behaviour. If people engaging in an addictive behaviour expect their actions to have negative consequences, then they are less likely to engage in that behaviour. For instance, Hansen et al (1991) found that those who abuse alcohol are likely to be people who perceive fewer negative consequences, while those who expect strong negative effects (perhaps on moral or religious grounds) are less likely to engage in the addictive behaviour.

Expectancy effects are also associated with the experience of the addictive behaviours themselves. Researchers have shown that expectancies about the effect of an addictive behaviour can sometimes have more of an influence upon the addict's experience than the actual changes it produces! It seems that what we expect to happen when engaged in the behaviour influences us even more than the behaviour itself. For instance, users of a hallucinogenic drug may have a good or bad trip depending upon their mood and expectations before taking it and how they interpret the symptoms of their experience as they occur.

On a similar note, expectancies do not have to be accurate in order for them to motivate our behaviour. For example, individuals may consume alcohol in part because they think (expect) that alcohol increases sexual arousal, when in fact it has just the opposite physiological effect (Crowe and George, 1989).

SELF-EFFICACY

Bandura (1997) says that self-efficacy refers to "beliefs in one's capabilities to organise and execute the courses of action required to produce given attainments". What this means is that self-efficacy refers to our beliefs in ourselves, and whether we believe that we are capable of dealing with the effects of a particular behaviour. According to self-efficacy theory, thought processes that are under our own control, particularly self-efficacy beliefs, also play an important role in determining human behaviour. The idea is that self-efficacy influences the decisions people make, the goals they pursue, the effort they expend to achieve them, how long they will persevere when confronted with obstacles and the likelihood that specified goals will be achieved (Bandura, 1999). Self-efficacy is thought to play a very important

role in whether or not we start engaging in addictive behaviours and whether we believe we can do anything about the addictive behaviour once it is established.

SMOKING – THE COGNITIVE MODEL

The three factors described earlier (coping, expectancy and self-efficacy) are all relevant to smoking behaviour. Each has a role to play in the cognitive description of how smoking is initiated, how it is maintained and how it might return after a period of abstinence.

Initiation

Whether smoking behaviour begins or not can be described in terms of *expectancy*. Smokers' expectancies regarding the effect of tobacco may be wide ranging. They may think that smoking reduces stress and negative feelings. They may believe that it makes them look attractive to the opposite sex, or that it will facilitate social interactions, relieve a craving for nicotine, control appetite and weight gain, and so on. All of these expectancies may motivate smoking behaviour regardless of whether they reflect reality. It is enough that the smoker *believes* that they are true.

In terms of coping, performance enhancement may explain why someone takes up smoking. It could be that people begin to smoke because they are having a hard time concentrating for some reason. Perhaps they are having to work long hours. Smoking can help people concentrate with increased attentional focus and enhanced performance of well-learned behaviours (Heishman, 1999). Once the difficult period is over, and the stress has passed, the person is left with an addiction to smoking. It could be that people begin to smoke because they are bored, and it relieves their mood (Brandon and Baker, 1991).

One reason that nicotine produces significant addictive effects is that people experience positive effects, including mild euphoria and mildly enhanced cognition. These positive subjective effects motivate further nicotine use (Kenny and Markou, 2001).

Finally we can consider self-efficacy as a reason for initiating the addictive behaviour. It could be that smokers know that the habit is dangerous and addictive but they believe that they are able to control the behaviour and any problems that may arise from it.

Maintenance

The maintenance of smoking behaviour can be addressed with reference to Beck et al's 'vicious circle' of addiction. The person may be unhappy, or may have difficulty concentrating in their stressful life. For this reason they engage in smoking behaviour. The addictive behaviour is initiated. This in turn leads to possible medical problems associated with smoking. It may also result in financial difficulties. Say, for example, a pack of 20 cigarettes costs approximately £7. A two pack a day person will spend almost £100 a week on cigarettes. That's £400 a month. This is a lot of money that could be better spent on food, rent or family. The smoker may also experience social problems. Many people regard smoking as socially unacceptable, and the law now bans smoking in enclosed spaces such as offices, pubs and clubs. Persons with this addiction may not feel able to visit such places any more, and if they do their behaviour there is heavily influenced by their need to leave the building to smoke. All of these things may result in a negative mood, and so the cycle continues.

The functions of coping may also explain why people maintain their addictive behaviour. It may be that people continue to smoke because the nicotine really does allow them to concentrate for longer, or engage in repetitive tasks without getting unduly bored.

Self-efficacy is also an issue in the maintenance of smoking behaviour. In the initiation of the smoking behaviour people may feel that they are capable of coping with the negative effects of smoking. It could be that once smoking behaviour has been initiated, they feel unable to cope with the withdrawal procedure associated with smoking and so they do not give up.

It is also worth noting that expectancies are important here. The smoker may expect the withdrawal experience to be extremely unpleasant, and this expectancy informs their self-efficacy. It may well be that some people find that it is relatively easy to stop smoking, whereas others find it extremely difficult. Expectancies are likely to influence whether someone continues to smoke or not. If all smokers expected it to be easy to give up then perhaps they would!

Relapse

Coping, expectancy and self-efficacy can all explain why a smoker may relapse. In terms of coping, the negative feelings of the withdrawal period can be relieved almost immediately by taking another cigarette. The symptoms of withdrawal include attention lapse, and smoking provides an immediate route to performance enhancement in this respect. Finally, the withdrawal process may well make the smoker feel extremely unwell, and even self-conscious. The symptoms may be obvious both to the person attempting to give up and to those around him or her. This is likely to make the person feel even more self-conscious. It is possible that a return to smoking is the easiest and most immediate way to escape from this feeling. It is also possible that self-efficacy is an issue in the cognitive explanation of relapse into smoking. It may be that relapsed smokers feel that, if they have given up once, they are able to do it again any time they want. Their reasoning is that a return to smoking will not be permanent as they have the experience of having given up previously.

GAMBLING – THE COGNITIVE MODEL

Gambling can also be approached from a cognitive perspective. Sharpe and Tarrier (1993) propose that the physiological effects of gambling, including excitement and a natural 'high' or buzz, come about because of cognitive influences. In their theory, whilst gambling is initiated by operant conditioning, the excitement generated by gambling, and occasional wins, encourages further gambling. If gambling continues, cognitive mechanisms become more important in maintaining the behaviour. The way that gamblers think about their own behaviour and interpret their experiences are key

MARLATT'S RELAPSE MODEL

According to Marlatt (1985), the cause of a relapse into the addictive behaviour is the presence of a 'high risk situation' which threatens an individual's sense of control and increases the risk of relapse. To avoid relapse, whether into smoking or gambling, the individual must carry out a coping response, which in turn produces an increase in self-efficacy. If a coping response is not used, the individual experiences a decrease in self-efficacy (they feel more out of control) and an increase in the expected positive outcome of engaging in the behaviour, be it smoking or gambling. These positive outcome expectancies are experienced as 'cravings' for the substance, and they lead to the initial re-use of the substance, referred to as a 'lapse'. The lapse, in turn, leads to a mismatch, called 'cognitive dissonance' ('I stopped smoking, and yet I smoked'). This also makes the person feel guilty and encourages the opinion that the failure and weakness is all their fault. These reactions then increase the likelihood of additional substance use, or full 'relapse'.

to understanding how this addictive behaviour is sustained.

Initiation

Gambling behaviour may begin because it provides the person with positive feelings, particularly if the gambling is successful. Positive feelings generate positive thoughts and, once created, these thoughts may be extremely difficult to change. The experiences associated with gambling (the buzz of excitement, the environment etc.) can provide the gambler with similarly enhanced positive feelings, further strengthening existing positive cognitions about gambling. Finally, just as with smoking, gambling may provide the gambler with a means of reducing boredom.

Maintenance

The maintenance of gambling behaviour can be described with reference to Beck et al's 'vicious circle'. Once initiated, gambling may provide the person with a method of improving his or her mood. The nature of gambling is such that people tend not to win all the time. Most gamblers lose money rather than win, and so they may very well find themselves in financial difficulties. This in turn leads to negative mood, which the pathological gambler escapes by gambling. They have entered the circle.

The functions of coping may also explain why people continue to gamble. It may be that they do so because the experience of excitement, and the possibility of the occasional win, makes them feel good. These events encourage gamblers to interpret their behaviour positively.

In terms of self-efficacy, gambling may be maintained because people do not see it as a problem at all. Many people gamble and do not realise it, such as those that play the National Lottery. It could also be that the perceived positive effects of not gambling are not great enough to make someone wish to stop. To put it another way, the withdrawal symptoms of gambling are not as serious as those from giving up smoking. That being the case, the person may not feel that there is any point in giving up as they really can stop at any time, since the physical effects of giving up are relatively easy to cope with.

Expectancy is extremely important here. The perceived benefits of gambling can be huge. Stories of people winning millions of pounds on the lottery, and hundreds of thousands of pounds betting on horse racing, are in the newspapers frequently. It follows that the gambler sees the possibility that

their actions will be life-changing: occasional wins will support these expectancies, so the gambler continues to gamble.

Relapse

In simple terms, the withdrawal effects from gambling may not be too serious. The gambler may not experience any feelings of illness and when compared with other addictions, the withdrawal symptoms can be very mild. The consequences of relapse are seen as being simply that the gambler returns to the possibility of winning money. Since the withdrawal may be comparatively painless, gamblers may feel that they can stop at any time. Moreover, as the gambler may feel able to stop easily, a relapse is not seen as too much of a problem. Similarly, the life the gambler leads without gambling may seem extremely dull to them. Relapse may happen because it reduces this boredom.

THE LEARNING MODEL

The learning model of addiction says that we can explain addictive behaviours in terms of learning theory. The types of learning in question here are classical conditioning and operant conditioning.

Social learning is also very important. Social learning theory is most associated with Albert Bandura who showed that children learn by observing others. Someone who is reinforced for their behaviour is more likely to be imitated. This is an example of *vicarious reinforcement* – a reinforcement which is received indirectly by observing another person being reinforced. Bandura said that we model our behaviour on that of someone we admire, or relate to in some way. For example, boys are more likely to model their behaviour on men, and girls on women. This issue is further explored later when we consider the role of the media in addictive behaviour.

"*Warning! You need to know about the learning model of addiction and how it is applied to initiation, maintenance and relapse for both smoking and gambling. Unless you are organised (like this chapter is organised!) you could get confused. So, first we explain what the learning model is, then we apply it to initiation, maintenance and relapse of smoking; and then to initiation, maintenance and relapse of gambling.*"

CLASSICAL CONDITIONING

This explanation of learning says that people and non-human animals learn because of the associations they make. The initial research was carried out by Pavlov. He demonstrated that dogs salivated to the sound of a bell because they 'associated' the sound with the presentation of food. Each time the dogs heard the bell, food was presented. Eventually, the bell itself could make them salivate. Salivation is a reflex action and requires no thought. It is a response to a stimulus. Here, the response is to an unusual stimulus. It is a conditioned reflex. A similar relationship can be said to happen in the learning of attachments. For instance, the caregiver acts caringly towards the child. This is called the **unconditioned stimulus (UCS)**. In response to this, the infant feels content. The feeling of contentment is called the **unconditioned response (UCR)**. After a while, and after the UCS has been presented a number of times, making the child feel content, the infant learns to associate feeling content with the actions of the caregiver. Classical conditioning can be regarded as a three-stage process, and can be summarised as follows.

STAGE 1	STAGE 2	STAGE 3
Pre-conditioning	Conditioning	Post-conditioning
The caregiver's actions (unconditioned stimulus – UCS) produce a feeling of contentment in the child (unconditioned response – UCR).	The caring behaviour is presented over and over again, making the infant feel content each time. The infant begins to associate the feeling with the stimulus.	The feeling of contentment has been learned (conditioned). It is a 'conditioned response – CR' to the now 'conditioned stimulus – CS' (the caring behaviour).

OPERANT CONDITIONING

In operant conditioning, we are said to learn because we are either rewarded for our behaviour, or the way we feel, or punished for it. If we do something and it makes us feel happy, then that behaviour is reinforced. We are more likely to do it again. If we do something and it makes us feel unhappy, or uncomfortable (such as putting a hand in a candle flame) then our behaviour will not be reinforced. In operant conditioning we talk about the unpleasant result of an action (the finger in the flame example) as punishment.

THE CUE-REACTIVITY THEORY

Research shows that when presented with a variety of cues associated with their problem behaviour, addicts show a distinct pattern of physiological and behavioural responses. In effect, addicts react to things associated with their addiction in similar ways to how they react to the object of the addictive behaviour. In the case of smoking these items might include lighters or matches, boxes of cigarettes and ashtrays. In the case of gambling they might include betting slips, betting shops and pages of newspapers displaying gambling odds. According to cue-reactivity theory, the mechanism underlying this behaviour is classical conditioning. Pavlov showed that a dog can be made to salivate to the sound of a bell once the bell has been paired with food. In addictive behaviour the experience of the craving is paired with the presence of the items associated with the behaviour. These paraphernalia are therefore able to elicit conditioned responses even in the absence of actual smoking or gambling behaviour (Carter and Tiffany, 1999).

Addiction-related cues acting as conditioned stimuli are therefore thought to play an important role in the emergence and maintenance of addictive behaviours (Tiffany, 1995).

SMOKING – THE LEARNING MODEL

Initiation

Smoking behaviour may begin because the person starts to associate the experiences of smoking with desirable outcomes or rewards. For instance, consider the issue of peer pressure. Friends and colleagues may encourage a person to take a cigarette: taunting, making fun and name-calling will not stop until they do so, and the person may feel embarrassed. This in turn reduces their feeling of self-worth. Accepting the cigarette, and taking up smoking allows them access to a social network, reduces or even eliminates the teasing or bullying and consequently makes them feel much happier. The new smoker associates the cigarettes with this positive feeling, reinforcing the link between smoking and feeling good.

A smoker may receive satisfaction from handling the pack, removing the cigarette, tapping one end against a firm surface to compress the tobacco more tightly, lighting the cigarette, and taking puffs at regular intervals. Such social and psychological factors are not to be overlooked in attempts to understand why people continue to smoke.

Maintenance

The pressures that people feel to take up smoking in the first place remain prevalent during their smoking life. The people they mix with are often themselves smokers. Giving up smoking makes it difficult to be around these people if the smoker is to stay away from cigarettes to reduce the craving they have for nicotine. The act of smoking can also become a highly ritualised habit – the routines described above are something many smokers find compelling and hard to resist.

At certain times the act of smoking, not just the addiction to the nicotine, forms an important part of the day. For instance, many smokers will tell you that they would give up – except for the cigarettes after a meal that they feel aid their digestion. In these situations smokers have associated the smoking process with a belief that the cigarette is improving their digestion. Many associate smoking with appetite reduction, and so the craving for food is replaced with the craving for nicotine.

If smoking no longer provides the positive feelings than it once did, then the relationship between the smoking and the desirable feelings begins to be extinguished. If this happens the smoker may be in a position to give up.

Relapse

The cue-reactivity paradigm is important here. Because smokers often link the materials associated with their addictive behaviour with the act of smoking itself, seeing or handling a lighter or a packet of cigarettes is enough to generate the craving for the nicotine. It may be that just seeing someone else smoking is enough to bring on familiar cravings for a cigarette. Since smoking is extremely prevalent in our society these pressures are there for everyone, including ex-smokers, to see. The pressures to return to their addictive behaviours are all around smokers every day, and it is not hard to imagine how difficult it is for those giving up cigarettes to avoid the things that tempt them back to their old habit.

GAMBLING – THE LEARNING MODEL

Initiation

In terms of the learning model, the start of gambling behaviour can be explained similarly to the start of smoking or any other addictive behaviour. Initially, the person may see others winning on slot machines or even on the lottery. Their expectations of the win may drive them to place their first bet, begin playing the lottery, or using slot machines. Once they have started, the excitement they experience is associated with the whole gambling process, reinforcing the positive feelings that gambling produces. This may be further reinforced by the occasional win, especially if there are early 'successes'. The gambler becomes addicted to the behaviour as this process continues.

Maintenance

The gambler continues the addictive behaviour because the rewards they receive, be they monetary (from winning) or physical (from the excitement of gambling), are reliable and relatively easy to come by. Placing a bet provides the encouragement and reward to continue gambling. This constant association of excitement with gambling reinforces the relationship between the two. Gamblers don't win *all* the time of course, but this only makes the compulsion to gamble stronger. This is because gambling provides a *partial reinforcement*, a schedule of reinforcement which produces very persistent learned behaviours. It may seem counter-intuitive, but it is in fact the infrequency of winning that maintains gambling behaviour. If gamblers were to win every time they bet, then the urge to gamble would not be as strong. For example, imagine the situation where putting ten pence into a fruit machine would result in a ten pence win each time. This would soon become tedious. However, fruit machines only occasionally pay out but (and this is important) they *will* reward a player with a win *at some point in the future*. Gamblers then are rewarded for their behaviour at fairly random intervals, and this means that they can go for a long time without winning and still have their urge to gamble undiminished.

In order for the gambling behaviour to be extinguished, it must be *consistently* associated with negative or neutral feelings. Given the many temptations and easy opportunities to gamble, this means that problem gambling is a very difficult thing to treat.

Relapse

Returning to gambling after a period of abstinence can be explained in terms of the cue-reactivity paradigm. The material associated with gambling is all around us, particularly with the easy way which people can now play the National Lottery, and not just by the usual selection of six numbers, but also the multitude of scratch cards available. Fruit machines are in many public places, and the internet is filled with online casinos and other opportunities to gamble. Gamblers attempting to give up the habit are surrounded with reminders of their addictive behaviour, and temptations to give in to the urge to gamble are everywhere. In terms of the cue-reactivity paradigm these reminders can be sufficient to generate the feelings associated with gambling, including the anticipation and the memory of the excitement associated with the behaviour, and a relapse may be the result.

FACTORS AFFECTING ADDICTIVE BEHAVIOUR

VULNERABILITY TO ADDICTION

The models of addictive behaviour all offer a different view of why people take up the behaviour in the first place, why it is maintained and why, after a period of abstinence from the behaviour, people return to it. While each of the models explains, in its own way, how the behaviour may be initiated, they do not explain why some people may be more vulnerable than others to the draw of addictive behaviours. Why is it that some people never take up smoking at all, never even trying a cigarette let alone maintaining a 20 a day habit for years on end? Why is it that some people can happily play the National Lottery once a month without becoming addicted, whereas others are particularly vulnerable to the perceived rewards of gambling? These people find it difficult to pass a fruit machine without playing, and constantly seek outlets for their gambling addiction. It seems that some are more vulnerable than others to addictive behaviours, and here we discuss three possible issues affecting this vulnerability; self-esteem, attributions for addiction and the social context in which the addictive behaviour takes place.

"Psychology in Action is all about applying knowledge. We are encouraging you to think this way by applying theory (self-esteem, attribution, social context) to smoking and gambling addictions. It's good to start thinking this way – it is how you get the best marks in the exam!"

SELF-ESTEEM

Self-esteem can be defined as a person's overall opinion of his or her worth. People with low self-esteem may regard themselves as worthless, or at least, not worth very much. They may feel incompetent, or out of control in some way. This can influence their emotions, making them feel a sense of despair, anxiety and shame. Self-esteem is a characteristic of our personality. Just as some people feel strong and confident, others feel weak, and unable to control what is going on around them. Other terms you may encounter that relate to this concept include self-respect, self-worth and self-regard. When these are low, then the person's self-esteem is said to be low.

Reaction to criticism

One reason we may suffer with low self-esteem is that other people's opinions of us or our behaviours may be negative. For instance, we may feel positive about ourselves if people congratulate us on our behaviour or performance. If we take examinations and do well then the feedback we receive from others around us, or the exam board, may make us feel good. On the other hand, if we do not do so well we may be criticised for not working hard enough, or letting ourselves down in some way. The result of this criticism may be a reduction in our feeling of self-worth.

Perceived ability to succeed

Those with low self-esteem are in a very unfortunate position as they see the possibility to achieve, to move away from their current positions in life, as very low or non-existent. They regard themselves as unable to change the things around them and see failure as the only likely result when faced with a difficulty. Some people regard tasks as challenges, but those with low self-esteem regard them as extremely intimidating and so doubt their abilities to overcome them. They are quick to say that they cannot do something, exhibiting what may be regarded as a negative attitude to an obstacle in their way.

SELF-ESTEEM IN SMOKING AND GAMBLING

A person suffering with low self-esteem may be particularly vulnerable to peer pressure, an extremely important influence in whether someone dabbles in an addictive behaviour such as smoking or gambling. For instance, if there is a social group that considers smoking as central to being a member, then access to that group will require a person to initiate smoking behaviour. Those with low self-esteem may be particularly vulnerable to this sort of pressure. They may see membership of the social group as rewarding, something that gives them a feeling of belonging. This belonging may well improve their feeling of self-worth. Here it is 'expectancy' of how the initiation of the addictive behaviour may change the way they feel about themselves that is driving them.

In terms of gambling, the person may regard the reward of winning money as a way to enable them to feel better about themselves. They can buy more fashionable clothes, perhaps a prestigious car. They can eat out more, see the latest movies or shows, spend time travelling and living a more glamorous life. Those with low self-esteem may see gambling as a way out of what they perceive to be a predicament of some kind – a dead-end existence that is making them feel unhappy. If only they had some more money they could really do something about their lives.

Once the person begins the addictive behaviour the feeling of self-esteem remains important. Both gambling and smoking are behaviours that receive criticism from society in general. The law has made it very clear that smoking is unacceptable, and smokers may be criticised daily for their habit. For those with low self-esteem, criticism is unlikely to spur them on to giving up their addictive behaviour: rather, it is likely to make them feel worse.

The same applies in terms of gambling. This addictive behaviour more often than not results in the gambler losing much or all of their money. They may be criticised for what others perceive as a selfish habit in which they prefer to spend time alone, risking money on chances of gain rather than being with family, using their money for more important things such as bills, or a household. Such criticism may deepen their sense of low self-worth.

As we have learned, those who suffer from low self-worth feel that obstacles are not challenges at all: they are regarded as extremely intimidating and as being probably insurmountable. Criticising a smoker or gambler who already suffers with low self-esteem is likely to make them feel even more worthless – and as such, even less likely to believe that they can overcome the huge difficulty of giving up their addictive behaviour. It is for this reason that those with low self-esteem are particularly vulnerable to maintaining these behaviours, as confidence and willpower are not available, to help to overcome them.

ATTRIBUTIONS FOR ADDICTION

The study of attribution in psychology looks at how people explain things and how they seek causes for events. The theory was put forward by Kelley (1967) and relates not only to why we think all sorts of external things happen, but also to why we think our own behaviours 'happen'.

Here's an example. Students may be asked why they did not pass the examination. They may respond in a number of different ways. They may say "I didn't pass because the exam was too hard". This is an 'external' attribution, meaning that the failure was not their fault – maybe it is the fault of the examiner, who set the questions.

They may also have responded that they did not pass the examination "because they were too stupid to be able to". This is an example of an 'internal' attribution. They are blaming their own inadequacies for their failure, and so it was all their fault that they did not pass.

In terms of addiction, attribution theory relates to the concept of 'control'. If things are beyond our control then we cannot be blamed for their happening. If our addiction is beyond our control then the behaviour is not our fault. If we regard something as being beyond our control we are making an external attribution. If, on the other hand, we consider ourselves as being entirely responsible for the addiction, and the reason we maintain the addiction is that we believe we are weak in some way, then we have internalised the reason or cause – we have made an internal attribution for the event.

"The best ways to show your knowledge of attribution theory is to give examples of it in action – remember you need to be able to apply your knowledge like this in the in this exam! To help you get started, the following diagrams are examples of how attribution might be applied to smoking and gambling."

ATTRIBUTIONS FOR SMOKING AND GAMBLING BEHAVIOUR

A basic understanding of attribution theory can be used to explain why some people are more vulnerable to engaging in addictive behaviours than others. Smoking and gambling are good examples of these. Consider the responses to the following questions:

Attributions for smoking behaviour

"Why did you start smoking?"

External attribution

Your response to this may be that you were under a lot of pressure from people in school to try a cigarette. This is an external attribution because you were somehow forced to begin smoking because the pressure to do so was so great. You regard your initial smoking behaviour as being beyond your control.

Internal attribution

You may have replied that you started smoking because you couldn't help it, you have no willpower and you always give in to things like that. This is an internal attribution because you explain your smoking behaviour as being entirely your own fault. You regard taking up smoking as being an issue of control and in your case you were too weak.

"Why do you maintain your smoking habit?"

External attribution

You may respond that you maintain your smoking habit because society makes it clear that we need to be thin, and you believe smoking somehow suppresses our appetite. You smoke because you have to be accepted in society. Here you blame your continued smoking behaviour on the norms of society and a belief, rightly or wrongly, that smoking will help you stay thin. The cause for your addictive behaviour is beyond your control. It is somehow not your fault that you have to smoke: it is society's fault.

Internal attribution

You may have responded that you continue to smoke because you are frightened of giving up. If you give up all your friends will leave you, and you will have to deal with horrible withdrawal symptoms. You are just not brave enough to stop. Here you are blaming your continued behaviour on your lack of bravery. It is all your fault that you do not stop: if you were braver then you would feel able to give up. As it is, you are unable to stop, and so you maintain your behaviour.

"You had stopped: why did you relapse and return to smoking?"

External attribution

You respond that the pressures of life just got too much and forced you back into your habit. If life had been less stressful you would not have relapsed. Your reason for the relapse is external. You regard the pressures of life as beyond your control and if things around you had just been different, a little easier, you would not have returned to your habit.

Internal attribution

You could have said that it was just that you are hopeless. You have no willpower at all. You are weak and just a bit useless. This is clearly an internal attribution. If you were less hopeless and had more willpower then you would have been able to remain away from cigarettes. As it is, you were just too weak. It is all your fault that you returned to your habit.

Attributions for gambling behaviour

Reasons for gambling can also be internally or externally attributed.

"Why did you start gambling?"

External attribution

Your answer may be something like "No one told me it was addictive; if they had done I would not have started". It's not your fault that you gamble because you were never told by doctors or professionals that it was addictive. If you had been you would never have started. Others are being blamed for not telling you the possible costs of gambling.

Internal attributions

It could be that you reply to this question by saying that you really liked the excitement of watching the drums on the fruit machine roll around. You found it great fun. You loved it in fact. You are blaming your initial gambling behaviour on your enjoyment of playing fruit machines. If you had found it boring you might not have engaged in gambling in the first place.

"Why do you maintain your gambling behaviour?"

External attribution	Internal attribution
You may respond that you continue to gamble because it is not your fault that you can't give up. You see reminders of your habit in every newsagent in the form of the Lottery, and it seems that every street corner has a betting shop. If there were no lottery and if betting shops were banned then you would give up. You are blaming your continued gambling on factors beyond your control, namely the presence of betting shops and the National Lottery.	Your answer to this may be that you continue to gamble because you are unable to give up, as you have no willpower at all. If you were stronger then you could stop. This internal attribution clearly indicates that you continue to gamble because you feel that you are too weak to stop.

"You had stopped: why did you relapse and return to gambling?"

External attribution	Internal attribution
You may say that you needed some money to pay your rent and because of your past as a gambling addict the bank would not lend you any money. You had to live somewhere, and so the only way to get the money was to gamble. It is not your fault that the bank was not willing to help you. Your relapse is due to others, not you. If the bank had helped you, you would not have been forced back to the betting shop.	Your answer may be that you just couldn't help it. You craved the lights of the fruit machines and the sounds of the racetrack and just gave in. Your attribution is internal. You feel that your relapse is your own fault, and you were not strong enough to resist your cravings.

THE SOCIAL CONTEXT OF ADDICTION

It is very important to consider the social context surrounding the addictive behaviour, since the pressures upon a person's behaviour can depend on their environment (Anthony and Chen, 2004). For instance, extremely wealthy people may be able to afford help to control their addiction, in the form of regular and costly visits to rehabilitation clinics, whereas these resources may not be available to those with a lower income. However, the role of social context in addictive behaviours can be much subtler than this.

"Smoking and gambling are by no means the only addictive behaviours, and there are times when it is useful to refer to other addictive behaviours in order to illustrate or explain what you mean. For this reason we have mentioned things like cocaine addiction, just in order to get a point across or explain something. Remember though, if the exam question explicitly mentions smoking or gambling, then you know what you must write about in your answer."

LIFE EXPERIENCES

Certain life experiences can make an individual more vulnerable to developing an addiction or more likely to relapse into addictive behaviour. It is also true to say that other types of experiences, such as being a member of a warm close family with low stress, may actually protect a person and reduce the risk of becoming addicted or relapsing. Events as different as sexual abuse, harassment, combat stress, occupational stress, marriage dissatisfaction, and physical traumas have all been linked to addictive behaviours. In particular, there is evidence that bad childhood experiences play an important role in susceptibility in this area. Turner et al (2002) indicate that with gambling, for instance, early experiences of attention deficit hyperactivity disorder may be present. They also indicate that many problem gamblers endured unpleasant life experiences the year before they began their gambling behaviour. The same report indicates that those from higher income families are less likely to gamble and those with a lower level of education are more likely to gamble.

ROLE OF PARENTS

Goddard (1990) carried out a longitudinal study investigating the elements of a child's world that might predict whether they began smoking or not. The main finding is that if parents smoke then children are more likely to smoke (Lader and Matheson, 1991). Further research showed that the parents' attitude to smoking was very important (Murray et al, 1984). If the child perceived their parents as being very anti-smoking they were up to seven times less likely to smoke. There is also evidence of gambling behaviour being related to the behaviour of parents. Wardle et al (2007) report, in the UK National Gambling Prevalence Survey, that problem gamblers are more likely to have had parents who gambled regularly.

SOCIAL ENVIRONMENTAL CUES

We have already seen that through conditioning and cue-reactivity theory, addicts react to things (cues) as though they were the objects of addiction. This also applies to social and environmental cues. Immediate environmental cues that would not otherwise be linked to addictive behaviours can acquire, through their association with gambling or smoking, the ability to trigger addictive behaviour. This can happen even after long periods of abstinence. For example, Volkow et al, (2006) demonstrated that cocaine addicts watching a video showing cocaine cues (i.e. things associated with cocaine use) experience increases in the transmission of dopamine in the brain (a chemical involved in reward). This can be related to other addictive behaviours such as smoking or gambling. If it is possible to understand the social environment associated with these addictions then we may be able to help addicts stop and stay away from their addictions.

The relationship between environmental cues and gambling was shown by Sharpe and Terrier (1993) who measured gamblers' perceived arousal (as skin conductivity) when watching a video of a poker machine. The more aroused or excited they were, the more they perspired and this lowered the resistance across the skin. The researchers showed that interrupting the video interrupted the increase in the gamblers' excitement, indicating that the environmental cue in the video was very important in this regard.

PEER PRESSURE

A great deal of behaviour is directly influenced by peers – that is, one's equals or age mates. Whilst the greatest influence of peers is felt during childhood and adolescence, they continue to exert an influence throughout our lives. Peers are an important source of information about acceptable behaviours and values. The groups with which people most associate or identify themselves (the peer group) are important in whether they take up smoking or gambling, since peer groups will contain individuals with similar interests, aspirations or attitudes towards the addictive behaviours. Indeed, it often the case that people with addictive

behaviours place some of the blame for their own behaviour on the influence of their peers.

According the 'life cycle' theory of addiction, peer influence is a crucial factor in whether a person becomes addicted. With this theory, a person encounters a problem that they have difficulty dealing with. Addictive behaviour somehow makes the problem easier to endure, and it is this sense of 'release' from the pressure that encourages the person to return to the behaviour. Before long the person is addicted: basically, the addictive behaviour – to smoking, illegal substance or whatever – is adopted as the solution to the problem. Peers are key because they can either help the person to deal with the initial problem, so easing the difficulty, or add to it by being a pro-addiction influence.

ROLE OF THE MEDIA IN ADDICTIVE BEHAVIOUR

"We all watch a bit of TV and we all think we know something about how such media influence our lives. This gives us the false impression that we know more than we really do, and often our response is to offer anecdote and personal opinion. Don't! Such responses in exams are not 'psychologically informed' and won't get marks. Be sure to embed psychology if you want your answer to be taken seriously."

The increased importance of the mass media in our society has had an impact on opinions about addictive behaviours as well as on how often the behaviours themselves occur. In recent years, the increased use of the internet and television, increased sales of celebrity magazines and development of popular culture have meant that we are now bombarded with images that may influence our behaviours (in both a positive and negative way) with respect to addiction. Celebrity 'endorsement' of certain lifestyles is particularly relevant in influencing addictive behaviour amongst young people, who are often most vulnerable to the cult of celebrity and the perceived glamour that goes along with it.

In the past, advertising for cigarettes and other nicotine-based products has portrayed the user as cool, sophisticated, independent, popular, physically attractive and fit. These are all concepts that teenagers, and those with low self-esteem,

THE TOBACCO BAN

Since 1991, the European Union has banned all tobacco advertising on TV. In the UK, this ban was extended in 2005 to all other media, including the internet, and newspapers: tobacco sponsorship of large sporting events was also banned. In addition to this, cigarette packets began to carry stark warnings of the dangers of engaging in this addictive behaviour.

are likely to aspire to. Bandura's social learning theory indicates that we may model our behaviour on that of someone whom we respect, or would like to be like, or who is an authority. The media can act as a source of this 'observational learning' by providing models which teenagers may seek to copy. It follows that exposure to media messages about addictive behaviours can provide direct reinforcement for whether or not a person takes part in those behaviours.

NEGATIVE EFFECTS OF THE MEDIA

It is claimed that much of what the media contain is what people want to watch. It seems that many people are interested in celebrity and so the media will naturally report the behaviour of a person if that report will help them sell their newspaper, or encourage people to tune in to their television programme. It is often the case that the media report problems that a celebrity is having with addiction, and how the law deals with this behaviour can form an important part of the report. The International Narcotics Control Board (INCB) have highlighted this issue. Young people are quick to pick up on messages from the media of celebrity addiction going unpunished.

They often react to the perceived leniency in dealing with such offenders by engaging in the addictive behaviour themselves. The INCB suggest that this raises questions about the fairness of the justice system and could undermine wider social efforts at reducing the demand for drugs (INCB, 2008).

Smoking

Strasburger (1995) reports that, despite tobacco adverts having been banned in America in 1971, up until the early 1990s tobacco was the most heavily advertised consumer product in the US. Much of this advertising is what he calls 'passive' or 'inadvertent', (for example brand logos on sports shirts or racing cars, specifically targeting young people). Whilst the practice of tobacco 'product placement' (manufacturers paying to have their products feature in movies) has, under government pressure, reduced significantly since the early 1990s, smoking is still an addictive behaviour frequently seen in movies.

Movies are a mass medium, designed to reach a large audience, and they deliver billions of impressions of smoking to adolescents each year. Hazan et al (1994) showed that since 1960 the top grossing films have shown their stars light up cigarettes at three times the rate of American adults. A recent study by Sargent et al (2007) using a national US adolescent sample, demonstrated that exposure to smoking in movies predicted the risk of the observer becoming an established smoker. The research shows that exposure to movies can influence smokers' responsiveness to tobacco. This can be called the 'movie exposure effect' and it is independent of other risk factors for smoking (Distefan et al, 2004). Are adolescents particularly sensitive in this way?

A longitudinal study by Hanewinkel and Sargent (2008) showed a clear 'dose-response' effect between viewing smoking in movies and rates of adolescent initiation of smoking.

They also demonstrated a correlation between the type of films being watched and smoking behaviour, with adolescents who watched films rated PG or R being 66% more likely to smoke than those who did not. It does not necessarily mean that the films *caused* those that watched them to smoke, but the result does suggest that the adolescents that watch these films are likely to engage in smoking behaviour, and it is in these films that more obvious smoking is permitted.

Gambling

The Responsible Gaming Council of Canada (2007) reported that 3.9% of adolescents in a sample of 15–17-year-olds could be classed as problem gamblers. A further 8.9% could be described as 'at risk'. Clearly the problem is one worth taking very seriously. Korn and Reynolds (2008) reported the impacts of commercial gambling advertising on young people, using Canada as an example. They indicated that there were over

120,000 gambling outlets in Canada, ranging from slot machines to racetracks, and including casinos and lottery ticket dispensers. Their research, using interviews and questionnaires, revealed that the interviewees were each able to recall one gambling marketing campaign; that they regarded gambling advertisements as influential; and that they felt that the advertisements were funny, showed 'cool' people, and indicated possibilities of financial gain – all things that are likely to be attractive to young people or those with low self-esteem.

The research went on to show that at-risk gamblers were extremely sensitive to gambling advertising, further exacerbating their problem. The key points from the work were that those interviewed were aware of, and had good understandings of, the prevalence and potential severity of gambling addictions. They felt that advertising 'normalised' gambling, making it feel like a regular, perfectly natural behaviour. The potential risks associated with such an attitude are highlighted by the fact that the interviewees were largely unaware of regulations governing the advertising of gambling. Other research, such as that of Hyung-Seok et al (2007), suggests that it is the nature of the gambling advertising that causes the problems, and that advertising that depicts gambling positively can, perhaps unsurprisingly, encourage people to engage in the behaviour, which may in time lead to the damaging effects we associate with problem gambling.

The negative effects of the media are thought to be magnified by the influence of peers. The Committee for Advertising Practice for example, who regulate advertising in the United Kingdom, recognise the influence of peer pressure on gambling. They regard the matter as so important that they have included a specific reference to it in their guidelines for gambling advertising in the UK. It states that:

'Advertisements for gambling must neither suggest peer pressure to gamble nor disparage abstention.'

POSITIVE EFFECTS OF THE MEDIA

The media can have a positive impact upon attitudes to addictive behaviours such as smoking and gambling. Studies have highlighted the role that mass media can play in reducing various addictive behaviours.

"This is often overlooked – media can be good! Exam answers look so much better when they contain a balance of views. It is easy to criticise the media as a negative influence but much more effective to balance that with a view of the positive effects of media."

Smoking

Since the 1950s, the portrayal of smoking on television has steadily decreased. For example, Signorielli (1990) reports that US TV characters were nine times more likely to smoke in 1964 than in 1982. At the same time the incidence of smoking in society has decreased, and although we can't jump to the conclusion that the reduction in TV smoking caused this change, it is likely that it made some contribution. Signorielli also points out that whilst TV is now much less likely to show smoking, it is no more likely to show characters taking an explicit anti-smoking stance.

Many studies have investigated the impact of anti-smoking media campaigns. Friend and Levy (2002) reviewed the impact of such campaigns in the United States. They showed that well-funded and implemented mass-media campaigns targeted at the general population, combined with a comprehensive tobacco control programme, are associated with reduced smoking rates amongst both adults and youths. Whilst youth-oriented media campaigns have shown more mixed results, the campaigns do nevertheless indicate a strong potential to influence underage smoking rates. Wakefield et al (2003) demonstrated that the media can help shape and reflect the social values of audiences about smoking whilst providing new information about the habit, such as its associated health risks. More recently, Klein et al (2005) concluded that, in adolescents at least, anti-smoking campaigns combined with telephone help services really can inform people, and help them work towards changing their behaviour. They also concluded that using media, such as the internet, can be a very effective way of communicating with young people for this purpose.

Gambling

Gambling advertising is becoming more and more obvious in our media. Of particular note is the huge increase in gambling online, including bingo, casino games, poker, and sports betting. In addition, mobile gambling is increasingly available. Gambling is, it seems, no further away than a click of a mouse or the press of a button on a mobile phone.

Just as with media campaigns on smoking, there is evidence to suggest, in the case of gambling, too, that it is the *nature* of the advertising that influences people's behaviour. Meserlian and Derevensky (2007) looked at the possibility of using 'social marketing' as a strategy for gambling prevention among adolescents. They concluded that using marketing campaigns with emotional messages, with real-life, engaging stories that showed the negative effects of gambling, could successfully raise people's awareness of the issues of problem gambling, and campaigns structured like this were recommended by the participants in the sample they used in their study. Their study raised the issue of perceptions of 'judgemental' campaigns. Just being told 'don't do it!' was regarded as likely to be unsuccessful, as adolescents would react badly to the perceived judgemental nature of the campaign. They recommend an approach that raises awareness, rather than telling people what

to do. Hyung-Seok et al (2007) showed that if the media representation of gambling was negative, then the effect was to influence attitudes and behaviour accordingly, i.e. viewers began to see gambling more negatively.

REDUCING ADDICTIVE BEHAVIOUR

Society regards addiction to smoking and gambling as unacceptable and as such we must consider how we might reduce these behaviours. The law can be used to make certain activities difficult (by banning them or taxing them to make them expensive) but psychology provides us with various models that can be used to describe how addictive behaviours can be reduced. Two of these are the theory of reasoned action and the theory of planned behaviour. One factor we must consider is the role of social cognition and how attitudes can influence addictive behaviours. It is acknowledged that people's behaviour in social situations is often greatly influenced by social factors (e.g. the opinions and expectations of others). The theories of reasoned action (TRA) and planned behaviour (TPB) provide a general framework which helps us to understand the relationship between attitudes

MEDIA CAMPAIGNS

Media campaigns have a long history. They have been used to inform the public of the dangers of many things, from smoking and heroin abuse to marijuana. One of the very earliest uses of the media to help inform and change people's involvement in a risky behaviour was a 1920s campaign on venereal disease. Lashley and Watson (1922) concluded that the campaign was good at informing people of the facts, but not so effective in changing their attitudes and behaviour. Giovino (2003) agreed, concluding that hugely expensive campaigns often have very little impact on people's behaviour. Randolph and Viswath (2004) say that this failure of many campaigns to change people's attitudes just highlights the need for careful psychological investigation into how people make and change their opinions and behaviours. This area of applied psychology finds its roots in the study of 'social influence'. This branch of psychology says that whether we alter our behaviour can depend on a number of things. It may not be, as Bandura described, direct observation of people that informs our decisions. Possibly, our decisions are based on such things as our understandings of whether people desire to be viewed in a positive light by others, our understanding of social norms, and how important these things are to us.

In contrast to these negative opinions about the ability of advertising to change people's attitudes and behaviour, some research on campaigns associated with smoking behaviour, including that of Wakefield et al (2003) and Klein et al (2005), indicates that the media *can* be used effectively to help people change their behaviours, particularly when combined with follow-up services such as quit-lines and other telephone support.

and behaviour, and to see how this understanding might be used to reduce addictive behaviour.

THEORY OF REASONED ACTION (TRA)

Developed by Azjen and Fishbein (1967), this theory attempts to explain the relationships between our attitudes to things (e.g. smoking and gambling) and our behaviours (e.g. whether we smoke or gamble).

The TRA can be summarised in four simple steps.

(1) ATTITUDE – As we go through life we accumulate beliefs about things. Some of these beliefs influence our attitude to behaviours such as smoking and gambling. These are called our *salient beliefs*. If the salient beliefs are positive, we feel positive about the behaviour, and we are said to have a positive attitude towards it.

(2) SUBJECTIVE NORMS – These are the norms that others use to evaluate the behaviours, in this case gambling and drinking.

(3) INTENTION – This is the likelihood that the person will actually carry out the behaviour. If a person has a high intention to smoke then the likelihood that he will do so is high.

(4) BEHAVIOUR – This is where intention is translated into action. Here the behaviour is the act of smoking or gambling.

APPLYING THE THEORY OF REASONED ACTION

The TRA can be applied to any number of actions and behaviours. The flow through attitude, norms, intention and behaviour for smoking might be summarised as follows:

> **1. Attitude**
> "In my opinion there is nothing wrong with smoking. Loads of my friends smoke, and none of them are ill from it."
>
> **2. Subjective Norm**
> "I bet all the boring teachers and adults wouldn't want me to smoke."
>
> **3. Intention**
> "I'd like to try a cigarette."
>
> **4. Behaviour**
> The person begins to smoke.

In terms of gambling, the steps through the TRA might be summarised as follows:

> **1. Attitude**
> "Gambling is a quick and easy way of making loads of money."
>
> **2. Subjective Norm**
> "They all play the lottery: that's just a form of gambling. It's perfectly normal."
>
> **3. Intention**
> "I wouldn't mind a gamble: it looks like fun."
>
> **4. Behaviour**
> The person begins to gamble.

THE THEORY OF REASONED ACTION

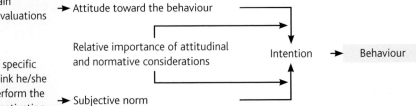

The person's belief that the behaviour leads to certain outcomes and his/her evaluations of these outcomes → Attitude toward the behaviour

Relative importance of attitudinal and normative considerations

The person's belief that specific individuals or groups think he/she should or should not perform the behaviour and his/her motivation to comply with the specific reference → Subjective norm

Intention → Behaviour

Adapted from Azjen and Fishbein (1975).

THEORY OF PLANNED BEHAVIOUR (TPB)

Azjen (1988) updated the TRA to include the possibility that not all actions and behaviours are completely under our control, and that people's perception of control is very important in our understanding of their behaviour. The TPB is very similar to the TRA except for the addition of 'control beliefs' – these are beliefs about factors that may help carry out the behaviour, or get in the way of carrying it out.

APPLYING THE THEORY OF PLANNED BEHAVIOUR

Just like the TRA, the TPB can be applied to any number of actions and behaviours. The flow through the TPB for smoking might be summarised as follows:

> **1. Attitude**
>
> "In my opinion there is nothing wrong with smoking. Loads of my friends smoke, and none of them are ill from it."
>
> **2. Subjective Norm**
>
> "I bet all the boring teachers and adults wouldn't want me to smoke."
>
> **3. Intention**
>
> "I'd like to try a cigarette."
>
> **4. Control**
>
> "It's my decision: I can make it for myself. I am completely in control of my actions."
>
> **5. Behaviour**
>
> The person begins to smoke.

In terms of gambling, the steps through the TPB might be summarised as follows:

> **1. Attitude**
>
> "Gambling is a quick and easy way of making loads of money."
>
> **2. Subjective Norm**
>
> "They all play the lottery: that's just a form of gambling. It's perfectly normal."
>
> **3. Intention**
>
> "I wouldn't mind a gamble: it looks like fun."
>
> **4. Control**
>
> "No one is forcing me to do this: I am making my own decision. I am fully in control of my actions."
>
> **5. Behaviour**
>
> The person begins to gamble.

APPLICATIONS OF TRB AND TPB

Using our knowledge of the TPB and TRA we can see that altering people's beliefs, attitudes, understanding of social norms, the social norms themselves and people's perception of whether they are in control of their behaviour, can all alter the incidence of the behaviour itself. For instance, if a person feels powerless to resist a behaviour then that behaviour is more likely to occur. Putting schemes in place that provide the person with support to resist in the first place, or support to remain away from their addictive behaviour once they have managed to stop it, may help reduce the incidence of such behaviour. Similarly, since it is experience and knowledge that give us our beliefs and norms in the first place, education and

THE THEORY OF PLANNED BEHAVIOUR

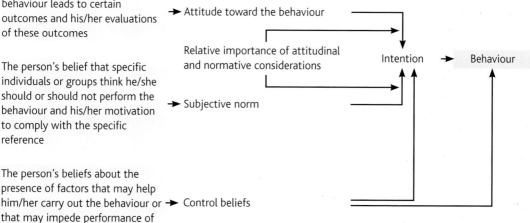

The person's belief that the behaviour leads to certain outcomes and his/her evaluations of these outcomes → Attitude toward the behaviour

Relative importance of attitudinal and normative considerations

The person's belief that specific individuals or groups think he/she should or should not perform the behaviour and his/her motivation to comply with the specific reference → Subjective norm

Intention → Behaviour

The person's beliefs about the presence of factors that may help him/her carry out the behaviour or that may impede performance of the behaviour → Control beliefs

Adapted from Azjen (1991).

information services can play a very important role, in influencing the formation of these beliefs. The TPB and TRA provide us with a way of looking at the mechanisms behind a behaviour and the influences upon it. This knowledge can help us modify the behaviour itself.

Both the TRA and TPB have been applied to a number of addictive behaviours. The potential of TPB for predicting the use and misuse of alcohol among school children was investigated by Marcoux and Shope (1997). The TRA and TPB were compared in their abilities to predict people's *intention* to drink alcohol, which was shown to be an extremely important factor in whether they took up the habit. Another important issue was peer pressure. Finally, the normative belief of parents was found to be significant. Students with parents who were very strict on alcohol use were less likely to use it. Issues such as reducing availability, decreasing peer pressure and encouraging parents to have discussions with their children about addictive behaviours and getting involved in prevention programmes are highlighted by this research.

Cigarette smoking in different groups of teenagers in the United States was investigated by Hanson, (2005). Attitude, subjective norm and perceived behavioural control all predicted smoking intentions in African-Americans. Attitude and perceived behavioural control were predictive of smoking in Puerto Rican, and non-white Hispanic teenage girls. It is clear, then, that the behaviours of different groups of people are influenced by different factors.

LIMITATIONS OF TRA AND TPB

Despite the wide application of the TRA and TPB, these theories have been criticised. The most common criticisms are:

1. Not always a role for all aspects of the models

In some studies there seems to be no role for subjective norms, while some show no role for perceived behavioural control, and some show no role for attitudes in determining behaviour (Ogden, 2004). It could be that these components of the models, although present, may not feature in all behavioural processes.

2. Behaviour measured by self-reports

Ogden (2004) goes on to indicate that behaviour in studies using the TPB and TRA is more often than not measured using self-report, rather than more objective measures. Self-report may suffer from a lack of accuracy and may be biased.

3. Are participants really acting as they say?

Ogden (2004) concludes by suggesting that asking participants about their thought processes after the event may only change the way that they are expressing themselves, the way they are thinking, at the time they are questioned. The questioning may not directly identify how someone was actually thinking in the first place that drove them to complete the action.

TYPES OF INTERVENTION

Support, to help an individual to stay away from addictive behaviours like gambling and smoking, can take many forms. These may include medical assistance to help with their cravings once they have stopped the activity; or psychological assistance in the form of support and counselling. On the other hand, intervention may have a wider focus than the individual, with public health interventions and legal restrictions imposed to help society reduce addictive activities.

"There are four types of intervention described here – make sure you learn them all, but also remember that you may have to comment on how effective each one is."

BIOLOGICAL INTERVENTIONS

There have been a variety of biologically-based approaches designed primarily to change the way addictive behaviours are experienced. People who design medicines are trying to find ways to prevent people from experiencing the pleasant 'high' associated with the addictive behaviour; or to find alternative substances that have some of the positive effects without their addictive properties.

Providing an alternative 'treatment' – agonist substitution

One method used in the treatment of substance addiction is called *agonist substitution*: this involves providing the person with a safer drug that is chemically similar to the addictive drug. The best known of these approaches is treatment of heroin addiction with methadone, but agonist substitution is also available for nicotine addiction. Like heroin, methadone is a very potent drug. Methadone programmes administer the drug in the form of a liquid, which the patient must drink in the presence of supervising personnel. Taking the drug orally means that the opiate level in the brain rises slowly and does not produce a high, in the way an

AGONIST SUBSTITUTION IN SMOKING – NICOTINE GUM AND PATCHES

Addiction to cigarette smoking is also treated using an agonist substitution method where the alternative, safer drug is provided to patients in the form of nicotine gum or a nicotine patch. Both methods maintain a sufficiently high level of nicotine in the brain to decrease a person's craving for nicotine in the form of cigarettes. Once the habit of smoking has subsided, the dose in the gum or the patch is gradually reduced over a period of several months to help the person give up cigarettes. In general, nicotine replacement via gum or a patch is successful in helping people to stop smoking, although both methods work best when used in combination with supportive psychological therapies such as cognitive behavioural therapy (Hughes, 1993).

injection of heroin would. The effect of methadone is extremely long-lasting, which means that if the drug user injects heroin while still under the influence of methadone it will have very little effect.

Zack et al (2003) have shown that the effects of gambling in the brain are very similar to the effects a psycho-stimulant such as amphetamine may have. They have successfully shown that a dose of amphetamine given to problem gamblers can stimulate their motivation to gamble. They go on to indicate that an agonist that targets the action of these drugs may well be useful in helping gamblers control their motivations to gamble.

Agonist substitution does have its critics. For instance, research suggests that some people who use methadone as a substitute for heroin really do benefit but they may actually become dependent upon methadone, possibly even for the rest of their lives (O'Brien, 1996). It follows that substituting nicotine agonist for nicotine may leave ex-smokers smoke-free, but the now ex-smoker may have become dependent on the agonist itself.

Providing an alternative drug – antagonist substitution

A second biological method used in the treatment of substance addiction involves *antagonist* treatments, where drugs are given that block or counter the effects of the drug that the person is addicted to. The most frequently prescribed antagonist drug is called *naltrexone*. This works by blocking the action of neurochemicals that provide the person with rewarding feelings when they take the drug.

Antagonist substitution is available for nicotine addiction as well as for a range of other addictive behaviours. It is a particularly effective treatment for alcohol addiction. O'Brien et al (1996) reported the results of two programmes using naltrexone along with more traditional behavioural treatments. In both programmes it was found that administration of naltrexone significantly improved the likelihood of success, decreasing the participants' craving for alcohol and increasing the number of participants who managed to abstain

from alcohol. Naltrexone has also been shown to be effective in reducing the gambling behaviour of problem gamblers (Hollander et al, 2000).

Immunotherapy – drug immunization

An interesting approach to managing addictive behaviour is suggested by a study by Carrera et al (1995), who managed to stimulate rats' immune systems to develop antibodies to cocaine. Antibodies are an important part of the immune system that help prevent infection, and their properties can be used for purposes of immunisation, for example from measles, mumps, rubella and malaria. In their approach, Carrera et al generated antibodies in the bloodstream that bound with molecules of cocaine and stopped them from crossing into the brain. As a consequence, these 'cocaine-immunised' rats were less sensitive to the effects of cocaine, and the levels of cocaine in the brains of these animals were lower after an injection of cocaine than in non-immunised rats.

Since this study was carried out, animal studies with vaccines against cocaine, heroin, methamphetamine and nicotine have all been undertaken, and several human trials for vaccines for cocaine and nicotine have taken place (Kosten and Owens, 2005). The results of these animal studies and human trials are very promising, and more extensive human trials are in progress. Theoretically, at least, treatment of addictions with immunotherapy should interfere only with the action of an abused drug and not with the normal operations of people's reinforcement mechanisms that allow them to feel happy for other reasons. Thus, the treatment should not decrease their ability to experience normal pleasurable situations. This technique is not just of use for drugs such as cocaine. In 2003, Janda identified a technique for stimulating the immune system to rid itself of nicotine. Immunotherapy for something as prevalent as smoking addiction may not be far away!

PSYCHOLOGICAL INTERVENTIONS

A number of psychological treatments have been developed for helping people with addictions.

Each approach is designed to address certain aspects of drug addiction and its consequences for the individual, their family, and for society in general.

Cognitive behaviour therapy (CBT)

CBT is a psychological technique used in the treatment of many kinds of psychological problems. For instance, it may be employed when someone feels anxious about flying, or when someone is suffering with mild depression. Essentially the goals of CBT are that the client is helped to think differently about the object or behaviour that causes them difficulty. Smoking and drinking are both behaviours that people may seek psychological help to overcome. In both cases the addict may be helped to change their thoughts and beliefs about their addictive behaviours, with the aim of helping them stay away from such behaviours in the future. The elements and principles of CBT appear in a number of strategies designed to help those with addictive behaviours, including *relapse prevention*, *the matrix model* and *addiction counselling*.

Relapse prevention

Relapse prevention is a cognitive-behavioural therapy that was originally developed for the treatment of problem drinking, and adapted later for cocaine addicts. Hajek et al (2005) have identified it as useful in helping people remain off cigarettes once they have managed to give up, and Echeburua et al (2000) have noted its value in helping pathological gamblers. Cognitive-behavioural strategies are based on the theory that learning and thinking processes play a very important role in the development of maladaptive behaviours – those behaviours that can cause the individual harm. During therapy, individuals learn to identify and correct problem behaviours.

Relapse prevention encompasses several cognitive-behavioural strategies that help the person stay away from their problem behaviour, as well as providing support for people who experience relapse. For instance, the relapse prevention approach to the treatment of cocaine addiction consists of a collection of strategies intended to enhance self-control. Hajek et al (2005) indicate that self-control in those in danger of relapse in smoking might be most necessary in counteracting the urge to seek out cigarettes. The techniques used include exploring the positive and negative consequences of continued use, and self-monitoring to recognise drug cravings early on. They might also be used to help the person recognise the situations where there may be a high risk of relapse.

Such situations, for smokers, may be particularly stressful times; or, for gamblers, periods of great excitement involving sporting activities. Once these high-risk situations have been identified, coping strategies can be learned. Anticipating the problems addicts are likely to meet and helping them develop effective coping strategies is a key element of this approach. Research indicates that the skills individuals learn through relapse prevention therapy remain after the completion of treatment. In one study, most people receiving this cognitive-behavioural approach maintained the gains they made in treatment, throughout the following year (Carroll et al, 1994).

The matrix model

The matrix model provides a framework for engaging those with problem behaviours in treatment and helping them stop and stay away from their addiction. The approach is eclectic, including elements related to the prevention of relapse, as well as to family and group therapies, drug education, and also self-help techniques. A number of studies have demonstrated that addicts treated with the matrix model demonstrate significant reductions in drug and alcohol use and improvements in psychological indicators, including feelings of self-worth and positive outlook. (Huber et al, 1997). Clients learn about issues critical to their addiction and relapse, receive support from a trained therapist, become familiar with self-help programmes, and, if appropriate, are monitored for drug use by urine testing. Education programmes for family members affected by the addiction are also included. The therapist's role is as teacher and coach, building and maintaining a positive, encouraging relationship with the patient and using that relationship as a powerful means of reinforcing positive behaviour change. The interaction between the therapist and the client is not confrontational or parental in any way. Therapists are trained to conduct treatment sessions in a manner that really develops the client's self-esteem, dignity, and self-worth. A positive relationship between client and therapist is vital to ensuring that the client remains in therapy.

Addiction counselling

Individualised addiction counselling focuses directly on reducing or stopping the addictive behaviour. Addicts are encouraged to attend sessions regularly, as often as one or two times a week. Related areas in the addict's life – such as their job, and any possible illegal activity, as well as their relationships with their families, friends and other associates – are also addressed.

Through its focus on short-term behavioural goals, individualised addiction counselling helps the client develop coping strategies and tools for abstaining from and staying away from their addictive behaviour. The addiction counsellor can refer the addict to doctors and other professionals for supplementary medical, psychiatric, employment, and other services if these are needed.

Addiction counselling can be very effective. In a study that compared heroin addicts receiving only methadone to those receiving methadone coupled with counselling, individuals who received only methadone showed very little success in reducing opiate use. The addition of counselling produced significantly more improvement (McLellan et al, 1988). When medical/psychiatric, employment, and family services were added, outcomes improved even further (McLellan et al, 1993).

Hazel et al (2006) assessed the effectiveness of a telephone addiction counselling service set up to help those who were trying to stop smoking. Their results showed that the line was effective in helping people to give up, but it was not terribly effective in protecting people from relapsing. Reid et al (1999) concluded that a dedicated helpline can be very useful for assisting people to give up smoking, if used in combination with other therapies, including biological therapies such as nicotine patches, as long as the client is motivated to give up. Bryant-Jefferies (2005) has indicated that careful addiction counselling can be extremely effective in helping those with gambling problems. In summary, it seems that the effectiveness of addiction counselling depends at least in part on the type of addiction being treated. It is nevertheless clear that, overall, it remains a useful tool in the fight against addiction.

Motivational enhancement therapy

Addicts are often poorly motivated to seek treatment for their behaviour. Motivational enhancement therapy is a counselling approach for encouraging behaviour change by helping to motivate addicts to become involved in their treatment. This approach employs strategies to bring about fast and internally motivated change in the addict, rather than guiding the client step-by-step through the recovery process. This therapy consists of an initial assessment session, followed by two to four individual treatment sessions with a therapist. The first treatment session focuses on providing feedback from the initial assessment session to stimulate discussion regarding drug use and to bring about self-motivational statements. Motivational interviewing principles are used to strengthen motivation and build a plan for change. Coping strategies for high-risk situations, such as periods when the addict would normally engage in drug taking, are suggested and discussed. In the sessions that follow, the therapist carefully monitors any changes; reviews and alters strategies being used to help the addict give up; and continues to encourage commitment to change or sustained abstinence from the problem drug. This approach has been used successfully with alcoholics and with marijuana-dependent individuals (Stephens et al, 1994).

PUBLIC HEALTH INTERVENTIONS

Drugs: the law

Most countries have laws to license and control addictive behaviours. These behaviours are of many kinds. Legislation may thus address a wide range of issues, from determining the punishments available for heroin use, to specifying where fruit machines may be placed (to exclude them from fast food shops, for example, where young people might otherwise be drawn into gambling). Typically though, such legislation covers any or all of the opiates (including heroin), amphetamines, (including speed) cannabinoids (including skunk and other forms of marijuana), cocaine, barbiturates (such as sleeping tablets and other tranquillisers), hallucinogens (such as LSD) and a variety of more modern synthetic drugs.

Using legislation to classify a substance is a common way of identifying how dangerous the substance is considered to be. The current drug classifications are summarised in the table on page 422. It is clear that legislation is important in the control of these substances, with the toughest punishments being the possibility of an unlimited fine and life imprisonment.

The classification and de-classification of substances under such legislation is not only related to the 'addictiveness' of the drug in question. The substances covered often have very different addictive properties. Some are highly likely to cause physical dependency, whilst others rarely cause any form of compulsive need. Typically, nicotine (in the form of tobacco) is hardly regulated at all, although it is well known as one of the most addictive substances ever discovered! You'll certainly not find it in the drug-classification table even though it is known to cause serious medical

		Possession:	Dealing:
Class A	Ecstasy, LSD, heroin, cocaine, crack, magic mushrooms, amphetamines (if prepared for injection).	Up to seven years in prison or an unlimited fine or both.	Up to life in prison or an unlimited fine or both.
Class B	Amphetamines, Methylphenidate (Ritalin), Pholcodine.	Up to five years in prison or an unlimited fine or both.	Up to 14 years in prison or an unlimited fine or both.
Class C	Cannabis, tranquillisers, some painkillers, Gamma hydroxybutyrate (GHB), Ketamine.	Up to two years in prison or an unlimited fine or both.	Up to 14 years in prison or an unlimited fine or both.

Classes of drugs and their legal implications. Source: The Home Office (2008).

problems and untold misery to those having to deal with the addiction.

Occasionally, legislation changes, to de-classify or re-classify a substance. This often depends on public pressure or new evidence from research that shows that the substance is more or less dangerous than was previously thought. Whether the addictive behaviour in question is socially acceptable plays an important role. Nicotine has been used in the UK for over 300 years, and as such it is part of the fabric of this society. It takes time, and a concerted effort, to alter public perceptions about a drug that has been so widely available for such a long time.

The smoking ban

In recent years, each nation of the United Kingdom has brought in a total ban on smoking in enclosed public spaces. In Scotland the law came into effect in March 2006, in Wales and Northern Ireland in April 2007 and finally in England in July 2007. What has been the impact of these bans on health, and nicotine use, in the UK?

» Researchers at the University of Dundee found significant improvements in the health of bar staff in the two months following the ban. They tested bar workers' lung function a month before the ban came in, and again two months after it had been introduced. The proportion showing symptoms related to passive smoking fell from more than 80% to less than 50%, with reduced levels of nicotine in the blood and improvements in lung function of as much as 10% (Menzies et al, 2006).

» A 2007 study of the effect of the ban in Scotland showed that there had been a 17% year-on-year drop in hospital admissions for heart attack since the ban was introduced in March 2006 (Pell et al, 2008).

» An analysis of the saliva of 39 non-smoking workers before and after the Scottish smoking ban came into force found a 75% fall in cotinine, which is a by-product of nicotine and is a good indicator of how much cigarette smoke has entered the body (Semple et al, 2007).

Smoke-free laws may also help smokers to quit. In places where some smoking restrictions already existed before the new laws came into force, as in the UK, the introduction of the law is estimated to have significantly reduced smoking rates. Smoking rates were estimated to be declining in England by 0.4% per year, but there is evidence that in the first year of the smoking ban this rate accelerated to 1%, over twice as fast as before. Almost half of all smokers tried to quit in 2007 and approximately 8% of smokers reported that the new law prompted them to make an attempt to quit (West, 2008). Smoking cessation services also saw a 12% increase in the number of people able to quit for at least four weeks in the three months before the ban, compared to the figure for the same three months in 2006, the year before the ban came in. The number of people setting a quit date in the two months immediately following the introduction of the smoking ban was also higher than in the same two months in previous years (NHS Statistics, 2007).

Not being able to smoke while in enclosed public places may help those smokers who have quit not to resume smoking. Amongst smokers in the Irish Republic who quit after the ban took effect there in March 2004, 80% reported that the law had helped them quit and 88% reported that it had helped them to remain as non-smokers (Fong et al, 2006).

Gambling

In 2007, The Gambling Act became law in the UK. With the exception of the National Lottery and spread betting (which are separately regulated), the Act applies to all commercial activities that might be regarded as gambling, from casinos to online betting organisations. It is clear that the scale of the task for those applying the law is huge. The media, the internet, and also more traditional outlets for gambling such as betting shops, offer, between them, constant encouragement to participate in this potentially addictive behaviour.

Evidence of how a change in legislation can influence the prevalence of gambling can be seen in recent alterations to the law, that were to permit the construction of so-called 'super casinos' in the UK. These were to be casinos in the style of those found in the gambling capital of the world, Las Vegas.

Legislation allowing these casinos was passed, and towns around the country successfully applied for the chance to build them. However, before building had even begun, the law was changed, removing the right to build the casinos and replacing it with the possibility of multiple smaller gambling establishments. In Manchester, for instance, the council indicated that the revised legislation, denying them the possibility of a new super casino, would cost the city up to 3,500 jobs. The government however felt that a huge venue of this kind would not be appropriate, even if many jobs would result from it. Although legislation is one way of controlling access to gambling, governments must take economic considerations into account when making their decisions. Addictive

behaviours produce many millions of pounds of government revenue, for example from taxes on tobacco, alcohol and betting.

There is also the issue of urban regeneration to consider. The attraction of gambling is such that the presence of a large casino in an economically deprived town can have an extraordinary impact, drawing gamblers in from miles around to spend their money, not only on gambling itself, but also on, for example, hotels and restaurants. The problem is, of course, that gambling may well have negative effects. It may encourage addiction, increase poverty and hardship among gamblers themselves, and cause misery for many who are associated with them. In framing legislation the government must weigh up the costs and benefits of allowing the increased development of casinos across the country.

The Gambling Act states that gambling is only allowed in the UK if specifically permitted by licence. If you want to run a gambling organisation, or use facilities that allow people to gamble, you must have a permit, or a licence to do so. If you do not have such permission you may be prosecuted and may face fines or imprisonment. The Act introduced a special regulator, the Gambling Commission, to oversee the implementation of the law, and supervise gambling businesses and the licensing of premises. However, gambling in private is outside the scope of the legislation. For instance, a private game of poker is permitted, and you may also play for things other than money. Private gambling is highly prevalent: it is not included in official government figures on gambling, and even if there was the will to act against it, it is hard to see how any kind of legislation would be effective.

The Gambling Act relates to the effect gambling may have on individuals and society when it refers to possible illegal activity linked to gambling. The Act requires the Gambling Commission to ensure that there is no link between gambling and crime or disorder. The law also notes that gambling presents a risk to children and what it describes as 'vulnerable adults'. These two groups of people are protected in several ways: firstly, as has been suggested earlier, by strictly controlling where gambling machines may be located; and secondly, by making it illegal for anyone under 18 to gamble. Moreover, it is an offence for any adult to encourage or entice someone under the age of 18 to gamble, and if adults do this they can face legal action.

EFFECTIVENESS OF PUBLIC HEALTH INTERVENTIONS

Public health interventions aim to encourage populations and individuals in activities and strategies for the improvement of health and prevention of disease. Public health interventions are not new, although it could be argued that government has become more engaged in such activities in recent years than ever before. One of the earliest public health interventions in the UK was probably the Sanitary Act of 1866 which made local authorities responsible for supplying water and disposing of household waste and sewage, thereby helping to prevent many diseases. In 1949 a law was passed making it compulsory to pasteurise milk, eliminating several thousand deaths a year that had been caused by bovine tuberculosis contracted through raw milk. Many more public health interventions have followed, which have cleaned air, discouraged drink-driving, enforced the wearing of seat belts in motor vehicles and controlled the range of additives in our food.

The most recent government statement on public health, however, was in 2004. This established the convention that the government should make a health intervention if an organisation's or an individual's actions were harming others. This has led to a number of recent health interventions, such as a ban on junk food advertising during children's television, and voluntary food labelling regulations. Probably the highest profile initiative, however, has been the drive to reduce smoking and tobacco-related harm. Smoking is, after all, the leading cause of preventable death, and costs the Health Service billions of pounds a year.

In much of the United Kingdom this guidance is produced by NICE (The National Institute for Health and Clinical Excellence). The Institute produces two types of guidance: public health intervention guidance (specific single measures, such as the guidance to GPs on the advice they should give patients for particular health issues) and public health programme guidance (broad strategies, for example encouraging sensible alcohol consumption). Evidence for the effectiveness of these public interventions is not as clear as we might hope. Research shows that whilst public health interventions can be very effective indeed at stopping or reducing behaviours in particular ways, people may change their behaviour to compensate for the intervention. Gomel et al (1993) for instance showed that a workplace ban on smoking was effective in stopping that specific

behaviour, but it had other more negative effects. In their study, smokers in the New South Wales Ambulance service in Australia were questioned over six weeks following the introduction of a smoking ban at their place of work. The results showed that the participants *reported* less smoking both during work and at home, but blood tests revealed that they may well have been compensating for non-smoking in work by smoking more outside work hours. The results also showed that the participants experienced an increase in craving and also stress levels.

Ogden (2000) reports other research into the effectiveness of public health interventions. She says that increasing the price of something, like cigarettes or alcohol, may well help people, particularly children and adolescents, to stop taking up the addictive behaviour in the first place. She says that an increase in the expense of smoking or drinking may make the perceived cost of the behaviour greater than the perceived benefits. Ogden goes on to predict that the UK smoking ban may well promote a reduction in smoking. However, she warns that, just because people are not allowed to smoke in public places, this does not mean that they will not increase their smoking elsewhere to compensate, as happened in Gomel et al's study of Australian ambulance service workers.

Whilst there is a downward trend in smoking, this trend is not evenly distributed. For instance, whereas adult male smoking is significantly reducing, the same cannot be said of adolescent female smoking, which actually shows signs of increasing.

Research consistently finds that people who begin smoking early in life are more likely to experience nicotine dependence as adults. Adolescence is also the time in life when an individual is most likely to begin smoking. Interventions focused on young people may therefore have the greatest long-term impact on smoking-related health problems.

Recent genetic research suggests that such interventions may one day be made more effective as it becomes possible to identify genetically high-risk individuals. Weiss et al (2008) studied 2,827 long-term smokers. They found that some individuals have genes which make them more prone to nicotine addiction in adulthood if they began smoking before the age of 17. Individuals with the same genetic variation who did not start smoking until 17 or later did not have an increased risk of long-term addiction. The implication is that there is potential in the future for developing methods of identifying particular subgroups of young individuals who are especially at risk of nicotine addiction.

Public health interventions might also be made more effective by recognising the social context of smoking. Research by Fowler and Christakis (2008) suggest that smokers who successfully quit tend to give up in groups rather than as isolated individuals. From data gathered as part of a large-scale longitudinal study on cardiovascular health, they found that whilst in 1971 smokers mixed equally with non-smokers in social situations, by 2000 smokers were being marginalised and tended to form separate clusters. The research also found that the closer the relationships between individuals in these clusters, the more influence one person who quits would have on the others. For example, a friend quitting decreased the chances of smoking in others by 36%, whilst a husband or wife who quit would decrease a spouse's smoking by 67%. Importantly, geographical distance was irrelevant – the key factor was the closeness of the relationship. Education also appeared an important factor. This research clearly has implications for the effectiveness of public health interventions in changing addictive behaviours.

A key finding from this study was that a quitter working in a small firm would decrease the smoking in co-workers by 34%, whilst the change in large firms was insignificant. NICE has in fact recognised the workplace as a key target area for reducing smoking. Employers are not legally obliged to help their employers stop smoking, though the ban on public smoking has made it more difficult for people to smoke at work. Smoking is not allowed in enclosed places, including vehicles used for work; nor is it permitted to set aside an enclosed room for smokers. Failure to comply with these regulations is an offence.

NICE provides employers with extensive guidance and support on how to encourage their employees to give up smoking. This ranges from information about access to local smoking cessation support to on-site counselling and guidance. Employers are encouraged to support staff by allowing them to attend cessation services without losing pay. Employers are also reminded that the health improvements associated with stopping smoking would benefit companies through reduced sickness and absence, and increased productivity.

A word of caution about public health interventions was sounded by Albarracin et al (2009). They found that weight loss campaigns promoting exercise actually had the effect of encouraging people to eat more! In their study, participants who viewed exercise ads ate one third more than participants exposed to posters with other types of message. This indicates that some campaigns which on the face of it present a clear message might have negative consequences by encouraging the opposite behaviour to that which is desired.

Anomalistic Psychology

CHRIS ROE

You are expected to develop knowledge, understanding and critical thinking in relation to the topic Anomalistic psychology.

This includes applying knowledge and understanding of research methods, approaches, issues and debates where appropriate. You must also show an appreciation of the relationship between research, policy and practices in applying psychology in everyday life.

WHAT YOU NEED TO KNOW

THEORETICAL AND METHODOLOGICAL ISSUES IN THE STUDY OF ANOMALOUS EXPERIENCE

- Issues of pseudoscience and scientific fraud
- Controversies relating to Ganzfeld studies of ESP and studies of psychokinesis

FACTORS UNDERLYING ANOMALOUS EXPERIENCE

- Cognitive, personality and biological factors underlying anomalous experience
- Functions of paranormal and related beliefs, including their cultural significance
- The psychology of deception and self-deception, superstition, and coincidence

BELIEF IN EXCEPTIONAL EXPERIENCE

Research into:
- psychic healing
- out-of-body and near-death experience
- psychic mediumship

WHAT IS ANOMALISTIC PSYCHOLOGY?

Anomalistic psychology is concerned with the study of extraordinary phenomena of behaviour and experience, including (but not restricted to) those which are often labelled 'paranormal'. We will define a paranormal experience here as one that seems to involve events or abilities that conflict with what C.D. Broad (1953) called the "basic limiting principles" of science. Broad described principles that he believed to be "so overwhelmingly supported by all the empirical facts…that it hardly enters our heads to question them". Some of these principles and the experiences that seem to contradict them are listed in Table 1. Prominent scientists have asserted that such phenomena are impossible and have no scientific basis. For example, Richard Dawkins (1998) concluded "The paranormal is bunk. Those who try to sell it to us are fakes and charlatans, and some of them have grown rich and fat by taking us for a ride."

Nevertheless the general public tends to believe that such phenomena are real and people frequently claim to have had personal experience of them. For example, two fairly recent representative surveys of UK residents conducted by the market research company MORI ('Paranormal survey', 1998; 'Three in five', 2003) found that up to two thirds of their sample reported that they believed in various paranormal phenomena (see Table 2). These might be usefully broken down into three types of belief: firstly that there is an immaterial part of the self that can function independently of the physical body and that might survive the death of that body; secondly that humans might have spontaneous experiences that suggest, in certain circumstances, that they are able to transcend the normal limits of space and time; and thirdly that some people may be able to have such experiences consistently enough to offer this ability as a professional service.

> **ASK AN EXAMINER**
>
> *"You'll notice that the word 'paranormal' is used a great deal in this chapter. As it says in the text, 'anomalous' and 'paranormal' are terms which are often used interchangeably by parapsychologists – for the most part they are* synonymous.*"*

Researchers working in the area of anomalistic psychology have attempted to provide explanations of those experiences that do not assume *a priori* that there is anything paranormal involved; instead they try to account for them in terms of known psychological and physical factors. They can then go on to test those explanations by designing studies that include controls to effectively rule out those factors or directly manipulate them to see if the phenomenon is affected – if it is, then it suggests that the 'known factors' explanation is along the right lines, but if it is not then the search

EXAMPLES OF BROAD'S 'LIMITING PRINCIPLES' AND EXPERIENCES THAT SEEM TO CONTRADICT THEM

Broad's principle	Apparent exceptions
Causes must come before effects	Premonitions, such as dreams that refer to (are caused by?) a future event
A person's mind cannot produce any direct change in the material world except those caused via the brain/sensorimotor system	Psychokinetic events, where people claim to have moved or distorted some object through an act of will
Any mental event is an event in the brain of a living body	Out-of-body experiences, where the centre of experience seems to be located away from the body. Near-death experiences, where mental events seem to occur when the brain is inactive Mediumship communications purportedly from deceased persons
All knowledge of the world comes to us through our conventional senses or by inference from known facts	Telepathy, where people seem to know directly what is in the mind of another person

Table 1

continues and researchers need to consider what further explanations are necessary.

In this chapter we will look at some of the explanations that have been put forward and evaluate them by looking at the kind of evidence that has been collected from surveys, field investigations and controlled experiments. In looking at this material we will adopt a position of scepticism. Michael Shermer defines a sceptic as "one who questions the validity of a particular claim by calling for evidence to prove or disprove it". In this sense all good scientists are sceptics and do try not to let their prior beliefs influence the judgements they make when presented with evidence for a particular claim. Shermer notes that, in science, facts are regarded as provisional and could potentially be challenged by future observations (much as, say, Newtonian physics has been superseded by quantum mechanics and relativity) so scepticism should be directed not only at the paranormal claims but also at the normal explanations that are put forward to explain them away, even if they seem more plausible given our current understanding of how the world works.

So what *kinds* of explanation should we be looking for? Schmeidler (1985) has suggested four ways in which paranormal beliefs might come about:

» firstly, they may be based upon careful analysis of research findings as presented in journals and other scholarly sources;

» secondly, they may be formed under the influence of a doctrine one accepts (such as a set of religious beliefs), or adopted from a person one respects who already holds those views, or reflect wider cultural assumptions (for example as communicated by the media);

» thirdly, they may have their origin in impressive experiences which the person was unable, after consideration, to account for in ordinary terms;

» and finally, they may fulfil some psychological need.

The first of these ways is unlikely to apply to the general population – few people have the time or inclination to become familiar with rather dry and difficult-to-get technical reports of experimental tests of paranormal claims (though later in this chapter we will present and critically evaluate some of the best evidence from these sources). Indeed, even people who are scientifically trained and are professionally involved in experimenting on and theorising about paranormal phenomena – usually described as parapsychologists – report

that personal experience was a more significant factor in their conviction that the effects were real than was the objective evidence from controlled experiments (McConnell, 1975). Some researchers have given graphic accounts of their own experiences which have helped shape their interest in and views of paranormal phenomena. There is also some suggestion that disbelief might come about as a result of particularly negative personal experiences (Roe, 1998).

"You will find frequent reference to culture throughout this chapter. You are expected to have an awareness of culture and paranormal belief, so don't ignore these: they are important."

Turning to the second of Schmeidler's explanations, it is certainly true that one's particular culture is likely to affect the range or type of experiences that are regarded as legitimate or proven, but belief in the paranormal *per se* does not seem to be a function of a particular culture. Gallup polls with US samples (e.g. Moore, 2005) give a similar profile of belief to that for the UK (see Table 3), and high levels of belief have been found in surveys in New Zealand (Clarke, 1991), Australia (Grimmer and White 1990), Iceland and Sweden (Haraldsson, 1985), South Korea (Haraldsson and Houtkooper, 1991) and China (McClenon, 1994). Some of this consistency may be due to the increasingly pervasive influence of the media, which can reach far beyond national boundaries.

It is certainly true that most media portrayals of the paranormal tend to be sympathetic to the claims rather than sceptical of them. Hollywood films such as *Ghost*, *The Sixth Sense*, and more recently *Ghost Town* rely on principal characters being able to interact with the dead; while others, such as *Minority Report*, *Premonition* and *Push* have plots that are driven by a central character's ability to glimpse the future. On the small screen we have television programmes that run from the ostensibly factual investigations of *Most Haunted* (from the UK) and *Ghost Hunters* (from the US) through to more clearly fictional series such as *Sea of Souls*, *Heroes* and *Medium*. Given that there are so few examples of shows that offer conventional explanations for these effects (the Steve Martin movie, *Leap of Faith* and the US series *Psych* are rare exceptions), then it seems likely that, despite

	February 1998			August 2003		
	Yes %	? %	No %	Yes %	? %	No %
A soul	67	9	24	68	6	27
Out-of-body experience	31	11	58	32	7	61
Near-death experience	51	12	37	60	7	34
Life after death	45	13	42	47	10	43
Ghosts	40	8	52	38	6	56
Reincarnation	24	12	64	23	9	68
Déjà-vu	66	4	30	57	5	38
Telepathy	54	9	37	42	7	51
Premonitions/ESP	64	7	29	54	6	41
That dreams can predict the future	30	10	60	25	6	69
Psychics/Mediums	28	9	63	28	6	66
Fortune telling/Tarot	18	7	75	13	4	83
Astrology	38	9	53	31	4	66
Faith healers	32	12	56	24	8	68

Table 2: Percentage of UK sample who believe in various paranormal phenomena (rounding may mean that some percentages do not total 100%).

	May 2001			June 2005		
	Yes %	? %	No %	Yes %	? %	No %
Reincarnation: that is, the rebirth of the soul in a new body after death	25	20	54	20	20	59
Ghosts/that spirits of dead people can come back in certain places/ situations	38	17	44	32	19	48
That houses can be haunted	42	16	41	37	16	46
ESP or Extrasensory Perception	50	20	27	41	25	32
Telepathy/communication between minds without using traditional senses	36	26	35	31	27	42
Clairvoyance/the power of the mind to know the past and predict the future	32	23	45	26	24	50
Channelling/allowing a 'spirit-being' to assume temporary control of body	15	21	62	9	20	70
Psychic or spiritual healing, or the power of the human mind to heal the body	54	19	26	55	17	26
Astrology, or that the position of the stars and planets can affect people's lives	28	18	52	25	19	55

Table 3: Percentage of US sample who believe in various paranormal phenomena.

the programmes being framed as fiction, the enduring impression will be that the claims they portray are plausible.

Perhaps unsurprisingly, the most influential factor in Schmeidler's list seems to be personal experience (Irwin, 1985). McClenon (1982) found that 54% of those who expressed a favourable attitude towards the reality of the existence of anomalous phenomena (psi) cited personal experience as influencing their opinion, and Blackmore (1984) reported that, of the 36% in her sample who professed belief in ESP, 44% cited their own

	February 1998			August 2003		
	Yes %	? %	No %	Yes %	? %	No %
Out-of-body experience	21	0	79	26	2	72
Near-death experience	17	1	82	20	0	80
Ghosts	37	4	59	49	19	32
Reincarnation	8	2	90	10	2	88
Déjà-vu	79	1	20	83	1	16
Telepathy	35	1	64	41	1	59
Premonitions/ESP	41	2	57	48	2	50
That dreams can predict the future	42	3	60	58	1	41
Psychics/Mediums	37	1	63	46	1	53
Fortune telling/Tarot	60	0	40	64	1	34
Faith healers	24	0	56	33	0	66

Table 4: Percentage of UK sample that believe in various paranormal phenomena who have had personal experience of it.

experience as the main reason. This pattern is also true for the MORI surveys cited earlier: of those who declared a belief in ghosts, a remarkably high 37% of the 1998 sample and an even higher 49% of the 2003 sample reported that they had had personal experience of ghosts; similarly high figures are reported for telepathy (35% and 41%), premonitions (41% and 48%), precognitive dreams (42% and 58%) among others (see Table 4), so clearly in attempting to account for paranormal belief we need to account for paranormal experience as well. Most of the explanations that we look at in the next section set out to do just that.

Towards the end of this chapter we will consider the possibility that people come to believe in at least some paranormal phenomena because they have some basis in reality: however, most research in psychology that is concerned with paranormal belief and experience has begun with the premise that we need to find an explanation in conventional terms; and only if this proves to be unsatisfactory need we go on to consider more unconventional explanations.

According to the 2008 UK Survey 64% of people believe in fortune telling.

FACTORS UNDERLYING ANOMALOUS EXPERIENCE

THE NEED FOR CONTROL AND SUPERSTITIOUS BEHAVIOUR

One explanation that has been put forward to account for the high levels of anomalous belief is that they need not be true if they are primarily need-serving (Krippner and Winkler, 1997). According to this view – termed the *psychodynamic functions hypothesis* by Irwin (1999) – some people are prone to see life as chaotic and unpredictable, and this provokes anxiety; anomalous beliefs develop as a means of alleviating this anxiety by giving the semblance of order or meaning to potential (particularly negative) future events (for example that those events should be thought of as challenges that are necessary for spiritual growth) or by offering the illusion of control over them, for example by practising certain superstitious rituals.

It certainly seems to be the case that paranormal belief is associated with elevated levels of anxiety, as a number of questionnaire studies have found these variables to be positively correlated (e.g. Wolfradt, 1997), although the magnitude of the relationships is relatively modest and they have not always been detected (e.g. Tobacyk, 1982).

There is also some independent support for the notion that an illusion of control or order in an uncertain situation can alleviate anxiety. For example, Sanderson, Rapee and Barlow (1989) found that participants who were given the false impression that they had control over an aversive (unpleasant) stimulus were less likely than controls to experience panic attack symptoms. Taylor and Brown (1988) provide a review of literature suggesting that such illusions of control may be beneficial in terms of mental health and wellbeing.

If the psychodynamic functions hypothesis is true then we might expect paranormal belief to be highest in those who feel most marginalised or disempowered, since they will have the clearest sense that key decisions that affect their lives are out of their control. However, there is little evidence of an overall relationship between social marginality or deprivation and paranormal belief, despite many attempts to find one (Irwin, 1993), though these studies have tended to use measures of marginality – such as age, ethnicity and marital status – that may be simply too crude.

When McGarry and Newberry (1981) asked students more directly whether they tended to perceive the world as largely unpredictable, difficult, or problem-laden and unjust, they did find that paranormal believers were more likely to hold this view than disbelievers. Keinan (1994) found that residents living in areas under threat of military action during the Gulf War (whose world genuinely was less predictable) scored higher on measures of magical thinking than those in areas that were not under threat: this finding would be consistent with Irwin's hypothesis. ('Magical thinking' refers to interpreting two or more events

SUPERSTITIOUS BEHAVIOUR

Have you heard that if you catch a falling leaf on the first day of autumn you will not catch a cold all winter? Or you should never turn a loaf of bread upside down after a slice has been cut from it? Perhaps the warning that you should not walk under a ladder is more familiar. These are all *superstitions*. A superstition is a belief that one thing affects something else even when this belief has no basis in reality. These superstitious beliefs influence the emotions and behaviours of those that hold them.

Superstitious behaviour was explained many years ago by B.F. Skinner using operant conditioning principles. For Skinner, a superstition is the formation of a false association between a reinforcer and a response when there is no cause-and-effect relationship between the two. He delivered food at regular intervals to pigeons kept separately in cages. He found that individual pigeons soon began to show their own odd behaviours just before the food arrived, for example one would bob its head, another would scratch the floor, and another peck the cage wall. It turned out that the pigeons were repeating the behaviour they had performed just prior to the 'reward' of food. They had associated the two events, even though they were coincidental and the food arrived regardless of the pigeons' behaviour. Humans appear to show superstitious behaviour for the same reasons. For example, a student uses a particular pen in an exam which goes well so she takes it to her next exam as her 'lucky pen'. Doing well in an exam whilst using this pen is a coincidence, but has become a causal association for the student. Such superstitions are extremely common.

More recent explanations have focused on why rather than how superstitions form. Research seems to show that superstitions tend to arise in situations that are uncertain, random and uncontrollable (Kida, 2006). According to Whitson and Galinsky (2008), superstitions develop because of misperceptions. They claim that misperceptions satisfy deep psychological needs for control and arise in order to minimise the threat that this lack of control poses. They demonstrated this in their study. Participants were asked to vividly recall a situation they had experienced in which they lacked control or had full control. They were then presented with three scenarios describing an important event preceded by an unrelated behaviour (e.g. knocking on wood before getting a business idea approved). The participants were then asked whether they thought the two events were related and how worried they were that the same behaviour should be performed in the future. Those who had recalled a no-control situation experienced greater belief that the two events were somehow connected, and were more worried about similar events in the future. People who perceive themselves to have less control over events are more likely then to develop superstitious beliefs.

Superstitions can become part of folklore and take on a cultural dimension. For example, in Greece and some Spanish-speaking countries Tuesday the 13th is considered unlucky. In the UK of course, it is Friday the 13th that is regarded as an inauspicious day, when bad luck may occur. When the film *Friday the 13th* was released in Argentina it was renamed *Martes 13* – Tuesday the 13th.

as causally connected with no concern for what the causal link is.)

We have to be wary here of inferring cause and effect from this kind of evidence because the study is not a true experiment and it may be that the (unmeasured) factors that determine which neighbourhood people choose to live in – such as class or religion – also affect people's levels of paranormal belief. If we want more direct evidence of a relationship between uncertainty and paranormal belief we need to be free to manipulate people's sense of uncertainty for ourselves, randomly allocating participants to different experimental conditions: only then can we be confident that any observed differences in paranormal belief are caused by that uncertainty.

Some studies of this kind have been conducted, usually by giving participants a task that in different conditions is more or less controllable, and they have found that paranormal beliefs and superstitious behaviours are indeed greater where the task is uncontrollable or the outcome uncertain (Matute, 1995). Dudley (1999) similarly found that levels of superstitious belief increased following work on an unsolvable puzzle, but decreased after a solvable puzzle; and paranormal believers have been found to be more likely to create an illusion of control when accounting for their performance at a chance-based task (Blackmore and Troscianko, 1985).

Away from the artificiality of laboratory manipulations, people's sense of control over the major decisions that affect them has been measured using Locus of Control scales. Where people feel they are responsible for their own destiny (for example that exam success comes from their own hard work rather than the whims of the examiner) they are described as having an internal locus of control; whereas if they feel that many of the major decisions are in the hands of others (teachers, politicians, and other people in authority) and there's very little they can do to change things, then they are described as having an external locus of control. As suggested by the psychodynamic functions hypothesis, there has been a relatively consistent tendency for high scores on belief in the paranormal to be associated with external locus of control (e.g. Irwin, 2000). However, many of these studies have measured locus of control using Rotter's (1966) scale, which may be somewhat removed from the sense of control over prospective personal events, particularly misfortunes, that paranormal beliefs were originally hypothesised to arise in response to.

A more direct measure was developed by Roe and Bell (2007), who asked participants to estimate the likelihood of various events happening to them in the future. These events ranged from the very positive to the very negative (such as getting married or being involved in a car crash where the car is written off). Participants were also asked to estimate how much control they felt they had over those events – did they feel that they could do anything to make the positive events happen

ARE CERTAIN TYPES OF PERSONALITIES MORE PRONE TO PARANORMAL BELIEFS?

Research has suggested a relationship between paranormal belief and a number of personality characteristics (Groth-Marnat and Pegden, 1998). Among the relevant characteristics appear to be the following:

Locus of control

A more external locus of control seems to be related to paranormal belief, though the extent of this relationship might depend on the type of paranormal belief. For example, Tobacyk et al (1988) found that greater internal locus was associated with less belief in superstition, but other categories of paranormal belief (e.g. spiritualism, alien life) were not associated with locus of control at all.

Sensation-seeking

People differ from each other in their need for excitement. Belief in paranormal phenomena might provide stimulation or arousal desired by people with a personality trait of sensation-seeking. Amongst other things, sensation seekers have a desire for novel and intense experiences. Kumar et al (1993) found that higher sensation-seeking personality scores were related to both a greater paranormal belief and a greater number of reported paranormal experiences.

Creativity

A high positive correlation appears to exist between belief in the paranormal and creative personality. This association has been found using a range of tests of creativity. For example, Gianotti et al (2001) asked participants to think up words which would meaningfully connect two others and found that the more original words came from those with high paranormal belief.

for them or to prevent the negative ones? As predicted, although there was no direct relationship between paranormal belief and estimates of likelihood and control, belief *was* related to anxiety; and anxiety in turn *was* related to expectancy and control (such that participants who were more anxious expected more negative events and fewer positive events to happen in their future, and did not feel that they had much influence over whether or not these events happened). This fits very neatly with the psychodynamic functions hypothesis, which suggests that perceived lack of control over one's life leads to anxiety and that paranormal beliefs arise as a response to that.

One final reservation in interpreting this research concerns the fact that much of it has used rather broad definitions of what counts as 'paranormal beliefs', using questionnaires such as Tobacyk's Paranormal Belief Scale (PBS: Tobacyk and Milford, 1983). This questionnaire includes items concerned with, for example, the existence of the Loch Ness Monster and the unluckiness of the number 13, so that any association identified using this measure may reflect a relationship between locus of control and superstitiousness rather than belief in the kinds of phenomena we have concentrated on here (psychic ability, evidence of survival after death, etc.).

When Tobacyk and Milford (1983) considered the relationships between scores on a measure of locus of control and the various subscales of the PBS, they found a significant relationship only for belief in extraordinary life-forms (such as the Loch Ness Monster), and suggestive correlations for belief in witchcraft and traditional religious belief, none of which have been considered of particular importance to parapsychologists. Tobacyk et al (1988) similarly found relationships only between locus of control and superstition and witchcraft.

COGNITIVE FACTORS UNDERLYING ANOMALOUS EXPERIENCE: CRITICAL THINKING

Sceptical researchers have tended to regard belief in the paranormal as evidence of some cognitive or logical error in which some people default to a paranormal explanation for an experience they have had because they do not have the cognitive resources to be able to work out how it could be explained in more mundane terms. Irwin (1993) has coined the term *cognitive deficits hypothesis* to describe the philosophy behind this approach, which characterises the believer rather unflatteringly as "illogical, irrational, credulous, uncritical, and foolish".

Researchers who are sympathetic to the cognitive deficits hypothesis would predict that believers should score significantly worse than disbelievers on a range of cognitive tasks. Indeed, a sizeable proportion of the empirical work looking for differences between believers and disbelievers has concentrated on exploring the nature of this supposed deficiency (see French, 1992, for a brief review). For example, some studies have tested the prediction that paranormal belief will correlate negatively with IQ (the more believing you are, the lower your IQ), but only some studies have confirmed this (e.g. Killen, Wildman and Wildman, 1974), while others have found no relationship (e.g. Watt and Wiseman, 2002), and yet others have found a positive relationship (Jones et al, 1977).

Why this pattern might be so inconsistent is not clear, though one suspicion is that it reflects a context effect, with brighter participants being more sensitive to the investigator's beliefs so that they complete the paranormal belief measure in a way that they believe will please them (so appearing more sceptical with a sceptical researcher and more believing with a researcher who believes some of the phenomena are genuine). However, when Smith et al (1998) varied the testing environment to produce situations that were pro-paranormal, neutral or anti-paranormal, they found that both the pro- and anti- situations still produced significant negative correlations between paranormal belief and intelligence.

Other researchers have measured performance on logical reasoning tasks called syllogisms: such tasks present participants with two statements (the premises) and ask them to judge whether a conclusion statement logically follows from them. For example, if the premises were 'all triangles are red' and 'this object is a triangle' then the conclusion 'this object is red' must follow – note that the conclusion can be valid even if it isn't true in the real world (for example because one of the premises is unsound) so that if we had the premises 'Santa visits on Christmas Eve' and 'This man is Santa' then it would be valid to say 'This man will visit on Christmas Eve' even if we don't really expect him to turn up.

Initial results with syllogisms suggested that again paranormal believers were less successful in deciding whether the conclusion was true (e.g. Polzella et al, 1975). Wiezerbiki (1985) replicated this effect but the difference was significant only for a subset of items which were concerned with parapsychological issues, and not for neutral items. When Irwin (1991) explicitly asked about *logical validity* he found no difference between believers and disbelievers, and this suggests that people were drawing on their personal beliefs or wider experience to decide whether something was *true* rather than *logically valid* (e.g. judging that ESP is real). Merla-Ramos (2000) similarly found that paranormal believers tended to have poorer syllogistic reasoning ability than disbelievers, but only for syllogisms that included paranormal or religious content.

Perhaps some people come to believe in paranormal phenomena not because of some general cognitive deficit but through ignorance of scientific principles that could help them better understand how the world operates so that they could recognise which kinds of explanation are legitimate and which are less so. It has been found that science students do have lower levels of paranormal belief than humanities students (Otis and Alcock, 1982) but it's not clear whether that is a consequence of learning how conventional science might account for paranormal phenomena or whether it reflects a process of *enculturation* where students have learned to take on the belief systems of the group that they want to be included in so as to be accepted by them.

Alcock and Otis (1980) tried to assess familiarity with scientific principles by asking participants to read descriptions of flawed experiments and evaluate the adequacy of the designs and the logic of the conclusions (which seems to be a good analogue of the skills needed to make best sense of a spontaneous experience or paranormal claim). They only found that sceptics *tended* to be more

critical than believers, rather than that they were *absolutely* more critical. Roe (1999) criticised these studies (perhaps ironically) for having flawed designs. He also suggested that any believer-disbeliever differences could be readily explained in terms of cognitive dissonance. This is a thought process whereby, when people are presented with new information that contradicts their personally-held views, they are motivated to look for reasons to be able to reject that new information so that they don't have to give up or modify the views that they are comfortable with. Where the articles to be assessed are pro-paranormal, it is the disbeliever who will be motivated to look for flaws and so will appear more critically aware. However, Roe found that if some participants were given an article that was actually very sceptical of the paranormal, then in this case cognitive dissonance would be felt by the believers and this time it would be they who responded by being most critical of the article.

In summary, there is some evidence to suggest that paranormal believers might fare worse on tasks that measure intellectual ability but the relationship between the two factors is quite weak and is influenced by a variety of context effects that need to be explored in more detail. At present it seems unlikely that individual differences in the extent of belief in the paranormal could be explained solely in terms of gross cognitive differences.

COGNITIVE FACTORS UNDERLYING ANOMALOUS EXPERIENCE: MEMORY AND PROBABILITY ESTIMATES

Some paranormal experiences involve the coincidence of events that seem so unlikely to have arisen just by chance that some other explanation is called for, so perhaps when looking for cognitive differences in believers and disbelievers it would make sense to concentrate on their ability to assess the likelihood of coincidences accurately. It seems that people are typically quite poor at appreciating how likely it is that coincidences could occur just by chance, particularly given that some of the most impressive cases are drawn from the population as a whole, massively increasing the likelihood of even quite improbable coincidences. Diaconis and Mosteller (1989) call this the *Law of Truly Large Numbers*, which simply put states that "with a large enough sample, any outrageous thing is likely to happen". For example, the chances of winning the lottery in the UK are infinitesimally small (13,983,816 to 1 according to the National Lottery website) yet one or more people do win most weeks because so many people have bought

CONFIRMATION BIAS

In psychology, confirmation bias (or confirmatory bias) is a tendency to search for or interpret information in a way that confirms our existing expectations and beliefs. This error of thinking can lead to distorted views of reality and faulty judgements.

This kind of cognitive bias pervades all aspects of our lives, and there is no reason to assume that anyone is immune from it. Like any other scientists, parapsychologists can be prone to it by selectively seeking out information which confirms their hypotheses. Russell and Jones (1980) found that when believers in ESP were shown experimental results which contradicted their beliefs they tended to have a poorer memory for this data than if the results supported their beliefs.

Confirmation bias is an important factor involved in the maintenance of paranormal beliefs. For example, someone who believes that they have predictive dreams will remember the minority of dreams which they interpret as having come true and ignore the majority of dreams which do not. This might also explain why, in psychic readings, people have a better memory for the hits than the misses – they are remembering only those things that confirm their existing beliefs.

Good critical thinking skills are important in combating confirmation bias as critical thinking involves challenging personal beliefs and analysing the reasons for having particular opinions or reaching certain conclusions.

tickets. Instead of asking "what are the chances of any particular person winning this week's lottery?" we should be asking "what are the chances of someone somewhere winning this week's lottery?" which of course is much more likely.

But coincidences don't just occur in the National Lottery. Those same individuals live full and varied lives when they are not playing the lottery so that there are ample opportunities for someone somewhere to witness other kinds of coincidence that also fall just by chance into this 'extremely unlikely' category. Some of those experiences will be subjectively labelled as paranormal. For example, Zusne and Jones (1982) note that since we all dream each night, it will be the case that,

simply by coincidence, some dreams will have the appearance of subsequently coming true. Vasiliev (1965, cited in Ullman et al, 1989) describes this explanation more prosaically:

> Prophetic dreams are more often founded on misunderstanding. Nearly everyone has dreams, sometimes many dreams in one night. In a week, a month, a person accumulates tens, if not hundreds of dreams. Do many of them materialise? Of course not. Dreams as a rule do not materialise; only in exceptional circumstances do they coincide, more or less, with future events. According to the theory of probability this is as it should be: many dreams,

THE ILLUSION OF CAUSALITY

For Blakemore (1992), many people believe in psychic phenomena because they have psychic experiences, and these experiences are a consequence of the way we think. She argues that paranormal experiences are like visual illusions – they are real experiences but occur as a result of internal cognitive processes rather than from 'peculiarities in the observable world'. These cognitive processes usually serve us well but in certain circumstances give rise to errors. Psychic experiences are basically illusions of causality – we assume that a causal explanation for an event is needed when this is not the case. Blakemore identified five types of illusion:

Illusions of Form: In recognising objects, some people are prone to see shape and form when none is there. This increases the likelihood of seeking a paranormal explanation when none is needed.

Illusions of Memory: Selective and constructive memory processes can make coincidences appear more meaningful than they are, and can cause people to misremember events.

Illusions of Pattern and Randomness: Seeking pattern and order is a basic sensory process and this can lead to seeing patterns that aren't there. In seeking a cause for a pattern that isn't there we may turn to paranormal explanations.

Illusions of Control: Where a coincidence occurs between a person's behaviour and some event external to them, personal control is assumed.

Illusions of Connection: Some things just happen by chance, but in unnecessarily seeking causal explanations for coincidences some people are likely to interpret the experience as paranormal.

many events – some of them must inevitably coincide. There is nothing wonderful in this.

French (2002) estimated that even if we take a conservative view and only include in our 'paranormal dream' category those coincidences that have a remote 1 in 10,000 chance of occurring by chance, and if we assume that people are able to recall just one dream from each night, then we should still expect 3.6% of the population to have such a dream in any given year. With a UK population of around 60 million this would give us a collection of over 2 million impressively unlikely cases each year.

Yet if that coincidence happens to us personally we are unlikely to regard it as a product of chance. People find stories of coincidences that happened to themselves far more surprising than the same stories occurring to others (Falk, 1989), perhaps because when it is someone else's story we encode it as an instance of a particular type or category of event, which draws our attention to the wide range of possibilities that could have occurred and which would have been equally impressive. For example,

if they describe dreaming of a childhood holiday and then meeting someone they haven't seen since that holiday, we can see that the dream could have meaningfully predicted their bumping into *any* of the people they met on that holiday, not just the one they did bump into. When the coincidence happens to ourselves we encode it in terms of its specifics, which blinds us to these alternatives.

The need to set a surprising coincidence in context is illustrated by the phenomenon of telephone telepathy, where people claim that they have been thinking about someone they have not thought of for a while, and soon afterwards that person calls (Sheldrake, 2000). Also, many people say that when the telephone starts ringing they sometimes know who is calling them, even when they had no reason to expect this person to call. They interpret it as evidence of telepathy, as if they had become aware at some level of the other person thinking of them as they dialled the number or thought about calling. This kind of experience is very common. Sheldrake (2000) found that 51% of a randomly selected London sample said this had happened

WHEN JACK PHONED JILL

Suppose a member of the public, Jack, tells us of his experiences of telephone telepathy when his friend Jill calls. We can't gauge how likely it is that Jack will think of Jill just as Jill calls without knowing about the factors that could make that coincidence more or less likely. For example, how often does Jill call? If she calls at least once a day, then we are less impressed by this conjunction. And how often does Jack think of Jill? If hers is the first name he thinks of every time the phone rings then again the coincidence takes less explaining. So, in order to gauge whether there's anything unusual about Jack thinking of Jill just as she's about to call we also need to ask: "How often does Jack think of Jill and she does not call (i.e. someone else calls)?" and "How often does Jack *not* think of Jill and (yet) she calls?". There is a fourth question we need to ask (adapted from Dean et al, 1992), namely "How often does Jack *not* think of Jill and *she does not call*?" This question seems counterintuitive and irrelevant so people rarely think to ask it, but we can illustrate with an example why it is important.

Suppose we ask Jack to keep a record over the next week of who he was thinking of every time the phone rings and of who was actually calling. His data are shown in the table below.

	Jill calls	Jill does not call (someone else does)
Jack thinks of Jill	45	25
Jack does not think of Jill	20	10

To show how easy it is to misinterpret the actual pattern if we don't consider all the data given in this table (and therefore all four questions posed above), let's only consider the times when Jill calls. In those cases Jack was thinking about her 69% of the time and wasn't thinking of her only 31% of the time, which looks like a meaningful association rather than random coincidence. And if we instead look only at the times when Jack thinks of Jill then it turns out that 64% of those calls were from Jill and only 36% came from other people; another clear majority that looks in need of explanation. But when we have all the data we can see that Jack was thinking about Jill 71% of the time *when the caller was someone else* (25 times out of 35) so proportionally he was actually thinking of her less often when she did call than when she didn't! Statistically, these are almost the exact pattern we would expect by chance alone. This is not something we could have been aware of if we paid attention only to the hits and ignored the misses.

to them (more frequently for women than men, at 56% and 41% respectively) and the figure was higher at 65% for a sample living in Bury, Lancashire (women were again higher at 71% compared with 53% for men). The incidence of telephone telepathy was even greater in an American survey (Brown and Sheldrake, 2001) at 71%. So we can have little doubt that the experience occurs, but what are we to make of it? Could it not have occurred by chance and thus illustrate a tendency to remember only the confirming occasions and forget the disconfirming ones?

It may be that some people are more liable to over-interpret coincidences as meaningful. Blackmore and Troscianko (1985) explored this suggestion by asking participants to assess how likely different chance outcomes were (see Box 1 for examples of the type of question used). In their first study Blackmore and Troscianko found that there was no difference between believers and disbelievers in their ability to estimate probabilities accurately;

but in a second, larger study believers did perform significantly worse, supporting the notion that some paranormal beliefs might arise from a misinterpretation of chance events.

Subsequent research has given mixed results, however (Blackmore, 1997), and it may be that apparent differences in performance at probability tasks simply reflect differences in more general cognitive ability. When Musch and Ehrenberg (2002) discovered an overall correlation between paranormal belief and error rates on probability reasoning tasks, they found that this relationship disappeared when they took into account the participants' grade point average over their last two years of secondary school, which they used as an indicator of cognitive ability. One reason why this plausible association might be so weak or inconsistent is because the probability questions posed are rather dry and abstract. They are not obviously related to the kinds of circumstances in which people can be expected to prematurely reject

ESTIMATING PROBABILITY

Try out the following questions to see how accurately you can predict the probability of different coincidences (answers are given in the footnote below).

1. How many people do you need for you to have a 50-50 chance that two of them will share the same birthday?
   23/43/63/83/103

2. A hat contains ten red and ten blue Smarties. I pull out ten and eight are red. What colour is the next one most likely to be?
   Red/Blue/Both equally likely

3. A box contains buttons that are either green or yellow in unknown proportion. Eight of the first ten buttons taken out are yellow. What colour is the next one most likely to be?
   Green/Yellow/Both equally likely

4. Which of the following is likely to happen more frequently: you roll five dice simultaneously and all five *roll a six; you roll one die five times and each time it rolls a six.*
   Five sixes simultaneously is more likely/
   Five sixes consecutively is more likely/
   Both equally likely

5. You flip a coin ten times. Which of the following sequences is more likely by chance?
   Series 1: HHHHHHHHHH
   Series 2: HTHTHTHTHT
   Series 3: HHTHTHTTHT
   Series 1/Series 2/Series 3/All are equally likely

Box 1

chance as an explanation in favour of a paranormal one (it seems unlikely that members of the public become paranormal believers because of a shared birthday or an unexpected run of heads or tails).

"It is worth developing a good understanding of probability and coincidence: they are core ideas in psychology. Not only will you be well-placed to answer a question should one appear in this section, but it is something you need to know about in the Psychological Research and Scientific Method section too."

A more pertinent test was conducted by Blackmore (1997) who published in *The Daily Telegraph* a questionnaire which she invited readers to complete and return to her. Participants had to say whether the ten statements listed in Box 2 were true for them (try this for yourself). Then Blackmore asked, "Suppose you stopped the first person you met in the street and asked him or her about the same ten statements. How many times would you expect him or her to say 'True'?" (Again, you could try this for yourself.) The probability misjudgement explanation of paranormal belief would predict that people would *underestimate* the number of statements that were true for others (i.e. think that they were much rarer than they actually are and be unduly impressed if they turned out to be true, say as part of a psychic reading). It would also predict that believers would be more susceptible to this bias than disbelievers.

Blackmore received a very substantial 6,238 responses and found that on average people

reported that 2.4 of the 10 statements were true for them, but their estimate of how many would be true for a random other person was significantly higher at 3.6, contrary to expectation. Believers and disbelievers did not differ from one another in their estimates so that Blackmore was moved to conclude, "the probability misjudgement theories are not supported by these data". It seems, then, that although probability misjudgements make for an attractive account of how paranormal believers might come to have impressive experiences, the experimental and survey data collected to date do not make a compelling case for their being influential in practice.

ANOMALOUS BELIEFS AND ENVIRONMENTAL TRIGGERS

Some paranormal experiences might be due to misinterpreting unexpected or unusual sensations that are triggered by features of the environment that we're not ordinarily aware of, and this could be a good starting point for explanations of haunt phenomena. Common experiences reported by witnesses at allegedly haunted locations include seeing apparitions, hearing anomalous sounds, having a strong sense of presence, and feeling sudden changes in temperature (Lange, 1996). Research has focused on the suggestion that witnesses might be misinterpreting ambiguous stimuli in line with expectation, or as a product of imagination, or as a (possibly neurological) response to environmental triggers (Houran and Lange, 2001).

Wiseman et al (2003) set out to test these ideas more systematically in an experiment conducted at Hampton Court Palace, a popular historical attraction that has been referred to as 'one of the

BLACKMORE'S (1997) TEN STATEMENTS

1. There is someone called Jack in my family
2. I have a scar on my left knee
3. Last night I dreamed of someone I haven't seen for many years
4. I travel regularly in a white car
5. I once broke my arm
6. My back is giving me pain at the moment
7. I am one of three children
8. I own a CD or tape of Handel's Water Music
9. I have a cat
10. I have been to France in the past year

Percentages answering yes to each item are: Q1, 21.3%; Q2, 33.5%; Q3, 9.7%; Q4, 24.1%; Q5, 16.4%; Q6, 26.9%; Q7, 26.4; Q8, 28.3; Q9, 28.7; Q10, 27.1

Box 2

most haunted places in England'. It includes the 'Haunted Gallery', where it is alleged Catherine Howard had to be dragged away from Henry VIII's quarters as she pleaded (unsuccessfully) for her life; and also the Georgian Rooms, in which visitors have commonly reported unusual phenomena. Floorplans of these two rooms were divided into 24 equal-sized areas: those areas that had previously been associated with anomalous experiences were marked as 'haunted' and those that had not as 'controls'. Researchers who interacted with participants in the study did not know which areas were haunted and which were controls, so that they could not influence the participants' judgements, for example by how they described the areas or how they behaved in them; this study would therefore be described as double blind (neither the participants nor the experimenters with them knew what was the 'expected' outcome).

Visitors to Hampton Court were invited to participate in the study. If they agreed they were asked to complete questionnaires about their prior belief in the paranormal and hauntings in particular, and about any unusual experiences they had while they walked around these rooms. The sample of 462 participants reported a total of 431 unusual experiences between them, of which approximately two thirds involved an unusual change in temperature, with the remainder involving feelings of dizziness, headaches, sickness, shortness of breath, some form of 'force', a foul odour, a sense of presence and intense emotional feelings. When those who had reported experiences were asked whether these were due to a ghost, 30 (14%) said that they were, 80 (37%) were uncertain, and 105 (49%) thought not.

The researchers found that experiences occurred significantly more often in the haunted areas than would be expected by chance but that the likelihood of sensing something unusual was not related to the participants' prior knowledge of the palace or its history. This would suggest that we can't explain people's experiences in terms of some expectancy effect. However, other data collected from these same participants bears more

directly on the issue of expectation and suggestion (Wiseman et al, 2002). As part of the initial questionnaire, participants were asked whether they believed in ghosts, whether they had previously experienced ghostly phenomena, and whether they expected to experience something unusual during their visit to Hampton Court. Based on their responses to these questions, participants were categorised as either believers or disbelievers. When researchers looked at the effects of belief they found not only that believers were more willing to interpret any experiences they had had as evidence of a ghost encounter (as we might expect), but also that they had more experiences in the first place. This might suggest that believers don't just differ in the attributions they make but that they also differ in their sensitivity to certain environmental or situational factors that could give rise to unusual sensations (Jawer, 2006).

Wiseman et al also tried to manipulate expectancy by telling some visitors that there had recently been increased number of reports of unusual experiences (Positive Suggestion condition) while others were told that very few people had recently experienced anything unusual in the location (Negative Suggestion condition). When they looked at the effects of belief and suggestion together they found an interesting pattern (see Table 5) where believers and disbelievers reported roughly the same number of experiences after the suggestion that there had been very little activity recently; but after the suggestion that there had been increased activity, believers reported more experiences whereas disbelievers reported fewer.

One environmental factor that might affect people's experience depending on their sensitivity is variations in the magnetic (referred to as 'geomagnetic') field that surrounds us. Gearhart and Persinger (1986) found that reports of hauntings seemed to be related to periods of heightened geomagnetic activity and it is known that geomagnetism can stimulate activity in the brain's temporal lobes, producing effects that seem similar to the haunt experience (such as sensing a presence). Although Wiseman and colleagues found

	Believers	Disbelievers	Overall
Positive suggestion	2.59	1.76	2.04
Negative suggestion	1.99	1.93	1.97
Overall	2.22	1.83	4.01

Table 5: Mean number of unusual experiences reported by believer and disbeliever groups in the Positive and Negative Suggestion conditions.

no significant differences in the mean strength of the geomagnetic field between haunting and control areas at Hampton Court, they did find that the degree to which the field fluctuated was significantly greater in 'haunted' than 'control' areas, and that there was a positive correlation between the amount of variance and the mean number of unusual experiences reported by groups of participants. Their findings that people tended to be consistent in reporting unusual experiences in some locations but not in others, and their discovery of measurable physical differences between those locations, does tend to support the idea that people are responding to some environmental stimulus.

In a second experiment Wiseman et al (2003) visited the South Bridge Vaults in Edinburgh, which consist of a series of small chambers, rooms and corridors built into the arches of South Bridge that were intended to provide accommodation for the poor. These lodgings became a slum, however, and were abandoned in the late nineteenth century, only to be rediscovered and reopened for public tours in 1996. Using a location with relatively small discrete chambers allowed the researchers to separate participants so that only one person would be present in each chamber (so their responses could not be influenced by the experiences of others). The rooms also had differing reputations for unusual activity so the researchers could see whether their participants confirmed that rank order and could try and identify features of the room that might be prompting those experiences. Participants were volunteers from the general public. They were randomly allocated to one of ten chambers and had to spend approximately ten minutes there on their own: if they experienced any unusual phenomena they had to keep a record and rate the degree to which they believed that a ghost had been responsible.

The site was clearly also effective in eliciting reports of haunting phenomena: of the 218 people who took part, 95 (44%) reported at least one experience and 172 unusual experiences were described, including unusual changes in temperature, descriptions of apparitions, a strong sense of being watched, burning sensations, strange sounds, and odd odours. When asked to rate whether experiences were due to a ghost, just 3% thought they were, and 58% thought they were not, although 39% remained uncertain.

The incidence of experiences reported in each room was very strongly correlated with their previous reputation, again suggesting that hot spots of haunting activity are quite stable. So what made some locations more likely to stimulate haunt experiences than others? The researchers reported that there was a positive correlation between paranormal activity and geomagnetic variance, but this trend was not significant so didn't replicate the pattern found at Hampton Court. However, the reputation of rooms as haunted was significantly correlated with the physical dimensions of the spaces, including height, floorspace and exterior lighting levels, which suggests that these contextual variables might influence the interpretation of experiences as paranormal or normal (Lange et al, 1996).

One of the chambers of the South Bridge Vaults in Edinburgh.

BIOLOGICAL BASES OF ANOMALOUS EXPERIENCES

"You are required to know about biological factors underlying anomalous experience, so don't pay this section any less attention because it has some biological and technical terminology! We have attempted to present material in an accessible way here, but you really must put in time and effort to learning it."

We saw in the last section that some people may show biological reactions to environmental triggers such as geomagnetism and that these might be interpreted as paranormal experiences. It has been suggested that out-of-body experiences might also reflect triggered disturbances to the brain's temporal lobes (Blanke, 2004). An out-of-body experience (OBE) is defined by De Ridder et al (2007) as "a brief subjective episode in which the self is perceived as being outside the body (disembodiment), with or without the impression of seeing the body from an elevated and distanced visuospatial perspective (autoscopy)". In other words, a person has the sensation of leaving their body, sometimes with the experience of looking down on it. OBEs are quite common, being reported by about 10% of the population – although for most OBE-rs they occur spontaneously just once or twice in their lifetime. They seem to be consistent across cultures (Blanke, 2004), and have been reported to occur more frequently in people who suffer from migraine or epilepsy (Blanke and Arzy, 2005), suggesting a common biological origin. Brain damaged patients who report OBEs have been described as having damage to the temporal and parietal regions of the brain (Devinsky et al, 1989) which is interesting given that the temporo-parietal junction (see Figure 1) is thought to be involved in the integration of information from and about the body to generate an internal map of self-perception (De Ridder et al, 2007). Recent brain stimulation studies involving this region have been able to create the perception of disembodiment (De Ridder et al, 2007), and in some cases autoscopy (Blanke et al, 2004).

> **"Out-of-body and near-death experiences are named anomalous experiences on the specification – make sure that you are able to offer some kind of explanation for them in case they appear in an exam question!"**

Near-death experiences (NDEs) share some features with the OBE and so attempts have been made to find a common cause. An NDE can be defined as "profound psychological events with transcendental and mystical elements, typically occurring to individuals close to death or in situations of intense physical or emotional danger" (Greyson, 2000). Parnia et al (2007) report that approximately 10–20% of cardiac arrest survivors report cognitive processes, including the ability to recall specific details of their resuscitation, during the period of cardiac arrest – at which time, they argue, the patients' brains should be incapable of constructing a lucid and coherent conscious experience.

OBE

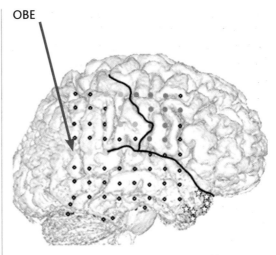

Figure 1: Site of stimulation producing OBE-like symptoms. (From Tong, 2003)

The near-death experience is now part of popular culture (even the Simpsons' dog, Santa's Little Helper, has had an NDE) but the core elements of the experience were only identified in Raymond Moody's (1975) book *Life after Life* which described a collection of 150 cases. Ring (1980) went on to identify a 'core experience' which consisted of five stages: feelings of deep peace and wellbeing; a sense of separation from the body; entering darkness/passing through a tunnel; seeing the light; and entering the light/beautiful garden. These stages tend to be described as if they unfolded in a particular order (and indeed the frequency with which they are reported does tend to diminish as you proceed through the list, much as one might expect if people are being resuscitated at different stages) but actual cases are much more varied than this (Greyson, 1998).

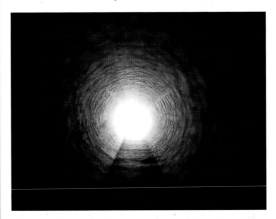

Biological explanations of the NDE have suggested that the feelings of deep peace and wellbeing are due to the release of endorphins, powerful naturally-produced painkillers, at times of threat or stress. The other features may come about as the brain reacts to the depletion of its oxygen supply. Whinnery (1997) noted that fighter pilots can sometimes lose consciousness for brief periods during aerial manoeuvres as their bodies are subjected to massive G-forces that reduce blood flow to the head. He found that pilots reported experiences during this time that included NDE features such as the tunnel experience and brief 'dreamlets', though Greyson (2000) commented that these experiences tend to be more fragmented and confused than typical NDEs.

Blackmore (1993) suggests that the brain cells most sensitive to lower oxygen concentrations are inhibitory cells so that surprisingly the brain initially produces more activity rather than less as control through inhibition is lost. What would the experience be like if one's neurons were firing at random? If this were to occur in the visual cortex, Blackmore makes a persuasive case that it should seem like moving from darkness towards a bright light until eventually being enveloped in it, which sounds like a classic tunnel experience.

It is also interesting to note that some of the experiences reported during temporal lobe seizures seem to be reminiscent of the NDE, including the out-of-body element. In support of this connection, Britton and Bootzin (2004) found that participants who had had NDEs had more epileptic-like EEG activity than did matched control participants, when their brain activity was continuously monitored over a normal sleep cycle. Epilepsy-like discharges through the hippocampus and amygdala brain structures could also conceivably give rise to the life review experience, since these areas are important for the storage of memories. However, it is difficult to see how these explanations could apply to the many NDEs that occur in circumstances where the experient's brain is clearly not suffering from oxygen depletion (Irwin and Watt, 2007).

It has also been argued that the particular features of NDEs reflect the experient's cultural expectations. Although the core features of the NDE have been recorded throughout history and across various cultures and religious groups, there do seem to be some culture-specific elements. For example, Schorer (1985) found North American NDEs included moccasins, snakes, eagles, bows and arrows as dominant imagery. Western NDEs place the experient right at the centre of events and they seem to be able to decide for themselves whether to return to their earthly body, which might accord with expectations of people from societies that emphasise the individual. In contrast, Asian Indians, who come from a more collectivist society, report being sent back to live because of an apparent supernatural bureaucratic mistake rather than through their own conscious choice, or because of earthly commitments (Pasricha and Stevenson, 1986). Differences such as this may suggest that whereas the process may be universal, the specific imagery and interpretation given to an NDE is determined by the expectations and beliefs of the individual (Roberts and Owen, 1988).

"Just a reminder – more material on culture! Remember what we said earlier – it is important that you pick up on these references to culture, as you might need to write specifically about culture in the exam."

ANOMALOUS BELIEFS AND EXPECTANCY EFFECTS

The South Bridge Vaults experiment draws attention to the possibility that people's experiences (or perhaps more likely their interpretation and recollection of ambiguous experiences) might be affected by the comments others make about what they are witnessing. In that study the effects of suggestion were controlled for by having people visit the locations alone, but in other studies the effects of suggestion have been investigated by manipulating this factor. The séance room offers an environment that is well suited to produce expectation and suggestion effects – the room is typically only dimly lit so that perceptions can be ambiguous; there can be a long delay before any phenomena occur so that it can be difficult to maintain attention; and because it is difficult to take detailed notes at the time, eyewitnesses' recollections are prone to distortion that might make the events seem more impressive than they actually were.

These problems were recognised in the heyday of interest in Spiritualism and Hodgson and Davey (1887) and Besterman (1932) investigated how susceptible to distortion people's recollections might be. They each staged mock séances in which they would know exactly what effects would occur (by trickery) and what methods had been used to achieve them. When they later asked their unsuspecting sitters to write a description of the séance they had just witnessed they found that the accounts failed to mention important events, including facts that could indicate how the effects had been produced (such as, for example, which objects had been inspected prior to the sitting, and even that the experimenter had briefly left the room!). More recently, Wiseman et al (1995) attempted a replication in which participants sat in a large circle in a darkened room, held hands and attempted to psychically move objects that had been marked with luminous paint and had been placed in the centre of the circle. During the sitting two of the objects were made to move via trickery. When asked to recall what they had witnessed, sitters often made errors, including misremembering details that were essential to understanding how the tricks were achieved.

In a follow-up study, Wiseman et al (2003) looked particularly at the effects of verbal suggestion. Using a similar design to their earlier experiment they extended it by including two objects (a table and a handbell) that did not actually move during the séance; however, the person leading the séance made statements about the table that suggested it had moved while he never gave any indication that the handbell had moved. When asked two weeks later about what they had witnessed, just over 30% reported that the table had moved while 10% thought that the handbell had moved, which does support the notion that people's perceptions and recall of an event can be distorted by false statements made at the time.

The tendency to falsely recall that the handbell had moved was associated with participants' prior belief in the paranormal, perhaps indicating that suggestions are more likely to be effective where people have an expectancy that the suggested event might happen. If that were the case then we might expect to find that disbelievers are more prone to suggestion if it involves an event that is consistent with their scepticism. Wiseman and colleagues tested this in a further séance experiment

in which an object (a slate) did move but the séance leader explicitly stated that it did not – since disbelievers would not expect to witness any paranormal movements perhaps here they would go with the suggestion rather than the evidence of their own eyes. In fact there was no difference between believers and disbelievers in their suggestibility, which might argue for individual differences in susceptibility to suggestion between both believers and disbelievers rather than some context effect. However, the overwhelming majority of participants in this study reported that the slate had not moved, which could mean that the movements that participants were supposed to notice were too subtle – it would have been preferable to counterbalance the objects used in case some are simply more noticeable than others.

But people don't seem to be prone to suggestion only in situations were perception is difficult and our sensations are ambiguous: similar effects can be produced under normal lighting conditions. For example, Jones and Russell (1980) gave a demonstration of extrasensory perception (ESP) that in one condition was successful (through trickery) but in another condition was not. They reported that believers in the paranormal tended to falsely recall that the unsuccessful demonstration had, in fact, produced evidence of ESP; disbelievers in the successful condition did not falsely recall that it had been unsuccessful.

Wiseman and Morris (1995) explored this further by having their participants watch a short video of a psychic claimant who produced an ESP effect (identifying which card had been taken from a deck) and a psychokinesis (PK) effect (taking a fork from a pile of cutlery and causing it to bend and then break by simply stroking it gently). Participants rated the 'paranormal' content of the videotape and then completed a set of recall questions. In order to distinguish between memory distortion effects that might occur at encoding from those that might occur at retrieval, participants were next told that the claimant was, in fact, a magician and the effects had been achieved through trickery. They then completed a second questionnaire to see if this affected the information they could retrieve from memory about the demonstration. Wiseman and Morris assumed that disbelievers would view the demonstrations as magic tricks from the outset, and so would recall significantly more details that were 'important' (i.e. that gave clues as to how the trick was effected); believers would view the demonstrations as genuine and so might overlook or forget those key details. They found that with the first questionnaire (before participants were debriefed about the claimant) disbelievers did recall significantly more 'important' information than believers. However, with the second questionnaire – completed when they knew that the videotape contained trickery – disbelievers and believers recalled equivalent amounts of 'important' information, suggesting that both groups had perceived and encoded the same information but that how they retrieved the information later depended on their beliefs about paranormal phenomena.

A second experiment was conducted that introduced a delay before recall to see if that affected how accessible the important information might be. The researchers also asked some 'pseudo-important' questions that if true could have pointed to particular ways of producing the trick but which did not in fact take place in this demonstration. This could catch out those observers whose scepticism might lead them to see trickery even where there was none so that they could reject the conclusion that something paranormal had occurred. The researchers found that after a delay disbelievers did recall significantly more 'important' questions than believers (by this time, debriefing them that the effect was a trick was not a sufficient aid to retrieval for them to recover the information they needed if they were to work out how the trick was done). However, there were no significant differences between believers and disbelievers in their recall of 'unimportant' questions or 'pseudo-important' questions, which Wiseman and Morris interpreted to mean that the better performance of disbelievers isn't simply due to their 'response set' causing them to 'remember' all sorts of features that might support their prior suspicion of fraud.

However, this comparison of important and pseudo-important information may not be the best way to determine whether sceptics will always perform more accurately when observing and recalling psychic demonstrations, since the situations investigated to date always involve a *pseudopsychic* demonstration in which the sceptics' general assumptions and expectations are always a more accurate reflection of what is observed. This stacks the cards against the believer. What is needed for comparison is a demonstration in which the appropriate conclusion is that paranormal phenomena *did* occur: in that case, it could be the disbelievers who are more susceptible to memory distortions.

Some informal studies of this type have been conducted at the University of Northampton by producing a version of the demonstration video in which all the effects are produced by prior preparation or video trickery. Nothing that appears on the tape itself is indicative that the effects are produced by fraud, so the reasonable conclusion should be that the claimant is demonstrating PK or ESP. In this case we have found that disbelievers tend to mis-recall the demonstration in ways that suggest that some sleight of hand was used, and it is the believers who have more accurate recollections of what they witnessed.

We saw earlier that in the séance room witnesses' accounts of events can be influenced by verbal suggestions made at the time. Recent work suggests that this can also be true for events that do not seem ambiguous at all, and in fact include camera close-ups that should make it clear whether the suggested event is happening or not. Wiseman and Greening (2005) showed participants videotape of psychic claimants in much the same way as Wiseman and Morris had done. During the demonstration the psychic claimant stroked the stem of a key and revealed that this had apparently caused it to become bent (it was clearly bent). He then placed the key on the table and the camera closed in to give a completely stationary shot that showed that the key did not continue to bend. Nevertheless, in one version of the tape the claimant said at this point that the key was continuing to bend, whereas in another version he didn't. When participants were later asked about the demonstration, one of the questions asked whether the key had continued to bend whilst it lay on the table. Among those who watched the video that included the suggestion 40% were confident that it had, whereas for the no-suggestion version only 5% thought so. There was no difference between believers and disbelievers, so susceptibility in this case is not simply a matter of wish fulfilment. This must give us some reservations about taking eyewitness testimony at face value, particularly where it relies on recall some time after the event.

SUGGESTION AND PLACEBO

One other area in which suggestion may play a role is with psychic, or distant, healing. Benor (1990) defines healing as "the intentional influence of one or more persons upon another living system without utilising known physical means of intervention", and it usually involves the aim of helping the patient recover from illness or injury through positive intention. Distant healing involves many approaches, including spiritual healing, prayer, therapeutic touch, Reiki healing, and external qigong. These therapies are very popular – Astin et al (2000) estimated that there are about 14,000 distant healers working in the United Kingdom, more than for any other branch of complementary and alternative medicine – suggesting that patients feel they are beneficial. However, when Schouten (1993) reviewed some of the evidence for the success of distant healing treatments he found that the health benefits were much stronger for subjectively experienced states of health than for objectively measured health criteria (i.e. patients might still be in pain but they feel it to be more tolerable now); and that it was important for success that the patient knew that 'treatment' was being applied. These suggest that healing may be effective in some cases by exploiting the *placebo effect*, a generally recognised phenomenon in conventional medical treatment where a patient shows improvement after being given a physiologically inactive treatment such as a 'sugar' pill. Patients have been found to respond to various kinds of placebo treatment, including that involving medical equipment (such as ultrasound) that seems functional to the patient but actually is not (Hashish et al, 1986); sham surgery that involves only superficial incisions rather than genuine excisions or repairs (Benson and McCallie, 1979); and application of acupuncture needles at ineffective acupuncture points (Kaptchuk et al, 2006). Radin (1997) estimated that, for clinical drug trials, between 20% and 40% of positive reactions may be placebo effects.

Modern clinical tests of the effects of healing take this into account by conducting double blind tests in which patients are randomly allocated to either a distant healing or a control condition but neither they nor their GP is told which condition they are in until the study is completed (e.g. Krucoff, et al, 2001). Recent reviews of this research suggest there may be a small beneficial effect of positive intentions from others that is in addition to the placebo effect (Schmid et al, 2004).

> **ASK AN EXAMINER**
> *"Psychic healing is a named anomalous experience on the specification – make sure that you are able to offer some kind of explanation for it in case it appears as an exam question! It is sometimes referred to as distant healing, so we've used both terms here."*

ANOMALISTIC BELIEF AND DECEPTION

Another type of paranormal experience that members of the public typically regard as quite impressive involves encounters with psychic readers and mediums. For example, Haraldsson (1985) surveyed people in a number of countries, including the UK, Sweden and Iceland. He found that of those who had attended a séance, a surprisingly high 83% had found the experience 'useful', whereas 28% of those who had visited a 'prophesy-psychic' had found it useful. Palmer (1979) conducted a survey in a university town in the USA that consisted of separate student and townspeople samples: he reported that among his student sample, 89% of those who had visited a psychic had found the experience 'very helpful' or 'somewhat so', and 78% claimed to have acted on the advice they had been given. For Palmer's townspeople, 45% found the reading very helpful or somewhat helpful. Roe (1998) surveyed a random sample of Edinburgh residents and found that 30% had attended at least one psychic reading, although very few could be classed as regular attenders. Over half of respondents (57%) regarded their reading as 'quite accurate' or 'very accurate', with fewer than 20% describing it as inaccurate. Of course the reading could be accurate because it is filled with general statements that could apply to most people, but in this study over half (52%) described their readings as 'very specific' or 'quite specific'. Nevertheless, almost half of this group (48%) found the reading to be of no value, although 50% did find the experience at least quite helpful, and this may simply suggest that although the information is commonly regarded as accurate and specific, it is trivial. (If I were to say to you 'you have two eyes and two ears but only one nose', that would be quite specific, accurate for most people, but hardly impressive evidence of ESP.)

"Psychic mediumship is a named anomalous experience on the specification – make sure that you are able to offer some kind of explanation for it in case it appears as an exam question!"

This generally positive picture contrasts quite sharply with much of the recent research investigating professional psychic readers, which provides little experimental evidence to support the view that they have paranormal access to information about their clients (O'Keeffe and Wiseman, 2005). Schouten (1994) reviewed some of the earlier research and concluded that "there is little reason to expect mediums more often to make correct statements about matters unknown at the time than…can be expected by chance". Although there have been some intriguing results from more recent and better controlled tests (e.g. Robertson and Roy, 2004), we still have to explain why members of the public come away impressed by their psychic readings in the real world when the results from controlled tests have generally been disappointing. In such cases, successes by psychics have often been explained not as a consequence of psychic ability, but in terms of the exploitation of common (but subtle) channels of communication using a technique that has been termed "cold reading" (Randi, 1981).

The classic account of cold reading is given by Hyman (1977) who defines it as "a procedure by which a 'reader' is able to persuade a client whom he has never met before that he knows all about

the client's personality and problems". Unfortunately, this does not give us much insight into the actual process of cold reading, and a perhaps more useful operational definition is given elsewhere by Hyman (1981):

> The cold reading employs the dynamics of the dyadic relationship between psychic and client to develop a sketch that is tailored to the client. The reader employs shrewd observation, nonverbal and verbal feedback from the client, and the client's active cooperation to create a description that the client is sure penetrates to the core of his or her psyche.

In practice, the techniques identified as examples of cold reading can vary from case to case, but many commentators have included the following elements:

Setting the stage: An important aspect of the persuasion process is to prepare the client for the reading, so that much of the early part of the interaction is intended to persuade the client that the reader is genuine, to engage their active participation in the reading process, and to provide plausible 'outs' should the reading nevertheless not be a success. The reader emphasises that they have a track record of successful demonstrations so their expertise is not in question – any 'failures' must inevitably be placed firmly at the feet of the client. The reader also emphasises that messages may come through them that are obscure or symbolic so that they are only meaningful to the client and cannot be deciphered without their help. Earle (1990), for example, notes

> The best readers always include a statement like, 'I only see pieces, as in a jigsaw puzzle. It is up to you to put them together', or, 'I may speak of a person being crushed by a house as in *The Wizard of Oz*, but you recognise it as a friend with overdue mortgage payments'.

Of course, suggesting that the elements of a psychic reading might be meant literally but could equally be symbolic or metaphorical can dramatically open up the possibilities for the elements to be interpreted in ways that the client regards as accurate. For example, if a reader were to give the statement "I see someone in your immediate family involved with a child or children", this could be regarded as a hit by someone whose sister has just announced that she is pregnant (where the child is barely formed) but it could also be impressive to someone whose mother teaches in a sixth form (where the 'children' are hardly children any more), and there are clearly lots of circumstances that fall between these examples that would work out equally well for the reader. Nevertheless, if that symbolic reference doesn't make immediate sense then the fault lies with the client.

The stock spiel: Also known as a psychological reading (Hyman, 1981), this is made up of prepared phrases, and can be delivered not only without feedback from the client during the reading, but also without the reader having any contact with her before the session begins. Such statements allow one to give a general description of the client, perhaps including some personal details but without focusing on any specific problems. The most common kinds of stock statements are known as Barnum statements because they seem to be effective because of the Barnum Effect. Dickson and Kelly (1985) have defined this effect as the tendency for "people to accept general personality interpretations as accurate descriptions of their own unique personalities". It is claimed that the descriptions are readily accepted because they are sufficiently vague for the subject to read into them what they want and are generally positive so as to make acceptance rewarding (yes, you really are a nice guy – though perhaps others may not always realise it). The Barnum effect is so-called in reference to the American showman Phineas T. Barnum who is alleged to have attributed the popularity of his circus to its including "a little something for everybody" (cf. Meehl, 1956), a comment which may also apply to Barnum statements themselves. The original Barnum Statements were collected by Bertram Forer (1949) from a newsstand astrology book and have been used with great success in psychology studies to show that people tend to accept them as true for themselves but don't recognise that they would be equally true for others. You may want to try this out for yourself, for example by having friends photocopy their hand for you to produce a graphology 'reading' which is in fact made up of Forer's list – the original statements are given in Box 3.

In trying to explain why people are susceptible to the Barnum effect researchers have focused on properties of the statements (vague and favourable items work better) and properties of the situation (people are more impressed when the method for generating the reading is obscure but seems specifically linked to the participant, and is produced by an 'expert') and these features can be found in the psychic reading situation (Roe, 1995). There are individual differences in acceptance of Barnum statements and at times this has been characterised as a 'susceptibility' that could be likened to gullibility. However, a more useful characterisation focuses on how people are geared towards making best sense of communications from others so that we are used to interpreting or filling in the gaps without perhaps realising that the gaps have been left there on purpose for us to fill in. To illustrate how good we are at doing this, read the following poem (taken from Marks and Kamman, 1980) and see how much sense you can make of it.

> With hocked gems financing him
> Our hero bravely defied all scornful laughter
> That tried to prevent his scheme
> Your eyes deceive he said
> An egg not a table correctly typifies
> This unexplored domain.
> Now three sturdy sisters sought proof
> Forging along sometimes through calm vastness
> Yet more often over turbulent peaks and valleys
> Days became weeks
> As many doubters spread fearful rumours
> About the edge
> At last from nowhere winged creatures appeared
> Signifying momentous success.

Now read the poem again but after checking what the poem means at the bottom of this page. This demonstrates how having a schema shapes our understanding of what is meant – the answer activates the schema for Christopher Columbus which is then used to help us understand the poem. With Barnum statements a schema is provided by the expectation that the material will describe ourselves and our circumstances so we make sense of it in relation to the vast amount we already know about those things. Randi (1981) gives a nice example of reading more into a reading than was actually said. As a guest with Paul Kurtz on a Canadian TV show he witnessed the psychic Geraldine Smith 'working the vibrations' from an object belonging to the host. She gave the rather vague prediction "I'm seeing the month of January here – which is now – but there would have to be something strong with the person with January as well." Although sceptical of the reading as a whole, the host of the show noted on reflection that Smith had actually determined that his birthday was in January. In fact no mention had been made of what type of association with January was being referred to – the client was left to fill in the gaps.

The poem is about Christopher Columbus.

FORER'S ORIGINAL BARNUM STATEMENTS

1. You have a great need for people to like and admire you.
2. You have a tendency to be critical of yourself.
3. You have a great deal of unused capacity which you have not turned to your advantage.
4. While you have some personality weaknesses, you are generally able to compensate for them.
5. Your sexual adjustment has caused some problems for you.
6. Disciplined and self-controlled outside, you tend to be worrisome and insecure inside.
7. At times you have serious doubts as to whether you have made the right decision or done the right thing.
8. You prefer a certain amount of change and variety, and become dissatisfied when hemmed in by restrictions and limitations.
9. You pride yourself as an independent thinker, and don't accept others' statements without satisfactory proof.
10. You have found it unwise to be too frank in revealing yourself to others.
11. At times you are extraverted, affable, sociable, while at other times you are introverted, wary, reserved.
12. Some of your aspirations tend to be pretty unrealistic.
13. Security is one of your major goals in life.

Box 3

As well as shaping our perception, this framework also helps determine what is remembered and what forgotten. Dutton (1988) describes this as follows "subjects have…a strong tendency to notice and remember only a percentage of available items. This is *selectivity of attention*. Given the considerable number of elements in any Barnum description, there will be wide latitude of response and agreement from any individual accompanied by a marked inclination to notice items that seem to fit more than items that seem inappropriate. Confirmations are remembered, often quite vividly, whereas less plausible aspects of the description are paid correspondingly less attention". There is indeed some (limited) empirical evidence to suggest that clients of psychic readings do tend to recall more of the reading elements which they rated as accurate than those items rated inaccurate (Roe, 1994).

Cold reading and fishing: The stock spiel gives the pseudopsychic material to begin the reading but this can be refined by taking advantage of information the client gives up during the interaction. For example, the general statement "You enjoy foreign travel" could be developed in lots of ways, and the decision as to how to proceed depends on an ability to "read" the client's reaction to this topic. In normal conversation, the speaker looks intermittently at the listener, especially toward the end of utterances, to see if the listener is still interested in what is being said, and to gauge whether the listener wishes to take a turn as speaker (Duncan and Fiske, 1977). The listener reacts to this cue by producing behaviours that indicate essentially whether they are happy for the speaker to continue, whether they wish the speaker to change the topic of conversation, or whether they wish to take a turn as speaker. These behaviours, known as 'back-channel signals' (Weiner et al, 1972), can be expressed in a variety of ways: these include vocalisations (including uh-huh's and similar nonverbal sounds – Argyle, 1988); facially through smiles (Brunner, 1979); and posturally through head nods, forward or sideways lean and drawing the legs back (Bull, 1987). Negative reactions can be signalled through frowning (Argyle, 1988), lowering the head or turning the head away, as well as by adopting characteristics of a closed posture, such as folded arms (Bull, 1987). Pseudopsychics can use these (generally unconscious) responses to gauge the appropriateness of what they are saying and steer the reading accordingly.

"There is little experimental support for the claims of psychic mediums. It is a good idea to develop an understanding of things like setting the stage, cold reading and fishing, as they can readily be used to explain how psychic mediumship appears to work. This is useful for the exam!"

However, this haphazard method is unlikely to produce, naturally, all the information the reader wants to know. Other data will have to be teased out through 'fishing', in which the client unwittingly gives information about themselves without realising they have done so. This can be in the form of direct questions (e.g., "Have you been thinking about a career change?") with the intention of storing away any response to be fed back to the client later in a different form as 'new' information. Another, equally useful form of fishing is the seeking of information about one topic while ostensibly giving information about another. For example, the statement "I get the impression that someone close to you, probably someone in the family, was quite ill recently, does that sound right?" apparently relates to health. In fact the client need only mention a spouse or partner, or son or daughter, for the reader to know that he can safely talk about relationship and family matters and events which only make sense in relation to them.

Cold reading can be very impressive to witness, and can lead to very specific readings for which the client can recall only the impressive endpoints in the reading without remembering the quite sophisticated manoeuvring that got them there. Some very interesting analyses have been given of psychic reading transcripts that seem to illustrate the use of cold reading in practice (Greasley, 2000). However, these analyses have been conducted after the fact and so haven't set out to test hypotheses about cold reading empirically in a way that allows for refutation. We have seen that there are few experimental studies of cold reading, which is disappointing, given that such work promises to tell us a great deal about the psychology of persuasion.

THEORETICAL AND METHODOLOGICAL ISSUES IN THE STUDY OF ANOMALOUS EXPERIENCE

Responding to paranormal claims

We have so far considered a number of explanations that have been offered to account for paranormal experiences in terms of conventional psychological processes. We have seen that unfortunately these have stimulated only a limited amount of controlled experimental work, and much of what has been conducted has adopted a quasi experimental or survey design so that it is not possible to infer cause–effect relationships. In some cases the results from those experiments have been mixed so that we can't confidently say that any of them has been definitively linked to

paranormal belief and experience. Nevertheless, they do provide us with the most plausible and likely explanations for people's spontaneous experiences and they also provide some guidance for how we might respond when someone describes to us a paranormal experience or makes a claim to have some form of paranormal ability. Morris (1986) provides an excellent guide to the ways in which we might be misled into believing that something paranormal has occurred that we should keep in mind, and Sagan (1997) gives us some useful questions to help direct us to the kind of information we need if we are to see whether (or which?) one of the normal explanations might be appropriate (see Box 4).

However, Sagan does go on to say that "the reliance on carefully designed and controlled experiments is key…We will not learn much from mere contemplation." Experiments can be designed both to test the original paranormal claim and to test more thoroughly the accounts of those who are sceptical of paranormal phenomena, to see if the reported phenomena can be reproduced in controlled conditions. If the claimed effect disappears in such conditions then it strengthens the case for believing that the normal explanations already mentioned in this chapter can account for the phenomenon. However, if evidence of an effect persists then we will need to look for alternative explanations.

EXPERIMENTAL PARAPSYCHOLOGY

The literature describing experimental tests of paranormal claims is quite extensive and could fill a book of its own (see, for example, Irwin and Watt, 2007). We can only give a flavour of that work here and so will concentrate on some of the attempts that have been made to investigate ESP and PK in the laboratory. ESP stands for extrasensory perception and refers to perception which occurs without the usual sensory processes, such as sight or hearing. PK stands for psychokinesis, which literally means 'motion produced by the mind', but is used to refer to the supposed ability of mind to affect matter.

PK research

Most modern PK research is on micro-PK. This is where an individual exerts an influence at a level which requires technical instrumentation or statistical analysis to measure the effect. Early studies of PK however focused on macro-PK. This term is used to refer to cases of PK which can be detected with the naked eye, such as levitation, metal bending and the movement of objects.

'BALONEY DETECTION KIT'

Carl Sagan described the fine art of baloney detection in some detail in his book *The Demon-haunted World* and listed a series of strategies for contending with dubious claims. The essence of Sagan's recommendations have been translated by Michael Shermer (2001) into ten basic questions that get to the heart of the validity of any claim and could prove useful when debating them. These are affectionately called the 'Baloney Detection Kit':

1. **How reliable is the source of the claim?**

Where can the evidence be found? Is it a source that is likely to verify its information and check credentials? Does it have a particular investment in the claim being true?

2. **Does this source often make similar claims?**

Is this source attracted indiscriminately to anomalous claims? Could there be some ulterior motive at work?

3. **Have the claims been verified by another source?**

Have independent persons or groups reported similar experiences or experimental effects? Have others found it difficult to replicate?

4. **How does the claim fit with what we know about how the world works?**

Is the phenomenon consistent with or share characteristics with any generally accepted phenomena?

5. **Has anyone gone out of the way to disprove the claim, or has only supportive evidence been sought?**

We have seen that the confirmation bias can be powerful and can lead us into error. Rather than seeking to confirm our hunches we should try and find tests that would disprove them; if they survive those tests then they are strengthened.

6. **Does the preponderance of evidence point to the claimant's conclusion or to a different one?**

Do we have all the evidence or just a selection? We would not expect every single experiment to confirm the theory (in the social sciences things are usually too complicated for us reasonably to expect that), but the pattern of reported evidence should be consistent with the claim.

7. **Is the claimant employing the accepted rules of reason and tools of research, or have these been abandoned in favour of others that lead to the desired conclusion?**

Has the evidence been gathered in ways that we can recognise as scientific? Is there an over-reliance on evidence that might not be reliable (e.g. anecdotal evidence) or open to interpretation (e.g. ambiguous photographs)?

8. **Is the claimant providing an explanation for the observed phenomena or merely denying the existing explanation?**

The case for an unconventional explanation of a phenomenon is not strengthened by being able to show that a conventional explanation is inadequate. Firstly, the unconventional explanation needs supporting evidence of its own, and secondly there may be any number of other conventional explanations that have yet to be tested.

9. **If the claimant proffers a new explanation, does it account for as many phenomena as the old explanation did?**

For new theories or models to replace older ones they need to be able to account for more observations or account for the same range of observations more efficiently or elegantly.

10. **Do the claimant's personal beliefs and biases drive the conclusions, or vice versa?**

All scientists hold social, political and ideological beliefs that could potentially slant their interpretations of the data, but how do those biases and beliefs affect their research in practice? Has the evidence been produced in a manner that includes the usual checks and balances to control for bias – peer-review to select articles for publication, critical debate among experts who disagree?

Further useful questions (From Marks and Kamman, 1980) shift the focus to the claimant:

1. **Why do you believe in the phenomenon?**
2. **What evidence would convince you that the claim was wrong?**
3. **Are there other explanations that could produce the same result?**

Box 4

Some of the earliest laboratory studies of macro-PK were conducted by J.B. Rhine in the 1930s. They involved experimental investigations into whether the fall of a die could be influenced by mental intention. The basic principle is straightforward. A die number is specified then dice are tossed, during which a person 'wills' the number to appear face up. The number of hits and misses over many trials are added up and if the number of hits exceeds that expected by chance then this is taken as evidence of PK. For example, if a target number is six and a die is rolled 60 times, then chance would dictate that a six appears about ten times. The likelihood of six appearing more than sixteen times is less than 1%, which statistically speaking is highly significant.

Throwing dice by hand inevitably introduces bias: for example skilled die throwers can toss die in a way which increases the likelihood of certain numbers appearing face up. Whilst rolling dice to rebound from a surface or throwing them from a cup reduces this bias, it doesn't entirely eliminate it. Rhine therefore invented a dice throwing machine, and improved methodology by introducing control conditions for comparison where dice would be rolled without PK influence, and reducing potential experimenter bias by having two separate experimenters record the results. Ultimately however, Rhine found the results of dice throwing studies were not as impressive as those of ESP, only occasionally showing some slight paranormal evidence. Such weak effects inevitably attracted criticisms of poor experimental design and statistical fluke. For example, critics of these studies however pointed to their flaws, not least with the nature of a die. Not every face of a die is equally likely to fall face up, as most dice are biased by their manufacture. If the die has

THE FEELING OF BEING STARED AT

Most people at some time have had the feeling that someone is watching them. Some psychologists suggest that this is an example of *distant intentionality*, where one person has an influence, at a distance, on the physiology of another. Parapsychologists refer to it as distant mental influence on living systems (DMILS). Macro-PK research of this kind of looks at whether it is possible to create a mental connection so as to influence another distant biological system. Studies have involved such things as whether or not someone's intense focus has a distant healing effect, influences the activity of small animals and insects, as well as giving the feeling of being stared at.

For Radin (1997), the feeling of being stared at is related historically to the notion of the 'evil eye', is endorsed by folklore, and is known in all cultures.

A typical procedure for studying this 'remote staring' effect involves the sender (or 'starer') watching the receiver (or 'staree') who is isolated in another room, on a video monitor. Some aspect of the receiver's physiology is measured (usually electrodermal activity, or EDA) to see if changes in their physiology occur during times of being stared at. A number of laboratory studies have found such an effect (e.g. Braud et al, 1993).

Baker (2000), however, criticises the use of physiological measures in remote staring studies. He pointed out that such measurements are vulnerable to experimenter effects, as demonstrated by Wiseman and Schlitz (1997). In that study, the sceptical researcher found no evidence for remote staring whilst the believer did, despite both researchers conducting their studies in the same way. Baker points out that a far more meaningful and reliable way of assessing this phenomenon is to measure conscious and overt responses – ask participants if they feel they are being stared at. For Baker, if remote staring exists then subtle physiological measures should not be needed to identify it, especially since it is something that 'is reported over and over'. In one study, he had participants sit at a table behind a one-way mirror for 20 minutes. During this time they were watched five times for one minute. None of the participants correctly guessed when they were being stared at.

A meta-analysis by Schmidt et al (2004) of 15 experiments involving 379 remote staring sessions found evidence for a small but significant effect. They point out however that not only did their meta-analysis include a small number of studies but these also tended to be of quite poor quality. They suggest that if higher quality studies had been included then the overall effect size might be reduced, perhaps even to a point where an effect did not exist.

'hollows' to indicate numbers, then the six face is much lighter than the other faces, especially the one face. Although this is likely to have only a very small effect on a single throw, the effect size will become much more important over many throws.

Studies of dice throwing showing a PK effect have proved very difficult to replicate – and this, combined with the many problems designing a fault-free experiment, means that doubt was always going to be cast on findings. Radin and Ferrari (1991) however conducted a meta-analysis of 128 dice throwing studies which collectively involved over 2,500 participants and over 2.5 million dice rolls. They found only a very small effect (50.02% hit rate in control studies where no one tried to influence the dice, against 51.2% in experimental studies with a PK agent). The difference may be small, but Radin and Ferrari point out that it equates to odds against chance of over a billion to one (compare that to the odds of winning the National Lottery!). Radin (1997) appears convinced that the results of dice-rolling experiments are evidence of mind-matter interaction. He also argues that this conclusion is corroborated by more recent and better controlled experimental research into PK using random number generators.

Micro-PK research began in the 1970s with the development of machines which could produce truly random events. Helmut Schmidt was the pioneer of this research, having developed a machine which created truly random events based on the emission of electrons from radioactive material. An electron would produce positive or negative signals equally, and depending on this signal, a light would move on a display. When stored on a computer they appear as 0 and 1. If the machine really is generating random numbers (it is usually referred to as an RNG) then by chance it should generate 1's and 0's an equal number of times.

A typical experiment involves a participant being asked to concentrate on moving the light on the display in a particular direction. Evidence for PK occurs when, over a number of trials (and given that chance levels are known), outcomes are biased in the intended direction. Latterly, computers have been used to produce random events, with audio stimuli also being occasionally employed. The advantage of using computers is that they eliminate participant bias and error in the recording of events, and checks can be made to ensure that they really are producing random events.

Whilst some studies appear to show an effect, many RNG studies fail to show any PK effect, even under the most rigid experimental conditions. Even when some effect is shown, it is only by a very small deviation from chance. Despite the fact that most experiments using RNG are generally well-designed so that they eliminate many of the problems associated with earlier dice-throwing studies, positive findings still tend to lack replicability. It also appears that particular researchers are more likely to report positive results than others.

Whilst RNG experiments may have advantages over dice throwing, some researchers have however criticised them on grounds of ecological validity. Over the years, the goalposts for proving PK have changed significantly. Early studies involved visual evidence of macro-PK (e.g. moving an object); then PK evidence was shifted to influencing the roll of a die; then latterly micro-PK evidence was required at an unobservable physical level. Braude (1997) among others has pointed out that these are quite different demands and it may be that PK occurs in quite specific forms and is not suited to every method used to test its existence.

In 1989 Radin and Nelson published the first major meta-analysis of nearly 600 PK studies using RNG. Whilst they found chance results in the control conditions (as would be expected) they found a very small but significantly above chance finding in the experimental condition. This for them was evidence that consciousness was having an effect on matter. Controlling for variations in procedure, statistics, type of data gathered and method of random generation, they found that evidence of PK was not dependent on the quality of the study. They also addressed the issue of extreme positive results being found only by select researchers. They found that excluding from their analysis 17%

of the most extreme results had little effect on the evidence for PK.

Nevertheless, most parapsychologists are not convinced by such claims and remain sceptical that these studies provide unequivocal evidence for psi. Also, meta-analyses such as that by Radin and colleagues have many pitfalls. For example, the emergent effect may have been magnified by a few flawed studies showing extreme success. Then there is the 'file drawer' effect, where non-significant findings are filed away and not made available for scrutiny. Responding to the file-drawer criticism however, Radin and Nelson (1989) calculated that for every published study with positive results there would have to be 90 unpublished ones in order to reduce their findings to insignificance – something that, they argue, is highly improbable.

This has not dampened debate however. For example, Steinkamp et al (2002) conducted a further meta-analysis, this time adding more studies, and found no significant evidence of PK. It seems that PK effects are sensitive to the inclusion or exclusion of particular studies. The fact that PK findings can be reduced to chance levels in this way casts serious doubt on the existence of micro-PK.

The most recent meta-analysis was conducted by Bösch et al (2006). This updated previous ones by adding more studies and also sought to uncover any variables that might be associated with success or failure in finding evidence for PK. Like Radin and Nelson before them, they found a small but significant effect for PK. As Wilson and Shadish (2006) point out however, the effect is so small that even a slight methodological flaw in the meta-analysis could produce it, and given the inherent problems of analysing data in such studies, this is the most likely explanation here. For Bösch et al, the PK effect is not proven and the indication of a PK effect in their meta-analysis is "due to selective reporting practices", i.e. the 'file drawer problem' again – the non-publication of small non-significant studies.

Evidence using RNGs can only ever be correlational, and it is a large step to infer a causal relationship when no known science is available to explain it. Also, effects when they are found tend to be so small that it is impossible to rule out the possibility that results could be an artefact (that is, caused by some aspect of the methodology). As Bösch et al point out: "If the answer is that the effect was parapsychological, it could form the foundation of a new or revised understanding of

the abilities of the human mind; it may provoke us to revisit Cartesian dualism or revise our understanding of the nature of matter. It is unlikely that our understanding of the world would remain unchanged." Occam's razor would suggest a parsimonious explanation for these events – "for the purposes of explanation, things not known to exist should not, unless it is absolutely necessary, be postulated as existing". That is, the findings are probably due to chance.

ESP research

The beginnings of systematic experimentation on ESP are usually associated with J.B. Rhine, who was interested in devising a method that addressed some of the problems in interpreting spontaneous experiences (Beloff, 1993). For example, with spontaneous cases there had really been no reliable means of assessing how likely a coincidence was just by chance, so Rhine decided on a method that had participants choose targets from a fixed array of alternatives, and so had a colleague Karl Zener produce the now-familiar ESP symbols (see Figure 2).

Figure 2: The five symbols that feature in the Zener card deck.

These allowed a participant's performance to be appraised statistically – with five different symbols there is a 20% likelihood of her guessing correctly just by chance, and if she makes enough guesses we can calculate exactly how improbable that degree of accuracy would be. The symbols themselves were preferred to playing cards or other images because they were thought to be more neutral and would therefore be less likely to give rise to preference biases. It was essential that the method for selecting targets was truly random so that participants could not use inference to improve their performance (for example in the way that card counters try to do in casinos). In the early studies this consisted of manual shuffling of the cards but in later studies mechanical shufflers were used. Finally, it was important to introduce barriers that effectively ruled out normal communication or cheating, so the participant and the experimenter would be separated by screens. Early work with ESP cards was very successful. In the first series in 1931/2, 800 guesses were recorded from 24 student volunteers and these resulted in

207 hits (by chance we should expect 160). This increase was highly significant.

Encouraged by this, Rhine and his colleagues conducted further experiments and a summary of these was published as a book called *Extrasensory Perception* in 1934. The main purpose of the book was to demonstrate (primarily to other academics) that this kind of claim could be tested empirically – although the claim might sound unscientific it was still amenable to testing using conventional scientific methods (Mauskopf and McVaugh, 1980). The book became a best-seller among the general public and started a fad for conducting ESP tests at home (Irwin and Watt, 2007). It also prompted a sceptical backlash. Certainly the early studies were not beyond criticism and over time improvements were made to control for subtle sensory cues (for example the person looking at the cards to 'send' them to the participant in a telepathy design might unwittingly make subtle changes in posture or breathing in response to different symbols; or, if the same cards are used too often, then participants might learn to associate wear-and-tear marks or creases on the backs with the symbols on the face). To eliminate these cues, in later studies participants would be placed in different rooms in different parts of the university campus (but see Hansel, 1989, for more detailed criticisms).

Critics wondered if the data could be explained by some misapplication of statistics or suppressions of contradictory results, and when these concerns were demonstrated to be unfounded some resorted to insinuating fraud on the part of the experimenters (Irwin, 1999). But while there have been occasional well publicised cases of experimenter fraud in parapsychology (Palmer, 1978) there is nothing to indicate that this problem is greater here than for other social sciences: indeed, there are grounds for expecting it to be less prevalent (Broad and Wade, 1983). As findings are replicated across laboratories any suggestion of fraud is made less tenable.

Experimental tests of Dream ESP

One criticism of the card-guessing research that was raised within parapsychology itself was concern about the ecological validity of this work, which seemed quite sterile and irrelevant to the kinds of spontaneous experiences of ESP that people actually reported (Rhine, 1981). In particular, as there was a tendency for those experiences to involve richer, more meaningful 'targets', and because they typically occurred during dreams or when the experient was drifting off to or waking up from sleep, it seemed sensible to concentrate on that altered state of consciousness. So in 1962 psychiatrist Montague Ullman established a dream laboratory at the Maimonides Medical Center in Brooklyn, New York that exploited the then recent discovery that there were certain periods during the sleep cycle when people exhibited bursts of rapid eye movements (REM), and these coincided with EEG readings indicating that the sleeper was in a mentally active state (Krippner, 1991). If woken during such periods, people were more likely to report having been dreaming than if woken at other times (Aserinsky and Kleitman, 1953).

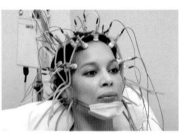

Ullman and colleagues would select participants who reported that they were able to fall asleep easily, dream frequently, remember their dreams, and had positive attitudes towards the possibility of telepathy. The participant would come to the sleep lab to spend the night as a percipient or 'receiver' and would spend time with the person who would later act as 'sender' so as to build some rapport between them. When the participant became tired she would have EEG electrodes attached to her head so that she could be monitored for REM and would go to bed in a soundproof room. After she had fallen asleep, the sender would be given a target image (usually an art print or postcard picture) that they were to concentrate on and try to 'send' to the receiver while she slept. The target for each trial was randomly selected by an independent member of staff from a large pool of images and had been sealed in an opaque envelope so that neither the receiver nor any of the researchers who interacted with her could have any idea of what the target was.

The sender went to a remote room in the building, or even in a separate building, so that it wasn't possible to communicate with the receiver by normal means. When the receiver began her first REM period, the sender was notified by the experimenter via a one-way buzzer and he then opened the envelope and concentrated on the target, attempting to communicate its contents to the receiver. Towards the end of the REM period the receiver was woken up from her dream and asked to describe what she could remember as well as any associations she might have to that dream. This dream report was tape-recorded and later transcribed, and the written version was called a *mentation*. The receiver then went back to sleep until the next REM phase, and the process was repeated (usually the same target was used throughout the night).

In the morning the researchers wanted to see if the receiver's dream had any correspondences to their target image that seem to go beyond what we might expect just by chance. However, if the receiver was simply shown the target image and asked to look for similarities, then this would capitalise on people's tendency to make lots of meaningful associations or see rather tenuous connections (perhaps motivated by expectation or a need to succeed) that would artificially inflate the impressiveness of the correspondences. Instead, the receiver was given twelve pictures consisting of a copy of the target and eleven decoys *without knowing which was which*, and she had to rate each of these for its similarity to her dreams. With this method it doesn't matter if you tend to see lots of connections between things (as might be the case for creative people, or believers in the paranormal) because you will be as likely to do this for the decoys as for the actual target and it shouldn't help you tell which is which.

Participants rank ordered the pictures, with the art print in first position being most like their dream and the one in twelfth being least like it. If the actual target was ranked in the top half of this ranking order (i.e. positions 1–6) then the trial was called a hit; if it was ranked in the bottom half (7-12) it was a miss: this is a rather crude measure of ESP performance since it gives no more credit for ranking the target a clear first than it does for ranking the target a mere sixth. If dream ESP is not possible then the participants' dreams will have only random, coincidental similarities to the pictures and they should tend to get a hit about 50% of the time, as expected by chance. Actual performance was quite a bit better than this. For example, in the first series with a selected participant (Ullman et al, 1966), the dreamer had seven hits and one miss, and in his second series (Ullman and Krippner, 1969) he achieved eight hits and no misses.

The Maimonides team built on this early promise and went on to conduct a total of 16 studies (13 formal studies and 3 pilot series) that were variations on the method described above. This programme has been reviewed by a number of researchers (e.g. Sherwood and Roe, 2003) and although the overall success rate of 63% does not seem to be enormously different from the 50% expected just by chance, over such a large number of trials this turns out to be highly significant. So, when we are able to calculate unambiguously how likely it is that our results could have occurred by coincidence, it doesn't seem plausible that they simply represent a statistical fluke. Neither can we easily account for them as a consequence of selective recall (all trials are reported, none are unpublished) or of selection bias (all targets were selected using random number tables) or of subtle cueing of the receiver (the sender was sensorially isolated some distance away and none of the staff who worked closely with the receiver knew what the target was at that time).

However, there are other criticisms that might apply. When they were originally reported, different Maimonides studies included different statistical analyses, and this could raise suspicions of selection or 'data mining' – the disreputable practice of conducting lots of extra statistical analyses if your initial prediction isn't confirmed, trawling through your data until (by chance) you find some significant effect somewhere and then present that as if it were the thing you were looking for all along, ignoring all the others. There certainly is some variability in the analyses conducted, which Child (1985) accounted for by noting that the data had been passed to various statistical consultants who may have differed in their preferred approach (psychologists were less statistically sophisticated then and didn't have access to powerful computer software to do the calculations for them, so it was not uncommon to have specialists do this). Nowadays we can see if this had an effect on the pattern of results, by converting each of the results into a common statistic: then there is no possibility of selection based on which analysis gives the 'best' result. Child (1985) did just this and concluded

The outcome is clear. Several segments of the data, considered separately, yield significant evidence that dreams (and associations to them) tended to resemble the picture chosen randomly as target more than they resembled other pictures in the pool.

Fraud has also been suggested as a possible explanation for the results (e.g. Clemmer, 1986) but no plausible mechanism for fraud has been given, and the onus is on the critic to demonstrate how it might have occurred in practice rather than on the researchers to prove their innocence (Sherwood and Roe, 2003). Nevertheless, insinuations of fraud can be readily refuted if the claimed effect could be reproduced by other research teams working at other laboratories (unless we suppose some grand conspiracy). Very few researchers have access to specialist dream laboratories but six replication studies did use EEG monitoring and deliberate awakening. Of these, only one could be regarded as a successful replication (see Sherwood and Roe, 2003) and, while the other experiments were later criticised for changing the procedure in ways that could have adversely affected performance (see Van de Castle, 1989), this does weaken the original claim to have captured a dream ESP effect.

Most replication attempts have been by researchers who did not have access to the specialist resources that were available to the Maimonides group. Instead investigators have improvised methods that typically sacrifice some degree of control over conditions in favour of greater ecological validity and participant convenience or comfort. For example, Child et al (1977) conducted two telepathy experiments with Sweeney acting as the only participant receiver and Child as the sender. Sweeney slept in her own home and awoke naturally in the morning. She knew that as she slept, Child would attempt to 'send' details of a randomly selected target for a short time in the evening. In the morning she would attempt to recall the content of her dreams, producing a dream diary.

After eight trials each of the three authors (i.e. including the sender) independently rated the eight dream transcripts against the eight pictures that had been selected as targets. In experiment two, judgements were made each morning rather than at the end of the series. Performance based upon the combined judgements in experiment one was better than chance but not significantly so, whereas in experiment two, performance was significantly better than chance – and when the results of these two studies were combined, the cumulative result was also significant. In studies that have a sender and in which judging is delayed by any length of time there is always the possibility that sender and receiver might meet by accident and that, perhaps unwittingly, the receiver could pick up on subtle cues that help them identify the target, even if the sender does his best not to leak information (perhaps the target image is quite frightening and they overcompensate by being too relaxed or warm, for example). This possibility can be avoided by adopting a clairvoyant design in which the target is selected automatically and no one knows its identity until after the participant's judgements have been made.

For example, Dalton et al (1999) developed a computer program that randomly selected and played a target video clip repeatedly during the night (between 3:00 and 4:00 a.m., so that it was likely to overlap with at least one REM period). During each of 32 trials, the three researcher-participants slept at home and kept a record of any dreams. In the laboratory the following morning, the computer presented them with four video clips (the target and three decoys) and they each ranked the clips for similarity to their dreams. They then shared their night's dreams and produced a joint rank order for the similarity of the clips to the group's collected dreams. Where the target clip was given a rank of 1 it was labelled a 'direct hit'; where it was ranked in positions 2–4 it was labelled a 'miss'. The group ratings and two of the three individuals achieved direct hit rates that significantly exceeded what could be expected by chance. The group had been more successful with emotional targets, particularly when they were negative, which is consistent with other work on emotional targets (Bierman, 1997).

Sherwood and Roe (2003) found 21 studies that qualified as replications of the Maimonides work. Fourteen of these studies reported above-chance results and six below-chance, and when combined the cumulative results are independently significant, so might be interpreted as supporting the original Maimonides claim – though it should be noted that they were also significantly *less* successful than the Maimonides studies had been. To account for this, Sherwood and Roe noted that the replications had been extremely varied in their methods and their outcomes were similarly variable, which might give pointers to good (and bad) practice for future replication attempts.

They made a number of recommendations, including that participants should be monitored and deliberately woken from REM sleep (equipment is now available to be able to monitor REM at home and to signal the dreamer with sounds or flashing lights). This should increase the amount and quality of dream material that participants recall – it is not uncommon for unselected participants to come to the lab for the judging phase with only the vaguest recollection of any of their dreams. Secondly, they noted that some experimenter-participant teams were more successful than others, which they interpreted in terms of establishing a warmer, more relaxed atmosphere that was more successful in putting the participant at their ease and enabling them to perform naturalistically. And thirdly they pointed out that the Maimonides researchers tended to recruit participants who had done well in screening studies or who had a track record of success in other ESP experiments, whereas many of the later replications involved unselected subjects. Future work might be more consistent if participants were selected for prior experiences, ability to regularly recall their dreams, or for certain personality factors that are regarded as psi-conducive, such as those discussed in the next section.

Experimental tests of ESP in the Ganzfeld

Despite some successes, dream research has not been an especially attractive proposition for researchers interested in testing claims for ESP effects in the laboratory, perhaps because the Maimonides approach requires prohibitively expensive equipment and facilities and the alternative approaches have relied on methodologically looser arrangements that have varied widely and carry no guarantee that participants will be asleep when the target is played or will remember their dreams when they do wake up in the morning.

A method was needed that would be much more reliable in reproducing the subjective experience of drifting off to sleep but at the same time allowed more experimental control over conditions and could be used in the laboratory during normal working hours. One technique that was adopted independently by three groups of researchers involved 'ganzfeld stimulation' (Braud et al, 1975). Ganzfeld means 'total field' and is a kind of sensory deprivation. This involves placing halved ping pong balls over the participant's eyes and shining a red (or sometimes pink) light on them (see Figure 3). The participant keeps his eyes open and the semi-translucent plastic of the ping pong balls diffuses the light so that he experiences a homogeneous visual field that seems warm and cosy, but because the light stimulus is unpatterned and unchanging his brain habituates to it and he may even experience 'blank out' periods in which it feels as if he has no visual experience at all.

Such an uninteresting visual experience can lead to 'sensory hunger', in which attention is drawn away from the visual system and towards more internally-generated sensations, in the form of mild hallucinations that have a dream-like quality. The ganzfeld is thought to facilitate the flow of ideation and imagery (Bertini et al, 1964) so that these impressions can seem very spontaneous, creative, and quite independent of any conscious thought processes. A similar auditory effect is achieved by having participants listen via headphones to 'white noise', a sound signal that evenly represents the whole audible frequency range to give an unpatterned hiss that sounds rather like the rush of cascading water. Again, sensory hunger can lead the participant to incorporate his own internally-generated material into the signal, giving the impression that certain sounds (such as noises, music, voices) can be heard in the white noise just on the edge of hearing.

Figure 3: The receiver in a ganzfeld session.

Meanwhile elsewhere the sender concentrates on a randomly-selected video clip.

The receiver then watches four clips and rates how similar they are to his impressions.

In a typical ganzfeld study, participants are recruited in pairs, with one to serve as the sender and one as the receiver. The sender's task is to watch a randomly selected target video clip during the time when the receiver is experiencing ganzfeld stimulation, and the prediction to be tested is that the receiver's internally-generated ganzfeld mentation will include elements that had somehow been communicated from the sender, and could be used to identify the target clip.

Sessions begin with sender, receiver and experimenter all present in a sound attenuated room (to further block out possible normal communication from the sender or other confederate) as the receiver is prepared for the session. The receiver lies back in a reclining chair and gets as comfortable as he can, removing his shoes and covering himself with a blanket if he wishes. He wears headphones with a microphone attached through which he can communicate with the experimenter and be heard by the sender during the session. Then halved ping-pong balls are placed over his eyes and held secure with medical tape and a red light shone onto his face.

The sender and experimenter then leave him, and the door to the receiver's room typically is locked, partly to ensure that it's not possible for him to be passed information about the target via normal means, and partly to reassure the receiver that no one will be in the room while he is in this vulnerable sensorially-deprived state (participants sometimes report a sense of presence which can lead them to believe someone is actually in the room with them). The sender is then escorted to her room, where she puts on headphones so that she can hear any comments from the receiver or experimenter as well as the soundtrack to the target clip when it is played. The sender's door is locked and then the experimenter goes to their own room to initiate the computer program that runs the session.

It's quite common for participants to feel a little nervous about this rather unusual procedure, so to encourage them to feel safe and relaxed they firstly follow a series of progressive relaxation instructions played by the computer over headphones. Once these are complete the program selects the target video clip and plays it to the sender repeatedly over the ganzfeld period as the receiver listens to white noise and reports on any impressions or sensations that she experiences. The sender can also hear the receiver's comments as feedback on her sending strategy. The receiver and experimenter would remain unaware of what target had been selected.

Most ganzfeld sessions last in the region of 25-30 minutes, and after this time the experimenter reviews the receiver's mentation with him to see if anything needs to be added, elaborated or modified while they are both still blind to the target identity. The receiver then removes his eye shields so he can view four video clips consisting of the target and three decoys, all selected and played automatically by the computer. These are rated or rank ordered for their similarity to the receiver's impressions, much as described for dream ESP studies, and once the ratings are saved the actual target is revealed as feedback.

Where the participant has to choose between four clips we would expect them to pick the actual target 25% of the time if they were just guessing, so what was the observed hit rate with this method? The first summary reviews of ganzfeld ESP research were concerned with *manual* ganzfeld studies. These had been conducted at a time when technology was not sufficiently advanced to allow computers to control parts of the procedure. Hence targets tended to be postcards and art prints placed in sealed envelopes and selected randomly using random number tables, and the smooth running of sessions relied upon research assistants who ensured that all the right materials ended up with the right people and all those who needed to be blind to the target remained that way. Nevertheless, these early studies were claimed to have a highly significant overall success rate of 55% where we would expect only 5% if chance alone were operating (Honorton, 1985).

Hyman (1985) was very sceptical of this conclusion. He felt that he had identified weaknesses in the design of some of these studies that would reduce the hit rate to chance levels once they were taken into account. The kind of factors Hyman had in mind included the following:

Adequacy of randomisation in selecting targets: because, as we have seen in this chapter, people's responses and judgements in an ESP study are likely to be biased, we need to be sure that the way in which targets were selected for them cannot be susceptible to the same biases. A truly random method needs to be used to pick targets and decoys, using for example, random number tables. Some studies however have used methods such as hand shuffling cards or flipping coins, which leaves some small opportunity for bias to creep in.

Security: it is also essential to ensure that there is no opportunity for the receiver to find out about the target via normal means (often that means by cheating). Some studies had weaknesses in the controls against normal communication, (for example in how closely the receiver was monitored) that could open the possibility for cheating by an especially ingenious person.

Selection in analysis and reporting: different studies had different preferred analyses and, as with the dream ESP work, this could allow researchers to have conducted a range of tests but only to report on the ones that 'worked out', giving a false impression of how positive the results had been. Hyman was also concerned about 'file drawer problems', where unsuccessful studies might never be written up or if they are submitted to journals they are rejected by referees as uninteresting. The upshot of this would be that we end up with a published record that is skewed towards those studies that were successful and all the others lie hidden in researchers' file drawers.

Hyman (1985) and Honorton (1985) each separately appraised the impact of these (and other) possible flaws on a database of 42 ganzfeld experiments contributed by ten independent research groups, and – perhaps not surprisingly – came to different conclusions. Hyman felt that the experiments had too many methodological weaknesses to justify the claim that ESP was responsible for any apparently above-chance scoring, whereas Honorton attempted to show that even where there were weaknesses, they could not be associated strongly enough to the outcomes to be able to explain them.

For example, when Honorton addressed the multiple analysis problem by converting all the different outcomes to a common measure (as Child had done for the dream ESP experiments), the cumulative outcome remained highly significant. He also calculated that there would need to be 423 unpublished studies to reduce the size of the effect to chance levels. It is highly unlikely that these studies could have been hidden away, given the very few people who were known to be using the ganzfeld method to test for ESP and the intensive nature of the method (each session takes a few hours from start to finish and it is extremely rare to run more than two sessions in any one day). In any case, when Blackmore (1980) surveyed the parapsychology community, she found that the hit rate in unpublished studies was no different from that for the published studies.

There was little possibility of Honorton and Hyman agreeing on their interpretation of these data as evidence of ESP, but the exchange did end very positively in a joint paper that concluded:

DO EXPERIMENTERS INFLUENCE ESP STUDIES?

Despite decades of research, there is still no credible evidence for the existence of psi, with research consistently failing to produce replicable results. It has been suggested that this is due at least in part to experimenter effects. For example, Honorton et al (1975) claim that experimenters who are friendly and supportive towards participants are more likely to get results supporting ESP than experimenters who behave in more negative, unfriendly ways. According to Schmeidler (1997), the attitude of the experimenter towards psi affects the outcome of studies, with psi-positive researchers more likely than sceptical ones to record evidence of psi. Presumably, the experimenter is somehow conveying this belief and expectancy to participants and thereby influencing the participants' own beliefs and expectancy about psi.

Researchers who consistently find evidence in favour of psi are often referred to as 'psi-conducive' whilst those who consistently fail to find such evidence are labelled psi-inhibitory'. This suggests that the results are somehow to do with the characteristics of the experimenter rather than experimental design. This was investigated by Wiseman and Schlitz (1999). Schlitz (a psi-conducive) and Wiseman (psi-inhibitory) conducted studies of remote staring under the same experimental conditions. They found that, as previous history would suggest, Schlitz's data supported a psi effect whilst Wiseman's did not. They argued that their findings were not due to poor experimental design as such, but probably reflected subtle differences in the way that the two experimenters responded to participants.

One consequence of this line of argument is that chance results could be attributed to psi-inhibition rather than a lack of psi. An implication is that research should only be conducted by those who are psi-conducive. This in effect makes psi scientifically untestable, as it prevents independent verification of results by replication, a vital feature of good science.

To complicate matters even further, it has also been claimed that the psychic abilities of participants in experimental studies of psi could be being influenced by the psychic abilities of the experimenter. This kind of 'unintentional psi' appears to be yet another barrier to reliably establishing a psi phenomenon.

> There is an overall significant effect in this data base that cannot reasonably be explained by selective reporting or multiple analyses. We continue to differ over the degree to which the effect constitutes evidence for psi, but we agree that the final verdict awaits the outcome of future experiments conducted by a broader range of investigators and according to more stringent standards. (Hyman and Honorton, 1986)

They went on to outline what those more stringent standards should be. Honorton took up the challenge of improving the methodology so that it addressed the various concerns that Hyman had raised; if the significant hit rates were still observed then it would cast doubt on the likelihood that these 'flaws' could explain earlier successes.

The new protocol placed many aspects of the procedure – such as random selection of targets, presentation of targets along with decoys during judging, and recording of all participant ratings before the target was revealed – under computer control, and so became known as an *automated-* or *auto-ganzfeld*, to contrast it with the earlier manual version. Bem and Honorton (1994) reported on the results of all the auto-ganzfeld experiments that took place at Honorton's laboratory, consisting of 329 trials involving 240 different receivers and 8 different experimenters. The overall hit rate for these trials was 32–35% (depending on how the experiments were divided), and even the lowest of these estimates is statistically significant, suggesting that eradicating the flaws that had been identified previously did not reduce performance to chance levels.

They also identified a 'recipe for success' by looking for internal patterns within this database: they found that dynamic targets such as video clips were more successful than static targets such as postcards; that participants who reported prior personal experiences and those who practised a mental discipline (such as meditation) fared better than those who did not; and that certain personality types or predispositions – particularly extraversion and creativity – seemed to be associated with more hits. Internal patterns such as these make it more difficult to account for the outcomes in terms of artefacts.

Hyman (1994) accepted that these experiments overcame many of the methodological weaknesses of the earlier series, describing them as "commendable experiments of high quality". He did however question the claim that they showed that the effect was replicable – although a number of experimenters had been involved, it was essentially Honorton's work and used the same basic method and participant pool; what was needed was truly independent replications using the autoganzfeld method.

Milton and Wiseman (1999) reviewed 30 such studies from 7 different laboratories that had been conducted since 1987 (after Hyman and Honorton's recommendations had been published). These studies achieved an overall hit rate of just 27.6% and so failed to confirm the above chance scoring reported by Bem and Honorton. In accounting for the discrepancy, Milton and Wiseman tended to focus on the possibility that Bem and Honorton's original result was due to some error or methodological weakness; although they were unable to provide any evidence of how that might have happened. For example, they claim "this failure to replicate could indicate that the autoganzfeld's results were spurious, with the main effect having been due to very weak sensory leakage" despite earlier conceding that "none of the opportunities for sensory leakage appear sufficiently strong…to explain away the positive results of the autoganzfeld in any immediately compelling way".

Ganzfeld researchers instead tended to focus on the possibility that there was something wrong with Milton and Wiseman's collection of studies (see Schmeidler and Edge, 1999), particularly that they had included some studies that should not have counted as ganzfeld studies and had not included others that they should have. Those changes would likely have been enough to make the replication studies significant in their own right (Milton, 1999). However, there is a danger that researchers' judgements of how 'standard' or 'appropriate' a published study is will be influenced by their knowledge of how that study worked out.

This issue can be resolved by having the ratings of 'standardness' made by judges who are unfamiliar with the studies and 'blind' to their outcomes. Bem et al (2001) did just this, giving three independent judges the original description from Bem and Honorton (1994) of how a standard autoganzfeld session should be conducted, along with just the method sections of the 40 autoganzfeld replication studies. The judges' task was to rate the extent to which these studies deviated from the standard ganzfeld method. As they hypothesised, these standardness ratings correlated with study outcome, with more conventional studies being more successful. When 'non-standard' studies were excluded, the remaining database gave a combined outcome that is highly significant. The rejected studies had a mean hit rate of 24% – very close to chance expectation.

This is a promising approach to understanding why the two reviews should have led to such different conclusions about the status of ESP. Nevertheless it is a concern that the effect seems so precarious that the inclusion or exclusion of individual studies can determine whether the null hypothesis is accepted or rejected. Even if the hit rate is accepted as significantly greater than chance expectation, it is also true that the effect size is significantly smaller than that reported by Bem and Honorton (Milton, 1999), and on this basis we may still say that the later database has failed to replicate the findings of the earlier one.

Perhaps a more telling criticism is the complaint that Milton and Wiseman had treated these replication studies as if they were intended simply to confirm the existence of an effect, when in fact many had been designed to investigate the mechanism of any effect by manipulating variables to see whether they might improve or perhaps impair ESP performance. These experiments could therefore include comparison conditions that were actually hypothesised to be unsuccessful. For example, Williams et al (1994) included a baseline condition that had no sender watching the clip and found, as they predicted, that performance here was significantly worse than for conditions with senders. Parker (2000) reported on a series of five studies: in the first of these the sender was not able to hear the participant's mentation and so received no feedback, and the hit rate was just 20%; whereas in the subsequent four studies senders could get feedback, and performance improved to an average of 40%. In both cases Milton and Wiseman's review simply combines the results of these different conditions, as if an equivalent ESP effect was expected to occur in all circumstances, which is flawed.

ANOMALISTIC PSYCHOLOGY AND PSEUDOSCIENCE

This brings us finally to the question of what status we should give to parapsychology – does it have the characteristics of genuine science or does it contain some suspect features that mean we should regard it as a pseudoscience?

"Learn the difference between a science and a pseudoscience, and learn to recognise a pseudoscientific claim when you see one. You will be laying the foundations of good critical thinking skills, as well as preparing for exam questions which might focus on this."

A pseudoscience is literally a 'false' science, and refers to activities that might have the superficial appearance of a respectable science (such as publishing results in journals, having professional credentials for practicing members, and so on) but doesn't include the fundamental features of reputable science that are intended to ensure that the claims it makes are valid. For example, Kurtz (1985) characterises pseudoscience as:

i. failing to use rigorous experimental methods in their inquiries – graphology (handwriting analysis) might fail on this count if supporters rely on personal testimonials from clients rather than scientifically controlled tests;

ii. asserting that they have achieved positive results though these have not been replicated by impartial observers;

iii. lacking a coherent theoretical framework that organises and explains the observations – astrology might fail this test in not having a coherent mechanism to explain how stars that are immensely far apart but happen to appear clustered together from our perspective on Earth could have a combined influence on human behaviour and destiny (Sagan, 1996).

Some commentators (e.g. Alcock, 1981) have claimed that parapsychology has the characteristics of a pseudoscience, so how does it fare against these three criteria? We have seen in this chapter that parapsychologists have attempted to design and conduct experiments that are rigorous and well controlled. Certainly these experimental designs have not been perfect, and a number of valid criticisms have been put forward, particularly for the earliest studies in any research programme – but we have also seen that attempts have been made to refine and improve procedures and to test whether the effect sizes observed are related to the 'quality' of the experiments. The mainstream psychological research on paranormal belief that we have looked at also has had various design flaws yet there is no suggestion that this makes the work pseudoscientific, so perhaps in practice this factor should not be used to consign parapsychology to the pseudoscience category.

Flew (1985) claims that the effects in parapsychology cannot be reliably replicated and it is this that separates it from the established sciences. Such replication failures may seem particularly suspicious if successful outcomes are produced only by a small band of proponents while replications by sceptics meet with failure. Martin Gardner (1983) makes this point when he complains

> How can the public know that for fifty years sceptical psychologists have been trying their best to replicate classic psi experiments, and with notable unsuccess? It is this fact more than any other that has led to parapsychology's perpetual stagnation. Positive evidence keeps coming from a tiny group of enthusiasts, while negative evidence keeps coming from a much larger group of sceptics.

If this were true, then there would have to be doubts about parapsychology's status as a science. However, when Honorton (1993) quotes Gardner as above, he goes on to say "Gardner does not attempt to document this assertion, nor could he. It is pure fiction. Look for the skeptics' experiments and see what you find…[the] lack of research by critics only serves to perpetuate the psi controversy". Little has changed since then, with most researchers who are sceptical of paranormal claims devoting their time to experiments that test or explore the counter-explanations that we have considered in this chapter, rather than testing the claims themselves.

That is not to say that parapsychological effects can be produced on demand in each experiment. It is clear that the effects we are dealing with are very small (so small, for example, that they could quite conceivably still be accounted for in terms of some as-yet unnoticed design weakness) and inconsistent, appearing in experiments on some occasions but not on others. Perhaps these two characteristics are related: Utts (1991) has shown that it is statistically naïve to think that if an effect is real and consistent then it should reliably lead to significant results – significance depends not only on there being an effect but also on its magnitude (small effects, such as the benefits for cardiac patients of taking aspirin, can still have real consequences); and crucially on the 'power' of the experiment (basically related to sample size, as bigger studies are capable of detecting smaller effects). Some failures to replicate parapsychological effects could therefore be due to researchers designing studies that were too small to detect the small effects they were dealing with.

SOME OF THE CHARACTERISTICS OF SCIENCE AND PSEUDOSCIENCE

Science	Pseudoscience
Findings are expressed primarily through scientific journals that are peer-reviewed and maintain rigorous standards for honesty and accuracy.	Literature is aimed at the general public. There is no review, no standards, no pre-publication verification, no demand for accuracy and precision.
Replicable results are demanded; experiments must be precisely described so that they can be replicated exactly or improved upon.	Results cannot be replicated and therefore not verified. Studies, if any, are always so vaguely described that one can't figure out what was done or how it was done.
Failures are searched for and studied closely, because incorrect theories can often make correct predictions by accident, but no correct theory will make incorrect predictions.	Failures are ignored, excused, hidden, lied about, discounted, explained away, rationalised, forgotten, avoided at all costs.
Over time, more and more is learned about the physical processes under study.	No physical phenomena or processes are ever found or studied. No progress is made; nothing concrete is learned.
Convinces by appeal to the evidence, by arguments based upon logical and/or statistical reasoning, by making the best case the data permit. Old ideas are abandoned when new evidence contradicts them.	Convinces by appeal to faith and belief. Pseudoscience has a strong quasi-religious element: it tries to convert, not to convince. You are to believe in spite of the facts, not because of them. The original idea is never abandoned, whatever the evidence.
Does not advocate or market unproven practices or products.	Questionable products marketed (such as books, courses, and dietary supplements) and/or pseudoscientific services (such as horoscopes, character readings, spirit messages, and predictions).

Adapted from http://www.quackwatch.com/01QuackeryRelatedTopics/pseudo.html

In the social sciences we are also aware of how sensitive an effect can be to other situational variables that are not adequately controlled (or indeed that researchers may not yet be aware of), which could cause effects to fluctuate from study to study in quite ordinary ways. For example, Irwin and Watt (2007) note that these concerns "might equally be applicable to other accepted areas of scientific research. In psychology, for example, many experimental results comprise small but statistically significant effects, and often the replicability of these effects is either poor or untested. That is not to say that effect size and repeatability are not important, but merely that critics' emphasis upon them in the parapsychology debate is fundamentally for rhetorical purposes". Again, this criterion seems unlikely to differentiate parapsychology from other social sciences in a way that would mark it out as pseudoscience.

Finally we should be aware that science does not consist solely of 'facts' (observations confirmed through repeated testing): crucially it also includes theories or models that organise and explain those facts and make predictions for future observations. Hyman (1995) has argued that "acceptable evidence for the presence of anomalous cognition [i.e. ESP] must be based on a positive theory that tells us when psi should and should not be present. Until we have such a theory, the claim that anomalous cognition has been demonstrated is empty. Without such a theory, we might just as well argue that what has been demonstrated is a set of effects – *each one of which could be the result of an entirely different cause.*"

Edge (1986) conceded "there is no generally accepted theory or set of theories in parapsychology which explains most of the phenomena and ties them together", and there seems to have been no greater consensus since then. However, Edge goes on to say that this "does not exclude parapsychology from the realm of scientific practice. There exists a network of core knowledge, accepted procedure, and some accepted lower level theories which guide parapsychologists in their research…Parapsychology does not lack for theories; the problem may be that there are too many theories!" These theories properly draw on advances in related fields, so that recent interest has focused on the physics of psi (e.g. Carr, 2008) and the neuroscience that provides its psychological foundation (e.g. Broughton, 2006). However, at present no single theory is widely accepted and experimental work is not consistently or obviously shaped by the theories that are available, which suggests that at best parapsychology might be regarded as an immature science.

In conclusion, then, there have been some attempts to test claims of ESP experimentally, using methods that are intended to rule out the kinds of normal explanation that we considered in the first part of this chapter. Collectively those studies have produced results that cannot be readily accounted for in terms of chance coincidence or subtle but normal communications. However, the effects are too small and inconsistent for us to conclude that we have a demonstrable and replicable ESP effect that might conceivably provide an alternative explanation of people's spontaneous experiences. On the whole the research is carefully done and further sceptical work (in the sense defined here) to test the claims themselves is certainly worthy of its place within anomalistic psychology as a complement to competent investigations of more mundane explanations of paranormal belief and experience.

Psychological Research and Scientific Methods

NIGEL HOLT

WHAT YOU NEED TO KNOW

This section builds on the knowledge and skills of research methods developed at AS level.

You are expected to be able to understand the application of scientific method in psychology, design investigations, understand how to analyse and interpret data arising from such investigations, and report on practical investigations.

THE APPLICATIONS OF SCIENTIFIC METHOD IN PSYCHOLOGY

- The major features of science
- The scientific process, including theory construction, hypothesis testing, use of empirical methods, generation of laws/principles
- Validating new knowledge and the role of peer review

DESIGNING PSYCHOLOGICAL INVESTIGATIONS

- Selection and application of appropriate research methods
- Sampling strategies
- Issues of reliability, including types of reliability, assessment of reliability, improving reliability
- Assessing and improving validity (internal and external)
- Ethical considerations in design and conduct of psychological research

REPORTING INVESTIGATIONS

- Appropriate selection of graphical representations
- Probability and significance, including the interpretation of significance and Type 1/Type 2 errors
- Choosing the correct statistical test, including levels of measurement
- Inferential analysis, including Spearman's Rho, Wilcoxon, Mann-Whitney, chi-square
- Analysing and interpreting of qualitative data
- Conventions of reporting on psychological investigations

THE APPLICATION OF SCIENTIFIC METHOD IN PSYCHOLOGY

RESEARCH METHODS IS NOT JUST MATHS

Research methods is one of the areas in psychology that some students find extremely difficult, and that most students have trouble with from time to time. Many people doing psychology confuse 'statistics' with 'research methods'. It's true that you do have to use some mathematical skills, but really methods are the vital skills that allow you to carry out research in psychology, and to look carefully and critically at the research that has already been done. A decent knowledge of research methods will enable you to look at the work of psychologists and to criticise their methods and findings. Evaluating research in this way allows us to think clearly about whether the work is *reliable* and *valid*, two terms that are extremely important in psychology, and which will feature later in this chapter.

Another problem people have is that they think that 'research methods' is just another separate area of psychology. That's partly the fault of textbook writers like us, and partly the fault of generations of psychologists. It just so happens that research methods tends to feature as a separate chapter and is therefore regarded as something you read about once, and forget about for the rest of the book. We would urge you to regard research methods as central to your study of psychology, with all the other bits (developmental, cognitive, social, etc.) as separate important extras. Methods will provide the backbone and the other areas will provide the fabulous and interesting covering. Without one you cannot have the other.

"If you are using this book as part of an A level course you will already be familiar with a good deal of the information you need to know about the scientific method, since it has been covered in the AS course. Much of it will be summarised as we go through this chapter. Methods can be tricky in places: there's no getting around the fact, but a sensible understanding and knowledge of where to find refreshment for an overworked memory can do wonders for confidence. There is nothing at all to say that you cannot flick back to your AS books, or even get a study guide to help you summarise what you need to know. Remember, research methods at A2 extends the knowledge and understanding of this area that you gained at AS."

THE MAJOR FEATURES OF SCIENCE

By now you should be quite accustomed to the idea that psychology is a science. Many people are not at all familiar or comfortable with our subject being described in this way. They feel that science is something that people in white coats do while locked up in laboratories housing dangerous chemicals or machines. They feel that because psychology often deals with opinions and emotions it is not a science at all. They are wrong. Psychology follows the principles of all good sciences. These are the application of the scientific method, with careful consideration of replicability and objectivity.

There is no great secret to identifying the scientific method. Your previous studies have already introduced you to the concept. The scientific method refers to ways of thinking about evidence and of carrying out research that allow us to develop what we already know. It is because of the scientific method that we now have the technology we do, and it is largely because of the application of the scientific method that we now know as much we do about psychology.

HYPOTHESIS TESTING

The scientific method progresses by hypothesis testing. You know by now that a hypothesis is a statement that can be tested in research. For instance, we might be interested in investigating whether people really do feel happier in the summer when there is more sunshine. Our hypothesis might be:

'People feel happier in the summer.'

We must now do our best to test this hypothesis. We must try everything we can to disprove it. Our efforts must be focused on finding out whether we can prove that people do not feel happier in the summer. If we can do that then we can reject our hypothesis. The process of trying to disprove a hypothesis is absolutely central to the progression of all sciences, and psychology is no different in that respect from physics, chemistry or biology.

REPLICABILITY

If we can carry out our research again at another time and find the same or similar results then we can say that we have managed to replicate our findings. Being able to do this is extremely important in the scientific method. If we find something on Monday and carry out the same research on Wednesday but find a different result we might, understandably, be a little cautious about Monday's hypothesis. After all, if we have found something on Monday, why *would* the effect not be there still on Wednesday? A high level of consistency (we use the term 'reliability' in psychology) means that we and those reading about our research can be confident that our findings are really what we say they are. Other researchers in our field (our *peers*) can then extend our research without having to carry out our work again. This process further improves our knowledge of psychology. Our subject is pushed on and on, developing every time a piece of work is carried out and published for others to read.

OBJECTIVITY

A good scientist should always be an objective scientist. This means that the findings of a piece of research should not depend on the person that did the research in the first place. The results should not be influenced by the person who designed the study, carried it out, analysed the results or drew the conclusions. A high level of objectivity increases other people's confidence in the results, as they are able to say that it would have made no difference who did the work, the results would have been the same. If the researcher was not objective then the results might have been biased or influenced in some way by his or her ideas and feelings. In cases like these we say that the research was subjective – the researcher's opinion influenced the study and the interpretation of the results. This means that another researcher doing exactly the same thing might not find the same results. For instance, a researcher is investigating the statements of people who said they had seen UFOs, to determine whether there was any consistency in the statements that might lead us to believe that UFOs really do exist. If the research is objective then true findings will result from this study. If the researcher's approach is subjective, the findings may be distorted or biased – for example, a researcher who believes that he has at one time been abducted by aliens might, if investigating the existence of UFOs, allow his conclusions to be influenced by this belief.

"In the exam you might be asked to comment on whether something is a science or not. You might be asked to explain why psychology is a science, or what makes something a science and something else not. To answer these types of questions you need to know what constitutes a science, so make sure you read this section carefully!"

THE SCIENTIFIC PROCESS

The process of science is always to strive for the truth. The end point of the scientific method is a theory that explains what it is that we are investigating. Building a theory is the end point of what can sometimes seem like a long process. Science does not stop there. Once a theory is built it is developed and modified by research that continues to be carried out. For instance, a well-known theory of memory, the working memory model, has been developed, added to and altered on many occasions since its original introduction.

EMPIRICAL METHOD AND DEDUCTIVE REASONING

An empirical method is one that allows us to collect data that can lead us to a conclusion. In psychology, an empirical method is one which permits us to observe or measure some aspect of behaviour and use our findings either to develop existing theories or to introduce new ones. This is central to our understanding of psychology as a science.

By employing empirical methods that allow us to develop hypotheses which we can go out and test, we are engaging in a process called *deductive reasoning* – we have a hypothesis or theory we assume to be correct and we test it in various ways to see if it stands up. It follows from this that psychology is only a science as long as its theories are actually testable, using the scientific method. This is why the issue of whether psychology is a science is still debated by scientists and philosophers, since many psychological theories cannot be tested empirically.

This process, often called the *hypothetico-deductive method*, is shown in the following diagram.

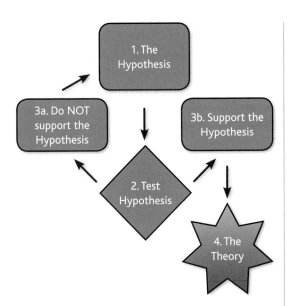

1. The Hypothesis

The scientific process begins with the hypothesis: this is the statement, based on the aims of our research, that will be tested.

2. Test Hypothesis

Appropriate methods of investigation are chosen that allow us to test the hypothesis.

3a. Do NOT support the Hypothesis

If the results of the tests are inconsistent with the hypothesis and therefore do not allow us to support it, we go back to the drawing board, and rethink the hypothesis itself. The procedure begins again, flowing through points 1, 2 and 3.

3b. Support the Hypothesis

If the results of the tests chosen in point 2 are consistent with the hypothesis then we can accept it and move on to our final goal.

4. The Theory

The findings of carefully constructed research that support the hypothesis allow us to begin to form a theory or modify one that already exists.

THEORY CONSTRUCTION

Theories are constructed by using the route of hypothesis testing, development and retesting that we have identified here as the scientific process. In the majority of cases a theory does not depend on one piece of research. It is the end result of a range of work, usually from a number of different sources and researchers. Once the theory is developed it continues to be tested – and this brings us to a very important point. The most important aspect of a scientific theory is that it must be testable and ultimately falsifiable. This may sound odd, but a good theory must always be falsifiable. By this we mean that researchers must be able to develop ideas that can ultimately end in the rejection or development of the theory. Some of the most famous theories ever developed in science are just theories and are still being tested. One day they too may be shown to be incorrect in some way, making room for new theories. For instance, Einstein developed the theory of relativity in a series of scientific works between 1905 and 1915. While a huge amount of research in science has taken place on the assumption that this famous idea is entirely correct, the theory may yet be shown to be wrong. If this is the case then it may be developed or rejected altogether. This is the hallmark of a good, scientific theory.

The problem of unfalsifiability is one of the criticisms of the work of Sigmund Freud. His theory of the subconscious is that it is made up of three interacting components – the id, ego and superego. This idea is unfalsifiable. It cannot be tested and as such is not regarded as truly scientific. It seems that some parts of psychology are more scientific than others!

THE GENERATION OF LAWS/PRINCIPLES

A scientific law, or principle, is a statement that describes the behaviour of things in the real world. For instance, Newton described a series of laws that tell us how items behave in the universe. Newton's first law, for instance, says that every object in a uniform state of motion tends to remain in that state of motion until an external force is applied to it. This means that if something is moving along it will continue to move along in the same way unless it is influenced by something else. This is a law. It always happens. A scientific law or principle can be thought of as a development of a scientific theory. The theory is tested and retested and, once there is enough evidence in its favour, it can be developed into laws and principles.

INDUCTIVE REASONING

Let's return for a moment to Newton's laws. How can we really accept Newton's ideas as laws when it is impossible to have tested every single incidence of an object bumping into another object. We cannot possibly know whether Newton's ideas hold true all the time so how can they be regarded as laws? The answer to this lies in the principle of *inductive reasoning*. If something usually works and if every observed case of something provides the same result, we can *induce* from this that the same thing will happen for all cases. In other words, we can *generalise* our law and apply it in many situations to explain other things. Here's an example. What colour are crows? You have not seen every crow in the world, but no doubt you have seen quite a few. The ones you will have seen are all black. You therefore induce from your observations that all crows are black. This example also demonstrates the value of inductive reasoning in science. Conclusions based on inductive reasoning are only ever generalisations based on limited evidence (for example, the evidence of your observations that all the crows you have ever seen are black). We can make inductive arguments more probable by adding evidence in their favour, or we can question them with contradictory evidence (for example, we go out and look for a crow that is not black). Either way, we are increasing our understanding through science.

PARSIMONY

There is often more than one explanation for a hypothesis. One of them might be quite complicated, requiring complex arguments and further untested assumptions. On the other hand, another explanation might be much more straightforward, with its assumption based firmly on what we already know. Despite the fact that both accounts explain the hypothesis, the principle of parsimony states that we should select the least complex one. In this way, parsimony ensures that our explanation does not go beyond the available empirical evidence. We can see the principle of parsimony in the logical principle of Occam's razor. This is a principle identified by a monk called William of Ockham in the 14th century which basically states that, given two or more explanations for an observed event, we should select the simplest one as the better. It's as straightforward as that.

GREAT THINKERS: KARL POPPER

Karl Popper (1902–1994) provided a vital way of thinking about science that has led to today's understanding of hypothesis testing and theory construction. It was Popper who said that a theory must be falsifiable in order to be considered as scientific. Any amount of evidence can be presented to support a theory, but only a single piece of evidence that shows the theory to be incorrect is needed for it to be falsified. Popper went on to use this central idea of science to attack the study of psychoanalysis and the work of Sigmund Freud as unfalsifiable and therefore not scientific.

GREAT THINKERS: THOMAS KUHN

Thomas Kuhn (1922–1996) wrote a very important book called *The Structure of Scientific Revolutions*. In it he says that science progresses quite happily most of the time but occasionally it undergoes a sort of shake-up, which is described as a *paradigm shift*. A paradigm is a way of thinking about something. If, perhaps because of the importance of a small group of researchers, people begin to think about their science differently, then the direction taken by science will change. Psychodynamic theory, behaviourism and biological ways of thinking about psychology, for example, can all be described as paradigms.

Kuhn says that each paradigm, or way of thinking, has its own framework of assumptions. Because of this, someone working in one paradigm cannot provide evidence in support of, or falsifying, a theory in another paradigm, because the principles upon which each paradigm is based are different. In psychology we can think of it as being illustrated by the example that research into the ideas of Freud under the paradigm of psychodynamicism cannot falsify research provided by medical psychologists in the neuropsychological paradigm. This is because the psychodynamic paradigm assumes the existence of the subconscious, and it is partly upon this assumption that the research is built. The neuropsychological paradigm is concerned with the physical activity of the brain and does not accept that the subconscious exists. It follows that information from the one paradigm cannot be used to falsify theories from the other.

The implications of this idea are huge for those interested in driving science forward and testing and building theories. Earlier in this chapter we discussed one of the principles of science, formalised by Popper, that a theory must be falsifiable. If the work of a researcher shows that a theory is incorrect, that theory will be rejected or changed to accommodate the new findings. If Kuhn's thinking is to be accepted, a paradigm shift will change this idea completely. If the discipline undergoes a change in direction, brought about by a paradigm shift, then the findings of a researcher, working under assumptions of an old paradigm, may be seen not as 'important, and falsifying the theory'. Instead they may be seen as a mistake made by the researcher, and the new paradigm theory continues, unchanged, simply because an old paradigm was used to derive the results that would otherwise have falsified the theory.

VALIDATING NEW KNOWLEDGE

Just because a researcher carries out some work that he or she is convinced will change the world, this does not mean that it will be accepted by the rest of the scientific community. Having work published really gives it a stamp of approval. If something appears in print then other scientists can have access to it, and thus have the chance to read and challenge it. Traditionally, research is published in scientific journals. These are magazine-like publications which appear one or more times a year. Getting research published however is not as easy as just sending it to the publisher. In science the principle of peer review is applied.

PEER REVIEW

When a psychologist completes a piece of research it is written in a generally agreed format and then sent to a psychological journal for consideration. If the journal thinks the work is good enough they will publish it for all to see. The process of assessing whether it is good enough for publication is normally peer review. The work is sent to one or more established scientists with similar expertise (who usually remain anonymous) for them to read and perhaps criticise its method and thinking. It is then sent back to the researchers with recommendations for revision. If the work does not meet the standards of the peer reviewers it will not be published. This system ensures that standards of quality are maintained in research and that unsubstantiated claims are not made.

The peer review system is certainly very highly regarded but it is not without its critics. For instance, just because something is not thought by a reviewer to be appropriate for publishing, this does not mean that others would feel the same way. It could be that the reviewer is providing a fair assessment, in which case the work should be rejected and looked at by the researchers again. It could be, however, that the reviewer is biased in some way. It may be that the paper under consideration is expressing an opinion that the reviewer disagrees with. If this is the case the reviewer may be approaching the review from a position of bias. In situations like these, research may not be widely seen by the community, just because of the opinions of a single reviewer.

Some peer reviewed academic journals are more highly thought of than others, and researchers try their best to have their work published in them. For instance, the journals *Nature* and *Science* are regarded as extremely prestigious. Universities

encourage their researchers to publish in such journals and not in less prestigious titles – and for this reason, some research, if rejected by highly respected journals, may never see the light of day because researchers feel "If it's not good enough for *Nature*, it's just not good enough."

Academic journals are extraordinarily expensive to buy. Many university libraries can only afford a relatively small number each year, and most provide the journals online through very expensive licensing agreements, with annual costs often running into hundreds of thousands of pounds. This means that the general public, or less wealthy colleges and universities, may not have access to the published research and so it remains relatively unread. Its use in advancing psychology is therefore limited. For reasons like these, exciting alternatives to traditional publishing have appeared – the latest of which is open access.

With open access, new knowledge can be viewed by the scientific community as well as the general public, allowing everyone to make up their own minds about the research. Open access can be combined with a form of peer review, as with the online journal *Philica.com*. On sites like these new ideas are rated by academics. Those rated as good contain ideas that might be trusted; those rated as bad are less likely to be trusted.

Despite numerous obstacles and sometimes long timescales involved in getting research published, the publication of psychological research is important for many reasons. Journals are international, which means that there will be widespread dissemination of the new research among peers. The work will therefore be more likely to be discussed and debated and the ideas possibly built upon with further research. The whole community will benefit from news of new developments, and

THE PUBLISHING PROCESS

Researcher submits an article to a journal. The choice of journal may be determined by:

● The journal's audience: is it the appropriate audience for the article?

● The journal's prestige: is it well known? Is it often cited?

The author is unpaid, but may pay 'page charges' (see terminology).

The journal selects two or more appropriate experts to peer review the article, without payment.

The peer reviewers assess:

● The quality of the research and the way it is reported

● The relevance of the article to the journal's readership

● Its novelty and interest

● Its content, structure and language.

Feedback from the reviewers determines whether or not the article is accepted. Acceptance rates vary from journal to journal.

The rejected article is returned to the author or the accepted article is passed to the editors employed by the publishers, either in-house or freelance.

The editors ensure that:

● The language of the article (particularly if it has been produced by a non-native speaker) is clear and unambiguous

● The standard style of nomenclature is adhered to

● Illustrative material is of a sufficiently high standard.

Editors also establish live links in the electronic version to the references cited and to other material such as data sets.

Where a journal exists in both paper and digital formats, the article is sent to the printer to produce a paper copy; and will be formatted for the online version of the journal.

Reproduced from: *Select Committee on Science and Technology: Tenth Report.*

---

because peer review ensures that only the best research gets published, the scientific community can be assured of the quality of the research.

Publication in peer reviewed journals can do a great deal to enhance the reputation of researchers. Not only are they more esteemed but, because of a good research and publication record, they also stand a better chance of obtaining funding for further research. Published research also provides enormous benefits for the institutions the researchers work for. Most research takes place in universities, which are funded by government grants. The amount of money a university gets is partly based on periodic audits of the university's research output, including the amount of published work they generate (the process is called the Research Assessment Exercise, or RAE). The publication of journal articles is therefore of crucial importance to both the researcher and their respective institutions.

DESIGNING PSYCHOLOGICAL INVESTIGATIONS

In AS psychology you will have had experience of a number of investigative methods and techniques that are available to psychologists. Which they choose will depend on the type of research they are doing.

CARRYING OUT RESEARCH

Psychology is a science and psychologists rely on scientific methods of knowledge acquisition in just the same way as do other scientists, such as chemists and biologists. The goal of psychology is to collect information about human behaviour and this is done by careful observation and measurement, which provides *empirical* evidence.

Research must be carried out carefully, and psychologists must be aware of issues that could influence their results: this includes the requirement to be as objective as possible. One way to be sure of taking appropriate care in our research is to follow certain steps to ensure we really are investigating what we want to investigate and asking the right sort of questions in our work. These steps are as follows:

Step 1: AIMS Be sure of the aim of your research. For instance, you might be interested in investigating whether those that smoke cigarettes have a worse memory than those that do not smoke cigarettes. Your *aim* here is to investigate the effects of smoking on memory.

Step 2: HYPOTHESIS Based on your aims, your hypothesis makes a statement that you can set about testing. It can be directional, and predict a certain type of influence on behaviour (e.g. smoking makes memory ability worse), or it can be non-directional, where a change in behaviour in either direction is not predicted, just that there will be a change (e.g. smoking will *alter* people's memory ability). In the latter case memory ability may get better or it may get worse.

Step 3: IDENTIFY VARIABLES Variables are things that change in the research. The one you control and change is called the *independent variable*. The one that you measure is called the *dependent variable*. Anything that *might* change the dependent variable other than the independent variable is called an *extraneous variable*. If the extraneous

variable *does* influence the dependent variable it has confounded your results and is referred to as a *confounding variable*.

Step 4: OPERATIONALISE VARIABLES This rather grand term simply means 'make them happen', i.e. make the variables measurable. So, if your independent variable is 'smoking', you will operationalise this by choosing some people who smoke and some who do not. Your dependent variable is 'memory ability' so you can operationalise this by designing a memory test, remembering a list of words perhaps, or a string of numbers – the more a person can remember, the better their memory.

Step 5: DECIDE ON A METHOD There may be a number of methods available for your study, and the choice depends in part on what it is specifically you are investigating.

Step 6: CONSIDER ETHICS Ethics are a vital part of research. Ethical principles include informed consent, deception, debriefing, the right to withdraw, confidentiality and protection.

Step 7: LOCATE YOUR POPULATION AND SAMPLE We choose a sample of a population. There are essentially three ways open to you: random, opportunity and volunteer sampling.

Step 8: PILOT IT and COLLECT YOUR DATA A pilot is a smaller scale version of the main study, used as a sort of 'dry run'. It helps you iron out any problems. When the pilot is complete and you are happy with the procedure, gather the data for real.

Step 9: ANALYSIS This means looking at what the data are telling us, i.e. what they mean. Later in this chapter we'll add more about this idea of analysis.

Step 10: PRESENT YOUR DATA There's more on this later on, but essentially you need to decide on the best way to present your data. You can do this with numbers, using tables to show your descriptive statistics (measures of central tendency and dispersion). You might also want to use a graph.

Step 11: FINDINGS AND CONCLUSIONS Look carefully at your results and decide what they show in terms of your hypothesis and psychological theory.

SELECTING APPROPRIATE RESEARCH METHODS

The good researcher is aware of a number of different methods and techniques. In reality, many professional researchers tend to concentrate on one or two methods because their research is very focused on particular areas, but for new psychologists a good overall knowledge is required.

It is useful to make sure that you know the difference between an experimental design and a non-experimental design. In a true laboratory experiment, it is the researcher who makes changes to variables and measures the result of those changes. For instance, in an experiment to measure the influence of chocolate eating on feelings of happiness it will be the experimenter who will give the participants one, two or three pieces of chocolate to eat, and who will measure, after each is consumed, how happy the person is. It is the experimenter who is in charge of the independent variable, in this case the chocolate. In a non-experimental design a variable is not manipulated by the researcher.

"Much of this material will be familiar to you from AS level. However, because it is vital that you understand all the research methods you cover on the A level course, we will now provide a useful overview. Remember – you are expected to know this stuff! Be prepared to revisit your AS work to expand on what we present here. For example, make sure you are aware of the advantages and weaknesses of the various methods."

EXPERIMENTAL DESIGNS

When we carry out an experiment, we change something and see what happens to something else. As we've already said, the something we change is called the independent variable, and the thing that changes as a result is the dependent variable. Once you've decided that you are running an experiment there are three designs open to you. Each has its advantages and weaknesses.

"Think carefully about the three different design choices. If you are asked in the exam to evaluate the methodology used in a piece of experimental research, displaying a knowledge of the different types of designs and the advantages and weaknesses of each would be an ideal way to gain marks."

To make things simpler, we will discuss three different designs for the same experiment. Imagine you were interested in investigating whether it was possible to stand on one leg longer in silence than when listening to music. You never know, you might be interested in something like that. Your independent variable would be whether there was music, or whether there was silence: it has two levels, music and silence. Your dependent variable (the thing you measured) would be the time the person managed to spend standing on one leg without falling over. The three possible designs for your experiment are identified and described below.

1. REPEATED MEASURES DESIGN

A repeated measures design is one where each participant takes part in each level of the independent variable. In our imagined experiment, this means that each participant does the test in silence and then each of them does the test with music.

Advantages

The same person takes part in each level of the independent variable and so there are no problems of individual differences, such as fitness and age. This means you do not need to use a huge number of participants, so the research can be completed sooner and, if you are paying your participants, for less money.

Weaknesses

There are possible order effects. This means that the time spent standing on one leg in silence may have influenced the time spent on one leg when listening to music. The person may have become tired and fallen over more easily on the second occasion. This is called a fatigue effect. Similarly, the person may have become more used to standing on one leg, lasting longer on the second occasion. This is called a practice effect.

2. INDEPENDENT GROUPS

An independent groups design uses two groups of participants. One group stands on one leg in silence and one group stands on one leg while listening to music.

Advantages

The major advantage of an independent groups design is that it completely eliminates order effects such as practice and fatigue.

Weaknesses

The difficulty with independent groups designs is that they are open to problems associated with individual differences. For instance, imagine the UK 'standing on one leg' Olympic team was in one group, and the old ladies' lawn bowls team was in the other group. That would hardly make a fair comparison! The way to avoid this is to have two huge groups. If you do that, the range of individual differences in one group would be similar to the range in the other group.

3. MATCHED PAIRS

The matched pairs design is like an independent groups design, but each person in one group is matched with a person in the other group. For instance, if you had an 82-year-old pensioner in one group, you should match them with an 82-year-old pensioner in the other group. Each person in each group has a matched person in the other group.

Advantages

The great thing about matching is that it controls for individual differences, and since it is a variation of an independent groups design, there are no problems with order effects either.

Weaknesses

Matching is extremely difficult, or even impossible. Even if you do have an 82-year-old pensioner in each group you are not to know whether one has had a huge amount of 'standing on one leg' experience while the other may be an absolute novice. In fact, even if you had identical twins, and allocated one to each group, you could not be sure whether their experiences and skills were identical. These individual differences have not been matched, and may influence your result. It is impossible to match people in different groups perfectly.

THE LABORATORY EXPERIMENT

In general, the laboratory experiment is run in carefully controlled conditions, and uses a standardised procedure. Variables are manipulated (the independent variable), are controlled (extraneous or confounding variables) and measurements are carefully taken (the dependent variable).

A good laboratory experiment has the following characteristics. It is…

Replicable – it can be repeated by other researchers

Generalisable – the results can refer to people outside the sample that you tested

Reliable – a repeat of the experiment will yield the same results

Valid – it measures what it says it measures.

THE FIELD EXPERIMENT

This is like a laboratory experiment, but the variables are manipulated by the researcher out in a more real-world setting. The advantages of this are that the real-world setting offers ecological validity and the people acting as participants in the experiment often need not know they are part of the study, eliminating any demand characteristics. The problem however is that these studies are often extremely expensive and time consuming to carry out.

THE NATURAL EXPERIMENT

Here the researcher makes use of a naturally occurring independent variable. For instance, the researcher may have the idea that towns near the seaside are perceived as more fun than towns inland. The researcher cannot change the position of the sea and so the independent variable, in this case proximity to the sea, is naturally occurring. The advantages of the natural experiment are those of the field experiment: it is high in ecological validity and there are few or no demand characteristics. The disadvantages are that the researcher has no control at all over the independent variable and so the chance of unwanted things influencing the experimental findings (confounding variables) is quite high.

THE QUASI EXPERIMENT

This looks rather like a lab experiment but it's not. Imagine you wanted to see whether Americans or English people were better at mathematics. You would locate a group of Americans and a group of English people and give each group a maths test. The allocation of participants to a group is done on the basis of their nationality, your independent variable. However, nationality cannot be manipulated, and so it's not a true experiment.

THE CASE STUDY

Some research offers a careful and systematic investigation of the case of an individual. Examples

LABORATORY EXPERIMENT	
ADVANTAGES	**WEAKNESSES**
● Replicability	● Cannot always use a lab experiment
● Easy to control variables	● More control means less natural
● Generalisability	● May be demand characteristics and experimenter effects, both of which may influence the results

might include Freud's investigation of Anna O, or the case of Phineas Gage.

The advantages of a case study are that it can be extremely detailed and may provide wonderfully rich and informative data about the person. The disadvantage of course is that generalisability is extremely low, as the case of that particular individual may well be unusual and unrelated to the rest of the population. Also, as case studies gather data from the past, the information may not be very reliable. Memory has an annoying habit of fading over time, and the responses a person may give regarding their past may not be entirely accurate.

THE OBSERVATIONAL METHOD

This is extremely obvious at first glance, and deceptively simple. It clearly means a method where researchers observe the behaviour of others. You will not be surprised to hear that it is not quite that simple. There are two main divisions of observational method. *Participant observation* is where the person doing the observing is part of the group they are observing. For instance, if observing the behaviour of a football team, the observer may be part of that team. *Non-participant observation* is where the observer is not part of the group they are observing. For instance, an observer may be investigating incidences of aggressive behaviour in the playgrounds of secondary schools. They themselves are not part of the group of students being observed. There are three things to watch out for in the observational method:

1. Awareness of the observer: If those being observed are aware of the person doing the observing then their behaviour may change and will not be natural.

2. Behavioural categories: The observer must decide what exactly they are looking for in the observation. These categories can form a checklist for use during the observation.

3. Bias: If the observer is not objective the results will be biased. Using multiple observers and

comparing their observations after each session can overcome this problem.

Finally, the observational method can be carried out in two different ways. Having chosen the behaviour to be observed – for example, aggression – the observer may count how many incidences of the behaviour occur during a period of time (*time sampling*), or may record all incidences of the behaviour (*event sampling*).

"When you think about observational methods, consider possible ethical implications of these methods. Is it ethically acceptable to observe someone who doesn't know they are being observed? Is it ethically acceptable to observe groups such as children, who may be regarded as 'vulnerable'?"

OBSERVATIONAL METHODS VS. OBSERVATIONAL TECHNIQUES

Observation can be a *method* and observation can be a *technique*. The observational method is a type of research in its own right. The observational technique, however, is something that you can use in any type of research. It's best to think of the observational technique as a tool that researchers use and the observational method as a style of research that they undertake. For instance, you might use the observational technique to count up how many people on the high street are carrying sales bags after an advertising campaign by a local shop. You are using the technique of observing to measure the impact of the campaign in a natural experiment.

CONTENT ANALYSIS

Content analysis is a form of observational method, but instead of watching people behave, the researcher analyses the content of a text or film. For instance, they may be investigating the use in newspapers of terms that might be regarded as racist, and how this might have changed over the years. They would decide on the racist terms

SAMPLING OF OBSERVATIONS	
ADVANTAGES	**WEAKNESSES**
● Natural settings, so natural behaviours are observed.	● Observer bias if researchers don't remain objective.
● Allows otherwise impossible or hard-to-example behaviours (e.g. aggression in children) to be investigated.	● Confounding variables may interfere, making it hard to determine the cause for something happening.
● Few demand characteristics because the observed are not put into a false situation and may not know they are being observed at all.	● Small groups are usually observed, making the results hard to generalise.

to watch out for and then look through newspapers marking down how often the terms were used.

SELF-REPORT TECHNIQUES

These include questionnaires and interviews. Here a participant records or expresses their own opinions and feelings about something. Both techniques have individual strengths and weaknesses, but both share the weakness that they are self-report and so the truthfulness of the answers may be in question as participants may respond in such a way as to make themselves appear socially desirable.

A questionnaire is a list of prewritten questions. These may be 'closed', where alternative responses are offered; or 'open', where free responses are offered; or possibly rank-order, where you are required to place things in some kind of order. The advantages of questionnaires are that they are a cheap way of collecting lots of data while retaining participant anonymity. The disadvantages are that those who agree to complete the questionnaires may be doing so because they like to help out, or the topic covered is of interest to them. The sample may, in this way, be biased. Also, some people chosen to complete the questionnaire at 'random' may decide not to do so, which means your random sample is no longer random, as you have to choose someone else to take part.

An interview is like a questionnaire, in that it provides self-report data drawn directly from a participant. Interviews may be 'structured', where the questions are very organised and rigid; they may be 'semi-structured', where the control and organisation is less rigid and the interviewer is offered more flexibility; or they may be 'unstructured', where the interview is completely free and uncontrolled. The advantages of the interview are that it can provide very rich and insightful data and can be very simple and fast to carry out, with generalisable findings if the sample is big enough. The disadvantages are those of the questionnaire. In addition to this, a person may provide quite different responses to the same questions in an interview on different occasions, thus threatening the validity of the results.

CORRELATION METHOD

Correlational analysis lets us see how two variables are related. For instance, height and shoe size; or ability at maths and ability at chess. Just as with observation, the correlational method is a research design option in its own right, but correlation analysis can be used with data from any other method where appropriate. The analysis provides a statistic called the correlation coefficient, which varies from −1 to +1.

A correlation coefficient of near to −1 indicates a strong negative correlation, which means as one variable increases in size the other decreases. For instance, the more money you spend, the less money you have to spend. This may not be a perfect negative correlation because we have not accounted for the amount of money you may be earning, so occasionally spending some money may not, in fact, result in a reduction in the amount that remains, if some wages have been paid to you.

A correlation coefficient of 0 means that there is no relationship at all between the two variables. For instance, there is no relationship between the amount of carrots grown in Israel and the number of cartoons on the TV between 3 and 4 p.m. on a Tuesday afternoon.

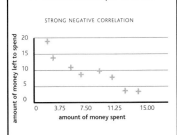

NEGATIVE (LESS THAN 0)
A 'downward slope' is seen.

The more perfect the line, the closer to −1 the correlation is. A strong negative correlation is one close to a perfectly straight downward-sloping line.

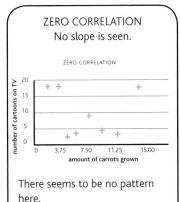

ZERO CORRELATION
No slope is seen.

There seems to be no pattern here.

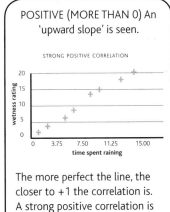

POSITIVE (MORE THAN 0) An 'upward slope' is seen.

The more perfect the line, the closer to +1 the correlation is. A strong positive correlation is one close to a perfectly straight upward-sloping line.

CORRELATIONS

ADVANTAGES	WEAKNESSES

● Naturally occurring variables can be measured and a relationship between the two identified. This may lead to future research.

● Cannot imply cause or effect, and variables are almost impossible to control. Even if the analysis indicates that there is no relationship we cannot be certain of that. It could be that something else that we have not measured or considered is happening that the analysis is not sensitive to.

A correlation coefficient of near to +1 means that there is a strong positive correlation between the two variables. As one goes up, so does the other. For instance, the longer it rains, the wetter you will get if standing outside. This may not be a perfect positive correlation because it may be that at some point your clothing becomes completely saturated and, however much more rain falls on you, you cannot possibly get any wetter.

Correlations are represented on scattergraphs (also known as scattergrams). On page 475 we have three scatterplots identifying the relationships described above.

Do not think that correlation means cause. It does not. Just because two variables are positively correlated does not mean that one causes the other. For instance, it is extremely likely that were you to collect the data you would find that the number of cars on the roads of the United Kingdom has risen steadily over the last ten years. You would also probably find that the number of people taking holidays abroad has gone up. The two variables (car sales and holidays abroad) are likely to be positively correlated. We cannot conclude, however, that increased car sales have caused people to take more holidays. There may be a third factor that we have not considered, such as 'amount of disposable income' that is related to both of these variables, but that we have not measured.

WATCH OUT! DEMAND CHARACTERISTICS AND INVESTIGATOR EFFECTS

There are a few things to keep in mind when designing research. Demand characteristics, investigator effects, reliability and validity can all cause problems for a researcher.

Demand characteristics – Something in a research design may change a participant's behaviour. If this happens then your data will not give you a true picture of what's going on in your study. For instance, participants who know something about the procedure may alter their behaviour to provide the researcher with the responses they *think* the researcher would like. Researchers often design 'single blind' procedures to eliminate, or at least attempt to eliminate, demand characteristics. These are procedures where participants are kept naive about the aims of the research. It is the job of the researcher to plan the study so as to minimise demand characteristics. Eliminating them is often very difficult indeed.

Investigator effects – These are a little like demand characteristics, but you should try not to mix them up! Research suffers with investigator effects when the researchers themselves influence the behaviour of the participant in some way. They may not do so on purpose, but they may give away their opinion in some way which may encourage

Investigator Effects

Demand Characteristics

the participant to respond differently for the rest of the session. Researchers may introduce a *double-blind* procedure to eliminate these effects. Here the researcher *and* the participant do not know of the aims of the research, and so neither can influence the results by inadvertently responding in certain ways.

"Demand characteristics, investigator effects, reliability and validity are extremely useful things to consider when you comment on the research you read about. Have these in mind when thinking critically about the methodology used. You can often pick up valuable marks by making one or two effective comments based on these issues when evaluating research."

SAMPLING STRATEGIES

Finding participants is something that all researchers have to do. A group of participants is referred to as a *sample*. A researcher cannot test everyone in the world, and would not want to. The idea is to select a sample of people who can be described as representative of the wider population. If the sample really is representative then we can say that we are able to *generalise* our results to the larger group. There are three sampling strategies, each with strengths and weaknesses that have implications for your research.

RANDOM SAMPLING

This is where all of the people in a population have the same chance of being selected.

Generalisability and bias

The vulnerability of random samples to dropouts means that the sample is easily biased, as the researcher must either go with a reduced sample or choose another random participant, who by the very fact that they were not originally 'randomly chosen' is not very random at all.

Similarly, it's very difficult to carry out a truly random sample if you have a very large population as it is unlikely that you will have a complete list of names from which to choose. This means that not everyone is equally likely to be chosen and so the sample is not truly random, but rather, it is biased towards 'people on your list'.

You must ask yourself how the names got onto the list in the first place. For instance, researchers may have used a telephone directory. If this was the case then the sample would be limited to those that own a phone and have their details listed. Some researchers may use the electoral register. If they do this then the sample is limited to those people who are 18 or over who have indicated that they wish to be able to vote in elections; and further limited because people whose names are on the full register are allowed to opt out of inclusion on the shorter version, to which researchers and others have access. In both these cases the sample is not generalisable to those in the population who do not meet these criteria.

OPPORTUNITY SAMPLING

This is where anyone handy is asked to participate. The most typical opportunity sample in psychology is one where researchers simply ask people in their department or college to take part. For instance, a researcher may put up a notice asking for people to help out in their research, or may simply approach people in the cafe and ask them for help.

Generalisability and bias

Typically, researchers choose people to take part from their own social group. They may, if not deliberately, choose people they would like to take part, whom they find attractive in some way. Or they may choose people who have taken part in previous research, and whom they trust. It may even be that the researchers only ask those who they think are least likely to reject their requests. Since choices are made, and the samples are drawn, from such a narrow population, the extent to which the findings can be generalised to the wider population is very limited.

Similarly, those who take part may have their own motives for doing so. At university, students may take part in their lecturer's research because they may feel that helping out will gain them more marks. This may leave the research open to bias in that the participant may attempt to provide data that will please the researcher in some way.

The other problem with an opportunity sample is that only those who want to take part do so. This means that you may find that the sample has a large proportion of 'helpful' or 'interested' participants, who may provide biased data. Obviously, this reduces the generalisability of the findings, as the sample is not reflective of the wider, general population. This means it has low ecological validity – we'll cover this more in a moment.

VOLUNTEER SAMPLING

This is also known as 'self-selected' sampling. Here people who want to take part do so. For example, a noticeboard or newspaper advertisement may be used to ask for volunteers to respond.

Generalisability and bias

The findings of the research may lack generalisability because a volunteer sample may consist of mostly helpful, interested, more motivated or obedient people and as such it may not be like the general population. In addition to this a volunteer sample may be open to bias as those who take part may do so in order to seem helpful and so please the researcher – who is often their psychology lecturer, and who therefore has the power to provide good marks on their work!

ISSUES OF RELIABILITY

Reliability refers to how well the research can be replicated at another time, or if two researchers carried out observations how well their opinions of what was observed agree. In short, reliability refers to the consistency of the research. As reliability increases so does our confidence in the results.

OBSERVER RELIABILITY

A widely used method and technique in psychological research is observation. Here the researchers observe behaviour, marking down what they see. Often they are looking for particular types or categories of behaviour. For example, researchers may be interested in investigating whether male children behave more aggressively at play when surrounded by other males or when in a mixed male/female environment. In this case researchers would observe the behaviour of males in a male-only play environment, recording the number of times they saw aggressive behaviour. They would then compare these results with similar observations made in a mixed male/female environment.

The results of research like this will not be of much use if the observations are not done in the same way – i.e. if they are not consistent. We need to ensure that another person observing the behaviour would come up with the same, or at least a very similar, result. For this reason two observers make observations at each session. Their results are compared for similarity. If the two sets of observations are similar then we can say that there is good observer reliability.

Assessing observer reliability

Comparing the observations of two observers is best done using correlation. This relatively simple statistical technique allows us to see how similar two sets of values are. A good positive correlation shows that the two observers provided similar results. If you can show a good positive correlation to two observations of the same event then you can say confidently that you had good observer reliability.

Improving observer reliability

1. Training

If the two observers are able to easily identify the type of behaviours they are watching then they will be able to record those behaviours efficiently. Practice certainly makes perfect as observation is a great skill. Until you try it, you'll not fully believe how fast the different behaviours come and how varied the behaviours that might be recorded are in different situations. For this reason, carefully training the observers before the research begins is advisable as a means of improving observer reliability.

2. Operationalisation

Both observers have to be clear exactly what they are looking for. For instance, if they are observing 'helping' behaviours then they must agree what this means. For instance, how 'helpful' does a behaviour need to be before they record it as 'helpful'? If the definitions of the behaviours to be observed are clear and carefully laid out then observer reliability will be better than if categories of behaviour are badly defined.

3. View of the behaviours

Each observer must have the same ability to see the behaviours being observed. The best way to do this is to have them both base their recordings of behaviour on exactly the same video film of the behaviours being recorded. This ensures that each observer sees exactly the same things. If the observations are recorded 'live', perhaps by watching behaviours in a school playground, then different sight lines may mean that incidences of a behaviour may be missed by one observer but recorded by the other. This would weaken the correlation between their results, and so weaken observer reliability.

TEST RELIABILITY

Various tests are employed in psychological research to measure behaviour. If a researcher is interested in assessing someone's personality then they can use a test carefully designed to do the job. These tests are often in the form of questionnaires and measurement scales that require the participants to indicate opinions of things, and how they might respond or behave in different situations.

Assessing test reliability

Assessing test reliability is very similar to assessing observer reliability. The method used here is *test–retest assessment*, or *test–retest correlation*. Here the test is given to the person again, on a different occasion. The person's responses to the test on each occasion are compared and a correlation carried out. If there is a high correlation between the responses on each presentation of the test then we can say that there is a high level of test–retest reliability. This means that the test measures what it says it does consistently.

Improving test reliability

Altering the test to improve correlation

If the test–retest correlation is low, then the reliability of the test is in question. This means that the researchers must alter the test to improve this reliability. They can do this by looking carefully at the test itself, and identifying the parts of it that did not correlate well on the two occasions it was given. They can then remove those components of the test that are weakening its reliability and replace them with alternative questions and tasks. This new test is then tested again, to see whether reliability has improved, using the test–retest correlation assessment. This process is repeated until a high level of test–retest reliability is shown by a strongly correlated first and second running of the test.

ASSESSING AND IMPROVING VALIDITY

Validity refers to how well the test or research actually measures what it says it measures. A tape measure, for instance, is a very valid tool for measuring height, but a stop-watch is not. Similarly, research that aims to measure the relationship between mathematics ability and age is valid if it does just that, but not if it actually measures the relationship between age and general intelligence.

INTERNAL VALIDITY

Internal validity is the extent to which we can say that our findings are truly to do with what we think they are to do with, rather than something that we have no control over. For instance, we may be interested in investigating whether memory ability is improved by eating chocolate. We must be sure that the person has not secretly drunk lots of cups of tea before the experiment. If the results of our research showed that their memory was indeed improved by chocolate eating we cannot be absolutely sure that the tea did not have

something to do with it, and so the task has low internal validity.

Improving internal validity

Anything that influences the dependent variable (in this case the score on a memory task) rather than our independent variable (here it's chocolate eating) reduces the internal validity of our research. In general these things are described as extraneous variables. If an extraneous variable (such as fatigue or practice) influences our findings, then internal validity is reduced. One of the most important aspects of research design is to minimise the influences of extraneous variables. Improved internal validity comes from improved resistance of your research to the influence of extraneous variables. This is best achieved by very careful research design and planning.

EXTERNAL VALIDITY

The results of our research have external validity if they can be generalised from our sample to the general population, in other settings beyond those in which the research was carried out and at different times.

ECOLOGICAL VALIDITY

This is a form of external validity. If the research has high ecological validity then we can say that the results relate to different situations from those in which the research was carried out. Some work carried out in a laboratory, for instance, may lack ecological validity, because outside the carefully controlled environment of the laboratory people may behave differently.

"Just because something is done in a lab does not mean that it lacks ecological validity. Findings from laboratory based research may transfer to other settings very well. Be careful of this in the exam. Don't just say 'It lacks ecological validity because it was done in a lab'. This won't get you marks. Be more specific. Explain what circumstances outside the lab might bring the ecological validity into question."

POPULATION VALIDITY

If research has high population validity then the findings can be said to relate to the general population. For instance, if a piece of research has used an opportunity sample of 10,000 people chosen from 20 countries worldwide, its findings are more likely to be relevant to the whole population of the world than if the sample had been three people taken from a cafe in Bristol. If we can say confidently that something has high population validity, then similar research carried out on a different sample elsewhere should provide similar results.

TEST VALIDITY

The validity of a test can be measured in three ways.

1. Content validity

The test being used is carefully scrutinised to see whether it really does test what it says it tests. This is usually done by experts who assess the theory behind the content to ensure that there are no omissions.

2. Face validity

This is like content validity but far less rigorous. Face validity refers to how valid a test seems to be 'on the face of it'. To be more certain, a content validity assessment should be made.

3. Predictive validity

This assesses how well a score obtained on the test at one point in time might predict a score obtained on the test at another time. For instance, if the test is carried out on a person when they are 20 years old, we might like to be able to predict their score on the test if carried out at 30 years old. A high predictive validity would allow us to do this.

ETHICAL CONSIDERATIONS IN PSYCHOLOGICAL RESEARCH

It is extremely important to design and carry out psychological research ethically. You will have covered ethical issues in research during your AS studies. A summary of the major issues is provided in the table below.

There is no reason why research should not be carried out ethically. In places where psychological research is conducted, work does not progress until a summary of the proposed investigation has been considered by a committee drawn from different disciplines and walks of life who look specifically at any ethical issues. This 'ethics committee' can agree to allow the research to go ahead as planned; it may opt to reject it until certain ethical issues have been considered; or it may decide to reject the proposal entirely. The committee acts as a safeguard to stop questionable research from taking place.

If ethically questionable research is conducted the penalties for the researchers can be severe. The work is unlikely to find a publisher, and the psychologists responsible may find themselves without access to further research funding: they may even be expelled from the British Psychological Society, the professional body for psychologists working in the UK. Other countries have their own professional bodies who take a similar view on unethical research.

SUMMARY OF ETHICAL CONSIDERATIONS WHEN DESIGNING A RESEARCH STUDY

ETHICAL ISSUE	EXPLANATION
INFORMED CONSENT	Participants must be told what they will be doing and why they are doing it so they can provide 'informed' consent.
DECEPTION	Participants should not be deceived unless absolutely necessary. If deception is required, great care and careful consideration must be given to the project.
DEBRIEFING	After the experiment is complete, participants must be 'debriefed' and informed of the motivations for the experiment. They must be given the chance to ask any questions they have.
RIGHT TO WITHDRAW	Participants should be free to leave the experiment at any time.
CONFIDENTIALITY	Any information and data provided by the participants must be confidential.
PROTECTION	The safety and well-being of the participants must be protected at all times.

DATA ANALYSIS AND REPORTING INVESTIGATIONS

APPROPRIATE SELECTION OF GRAPHS

Data can be presented as graphs, tables or statistics. Always remember that the point of presenting data is to make your results easy to read for those interested in your research.

A graph should be simple and clear, and should be the appropriate type of graph for the data you have. A table should not be messy or complicated, or include too much information, and your statistics should be presented simply and as obviously as you can. Experience has shown us that some people, including professional researchers, do not take nearly enough care when presenting their data and it can really spoil what would otherwise have been an elegant and careful piece of work. Professional researchers will tell you that when looking over the many hundreds of papers that are produced in their field each year, they first look at the title of the article, then the summary at the start, then the results section where the research data is presented. If they find the presentation of the data interesting they may spend time reading the whole article from start to finish. If they do not find the presentation of the data clear then they may put the article to one side, maybe not returning to it at all. It is for this reason that the importance of data presentation should not be underestimated.

There are four types of graph to know about. We have already discussed one of them – the scattergraph – when we talked about correlations. Each type of graph is appropriate for different types of data. Do not draw all of them for all data sets, and do not make the mistake of just drawing your favourite type of graph. It may well not be appropriate.

> *"It is important that you are familiar with graphs. It is much more likely that you will be required to read and interpret the information contained in graphs, rather than draw one. Make sure you practise this skill."*

BAR CHART

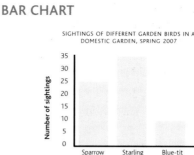

SIGHTINGS OF DIFFERENT GARDEN BIRDS IN A DOMESTIC GARDEN, SPRING 2007

The bar chart is an extremely useful and common way of presenting data. It is used to depict the number of incidences in a particular 'discrete' category. This means that the categories identified do not overlap in any way. In our example we have 'types of bird'. You cannot have a starling that is also a blue-tit. There is no overlap. You might also use this type of graph if you were depicting data separated by gender – for instance, the number of boys enrolled on a football summer school and the number of girls. You cannot have a boy who is also a girl. The two categories do not overlap: they are discrete. Bar charts have:

» Gaps between the bars

» Frequency (number) on the y-axis

» Category labels on the x-axis.

HISTOGRAM

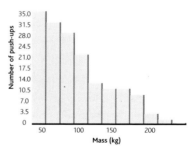

NUMBER OF PUSH-UPS POSSIBLE AT DIFFERENT MASS

The histogram is similar in many ways to the bar chart. The major difference is that in a histogram the x-axis does not depict discrete categories, rather it shows a continuous scale. In our example that scale is mass (kg). If, on the other hand, your data were concerned with temperature and fatigue, you would measure 'degrees Celsius' on the x-axis. Histograms have:

» No gaps between the bars

» A continuous variable on the x-axis.

FREQUENCY POLYGON

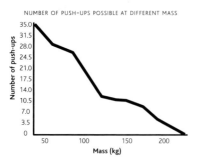

NUMBER OF PUSH-UPS POSSIBLE AT DIFFERENT MASS

The frequency polygon is very similar to the histogram. Imagine a histogram with a point drawn in the centre of the top of each bar. Now, remove all the bars and join up the points. A frequency polygon has:

» A continuous variable on the x-axis

» A continuous line, no bars.

TABLES

The whole point of a table is to present otherwise complicated information in as simple a way as possible. A table should allow readers to find the information they need with as little effort as possible. Tables can be large, containing lots of data, or they may be small, containing data in the form of summary statistics, such as mean, mode and median. In the case below, we have a table showing the mean scores of male and female students in maths, English and science examinations.

	Male	Female
Maths	56	44
English	43	67
Science	51	52

When drawing a table make sure you follow the most important rule: be as clear and straightforward as you can.

WHICH IS BEST?

Each measure of central tendency and dispersion has its good and bad points. A strong descriptive statistic is generally one that takes in a good deal of the raw data in its calculation, so bear that in mind when thinking about which is most suitable. The strengths and weaknesses of each are described below.

	Mean	Mode	Median	Standard deviation	Range	Semi-interquartile range
Strength	Most powerful measure of central tendency as it uses all of the data	The best measure to use if you want to know how often things happen	Not heavily influenced by rogue scores	Uses every value in the data set, not heavily distorted by extreme values and is the most sensitive	Takes extreme scores into consideration and is simple to calculate	Less distorted scores than the range
Weakness	One rogue score (large or small) can heavily influence it. For instance, the mean of 3, 4 and 8 is 5. The mean of 3, 4, 8 and 1,005 is 255. The extreme value has seriously influenced the mean	Sometimes a data set does not have a most common value and sometimes it has lots of common values	Not good for using with small data sets. For instance, if you only have the numbers 1, 17 and 2,000 in your data set the median is 17. Not very informative	The most laborious of the measures of central tendency to calculate	If either of the two scores are extreme, range will be distorted. It tells us little about how spread out or clustered together the data are	Uses only 50% of the data in the calculation and is quite laborious to calculate

It's not really useful to ask which of the measures is best and which is worst. Each is appropriate in different circumstances, depending on the data you have and what you are looking for in your research.

DESCRIPTIVE STATISTICS

Descriptive statistics are ways of representing raw data simply. Measures of central tendency and measures of dispersion are the two types of descriptive statistic with which you are familiar from your AS studies.

A measure of central tendency is sometimes referred to as an average. An average is the score that is typical of all the data you have in your set. Measures of dispersion tell us how spread out the data are. The larger the measure of dispersion, the more spread out the data.

Each measure of central tendency (mean, median and mode) has an appropriate measure of dispersion: this is easily described in a table.

"when using a...	use a..."
Mean...	Standard deviation
Median...	Semi-interquartile range, or range
Mode...	Range

Calculating these values is not very difficult: it just takes a little time. This is how you make the calculations. It is worth refreshing your memory.

MEAN

1. Add up the numbers in your data set (call this number A).
2. Count up the number of values in your data set (call this number B).
3. Divide A by B.

MODE

1. Identify the most common value in your data set. This is the mode.
2. If there are two equally common numbers you have a 'bi-modal' set (two modes).
3. If you have three equally common numbers you have a 'tri-modal' set (three modes).

MEDIAN

1. Put your data in order (smallest to largest).
2. The data value in the middle is the median.
3. If you have an even number of values, take the mean of the two in the middle.

STANDARD DEVIATION

1. Calculate the mean of the values in your data set.
2. Subtract the mean from each value in turn and square the result in each case.
3. Add up all of the squared values from step 2.

MATHEMATICAL SYMBOLS – A HANDY GUIDE

The problem with maths is that it sometimes uses symbols that make it look more like Ancient Greek than something we might possibly understand. It's not that complicated actually. Here's a handy guide to what each symbol means.

Symbol	Meaning
$\sqrt{}$	square root
Σ	sigma. This just means 'the sum of'
N	the number of items in your data set
x	the value you are working with
$\bar{x}$	x-bar. This just means 'the mean of your data set'
2	multiply by itself. Also known as 'squared'
σ	lower case sigma. This means standard deviation
=	equals. What's on the left of the symbol equals what is on the right
<	less than. What's on the left is less than what's on the right
>	greater than. What's on the left is greater than what's on the right
<<	a lot less than. What's on the left is a great deal less than what's on the right
>>	a lot greater than. What's on the left is a lot greater than what's on the right
~	approximately. What's on the left is approximately the same as what's on the right

4. Divide the result from step 3 by the number of values in your data set.

5. Take the square root of the figure you calculated in step 4.

RANGE

1. Find the largest and smallest values in your data set.

2. Take the smallest from the largest.

SEMI-INTERQUARTILE RANGE

1. Put your values in order (smallest to largest).

2. Count up how many values you have. Call this 'N'.

3. Calculate N+1 and divide by 4. Call this 'L'.

4. In your ordered data set, find the number at position L.

5. Calculate N+1, multiply it by 3, then divide it all by 4. Call this 'U'.

6. In your ordered data set, find the number at position U.

7. Take the value in step 4 from the value in step 6.

8. Divide the result of step 7 by 2.

When you take each step at a time, the mathematics are not too difficult at all. It's important to be organised when making these calculations. Make sure your working-out paper does not become muddled, and that you keep track of the values. If you do that then life will be much simpler.

EQUATIONS

Before writing this we asked as many students as we could what they would find useful, and what they would like, when learning about research methods and statistics: 82% of them told us that they would like to avoid equations at all costs, and 87% said that learning how to use equations would be extremely useful. It is clear then that most students hate equations and at the same time most of them think that it's a good idea that they know how to use them. How right they are!

$$\sqrt{\frac{\sum (x - \bar{x})^2}{N}}$$

This is the equation for working out standard deviation. The trick with these things is to understand what each part means, and to do one thing at a time. Let's split it up into its parts and then work out how to use it. Armed with your knowledge of the more common symbols used in mathematics, let's take a look at the equation again. Look at the line right in the middle for the moment:

$$\sum (x - \bar{x})^2$$

1. Calculate the mean value (x) of your data set.

2. Take your value (x) and subtract from it the mean of the data set ($\bar{x}$).

3. Multiply what you get in step 2 by itself.

4. Do this for all of the values in your data set in turn, writing the result down each time. If you have 20 values then you will end up with 20 numbers.

5. Now add up ($\sum$) all the numbers you calculated in step 4.

You may get a negative number in step 2, but that doesn't matter at all, because once you've squared it (multiplied it by itself) you always have a positive number, much easier to deal with. Tedious and some might even say very boring, but not terribly complicated so far. The rest is even simpler.

6. Take the total you get in step 5 and divide it by the number of values in your data set (N).

7. Put this number into your calculator, find the square root button marked $\sqrt{}$ and push it. The result you get is σ, the standard deviation for your data set.

If you do one thing at a time, equations are not very complicated at all. The best thing to do is just practise a little, take your time and be organised. Get to know what each part of the equation means. It's a bit like learning another language, but there's not too much to know. Each equation uses pretty much the same information in a slightly different order. If you know the basics, any equation is child's play. Oh, and if you feel a little daunted by this type of thing, so do 82% of our students: and some of them are at university – you are not alone.

PROBABILITY AND SIGNIFICANCE

We've already let you in on a few secrets about statistics. Here's another. All they are for is for showing that your result didn't occur by chance. That's pretty much it. Don't let anyone fool you into thinking they are any more complicated than that. When we do some statistics all they give us after we've finished adding, multiplying, dividing and things is a single important number, which we refer to as 'p'. It stands for 'probability'.

The p value gives us an idea of how likely it is that our results happened by chance or not. The p value can be anywhere between 0 and 1. A p of 1 means that something is definitely, absolutely going to happen. For instance, there is a probability of 1, an absolute certainty, that in the UK Christmas Day will fall on December the 25th. A p of 0 means that something is never ever going to happen. For instance, there is a probability of 0 that this book will turn into a badger.

The nearer to 1 your value of p is, the more likely it is that the results happened by chance. The smaller the value of p, the more likely it is that we can confidently accept our hypothesis, and reject our null hypothesis. A p of 1 means that we are 100% certain that something will happen. A p of 0.9 means that we are 90% certain that something will happen by chance. A p of 0.8 means we are 80% certain that something will happen by chance and so on. The smaller the p the less likely it is that something will happen by chance. Remember:

Small p – Good

Big p – Bad

If we can reject our null hypothesis we can say that our results were 'significant'. By this we mean that our findings did not occur by chance. Statistics let us measure how 'significant' our results are. Statistical tests are used to analyse the data gathered in research to tell us the p value (we will describe these tests in more detail shortly). The smaller the p value, the more significant the result. For example, the statistical analysis might tell us that we have a p value of 0.02. This is the significance level. When we report 'p' in research papers and books it is more often than not written like this: $p \leq 0.02$.

What this means is that the level of p we have found is less than or equal to 0.02. This means that we are at least 98% certain that our results did not happen by chance. Is 98% enough though? For this we need to check the level of significance selected for our research, and this is given by a number referred to as 'alpha'.

ALPHA ($\propto$)

It is important to decide just how sure we need to be that our results did not occur by chance for us to go ahead and conclude that the hypothesis is to be supported and the null hypothesis rejected. In other words, just how small does p need to be?

The level that p needs to be for us to accept it is called the 'alpha' level. In psychology we say that we need to be at least 95% certain that our results did not happen by chance; 95% certainty translates to a p of 0.05. This means that if our p value is less than or equal to 0.05 then we can reject our null hypothesis and say that our results are significant at the 0.05 level.

You may ask why it is that we choose an alpha of 0.05. The answer to this is that this level is an accepted convention right across the behavioural sciences as it gives us the best chance of avoiding both type 1 and type 2 errors (see below for a description of these). In some cases however we might want to be even stricter. For instance, in situations where people's quality of life may be harmed if we are not very sure that our results did not happen by chance we may choose an alpha of 0.01. That is to say, we would need to be at least 99% certain that our results did not happen by chance. This would allow us to say that our results were significant, not only at the 0.05 level but also at the more demanding 0.01 level we require in such a case. You might employ an alpha like this,

---

THINGS HAPPEN BY CHANCE!

Things happen by chance all the time. For instance, you might recover from a cold the day after you happened to have a banana for breakfast. Does this mean that the banana caused the cold to go away, or did it just happen by chance? You would need to do some research to see. Let's say you have carried out your research, drawn the graph and worked out the descriptive statistics. The results seem conclusive. It really does look as if bananas are the cure for the common cold. More people who had a banana recovered than people who did not have a banana. However, you cannot yet conclude anything as you are not sure that your result did not happen just by chance. It may look as though a chance result is very unlikely, but you need to check, and we do this by significance testing.

for instance, if you had been investigating how well an experimental drug influenced the memory of elderly people with Alzheimer's disease. In order to put your drug onto the market and allow people to start taking it, you need to be very sure that it does what it is supposed to.

If the p value you find does not fall at or below your chosen alpha, then you are unable to accept your hypothesis. Instead you are unable to reject the null hypothesis and you cannot say that your results were significant. In these circumstances, you have to say that your results were non-significant. This is quite different from *insignificant* by the way! Your findings were not at all insignificant. Even a result that does not support the hypothesis is interesting to scientists, but statistically speaking, it is a non-significant result.

Investigation	Hypothesis and null hypothesis	Alpha	Calculated p value	Correct decision	Incorrect decision
Does eating crisps make you feel sick?	Hypothesis: The more crisps you eat the sicker you feel. Null hypothesis: You do not feel sicker by eating more crisps.	0.05	$p \leq 0.02$ (p is less than or equal to 0.02)	The p value is less than alpha. We can reject the null hypothesis and say that the result supports our hypothesis. We can confidently sat that we are 95% certain that our results did not occur by chance. Our results are significant.	A type 2 error: We cannot reject the null hypothesis and must reject the hypothesis. The implications of an error like this may result in people eating loads of crisps because they believe it will not make them feel sick when in fact it does.
Does wearing perfume make females more attractive to males?	Hypothesis: Wearing perfume makes females more attractive to males. Null hypothesis: Wearing perfume does not make females more attractive to males.	0.05	$p \leq 0.09$ (p is less than or equal to 0.09)	The p value is larger than alpha. We cannot accept our hypothesis and must retain our null hypothesis. We can only say with 91% confidence that our results did not occur by chance. Our results are non-significant.	A type 1 error: We can reject the null hypothesis and accept the hypothesis. The implications of this error may be serious for the perfume industry. Sales of perfume may drop because women may feel that wearing it makes no difference to their perceived attractiveness.
Should we prescribe a potentially dangerous experimental drug to those with schizophrenia?	Hypothesis: Treatment with the experimental drug improves the quality of life of those suffering with schizophrenia. Null hypothesis: Treatment with the experimental drug does not improve the quality of life of those suffering with schizophrenia.	0.01	$p \leq 0.017$ (p is less than or equal to 0.017)	The p value is less than alpha. We can reject the null hypothesis and say that the result supports our hypothesis. We can coincidentally say that we are 99% certain that our results did not occur by chance. Our results are significant at the 0.01 level.	A type 2 error: We cannot reject the null hypothesis and must reject the hypothesis. The implications of this error are potentially very serious. Millions who suffer from schizophrenia will not benefit from this wonderful new drug.

TYPE 1 AND TYPE 2 ERRORS

After you have carried out some statistical tests, you must decide whether you accept or reject the null hypothesis. There are two major errors that can be made when doing this. These are described rather confusingly as type 1 and type 2 errors.

TYPE 1 ERROR

This is also known as the 'false positive' error. It is the mistake of rejecting the null hypothesis when it is actually true. You have made the decision to accept your hypothesis by mistake. A very strict alpha value makes this kind of mistake less likely.

TYPE 2 ERROR

This is also known as the 'false negative' error. This is the mistake of accepting the null hypothesis when it is in fact false, and you should have rejected it in favour of your hypothesis. A very strict alpha value makes this kind of mistake more likely.

"Do not underestimate the importance of learning about probability, significance, and type 1/type 2 errors! They are a crucial aspect of data analysis and you can bet that they will feature frequently in exam questions!"

CHOOSING THE CORRECT STATISTICAL TEST

The choice of your test is influenced by the type of research you have done, and the type of measurements you have made.

LEVELS OF MEASUREMENT

There are three types of measurements you can make in psychological research. These are nominal, ordinal and interval. The best way to describe each is with an example.

Nominal level

If you have nominal data you have data that can be classified in categories. By this, we mean that if something is in one category it cannot be in another category also. For instance, if you are counting up the number of men and women at a rugby match, you cannot have someone who counts as a man and also as a woman. Similarly, if you make a trip to a safari park to carry out a survey on animals you may want to count the number of monkeys you see and the number of hippos. You cannot have a monkey that is also a hippo –

they exist as discrete categories. If your data is like this, it is described as nominal level data.

Ordinal level

The clue for this one is in the name. Ordinal suggests that there is an *order*. Horse racing is a good example. Horses are recorded as finishing first, second, third, fourth and so on. The order in which they finish is the important thing, not the distance between them. If your data is like this, in some kind of order or rank, then it is described as ordinal level data.

Interval level

If you are measuring something on a scale, perhaps the height of something or the time it takes someone to do something, then you are using an interval scale. Time, temperature, weight and height are all examples of interval levels of measurement.

A knowledge of your experimental design and the level of measurement used will allow you to answer three simple questions, which will lead you to the appropriate statistical test.

EXAMPLE 1

Our research is concerned with the relationship between a person's level of sadness and the amount of chocolate they eat. Here we are measuring sadness ratings and volume of chocolate consumed in ten different people.

Question 1: Do I have correlation data?

The answer to this is YES. You are looking for a relationship between variables and so your choice of test is the Spearman's Rho.

EXAMPLE 2

Our research is concerned with investigating whether males are better at science subjects than females. We collect science test scores from ten males and ten females and want to compare them.

Question 1: Do I have correlation data?

The answer here is NO. You are looking at differences.

Question 2: Am I looking at numbers in categories?

The answer is NO. You are looking at differences.

Question 3: What type of design did I use?

The answer to this is an independent samples design. You have two groups, one male and one female. A comparison is made of the scores of different participants in the different conditions. The test for you is the Mann-Whitney test.

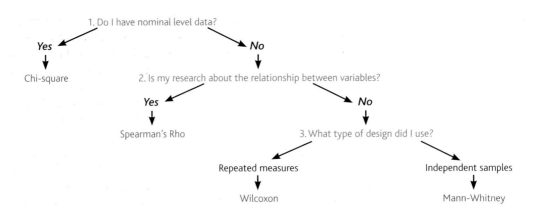

EXAMPLE 3

Our research is investigating whether memory is better after a high-protein meal than before. Each participant carries out a memory task before a high protein meal of fish and chicken, and again after the meal.

Question 1: Do I have correlation data?

The answer is NO. You are looking at differences.

Question 2: Am I looking at numbers in categories?

The answer is NO. You are looking at differences.

Question 3: What type of design did I use?

The answer to this is a repeated measures design. Each participant provided information before the meal and also after the meal. A comparison is made of the same participant's scores in the two conditions. The test for you is a Wilcoxon test.

EXAMPLE 4

Researchers are investigating whether psychology students and maths students revise differently and whether this influences test scores. The two methods used are cramming information or organised revision. Students can be either psychology or maths students (not both) and they may be organised learners or crammers (not both).

Question 1: Do I have correlation data?

The answer is NO. You are looking at categories of behaviour.

Question 2: Am I looking at numbers in categories?

Yes you are. You are looking at whether test score is influenced by the type of learning and the subject. Each person cannot be in more than one category. They are either psychologists or maths students, and they are either crammers or organised learners. The test for you is a chi-square test.

INFERENTIAL ANALYSIS

DATA ANALYSIS: TEACHERS LOOK AWAY NOW

Let's be absolutely honest about this: most people are not terribly fond of mathematics. In psychology, we spend quite a lot of time using numbers and talking about statistics. Why? Because we need to know whether our findings allow us to conclude anything about our hypotheses. Because statistics are seen as extremely complicated they tend to get more than their fair share of coverage in books and in lessons. This is because people find them hard to understand and so authors and teachers spend a great deal of time explaining them.

It may come as a shock to you, but most psychologists working professionally are also not very fond of statistics. Most of them, however, have realised three very important secrets that we are about to let you in on here. Don't tell anyone though.

1. Statistics are just a tool.

It's as simple as that really. Statistics are the end point of your research. Nearly all of your time as a researcher is taken up deciding what you want to do, how you are going to do it and actually doing it. The statistics come right at the end. They are only a tool for finding out which conclusions you can make from your data. Just as a hammer is a tool for making nails go into walls and an iron is a tool for making clothes flat, statistics are tools to let us weigh up our findings.

The second secret you need to know about statistics is a pretty controversial one. We include it here because we have found it very useful in our learning over the years.

2. Statistics ARE often hard to understand.

There, we've said it. There are two reasons for finding things hard to understand. The first is that you think you are not very smart, and so if something is tricky, then it's your fault. The second, just as valid, reason that something seems hard is that it IS hard. Anyone who tells you that statistics are always simple would be lying to you. They do require some thought. However, the reason most people find them hard is neatly side-stepped when we let you in on secret number 3.

3. You do not *have* to understand it all.

At this point, teachers all over the country are fainting with the realisation that this, the most controversial of their secrets, has been told to their students. Here's an example of what we mean: stick with us here, it's worth it. Sometimes psychologists may use equations when working something out. In these equations they may need to divide by things, multiply numbers or add a lot of numbers up. Here's where secret number 3 comes in.

The reason many students setting out to learn how to use statistics in psychology find it hard is because they are naturally thoughtful and inquisitive people. They are used to asking questions like "WHY am I doing this?" and "WHY do I need to divide by this number?" The problem is that the answers to these questions are often much more complicated than you might expect, and so the student psychologist can become bogged down and sometimes confused. They learn that statistics can be hard and confusing and then everything that involves them is to be hated and avoided.

Now, rewind a little. What might have happened if the student psychologist had not asked the WHY questions? If they had not needed to know why something needed to be divided by something else? In fact, in many cases, most psychologists do not know why certain things are done when applying the tests, they just do them. Here's the most controversial tip of all. Just for the moment, and just where following instructions on statistics are concerned, switch off the bit of your brain that makes you ask 'Why?' Just do it, in the firm knowledge that it works. Remember, statistics are a tool, just like any other. You do not need to understand the physics that go along with the act of hammering a nail into a wall do you? You do not consult textbooks to understand how the thermostat works in an iron when smoothing your clothes do you? Then don't worry about why we divide by something, or why you are told to multiply two numbers together.

An often overused but really good example is cake making. Following a tried and tested recipe one step at a time will result in a good cake. Changing the recipe might improve the cake, but it may well ruin it, so it's safer to stick to the recipe as it always gives successful results. Cooking is basically chemistry with food. When you mix things together and apply heat you change the structure of the ingredients, turning them magically into wonderful cakey goodness. You do not need to be an expert in molecular chemistry to know how to make a cake. You do not need to know how molecules are broken and re-formed during the cooking process and why these molecules are easy to digest. You do not ask 'why' questions in cake making, so there is no need to ask them in statistics.

We have been as careful as we can to set out the statistics you need to know in a form that is easy to follow and reproduce. Where appropriate we'll tell you what's happening and why, but the rule is, if you follow each step carefully you will be provided with the information you need in your research.

USING INFERENTIAL STATISTICS

Descriptive statistics allow us to *describe* the data we are using. They include presenting data in the form of graphs and tables or summarising them as measures of central tendency or dispersion. In this section we will describe how to carry out four different statistical tests that allow us to *infer* something about our data. By that we mean that they allow us to deduce or conclude something about the research we have carried out, not just describe the data. Inferential statistics are often used right at the end of the research process to allow researchers to conclude things about whether their results have occurred by chance or not. Remember, the tests are only tools to allow you to arrive at a p value for your research. The various tests may seem a little confusing at first, but stick with it, and they will become much easier to handle.

"You are required to know about the use of four inferential tests: Spearman's Rho, Wilcoxon, Mann-Whitney and chi-square. Don't learn every step of each test – instead, develop an appreciation of the logic of inferential analysis. Understand why you would use a particular test, how the score from each test leads to a p value and how this is interpreted for significance. A good understanding of these things will serve you well in the exam."

SPEARMAN'S RHO

This test is used in correlation research. If you are looking at the relationship between two variables and have drawn a scattergraph, then Spearman's Rho is the test to use. We'll start by summarising some research involving correlation and using the real data in our calculation.

Aim:

To investigate the relationship between ability at mathematics and ability at playing chess.

Hypothesis:

The better you are at maths, the better you will be at chess.

Null hypothesis:

Being good at maths does not mean that you will be good at chess.

Operationalising the variables:

Maths ability was operationalised as 'score out of 100 on a maths test'.

Chess ability was operationalised as 'number of chess problems out of 100 successfully solved'.

The raw data:

	Maths Score	Chess Score
1	58	67
2	34	43
3	77	72
4	59	61
5	46	50
6	90	99
7	22	20
8	78	73
9	89	90
10	67	70

The graph:

This is correlational research investigating the relationship between one variable and another. The appropriate graph to draw is a *scattergram*.

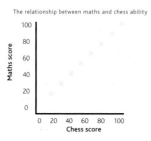

The relationship between maths and chess ability

The descriptive statistics:

	Maths Score	Chess Score
Mean	62	64.5
Standard deviation	22.81	22.78

It seems from these data that there is indeed a strong positive correlation between maths ability and chess ability. This is shown most clearly in the graph. As maths score increases so too does chess score, typical of a positive correlation. To be more certain, and to see whether the correlation is significant, we need to carry out the *Spearman's Rho statistical test*.

Doing Spearman's Rho

Step 1: Rank the scores for each variable

Ranking will become extremely straightforward as you have to do it for three of the tests you are required to understand. It is simple enough, but take care to get it right. Take your original table and add two more columns. Ranking means putting the scores in order, smallest to largest, and giving the smallest the rank of 1, the next smallest the rank of 2 and so on. You can see how this is done by looking at the ranks for maths scores in the table below. Notice, the smallest maths score was 22. This gets the rank of 1. The next smallest was 34. This gets the rank of 2 and so on, right up to the highest score of 90, which gets the rank of 10.

	Maths Score	Chess Score	Maths Rank	Chess Rank
1	58	67	4	5
2	34	43	2	2
3	77	72	7	7
4	59	61	5	4
5	46	50	3	3
6	90	99	10	10
7	22	20	1	1
8	78	73	8	8
9	89	90	9	9
10	67	70	6	6

The ranking of our data is uncomplicated. In other circumstances, though, you may find that two participants score the same on the same task. This common problem makes the ranking slightly more difficult. Take a look at the section on tied ranks below for more on this.

Step 2: Work out differences and square them

In our case we need to work out the difference between maths score and chess score for each of our participants. To start you off:

Participant number 1 was ranked at 4 for maths and 5 for chess.

$$4-5 = -1$$

For each participant, the 'difference' number, and then the figure which is the result of squaring that number, are recorded in two new columns, to the right of those shown in the table above. When you've done this for all your participants you should end up with a table like this:

	Maths Score	Chess Score	Maths Rank	Chess Rank	d (difference)	d² (d squared)
1	58	67	4	5	-1	1
2	34	43	2	2	0	0
3	77	72	7	7	0	0
4	59	61	5	4	1	1
5	46	50	3	3	0	0
6	90	99	10	10	0	0
7	22	20	1	1	0	0
8	78	73	8	8	0	0
9	89	90	9	9	0	0
10	67	70	6	6	0	0

Step 3: Add up the numbers in the d² column (Σd² – 'sigma d²' in English)

You need this number for working out the equation. In our case all we do here is add up the numbers in the far right column:

$$1+0+0+1+0+0+0+0+0+0 = 2$$

Step 4: Identify N and N²

N refers to the number of pairs you have in your data. In this case we have 10. N² is simply that number squared: in your case that's (10 x 10) which is 100.

Step 5: Get organised

Get all the numbers you need for your equation.

$$r_s = 1 - \frac{6(\Sigma d^2)}{N(N^2-1)}$$

r_s – this is the statistic we are after – Spearman's Rho.

N – the number of people who provided data in your correlation research.

d – The difference between each rank of one variable and the corresponding rank of the other variable.

Your equation requires Σd^2, N^2 and N. Make sure you know what these are and write them down on the top of the paper on which you will do your calculations.

$$\Sigma d^2 = 2$$
$$N = 10$$
$$N^2 = 100$$

Step 6: Insert your numbers into the equation

With your numbers it looks like this:

$$r_s = 1 - \frac{6(2)}{10(100-1)}$$

This looks a little less frightening and gets even simpler. The first rule is to work out everything within the brackets first. When you do that you get the following:

$$r_s = 1 - \frac{6(2)}{10(99)}$$

You'll know this from maths, but it won't hurt to remind you that you need to multiply the number inside the brackets by the number on the outside: i.e. you need to calculate 6 x 2 and 10 x 99. When you do that, your equation looks like this:

$$r_s = 1 - \frac{12}{990}$$

Next, work out the fraction. Remember, you divide the top number by the bottom number, (in other words, 12÷990) to give you the statistic we need which will indicate the strength of your correlation.

$$r_s = 1 - 0.012$$
$$= 0.988$$

This is your *correlation coefficient*. You will recall that anything positive means that as one variable increases so too does the other (the absence of a sign in front of the number means that it is positive). You will also know that the nearer to 1 your coefficient is, the stronger the correlation. It is clear that we have an extremely strong correlation here, but is it significant? Might it have occurred by chance?

Step 7: Finding the critical value

To see whether the calculated r_s is large enough for you to say that your results did not occur by chance you need to look in statistical tables. At the end of this book you will find an appendix with the table you need for this test. To use it, you need to know:

N   The number of participants in your task: 10

r_s The value of Spearman's Rho that you calculated: 0.988

The type of hypothesis

Whether you chose a directional (one-tailed) or non-directional (two-tailed) hypothesis. In this case our hypothesis was directional, as we predicted that better maths scores would go along with better chess scores.

Your level of alpha ($\propto$)

The level of significance (alpha) you are using. Remember, this is usually 0.05, but may in other cases be much lower.

What you need to do now is compare the calculated number (sometimes called the *observed* value) to a number in an appropriate statistical table (sometimes referred to as the *critical* value). You look up the relevant number in the table and see if your observed value is *equal to or larger than the critical value from the table*.

The full table can be found in the appendix, but for simplicity, the section from the table that refers to your research is as follows:

Levels of significance for a one-tailed test

N	0.05	0.025	0.01	0.005
10	0.564	0.648	0.745	0.794

What we can see is that our calculated level of 0.988 is much larger than the level required for a significance (p) level of 0.05, or any other significance level for that matter! We can clearly be 95% certain that our results did not occur by chance. We can definitely reject our null hypothesis and say that our results provided clear support for the hypothesis that there is a strong relationship between maths and chess ability.

> **ASK AN EXAMINER**
>
> "Remember, just follow the logic of these tests, don't try to remember how to do them. You start research with a hypothesis and the inferential analysis allows you to see whether or not it is supported by the data you have gathered in your research. If the analysis says that your findings might be due to chance then you have supported the null instead of your hypothesis!"

DEALING WITH TIED RANKS

Take a look at the following data. The ranking has already been done for you.

	Spelling Score	Memory Score	Spelling Rank	Memory Rank
1	3	7	3.5	9
2	0	6	1	8
3	8	3	9	4
4	7	4	8	6
5	6	4	7	6
6	9	0	10	1
7	5	8	6	10
8	3	1	3.5	2
9	4	2	5	3
10	1	4	2	6

Look at the first column where spelling scores are indicated. Participants 1 and 8 both scored 3 on this test. Now look at the 'Spelling Rank' column. When ranking a column of scores like this, each tied score gets an average of the rank positions that they would normally be in. In this case, the scores would be in rank positions 3 and 4. The mean rank value for these two positions is $(3+4)/2 = 3.5$.

Look now at the 'Memory Score' column. Notice that three participants scored 4 on this test. These scores would occupy rank positions 5, 6 and 7 and so each receives the mean rank of $(5+6+7)/3 = 6$.

The rest of the test progresses in exactly the same way as usual. The only slightly tricky thing here is making sure that you get the ranking right.

THE WILCOXON TEST

The Wilcoxon is used when you are looking for differences, rather than a relationship, with a repeated measures design. This means that the same participant provides data for the different conditions in your research. We can use a simple example of comparing memory in silence and memory with music. In the experiment we could see how people perform on a memory test in silence and how they perform on the memory test while listening to music. The test can be as simple as remembering a list of numbers.

Aim:

To investigate whether memory is influenced by music.

Hypothesis:

Memory for numbers will be worse while listening to music than in silence.

Null hypothesis:

Memory for numbers will NOT be worse while listening to music than when in silence.

Here are some results.

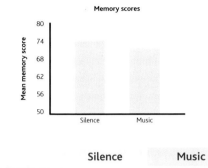

Memory scores

	Silence	Music
Mean	72.55	64.55
Standard deviation	15.15	16.36

It seems that silence does indeed provide better conditions for memory than music. Unfortunately we cannot yet reject our null hypothesis and accept our hypothesis. We cannot be sure that our results did not occur by chance and so we need to test the significance of our findings.

DOING THE WILCOXON TEST

Step 1: Take the scores on one condition from the scores on the other condition

In this case, we simply subtract the memory score while listening to music from the memory score in silence. In this test we must be careful to mark down whether the difference is positive (+) or negative (−).

Step 2: Rank the differences

Here we rank the differences, not the scores themselves. There are two rules to remember for ranking in this test.

1. Ignore all the ties when ranking.

2. Ignore the sign when ranking.

Once you've done this you should end up with a table that looks like this:

	Silence	Music	d (difference)	Ranks of d	Sign of the rank	Negative ranks	Positive ranks
1	76	80	-4	4	−	4	
2	76	67	+9	10.5	+		10.5
3	55	54	+1	1	+		1
4	89	78	+11	14	+		14
5	76	65	+9	10.5	+		10.5
6	87	81	+6	7	+		7
7	67	64	+3	2	+		2
8	34	27	+7	8.5	+		8.5
9	67	45	+22	19	+		19
10	65	51	+14	17.5	+		17.5
11	59	55	+4	4	+		4
12	91	87	+4	4	+		4
13	99	99	0	(tie)	..		
14	56	51	+5	6	+		6
15	68	55	+13	15.5	+		15.5
16	89	76	+13	15.5	+		15.5
17	78	64	+14	17.5	+		17.5
18	74	67	+7	8.5	+		8.5
19	65	55	+10	12.5	+		12.5
20	80	70	+10	12.5	+		12.5

Notice that in our data there is one tied score, and only one negative difference, ranked at position number 4.

Step 3: Add up the negative and positive ranks, and choose the smaller of the numbers

In our data, the total sum of the negative ranks is 4. The total sum of the positive ranks is a lot more, and comes to 186. The number we want is the smaller of these, 4. This is your Wilcoxon statistic, referred to as T. It is your observed value.

Step 4: Finding the critical value

You must now compare the observed value to the critical value in the relevant table. It is included in an appendix at the back of this book. To do this, you need to know:

N The number of participants in your task: 20
T The observed value you calculated: in this case it is 4.

The type of hypothesis

Whether you chose a directional (one-tailed) or non-directional (two-tailed) hypothesis.

Your level of alpha ($\propto$)

The level of significance (alpha) you are using. Remember, this is usually 0.05, but may in other cases be much lower.

The first thing to do is look down the first column for your value of N. Next, read across to the relevant column that refers to your level of alpha. Here you will find the number you are looking for. For simplicity, only the relevant line in the table is reproduced here.

Levels of significance for a one-tailed test

N	0.05	0.025	0.01	0.005
20	60	52	43	26

If *your* value is *smaller than the value in the table* you can say with confidence that your results did not occur by chance. Here, the critical value from the table is 60, for the significance level of 0.05. Your value (4) is definitely smaller than this.

This means that you can say that your results are significant. We report this as follows: 'The difference between memory in silence and when listening to music is significant (p<0.05)'.

THE MANN-WHITNEY TEST

If your research investigates the difference in performance on a task by two different groups then this is the test to use. In other words, if you have used an independent samples design, and you are looking for differences, then use the Mann-Whitney. Here's an example of where this test is appropriate.

Aim:

To investigate whether women are more able at doing two tasks at once than men.

Hypothesis:

The ability to do more than one task at once is different in women and men.

Null hypothesis:

The ability to do more than one task at once is *not* different in women and men.

Operationalising the variables:

Two tasks were operationalised by doing sums while copying a rhythm by tapping the feet.

The raw data:

Men (N = 8)	Women (N = 10)
12	9
4	5
17	8
11	4
8	10
12	9
10	4
9	5
	3
	12

Notice, we have eight men and ten women. That's not a problem for the Mann-Whitney test as it conveniently handles both equal and unequal group sizes.

We refer to each different group as group A and B, so the number in group A is N_A (8) and the number in group B is N_B (10)

The graph:

We have two different groups. The appropriate graph to draw here is a simple bar chart.

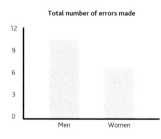

Total number of errors made

The descriptive statistics:

	Men	Women
Mean errors	10.38	6.9
Standard deviation	3.74	3.07

From the graph and the descriptive statistics it looks very much as if women make fewer errors when doing more than one task at once than do men. We'll need to do some statistics, in this case a Mann-Whitney, to assess the likelihood that these results have occurred by chance.

Doing the Mann-Whitney Test

Step 1: Rank the data

In the Mann-Whitney, we rank all the data together. By this we mean that the men's scores and the women's scores are all ranked at the same time. We've done this for you here. Notice the usual problem of tied ranks. If you are not sure about this, look back to the section above.

Men (N = 8)	Rank	Women (N = 10)	Rank
12	16	9	10
4	3	5	5.5
17	18	8	7.5
11	14	4	3
8	7.5	10	12.5
12	16	9	10
10	12.5	4	3
9	10	5	5.5
		3	1
		12	16

Step 2: Add up the ranks in each group, calling them Rank A (R_A) and Rank B (R_B)

Sum of ranks for men (R_A)

$$16+3+18+14+7.5+16+12.5+10 = 97$$

Sum of ranks for women (R_B)

$$10+5.5+7.5+3+12.5+10+3+5.5+1+16 = 74$$

Step 3: Use your values to calculate the results of two formulae

For the Mann-Whitney, we need to calculate two values, referred to as U_A and U_B. Here are the formulae. They are very similar indeed, so be careful you are using the right numbers when you calculate them!

1.
$$U_A = N_A N_B + \frac{N_A(N_A+1)}{2} - R_A$$

2.
$$U_B = N_A N_B + \frac{N_B(N_B+1)}{2} - R_B$$

These look a little frightening at first, but let's take one at a time and see what they look like when we insert our numbers. As usual, begin by identifying the numbers you need and organising yourself carefully.

U_A – the number we are calculating with the formula

U_B – the number we are calculating with the formula

N_A = the number in Group A (men) = 8

N_B = the number in Group B (women) = 10

R_A = the sum of ranks in Group A (men) = 97

R_B = the sum of ranks in Group B (women) = 74

1.
$$U_A = N_A N_B + \frac{N_A(N_A+1)}{2} - R_A$$

Inserting our values, the formula now looks like this:

$$U_A = 8 \times 10 + \frac{8(8+1)}{2} - 97$$

A little basic mathematics can simplify it further to:

$$U_A = 80 + \frac{8(9)}{2} - 97$$

This is equal to:

$$U_A = 80 + \frac{72}{2} - 97$$

which equals:

$$U_A = 80 + 36 - 97$$

so finally

$$U_A = 19$$

2.
$$U_B = N_A N_B + \frac{N_B(N_B+1)}{2} - R_B$$

Inserting our values, the formula now looks like this:

$$U_B = 8 \times 10 + \frac{10(10+1)}{2} - 74$$

Again, some straightforward mathematics can simplify it further to:

$$U_B = 80 + \frac{10\,(11)}{2} - 74$$

This is equal to:

$$U_B = 80 + \frac{110}{2} - 74$$

which equals:

$$U_B = 80 + 55 - 74$$

so finally

$$U_B = 61$$

Step 4: Select the smallest value of U and consult the tables for a critical value

In our case, the smallest value of U calculated was U_A: this is our observed value at 19. We now need to consult the table of critical values for the Mann-Whitney. To do this we need to know the number of participants in each group. We had eight males and ten females, so we read across the top of the table until we reach 8, and we then read down to the N = 10 line.

A portion of the table is reproduced for you here, but make sure you refer to the real table in the appendix of this book to be sure you know how to read it.

		N2				
		7	8	9	10	11
	7	4	6	7	9	10
	8	6	7	9	11	13
	9	7	9	11	13	16
N1	10	9	11	13	16	18
	11	10	13	16	18	21

You can see that the critical value of U for N of 8 and N of 10 is 11. If your value of U is equal to or less than the critical value then you can say confidently, with 95% certainty, that your results did not happen by chance.

Our value of U was 19. This is not smaller than 11, so we cannot reject our null hypothesis. Even though the graph and the descriptive statistics suggested that it might be the case, we cannot say with confidence that women are indeed better at doing more than one task at once. This is a very good example of why we should always do the statistics! If we had not done so, we might have made the error of rejecting our null hypothesis by mistake, and accepting our hypothesis even

though the difference could well have happened by chance.

CHI-SQUARE (χ^2)

Chi-square test (pronounced 'ky square') is often written as χ^2. We use this test when we have numbers of people in different categories. Here's an example from earlier, to help clarify what we mean:

'Researchers are investigating whether psychology students and maths students revise differently and whether this influences test scores. The two methods used are cramming information or organised revision. Students can be either psychology or maths students (not both) and they may be organised learners or crammers (not both).'

In this case we have a group of psychology students and a group of maths students. The rule is that we cannot have a student studying both. Each of our subject groups is split into two according to the revision style of its members: those that cram for exams (crammers) and those that revise in an organised way (organised).

To summarise, students can be in one of four completely separate categories. These are as follows.

1. Psychology: Crammers
2. Psychology: Organised
3. Maths: Crammers
4. Maths: Organised

What's important here is that no one can be in more than one group. The chi-square test looks at whether the number of students in each category is different from what we might expect just by chance. In this way the test tells us whether the null hypothesis (that something happened by chance) can be rejected or not, thus allowing us to make a decision about our hypothesis.

Aim:
We are interested in whether the type of revision (cramming or organised) works differently for different subjects.

Hypothesis:
There will be a difference in the effectiveness of different types of revision depending on the subject.

Null hypothesis:
There will *not* be a difference in the effectiveness of different types of revision depending on the subject.

Operationalising the variables:
A self-report questionnaire of psychology and maths students asks them to identify the type of revising they do, cramming or organised revision.

The raw data:

	Psychology	Maths
Crammers	5	50
Organised	35	10

Each square relating to each of the four categories is referred to as a 'cell'. Each 'cell' contains a number which relates to the number of students in that category and is referred to as the *observed frequency*.

The graph:

We have two different groups. The appropriate graph to draw here is a simple bar chart.

The question is, are the numbers of students in these categories different from what we might expect to see just by chance The way to find out is to carry out a chi-square test.

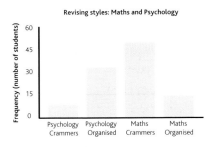

Revising styles: Maths and Psychology

DOING THE CHI-SQUARE TEST

Step 1: Add up the values in the rows and the columns of the results table, and calculate an overall grand total

The easiest way to do this is to reproduce the results table, adding the totals of the rows and columns and the grand total, like this:

	Psychology	Maths	Total
Crammers	5	50	55 (5+50)
Organised	35	10	45 (35+10)
Total	40 (5+35)	60 (50+10)	Grand total 100 (5+50+35+10)

Step 2: Work out what might be expected just by chance

To work out the number in each cell that might occur by chance is easy, and the result is referred to as the expected frequency. We use the following very basic formula:

$$E = \frac{RC}{T}$$

The expected frequency for the cell (E) equals the row total (R) times the column total (C) divided by the grand total (T).

The four sums are easy to calculate. Make sure you work out the row total times the column total before dividing by the grand total though, and make sure you use the correct row totals and column totals in each calculation.

Observed frequency = 5
Expected frequency = (55x40)/100
= 2200/100 = **22**

Observed frequency = 50
Expected frequency = (55x60)/100
= 3300/100 = **33**

Observed frequency = 35
Expected frequency = (45x40)/100
= 1800/100 = **18**

Observed frequency = 10
Expected frequency = (60x45)/100
= 2700/100 = **27**

To summarise, the expected frequencies for our data look like this:

	Psychology	Maths
Crammers	22	33
Organised	18	27

Step 3: Use your observed and expected frequencies to calculate chi-square

Now that we have observed and expected frequencies for each cell we can calculate chi-square using this equation:

$$x^2 = \sum \frac{(O-E)^2}{E}$$

To calculate chi-square (χ^2) we have to calculate $(O-E)^2/E$ for each cell, then add up (Σ) the results of the sums.

We've done this for you here. Each cell contains a single calculation, using the observed and expected frequencies for that cell.

	Psychology	Maths
Crammers	Observed frequency = 5 Expected frequency = 22 $(5–22)^2/22$ $=-17^2/22$ $=289/22$ **= 13.14**	Observed frequency = 50 Expected frequency = 33 $(50–33)^2/33$ $=17^2/33$ $=289/33$ **= 8.76** (2 decimal places)
Organised	Observed frequency = 35 Expected frequency = 18 $(35–18)^2/18$ $=17^2/18$ $=289/18$ **= 16.06** (2 decimal places)	Observed frequency = 10 Expected frequency = 27 $(10–27)^2/27$ $=-17^2/27$ $=289/27$ **= 10.70** (2 decimal places)

To complete the calculation of chi-square, add up the results of the individual calculations:

chi-square = $13.14+8.76+16.06+10.70$
= 48.66

Step 4: Using the table, find the relevant critical value of chi-square

To find the correct number you must know whether you chose a directional (one-tailed) or non-directional (two-tailed) hypothesis. In our study we simply stated that there would be a difference between the revising styles: we did not say whether one would be larger than another, so we have a non-directional hypothesis.

Before you can use the table you must calculate a value called 'degrees of freedom', shortened to 'df'. This is done using the following simple formula:

df = (number of rows – 1)
x (number of columns – 1)

For our data it could not be simpler

df = $(2–1)x(2–1)$
= $1x1$
= 1

Finally, consult the relevant table. It's printed at the end of this book for you, but for convenience, the key portion of it is reproduced here. As usual, make sure you consult the table itself, so that you know how it works.

Levels of significance for a two-tailed test

	0.20	0.10	0.05	0.02	0.01
1	1.64	2.71	3.84	5.41	6.64
2	3.22	4.60	5.99	7.82	9.21
3	4.64	6.25	7.82	9.84	11.34

The value for chi-square that you calculated must be the same as, or larger than, the critical value you read from the table. Your calculated value was 48.66. The critical value for the significance level of 0.05 is 3.84. It seems that you can very confidently reject the null hypothesis and say that your data did not occur by chance. Your result is significant ($p<0.05$).

ANALYSING AND INTERPRETING QUALITATIVE DATA

The purpose of research is to provide data of some kind that can be analysed to help support or reject a hypothesis. The data can be in many different forms, but it will either be quantitative or qualitative. The distinction is quite easy to remember. Quantitative data is to do with quantities (numbers, amounts). Qualitative data is to do with quality (opinions, feelings). Which kind you use will depend on the type of research being conducted. In some cases you might even collect both quantitative and qualitative data. For instance, you might be interested in measuring stress levels in relation to maths problems. The result of a maths test would be quantitative; asking people how they feel about the maths test would be qualitative.

How then, do you present qualitative data? It's actually more straightforward than you may think. Consider the following example. A researcher is carrying out a kind of analysis called 'discourse' analysis on interviews with politicians which involves investigating samples of speech. He is interested in seeing how often politicians comment on matters that are local to the United Kingdom, or matters relating to international issues. The speeches of ten politicians are identified and investigated. The comments recorded by the researcher include:

'The US elections have huge implications for the wars in the Middle East'

'The Scottish parliament can work hand in hand with the parliament in Westminster'

'The floods in the West Country were devastating. We must do all we can to stop this happening again'

'The crisis in central Africa is worsening. I fear for the lives of these people'

'Rebel fighters in parts of the Russian Federation have grown in strength over the last two years'

'House prices in the UK are, frankly, ridiculous'

While a list of comments like this is interesting, it is not very well organised. We can use a table to help present some of the data in such a way that the reader does not have to sort through a list to work out what has been said about the UK and what has been said about issues outside the UK. There may be many more comments, and these may be included in another table, but a good summary table with samples of the comments will be very useful to readers interested in seeing the kind of comments that have been made. The table may look like this:

Category	Examples
Comments directly relating to UK issues	*'The Scottish parliament can work hand in hand with the parliament in Westminster'*
	'House prices in the UK are, frankly, ridiculous'
	'The floods in the West Country were devastating. We must do all we can to stop this happening again'
Comments directly relating to international issues	*'The US elections have huge implications for the wars in the Middle East'*
	'The crisis in central Africa is worsening. I fear for the lives of these people'
	'Rebel fighters in parts of the Russian Federation have grown in strength over the last two years'

The table makes it much easier and faster to find the relevant information. Tables like this might also include the total number of comments in each category. If we have a total number we can draw a graph, like this:

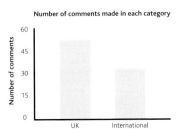

Number of comments made in each category

It is immediately clear from this graph that the speeches of the politicians used in this research had many more comments that directly related to UK issues than ones that dealt with international matters. This is a perfect example of what a graph is for. Graphs allow readers to access a good summary of the data in an immediate, visual way.

CONVENTIONS OF REPORTING ON PSYCHOLOGICAL INVESTIGATIONS

Once we have completed our research we need to write it up before sending it for peer review and

(we hope) publication. There are certain conventions that should be followed when reporting psychological research. These are conventions rather than 'rules' because some scientific journals require a slightly different style, but generally speaking, psychological research should be presented in a certain way. Imagine that we wanted to present our research into whether memory is worse with music playing than in silence. Our report should be organised into the sections we identify here.

1. TITLE

It seems obvious to say it, but a strong and clear title is extremely important. Thousands of pieces of research are published every year. Researchers pore through the titles of this new research to see if anything grabs their interest and is relevant to their own work. A title that clearly expresses what the research is investigating is extremely helpful. In our study of whether memory is worse in music or in silence we may choose the following title:

'Memory: An investigation into why music really makes it rubbish'

However, this is not very informative, or formal. A better title might be:

'An investigation into how memory for numbers is influenced by music'

This is more like it. From this title the reader is able to see that the research is into memory: it investigates memory for numbers, and music is used to disrupt it.

An even better title might be:

'The irrelevant sound effect: The disruption of memory for serially presented digits in conditions of music and silence'

The phenomenon we are investigating here is actually called 'the irrelevant sound effect'. It has been widely studied and refers particularly to memory in silence compared to memory with sound presented at the same time. This title clearly indicates to the reader what type of research is in the report.

In this section of the book we have the permission of the authors to use sections of a real paper which appeared in a publication called the *Journal of Applied Psychology* in 2007. The authors were Beaman and Holt, and the copyright for the paper belongs to the publishers, John Wiley and Sons. The title was:

'Reverberant auditory environments: The effects of multiple echoes on distraction by "irrelevant" speech'

In their research, Beaman and Holt looked at how sounds with an echo (reverberation) influenced memory differently than places without an echo.

2. ABSTRACT

The abstract is a short summary of the research paper placed at the very start. A good abstract should provide a little background, some details of the method, a statement of results and a short conclusion. All this in fewer than 150 words. The abstract comes first, straight after the title, but you should always write it last. The reason is that it includes a very brief summary of the information you have included in every section of your report and so it's much easier to write when you have finished the rest of the research report!

Here's an abstract that, unfortunately, is actually better than some we have seen over the years! We really hope you agree that it is not terribly good.

> We did some research that was looking at whether people were more rubbish at remembering stuff when they had music coming through headphones. We gave them things to remember and they remembered them. We worked out some maths and decided whether their remembering was better when they couldn't hear anything. It was. There were about 10 people we tested. At the end of it we decided that it was useful to know this, for instance, that's why we think it should be quiet in libraries mostly. Right at the end we thought about some other research and we think we will now investigate whether listening to old-fashioned music like your dad listens to will make memory worse than listening to stuff you have on your own iPod.

There is very little detail in the abstract. The background to the research is not clear at all. We do not know what the task itself was, what the hypothesis was, what the variables were or how they were operationalised. We do not have a clear understanding of the statistical tests carried out or what exactly was found, and the suggestions at the end for further research are vague to say the least! Not very good at all. Now look at the version below.

> The research detailed here is an investigation into whether memory for digits presented in series is influenced more by the presentation of music during the task than when participants proceeded in silence. Previous research has suggested that any kind of sound interferes with recall of numbers presented in series, suggesting the hypothesis that memory would be worse when listening to music. An opportunity sample of 10 participants took part in an independent samples design and provided data that supported the hypothesis ($p \leq 0.05$). How the sound influences memory is discussed, with reference to the working memory model. Concluding comments included possibilities for further research.

This abstract is much better. Here we have some background, some detail of our design, the result and even something of our discussion and conclusion – all in fewer that 150 words. Finally, here is the real abstract from the Beaman and Holt research. It's quite complicated, but it does give you an idea of the kind of information and detail you find in professionally produced work.

> Two experiments examine the effect on an immediate recall test of simulating a reverberant auditory environment in which auditory distracters in the form of speech are played to the participants (the 'irrelevant sound effect'). An echo-intensive environment simulated by the addition of reverberation to the speech reduced the extent of 'changes in state' in the irrelevant speech stream by smoothing the profile of the waveform. In both experiments, the reverberant auditory environment produced significantly smaller irrelevant sound distraction effects than an echo-free environment. Results are interpreted in terms of changing-state hypothesis, which states that acoustic content of irrelevant sound, rather than phonology or semantics, determines the extent of the irrelevant sound effect (ISE).

3. THE INTRODUCTION

The introduction is a really important part of the write up. It's here that you get the chance to describe the background to your research and how you really came up with your idea in the first place. This is where you place your work alongside other research in the same field. All introductory sections differ slightly in length, depending on what it is that we need to cover and how much background research there has been in the area. Introductions, however long, should nevertheless follow the golden rule.

Start Wide

End Narrow

Think of your introduction as a funneling system. You should start with all of your background information and details of research that has already been done. You really need to provide a good general overview in the introduction. As you proceed, you should begin to focus your ideas on your research. Towards the end of the introduction, talk about the aims of your research, ending finally with your hypothesis. Take a look at some excerpts from Beaman and Holt (2007).

> The use of virtual environments (VE) in psychology is now well-established. Studies of spatial navigation (Ruddle, Payne, & Jones, 1998), spatial memory (Ruddle, Payne, & Jones, 1999)…and neuropsychological rehabilitation (Wann, Rushton, Smyth, & Jones, 1997) have all benefited from these VE techniques… However, virtual auditory environments are much less common than virtual visual environments. When virtual auditory environments have been created, however, they have proved useful to the study of the 'sense of place' associated with particular buildings and historic sites…The purpose of the current study is to apply similar techniques to the study of auditory distraction by so-called 'irrelevant sound' known to disrupt working memory.

The introduction begins very generally, and quickly proceeds to a statement of the broad aims of the research. The authors have really told the reader what to expect, the background and the general ideas behind their study. Later in the introduction Beaman and Holt begin to be more specific.

> In a reverberant environment the direct signal is overlayed (sic) with multiple reflections, the intensity of each reflection and the delay imposed upon it being a function of the intensity of the original signal and the nature (e.g. the size, surfaces and contents) of the room…It follows that larger spaces with more reverberation may intrinsically be less distracting environments (in acoustic terms) than small rooms with low levels of reverberation. This prediction follows from the changing-state hypothesis of Jones and colleagues…we propose to take a different approach and ask whether extreme values of reverberation, which we expect to represent a powerful manipulation, will affect the results obtained for a much smaller sample size. The advantage of this approach is that it makes positive, rather than null, predictions

> and provides a direct test of the changing-state hypothesis.

Here, the introduction is really setting the scene, explaining that certain hypotheses and theories described in other research will be investigated. The authors finish by explaining that predictions will be made to test a hypothesis. We can see that the introduction covers a great deal of ground. We've only included a few excerpts here: much more is described in the original article. We can see from the sections we have reproduced that the introduction begins very generally, then focuses, using the 'start wide, end narrow' rule, funneling the information down from a general discussion to a much more focused one.

4. THE METHOD

When writing a method section, you need to ask yourself one simple question: 'Would someone else be able to do exactly what I did from reading my method?'

If the answer to this is 'No', then your method is not good enough. A good method has just the right amount of information for someone who has never watched you work before, and who may never have carried out research in the area, to carry out a 'replication' of your study. Replication is a very important aspect of scientific research. If a study can be replicated then we can be more certain that the findings are to be trusted. Replication adds to the reliability of the research, with unreplicable research being regarded as unreliable. A good method provides other researchers with the information they need to repeat your work closely enough that they can hope to replicate your findings. A method might include a number of sections. Not all methods include all of these sections, but we'll include them here for reference.

Design: A statement of the design used may be included. Here you might indicate the different conditions in your research and if appropriate you might say whether a repeated measures or independent samples design was used, or even include the independent and dependent variables /IV and DV/.

> Four conditions were presented, each with 15 trials, giving a total number of 60 experimental trials per participant. Presentation order for each candidate was chosen randomly from the 24 possible condition orders…The four conditions were…three levels of reverberation…and a 'no sound' control condition.

Participants: In this section you would give details of your sample, including how many men and women there were and the age range. You should also indicate how the sample was identified, perhaps using an advertisement for a volunteer sample, or the phone directory for a random sample. It may also be appropriate to indicate where the research was conducted and from what country the participants came. You must be very careful to make sure that the participants remain anonymous as this is their right, and it is also one of the principles of ethical research. This is from Beaman and Holt (2007):

> Eleven students of…University volunteered to participate in this study. All participants reported normal hearing levels and normal or corrected-to-normal vision. All had English as their first language.

Apparatus and stimuli: In this section researchers would indicate the apparatus they used in their research. If they used certain sounds, or visual stimuli, then they would give details of these, perhaps indicating how each was produced.

> Sounds were digitally recorded on MiniDisc and presented from a Sony MiniDisc player at a comfortable listening level to students through Sennheiser HD570 headphones. Listening levels were set to a comfortable level with a test recording before the experiment began and kept at the same level for the duration of the experiment. Stimuli were presented on a Pentium Class PC running Windows XP and MS PowerPoint software…using Cool Edit sound editing suite (Syntrillium Software Corporation).

Procedure: This section of the report is particularly important for those wishing to replicate the research. It is here that researchers show exactly what they did.

> Each participant was tested individually in a quiet room. The irrelevant sound was presented continuously…throughout the presentation… directly from the digital recording. Participants were instructed to ignore anything they might hear and were reassured they would not be tested on it in any way. In each trial…the seven numbers were presented in succession on a VDU. After the presentation the instruction 'recall now' was presented. Participants recorded the numbers manually on response sheets provided, writing from left to right. They were asked not to omit any responses and, if they could not remember a particular item, to write down their best guess and move onto the next item. They were asked not to go

back and amend previous answers if they felt they had made an error. The visual instruction 'Push space for next trial' cued participants to progress through the experiment.

5. THE RESULTS

After researchers have identified their method, the results are presented. The presentation of results may be in the form of descriptive statistics, tables, graphs and also inferential statistics. In the case of Beaman and Holt (2007) a more complicated statistic called an ANOVA (Analysis of Variance) has been used. Excerpts from the results of this research are shown below.

> …analysis of variance (ANOVA)…showed a significant effect of…speech condition on the mean number correctly recalled…, p<0.013.

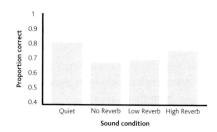

> Overall, the results do not support the general claim that attempting to absorb noise and reduce echo in workplace environments reduces the likelihood of observing auditory distraction effects.

6. DISCUSSION AND CONCLUSION

Sometimes the discussion and conclusion are split into two separate sections, but more often than not, they are included as a single section in published research.

This section follows the general rule that it should be a discussion.

> 'of the issues presented in the introduction *in light of your results*'

This means that the discussion should look again at what was said in the introduction about the claims of past research and to see if your results allow you to say anything about those claims and hypotheses. Your results may allow you to reject a well-known and widely accepted hypothesis, or they may provide evidence that supports it all the more. You can use the discussion to talk in detail about why you found the results you did.

> The results of these experiments are supportive of the view that the extent of auditory distraction observed is dictated by the number of 'changes in state' that occur within the

irrelevant sound stream and that anything which acts to reduce the number or extent of these changes will reduce the size of the distraction effect.

The words in the irrelevant stream in these experiments were not, so far as can be ascertained by passive listening, rendered unintelligible by the process of adding reverberation, although no formal tests were carried out on whether the relative levels of intelligibility varied between the conditions and that remains a limitation of the current study.

The present results are inconsistent with the view that it is always helpful, when aiming to optimise cognitive efficiency, to reduce the level of reverberation within the environment…

These experiments are the first to demonstrate that intrinsic factors of particular environments can modify the extent of auditory distraction objectively observed in such environments.

Concluding remarks can be brief and clear. They summarise what the researchers feel can sensibly be concluded from their results.

In conclusion, we have established that reverberation can reduce the auditory distraction effect produced by irrelevant speech.

At the end of the discussion you might decide to identify other things that could now be investigated that relate to your research.

Further research looking at the subjective experience of such noise should, in addition, lead to a greater understanding of how auditory environments can be made more conducive to efficient cognitive function both objectively and subjectively.

7. REFERENCES

The final section is a reference list. Here the researchers give full details of the other research in books or academic journals that they have referred to in their investigation. This is very useful for those reading the work as they may be interested to extend their reading to the articles and books indicated by the researchers who wrote the paper. The reference section from Beaman and Holt (2007) includes the following:

1. Ruddle, R. A., Payne, S. J., & Jones, D. M. (1998). Navigating large-scale 'desk-top' virtual buildings: Effects of orientation aids and familiarity. *Presence: Teleoperators & Virtual Environments, 7,* 179–192.

This is a research paper by Ruddle, Payne and Jones. It was published in 1998, in the seventh volume of an academic journal called *Presence: Teleoperators & Virtual Environments* on pages 179 to 192.

2. Ruddle, R. A., Payne, S. J., & Jones, D. M. (1999). Spatial knowledge and virtual environments. In J. M. Noyes & M. Cook (Eds.), *Interface Technology: The Leading Edge* (pp. 135–146). Baldock, England: Research Studies.

This is a chapter of a book called *Interface Theory: The Leading Edge.* The book was edited by Noyes and Cook, and was published in 1999 by a company called Baldock, based in England. The chapter was written by Ruddle, Payne and Jones and is titled "Spatial knowledge and virtual environments".

3. Wann, J. P., Rushton, S. K., Smyth, M., & Jones, D. (1997). Rehabilitation environments for attention and movement disorders. *Communications of ACM, 40,* 49–52.

This is a short article, written by Wann, Rushton, Smyth and Jones in 1997, called 'Rehabilitation environments for attention and movement disorders'. It appeared in volume 40 of an academic publication called *Communications of ACM,* on pages 49–52. ACM stands for Association of Computer Machinery.

CREDITS

INDEX

NEW 2008 AQA 'A' SPECIFICATION

Crown House Publishing Limited
www.crownhouse.co.uk

A2 LEVEL

Psychology

the study
guide

THE COMPLETE STUDY AND REVISION GUIDE

Nigel Holt and Rob Lewis

A2 Level Psychology: the study guide

All you need for exam practice and preparation

Exam-style questions and practice exam paper with example answers, ideas for practical work, a comprehensive glossary, Examiner tips, revision advice and more!

ISBN: 9781845901011 available from all good book stores